D0852179

Human Change Processes

HUMAN CHANGE PROCESSES

The Scientific Foundations of Psychotherapy

MICHAEL J. MAHONEY

BasicBooks
A Subsidiary of Perseus Books, L.L.C.

The author gratefully acknowledges permission to reprint excerpts from the following sources:

F.A. Hayek, *Studies in Philosophy, Politics, and Economics.* © 1967, University of Chicago Press.

F.A. Hayek, *New Studies in Philosophy, Politics, Economics, and the History of Ideas.* © 1978, University of Chicago Press.

F.A. Hayek, *Law, Legislation, and Liberty.* Vol. 1. *Rules and Order.* © 1979, University of Chicago Press.

Library of Congress Cataloging-in-Publication Data
Mahoney, Michael J.
    Human change processes : the scientific foundations of
psychotherapy / Michael J. Mahoney.
      p.   cm.
    Includes bibliographical references and index.
    ISBN 0-465-03118-8
    1. Change (Psychology)   2. Developmental psychology.
3. Psychotherapy. I. Title.
BF637.C4M29 1991
155—dc20   90-80675
                                              CIP

To Walter B. Weimer,
long-time friend, valued critic,
and the scholar most responsible
for awakening me from the dogma
of authoritarian epistemologies;

and to Vittorio F. Guidano,
both friend and "familia," who helped
teach me that psychotherapy, like life,
is always applied epistemology.

Contents

Preface

This book represents the culmination of ten years of research and writing about basic principles and processes of human psychological change. It has been my most intense and sustained project as a scientist and health professional. There were, to be sure, times when its scope felt almost overwhelming. Motivated by a desire to be comprehensive and integrative, I was drawn into literatures that were humbling in both their expanse and difficulty. As often as I felt overwhelmed, however, I was even more often inspired by the ideas and experiences generated in the process of exploration. Whatever the ultimate contributions of this work may be, I have richly enjoyed the paths of inquiry that it has afforded me.

A central assertion of this book is that we are participant observers in an era of dramatic change in human experience. Increasing numbers of individuals are reporting fundamentally novel ways of knowing and experiencing their lives, their selves, and their relationships to other people and our shared planet. Among many other expressions of this "axial" (pivotal) shift in human understanding, recent developments in both theory and research suggest that consciousness, affect, personal identity, and intentionality can (again) be examined as important expressions of human activity. I believe that this shift has important implications for our understanding and facilitation of individual and collective adaptation and development.

My goal in this book has been to examine our basic assumptions about human change processes. I have also tried to practice an intentional self-awareness in the process of that examination, so that specific assumptions could be constructively reviewed (for example, the assumption that there are basic assumptions). In so doing, I have emphasized that our theories and therapies of human change are also theories of human nature and psychological possibility. This is not to imply that human ideas dictate all else: I do not subscribe to the doctrine of "rational supremacy" (the notion that the head rules over the heart). Rather than simply reverse the arrow of causality, however, I suggest that the phenomenon of change is much more complex and dynamic than traditional models have allowed.

Throughout my writing I have had three broad clusters of persons in mind as my imagined readers: graduate students in psychology, psychotherapists, and research scientists. I have further imagined that the primary interest of each group might represent a mixture of motives ranging from preparations for comprehensive examinations and reviewing the scientific foundations of psychotherapy to developing a more constructive dialogue between researchers and practitioners. In the interest of serving as a resource for such readers, I have made extensive (though hardly exhaustive) references to existing literatures in a variety of fields. I have also ventured summary tables, technical appendices, and approximations to some general principles relevant to research and professional practice. I can only hope that the possibilities suggested by these ventures are sufficient to counterbalance their undeniable limitations.

A project of this magnitude is not achieved without generous encouragement, both personal and professional. Over the decade of research and writing that this book has involved, I have enjoyed the welcome support of many more students, colleagues, and friends than I can possibly name here. Some have offered words of encouragement after a workshop or lecture; some have written notes of appreciation. Across conferences and continents, I have been touched and inspired by their interest and good wishes. I am also indebted to the institutions that have supported my work during that period: The Pennsylvania State University, the University of California at Santa Barbara, and the University of North Texas. I spent a formative six months at the University of Rome Psychiatric Clinic, thanks to a 1984 Fulbright Research Scholar Award from the Council for the International Exchange of Scholars. Encouragement was also rendered in honors awarded me by the American Psychological Association and the American Association for the Advancement of Science.

The partial list of friends and colleagues who have supported me in this work would include Neil McK. Agnew, Giampiero Arciero, Diane B. Arnkoff, Albert Bandura, Aaron T. Beck, George and Judith Brown, James F. T. Bugental, Donald T. Campbell, Antonio Caridi, John W. Cotton, Gerald C. Davison, Viktor E. Frankl, Oscar F. Gonçalves, Judith Gordon, Leslie S. Greenberg, Vittorio F. Guidano, Gail Hackett, John J. Horan, Robert Landheer, Ed Lewis, G. Alan Marlatt, Andrew W. Meyers, Mayte Miro, Luis Joyce Moniz, Bert S. Moore, Thomas Pruzinsky, James

E. Pumphrey, Mario A. Reda, R. Murray Thomas, Holly Van Horn, Frances Vaughan, Roger N. Walsh, Walter B. Weimer, Barry E. Wolfe, and Jules Zimmer. The special contributions of Vittorio Guidano and Walter Weimer are reflected in the dedication.

It does not take much experience as a clinical practitioner to realize that helping is considerably more challenging than most textbooks and treatment manuals admit. The quick-fix miracles promised by popular prescriptions for happiness are often an insult to the pain, struggle, and perseverance exhibited by many psychotherapy clients. This lesson has been taught me repeatedly over the years, and I have learned it most convincingly from the people I have served clinically. My clients have been some of my most powerful teachers, especially regarding the complexities of life and the fundamental importance of human caring. I honor their "courage to be," as Paul Tillich put it, as well as their trust in self, in me, and in the processes of personal development. For sharing with me the secrets of their hearts and the struggles of their private lives, I am deeply grateful.

The ultimate time and energy that were required by this project could not have been known to JoAnn Miller when she first offered a contract with Basic Books. Her patience with me and her faith in this book helped us through multiple *livelines* (my preferred term for deadlines). The extensive revisions that caused so many delays were, I believe, wise and worthy labors, and I thank JoAnn for her support throughout. Robert A. Neimeyer, Mary Alice Flint, and Phoebe Hoss read the entire manuscript and offered valuable suggestions for its refinement. I am also grateful to Mary McConkey and Mary Hayman for their invaluable help on the manuscript and their spirited encouragement of its very human author.

Finally, this work would not have been possible without the help and caring of a loved and loving "secure base" made up of my family, especially my wife, Teresa, and my two most precious begottens, Sean Michael and Maureen Elizabeth Mahoney. My greatest fortune has been the joyful privilege of sharing my life with them.

MJM

1

Human Change: The Ultimate Ethical Frontier

If we know the laws of change, we can precalculate in regard to them, and freedom of action thereupon becomes possible.
                                                                                                    —I Ching

Although the technologies for producing change have accelerated substantially in the last few centuries, fascination with the "laws of change" has been around much longer than written history. Likewise, as reflected in this crystal from the ancient Chinese classic, the *I Ching,* or Book of Changes, our fascination with those laws has practical motivation. We wish to understand change in large part because we want to control it or—at the very least—to be prepared for its impact when it lies beyond our control. Francis Bacon rallied the "natural philosophers" of the seventeenth century around a simple equation that came to form the cornerstone of all subsequent science, pure and applied: *knowledge is power.* It is, indeed—but we have since learned that there are different kinds of knowledge and that there can be power in acceptance as well as in control. Moreover, there is an important difference between conceptual and practical knowledge, as is demonstrated by the fact that "knowing" the laws of motion expressed in the balance of a moving bicycle does not amount to actually "knowing how" to ride one.

Abuses of power are also easy to demonstrate, particularly in our own century. No child of the twenty-first century will, for example, be spared the consequences of the nuclear power developed in our era (Newcomb 1989). For the first time in human history, the regretfully real threat of planetary self-destruction has become an element of everyday existence.* The many inspiring achievements of the life sciences remain overshadowed by that threat, and the hopes we harbor for the generations to follow us have never been so clearly anchored in the urgent need for human change. Such change involves new ways of relating to one another, to ourselves, and to our shared planet, as well as new means of resolving human conflicts (many of which center on power). Unless and until our moral development becomes sufficient to balance our knowledge and power with wisdom and responsibility, all other potential developments will remain jeopardized.

This is a book about human change, and specifically the kinds of change usually sought in the context of psychotherapy and "self-development" projects. These kinds of change are, I believe, directly related to such earth-shaking issues as world peace. The principles and processes of human psychological change are not different inside or outside psychotherapy; and the demands of life, although individually experienced, are ultimately universal at some levels. Moreover, many of the issues that constitute the core concerns of the psychotherapy client are identical to those at the heart of all human relations—issues of power, for example, as well as the struggle after meaning, the reduction of suffering, and having enough peace and security to allow ample opportunities for recreation and development. Finally, I believe that the helping professions must address issues that link our individual lives and our collective responsibilities. The protection and development of cultures and societies that bear promise for human rights and world peace are all rooted in individual human conduct and the quality of our everyday lives "at home, up close and personal." In other words, personal change lies at the heart of collective change, and the interactions between individuals and their worlds are complexly reciprocal. Changes in either will trigger changes in the other, even when the persons involved are relatively unaware of or apparently uninterested in the larger spheres they influence.

SELF-FOCUS AND SOCIAL RESPONSIBILITY

Future accounts of human activity that look back at the twentieth century are likely to note that much more than "the times" were changing. The people were changing, too, one by one and in masses. Were there ever any doubt that human beings are capable of substantial psycholog-

---

*This dire possibility has emerged out of quests for and abuses of power, and can be averted only if we revise our ways of resolving conflicts, "raising" children, and integrating personal and planetary responsibilities (see Bandura 1986; Broughton and Honey 1988; Doctor et al. 1988; Ferencz and Keyes 1988; Jacobs 1989; Kramer 1989; Migdal 1988; Ornstein and Ehrlich 1989; Staub 1988; Walsh 1984, 1989; Watkins 1988; and Wollman 1985).

ical change, the events of the twentieth century would offer ample and diversified testimony. In no other period of history have so many aspects of human experience been so dramatically changed. We "moderns" experience ourselves and our worlds in ways far different from our ancestors. Many of those changes have involved vigorous assertions of basic human rights. The human rights movement, for example, was itself expressed in the suffrage, the civil rights, the women's, the senior citizens, and the child protection movements, as well as in the sexual and communications revolutions. The "human potential" movement helped link rights to responsibilities and encouraged the continuing exploration of human possibilities. Whatever else may be its legacy, the twentieth century will be remembered as an era of dramatic personal and planetary change.

On several levels, of course, we are all seeking—and achieving—some form of change every moment of our lives. Whether it be the transition from inhalation to exhalation or from one thought to another, we are each constantly engaged in the dynamic movements of a life in process. At the biological level, a moving balance of change and exchange are inherent in all life maintenance. We are forever "adjusting" to the shifting demands of each micromoment, demands that change with the flux of our worlds and with our never-ending adjustments to our own adjustments. Moreover—although their organizational continuity is maintained—the makeup of the cells in our bodies is totally "renovated" (physically reconstituted) many times in a lifetime (Rose 1988). It is, in fact, our incapacity to maintain that self-renewing process endlessly that forces each of us ultimately to deal with death (Becker 1973).

At the psychological level, our perennial pursuit of change is also readily apparent. The psychotherapy client and the seeker of personal development may seem the most obvious examples, but there is more change in our lives than most people appreciate. Research on daydreaming and fantasy, for example, indicates that our "thought segments"—the endlessly changing focus of our personal "streams of consciousness"—are often no more than ten seconds in length. We spend the vast proportion of our waking lifetime unconsciously absorbed in the changing patterns of our private experience (Csikszentmihalyi and Csikszentmihalyi 1988; Klinger 1971, 1977; Pope 1985; Pope and Singer 1978; Singer 1966; Singer and Pope 1978). Yet amidst this flux there is undeniable continuity and stability. Change processes are somehow inseparable from and essential to the order-preserving processes that permit us to function as we do. In other words, we cannot talk about human change processes without simultaneously addressing human stabilizing processes. As we shall see, many of the great debates in psychology have dealt with only partial acknowledgments of that complementarity.

Whether our interest lies more with psychological change or stabilization, it involves an inevitable amplification of self-study. Although psychological self-focus may not be universal, it has clearly become one of the cardinal characteristics of twentieth-century humanity. Living in the most complex and changing environment in Earth's history, we humans have exhibited a growing fascination with ourselves, our self-awareness, and our awareness of our awareness. As I shall elaborate in the next chapter, some of this reflexive interest has emerged from philosophical developments in hermeneutics (the study of interpretation), in phenomenology (the study of experience), and in the poststructuralist and the deconstructionist movements. Still other expressions of the "inward arc" of human inquiry have come from the sciences themselves and from science studies. Research on the "subjective side of science," for example, has shown psychological processes to be pervasive in all human inquiry. Likewise, these processes are themselves embedded in cultural and social contexts (Gholson et al. 1989; Knorr-Cetina 1981; Knorr-Cetina and Mulkay 1983; Latour and Woolgar 1979; Mahoney 1976, 1979a, 1987, 1989a; Mitroff 1974; Woolgar 1988). From astrophysics to quantum mechanics, scientists have increasingly encountered themselves as "variables" or "factors" in their own inquiry. The astronomer and the microbiologist may rarely notice their own reflection in the lens pieces of their respective instruments, but confrontations with self and the humbling limits of human knowing have become commonplace issues across the sciences.

But beyond the scientists, philosophers, and psychologists who encounter themselves in their studies and practice, the self-focus of the twentieth-century has involved large numbers of people from all walks of life: they also have become absorbed in the looms of their individual (and, for some, collective) minds. Indeed, interest in self-exploration and personal development has become so strong and pervasive that it has elicited harsh criticism from some social commentators (Bellah et al. 1985, 1987; Caporael et al. 1989; Doi 1985; Glasser 1972; Kolbenschlag 1988; Lowen 1983; Seligman 1989; Yankelovich 1981). Lamenting the self-preoccupation of the "me generation" and the human potential movement, these critics have argued that our "obsession" with self may well be one of the most disastrous phenomena of the century. In *The Culture of Narcissism,* for example, Christopher Lasch offered an exemplary scolding:

The growing despair of changing society, even of understanding it . . . underlies the cult of expanded consciousness, health, and personal "growth" so prevalent today.

After the political turmoil of the sixties, Americans have retreated to purely personal preoccupations. Having no hope of improving their lives in any of the ways that matter, people have convinced themselves that what matters is psychic self-improvement: getting in touch with their feelings, eating health food, taking lessons in ballet or belly-dancing, immersing themselves in the wisdom of the East, jogging, learning how to "relate," overcoming the "fear of pleasure." (1979, p. 29)

Lasch contends that this infatuation with our personal experience has produced little genuine self-understanding. Like other critics, he warns about the dangers of selfish preoccupation and private survivalism, both of which are portrayed as inimical to social involvement and civil responsibility. Despite these criticisms, however, our bookstores and supermarkets are flooded with manuals on how better to know, to be, and to nurture ourselves.

Although I share the concern of some observers regarding the possible erosion of "old-fashioned" values—for example, the importance of the family and human relatedness—I do not believe that our increasing self-focus is "bad for society," or necessarily incompatible with social sensitivities and commitments. Rather, with Socrates, I believe that "the unexamined life is not worth living," and, at the same time, that "the unlived life is not worth examining" (Kopp 1978, p. 72). Our attempts to better understand and to care for ourselves are basically healthy and valuable activities, but we are well advised to appreciate the differences between "knowing" and "being and becoming" ourselves.

Critiques of psychotherapy, self-study, and other attempts at self-development are often sprinkled with claims that such endeavors lack either scientific backing or genuine caring. Moreover, such critiques often portray the modern psychological pilgrim as a whining neurotic solely preoccupied with selfish interests. Their well-worded rhetoric rarely reflects much compassion for the pain and struggles of the person in process. I find such portrayals offensive and demeaning to the many individuals for whom self-examination (not to mention psychotherapy) is a courageous and commendable venture. As I shall document in the chapters to come, our relationships with ourselves—that is, our forever imperfect self-knowledge, self-appraisal, and active self-care— emerge out of and influence all other relations in our lives, especially those we consider intimate. I thus concur with Kopp's observation that "all of the significant battles are waged within the self" (1972, p. 224). I would add, however, that the domain of that self and the dynamics of waging or waiving those battles are themselves embedded in social and cultural foundations (Batson 1990; Hui and Villareal 1989).

What I am driving at here is that self-care and social responsibility are not separate domains. Moreover, both are imbued with ethical complexities. As Donald T. Campbell aptly noted in his presidential address to the American Psychological Association in 1975, we cannot afford to ignore the wisdom embedded in many of our social and cultural traditions. At the same time, however, we must be willing to venture risks that take us beyond dehumanizing and destructive dogmas. Although major strides have been made in reducing racism, sexism, and other affronts to human rights, prejudice and oppression are still all too common (Eliou 1988; Kolodny 1988; Komada 1988; Longino 1988; Prilleltensky 1989; Ragins and Sundstrom 1989; Rokeach and Ball-Rokeach 1989; Russo 1990; Sutherland 1988). At both individual and collective levels, some important battles have been won, but the wars are far from over. This last statement is, in fact, illustrative of the distance we have yet to travel: our language is still filled with metaphors of conflict and war at a time when we are in dire need of a rhetoric conducive to compassion and peace.

To summarize, our increasing self-focus is not, in my opinion, a regrettable phenomenon reflecting the erosion of social values and transpersonal commitments. I do not, on the other hand, deny the urgency of the issues we face in balancing our personal concerns and our public responsibilities. Human rights, personal well-being, and peaceful coexistence are each embedded in both individual and extended contexts:

The self is self only because it has a world, a structured universe, to which it belongs and from which it is separated at the same time. Self and world are correlated, and so are individualization and participation. . . . The courage to be is essentially always the courage to be as a part and the courage to be as oneself, in interdependence.

Separation is not estrangement, self-centeredness is not selfishness, self-determination is not sinfulness. (Tillich 1952, pp. 87–88)

It is therefore time to cease "jumping with moral indignation on every word in which the syllable 'self' appears" (p. 87). We are both part and whole; and, as Cris Williamson poignantly reminds us, we are both "the changer and the changed" (1975).

Despite occasional laments to the contrary, we are also active and responsible agents in the developments that characterize both our person and our planet. What we do is necessarily a reflection of what we value; and the latter, in turn, is often a humbling lesson in self-awareness. I believe that the kinds of changes we are seeking—human rights, personal and planetary peace, the reduction of suffering—are themselves a reflection of sweeping changes in our views of ourselves and our worlds (chapter 2). I also believe that psychotherapy and personal development projects hold great potential value for our times and those of our successors. In our private and often painful pursuits of change, all humans participate in a project that reaches far beyond the boundaries of our individual lives. It is to those lives and to that project that I address this book.

BASIC QUESTIONS ABOUT HUMAN CHANGE

The fundamental questions that guide all inquiries into human change fall into two broad and overlapping families: questions about the nature of change in general, and those about the principles and processes of human change in particular. I shall deal only briefly with the former; the latter will consume the remainder of this book.

The Nature of Change

The concept of change is so fundamental and pervasive in modern thought that it often escapes our scrutiny. We casually speak of changing our clothes, changing light bulbs, changing weather, and changing minds, all such utterances sharing the same term but diverging significantly in their intended meanings. We often talk about change as if there were little to explain or understand. As we shall see, however, our conceptualization of change has never been so central to our understanding and conduct of science. The recent escalation of interest in the study of order, chaos, and complexity in all sciences is testimony to the importance of those ideas (appendix E). We are only now beginning to appreciate the complexity and dynamics of change processes in even the simplest of "open systems," and our engineered technologies for producing human change have never before seemed so utterly naïve and oversimplifying.

The earliest recorded writings on the nature of change are scattered across several centuries in the first millenium B.C. In Western civilization the pivotal writings were those of two pre-Socratic Greek philosophers. Parmenides (c. 510–450 B.C.) is perhaps best known for his assertion that there is no change (either in ourselves or the universe). He maintained that all change is an illusion concealing the fundamentally timeless, permanent, and static (fixed) nature of reality. This view was opposite to that proposed by his contemporary, Heraclitus (c. 535–475 B.C.), who argued that stability and permanence are an illusion and that there is nothing but change (again, in ourselves and in the universe at large). It was Heraclitus who posed the paradox that "one cannot step into the same river twice": the reason is that both the river and the individual will have changed in the meantime, if only by their having once come together. According to Heraclitus, "all is flux." He was the first Western thinker to suggest the primacy of opposing forces or essential tensions in the generation and maintenance of dynamic stabilities. Heraclitus compared this "unity of opposites" with the attunement of tensions in the bow and the lyre. This idea, which was then more prevalent in Asian thinking, would later find expression in the dialectics of Hegel, the theories of dynamic equilibration (balance) developed by Johann Herbart and Jean Piaget, and the multiple theories of "opponent processes" in biology, perception, and human motivation.

Beyond their own ideological opposition, Parmenides and Heraclitus are noteworthy for their joint assertion that everyday experience—especially as revealed by the senses—is not an accurate reflection of reality. This need to mistrust the senses had already been proposed by Pythagoras (570–500 B.C.) and would be further elaborated by Plato (427–347 B.C.) and his followers (chapter 2). Meanwhile, however, that same general idea had long since been formalized by Asian writers. According to them, the experiences of the body and the "outer mind" (including the senses) are inferior and illusory relative to those of more refined (and spiritual) "inward" reflections. The earliest and most influential Asian work on the nature of change was the *I Ching* (or Book of Changes), which is one of the classics of Confucian thought and a central expression of the religious systems of Taoism and Buddhism. The essence of the *I Ching* is said to have been discovered on the back of a tortoise by the legendary emperor Fu Hsi (twenty-fourth century B.C.), but the book is thought to have been written much later. It is, in fact, possible that the dynamic "opposite tensions" perspective developed by Heraclitus may have reflected this much-earlier view in which nothing is static and two complementary, opposite forces (the passive *yin* and the active *yang*) create a dynamic and developing whole (the *Tao*).

These early inquiries into the fundamental nature of change are particularly noteworthy for their joint recognition that contrast and opposition are central considerations. That later Asian and European philosophers would carry that insight in opposite directions (chapter 2) serves only to reiterate its basic assertion. Aristotle, for example, would base his influential theory of logic on the requirement of self-consistency, while later Asian thinkers would acknowledge the centrality of paradox and (apparent) self-contradiction in the nature of enlightened knowing. A second and related insight from these early divergences of thought was the acknowledgment that change and stability are *co-dependent* concepts: one cannot discuss one without the other; they are integrally relative. Thus, one cannot hope to understand the processes of human psychological change without simultaneously addressing the processes of stabilization. Order and disorder are maintained and changed by the same principled dynamics.

Principles and Processes of Human Change

Three fundamental questions lie at the heart of all that we now know as psychotherapy, counseling, and education:

1. Can humans change?
2. Can humans help humans change?
3. Are some forms of help better than others?

The diverse responses to these questions from scientific theories and research constitute the central theme of this book. The third question—the issue of how best to help—assumes a positive response to the first two. And any affirmative answer to all three (no matter how cautious in tone) necessarily invites additional questions: for example, by inserting *how* or *why* at the beginning of the main questions, by questioning the limits and kinds of change, by asking how change is experienced, and, ultimately, by pondering the practical implications of our inquiries (what should we do in parenting, education, psychotherapy, and professional training?).

These issues have pervaded ideological battles between various schools of thought in psychology. The first question, for example, is technically known as the issue of human *plasticity*, or the human capacity to change. Prior to recent work demonstrating considerable flexibility among older persons, the *funnel hypothesis* was a widely accepted representation of the relationship between age and psychological flexibility across a human life. Figure 1.1 offers a graphic depiction of the relentless narrowing of plasticity previously thought to be associated with time and experience. According to this view, living, learning, and aging involve an inescapable contraction of possibilities over the lifetime. We now know

Figure 1.1   Funnel Theory

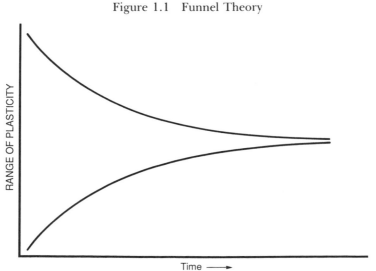

SOURCE: © 1989 M. J. Mahoney

that the funnel theory is a presumptuous insult to the lifespan potential for human psychological development (Alexander and Langer 1989; Baltes 1987; Bandura 1982; Brandtstädter 1989; Bühler 1935; Dacey 1989; Frenkel 1936; Hareven and Masaoka 1988; Heckhausen et al. 1989; Honzik 1984; Hooper and Moulins 1989; Kliegl, Smith, and Baltes 1989; Lerner 1984; Levinson 1986; Neugarten 1977; Piolat 1988; Purves 1988; Woodruff-Pak 1989).

Two other responses to the question of how much change is possible offered more divergent conceptualizations of human plasticity. In the tenets of radical behaviorism, a skilled and powerful "environmental engineer" could exhibit virtually infinite "behavior control" over an organism at all points in its "reinforcement history." Hence John B. Watson's infamous arrogance about the malleability of the human form:

Give me a dozen healthy infants, well-formed, and my own specified world to bring them up in and I'll guarantee to take any one at random and train him to become any type of specialist I might select—doctor, lawyer, artist, merchant-chief and yes, even beggar-man and thief, regardless of his talents, penchants, tendencies, abilities, vocations, and race of his ancestors. (1924, p. 104)

As discussed in chapter 3, the decline of radical behaviorism may well have been accelerated by such sweeping and readily falsified claims as these.

Another well-known response to the question of human plasticity was that offered by orthodox psychoanalysis. According to Freud, humans are most psychologically malleable during their first six years and, to a lesser degree, during adolescence. For the most part, however, he believed that personality patterns are formed primarily by experiences in early psychosexual development, and that dramatic personality change in adulthood is rare. The contrasting portrayals of radical behaviorism and orthodox psychoanalysis are illustrated in figure 1.2. In recent surveys involving behaviorists and psychoanalysts, these different assumptions about plasticity have been reflected in different opinions about the difficulty of psychological change.

As it turns out, the question of human plasticity is much more complex than the foregoing responses have acknowledged. Indeed, modern studies of human plasticity go far beyond the traditional and simplifying questions of whether and how much change is possible. More interesting questions have emerged: What changes when a person changes? What are the forms of change? Are there basic patterns and processes? What are the general principles of change? And what can and should be done with refined knowledge about all of the above? For the most part, these more advanced questions have emerged out of a growing consensus that human plasticity is formidable, albeit finite:

Figure 1.2   Human Plasticity as Viewed by Orthodox Behaviorism and Psychoanalysis

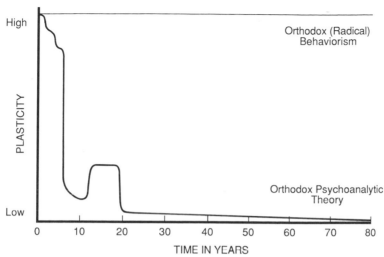

SOURCE: © 1989 M. J. Mahoney

Human beings are made neither of glass that breaks in the slightest ill wind nor of steel that stands defiantly in the face of devastating hurricanes. Rather . . . humans . . . bend with environmental pressures, resume their shapes when the pressures are relieved, and are unlikely to be permanently misshapen by transient experiences. When bad environments are improved, people's adaptations improve. Human beings are resilient and responsive to the advantages their environments provide. Even adults are capable of improved adaptations through learning, although any individual's improvement depends on that person's responsiveness to learning opportunities. (Scarr 1982, p. 853)

This viewpoint places considerable emphasis on the capacities and the agency of individuals, who not only survive but also select and transform the social and physical environments that form their medium of exchange.

Also relevant here are technical points (see chapter 6 and appendix F) about the phenomenon of *neoteny*, which can be loosely defined as a lifelong childlike flexibility and resilience. Indeed, the human abilities to survive and to thrive are inherently related to our developmental flexibility. In human evolution, we "purchased" that flexibility at the price of extensive and extended sensitivity to the social and cultural dimensions of our worlds. Cultural evolution and the transmission of (tacit) beliefs and skills across generations have had far greater significance for human development than have the genetic changes that led to the human body as we know it. This point is most dramatically illustrated in studies of early psychological development in the context of a primary caregiver (chapter 7), which, in turn, emphasize the significance of the second and third basic questions about human change.

CHANGING VIEWS OF HUMAN CHANGE

Psychologists' views of human change are themselves in the process of changing. These changes are, I believe, part of an even broader and deeper shift in the sciences and humanities. As I discuss in chapter 2, we are in the midst of a pivotal period in the history of ideas, and the directions we take (or fail to take) in the coming years have special significance for the quality of life that many generations to come will enjoy or endure. In the more circumscribed domain of psychotherapy and theories of psychological development, some of those changes are readily apparent. The theoretical orientations of U.S. psychologists have, for example, changed dramatically over the last three decades. Figure 1.3 summarizes the results of fifteen surveys published between 1953 and 1988.* The apparent decline of psychodynamic perspectives is noteworthy (Reiser 1989), as is the widely fluctuating popularity of eclectic perspectives and the recent emergence of cognitive psychotherapies. There are many possible interpretations of these data, of course; but their variability suggests that some of the most striking evidence of human change may come from the reports of professional change agents.

This point is corroborated by the results of a recent survey on psychotherapists' views of basic principles of human development and optimal practices in psychotherapy (Mahoney et al. 1989). Debates about the relative effectiveness of the various psychotherapies have traditionally highlighted their differences, but the findings from this study suggested

---

*This figure is based on the following surveys: Barrom, Shadish, and Montgomery 1988; Garfield and Kurtz 1976a; Goldschmid et al. 1969; Kelly 1961; Kelly et al. 1978; Lubin 1962; Mahoney and Craine 1988; Norcross and Prochaska 1982; Norcross, Prochaska, and Gallagher, in press; Norcross, Strausser, and Faltus 1988; Prochaska, Nash, and Norcross 1986; Prochaska and Norcross 1983a; Shaffer 1953; Smith 1982; and Watkins et al. 1986. The results of four other surveys were not included due to small sample sizes or emphases on occupational roles rather than theoretical orientations per se (Beitman and Maxim 1984; Marmor 1975; Strauss et al. 1964; Wogan and Norcross 1985). When two or more surveys appeared in the same year, their results were averaged. Since, regrettably, these surveys were comprised predominantly of clinical psychologists in the United States, they may not reflect changes in other countries, cultures, and professional specializations.

In figure 1.3, psychodynamic (PA) included views labeled psychoanalytic, neo-analytic, Jungian, Adlerian, neo-Freudian, and transactional analysis. Behavioral (B) perspectives included behavior therapy, behavior modification, and learning theory. Humanistic (H) respondents included existential, Rogerian, client-centered, Gestalt, Frommian, and nondirective subtypes. Cognitivists (C) included adherents to cognitive behavior modification, logotherapy, rational-emotive therapy (RET), and reality therapy. Systems (S) respondents included those associated with family therapy, Sullivanian, and communications approaches.

Figure 1.3   Primary Theoretical Orientations of U.S. Clinical Psychologists

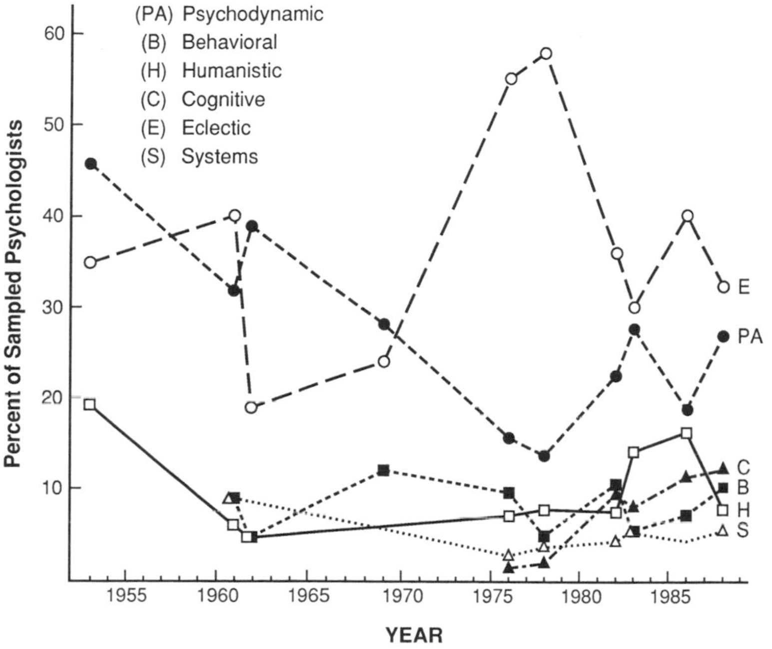

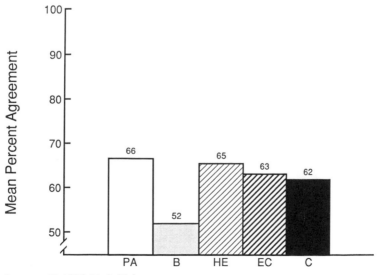

SOURCE: © 1989 M. J. Mahoney

Figure 1.4   Difficulty of Change Estimated by U.S. Clinical Psychologists of Different Theoretical Orientations

SOURCE: © 1989 M. J. Mahoney

substantial areas of agreement across theoretical orientations. Behaviorists did set themselves apart from other practitioners by rating psychological change as less difficult than did their nonbehavioral colleagues (figure 1.4). In an interesting exception to this pattern, behaviorists who reported having been in therapy themselves were less sanguine about the ease of effecting significant personal change. Also of interest was the strong agreement across theoretical orientations that such change generally entails the active exploration of novel experiences on the part of the changing individual (figure 1.5). Regardless of their theoretical leanings, therapists also agreed that psychological development involves changes in the self system (figure 1.6), and that such changes are facilitated by a safe and caring human relationship. Finally, there was strong agreement that optimal psychotherapy involves encouragement toward self-examination (figure 1.7).

Whatever the nuances of meaning that might be attributed to these illustrations, it seems clear that more than the times are changing. Like the humans they strive to understand, psychologists are also exhibiting substantial capacities for change. For psychotherapists, of course, this reflexivity is still further amplified. As the socially sanctioned agents of change, psychotherapists bear unique privileges and responsibilities in their enactments of that professional role. A central assertion of this book is that our professional aspirations in the realm of human helping and our

Figure 1.5   Perceived Incidence of Novel Exploratory Activity in Psychological Development

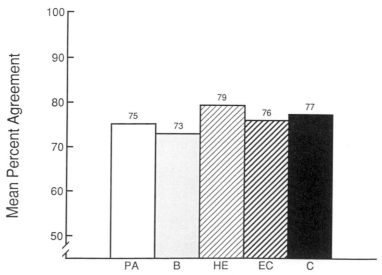

SOURCE: © 1989 M. J. Mahoney

Figure 1.6   Perceived Self System Change in Psychological Development

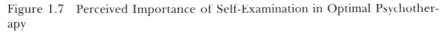

Figure 1.7   Perceived Importance of Self-Examination in Optimal Psychotherapy

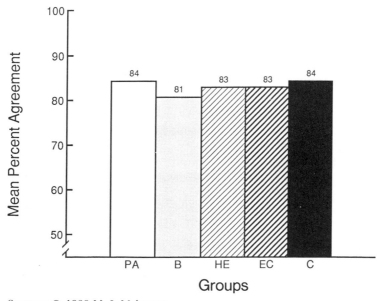

efforts to facilitate development in those we serve are inseparable from
our assumptions about human change processes. Since many of those
assumptions lie deeply buried in our cultural, familial, and personal histories, it is important that we continue to examine and expand our awareness of all three.

ANSWERING THE BASIC QUESTIONS ABOUT HUMAN CHANGE

Throughout this book, greater emphasis is placed on the quality and
continuation of our quests and questions than on any concrete arrivals
or simple answers. Still, the theory and research I hereafter survey yield
a qualified yes in response to each of the basic questions.

Can Humans Change?

Yes, humans can change—but doing so is much more difficult than many
theories have admitted. This is, in fact, one of the important points of
convergence across contemporary schools of thought in psychotherapy.
Significant psychological change is rarely rapid or easy. There are also
limits to how much and how quickly an individual can change without
jeopardizing his or her psychological integrity (that is, sense of self and
reality). What I shall term *core processes*—those involved in a person's
experience of reality (order), self (identity), value (valence), and power
(control)—are much more resistant to change than are more peripheral
aspects of that person. The self system, for example, is central to all
aspects of an individual's experience and yet is particularly resistant to
rapid or dramatic change. That resistance is not, however, an enemy or
obstacle in the therapeutic enterprise. In contrast to negative models of
resistance, I shall argue for a *self-protective theory of resistance* in which the
processes associated with reluctance to change are shown to reflect the
central importance of personal coherence (systemic integrity) in living
systems. It is natural and, indeed, healthy for an individual to resist
moving too far and too quickly beyond his or her familiar sense of self
(even when that self-sense is painful). When this self-protective tendency
is respected and worked with, rather than against, the consequences for
the individual are more likely to be positive and developmentally progressive.

The processes and experience of psychological change will also be
shown to reflect complex, nonlinear dynamics. In other words, such
change is not a simple and smooth accumulation of small changes, yield-
ing a neatly predictable outcome. Rather, human change reflects a dy-

namic and "punctuated" equilibrium in which phases and forces of change alternate and intermingle with phases and forces of stabilization. In my discussions of the nature of change, I will repeatedly touch on the dynamic, developmental processes that make up the "moving balance" of a life in progress. Emotionality and episodes of disorganization and experienced disorder will be destigmatized in these discussions, and I shall invite a deeper appreciation for the role of these dynamics in life-span personal development.

Finally, I shall repeatedly emphasize the need to acknowledge and respect individual differences. Although the principles and processes of human psychological change are universal at some level of abstraction, the particulars of each individual life in process are truly unique. Hence, all generalizations about psychotherapy are necessarily tentative and conjectural. There is no single system or therapy that is "best" for everyone. Moreover, the ultimate effects of any engineered change (planned intervention) are never certain and never fully knowable beforehand.

Can Humans Help Humans Change?

Yes, humans can help humans change—but they can also hinder such change, particularly when the change agent occupies a position of relative power and the helping relationship involves strong emotional attachments. On the negative side, the power and primacy of human relations will be most apparent in cases of early, intense, and repeated psychological trauma, most often experienced as neglect, rejection, and abuse. Here I shall argue strongly for the importance of primary prevention and responsible parenting and education in the ultimate improvement of life quality. On the positive side, here also I shall emphasize the critical importance of human relationships in helping. The optimal therapeutic relationship is secure, developmentally flexible, and fundamentally caring. Such a relationship is also sensitively tuned to the individuals involved, so that a special human context is created—a context in and from which the client can explore and experiment with old and new ways of experiencing self, world (including other people), and their possible relationships.

The importance of active exploratory behavior on the part of the changing individual will be a central point here. As many literatures document, there can be no real learning without novelty—that is, without a challenge to or elaboration of what has become familiar. Novel experiences are rarely sought when an individual feels anxious, vulnerable, or depressed, but a caring human relationship can provide what John Bowlby (1988) calls a "secure base" from which to explore. In and from such a base, the individual can be encouraged to learn and explore in self-caring and socially responsible ways.

Are Some Forms of Help Better than Others?

Yes, some forms of help are better than others—but we are just now beginning to understand some of the complexities inherent in that question. Are professionally trained helpers better than nonprofessionals? Are some forms of therapy more effective than others with certain problems or individuals? And what, after all, do we mean by "better"? How, for example, do we reconcile the frequently different change goals of the client, the psychotherapist, and various subcultures and societies?

In considering responses to this question, I shall address the issue of prime movers, or first causes, in human experience. Until recently psychological theorists and researchers believed that human experience could be neatly divided into three parts: thought, feeling, and action (figure 1.8). They have disagreed vigorously, however, about the relationships among these realms, and a substantial portion of their professional energies have been invested in defending or attacking a particular pattern of relationship. The major theories on the topic have basically been *prime mover* arguments, asserting that one of the three domains exerts primary influence over the other two. Behaviorists have favored behavior as the primary force in human experience and argued that changes in motoric activity produce changes in attitudes and affect. Cognitivists have rallied around the primary power of thought and argued that changes in thinking produce changes in both behavior and feeling. The third group—variously called "humanists," "experientialists," and "evocative" therapists—have asserted the primacy of emotionality in driving the other two realms.

Not surprisingly, each group has endorsed a different emphasis in

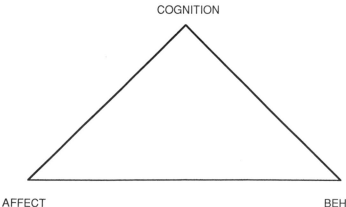

Figure 1.8   Three Domains of Human Experience

COGNITION

AFFECT   BEHAVIOR

Source: © 1989 M. J. Mahoney

psychological services. Behaviorists have emphasized action, cognitivists have been partial to insight and reflection, and humanists have encouraged emotional experience and expression. Only in the last decade, however, have there been genuine dialogues among the rival groups and a growing appreciation for the complex interdependence of their respective realms of preference. It has taken psychology a long time to put the person back together, and we are just now beginning to sense the complexity and individuality of human experience. Moreover, only recently have we begun to recognize and value the contributions of each of the major theoretical perspectives. With increasing dialogues across old ideological fences, there is under way a welcome mending and integration that bodes well for the refinement of both our understanding and our professional services.

Although our knowledge in the area of human helping remains rudimentary, there are now some warranted generalizations that can tentatively guide our training and practice. This book is an attempt to identify and harvest the lessons of science as they bear on service and the lessons of clinical experience as they bear on theory and research. Part I offers a conceptual introduction and historical context for understanding the expanse of theory and research that deal with human learning and development. Part II offers integrative reviews of the existing literature on processes and principles of order and disorder in human experience. In part III, I shall venture to outline some general principles bearing on human psychological development and optimal psychotherapeutic practice. I shall conclude on a note sounded here at this book's beginning: namely, that our relationships with ourselves critically affect the quality of life we experience, and that that quality emerges from and returns to influence our relations with others. One's ability to relate to other human beings is based on one's experiences of and relationships with one's "innermost" self; and these, in turn, grow out of one's most intimate relations with other people. Tolerance, respect, forgiveness, compassion, and heartfelt affection are all made more or less possible by a dynamic reciprocity of influence between individuals and their "care sharers."

I shall discuss this crucial connection between self and others in my final emphasis on the psychotherapist's needs, rights, and responsibilities to seek ever-richer qualities of personal self-knowledge, self-affirmation, and active self-care. The personal life of the psychotherapist is, indeed, a microcosm of psychological complexity, filled with a host of burdens and blessings, and characterized by precious privileges and sometimes-overwhelming responsibilities (chapter 13). The optimally helpful psychotherapist, I shall conclude, is generously aware of those complexities and deeply committed to taking good care of that valuable human self that presumes to counsel other selves in their own lifelong becomings.

2

A Brief History of Ideas

All history is the history of thought.   —Robin G. Collingwood

Written documents show that the human mind has found itself fascinating for at least the last three millennia. The evolution of our thinking about the world clearly reflects a deepening reflection on *how* we know, and we have finally begun to study ourselves as intensely as we have studied our surrounding worlds. This increasing self-examination emanates, at least in part, from an emergent awareness that, as Friedrich Hayek, Nobel laureate in economics, tersely put it, "much that we believe to know about the external world is, in fact, knowledge about ourselves" (1952*b*, pp. 6–7). Herein lies the relevance of philosophical issues for theory, research, and practice in psychology.

PHILOSOPHY AND THE QUESTIONING PROCESS

As a field of study, the history of ideas has been until recently a rarefied source of fascination for relatively few specialists. Moreover, only in the last few decades have scholars come to acknowledge the extent to which all writings about history involve extensive interpretation (Collingwood 1972; Robinson 1981; Weimer 1974*b*, 1974*c*). It is common to find the same events rendered differently by different writers. The past is seldom portrayed identically by conservatives and liberals, for instance, or by naturalists and mystics. For this reason, *historiography*—the act of writing about the past—must be distinguished from the concept of *history* itself, that abstractly perfect record of what actually took place in the past. Since a perfectly objective historiography is impossible, every simplification being—as Alfred North Whitehead (1957) once commented—necessarily an oversimplification, one should consult both original sources and other possible interpretations of our collective conceptual past (Dennett 1984; Durant 1926; Durant and Durant 1935–75; Hamlyn 1987; Hoffding 1900; Hofstadter 1979; Hofstadter and Dennett 1981; Langer 1967, 1972, 1982; Langer 1980; Onians 1951; Reese 1980; Robinson 1981; Russell 1945; Sahakian 1976; Stone 1988; Wiener 1974).

Philosophilia and Philosophobia

The word *philosophy* literally means "love of knowledge," and there seems to be little disagreement that the heart of philosophy is inquiry—active, exploratory questioning. Nevertheless, reactions to and interest in philosophy are not uniformly positive. There are, of course, a few "philosophiles" who exhibit reverent regard and insatiable appetite for both classical and modern philosophy. At the same time, however, there are many more "philosophobics," people who avoid or abhor anything remotely associated with reflective studies. Mere mention of the word *philosophy* may motivate them to skip a chapter, avoid a book, or nod off in resolute lack of interest—a regrettable and costly pattern of avoidance.

All modern sciences are the unmistakable descendants of what was once a relatively undifferentiated love of study called philosophy. Beyond the sciences, our modern viewpoints in aesthetics, ethics, economics, hermeneutics, the humanities and liberal arts, logic, rhetoric, and sundry other areas all have their roots in the history of ideas and, therefore, in philosophy. As different disciplines carved out their own identities from the background of philosophy, however, many exhibited an intentional distancing and disdain for their conceptual parent. Philosophers themselves have made some of the most damaging remarks about their own endeavors. The Roman philosopher Cicero, for example, remarked that "there is nothing so absurd that it has not been said by philosophers"; and twenty centuries later, Bertrand Russell concluded that "philosophy . . . has made greater claims and achieved fewer results than any other branch of learning" (both cited in Kline 1985, p. 3).

The most common complaint of those who have been vigorous in their attacks on philosophy has been that some philosophers obscure rather than illuminate the matters they are investigating. Its critics essentially agree with the physicist R. C. Tolman's caricature of philosophy as "the systematic misuse of a terminology specially invented for that purpose" (cited in Dukas and Hoffman 1979, p. 106). More often than can be ignored, philosophy has tolerated and even glorified obfuscation and irrelevance. Its "signal-to-noise ratio" has been pitiful at times, and its practical value has rarely been explored. Despite its excesses and eccentricities, philosophy remains a vital fascination for significant portions of each new generation. We long to know, and our longing has recently found us confronting the paradox that knowledge, knowing, and the individual knower are inseparable aspects of an endless pursuit. As we shall see, knowledge is neither a disembodied collection of information nor a possession. From the perspective developed here, knowing is inescapably open-ended, dynamic, and simultaneously personal and collective.

In Defense of Reflective Inquiry

Philosophy permeates the living of all lives, whether consciously or otherwise; and its relevance should therefore require little defense. (There are several readable overviews of philosophy and the history of ideas [Boorstin 1983; Durant 1926; Stone 1988].) Psychologists should also be aware of the fact that their discipline evolved out of eighteenth- and nineteenth-century philosophy (Curti 1974; Hilgard 1987; Long 1974; Mueller 1974). This fact is, though unequivocal, often overlooked or diminished by some modern psychologists (Bartley 1987*b;* Blackmore 1979). A recent study by the psychologist L. Zusne (1987) offers ample documentation of the extensive debt psychology owes to philosophy. In analyzing 16 U.S. and 8 European books on the history of psychology published since 1950, Zusne found that on average 60 percent of the pages in those books was devoted to individual scholars, and that 190 individuals accounted for almost 86 percent of the total pages devoted to such personages. In a further analysis of his data, I found that close to 40 percent of those "most important" 190 individuals in the history of psychology were, in fact, philosophers. Table 2.1 lists the 13 most extensively discussed philosophers in those 24 texts. Their ideas and those of their less visible colleagues have significantly influenced all modern psychological theories and therapies.

Recent developments in the physical, biological, and social sciences have also demonstrated that the interface of philosophy and psychology is at the "cutting edge" of our understanding. The recent (albeit belated) convergence of epistemology (theories of knowing), cognitive science, and science studies is a case in point. The essence of that convergence reflects an acknowledgment that an adequate understanding of human knowledge requires an understanding of both the human knower and the human learning/knowing processes. Psychology is essential to philosophy; and both are central to developments in all sciences, past, present, and future.

The philosophy I am talking about here is not a cold, antiseptic expression of logical analysis or a technical literature to be digested by the

Table 2.1   Philosophers
Influential in the History of
Psychology

Name	Citation Index[a]
Aristotle	107.64
Descartes	53.36
Plato	45.76
Locke	37.44
Hume	34.08
Kant	32.16
Augustine	30.24
Leibniz	27.37
Berkeley	25.76
Herbart	23.69
Aquinas	22.86
Brentano	20.64
Spinoza	20.52

[a]The Citation Index reflects the simple product of the number of texts in which an individual was discussed (12–24) and the average percentage of pages in that text on which they or their work was discussed.

intellect. It is, rather, an active, exploratory, self-examining attitude that embodies a passionate commitment to knowing. Such a philosophy is the "mission" to which Socrates devoted and sacrificed his life. It is not a collection of words or even a system of explicit beliefs, but an ongoing integration of thinking, feeling, and action. "The magic of real philosophy is the magic of the specifically human act of self-questioning—of being in front of the question of oneself" (Needleman 1982, p. 13).

A core assertion of this book is that our private and personal theories about ourselves and our worlds lie at the heart of all of our experience. *The moment-to-moment processes that constitute personal experience are themselves inseparable from and dramatically influenced by our active personal knowing processes.* In other words, there is a powerful and synergistic relationship between the quality of our life experiences and the structures and processes of our private and predominantly tacit (nonverbal, unconscious) theories of ourselves, our worlds, and their possible interactions. Our private assumptions and ingrained beliefs constitute everpresent anticipations and constraints on what and how we experience. As we shall see, personal knowing processes are themselves complex and dynamic, endlessly constructing, perpetuating, and revising our personal realities.

To understand what is meant by a *personal reality*, one must first reflect on the sense of contrast, if not contradiction, in the pairing of these terms. Reality is generally considered a public, "out there" realm comprised of "things" (the Latin *res* means "thing," and the early Indo-European word *rei* means "property"). In general use, then, reality is definitely not personal. Likewise, it is unusual to employ the plural form of reality, since plurality flies in the face of there being only one *real* (genuine, stable) reality. Nevertheless, there are as many (experienced) realities as there are individuals, and these personal or private realities lie at the heart of all human experience. Indeed, those who teach, parent, or counsel are, with or without their own awareness, attempting to facilitate changes in the personal realities of their respective apprentices. We are all—literally—living, embodied theories of ourselves and our worlds, and this was true long before our "higher" intellectual processes came into either being or fashion. Our theories of self and life develop spontaneously in our efforts to survive and adapt. Most important, those efforts frequently involve thought, felt, and enacted interactions with other human beings, and it is in the context of our relationships with others that these "assumptive worlds" and "working models" are most formatively influenced.

At the personal and practical level, the assertion that personal knowing processes are integral to personal experience also implies that changes in the quality, the meaning, or the "movement" of a life are necessarily associated with changes in the ordering or organizing processes that actively maintain or elaborate that life. These processes are central to personal knowing and tend to insulate us from dramatic changes in our experiences of self and world. Metaphorically, we are both unwitting guards *and* prisoners of our tacit theories of what life is and how best to negotiate it. As much as we may wish or work to be different, we are naturally resistant—as is vividly illustrated in clinical literature—to life developments that take us too far or too quickly beyond the person or reality we currently define as our own. It is therefore not accidental that significant personal change is often a slow and challenging process. As later discussions will illuminate, there is unmistakable evolutionary wisdom in our caution and ambivalence in renovating the delicate heart of our island of being. It is in the realm of our personal ordering processes that our experiential continuity is maintained or modified. Moreover, *all significant psychological changes involve changes in personal meanings, and those meanings reflect the dynamic interdependence of our thoughts, feelings, and actions.*

Finally, all theories of psychological change are fundamentally theories of learning, and all theories of learning ultimately entail a theory of knowing. As we shall see, all knowing is active, embodied, and fundamentally emotional. Significant changes in a life in process are imbued with episodes of extreme affective intensity and overall (systemic) disorganization. Those who would counsel on the complexities, choices, and struggles of the living of a life can offer optimal help only to the extent that they appreciate—at both conceptual and experiential levels—the operation of such processes in each unique person-in-process. Besides the individual circumstances and experiences that shape how we think, act, and feel about ourselves and our worlds, our philosophies reflect the unmistakable legacy of hundreds of thousands of years of our ancestors' efforts. Their experiences, and the ideas they offered by way of ordering those experiences, constitute a valuable heritage in our own efforts.

FORMATIVE BEGINNINGS IN THE QUEST FOR KNOWLEDGE

The burning questions about knowledge and human existence have not changed much over the centuries, although the many answers offered have recently begun to assume novel forms. Taken together, *our philosophical heritage chronicles an abiding quest for order and systems of order,* as well as for the power, meaning, and purpose such order might convey (Foucault 1965, 1970; Frankl 1959, 1978).*

Prehistoric Mentation

The history of ideas is a history not just of conceptual abstractions, but rather of human *activity* related to understanding and influencing the order and disorder of daily experience, personal and collective. Likewise, although the emergence of spoken and written languages literally transformed some of our ways of thinking about the world, it would be naïve to assume that humans did not experience "ideas" before they were able to express them. This prehistoric mentation played an undeniable role in forming our earliest conjectures about who and where we are (not to mention why and other such queries). Unfortunately, our current understanding of such mentation is crude, and may ever remain so. The idea that we, as modern humans, can fully comprehend the evolution of our own ideas is itself preposterous. The leaps we have made over millions of years of evolution have undoubtedly transformed much of the process (as well as the content) of our moment-to-moment experience, so that our twentieth-century verbal hemispheres can only hope to see "through

*Regrettably, the history of Western philosophy has all too often been rendered as the history of (all) philosophy. More often than not, it has been the history of philosophy as rendered by male Caucasians in the western hemisphere. For informative overviews of the extensive contributions and main themes of Asian philosophy, see volume I in Durant and Durant 1935–75, as well as Fischer-Schreiber et al. 1989; Murphy and Murphy 1968; Radhakrishnan and Moore 1957; Tomlin 1963; Wiener 1974; and Yu-lan 1934. For discussions of gender issues in epistemology, see Anderson and Zinsser 1988; Belenky et al. 1986; Keller 1983, 1985; J.R. Martin 1989; and Tuana 1989.

a glass darkly" the vestiges and legacies of our own conceptual development.

The first scholar to recognize this point was Giambattista Vico, a professor of rhetoric at the University of Naples in the early part of the eighteenth century. Lamenting the "conceit of scholars" who had assumed that human thought had always been formal and formalizable, Vico noted that "we can now scarcely understand and cannot at all imagine how the first men thought" (1948 [1725] p. 265). He puzzled over how human mentation might have emerged out of animal intelligence, and concluded that the cardinal feature of human thought was its ability to transcend immediate reality: that is, its ability to develop means for suspending or (symbolically) altering present time and space. Anticipating developments that are now on the cutting edge of twenty-first-century thinking, Vico also emphasized the *embodiment of mind,* which he meant literally:

The first men lived in a world of "real words," of the passionate action of the bodies of nature moving in relation to each other. . . . Vico asks us to imagine a beginning point of human experience in which all was body and bodily motion, in which meaning was an action between bodies, and in which human thought was nothing more than the bodily act of sensation. There is no mere sensation for Vico. Sensation is the act that underlies or is the first moment in any act of knowing. It is a necessary act through which the mind initiates for itself what is to be known or thought. (Verene 1981, pp. 84–85)

Vico believed that the earliest humans created order in their experience. In words that anticipated Jean Piaget two centuries later, he said that "to know" is "to make" *(facere).* Given that we fabricate the experiential worlds we inhabit, it is little wonder, he said, that those worlds appear stable. Some of our favorite and most formative fabrications are conveyed in the fables and myths that continue to fascinate us to this day. Indeed, Vico suggested that mythology should be the first science because myths express the most primitive and powerful human constructions of worldly order. With his embodiment of cognition and emphasis on active, constructive processes in the creation and maintenance of realities, it is not coincidental that Vico is credited as being the founding father of constructivist psychology (chapter 5).*

*Outside psychology, Vico is remembered primarily for his founding of the philosophy of history and, more specifically, for his cyclical theory of history. Parallel to the pendular oscillations of life proposed by Machiavelli *(corsi e ricorsi,* course and recourse), Vico suggested that human history reflects an endless repetition of three "ages" of mental development. In the first, the "age of gods," humans ordered their lives through divine rules, which were primarily conveyed by myths and enacted in the strict polarization of the sacred and the profane. In the "age of heroes," the myths began to portray and glorify a superhuman hero, often expressed as aristocracy, who was capable of at least surviving skirmishes with the gods. The third and final stage of mental development, according to Vico, was the "age of men," in which supernatural forces give way to expressions of human agency and,

The First Axial Period

Although it was not formally recognized until the nineteenth century, most observers of human history now acknowledge that a profound change appeared in human mentation sometime around the sixth century B.C. The nature and causes of that change are still a matter of scholarly discussion, but there is general consensus on its appearance and apparent significance. As Vico had noted, the earliest human accounts of nature and life were dominated by mystical, mythical, and supernatural metaphors. Many of those same metaphors remain powerfully active today. What happened in the sixth century B.C. was not so much the overthrow of those primitive beliefs, but rather their transformation into two major and divergent paths of conceptualization: organized religion and rational philosophy. In a period of less than two centuries, humans in Europe and Asia independently founded the first world religions, Buddhism and Zoroastrianism, and thus laid the groundwork for Islam, Christianity, and other religions that would follow.

At the same time, the earliest Greek philosophers—including Thales and Pythagoras—were drawing attention to the power of the intellect and reason. The invitation, from both the religions and the philosophies, was to look inward and reflect, with the assurance that such practice would lead to an enlightened awareness. Like Confucius and Buddha, Heraclitus preached that the stability of the "apparent" world was an illusion, and that all was perpetual change. Counterbalancing this assertion came the assurances of Parmenides and others that nothing ever really changes. From the spiritual angle, *this* life and *this* world came to be diminished as trivial relative to *eternal* life and an *other* world.

Body and soul had been previously separated by ancient mystics, but their separation had never been given the formal scaffolding now offered by what philosopher Karl Jaspers (1951) called the "axial religions" and "axial philosophies" (Mumford 1956). It was a time of "turnings," so to speak; an era of unprecedented reflective and spiritual activity, accelerated and expanded by dramatic increases in written communication. Formative boundaries were drawn between this world and another, between body and mind/spirit, between the "real" and the illusory (eternal/transitory), and between the individual and the universe. Moreover, these boundaries formed the core of many questions that would face humanity for thousands of years to come. It is fascinating to realize that the major belief systems we honor today, whether in modern robes of science or of spiritualism, were germinated in such close proximities of time and yet across such a wide range of places and cultures. In retrospect, the first axial period can be described as that era in our psychologi-

---

inevitably, the power of economic issues leads to eventual degeneration of the civilization and a return to divine guidance.

cal emergence when humans first "formally" discovered the universe within themselves and the powers of faith and reason. In doing so, they dramatically transformed the quality and range of their relationships with what lies beyond them in time and space.

Western philosophical thought emerged out of the mysticism that had prevailed before the axial period in the sixth century B.C. (Frankfort et al. 1946; Kirk, Raven, and Schofield 1983). With Thales and the pre-Socratic philosophers came the application of "natural" reason to the formerly supernatural mysteries of life. But Thales was relatively insignificant compared with four of his successors. The contributions of Pythagoras, Socrates, Plato, and Aristotle have been among the most influential in shaping the contours, questions, and methods of subsequent reflective inquiry (figure 2.1, table 2.2). Together they spun conceptual webs that both tethered and freed inquiring minds for almost twenty-five centuries. Four of the most dominant and influential philosophical traditions of all time were formalized in their thinking:

1. *Rationalism,* which argues that knowing is fundamentally based in reason, which is epitomized in mathematics and logic.

2. *Dualism,* which divides reality into two distinct dimensions—the physical (material) and the nonphysical (mental, spiritual, or "metaphysical").

3. *Idealism,* which argues that reality is based in ideation and abstraction.

4. *Realism,* which argues that reality is a singular and stable order of things external to and independent of human mentation.

These four ism's have permeated subsequent assumptions and assertions about the nature of our world and the nature of our methods for knowing it. Their influence is most apparent when one looks at some of the great debates within selected specializations (tables 2.3, 2.4, and 2.5).

The Great Debates in Traditional Philosophy

For all its diversity, philosophy can be ordered in terms of the domains of its questions. There are at least five broad arenas of philosophical questioning: *ontology*—the study of the nature of reality and existence; *epistemology*—the study of the nature of knowledge and knowing; *hermeneutics*—the study of interpretation and communication (with a variety of emphases including rhetoric, semiotics [the study of signs and symbol systems], and semantics); *axiology*—the study of values, ethics, and aesthetics; and *praxis*—the analysis and guidance of actual practice (the "conduct of life"). Loosely interpreted, these specializations suggest that the bulk of scholarly reflection to date has organized itself around five broad clusters of questions: What is real, true, or enduring? How do we know? How can and do we share our experiences? What is good, moral, or

Table 2.2   A Selective History of Western Philosophy
600 B.C.–1800

Greek Classics (c. 600 B.C.–325 A.D.)		
640–546 B.C.	Thales	First Western philosopher; brought geometry to Greece after travels in Egypt.
570–500 B.C.	Pythagoras	Pioneer in mathematics; primary founder of Western rationalism; deemed thought more powerful than the senses as a source of knowledge.
540–475 B.C.	Heraclitus	Pioneer in *process thinking* ("nothing is static; all is becoming"); pioneer in *opponent process metatheory* (that is, unity or complementarity of "opposite tensions").
539–469 B.C.	Parmenides	Pioneer in "stasis thinking"—"there is no change; reality is fixed and timeless; all change is illusion."
490–410 B.C.	Protagoras	Most important of Sophists (early rhetoricians who taught for a fee); argued that truth is relative.
460–370 B.C.	Democritus	Founder of atomism; advocate of materialism; proto-empiricist.
469–399 B.C.	Socrates	Patron saint of philosophical inquiry; mentor of Plato; the "Socratic mission" entails a never-ending search for truth and an abiding humility about current knowledge; emphasized value of self-knowledge: "know thyself"; "the unexamined life is not worth living."
427–347 B.C.	Plato	Most influential Western philosopher; rational theories of ethics, immortality, and utopia; formalized dualism between reality and appearance; visual metaphor of knowing; cave metaphor of truth/appearance contrast; mentor of Aristotle.
412–323 B.C.	Diogenes	Pioneer of Cynicism; forerunner of Stoicism.

Table 2.2   *(Continued)*

Greek Classics (c. 600 B.C.–325 A.D.)		
384–322 B.C.	Aristotle	Formalized (deductive) logic; formalized classification as a form of knowing; correspondence theory of truth; theories of ethics, politics, and physics.
367–275 B.C.	Pyrrho	Pioneer of Skepticism, which challenged trustworthiness not only of senses but also of rationality and morality; doctrine of dogmatic doubt.
342–270 B.C.	Epicurus	Materialist; proto-empiricist; founded Epicurean philosophy ("pleasure is the beginning and end of the blessed life"); argued for the validity of sense perception and natural (versus supernatural) theories of life and death; embraced Democritus' atomism; the goal of wisdom is *ataraxia* (freedom from anxiety).
336–264 B.C.	Zeno (of Citium)	Founder of Stoicism; doctrines of cosmic determinism and the degradation of feeling; viewed emotions as false judgments; idealized *apatheia* (freedom from passions).
106–43 B.C.	Cicero	Roman pioneer in eclecticism; aspired to integrate best parts of rival schools of thought; endorsed moderation and rejected extreme forms of both dogmatism and skepticism.
99–55 B.C.	Lucretius	Materialist; refined ideas of Epicurus and Democritus on atomism; proposed prototype theory of organic evolution.

Dark and Middle Ages (c. 300–1300 A.D.)		
354–430	Augustine	Rationalist theologian; used Plato and Aristotle to defend Christian doctrines; emphasized wisdom of faith and pursuit of self-knowledge; believed that evil emanates from perversity of will; formalized the act of confession.

Table 2.2   *(Continued)*

Dark and Middle Ages (c. 300–1300 A.D.)

1214–92	Roger Bacon	Endorsed mathematics as foundation of all science; anticipated Francis Bacon's call to observation and experimentation.
1225–74	Thomas Aquinas	Integrated and revised the ideas of Aristotle to accord with Christian theology; made influential distinctions between essence and existence, as well as between faith and reason.
1266–1308	Duns Scotus	Anticipated empiricism by arguing that all knowledge arises from the senses; he believed the newborn's mind to be a *tabula nuda,* a concept later championed by Locke.

Renaissance (c. 1350–1600)

1304–74	Francesco Petrarch	Revived interest in Greek and Roman classics; pioneer in writings on individualism and humanism.
1467–1536	Desiderius Erasmus	Opposed dogmatic scholasticism and appealed to integration of rationality and spirituality; contributor to humanism.

Scientific Revolution and Age of Reason (c. 1500–1700)

1561–1626	Francis Bacon	Emphasized observation, experimentation, and induction in knowledge development; father of modern empiricism.
1596–1650	René Descartes	Father of modern rationalism; pioneer in mathematics; formalized mind-body dualism and the method of doubt in epistemic inquiry; proposed *cogito, ergo sum* ("I think, therefore I am") and placed cognition at the center of knowing; idealized mathematical reasoning and certainty as the heart of rational inquiry.
1588–1679	Thomas Hobbes	Pioneer empiricist ("all thought is ultimately derived from the senses").

Table 2.2   *(Continued)*

Scientific Revolution and Age of Reason (c. 1500–1700)

1632–77	Baruch Spinoza	Vigorous rationalist who emphasized the deductive nature of all explanation; proposed "psychophysical parallelism" (or "prearranged harmony") to account for the separate but synchronized activities of mind and body.
1632–1704	John Locke	Pioneer empiricist; criticized the rationalist tradition; proposed *tabula rasa* ("blank tablet") model of mind at birth and distinguished primary and secondary qualities in perception.
1646–1716	Gottfried Leibniz	Rationalist and realist; doctrine of monads; proposed the Principle of Sufficient Reason (nothing happens without a reason); extended earlier arguments for the existence of God.

Enlightenment (c. 1700–1800)

1668–1744	Giambattista Vico	Founder of philosophy of history; proposed that history reflects repeating cycles; pioneered speculations on prehistoric mentation and wrote first treatise on constructive nature of human knowing.
1685–1753	George Berkeley	Founder of Idealism (*esse est percipi,* "to be is to be perceived"), arguing that all that exists is ultimately mental.
1711–76	David Hume	Father of modern skepticism; an empiricist, he identified problems in traditional notions of causality and induction.
1694–1778	François Voltaire	Vocal critic of the clergy and nobility; encouraged liberal thought and social reform.
1712–78	Jean Jacques Rousseau	Father of romanticism; argued that civilization has distorted the natural wisdom and well-being of the "noble savage."

Table 2.2   *(Continued)*

Enlightenment (c. 1700–1800)

| 1724–1804 | Immanuel Kant | Father of modern critical philosophy; proposed innate (a priori) knowledge and argued that the mind imposes its own structures ("categories") on the particulars of thought and perception. |

---

beautiful? And how do belief systems inform or guide practice (for example, how should one live one's life)? Simple as they may sound, these questions have invited diverse and often polarized answers, as is reflected in the many schools of thought across and within questions. The first two alone—the nature of reality and the nature of knowing—reflect the evolution of human questioning.

Idealism and Realism.   In ontology, for example, the two most enduring debates have focused on the nature of reality (with idealism and realism as

Figure 2.1   Major Systems of Philosophical Thought

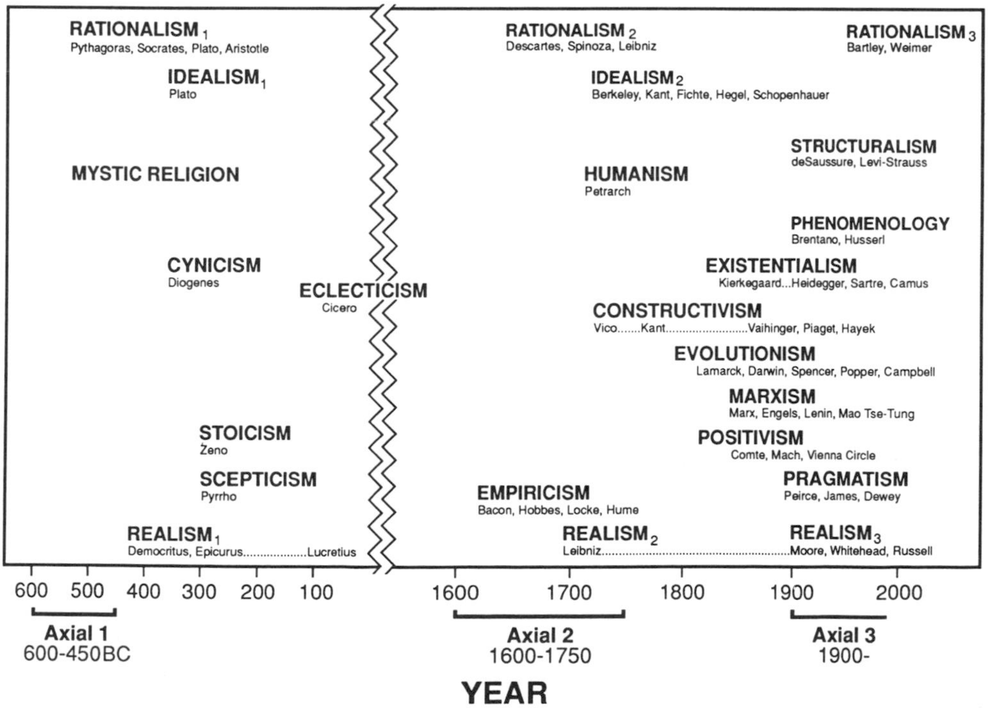

Source: © 1989 M. J. Mahoney
Note: Subscripts reflect different expressions of a given system.

as opposite poles) and on the related issue of how (and whether) physical and nonphysical realms can relate to one another (a problem created by the assumption of dualism) (see table 2.3). The latter is best known to psychologists as the mind-body problem, which I discuss in the next section. My narrative is necessarily complicated at this point by the fact

Table 2.3   Major Theories of Reality (Ontology)

Idealism (400 B.C.–present)	All of reality is based in ideation; in its first, classical formulation by Plato, ideas are fundamentally real by being pure and perfect "forms." In its second formulation by Berkeley in the eighteenth century, the act of perception is a prerequisite to objective existence (*esse es percipi*, "to be is to be perceived"); therefore, no material objects or "external" realities exist apart from their creation and maintenance in minds and mental processes. Key figures: Plato, Berkeley, Kant, Fichte, Hegel, Schopenhauer, Croce, Royce, Cassirer, Unamuno, Ortega y Gassett.
Realism (400 B.C.–present)	Reality is a singular, stable order of events and objects external to and independent of mind and mental processes; in *empirical realism,* the senses and other technical methods of observation are said to reveal, albeit imperfectly, regularities and principles of reality; in *naïve realism* (believed by no one), the senses reflect reality perfectly (the doctrine of Immaculate Perception); in *representative realism,* the senses are said to represent reality. Key figures: Plato, Aristotle, Moore, Russell, Whitehead, Santayana.
Dualism (400 B.C.–present)	Reality is comprised of two separate and distinct dimensions: the physical or material and the mental or conceptual; dualism fostered energetic debate over mental-physical interaction in the famous mind-body problem, solutions to which included *monism* (there is only one dimension), the physical (*materialistic* monism) or the nonphysical (*idealistic* monism), as well as *interactionism* (mind and body interact), psychophysical parallelism, and *epiphenomenalism* (mind is an epiphenomenon of the physical activity of the brain). Key figures: Plato, Descartes, Spinoza, Fechner, Popper, Eccles, and many moderns.
Process philosophy (500 B.C.–present)	All being is becoming; reality is an implicate, emergent order, self-organizing and unfolding dynamically; the mind and mental development illustrate this point. Key figures: Heraclitus, Spencer, Huxley, Bergson, Whitehead, Dewey, Bohm.

Table 2.4   Major Theories of Truth

Relativism (450 B.C.–present)	Truth is relative; theories vary regarding "relative to what." The basic assertion is that there are no absolutes, including truth; and that we must therefore abandon the search for such absolutes as truth and certainty. Key figures: Protagoras, Pyrrho, and the Skeptics in general (early and modern).
Correspondence theory (400 B.C.–present)	The "true" *corresponds* to *reality,* which is, in turn, separate (external to humans and independent of sense experience), singular, and unchanging; from this view, truth and reality converge in an absolute and ultimate order. Key figures: Plato, Aristotle, Plotinus, Aquinas, Santayana, Moore, Whitehead, Russell, Broad, Sellars.
Coherence theory (400 B.C.–present)	Truth is the coherence of ideas, and ideas (and philosophic reflection) are better paths of inquiry than are lessons of experience; truth is Perfect Order; logical consistency and formal (deductive) implication *justify* (authorize) truth claims. Key figures: (early) Plato, Aristotle, (recent) Spinoza, Leibniz, Kant, Hegel.
Subjectivism (1850–present)	Truth is subjectivity and hence infinitely individualized; the true is that which is *immediate* and *real for the individual* at a given point in time. Key figures: Kierkegaard, Brentano, Husserl, Binswanger, Merleau-Ponty.
Pragmatism (1900–present)	Truth is the ultimate set of beliefs held by a community of inquirers after an infinite interval of practical (behaviorally enacted) inquiry; truth is therefore viable, working knowledge. Key figures: Peirce, James, Dewey.

that there have been two distinguishable forms of idealism, the first stemming from Plato and the second associated with Bishop George Berkeley and Immanuel Kant (figure 2.1 and tables 2.2 and 2.3). Without belaboring the technicalities of that distinction, note that the more modern form (Idealism² in figure 2.1) denies the existence of anything other than mind and mental phenomena.* It is the "all in your mind" school

---

*Plato's student, Aristotle, uses the term Universals rather than Forms, but both meant to refer to an immutable and perfect reality of essences. Although paradoxical to present usage, Plato was thus both an idealist and a realist. Plato's Doctrine of Ideas integrated the dichotomy represented by his predecessors Heraclitus and Parmenides (table 2.2). In the realm of sensory experience, Plato agreed with Heraclitus that change is pervasive ("all is becoming"); in the realm of ideas, however, he concurred with Parmenides that "there is no change."

Table 2.5   Major Theories of Knowing (Epistemology)

Rationalism (500 B.C.–present)	Knowing and knowledge are essentially based in reason, mathematics, and formal, logical thought; the senses are illusory and inferior to reason; some, if not all, knowledge of principles and particulars in "real time and space" is innate and independent of experience. Key figures: Pythagoras, Parmenides, Plato, Aristotle, Aquinas, Descartes, Spinoza, Leibniz.
Empiricism (1600–present)	Knowing and knowledge are essentially based in sense experience; in its modern "rationalized" and "logical" forms, empiricism emphasizes the power of careful observation, accurate measurement, and systematic and strategic intervention (experimental "manipulation") when paired with "strong (inductive) inference" processes in the never-ending dialectic between reason and experiment. Key figures: Roger Bacon, Francis Bacon, Hobbes, Locke, Hume, Condillac, J. S. Mill.
Evolutionary epistemology (1850–present)	Knowing is both the process and product of ongoing activity in which variations are differentially influenced by selection processes; knowing and knowledge cannot be justified or authorized as valid; viability is more apt a concept than validity. Key figures: Lamarck, Darwin, Spencer, Huxley, Baldwin, Popper, Hayek, Campbell.
Pragmatism (1900–present)	Knowledge is what works; a belief is a willingness to act; meaning inheres in the practical consequences of action. Key figures: Peirce, W. James, Dewey, Royce, Schiller. G. H. Mead.

of thought, if you will. The polar contrast to idealism has been realism, which has also assumed different forms. In essence, however, modern realism (Realism[3] in figure 2.1) simply asserts that there are "things out there"—what A. N. Whitehead (1957) called "furniture in the universe"—independent of our knowledge, perception, or imagination of them (Leplin 1984; Popper 1983; Weimer 1982a; Wheeler 1982).

The debate between realists and idealists has gone on for centuries, exhibiting conceptual evolution in the process of its perpetuation. As we will see in later chapters, it continues to be a lively topic in some controversies regarding the nature of cognition and cognitive processes. Because it has been so central a theme in the history of ideas, its conceptual contrasts warrant careful examination.

The Mind-Body Problem.   By drawing a sharp and static distinction between the realms of mind and matter, the doctrine of dualism forcefully discouraged theoretical and technological integrations in the cognitive and brain sciences for many years. Because dualism was formalized by René Descartes in the seventeenth century, some modern writers refer to it as "Cartesian dualism," without noting that Descartes was picking up where Plato and his cohorts had left off. The attempted resolutions to the problem of mind-body dualism have taken several major forms (Broad 1925). *Monism* may be the simplest, in that it denies the problem itself by asserting that there is only one kind of "stuff" of reality. Monists have disagreed, however, as to the nature of that singular "stuff." Materialistic monists have argued that reality is exclusively physical—the assertion of such writers as Democritus, Thomas Hobbes, and the radical behaviorist John B. Watson. Radical idealists contend just the opposite: that the stuff of reality is exclusively nonphysical.

Another suggested resolution to the problem of mind-body dualism is called *psychophysical parallelism* and was suggested by Spinoza and Leibniz (it received this title from Gustav Fechner in the nineteenth century). Parallelism suggested a "pre-arranged harmony" between physical and nonphysical realms, so that mind and body—although separate entities— were perfectly synchronized, events in one realm being perfectly mirrored in the other even though they never interact. A variation on this same argument was called *occasionalism,* as proposed by Nicolas de Malebranche, Arnold Geulincx, and others: in it, mind and body were said to be two independent processes which are "occasionally" synchronized by supernatural intervention.

The most popular resolution of the mind-body problem among modern philosophers and neuroscientists is *interactionism,* which contends that the phenomena referred to as mind and mental processes can, in fact, influence their own biological substrate (that is, the body and brain that undergird them), and vice versa (Popper and Eccles 1977; Pribram 1986; Sperry 1988). In addition, analyses of the language and concepts used in discussions of both mind and body have pointed toward resolutions that transcend the dualism that has dominated thinking in this area (Clark and Paivio 1989; Johnson 1987; Lakoff 1987; Lakoff and Johnson 1980; Ryle 1949).

Rationalism and Empiricism.   The great debate in epistemology has focused on the relative contributions of thought versus experience in our efforts to know. The term *versus* again reflects a dualistic approach, and the dualism inherent in this debate has only begun to be challenged in the last two centuries. With rare exceptions, however, the side of the argument emphasizing the experiential base of knowing (empiricism) did not really emerge until the scientific revolution in the seventeenth and eighteenth centuries—the second major turning point in the history of ideas (figure 2.1). Until then, rationalism was the dominant view in philosophy. Since the modern (and ongoing) revolution in epistemology involves a reappraisal of traditional views of rationality, it is worth elaborating the early roots and conceptual legacy of rationalism.

The primary founder of rationalism was Pythagoras, and it is not coincidental that he was also the father of mathematics. To this day, our notions of reason, logic, and rationality are closely aligned with mathematical ideas. Pythagoras was the first to recognize the mathematical regularities of musical harmonics, and his insight into the relationships among the sides of a right triangle—the famous Pythagorean theorem—offered a practical example of the power of mathematics and, hence, of reason in the realms of everyday life. It is primarily thanks to Pythagoras—with later help from the likes of Descartes, Russell, and Whitehead—that modern views of science are so thoroughly mathematical in flavor. To be "scientific" in these times is almost inherently to be mathematical (Bannister 1987; Davis and Hersh 1986; Hornstein 1986; Kline 1985). But the emergence of rationalism begot much more than mathematics; it also invoked the concept of a perfectly ordered reality beyond our local awareness and a belief in eternal and exact truth. Pythagoras had argued that "thought is superior to sense," and his call to rationalism set the stage for the later reflections of Plato and Aristotle (Russell 1945).

The glorification of the human intellect and the denigration of the body and senses inherent in rationalism were forcefully conveyed in Plato's metaphors. He regarded the soul as a microcosm of the universe, divided into three parts. The movement of the soul, according to Plato, is comparable to that of a charioteer and his charges. The driver is our intellect or reason, located in the head, whose job it is to control and coordinate two horses, one more manageable than the other: a well-mannered white steed (representing emotionality and will) and an unruly black horse (representing desire and base appetites). Emotionality and will were thought to be active and located in the heart, while desire was described as passionate (hence rendering us "passive" to its demands) and centered in the abdomen and loins. That this most base of energies is indeed fundamental to human nature was made clear by Plato in a passage about dreams that sounds eerily Freudian:

Those desires which are awake when the reasoning and taming and ruling power of the personality is asleep [are] the wild beast in our nature, gorged with meat and drink. [It] starts up and walks about naked, and surfeits at its will; and there is no conceivable folly or crime, however shameless or unnatural . . . of which such a nature may not be guilty. . . . In all of us, even in good men, there is such a latent wild beast nature, which peers out in sleep. (Cited in Durant 1926, p. 23)

In the charioteer metaphor, mind and body were officially separated; and given the animal legacy of the body, Plato thought that control of the body by the powers of the intellect was essential to civilized conduct. It was with Pythagoras, Plato, and Aristotle that the doctrine of *rational supremacy* was initiated; that is, the doctrine that reason can and should rule over voluntary action and feeling. For better and for worse, that idea has had a profound impact on all subsequent Western thinking, and remains a central issue in modern cognitive science. This last point is elaborated by Walter B. Weimer in a discussion of Plato's famous "paradoxes" of the *Meno* (Weimer 1973).

Aristotle, who also significantly influenced our thinking, founded the field of logic, basing meaningful communication and formal rationality on a foundation of self-consistency (the absence of contradiction). In laying the foundations for Western logic, Aristotle moved humanity in the direction of a shared system of knowing characterized by formal rules accessible to every reflective being.* Aristotle also encouraged the sciences and, in this sense, stepped beyond his training with Plato to make room for natural observation. He imbued science with both *justificationism*—the reliance on authority to "justify" an assertion—and *correspondence theory*—the assertion that truth is the correspondence between an idea and reality (see table 2.4). In the psychological realm, Aristotle further glorified rationality, making reason the rightful guide in all human action. He thus joined Plato in advocating the doctrine of rational supremacy—a view that figures prominently in modern rationalist (cognitive) therapies. Aristotle also anticipated *associationism,* arguing that learning involves principles of similarity, contrast, and contiguity. Believing that the brain served primarily to cool the blood, however, he located the intellect and soul in the heart (see appendix D).

In one sense, Aristotle straddled what would later become the great debate in epistemology—that waged between rationalism and empiricism (see table 2.5 and the next section). After Pythagoras and Plato, Aristotle defended the intellect and mentation as potential and perhaps primary sources of knowledge, but he also suggested that observation and classification are important in discerning the order of things. Reality—the eternal and unchanging order behind the flux of appearances—was deemed accessible only by means of "perfect" or "universal" ideas that are themselves absolute and unchanging. Truth was defined as correspondence between thought and its object, while rationality was defined

---

*Aristotle's categories were a first attempt to classify the whole of creation—to establish a formal order to things. There were ten such categories: substance, quantity, quality, relation, location, time, position, possession, active, and passive.

as the internal consistency of a set of assertions. These core assumptions in Western rationality are at the heart of many modern questions about knowing.

The Second Axial Period: Empiricism and the Scientific Revolution

With such exceptions as Augustine, Aquinas, and perhaps Duns Scotus (table 2.2), the next significant development in Western philosophy after Aristotle did not occur for about nineteen centuries. Relative to what preceded and followed it, this period was characterized by intellectual scholasticism and somnambulism. Indeed, during the centuries labeled the Dark and Middle Ages (roughly, the fourth to the fourteenth centuries), there was active—and often violent—suppression of open inquiry.

Then, in the Renaissance (literally "rebirth"), between the fourteenth and the sixteenth centuries, a series of revolutions began to transform the quality and contents of everyday life in much of Europe—exemplified by the Protestant Reformation begun in Germany by Martin Luther in 1517. Everywhere, authority was being questioned, and the human rights to inquire and reflect—to think for oneself—were being defended. Although this revolution in the history of ideas was hardly peaceful, it did eventually prevail.

If the first turning point in the history of ideas (Axial[1] in figure 2.1) involved a turning inward toward reason and religion and a detachment from sensation and embodiment, the second (Axial[2]) involved a dramatic shift back to sensation and toward an expanding engagement with the world. It was reflected first in naturalistic observations about two highly interesting topics: the heavens and the human body. Vesalius and William Harvey, for example, drastically changed how humans viewed their embodied selves (see table 2.6), while Copernicus boldly transformed the appearance and harmony of the skies. The Copernican revolution remains one of the single most fascinating stories in the history of thought: the "firmament" has not felt so firm ever since he told us that we were in movement. Likewise, the Newtonian revolution, which followed soon after, has left a legacy that is still not fully appreciated (Bernal 1954; Cohen 1980; Kuhn 1957, 1962, 1970a).

From the standpoint of philosophy and particularly epistemology, the single most important person in this early reappraisal of the rationalist tradition was Francis Bacon. In 1620 he published his pivotal *Novum Organum* (New Instrument), emphasizing induction, observation, and careful experimentation as a new method of knowing separate from the deductive scholasticism associated with Aristotle. The rallying cry was back to the lessons of experience—a cry once voiced by Democritus and Epicurus—but now with the added power of careful observation and

Table 2.6   Selected Events in Science, 1543–1700

1543	Vesalius performed dissections on human cadavers and published illustrations of human anatomy.
1543	Copernicus published his revolutionary (heliocentric) model of the solar system.
1572	Tycho Brahe published extensive data on the movements of stars and planets.
1600	Bruno was burned alive for refusing to recant his heretical views in astronomy and philosophy.
1609	Kepler announced his laws of planetary motion.
1610	Galileo's telescopic observations supported the Copernican model.
1620	Bacon's *Novum Organum* published.
1621	The slide rule invented by Oughtred.
1628	Harvey published his work on blood circulation.
1633	Galileo forced publicly to recant his views.
1634	Kepler wrote science fiction (about lunar life).
1637	Descartes published his *Discourse on Method.*
1642	Pascal invented the first adding machine.
1662	Boyle's law of gases published.
1664	Descartes's mechanistic theory of the body published posthumously.
1665	The first two scientific journals launched.
1676	van Leeuwenhoek announced his discovery of protozoa in rain water.
1684	Leibniz offered his differential calculus; the integral calculus followed in 1686.
1687	Newton published his laws of motion and gravitation.
1690	Huygen developed the wave theory of light.
1691	Ray classified all organic life forms.

logical inference. *Empiricism,* the doctrine making experience the source of all knowledge, was reborn in Bacon's writings, and would later be elaborated in the works of Locke, Berkeley, Hume, and Mill. Not coincidentally, these appeals to experience overlapped with the scientific revolution (table 2.2).

Bacon had asserted that *knowledge is power,* and the Industrial Revolution soon showed that technical knowledge could be both powerful and profitable. With increasing swiftness, "progress" was wrought, and Newton's world was soon put to work in the service of economics, if not humanity (Boorstein 1983; Braudel 1979a, 1979b, 1979c; Bronowski 1973; Parkinson 1985). Ideas were put to work, often in the service of military offense and defense. And, for the most part, they did work. These were the relatively simple ideas of a machinelike universe, with clean vectors of force and direction and independent dimensions of absolute time and space as well as matter and energy.

It is perhaps not surprising to learn that Newton had been trained as a clockmaker: his was definitely a clockwork universe. And the philosophy that undergirded science was a hybrid of a new rationality *(inductive inference)* combined with systematic observation and experimentation. It was *rational objectivism* at its finest hour, with the grand machine of science grinding out a rich supply of facts to form the brickwork for the edifice of knowledge. Rational objectivism is still the dominant metatheory in science, and only recently has it begun to erode under the challenges of both theory and research. Briefly stated, rational objectivism presumes *(a)* the existence of a single, relatively stable, external reality that is totally independent of human perception and conception (realism); *(b)* the primacy of explicit reason and mathematics in rendering valid knowledge (rationalism); *(c)* a sharp distinction between the subject and the object of knowledge, with an emphasis on establishing knowledge independent of the knowing subject (objectivism); *(d)* a sharp distinction between physical (spatiotemporal) and nonphysical (or metaphysical) phenomena and processes (dualism); and *(e)* the veracity of the assumption that true or valid knowledge about reality is ultimately rendered through rational interpretations of sensory experience (logical empiricism). As we shall see, this theory has led to thorny problems for psychologists and cognitive scientists in that it has encouraged them to conceptualize knowledge as a process of discovering and internalizing an external realm. The essential argument of rational objectivism is that there is one true (that is, valid, right, or accurate) way to view reality, and that all other interpretations are in error.

Observability remains a pivotal criterion of objectivity in the social sciences, even though it has long since been abandoned (and replaced by other criteria) in the physical and biological sciences. When common psychological terms were recently rated by psychologists (Clark and Paivio 1989), there was a near-perfect inverse correlation ($r = -.89$) between their observational and theoretical nature. Scientific objectivity—at least in the behavioral sciences—remains tethered to concrete and simplistic notions of observation. If the physical and biological sciences had employed a similar strategy and postponed their inquiries until they could literally see the objects and processes proposed in their evolving theories, their conceptual horizons would have been frozen for the greater part of the last century.

Until the second half of the present century, it was generally assumed that scientific knowledge was grounded in empirical facts which are fixed and absolute in their meaning. Scientific progress was thought to be an accumulation of such facts in such abundance that eventually truths would fall out in patterns. Induction was still believed to be a logical (rather than psychological) process, and data were thought to be impartial arbiters in answering any and all well-put questions. Each of these assumptions has come under serious challenge in the last half-century.

The Age of Science is still tangibly with us, of course, and the foregoing assumptions are still defended by some. But much has happened in the last century, particularly in its last half. Indeed, I believe that the magnitude of some of those changes is far greater than we yet realize. The pace of our change has accelerated tremendously. And while Newton's world has remained well behaved in the realms of physical engineering, at the turn of the century it began to show its limitations—particularly at the edges of living systems and in the microstructure of reality—quantum mechanics. New ideas were gestating and soon ushered in a third major evolution (Axial[3] in figure 2.1) in the history of ideas. This third "turn" is still in progress, of course, and in it we are participant-observers.

The Third Axial Period: Relativity and Criticism

From its inception, the twentieth century has been and continues to be a palpable turning point in the history of human ideas. In one sense, of course, the changes rippling through modern life had their germination in the Renaissance and what followed in the second axial period (table 2.2). Although there was no private life in the modern sense of the term until the thirteenth and fourteenth centuries, the notion of privacy and the public realms defining it jointly set the stage for the emergence of personal identity, the sense of self, and the ideas and issues that would later constitute the human freedoms and rights movements of modern societies (Duby 1988; Hamowy 1987). With the strengthening of the sense of self by natural scientists at the end of the nineteenth century, there also emerged a more vocal intolerance of the authorities who had previously dominated "acceptable" thinking about thinking. In analyzing the emergence and development of "women's ways of knowing," for example, feminist scholars have documented the extent to which women's experiences and ideas have, until recently, been ignored and/or suppressed by scientists and scholars (Belenky et al. 1986; Deaux 1984; Gilligan 1982; Gornick 1983; Keller 1983, 1985; Tuana 1989).

The physicists Max Planck, Niels Bohr, and Albert Einstein opened the century by recasting the nature of reality and demonstrating the relativity of time, space, and perspective. Heisenberg would later argue that observation is a posture of choices, and that basic choices are binary. Epistemology was no longer distinct from ontology—a point that would be personalized in the captivating analyses of existentialism, phenomenology, and hermeneutics. Meanwhile, the Industrial Revolution was also transforming the nature of everyday experience for increasing numbers of people. As Fernand Braudel (1979a, 1979b, 1979c) and other historians would later note, in the nineteenth century the average citizen of the planet was born, lived a lifetime, and died within an eight-mile radius. The number of people who shaped one's social and personal worlds was limited by modern standards. But all that changed with technological improvements in transportation and communication. The planet became phenomenologically smaller, and its average citizen was increasingly immersed in a sea of changing faces, communication media, and opportunities to interact.

Early in the century, Freud challenged the rationality of the human intellect; and Kurt Gödel later demonstrated that formal (Aristotelian) systems of axiomatic logic are necessarily incomplete, and, moreover, that such systems are inconsistent in that they presume their own derivation without logical justification. Positivism—formalized as logical positivism in the first quarter of the century by the "Vienna circle" (Ayer, Carnap, Feigl, Neurath, von Mises, Schlick, and Schrödinger)—was the epitome of the objectivist tradition. But the objectivity these philosophers sought denied the inseparability of knower, knowing, and known. The criterion of verification that positivists specified as a demarcation between scientific and nonscientific propositions was soon recognized to be self-contradictory and meaningless on its own criterion. There was no potentially verifying experience to confirm the core assertion of logical positivism.

Meanwhile, linguistics was being born, the neuronal theory of brain function was emerging (appendix D), and Darwin's ideas were affecting all the sciences. *Justificationism*—the stubborn quest for "authorized" knowledge and the dream of ultimate, absolute certainty—began to erode from within, but not until the latter half of the twentieth century. Three influential works that appeared in 1962 served to hasten that erosion: Thomas Kuhn's *The Structure of Scientific Revolutions,* Karl Popper's *Conjectures and Refutations,* and William Bartley's *The Retreat to Commitment.* Limited rationalism fell into disrepair, and the "comprehensively critical rationalism" endorsed by Bartley and Walter Weimer represented a clear shift in epistemological assumptions (Bartley 1984 [1962], 1987*a,* 1987*b,* 1987*c;* Mahoney 1976; Radnitzky 1987*a;* Weimer 1979, 1983, 1987). Approaches to theory, research, and scholarly communication have undergone significant and accelerating changes over the last few decades (Allen 1989; Bazerman 1988; Feyerabend 1981*a,* 1981*b;* Fiske and Schweder 1986; Fuller 1988; Olby et al. 1990; Skinner 1985).

In ontology, there has been considerable effort to transcend the long-standing dualism of idealism and realism, and the perspective of *constructivism* has begun to draw increasing support for its attempts to integrate the dynamic reciprocity between living systems and their environments (chapter 5, appendix C). There has also been a decline in the popularity of simple, linear ("billiard ball") determinism and reductionistic causal analyses and an increase in the study of complexity, especially spontaneously self-organizing varieties (such as that exhibited by living systems). In epistemology, there has been a shift away from classical rationalism and its emphasis on explicit knowledge expressed in concrete and unambiguous terms (both linguistic and mathematical). The meaning of *rationality* has been reappraised, and there has been a decline in authority-based (justificational) epistemologies and an increase in the popularity of critical and *postcritical* (nonjustificational) alternatives. Modern scholars exhibit an increasing interest in exploring general principles (as contrasted with concrete particulars) and "evolutionary" or "developmental" epistemologies that emphasize the roles of variation, selection, and differential retention in the growth of knowledge (chapter 6).

In psychology and the social sciences, there has been a reappraisal of traditional assumptions about human neural organization as well as about the nature of cognitive processes, with a shift away from centralized control and representational models, and a shift toward decentralized (coalitional) control models and "embodied" theories of mental representation (chapters 4–5), as well as a growing appreciation for the dynamic interdependence of "systems within systems" (such as neural, endocrine, musculoskeletal, and immune) (appendix D). Traditional debates about the relationships among cognition, affect, and behavior have been reframed, with many psychologists abandoning prime-mover (first-cause) models in favor of more integrative and holistic ones (chapters 5–8). There has also been a resurgence of both scientific and practical (applied) interest in lifespan developmental processes, with growing acknowledgment of the importance of emotionality (chapter 8), and the centrality of self (personal identity) processes in organizing (and resisting) that development, and of the role of human relationships in either thwarting or facilitating such development (chapter 9).

Finally, there appears to be growing interest in the integration or "convergence" of knowledge and in the merits of studying *metatheory* (families of theories). Significant portions of that interest within psychology have been exhibited in the exploration of psychotherapy integration. Both within and beyond psychology, other expressions of such interests can be found throughout the literature of hermeneutics (studies of interpretation). In parallel with the developments of poststructuralism and deconstructionism, these studies have emphasized the complex recursiveness of all knowing. They have also highlighted narrative structure, cultural and historical contexts, and personal embeddedness in all efforts to know (Attridge, Bennington, and Young 1987; Fischer 1987; Gadamer 1988; Harland 1987; Kurtzman 1987; Madison 1988; Melville 1986; Messer, Sass, and Woolfolk 1988; Skinner 1985; Spencer-Brown 1972).

CONCLUSION

Overall and across the three millennia, human ideas have reflected primitive and dynamic "essential tensions" in our thinking. We have struggled, for the most part, with powerful dichotomies—the boundaries between what is real and illusory, good and bad, internal and external, and physical and mental. Much of what has transpired in philosophy over the last century has, in fact, been related to the problems and potentials generated by such traditional dualisms. There are many indications that we are now in the midst of sweeping conceptual shifts that mark a clear turning point in the history of human understanding. It is an exciting and challenging time for the sciences, and a period of dramatic conceptual development in psychology.

3

·▲▼▲▼▲▼▲▼▲▼▲▼▲·

The Foundations and the
Future of Scientific Psychology

The first fact for us, then, as psychologists, is that thinking of some sort goes on.
— William James

Although psychology has been recognized as a discipline in its own right for little more than a century, its emergence and development reflect considerable diversity and undeniable complexity. A complicating factor in rendering its history is the fact that that history is now in the process of being rewritten. The old history has been characterized as having reflected "parochial and amateurish scholarship" and "whiggish tales of [psychology's] emergence from subjectivity and speculation into the objectivity of experimental facts" (Samelson 1988, p. 1837). The new history appears to be less simplistic and naïve, more attuned to primary sources, and less exclusive in its preoccupation with male psychologists in the United States (Ash and Woodward 1988; Furomoto 1989; Scarborough and Furomoto 1987). In the process of this rewriting, it has also become clear that the discipline of psychology has already moved through a conceptual spiral remarkably similar to that exhibited in the overall history of ideas. The primary emphases of theory and research have moved from an initial focus on the inner person, through a long period of exclusive focus on ostensibly external factors (behavior-environment relations), and then on to a more distributed balance that still leans toward the insides of the organism (as in the cognitive revolution and the modern resurgence of phenomenology). These changing emphases have been marked by heated debates about the nature of "truly" scientific psychology, and bear directly on theory and practice.

What William James considered a "first fact" for psychology—the fact that thinking occurs—was all but abandoned when experimental psychology later came to be dominated by behaviorism for almost half a century. Indeed, some observers of psychology have cast its advances and retreats in terms of its early submission to and belated emergence from the strict determinist (mechanist) view enshrined by radical behaviorism. The decline in the popularity of behaviorism as a comprehensive theory of human experience coincided with the emergence of the cognitive sciences and the maturation of modern varieties of humanism. But the developmental picture was more complex than the simple eclipse of one paradigm by two others. Other promising approaches existed before and during the reign of behaviorism, and many of the leading developments in modern psychology can trace their legacy to the rich insights of the likes of James, Wilhelm Wundt, Leo Wertheimer, Charles Sherrington, and Freud, to mention a few.

EARLY PSYCHOLOGICAL INQUIRY

The discipline of psychology emerged from the diverse contexts of philosophy, experimental physiology, and the life sciences. The dimensions of mind and its relation to feelings and conduct had, of course, been discussed by many philosophers over the centuries. It was not until psychology became experimental, however, that it came to be viewed as a science, even though several of its pioneers recognized that research methods in psychology would have to involve much more than the kinds of experimentation developed by the physical and biological sciences. The birth of psychology is conventionally dated 1879, when Wilhelm Wundt established his experimental laboratory at the University of Leipzig. Wundt's insights have only recently been rediscovered and appreciated for their modern relevance, but others before him also made real contributions (Furomoto 1989; Hearst 1979; Webb 1988, 1989; Weimer 1974b, 1974c).

Modern psychology and the cognitive sciences, for example, have been significantly influenced by the English philosopher Thomas Hobbes and the French philosopher René Descartes. The perennial tension between reason and experience (rationalism and empiricism) was personified in the writings of these two men. Philosophy and science began to differentiate in their methods (and madnesses) thanks in part to the formal reiteration of mind-body dualism and the revived respect for mathematics and logic. Psychology borrowed heavily from their full range, and only recently has the dominance of dualistic thinking and logical empiricism receded in the face of developments associated with the "modern synthesis" in the field.

Awakened by the writings of David Hume, Immanuel Kant was also to influence both the philosophy and the psychology of the nineteenth century. Hume and Kant were jointly responsible for the "selfless" psychology William James would later work to rectify. Because of their insights into the limitations of inductive inference and experience, both Hume and Kant had a negative view of the possibility and promise of experiential (empirical) psychology. They also agreed that a psychology of self would be impossible. But both writers had left open conceptual loopholes that their successors would use in later efforts to join the realms of reason and experience. Jakob Fries took the first step in that direction by pointing out that Kant could not have contributed what he did without having first observed and analyzed his own experience. Fries defended psychology as "the fundamental science, and the foundation for other sciences" (cited in Hilgard 1987, p. 27).

Then Johann Friedrich Herbart, the successor to Kant's position at Königsberg, introduced several ideas and methods that remain alive in contemporary studies. He was largely responsible for: (1) the introduction of mathematics into psychological theory (including the depiction of learning curves mathematically equivalent to those later developed by Hull and Estes); (2) the first statement of the *opponent process* theory of learning, which involves dynamic, ongoing equilibration via the assimilation and accommodation of psychological schema; and (3) one of the first explicit conjectures about unconscious processes—an idea embraced by T. H. Meynert and later conveyed by him to his student Sigmund Freud.

After Kant and Herbart, Friedrich Beneke and Hermann Lotze paved the philosophical path for Wundt to establish an experimental psychology. (A converging path came from experimental medicine and physiology, exemplified by the studies in "psychophysics" by Gustav Fechner and Ernst Weber.)

Perhaps no other influential psychologist has been as poorly represented or belatedly appreciated as Wilhelm Wundt (Blumenthal 1975, 1980, 1985; Weimer 1987). At the turn of the century, he and William James loomed large as the two most imposing figures in the fledgling science of psychology. Hilgard (1987) has noted some of their similarities and differences, both personal and theoretical. Both were empirical, although only Wundt was experimental. (Empirical inquiry relies on observations and is grounded in experience; experimental inquiry is also empirical but adds systematic manipulations or interventions to its methodology.) Both Wundt and James were impressed with the creative or generative capacities of mind and opposed associationism. Having survived troubled childhoods, both experienced what were later termed "creative illnesses" and struggled with psychological problems—respiratory difficulties and shyness in the case of Wundt, back problems and depression in the case of James. Both wrote about a wide range of psychological phenomena, but Wundt was more systematic while James enjoyed tackling the "pluralisms" of reality and experience (Viney 1989). James's writings often exhibited the meanderings of the "stream of consciousness" about which he wrote. But the most important dimension on which these men differed had to do with a significant issue in approaching the study of consciousness: namely, whether psychological studies should be aimed at identifying the contents and structure of experience rather than mental acts and their functions. The distinction and the debate remain active to this day. These outlooks began as the approaches of structuralism and functionalism, but their ideological successors included associationism, behaviorism, gestalt psychology, and psychoanalysis (figure 3.1).

Structuralism and functionalism emerged out of a debate over the proper focus and methods of scientific psychology. Wundt had distinguished two branches of scientific inquiry: *Naturwissenschaft* and *Geisteswissenschaften*. The former referred to "natural science" and was experimental in method; while the latter was "historical-cultural" and, although empirical, not experimental. It was through the writings and teachings of E. B. Titchener that early American psychologists were to become familiar with Wundt's work, and Titchener allowed his own strong opinions to distort his translations of his German colleague's assertions. The structuralism Titchener adamantly endorsed was not faithful to his mentor's ideas, however, and made that school of thought rigidly *sensationalist*. "It was Titchener, loyal to Wundt's experimentalism but not sticking to his systematic views, who gave sensation its central place (Hilgard 1987, p. 73).

Figure 3.1   Major Systems of Psychological Thought, 1880–1950

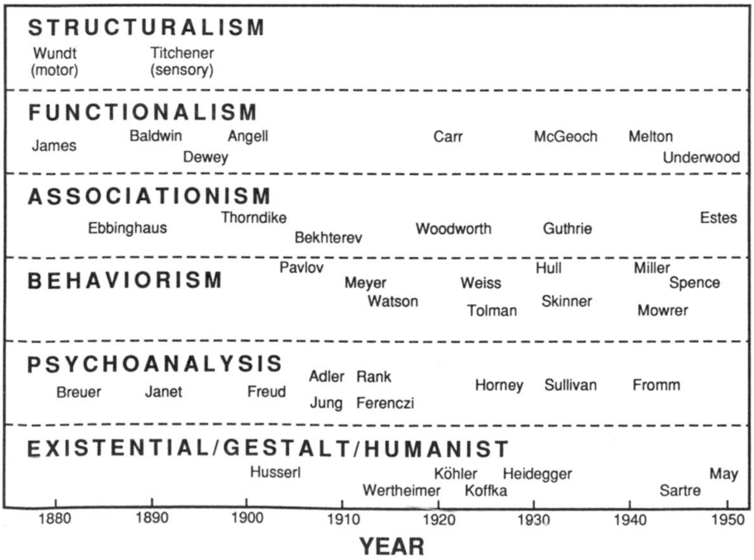

SOURCE: © 1989 M. J. Mahoney

The term *structuralism* has been (and is) used, of course, with distinctly different meanings both within and beyond psychology. U.S. psychologists, for example, have used *structuralism* in reference primarily to the tradition associated with Wundt and Titchener and their attempts to identify the (static) "architecture" of mind and the structural properties of experience. Contemporary philosophers, on the other hand, use the same term to refer to a tradition of inquiry associated with literary interpretation and such writers as deSaussure, Jakobson, Lévi-Strauss, Marx, Greimas, and Barthès. This latter (philosophical) structuralism has also been the reference point from which have emanated the poststructuralist and deconstructionist writings of such people as Jacques Lacan, Michel Foucault, and Jacques Derrida (chapter 5). It was in contrast to psychological structuralism that functionalism was defined.

The functionalists were emerging out of the "act psychology" of Franz Brentano and the emphasis on adaptation and function that had become increasingly popular since the publication of Charles Darwin's *On The Origin of Species* in 1859 (Richards 1987). William James, James Mark Baldwin, John Dewey, James McKeen Cattell, and James R. Angell were among its most influential early representatives. Their focus was on habit, action, and functional significance—the how and why of consciousness rather than its contents and structure. It was one of Angell's graduate students, John B. Watson, who would soon thereafter try to purge psychology of its interests in introspection and consciousness.

RADICAL BEHAVIORISM: THE RISE AND FALL OF MINDLESS PSYCHOLOGY

Behaviorism arose in its modern form out of a legacy of evolutionary functionalism, on the biological side, and of rationalist objectivism, on the philosophical side. As I have noted, the polarization between structuralist (sensationalist) and functionalist models had itself emerged out of a controversy over whether consciousness was better studied via its elemental parts (contents, sensations) or its acts (the sequence of events that characterize person-environment adaptations). The functionalists proliferated over the first half of the twentieth century, influencing and encouraging the parallel developments of associationism and behaviorism as theories of learning (figure 3.1).

Objectivism: The Quest for Certain Knowledge

Part of the revolt against Wundt's introspectionism at the turn of the century came from the writings of Titchener and Oswald Kulpe, both of whom had been impressed with the strict sensationalism of the positivist philosopher Ernst Mach. The newborn and aspiring science of psychology was also getting caught up in the "positivist" and "objectivist" movements that would later embrace the "operationism" outlined by the theoretical physicist Percy Bridgman (1927). In its struggle to find a respectably scientific methodology to study human activity, much of experimental psychology fell victim to the illusory dream of absolute and perfect objectivity. That illusion was most tersely expressed in Watson's manifesto, in which he claimed, "Psychology as the behaviorist views it is a purely objective experimental branch of natural science" (1913, p. 138).

The impact of this view on definitions of psychology was readily apparent, as was documented in a recent study by Henley and his colleagues (1989). They examined the definitions of psychology offered in 233 introductory texts published between 1887 and 1987. Before 1929, the bulk of those definitions emphasized mind, mental life, and consciousness. By 1969, however, 60 percent of the sampled texts defined psychology as the science of behavior. (Of the texts printed in the 1970s, 22 percent offered no definition.) Behavior remained the most prevalent focus of definitions offered between 1980 and 1987, but mind and mental processes had by then returned as popular alternatives. These findings reflect the conceptual spiral mentioned earlier. In their zeal to achieve the objectivity of the physical sciences, many early psychologists abandoned the concepts of mind and consciousness in favor of the relatively simpler realm of publicly observable activity. They "came back to their senses," as some behaviorists would later quip, "in losing their minds." Avoidance of the "inner organism" was expected to solve the problems of interpretation, complexity, and subjectivity associated with introspective methodologies. The preferred experimental subject for studies of learning soon became animals rather than humans. In either form, the whole-bodied organism was allegedly objectified by being sliced into more manageable pieces of outwardly observable activity. The objectivist movement—which was also diverting the development of U.S. sociology at about the same time—insisted on public observability and thereby foreclosed on the rich domain of the "inner person."

Although John B. Watson was not the first to suggest that psychology confine itself to observable behavior, he was unquestionably the most visible and outspoken. His position of *radical behaviorism* entailed both an ontological claim of materialistic monism (often termed *metaphysical behaviorism*) and an epistemological prescription to deal only with observable events and behaviors *(methodological behaviorism)*. The first scholarly biography of Watson is very recent (Buckley 1989), primarily because he destroyed most of his personal and professional papers shortly before he died. Some of his correspondence survived, however, and his popular writings were filled with cynical attacks on marriage, the family, religion, philosophy, and the concept of consciousness. His most popular book on childrearing, for example, was dedicated to "the first mother who brings up a happy child" (Watson 1928). According to Reed, Watson's writings "reveal his deep cynicism, personal insecurity, and distrust of emotional intimacy" (1989, p. 1386), and his "science was an expression of his energetic and tortured search for self-control and social status" (p. 1387). For these and other reasons, it is not surprising that later advocates of behaviorism have been careful to distinguish their views from those of Watson (for example, Rachlin 1989; Skinner 1953, 1974).

Although methodological behaviorism, in considerably liberalized forms, continues to be respected by many modern experimental psychologists, metaphysical behaviorism and the most orthodox forms of radical behaviorism appear to be represented by a shrinking minority among contemporary psychologists. Even within that minority, there appear to be increasing differences in definitions and views. In a longitudinal study of the beliefs of leading behaviorists and cognitivists, for example, it was recently found that orthodox views—although still held by a few—have lost much of the appeal and support they enjoyed in the first half of the century (Mahoney and Gabriel 1990). This decline was also reflected in B. F. Skinner's (1977, 1987) recent laments over the changing emphasis in the field. "What happened to psychology as the science of behavior?" was the title of his 1987 article, where he applauded a recently published biography of the biologist Jacques Loeb. Loeb's turn-of-the-century emphasis on an atheoretical, nonmediational approach to life had significantly influenced the later thinking (behaving) of both Watson and Skinner. Loeb's biography was titled *Controlling Life: Jacques Loeb and the Engineering Ideal in Biology* (Pauly 1987). Its portrayal of an unreflective technician was captured by Servos in his review of that book:

Loeb stands at the fountainhead of a new tradition in the biological sciences—a tradition that places more emphasis upon the control of organisms than on a formal or complete understanding of their nature. Whereas his contemporaries, like Francis Bacon before them, believed that power and knowledge were inextricably linked, Loeb thought it possible to manipulate life without understanding it, to treat the organism as a black box from which all manner of behaviors could be coaxed by environmental cues. . . . [He believed] that scientists, rather than searching vainly for true causes, should really be concerned with producing effects. By 1891, Loeb had come to see himself as an engineer of living substance . . . [and his] experiments . . . were attempts to manipulate life processes in the absence of an understanding of mechanisms. (1987, p. 305)

That strategy appealed to both Watson and Skinner, whose dream of a "purely objective" science also encouraged a strong aversion to any impurities in the inquiry process.

Embedded in that aversion is the dichotomous implication that one is either objective and scientific or subjective and unscientific. As research in science studies and cognitive processes has now documented, pure objectivity is theoretically inconceivable and pragmatically impossible. Reckless subjectivity is not, however, the only alternative. With the anthropologist Clifford Geertz, I have "never been impressed by the argument that, as complete objectivity is impossible in these matters (as, of course, it is) one might as well let one's sentiments run loose. As Robert Solow has remarked, that is like saying that as a perfectly aseptic environment is impossible, one might as well conduct surgery in a sewer" (1973, p. 30). The "sewers" of psychology for Skinner appear to have been cognitive and humanistic approaches along with psychotherapy in general, which he termed three "formidable obstacles" to the progress of psychology as a science.

Scientism and the Decline of Orthodox Behaviorism

The legacies and liabilities of behaviorism as a theory of human experience and as a prototype of psychological science have drawn wide-ranging evaluations (Boakes 1984; Fiske and Schweder 1986; Mahoney 1989c; Manicas 1987; J. Moore 1987; O'Donnell 1985; Rachlin 1989; Rescorla 1988; Smith 1986). The chapters that follow will convey my respect for the spirit of the scientific commitments of behaviorists, past and present, and for their conceptual heritage in functionalism and evolutionary epistemology. Organismic activity, emotional "behavior," and the influence of "real-world" consequences are of central importance to any adequate understanding of the adapting and developing individual. At the same time, however, I believe that Watson, Skinner, and some of their conceptual compatriots have not served their theoretical mission well by their zealous denigration of models and methodologies that do not conform to their own preferences. Such dogmatically self-righteous and exclusionary perspectives on science are called "scientistic" by philosophers to distinguish them from approaches more congruent with the openness traditionally associated with scientific philosophy (Hayek 1952a; Koch 1959; Mahoney 1989c; Weimer 1982a, 1982b).

Scientistic perspectives propose an exclusive set of assumptions, methods, or legitimate questions as proper to genuine science and energetically ignore, denigrate, or discredit alternative viewpoints. They therefore deviate from the "open exchange" traditionally deemed central to epistemic progress (Campbell 1975; Conway 1984; Kuhn 1977; Mahoney 1985a). As I have noted elsewhere,

radical behaviorists . . . are free to claim to be the only truly scientific students of human experience, but in so doing they jeopardize their warrant for that very claim by demonstrating a failure to appreciate some essential aspects of the "true" science to which they aspire. Naive objectivism is a misguided (and misguiding) ideal in modern science, and scientism is a dogmatic form of myopia "which is decidedly unscientific in the true sense of the word" (Hayek 1952*a*, p. 15). Thus, in response to the question "What happened to psychology as the science of behavior?" (Skinner 1987), I concur with Hilgard (1987) that the discipline has matured enough to recognize the limitations of that equation. (1989*c*, p. 1376)

The fall of behaviorism from its position as the most popular perspective among scientific psychologists has been multiply determined. Its problems in dealing with the complexities of "conditioning" and learning have contributed at least as much as other variables. The "laws of learning" have had to be revised to account for the "misbehavior of organisms," hereditary "preparedness" toward some kinds of associations, animals responding in the presence of free food, and reinterpretations of Skinner's early work on the automaticity of reinforcement effects. These and other reports took their toll on some behaviorists' confidence in the adequacy of their first principles (Bolles 1972; Breland and Breland 1961; Gardner and Gardner 1988; McKeachie 1974; Neuringer 1969, 1970; Seligman 1970; Staddon and Simmelhag 1971; Timberlake and Allison 1974).

Conditioning theories of learning have been forced toward choice points involving conceptual revision or rejection. Revisions and reconceptualizations of behaviorism have been offered with increasing frequency over the last decade, many cast as possible reconciliations with cognitive approaches (Amsel 1989; Hayes 1987; Herrnstein 1990; Killeen 1984; Kleinginna and Kleinginna 1988; Martin and Levey 1985; Rachlin 1989; Turkkan 1989; Zuriff 1985). At least some of the suggested reconceptualizations of behaviorism have been influenced by the studies of animal cognition (Dore and Dumas 1987). Herrnstein and Loveland (1964), for example, demonstrated that pigeons can readily learn to discriminate between photographs with or without humans in them. Later work showed that pigeons could also discriminate and categorize a wide variety of photographic stimuli: trees, leaves of different types, water, other pigeons, the letter "A" and the number 2 (regardless of font), and aerial photographs with and without human-made objects in them (Bhatt et al. 1988; Wasserman, Kiedinger, and Bhatt 1988). As Roberts and Mazmanian put it, studies of "natural concept learning" in animals "have demonstrated that monkeys and pigeons can conceptualize at a more abstract level than has been revealed in previous animal studies, but the basis for this ability remains unclear" (1988, p. 259).

It is increasingly clear, however, that these studies reflect a deeper appreciation for the complexity of living systems and an openness to new possibilities in their study. In developing novel methods and questions, such research has generated provocative new findings suggesting that our prior assumptions had unnecessarily limited both theory and research.

Indeed, aspects of the "new" (reconceptualized and revitalized) behaviorisms of Hayes, Killeen, Rachlin, and Zuriff are not entirely at odds with recent developments in the cognitive sciences.

Studies of Attitudes, Awareness, and Abstraction

Not all of psychology had, however, abandoned the study of mediational processes. Experiments on associative and verbal learning had continued, and several of the major learning theorists had laid important foundations for cognitive studies in the second half of the century. Clark L. Hull's doctoral dissertation in 1920, for example, focused on the human learning of concepts; and Neal Miller's 1935 dissertation demonstrated that thoughts could influence responses to physically identical stimuli. Edward C. Tolman's "expectancy theory" and "purposive behaviorism" (1932) were decidedly cognitive; and the important work of Wolfgang Köhler (1925) and other gestalt researchers helped to elevate estimations of the mentality of animals and to show the holistic features of human perception. By 1950, William K. Estes (1971) and others were beginning to develop mathematical models of learning, and these models accelerated the transition to what would later be termed "cognitive psychology." Verbal learning researchers were also encountering semantic generalization in their studies, suggesting that their human subjects were responding not to an inert external stimulus but, rather, to "meanings" and associations—that is, to "the stimulus as perceived." This fact was dramatically demonstrated in a series of experiments on the role of awareness in human learning, where perceived contingencies often exerted greater influence on performance than did those actually programmed by the experimenter (Bandura 1969; Brewer 1974; Dulany 1962, 1968; Kaufman, Baron, and Kopp 1966; Mahoney 1974; Spielberger and DeNike 1966; Weiner 1965).

Beyond these important developments in experimental psychology were some parallel movements in social psychology and personality research. There was a strong surge of interest in attitudes and beliefs, along with innovative efforts to measure mood, personality, and a variety of aptitudes and attributional processes. Theories of psychopathology and psychotherapy were likewise moving toward "multiply determined" (or interactive) models that included organismic variables as important parameters.

FROM MIDCENTURY TO THE PRESENT

From the scientistic expressions of behaviorism, which dominated the self-acclaimed scientific form of psychology until just after midcentury, psychoanalytic, gestalt, and humanistic-existential perspectives were all classified as unscientific and hence belittled and ignored as less legitimate or valuable. That there were (and still are) hard feelings between these "two cultures" within psychology is readily documented (Altman 1987; Conway 1984, 1989; Kimble 1984; Krasner and Houts 1984; Snow 1964; Viney 1989). Indeed, at least part of the estrangement that forced U.S. psychology to splinter along scientist-versus-practitioner loyalties in 1988 can be traced directly to the legacy of tensions among the handful of rival metatheories that have differentiated within psychology.

Rival Siblings at Midcentury

Animosities between representatives of different schools of thought in psychology were particularly apparent in the third quarter of the twentieth century. Harsh words were exchanged often, and predictions about the demise of a rival paradigm were common. In 1949, for example, the behaviorist Andrew Salter suggested that psychoanalysis was a dying and useless encumbrance:

It is high time that psychoanalysis, like the elephant of fable, dragged itself off to some distant jungle graveyard and died. Psychoanalysis has outlived its usefulness. Its methods are vague, its treatment is long drawn out, and more often than not, its results are insipid and unimpressive. (P. 1)

Ironically, it was only a few years later that the historian Sigmund Koch used even harsher words in welcoming the impending demise of behaviorism:

I would be happy to say what we have been hearing could be characterized as the death rattle of behaviorism, but this would be a rather more dignified statement than I should like to sponsor, because death is, at least, a dignified process. (1964, p. 162)

Behaviorism was, however, hardly defenseless against this rhetorical bantering. B. F. Skinner was its most vocal champion, having harshly denigrated the "inner person" appeals to dignity and freedom made by "mentalistic" approaches (Skinner 1953, 1959, 1971, 1977, 1987). The "inner world" accessible to each of us only by self-observation was labeled by Skinner as unessential and unimportant; he added, "It is impossible to estimate the havoc [that theories about internal states and processes] have wreaked . . . [upon] effort[s] to describe or explain human behavior" (1974, pp. xii–xiii). In a later article explaining why he was not a cognitive psychologist, Skinner reiterated his hard-line stance:

I see no evidence of an inner world of mental life. . . . The appeal to cognitive states and processes is a diversion which could well be responsible for much of our failure to solve our problems. We need to change our behavior and we can do so only by changing our physical and social environments. We choose the wrong path at the very start when we suppose that our goal is to change the "minds and hearts of men and women" rather than the world in which they live. (1977, p. 10)

In the face of such affronts, many psychologists have been stirred to passionate statements and counterattacks. The famous debate between Carl Rogers and Skinner (1956) was a commendable attempt at dialogue, but such dialogues have often broken down or deteriorated into diatribes (Matson 1973; Wandersman, Poppen, and Ricks 1976). Floyd W. Matson voiced his frustrations over this state of affairs and the issues that continue to separate humanism and behaviorism:

Plainly, the differences between us must be very deep—not just technical or strategic or methodological, but philosophical, and perhaps moral. For my part, I believe that Skinner and his gentle friends state the case against their own philosophy so openly and candidly that one need only cry "Hark! See there? They are exposing themselves (the Grand Conditioner has no clothes)!" On the other hand, the Skinnerians perceive themselves as not only warmly clothed but gorgeously arrayed: Wrapped in the mantle of Science, armed with the tools of the "technology of behavior," they walk the green pastures of Walden Two and marvel at their adversaries, who speak a gibberish compounded of nonsense syllables such as "freedom," "choice," "responsibility," "mind," and so on. (1971, p. 2)

The differences, it seems, are deep, and recent efforts to reconcile behaviorism with psychodynamic perspectives have also encountered formidable difficulties and criticisms (Arkowitz and Messer 1984; Feather and Rhoads 1972; Liotti and Reda 1981; Locke 1980; Marmor and Woods 1980; Messer and Winokur 1980; Wachtel 1977, 1982, 1987). It has been the spirit of those efforts, however, more than their success that has marked a significant development in contemporary psychology.

Changing Theories of Change

If we confine our focus to theories of psychotherapy, it is evident that a lot has gone on in a relatively short period of time. Moreover, it is also clear that the possibilities for significant development have never been as extensive as they are in modern psychology. Before the First World War there were only two major theoretical perspectives: psychoanalysis and behaviorism. At the end of the 1980s, however, there were published estimates of more than four hundred distinguishable forms of psychotherapy—a number that has yet to show signs of leveling off or declining (Feder and Feder 1981; Feiss 1979; Gutsch, Sisemore, and Williams 1984; Herink 1980; Hill 1978). The vast majority of these varieties have, to be sure, involved differentiations of prior approaches, so that the entire multitude can probably be classified into no more than half a dozen *metatheories* (families of theories) without leaving too many in a "miscellaneous" or "other" category. Even so, the continuing proliferation of such systems reflects the considerable activity within professional psychology.

In the midst of this rapid and ongoing differentiation of therapeutic psychologies, however, there has also been an impressive growth of interest and activity in unifying or integrating that same diversity. As we saw in chapter 1, recent studies have suggested that between one third and one half of U.S. psychotherapists now characterize their theoretical stance as eclectic, although the majority of them prefer the term *integrative* (Babcock 1988; Garfield and Kurtz 1976*a*, 1977; Goldfried 1980*a*, 1980*b*, 1982; Norcross and Prochaska 1988). This trend represents a significant development in contemporary theory and practice. But there have been other signs of theoretical and practical integration, or "convergence," as well.

In 1982, for example, the followers of Alfred Adler's Society for Individual Psychology organized their world congress in Vienna around "the contacts of Individual Psychology with other approaches." In a gesture of maturity previously rare to the discipline, they invited representatives of the major metatheories and opened a valuable dialogue about human nature and the nature of human helping. It was the first time in seventy-one years—since Adler split with Freud in 1911—that the followers of these great pioneers had come together to talk (Reinelt, Otalora, and Kappus 1984). I was honored to be one of the participants in that congress, and it was from there that I began my continuing correspondence and friendship with Viktor E. Frankl.

A similar event occurred in Bogotá, Colombia, in 1983. Inspired by the transtheoretical visions of a small group led by Augosto Pérez Gomez, an international congress was organized on the convergence of psychotherapies. Again, representatives of different theories within psychotherapy were invited to the dialogue (Simek-Downing 1989). Meanwhile, in the United States and elsewhere, there were many other efforts to explore the possible meanings of consensus and compatibility. The Society for the Exploration of Psychotherapy Integration began as an informal network of scholars in 1980 and held its first congress in 1985. The *Journal of Psychotherapy Integration* now provides a forum for studies of convergence. The rationale for these developments was straightforward. To the extent that individuals trained in different theoretical traditions still see similar patterns or processes despite very different conceptual bifocals, those patterns or processes may be robust phenomena (or, at the other extreme, powerful illusions). Genuine dialogue and the dialectic exchange it affords came to be recognized as more generative and interesting than rigid isolationism and parochial rivalries.

Over all, then, there are multiple signs that both psychology as a discipline and psychotherapy as a specialty are in the throes of major changes as they enter their second century of recognized existence. Depending on one's choice of emphases, those changes may be portrayed as both problematic and promising. The growing interest in transtheoretical dialogue and in theoretical convergence is a welcome sign of professional maturation, for example; whereas the failure of the American Psychological Association to prevent a major split between scientists and practitioners may be more costly than has yet been appreciated.

SCIENCE AND SERVICE IN THE FUTURE OF PSYCHOLOGY

Even a cursory glance at the history of thought within psychology reveals how much that field has changed. Likewise with the range and complexity of modern expressions of psychology and psychotherapy, which also suggest that major changes are still in progress. This is not to deny the fact that some orthodoxies have survived more than a century with relatively little change, or that substantial energy has been invested in the perpetuation of original theoretical formulations. At the same time, however, the unchanging orthodoxies in psychology have lost ground in relative popularity, and the continuing differentiation of "new views" has never been so robust.

For many years there has been tension between those psychologists who consider themselves primarily researchers and those whose primary emphasis is on clinical services. Consider the opening paragraph of a book on this topic:

It is clear that research and clinical practice have a synergistic relationship, with each informing the other. It is clear that effective clinical psychologists will guide their practice on the basis of established research findings. It is clear that contributing research clinicians will be actively involved in practice, deriving hypotheses from clinical experience in order to better their research which, in turn, will influence their practice. And it is clear that each preceding statement is a romantic platitude, more honored in the breach than in performance. More likely, the practicing clinician does not read research journals very often, having discovered, early on, the irrelevance of the findings to practice. More likely, the research clinician has not treated a clinical patient for years, so the lack of apparent relevance of the findings is of little surprise. And most likely, the practitioner will register disdain for the researcher, who will complain about the disregard of the practitioner for the evidence of science.

The tension between research and practice in psychotherapy has a long history. (Stricker and Keisner 1985, p. 3)

Since the 1970s, an increasing proportion of new psychologists have chosen to specialize in therapeutic services. During that same period there has been a steady decline in the number of new Ph.D.s who have chosen careers in research or academia. The gap between science and service has widened substantially, and academic researchers have resigned from (or declined to join) the American Psychological Association over the past two decades.

Finally, in 1988, a majority of the ninety thousand members of the APA voted to reject a reorganization plan "designed to heal the schism between clinical and research psychologists" (Holden 1988, p. 1036). The result was a significant splintering, with the researchers and "scientist-practitioners" founding the American Psychological Society, an organization expressly devoted to maintaining the scientific foundations and research emphases of the profession. The net impact of this discord is not yet known, but it peaked at a time when the profession was in dire need of cohesion. That psychology is paying a hefty price for its failure to resolve its internal dissension is easy to discern. Federal funding for basic research in other sciences has increased substantially in the last fifteen years, for example; whereas, during that same interval, funding for research in the social and behavioral sciences has been reduced by 25 percent (National Research Council 1988).

Needless to say, one of the major challenges facing modern psychology is to move beyond self-handicapping internal schisms and paradigm rivalries. I do not believe that such a movement requires the elimination of diversity in psychological theory and practice. Nor do I foresee the imminent development of a "grand unifying theory" or methodology that will unite psychology and accelerate the resolution of differences between basic researchers and practitioners. At the same time, I believe it is imperative that theory, research, and practice be intimately connected and interactive. In this sense, I remain faithful to the ideals of the "scientist-practitioner" model in which research and professional services are reciprocating influences. In spite of the problems such a model presents for training, the policy of separating science from service is not a viable alternative (Altman 1987; Fiske and Schweder 1986; Kasschau, Rehm, and Ullmann 1985; Meehl 1978; Stricker and Keisner 1985). Future psychologists will, however, need to address their differing definitions of *science* and *scientific,* as well as the different meanings of *experiment, empirical, research,* and *scholarly contributions* to the literature. Also needed will be new methodologies for bridging the gap between research and practice and new guidelines for written communication in the field (Bazerman 1988; Garfinkel 1985; Heelen 1989; Morawski 1989; Reason and Rowan 1981; Valle and Halling 1989). A major purpose of the chapters that follow is to outline the implications of selected research areas for psychological practice and, reciprocally, to identify lessons from life counseling that bear on our developing theories and research on human change processes. Selected priorities for future research, training, and service are presented in appendix H.

To conclude, the refinement of our knowledge and our services in psychology are dependent both upon a mutual respect for the contributions of each to the other and upon an active engagement in dialogues that reflect that respect. The words that follow, although originally written in reference to possible obstacles to scientific progress, are just as pertinent in terms of the service dimensions of applied science:

As our priorities and values mature in the unknown crucible of future developments, let us hope that we deepen our appreciation for the collective enterprise of science and the personnel dedicated to its development. Ours is a privileged profession, indeed, and that very privilege demands a corresponding sense of responsibility and commitment. As we come to more deeply appreciate that one of the cardinal features of science is its perennial openness—its freedom to grow—it is to be hoped we will examine the most salient constraints on that openness. Whatever paths and policies we pursue in our quest for knowledge, however, we can only hope to grow by remaining open to change, and that, in itself, is a most formidable challenge. (Mahoney 1985c, p. 37)

II

SCIENTIFIC STUDIES
OF HUMAN
LEARNING AND
DEVELOPMENT

4

**The Cognitive Sciences:
Revolutions and Evolutions**

The cognitive revolution is now in place. Cognition is the *subject of contemporary psychology.*
—J.E. LeDoux and W. Hirst

The cognitive sciences represent one of the most powerful developments of the twentieth century. The "inside stories" of sensing, learning, remembering, choice, and action have generated fascinating conjectures and studies about how human knowing develops and changes. I am, of course, biased in my appraisal, and aware that my awareness probably does little to reduce even those biases I can communicate. Human knowing is necessarily imperfect, and its metaphorical illumination is thus very partial. The quality of that illumination probably ranges between the pure light of Plato's Ideas and the dark lie that denies the existence and power of any "inner life." What the cognitive sciences have taught us, and what the cognitive psychotherapies are attempting to practice, are lessons in understanding and influencing the fundamental processes by which individual humans attend to, learn, remember, forget, transfer, adapt, relearn, and otherwise engage with the challenges of life in development.

As I disclose my enthusiasm for the promise of the cognitive sciences, I hasten to add some important reservations about the adequacy of those inquiries as they now exist. Recent research has documented, for example, that knowing and experiencing processes are influenced by some of the same things mainstream cognitive science has systematically ignored (such as feelings, mood, context, culture, and history). Moreover, it is increasingly clear that we must distinguish between levels or forms of knowing, and abandon the illusion that "knowing is thinking" (or that thinking is the main form of knowing). Evidence on the "tip of the tongue" phenomenon and the "feeling of knowing," for example, illustrates the extent to which our everyday experiences reflect complex and dynamic "attention- and movement-guiding" systems that operate well beyond our awareness (Bradley, MacDonald, and Fleming 1989; Brown and McNeill 1966; Butterfield, Nelson, and Peck 1988; Greenwald, Klinger, and Liu 1989; Hart 1965; Jones 1989; Nisbett and Wilson 1977; Shevrin and Dickman 1980; see also appendix A and chapter 5). In spite of my reservations, however, I share a deep commitment to studies of knowing—especially those that speak to the daily experience of every person. As a professional helper, I am also keenly interested in what those studies have to say about the living of a life, the nature of human change processes, and the most effective means for counseling persons in process.

THE COGNITIVE REVOLUTION

Although it was not hailed as a major turning point until much later, what has come to be called the first cognitive revolution in psychology had its beginnings between 1955 and 1965. There is, in fact, some warrant for asserting that the revolution was officially "born" in 1956. It was in September of that year that a symposium on information theory was held at the Massachusetts Institute of Technology. Among the presenters there were Noam Chomsky, George A. Miller, Allen Newell, and Herbert Simon, all key figures in early theory and research. Five influential works in cognitive science were also published in 1956: Bruner, Goodnow, and Austin's *A Study of Thinking,* Chomsky's "Three Models for the Description of Language," Miller's "The Magical Number Seven, Plus or Minus Two," Newell and Simon's "The Logic Theory Machine," and Benjamin Whorf's *Language, Thought, and Reality.* In Russia, Vygotsky's *Thought and Language,* which had been suppressed since 1936, was again allowed to be printed. Moreover, a small conference at Dartmouth signaled the burgeoning interest in artificial intelligence.

In an ironic coincidence, the following year (1957) marked the publication of Chomsky's *Syntactic Structures* as well as B. F. Skinner's *Verbal Behavior.* In his review of Skinner's book, Chomsky argued convincingly that stimulus-response analyses of language were necessarily inadequate, and in doing so helped challenge the longstanding reign of behaviorism as the dominant metatheory in experimental psychology. Table 4.1 shows both the historical legacy and the dramatic acceleration of research and theoretical activity in the cognitive sciences, especially in the 1960s and 1970s. With some valuable help from colleagues in linguistics, computer science, philosophy, and the neurosciences, mainstream psychology reoriented toward understanding those processes within the organism

Table 4.1   Selected Events in the Cognitive and Cognitive-Clinical Sciences,
1860–1988

1860

Gustav Fechner published the first quantitative "law" on the relation between stimulation and perception.

1874

Franz Brentano and Wilhelm Wundt, in separate books, highlighted the question whether to study mental "acts" or "contents"—a precursor to the later differentiation of functionalism and structuralism as schools of thought.

1879

Wundt established his experimental laboratory at Leipzig.

1880

Francis Galton published the first study of memory (for everyday events such as the appearance of one's breakfast table).

1885

H. Ebbinghaus published his famous self-studies of memory; he later engaged in a debate with Wilhelm Dilthey (his former mentor and the founder of *hermeneutics*) on the merits of quantitative/reductionistic experimental studies versus naturalistic/holistic analyses.

1887

The term *philosophy* began to be dropped from the titles of several early journals, signifying the intention to separate experimental psychology as a scientific discipline.

1890

William James's two-volume *Principles of Psychology* outlined and anticipated many of the central issues in the cognitive sciences.

1895

The separation of "structuralist" and "functionalist" approaches was formalized in a series of exchanges between E. B. Titchener, J. M. Baldwin, and J. R. Angell over the interpretation of reaction time experiments; Baldwin published his evolutionary-developmental volume, *Mental Development in the Child and the Race.*

1896

John Dewey published his famous critique of the reflex arc concept.

1907

Henri Poincaré demonstrated the phenomenon of "incubation" in problem solving.

1912

Max Wertheimer published his early work on the "Phi" phenomenon (Kurt Koffka and Wolfgang Köhler were his research assistants).

1916

Ferdinand de Saussure laid the foundations for modern linguistics.

Table 4.1   *(Continued)*

1926

The Language and Thought of the Child, by Jean Piaget, was translated into
English; after some brief interest, Piaget's work would not resurface as
theoretically important until 1950.

1929

Ernst Cassirer's *Philosophy of Symbolic Forms* emphasized the importance of
symbolic processes in experience; Alfred Korzybski founded the Institute
for General Semantics in Connecticut.

1931

Kurt Lewin began publishing an influential series of works on "field theory"
and "topological" psychology.

1932

E. C. Tolman published *Purposive Behavior in Animals and Men,* a pioneering
expression of "cognitive behaviorism;" F. C. Bartlett's *Remembering* argued
for reconstructive processes in memory; John McGeoch argued for an
interference theory of forgetting.

1934

The Russian psychologist L. S. Vygotsky published *Thought and Language,*
which was suppressed two years later and did not reappear in Russian until
1956.

1940

Ludwig von Bertalanffy published his early thoughts on "general systems
theory," to be elaborated in 1968.

1942

Karl Lashley stated that the problem of "stimulus equivalence" is central to a
genuine understanding of nervous integration.

1943

Norbert Wiener and colleagues published an influential paper on "behavior,
purpose, and teleology" which proposed self-corrective "cybernetic"
modeling of adaptation; Warren McCulloch and Walter Pitts published a
"logical calculus of the ideas immanent in nervous activity."

1944

The Thorndike and Lorge word-frequency tables were published.

1945

Max Wertheimer's *Productive Thinking* emphasized the role of (often sudden)
insight in problem solving.

1946

Fritz Heider published an influential paper on the role of "balance" (later
termed "consistency" by social psychologists) in attitudes and cognitive
organization.

1947

Jerome Bruner and Leo Postman inaugurated "The New Look in Perception"
via a series of studies on perceptual set and emotionally biasing variables.

Table 4.1 *(Continued)*

1948

Norbert Wiener published *Cybernetics,* emphasizing feedback mechanisms in information theory; at the Hixon Symposium on "Cerebral Mechanisms in Behavior," John von Neumann noted parallels between the computer and the brain, Warren McCulloch spoke of "information processing"; Newell, Shaw, and Simon developed a computer capable of proving some of the theorems of the *Principia Mathematica* (1913) by A. N. Whitehead and Bertrand Russell; Karl Lashley challenged the tenets of behaviorism and asserted that organization is not imposed by the external environment but emanates instead from within the organism.

1949

C. E. Shannon and W. Weaver published *The Mathematical Theory of Communication,* setting an important precedent for the use of "information theory" and serial (linear) models in information processing; Donald O. Hebb's *The Organization of Behavior* suggested aspects of neural interaction that would later influence connectionist models of cognition.

1950

A. M. Turing published his influential piece on computers and the mind; T. Adorno and colleagues published *The Authoritarian Personality,* setting the stage for later theories of "cognitive style."

1951

Leo Postman published "Towards A General Theory of Cognition"; George Humphrey published *Thinking* and challenged traditional associationist models; von Neumann published his theory of automata in the volume based on the Hixon Symposium; G. A. Miller published his *Language and Communication;* the National Committee on Linguistics and Psychology was formed.

1952

Friedrich Hayek published *The Sensory Order,* arguing that the nervous system organizes itself into patterns of activity which are predominantly tacit and functionally embodied; Charles E. Osgood began his work on the nature and measurement of meaning.

1953

E. C. Cherry published his work on selective attention and "shadowing."

1955

Jerome Bruner and Sir Frederick Bartlett organized a conference on cognition in Cambridge, England; George A. Kelly published *The Psychology of Personal Constructs.*

1956

A seminal conference was held at MIT; George Miller, Herbert Simon, Allen Newell, and Noam Chomsky were among those participating. Five influential works were also published that year (see text); a conference at Dartmouth drew pioneers in artificial intelligence.

Table 4.1   *(Continued)*

1957

Benton J. Underwood demonstrated the importance of "proactive inhibition" in learning; Chomsky published *Syntactic Structures,* and Skinner published *Verbal Behavior;* Leon Festinger published his theory of cognitive dissonance; Charles E. Osgood and colleagues introduced the "semantic differential" for measuring polarized aspects of meaning (good/bad, strong/weak, active/passive).

1958

Donald E. Broadbent announced his "funnel" (filter) model of attention; Roger Brown published *Words and Things;* Frank Rosenblatt's Perceptron program offered a pioneering breakthrough in computerized pattern recognition based on a neuronlike network.

1959

Chomsky published his critical review of Skinner's *Verbal Behavior;* Viktor E. Frankl published his introduction to logotherapy.

1960

G. Miller, E. Galanter, and K. Pribram published *Plans and the Structure of Behavior,* suggesting that a cybernetic process replace the reflex as the fundamental mechanism of self-regulation; George Sperling demonstrated brief iconic memory.

1961

Alexander Luria published *The Role of Speech in the Regulation of Normal and Abnormal Behavior,* a volume that influenced some early expressions of "cognitive behavior modification."

1962

Bruner and Miller established the Center for Cognitive Studies at Harvard; Frank Rosenblatt published his influential theory of "perceptrons" in *Principles of Neurodynamics;* Albert Ellis published *Reason and Emotion in Psychotherapy.*

1963

Albert Bandura and R. Walters published *Social Learning and Personality Development,* emphasizing vicarious learning processes.

1965

In social psychology, "attribution theory" began to be outlined by H. H. Kelley, E. E. Jones, K. E. Davis, and J. Rotter.

1966

James J. Gibson published *The Senses Considered as Perceptual Systems;* in a series of experiments, C. D. Spielberger, D. E. Dulany, and others demonstrated the powerful role of "awareness" in human learning.

1967

Ulric Neisser's *Cognitive Psychology* offered an integrative overview of the field; Aaron T. Beck's *Depression* emphasized cognitive factors in its etiology and treatment.

Table 4.1   *(Continued)*

1968

Atkinson and Shiffrin published their influential model of information processing; in a brief piece, T. G. Bever, J. A. Fodor, and M. Garrett noted the formal limit of all associationist models of anything.

1969

Marvin Minsky and Seymour Papert published *Perceptrons,* an important evaluation of Rosenblatt's theory by that name; Saul Sternberg published influential studies on short-term memory; Donald A. Norman's *Memory and Attention* integrated the extant research in those areas; Louis Breger published *Clinical-Cognitive Psychology,* and Albert Bandura's *Principles of Behavior Modification* argued for central mechanisms in change.

1970

Gordon Bower reported his findings on interactive imagery in memory; the journal *Cognitive Psychology* was founded.

1971

William K. Estes, a former student of Skinner, defected into cognitive psychology where his mathematical modeling was influential; the journal *Cognition* was founded; Roger Shepard published his first studies of the mental rotation of images; Bransford and Franks showed that individuals abstract and recall meanings rather than specific details; Karl Pribram's *Languages of the Brain* previewed his "holographic model of mind"; Arnold A. Lazarus introduced "multimodal" therapy, with an emphasis on imagery and cognition.

1972

Endel Tulving developed his model of episodic and semantic memory (a third form, procedural memory, was added in 1983); Gregory Bateson published *Steps to an Ecology of Mind,* an important early bridge between biological, psychological, and systems approaches.

1973

The journal *Memory and Cognition* was founded; William Powers's *Behavior: The Control of Perception* lent support to active (motor) models of perception.

1974

A. Tversky and D. Kahneman published their work on heuristics and biases in human judgment; Michael J. Mahoney published *Cognition and Behavior Modification;* W. Dember argued for the interdependence of cognition, emotion, and motivation; W. F. Brewer argued that there was no convincing evidence of operant or classical conditioning in adult humans; J. J. Jenkins encouraged the shift from S-R to cognitive analyses of memory in an influential paper entitled "Remember That Old Theory of Memory? Well, Forget It!"

Table 4.1   *(Continued)*

1975

Eleanor Rosch and Carolyn Mervis pioneered a radical reformulation of categorization processes and research methods, emphasizing naturally existing (rather than artificially constructed) categories; Humberto Maturana published a seminal article on "the organization of the living" that set the stage for later developments in the study of cognition from the perspective of "self-organizing complexity."

1976

Neisser's *Cognition and Reality* moved away from computer models and constructive processes in perception and argued for more ecological validity and realism in research topics and methodologies; Beck published *Cognitive Therapy and the Emotional Disorders.*

1977

The *Journal of Mental Imagery* and the journals *Cognitive Science* and *Cognitive Therapy and Research* were founded; Donald Meichenbaum published *Cognitive Behavior Modification;* Walter B. Weimer's "motor metatheory" highlighted the debate between traditional (sensory) and emerging (constructivist) models of cognition; Hazel Markus reported research on differential processing of information about self; Bandura published his theory of "self-efficacy."

1978

The connectionist movement gained momentum from the works of such individuals as J. R. Anderson, M. A. Arbib, D. H. Ballard, J. A. Feldman, G. E. Hinton, T. Kohonen, J. L. McClelland, R. A. Ratcliff, and D. E. Rumelhart; the properties of connectionist models, later outlined by Feldman and Ballard in 1982, included "massively distributed parallel processing" and interactive neuronlike networks reminiscent of D. O. Hebb's learning theory.

1979

Stephen Kosslyn and Zenon Pylyshyn began a debate over the nature and functions of mental imagery; Bateson published *Mind and Nature: A Necessary Unity.*

1980

Richard S. Lazarus and Robert B. Zajonc began a debate on the relative primacy of cognition and affect in experience; George Lakoff and Mark Johnson published *Metaphors We Live By,* an important invitation to embodied cognition, metaphor, and a reappraisal of the nature of mental representation; Humberto Maturana and Francisco Varela published their reformulation of cognition based on autopoiesis (biological self-organization); Terry Winograd reported his personal "breakthrough" to approaching language via the ideas of Maturana, Martin Heidegger, and Hans-Georg Gadamer.

1981

The journals *Brain and Cognition* and *Imagination, Cognition, and Personality* were founded; Bower drew attention to the relationship between mood and memory.

Table 4.1   (Continued)

1983

Ralph N. Haber challenged the concept of iconic storage in visual information
processing; V. F. Guidano and G. Liotti published *Cognitive Processes and
Emotional Disorders,* emphasizing a developmental, constructivist approach.

1984

In the preface to *Cognitive Psychotherapies,* Mario A. Reda and Michael J.
Mahoney made reference to the distinction between rationalist
(associationist) and constructivist cognitive therapies.

1985

David Foulkes published the first cognitive *process* (versus content) and
developmental analysis of human dreaming; Howard Gardner published a
history of the (nonclinical) cognitive revolution.

1986

Several cognitive scientists (for example, Barclay, Brewer, and Rubin)
reported studies of personal (everyday) memory and autobiographies; B. J.
Baars published a history of the (nonclinical) cognitive revolution.

1987

The journal *Cognition and Emotion* and the *Journal of Cognitive Psychotherapy* were
founded; Maturana and Varela, in *The Tree of Knowledge,* and Donald Ford,
in *Humans as Self-Constructing Living Systems,* expanded on the autopoietic
approach to cognitive processes; Guidano's *Complexity of the Self* emphasized
"selfhood" processes as the center of personal psychological organization.

1988

The *International Journal of Personal Construct Psychology* was founded; Katherine
Nelson published a pioneering study of very early memory development.

---

that contribute to the phenomena of attention, perception, learning, and
memory. Borrowing from the terminology and concepts of information
theory, computer science, and general systems theory, cognitive scientists began to develop models and methodologies that allowed them to
pose increasingly sophisticated questions about human mentation. I shall
leave the specifics of those models and methods to other resources (Anderson 1980, 1983, 1984; Baars 1986; Blakemore and Greenfield 1987;
Boden 1981; Bolles 1975; Bower and Hilgard 1981; Bransford 1979;
Bruner 1979, 1986; Cowan 1988; DeMey 1982; Dennett 1978, 1984,
1988; Dretske 1981; Falmagne 1975; Fodor 1981; Ford 1987; Friedman,
Das, and O'Connor 1981; Gardner 1985; Goldman 1986; Haugeland
1981, 1985; Heims 1980; Herrmann and Chaffim 1988; Hunt 1989; Jackendoff 1987; Klatzky 1984; Mayer 1983; Neisser 1967, 1976; Norman
1969, 1981; Posner 1982; Rieber 1983; Scheerer 1988; Shaw and Bransford 1977; Weimer and Palermo 1974, 1982).

Most pertinent for this volume are the possible contributions of cognitive science to theory and practice in facilitating human change. Since

recent developments have begun to highlight differences in the basic
assumptions and methods of cognitive scientists, it is appropriate to
begin by examining the conceptual underpinnings of traditional cognitive research.

The Sensory Metatheory of Mind

According to the empiricist portrayal of the mind, the world is revealed
to us through our senses, and it is the "traces" of our sensory experiences—our ideas, memories, and the like—that form the foundations of
our knowing. The eighteenth-century contemporaries David Hume and
David Hartley extended Aristotle's earlier speculations about how experiences (and ideas) come to be linked together—the theory of associationism—leading to what Karl Popper would later call "the bucket theory of
mind" (1972a). As we saw earlier, the sensation-preoccupied structuralism of Titchener and the "reflexology" of radical behaviorism lent even
further support to this trend toward studying organisms "from the outside in." In the case of orthodox behaviorists, of course, what mediated
between the stimulus ("input") and the response ("output") was considered irrelevant.

When the cognitive revolution hit, it was viewed by many as a reflection
of the growing realization that behavioristic, stimulus-response models of
learning were simply inadequate. What few realized at the time was that,
with rare exceptions (such as Chomsky's work in linguistics), the earliest
cognitive models were little more than internalized versions of the same
metatheory that had been assumed by behaviorists. That perspective has
been dubbed the *sensory metatheory of mind* because of its basic assumption
that the organism is a relatively passive repository of sensations. In the
sensory metatheory, for example, perception is studied as if it were predominantly stimulus-initiated (appendix A), and memory is generally
rendered via storage metaphors that emphasize "mental representations" of experience. The associationistic parallels between stimulus-
response and information-processing models of learning are illustrated
in figures 4.1 and 4.2. The main alternative to the sensory metatheory is
the *motor metatheory of mind*, which also lies at the heart of constructivist
approaches to cognition and counseling (chapter 5).

The earliest mediational models were, in fact, those of the now-classic
learning theorists (Guthrie 1935; Hull 1943; Tolman 1932), and they
imagined miniature prototypes of stimuli and responses operating inside
the organism. The purpose, of course, was to maintain an unbroken chain
of causally determined events. In the next generation of mediational
models, these "covert" stimuli and responses were replaced by constructs with different names, but their essential function remained intact
(see figure 4.2). A stimulus, now endowed with something called "infor-

Figure 4.1   Linear Association in Stimulus-Response Models of Learning

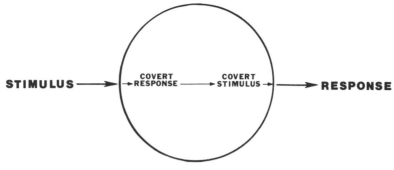

SOURCE: © 1989 M. J. Mahoney

Figure 4.2   Linear Association in Information Processing Models of Learning

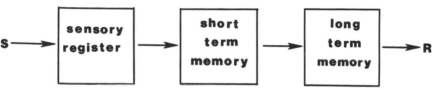

SOURCE: © 1989 M. J. Mahoney

mation," was said to enter the organism by impinging upon its sensory receptors. It left a brief trace of itself on a "sensory register," and lingered a bit longer in a new internal domain—"short-term memory." If rehearsed soon enough and properly, it could extend its metaphorical little life by being "encoded" or "consolidated" into the protective vaults of "long-term memory." Some of these second-generation mediational models did not bother to speculate on response generation. Others proposed that the "registration" of an "incoming" stimulus that "corresponded" to a memory trace could result in a behavioral response associated with that trace.

Subsequent versions of mediational models became more complex, particularly when cognitive scientists began to assert that there were "executive programs" and "executive routines" that coordinated the manipulation of the various species of "mental representations." These executive processes were also said to be ultimately responsible for action. Eventually the mind/brain was populated with *schema* (*schemata* in plural form), a concept resurrected from Kant and Herbart. Brewer and Nakamura assert that "schema theory is one of the most intellectually exciting areas of current cognitive psychology" (1984, p. 120). As they point out, most modern conceptions of schema were inspired by Bartlett's *Remembering* (1932). (For examples and overviews of the use of schema in both education and clinical work, see Beck 1967, 1976; Goldfried and Robins 1983; Hollon and Kriss 1984; and Spiro 1977.)

Although definitions vary, schema generally refer to abstract cognitive "structures" that comprise and/or generate patterns or themes of experience. As we will see, they reflect an important step beyond concrete "copy" theories of mental representation, and recent dialogues in the cognitive sciences suggest that their abstract and unconscious properties have signaled a major development in contemporary theories of knowing. (For interesting reading on the history of studying "abstraction" and the impact of such studies on stimulus-response and information-processing models, see Baars 1986, especially the interview with James Jenkins; Bransford and Franks 1971; Posner and Keele 1968; and Weimer 1973.) The concepts, methods, and models of the cognitive sciences have been undergoing some significant revisions in the last two decades, however, and the popularity and different meanings of *schemata* are only part of the story.

As I have noted, the first cognitive revolution was heavily steeped in the models and methods of cybernetics and computer science (table 4.1). *Information processing* became a synonym for cognitive psychology, and computation was the preferred metaphor for knowing. The sophistication of these conceptual metaphors grew with advances in technologies— from cameras and switches to switchboards, cybernetic machines, and ultimately supercomputers. These technologies and the conceptual models they fostered lent significant momentum to the shift from radical behaviorism to cognitive science. But cognitive scientists are also human, and at least as fallible as the grand machines they have come to love.

Reappraising Some First Assumptions

In his partial history of the cognitive revolution, Howard Gardner (1985) aptly enumerated some of the core assumptions of mainstream cognitive science. I emphasize the terms *partial* and *mainstream* because Gardner was at least forthright about his biases, and those biases were clearly mainstream in their glorification of the computer and its "representational" metaphors for mind and knowing. Besides being partial to the mainstream tradition of computer science, Gardner's history of the cognitive revolution makes no mention of the significant contributions of pioneering work in cognitive approaches to counseling and psychotherapy (for example, Bandura 1969; Beck 1967; Breger 1969; Ellis 1962; Frankl 1959; Kelly 1955; Lazarus 1971; Mahoney 1974; Meichenbaum 1977; Raimy 1975). Baars's (1986) history originally included interviews with many of these clinical pioneers, but these chapters were regrettably deleted from the final manuscript when his clinical co-editor withdrew from the project. (For a sketch of clinical contributions to the cognitive revolution, see Dobson 1988; Mahoney 1977*b;* Mahoney and Arnkoff 1978; and Mahoney and Lyddon 1988.)

According to Gardner, the first three "key features of cognitive science" are: its necessary reliance on the concept of mental representation, its reliance on computation and computer simulation, and its "de-emphasis on affect, context, culture, and history," which he refers to as "murky concepts" (1985, p. 42). Gardner considers mental representations and the use of computers as "core assumptions" of the field; while the avoidance of feelings, cultures, and histories is rendered as a methodological or strategic emphasis. These "key features" of cognitive science are, however, no longer so central or unequivocal. They are, in fact, at the heart of ongoing reappraisals of theory and method in studies of knowing, and the repeated and salient *inadequacies* of these emphases have stimulated some of the most exciting recent developments in the mind sciences.

What I am driving at here is that there has already been some significant development within and alongside the cognitive sciences—some noteworthy "evolution within the revolution." The "second cognitive revolution," for example, has involved the emergence of modern "connectionism" and the rejection of earlier computer models in favor of the more powerful massively distributed parallel-processing capacities of modern supercomputers (see appendix B). The "third cognitive revolution" has been that of modern "constructivism," which rejects the computer analogy entirely and appeals to active (participatory) processes in knowing (chapter 5). These developments suggest, among other things, that the computational, representational, and sensationalist traditions that have dominated information-processing models must now compete with more holistic and "embodied" theories of knowing. Moreover, these newer approaches have made it clear that what Gardner called "the murky concepts" of affect, context, culture, and history are, in fact, all essential to an adequate understanding of knowing.

SELECTED PROBLEMS IN MODELING MINDS

Thus, while psychology and the social sciences were going through their specialized versions of the cognitive revolution, the cognitive sciences have been in the throes of their own dramatic developments. As is often the case with scientific progress, these developments have emerged primarily out of efforts to clarify and resolve problems encountered in the intensive study of preceding paradigms. Three of the main problems faced by early models of mind have been the control structure of the mind, the nature of memory and mental representation, and the problem of meaning. The second revolution (connectionism) emerged partly out of efforts to resolve the first problem, and the third revolution (constructivism) has reflected a response to all three. All of these problems are central to our conceptualizations of professional counseling.

The Control Structure of the Mind

Until recently traditional information-processing metaphors have preferred linear (serial) chains of operations, with relatively less emphasis on simultaneous (parallel) and interdependent operations. It is in this sense in particular that these metaphors reflect the legacy of traditional (linear) associationism. As rendered by some early empiricist philosophers and many radical behaviorists, all human knowing—indeed, all human experience—is comprised of discrete links in a linear sequence (usually time). This simplest notion of association is essentially two-dimensional and sequential.

The first alternative to the linear chaining (associationist) model of the operations and control structure of the mind was offered by *hierarchy theory,* which has since become popular in biological, evolutionary, and some philosophical portrayals of nervous system organization (von Bertalanffy 1967; von Foerster 1962; Hayek 1952*b;* Lashley 1951; Mountcastle 1978; Pattee 1973, 1981; Polanyi 1951, 1958, 1966; Salthe 1985, 1989; Shaw and McIntyre 1974; Weimer 1987). In a linear (nonhierarchical) sequence, interruption of a "signal" at a given point results in the cessation of activity—the nonoccurrence of those links that occur later in the chain. This is clearly *not* how the nervous system works, as has been repeatedly demonstrated by both experimental psychologists and neuroscientists. My favorite illustrations of this point occur in early work with rats in mazes. If—after a rat has learned the appropriate sequence of left and right turns that lead to the goal box—the maze is then modified, the rat does not simply stop in its tracks and abandon its mission. One can put up barriers, add distracting stimuli, or even fill the maze with water— and still the enterprising rodent will succeed in finding an alternate route to its reinforcer! In a hierarchically structured organization (figure 4.3), an interruption at any given point in the hierarchy still leaves other paths of operations, resulting in a clearly more powerful control structure.

To their credit, early information-processing models of cognition stepped beyond the two-dimensional linear chaining of classical associationism when they postulated a vertical chain of command, with executive or "central processing" mechanisms coordinating operations that occur below them in the hierarchy (figure 4.4). Like the early computers used to simulate human knowing, early cognitive models of that knowing were imbued with the limits of available technology. It was therefore understandable that early cognitive scientists readily embraced the idea of a

Figure 4.3   An Example of Hierarchical Organization

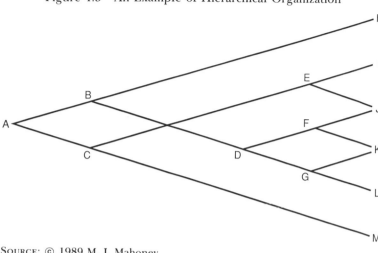

Figure 4.4   The Centralized Control Structure Common to Information Processing Models

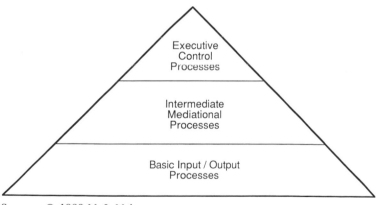

centralized control structure. Yet a vertical linearity is forced upon us by this specification of components. With only a single and simple vertical hierarchy, the implication was that the mind is organized and managed centrally—an unwarranted assumption that may have emerged from Victorian and rationalist models of the nervous system and its operations (appendix D).

Connectionism.   It was, in fact, this dawning awareness that made *connectionism* one of the most highly publicized developments in mainstream cognitive science over the last decade. Enthusiasm over this perspective has been widespread, its most ardent advocates claiming that it represents a genuine Kuhnian "paradigm shift" in cognitive studies. That it represents a shift is less equivocal than whether that shift is a significant advance in our understanding.

The basic features that define connectionism as a novel approach to our understanding of knowing can be summarized as follows:

1. A reliance on models and theories in neuroscience (rather than computer science) in model building
2. A rejection of traditional serial (linear) models of information processing in preference to multiplex "massively distributed parallel processing" models
3. In some versions, the acknowledgment of "subsymbolic" processes that cannot be expressed in explicit symbolic form.

Connectionism is thus revolutionary in relation to traditional information-processing approaches to cognition. It relies on neuroscience as a source of its assumptions about the distributed "networks" of knowing, and rejects the serial operational structure previously dominant in computer science and artificial intelligence—a structure built upon the limiting assumptions of the classical von Neumann and Turing models. This has meant a liberation from a "30-year-old framework of the 'von Neumann' machine, with its Central Processing Unit connected to its passive array of memory by a small bundle of wires" (Waltz and Pollack 1985, p. 69). Instead of confining themselves to the computational speeds and constraints of traditional programs, connectionists have appealed to "massively distributed" processing going on simultaneously (in "parallel") rather than sequentially (that is, in "serial" or "linear" fashion) within multiple "modules." Among other things, this arrangement amplifies the absolute power of the system as a whole, in part by multiplying its constituency of semi-independent processing circuits. I say "semi-independent" because most connectionist models also assert that the various modules are somehow all connected, with the "strength" and nature of the connections influenced over time by the frequency of their co-activation. Moreover, many forms of connectionism are still imbued with the metaphor that all mentation is computational; it is not yet clear what future contributions can be expected from this approach. (For a more detailed discussion, see appendix B.)

Coalitional (Decentralized) Control.   A more promising candidate for alternate control structures for the mind is offered by the distinction between "monocentric" and "polycentric" orders. Figure 4.5 is based on one of Michael Polanyi's early attempts to portray the latter. In a finite complex system (such as ourselves), no single or "central" part could possibly access the extensive information distributed throughout the entire system (not to mention the added complexity that such information is itself always characterized by being in varying states of flux). Based on current estimates of the number of neurons in the neocortex alone, the human brain "constitutes a far larger aggregation of interacting units than the entire world population" (Weimer 1987, p. 264). The number of connections among those units is also staggering—our neural architecture is extensively recursive—so that "the order of complexity is out of all proportion to anything we have ever known" (von Neumann 1951, p. 24). The important works of Mountcastle (1978) and Edelman (1987) have recently rendered convincing evidence that our nervous systems are, indeed, "decentralized" or "coalitional" in both structure and function (appendix D). That is, the brain and the body are most adequately modeled as a complex unity of distributed systems and dynamic (ever-shifting), multiple control centers. The portrayal of such a model would require figure 4.5 to be three-dimensional—with multiple connections

Figure 4.5   A Decentralized (Coalitional) Control Structure

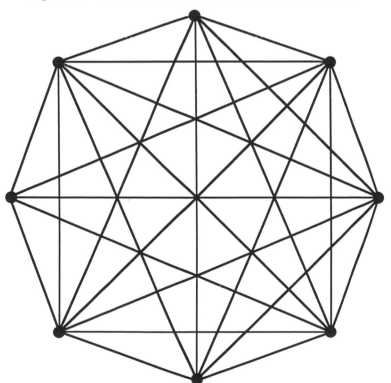

SOURCE: © 1989 M. J. Mahoney

through the interior; and the various "centers" or "nodes" of control would change over time. This is *heterarchical* control, a *heterarchy* being a system of distributed and interactive hierarchical subsystems (Ford 1987). Among other things, coalitional (decentralized) models of neural organization and psychological functioning suggest that researchers and practitioners must eventually address the dynamic complexities of "consciousness" and "conscious" (voluntary) control, as well as the inescapable fact that "unconscious" processes are pervasive in human experience (Higgins 1989; Hilgard 1977, 1987; Weimer 1977, 1982*b*, 1987; see chapter 5).

The Nature of Memory and Mental Representations

A second major problem for traditional theories of mind has been the nature of memory, which has been conceptually inseparable from the nature of mental representation. That this is a hot topic in current studies of cognition is reflected by the range of views it has fostered (Fodor 1981; Georgopoulos, Lurito, and Masey 1989; Haber 1983; Hanson 1970; Mahoney, Miller, and Arciero, in press; Maxwell 1970; Mehler, Garrett, and Walker 1982; Oakley 1983; Roitblat 1982; Shanon 1987, 1988*a*, 1988*b;* Shepard 1987; Smolensky 1988; Weimer 1977, 1982*a*, 1982*b*, 1987). The debate over the nature of mental imagery has been an illustrative forum for elaborating different perspectives (Fodor and Pylyshyn 1988; Hilgard 1981; Kosslyn 1980; Pylyshyn 1984). The need to reappraise traditional assumptions in this area is highlighted by their centrality in models of learning, memory, and cognitive processes:

Practically all of contemporary cognitive science—both natural and artificial—is conducted within the representational-computational framework. This perspective may be defined by the following three tenets:

1. Man behaves by virtue of knowledge.
2. Knowledge consists of mental representations, i.e., of well-defined symbols organized in well-formed semantic structures.
3. Cognitive activity consists of the manipulation of these symbols, i.e., computations. (Shanon 1987, p. 33)

This brief summary notes that the whole package of computational models and symbolic representations is now being reappraised in the cognitive sciences. Computation requires discrete elements and operations that can be expressed in explicit symbols or quantitative terminology. However, the thrust of the evidence—both historical and recent—is that the nervous system is not that simple, its activities are not comprised of discrete events, and computation is but a small part of its operational functioning.

To simplify, the great debate over the nature of mental representation has been yet another expression of some of the essential tensions in the history of ideas reviewed in the last two chapters. Just as the concepts of *schema* and *constructivism* ran against the current of concrete, operational research themes, the concept of *abstract, tacit,* or *unconscious* mental processes has met with resistance from traditional (rationalist) cognitive researchers. It is as if there were two barely overlapping perspectives, the one organized around the legacy of British empiricism and the other more Continental in its embrace of classic and Kantian idealism. As adapted from Brewer and Nakamura (1984), the British empiricist tradition can be characterized as: (1) maintaining that all knowledge derives from experience (empiricism); (2) asserting that the mind is composed of simple elements (atomism); (3) recommending simple interpretations of mind and mentation rather than more complex ones (parsimony); (4) identifying the fundamental mechanism of learning (and knowing) as association—contiguity (connection) in space and/or time (associationism); (5) portraying the mind as basically passive and/or reactive/retentive (sensory metatheory); and (6) portraying mental operations as mechanistic and determined (determinism, mechanical theory). The Continental position, on the other hand, has traditionally taken the opposite stance to each of these contentions.

Prior to the recent acceleration of challenges to the traditional view, it was assumed that the mind/brain "picks up" and "stores" information about the world. Such information was said to be stored in the form of mental representations, which were thought to be literal copies of either the world or prior sensory experience. (This assertion has sometimes been called *copy theory* to emphasize its insistence on the existence of mental units that correspond either to the external world or to the sensory experiences that are thought to reveal that world). Terms for and treatments of the units of storage have varied, with visual and verbal metaphors being predominant (as in mental "images" and [semantic] "propositions"). Even Neisser, whose influential 1967 and 1976 books were basically representational, has recently disavowed the use of representational concepts in human perception:

Some have suggested that new objects are systematically compared to stored category prototypes. . . . For my part, I suspect that no comparisons with stored representations are necessary at all. Previous experiences may simply have tuned the perceptual systems so that a new object can be directly seen as a member of the appropriate category. Unfortunately, these processes are not yet well understood. (1987a, p. 23)

Recent contributions by George Lakoff (1987) and Mark Johnson (1987) are relevant here. Besides criticizing objectivist proposals of mentation and mental representation, these writers have gone a long way toward "embodying" the mind and its operations (Lakoff and Johnson 1980). After outlining the five most common definitions of *propositional,* for example, Johnson adds a sixth in which *"propositional content is possible only by virtue of a complex web of nonpropositional schematic structures that emerge from our bodily experience"* (Johnson 1987, p. 5). In this view, schemata are neither (mentally) represented nor propositional in the traditional sense: that is, they are neither mental "pictures" nor subject-predicate structures that specify truth conditions. They operate, instead

at a level of mental organization that falls between abstract propositional structures, on the one side, and particular concrete images, on the other.

The view I am proposing is this: in order for us to have meaningful, connected experiences that we can comprehend and reason about, there must be a pattern and order to our actions, perceptions, and conceptions. *A schema is a recurrent pattern, shape, and regularity in, or of, these ongoing ordering activities.* These patterns emerge as meaningful structures for us chiefly at the level of our bodily movements through space, our manipulation of objects, and our perceptual interactions. (Neisser 1987*b,* p. 29)

As structures for organizing our experience, it is important to emphasize that this view of schemata portrays them as dynamic—rather than fixed—"preconceptual" ordering processes. They are, in other words, structures of activity that are themselves active and malleable. Schemata are also "the primary means by which we construct or constitute order and [they are] not mere receptacles into which experience is poured. . . . Unlike templates, schemata are flexible. . . . Insofar as meanings involve schematic structures, they are relatively fluid patterns that get altered in various contexts" (Neisser 1987*b,* p. 30). Bodily experience is thus the basis for primitive, preconceptual structures that constrain and construct all manifestations of "higher-level" mentation. Lakoff and Johnson offer numerous examples from their research, emphasizing such basic dimensions as up/down, in/out, and light/dark in their illustrations of embodied experiences that contribute to schemata and metaphors pervasively involved in our efforts to learn and know (Burke 1962, 1965, 1966; Osborn 1972).

Representation is a term appropriate only in formal symbol systems such as language and mathematics, and it is misleading to suggest that the nervous system—which can *work with* such systems—is itself *comprised* of such formal systems and symbols. "Rather than constituting the basis for (human cognitive) activity, representations are the products of it" (Shanon 1987, p. 34). The misleading terminology of *mental representation* is thus only a surface expression of more basic assumptions about the perennial problem of memory—its ecological and personal aspects as well as its "laws" or principles. As the extensive literature on that topic shows, we remain perplexed in our attempts to understand how we learn from experience and how we "retain" and transfer the lessons of such learning to our ongoing activities (Brewer 1986; Bruce 1985; Cofer 1979; Dudycha and Dudycha 1941; Horton and Mills 1984; Neisser and Winograd 1988; Oakley 1983; Rubin, Wetzler, and Nebes 1986; Tulving 1984, 1985. Critical reappraisals of representational theories of memory are presented in Casey 1987; Johnson 1987; and Rosenfield 1988).

Longitudinal research on human dream processes offers a relevant real-life illustration of this point. Using a process-oriented approach (as contrasted with more traditional content analyses), for example, David Foulkes (1985) studied the dreams of 150 children between the ages of three and fifteen years. That research has portrayed dreams as involuntary but organized symbolic acts predominantly based in (or drawing upon) what we know and remember. Foulkes believes that the same processes operative in waking cognition are also involved in dreaming, although the latter appear to reflect more extensive reorganizations. Critical of the research on dream interpretation and content analysis, Foulkes is convinced that dreams are indeed potentially important sources of information about self. His reason is partly that the single most frequent character in REM dreams is the self—a pliable self, to be sure— who appears, observes (without visually appearing), and otherwise serves as a character in roughly 95 percent of REM dreams.

More pertinent to the nature of mental representation, Foulkes's research has led him seriously to question representational models of imagery and memory in general. He has come to view both the waking and the dreaming mind as constructive and interpretive, and describes it as oriented toward organizing experience rather than preserving it "photographically or phonographically" (1985, p. 26). Some of his most interesting data on this assertion have come from studies of the dreams of blind persons. The dreams of the congenitally blind, for example, are as rich as those of their sighted peers, even though the blind dreamers have never seen the landscapes of their mind's creation (and there is little evidence that this could be due to compensatory reliance on other sense modalities). Even more intriguing are the studies of individuals who have lost their sight after the age of seven. Their dreams indicate that they retain the skills involved in generating mental images (whatever they are) despite their loss of vision. They "dream coherent visual representations of people and places they've never known visually—that is, of people and places they've experienced only since their loss of vision" (p. 38). In individuals blinded before the ages of five to seven, however, this capacity is absent. Important skills involved in the construction of what we call mental images may therefore require the visuomotor experiences of those years for their adequate development.

To sum up, there is no question that memory and what we experience as mental representations are important phenomena in our lives. Our efforts toward knowing are ongoing attempts to bring the past (personal

and collective) to bear upon the present and the future; no one is denying
the phenomena of memory and learning. But, as we have seen, it is a
mistake to assume that the imperfect concepts we invoke to talk about
these phenomena are operationally existent in or fundamental to those
phenomena. Mental representation, to the limited extent that it is currently understood, involves complex, dynamic, and abstract patterns of
activity in and beyond the nervous system. From the perspectives developed in constructivism and self-organizing complexity (chapters 5 and 6),
humans do not "have" mental representations (in the sense of internal
possessions) so much as humans *are* interpretations of their worlds: we
are, to say it again, embodied tacit theories whose actions do not reflect
internal representations so much as our ongoing negotiations with the
"edges" that define our experience (of self/world, figure/ground, and so
on).

The Problem of Meaning

A third major problem for computational and representational models of
mind is, in fact, the single most significant problem facing all of theoretical psychology: namely, the problem of meaning.

There is only one problem that has ever existed in psychology, and everything
the field has investigated is merely a manifestation of that problem, a different
aspect of the same elephant, an elephant that we have grasped at since the dawn
of reflective thought without ever reaching at all. . . . The problem, "When are
stimuli equivalent?", *is* the problem of stimulus recognition, which *is* the problem
of concept formation, *ad infinitum,* all of which together constitute the problems
of meaning. Stimuli are equivalent, in the final analysis, only because they mean
the same thing. No matter where one goes in psychology there comes a point at
which one runs straight into an insurmountable wall that is, conceptually speaking, infinitely high and wide. All we can do is look up and see that written on that
wall are all the problems of the manifestations of meaning. (Weimer 1974a, pp.
427–29)

Indeed, all psychological change—including that subtyped "cognitive"—involves
changes in meaning—specifically, changes in personal meaning(s). Let us therefore look more closely at meanings and their dynamics.

The Major Theories of Meaning.   There are, at least to my parsing of the
matter, perhaps four main metatheories of meaning. The first might be
called *physical associationism* and is exemplified by the many varieties of
behaviorist and reductionist research programs. From this perspective,
the meaning of anything amounts to its net momentary associations with
prior sensory experience. Discrete stimuli are said to be differentiated by

organisms for whom they signify different sensory associations (as in reinforcement and punishment). In this tradition, then, meaning is only a matter of behavioral or neurophysiological history. While there may be good reason to believe that meaning is, indeed, related to such experiential history, associationist models have failed to account for the many complexities involved.

The second major bundle of theories of meaning might be called *representationalist,* in that they include cognitive mediation in the phenomenon of meaning. From this perspective, meaning is a matter of correspondence between mental representations and the world "as it is in itself." As noted in the preceding section, these representations were generally assumed to be sensory (for example, visual) or (begging the question) semantic (Brewer 1974*a*). The early representationalists were also rationalists and idealists (Pythagoras, Plato, and Aristotle). In the seventeenth and eighteenth centuries, however, the nature of representation (and of knowing, for that matter) was polarized by the contrast between empiricism and rationalism, with Kant's idealism appealing to universal categories of knowing independent of experience. Empiricists and rationalists alike invoked some form of mental representation, but with differential emphasis on the origin or basis for these internal replicas (experience versus ideation). The meaning of meaning was later influenced in the nineteenth century by the concepts of evolution and adaptation. The functionalists, who would become the behaviorists of the twentieth century, translated meaning into dimensions of instrumentality, function, and efficiency. The structuralists, on the other hand, tended to remain closer to aspects of the rationalist tradition.

After representationalism (which remains popular today in a variety of forms), the next major development in theories of meaning might be called *contextualism.* The basic assertion of contextualism is that meaning is dependent upon context. The term *contextualism* was coined by Stephen C. Pepper (1942) in his classic *World Hypotheses.* There he developed the theory of "root metaphors," arguing that the major families of theories about the world could be distinguished according to their expression of four basic metaphors: formism, mechanism, contextualism, and organicism. (See Conway 1989, for a valuable review of literatures relevant to this assertion; and Lyddon 1989, for an illustration of its relevance to psychotherapy.) Jenkins (1974) drew upon Stephen C. Pepper's work in his presentation of a contextual theory of meaning. (Other illustrations of contextualist approaches are offered in Bransford and McCarrell 1974; Goffman 1974; and Lee 1989.)

Although contextualism may not appear an earth-shaking proposal by modern standards, it was a significant step beyond the notion that meanings are universal and independent of either the situation or the knower. Thus, for example, a vertical line is likely to be accorded different meanings depending on whether it is sandwiched between numbers or letters.

The same physical stimulus ("1") is readily perceived as the digit "1" when bordered by other digits (as in "413") and just as readily viewed as the twelfth letter in the English alphabet when it is bordered by other letters (as in "elm"). What contextualism forced us to see was that meaning does not reside "in" a stimulus, and that stimuli (including words, sentences, and so on) are embedded in contexts or backgrounds that color their interpretation. In a less direct way, contextual theories of meaning also helped to pave the way for later appreciations of the importance of ambiguity in cognition and the relevance of hermeneutics in analyses of knowing.

The fourth and final metatheory of meaning that I address here is *contractualism*. Less well known than contextualism, it represents a significant contribution to this area primarily because of its assertion that the individual is an active participant in the processes involved in the experience and modification of meaning. The term *contractualism* was suggested by D. R. Proffitt in his 1976 doctoral dissertation and employed by Weimer in his subsequent discussions of the problem of meaning (Proffitt and Halwes 1982; Weimer 1977). (For a discussion of meaning making in adult development, see Carlsen 1988.) The verb *contract* seems particularly appropriate since its Latin root *con tractare* denotes the "handling" or "management" of something or a commitment to action. The same term also denotes a "drawing" or pulling together—a meaning I shall touch on in a different context when I discuss the metaphor of episodic "contraction" (tightening inward) in people's experience of significant psychological change (chapter 12).

Contractualism maintains that meaning is, indeed, context-dependent, but adds the assertion that the individual is actively involved in making and changing "contracts" with regard to those contexts. As a member of the audience at a play, for example, individuals tacitly agree to "go along with" imaginary boundaries and/or "props" as if they were real. Indeed, the playwright, director, and actors are deemed successful in their art form to the extent that they "engage" their audience—that is, make it possible, easy, or enjoyable to *participate* in the tacit contract involved. From this perspective, learning involves changes in meanings that are brought about by active changes in our (predominantly tacit) contracting processes. Meaning does not reside in the stimulus or even in the relationship between the stimulus and its context. It does not, in fact, "reside" at all so much as it "reflects" the ongoing relationship between the individual and her or his life "text" (Gonçalves 1989).

EVOLUTION WITHIN THE REVOLUTION

As the foregoing summaries illustrate, there has, indeed, been significant evolution within the revolution labeled "cognitive." I have rendered those developments as secondary and tertiary "revolutions," although I must confess that I prefer the less adversarial metaphor of "evolution." Because I both respect and suspect the promise of computational connectionism, I have conveyed its facets in a technical appendix (B). Constructivism and its parallels in human development and self-organizing, evolutionary complexity are dealt with in chapters 5 to 7. Before moving on to those fields of inquiry, however, I shall comment on the contours of what some are now considering the fourth revolution in modern epistemology.

Hermeneutics and Human Understanding

There are signs of a possible fourth revolution in our understanding of human knowing. The new contender is hardly new at all, however, in that it involves the modern recognition and expansion of the perspective called hermeneutics in rhetoric, the humanities, and, most recently, the social, behavioral, and mind sciences. *Hermeneutics* is that field of study pioneered by Biblical scholars whose specialization was textual analysis or interpretation—rendering the meaning of religious text. The term comes from the Greek *hermeneutikos,* meaning "interpretation." (It was the task of the mythical figure Hermes to interpret and explain to humans the implicit meanings hidden in the messages of the gods.) In recent years, scholars in the social sciences and philosophy have extended the scope of hermeneutics to encompass the interpretation of secular texts. This application has reflected the realization that there are implicit meanings in the messages exchanged among humans, and hermeneutics has become a major voice in modern epistemology and in several realms of psychology and psychotherapy (Arciero 1989; Bubner 1981; Dilthey 1976; Frank 1987; Gadamer 1975, 1976, 1988; Gonçalves, 1990; Heidegger 1962, 1971; Madison 1988; Mendelson 1979; Messer, Sass, and Woolfolk 1988; Palmer 1969; Stent 1985; Wachterhauser, 1986; Winograd and Flores 1986). I can here do little more than sketch its basic contentions.

Although hermeneutics originated in the interpretation of religious texts, a sizable portion of the scholars responsible for rendering those interpretations were struck by the historical difficulties of interpreting a text whose words may have meant very different things in very different times. Wilhelm Dilthey was the central figure in establishing hermeneutics as a field relevant to virtually all others. As its methods (and difficulties) were incorporated into secular philosophy and the social sciences, hermeneutics was itself enriched from its many encounters with literature, history, and cultural studies. According to Winograd and Flores (1986), there is an ongoing debate in hermeneutics between the *objectivists,* who locate meaning in the text and consider it to be independent of interpretation; and those advocating a different view that has been most forcefully presented by Hans-George Gadamer. Although coming from a different conceptual heritage (which included Hegel and Heidegger), Gadamer has proposed views on "truth and method" that are remarkably parallel to those expounded by the psychological "constructivists" (chapter 5). For example, Gadamer sees active interpretation as primary to all understanding. Using a powerful metaphor that includes edges, movement, and change, he claims that understanding is the interaction of the "horizon" provided by the text and the personal horizon of its reader.

Finally, Gadamer and others have argued that something called the *hermeneutic circle* is inevitable: that is, the meaning of a text is determined (contextualized) by the horizon of its interpreter and the moment of interpretation. But the interpreter's horizon is itself the unfinished product of a history of prior language interactions, each of which can represent a text in itself that can now (historically) be understood only in the dim light of the interpreter's pre-understanding at that time. As Winograd and Flores put it, "What we understand is based on what we already know, and what we already know comes from being able to understand" (1986, p. 30). Ironically, the hermeneutic circle comes close to the paradoxes of Plato's *Meno* in that "On the one hand, the words and sentences of which a text is composed have no meaning until one knows the meaning of the text as a whole. On the other hand, one can only come to know the meaning of the whole text through understanding its parts" (Stent 1985, p. 214). (See Shanon 1984 and Weimer 1973 for more elaborate discussions of the paradoxes of the *Meno.*)

Following the earlier contributions of Rudolf Bultmann and Martin Heidegger, Gadamer's analysis proposes that the only way out of the hermeneutic circle is through the doctrine of *pre-understanding.* This pre-understanding reflects the life experience and expectations that the individual brings to all interpretations. Although we are existentially "thrown" into ever-new situations, the doctrine of pre-understanding maintains that we remain fundamentally historical beings. The very nature of our being is embodied in a personal history lived within the contexts of our culture, our language, *our* body, and our time. Needless to say, our understanding—particularly of ourselves—must be necessarily limited and only partially expressible. We cannot know ourselves completely and we cannot fully express our knowledge.

Contributions from hermeneutics are beginning to demonstrate their relevance for the cognitive sciences and psychotherapy, and lend a bit of cross-disciplinary convergence to the "active organism" metatheories to be discussed in chapters 5 to 7. From the hermeneutic perspective, then, "significance does not lie in the meaning sealed within the text, but in the fact that the meaning brings out what had previously been sealed within us." Thus, "each text constitutes its own reader" (Iser 1978, pp. 157–59);

and subject/object distinctions become both ambiguous and dynamic with "the reader in the text" (Suleiman and Crossman 1980). New or changed meanings arise from the active *encounter* of the text and its reader so that, as Fischer put it, "we constitute ourselves . . . through narrative fiction, fictions that reflect both the structure of man's brain as a process and man as a structure of the stories that the brain tells to itself about itself" (1987, p. 350).

In conclusion, the problem of meaning remains central to developments in our understanding of how and what we know, and our knowing processes cannot be separated from the "raw feel" and existential tone of our moment-to-moment experience. Whatever else it may be, meaning involves relationships; and it has become increasingly clear in this century that our "engagement" with life entails a lifelong "effort after meaning." This insight—long familiar to existential and humanistic scholars—was formalized by Viktor E. Frankl (1959, 1978, 1985) in his establishment of *logotherapy* (literally, "meaning therapy"). Research ranging from health psychology, trauma counseling, and psychotherapy has extensively corroborated the assertion that personal meanings and their change lie at the heart of psychological well-being and resilience (Antonovsky 1979; Aron and Aron 1987; Beiser 1974; Carlsen 1988; Dollinger 1986; Friedman and Booth-Kewley 1987; Klinger 1977; Kobasa, Maddi, and Kahn 1982; Laderman 1987; Perloff 1983; Warr 1978).

The (R)Evolution(s) in Progress

Whether viewed from the perspective of connectionism, constructivism, or hermeneutics, however, it is increasingly clear that scientists studying complex phenomena have been jointly acknowledging the range and role of "individual differences" in human knowing processes. Previously ignored as "measurement error" or "error variance" in the social and behavioral sciences, individual differences have come to be recognized as importantly unique and undeniably powerful. An adequate understanding of (and all generalizations about) human experience patterns will therefore require an acknowledgment of "person variables." Traditional models of knowing, as expressed in the first generation of modern cognitive theories, have portrayed humans as "way stations" for information. The linearity of that input-output function was challenged by the connectionist shift to "massively distributed parallel processing" in the second cognitive revolution. Constructivists have invited an even more radical shift in assumptions and assertions about human knowing, and hermeneutic scholars have sponsored additional challenges to objectivist, rationalist, and justificational approaches to understanding.

Although some of these scholars have advocated radically "subjectivist" or "relativist" perspectives, others have struggled with the metaphors of correspondence and influence between private and public realities. Thus, as previewed in chapter 1, a significant part of the challenge facing modern psychological research and practice is both empirical (experiential and public) and ethical (value-laden). To the extent that mental health professionals believe that their role is to "correct" perceptions of or adaptations to an objective reality, their services will be necessarily patronizing in connotation. To the extent that those professionals appreciate the complexity and individuality of personal experience, they may feel paralyzed by the limits of their powers to "know what is best" for any given seeker of their counsel. These are only a few of the problems acknowledged and preliminarily addressed by some of the recent developments in cognitive science and psychotherapy.

5

Constructivism and Self-Organization

[The world] is patently not a fixed reality and even less a particular physical environment, but most definitely a world of ever-changing individual constructions, or better . . . a world of social co-constructions.   —Hans G. Furth

As used here, *constructivism* refers to a family of theories about mind and mentation that (1) emphasize the active and proactive nature of all perception, learning, and knowing; (2) acknowledge the structural and functional primacy of abstract (tacit) over concrete (explicit) processes in all sentient and sapient experience; and (3) view learning, knowing, and memory as phenomena that reflect the ongoing attempts of body and brain to organize (and endlessly reorganize) their own patterns of action and experience—patterns that are, of course, related to changing and highly mediated engagements with their momentary worlds. It is with this perspective that we begin to see, again, the swing in the conceptual pendulum between organism and environment.

Although part of the promise of the third axial shift has involved its emphasis on the relativity of all absolutes (see chapter 2), parts of that shift are difficult to accommodate. The loss of such hoped-for goals as absolute truth—objectivity, validity, and rock-solid proof—entails its own existential form of mourning. It also requires a re-examination of what we mean by empirical and scientific. But on the other side of these "losses" there are significant "gains," which include a deeper appreciation for the individual "in process"—not just the organism developing, but the infinitely unique "social/symbolic selves in process" that populate our lives. And, as is the case in all conceptual shifting, there is the danger of going too far toward an opposite pole of some dualism. This potential risk is outlined by Allan Buss (1978) in an analysis of the four major revolutions within psychology: behaviorism, psychoanalysis, humanism, and the cognitive revolution. He concluded that the conceptual traditions associated with each involved transformations of the subject-object relation where the terms *person* and *reality* are connected by the verb *constructs.*

THE MULTIPLE MEANINGS OF CONSTRUCTION

The term *constructivism* derives from the Latin *construere,* which means "to interpret" or "to analyze," with emphasis on a person's active "construing" of a particular meaning or significance. In English usage, of course, the verb *construct* is frequently used to denote acts of building, synthesis, and form giving. As a modifier, the term *constructive* implies a positive or progressive nature. Beyond these common uses, in the field of law a *constructionist* is one who renders rigid or strict interpretations of codes or rules; and in mathematics *constructivism* refers to a corollary of the doctrine of *formalism,* which requires that real or true mathematical assertions be capable of formal proof or apprehension (Flew 1979). Moreover, in philosophy and hermeneutics, the terms *constructionism, deconstructionism,* and *constructivism* have been used with widely varying denotations (Madison 1988).

In the social sciences *constructivism* has been used with two different meanings: as a portrayal of the organism as an active agent in its own ongoing development, and as a means of highlighting the social contexts that construct and orient our efforts at knowing, communicating, and becoming (Doise 1989; Gergen 1985; Holmes 1986; Kegan 1982; Scarr 1985; Segal 1986; Watzlawick 1984). In modern German philosophy, constructivism is associated with "the demand for a *construction, rigorously regulated by a method,* of all concepts and procedures that are important for a specific science" (Bubner 1981, p. 142). As we saw at the end of chapter 2, aspects of "poststructuralism" in philosophy have been dubbed "deconstructionism" to emphasize their "undoing" of some assertions of classical structuralism (Attridge, Bennington, and Young 1987; Harland 1987; Kurtzman 1987; Lichtman 1986; Madison 1988; Melville 1986; Sheridan 1980).

In economic philosophy, *constructivism* has been used as a synonym for something called *rationalist interventionism*—the practice of attempting to regulate or control complex phenomena through explicitly rationalized intrusions into (that is, "interventions in") their operations (Hayek 1964, 1978; Weimer 1982a). This last usage is most problematic for my narrative because it creates an unavoidable semantic complexity. Friedrich Hayek and Walter Weimer, for example, are opposed to rationalist interventionism (what we might call *social constructivism*) and, at the same time, these two individuals are major proponents and representatives of active, motoric theories of mind (what might be termed *psychological constructivism*). Despite this unfortunate semantic paradox, and for lack of a more adequate alternate term, I shall retain the term *constructivism* in what follows and delimit its meaning to the psychological features elaborated below. But first a bit of historical context.

A BRIEF HISTORY OF CONSTRUCTIVISM

Although better known for his role in the emergence of empirical philosophy and the scientific revolution, Francis Bacon was also among the first to note the phenomenon of *confirmatory bias:* that is, the human tendency to distort experience in order to make it "fit" our memories and expectations. In 1621 he made this insightful comment:

The human understanding when it has once adopted an opinion . . . draws all things else to support and agree with it. And though there be a greater number and weight of instances to be found on the other side, yet these it either neglects and despises, or else by some distinction sets aside and rejects, in order that . . . the authority of its former conclusions may remain inviolate. (1960 [1621], p. 50)

Bacon believed that confirmatory bias and "self-fulfilling prophecies" lay at the heart of all superstitions. (For contemporary examples of such bias, see Greenwald 1980; Jones 1977; Jussim 1986; and Nisbett and Ross 1980.) Furthermore, he was quite prescient (relative to modern notions, at least) in noting that "it is the peculiar and perpetual error of the human intellect to be more moved and excited by affirmatives than by negatives; whereas . . . in the establishment of any true axiom, the negative instance is the more forcible of the two" (p. 51).

Hints that Francis Bacon may have been a protoconstructivist are offered in his doctrine of the "idols," in which he outlined four categories of fallacy to which the human mind is vulnerable. It was, ironically, his quest for a "real and correct view of the world" that led Bacon to insist that these psychological distortions need to be eliminated to achieve scientific objectivity. He was therefore an influential early voice in the tradition of objectivism in human inquiry. After his elegant outline of some important ideas about limitations and biases in human cognitive functioning, Bacon went on to urge that those same limitations and biases could be overcome and eliminated. In his focus on absolute objectivity (knower-independent knowing), he laid the foundations for logical empiricism and its objectivist agenda. Reality, for Bacon, was not a constructed phenomenon; his emphasis was on removing the distortions that handicap our ability to "really" and "correctly" perceive it. He was a catalyst, to be sure; but Francis Bacon was no constructivist.

Vico, Kant, and Vaihinger

The Italian founder of the philosophy of history, Giambattista Vico (1668–1744), might also be credited with being the founder of constructivism. His was certainly the first organized presentation on the role of powerfully constructive processes in perception, imagination, and knowing (Berlin 1976; Mahoney 1988a; Pompa 1975; Verene 1981; von Glaserfeld 1984). Vico was also an early speculator on prehistoric mentation and the evolution of human cognitive processes. In his 1725 book *Scienza Nuova,* he emphasized that humans create order in their experience by projecting familiar categories onto unfamiliar particulars. Vico said that "to know" is "to make" *(facere),* anticipating by more than two centuries the assertion of the constructivist Jean Piaget that to know an object is to act upon it.

After Vico, Immanuel Kant's *Critique of Pure Reason* (1781) was the next major expression of constructivism (in the form of Kantian idealism). Kant argued that the human mind imposes its own inherent structure on the particulars of thought and experience. It was his "great thesis," as Will Durant put it, that

the mind . . . is not passive wax upon which experience and sensation write their absolute and yet whimsical will; nor is it a mere abstract name for the series or group of mental states; it is an active organ which moulds and coordinates sensations into ideas, an organ which transforms the chaotic multiplicity of experience into the ordered unity of thought." (1926, p. 291)

The next major constructivist was Hans Vaihinger, the Kantian scholar whose dissertation on "the philosophy of as if" would later influence the theories and therapies of both Alfred Adler and George Kelly. Vaihinger believed that human mentation serves a purposive, organic function, and that

consciousness is not to be compared to a mere passive mirror, which reflects rays according to purely physical laws, but "consciousness receives no external stimulus without moulding it according to its own nature." The psyche then is an organic formative force, which independently changes what has been appropriated, and can adapt foreign elements to its own requirements as easily as it adapts itself to what is new. The mind is not merely appropriative, it is also assimilative and constructive." (1924 [1911], p. 2)

Emphasizing the instrumental and functional significance of cognitive processes for the biological survival and activity of the individual, Vaihinger argued that "the object of the world of ideas as a whole is not to portray reality—an utterly impossible task—but rather to provide us with *an instrument for finding our way about more easily in this world*" (p. 15). As reflected in this instrumentalist statement, he was in agreement with evolutionary epistemologists in emphasizing the relative viability of fallible efforts after knowledge over now-primitive illusions of ontological validity.

Modern Constructivists

Constructivist views of mind and mentation are scattered across many works in the twentieth century. Although Wilhelm Wundt had outlined an essentially constructivist theory of human experience at the turn of the century, his ideas did not achieve the same visibility or impact as those of his North American contemporaries, in part because of Titchener's distortions (Blumenthal 1975, 1985; Buss 1978; Hilgard 1987; Weimer 1987). Bühler and Brentano at Würzburg were also amiable to constructivist notions, as were some of the early workers in gestalt psychology. There was also a constructivist thread in the work of pioneer neuroscientist Charles Sherrington and in the later studies spawned by motor theories of mind (Held and Hein 1963; Smith 1969; Washburn 1926; Zajonc and Markus 1984). Frederic Bartlett's *Remembering* (1932) was an explicit invitation to constructivist thinking, but was viewed as being "outside the current of contemporary American research on memory" (McGeoch 1933, p. 774). Bartlett's assertions about abstractive processes and the perpetual "effort after meaning" in mentation would not be appreciated until several decades later. This was also true of the works of the most visible and influential twentieth-century constructivist, Jean Piaget, whose work had extensive impact on research in the last half of the century (Ginsburg and Opper 1969; Piaget 1926, 1928, 1929, 1930, 1932, 1950, 1970, 1981, 1987a, 1987b; Piaget and Inhelder 1963). His prolific contributions to "genetic epistemology" and developmental psychology were permeated with the assertion that "intelligence organizes its world by organizing itself" (cited in von Glaserfeld 1984, p. 24). And finally, at least in terms of theoretical contributions in cognitive science, Hayek's *The Sensory Order* (1952) stands out as perhaps the single most elegant expression of constructivism.*

*Expressions of constructivism have not, however, been confined to cognitive and clinical psychology; they are increasingly apparent in many specialties within the field as well as in the literatures of anthropology, biology, neurophysiology, physics, science studies, and sociology (Arbib and Hesse 1986; Berger and Luckman 1966; Eccles 1977; Granit 1977, 1982; Hamowy 1987; Held and Hein 1963; Jantsch 1980, 1981; Knorr-Cetina 1981; Kozulin 1986; Magoon 1977; Mahoney 1976, 1988a, 1988b, 1988c; Maturana 1975, 1988, 1989; Maturana and Varela 1980, 1987; Overton 1976; Schutz and Luckmann 1973; Smith 1969; Varela 1979, 1986; Weimer 1977, 1982a, 1987; Zeleny 1980). In the realms of personality

PROACTIVE COGNITION AND PARTICIPATORY KNOWING

The single most distinctive feature of constructivism is the assertion that all cognitive phenomena—from perception and memory to problem solving and consciousness—entail active and proactive processes. In less technical terms, the organism is an active participant in its own experiences as well as in learning. We are, to repeat a theme, co-constructors of the personal realities to and from which we respond. Rather than just being a passive repository of sensory experience or a mechanical way station for information processing, the organism is portrayed as an active, anticipatory "embodied theory."

Motor Metatheory and Feedforward Mechanisms

In psychological constructivism, cognitive processes are viewed as inherently "instrument-al" or "motoric," as Weimer makes explicit in contrasting this approach to traditionally passive sensory models:

What the motor metatheory asserts is that there is no sharp separation between sensory and motor components of the nervous system which can be made on functional grounds, and that the mental or cognitive realm is intrinsically motoric, like all the nervous system. The mind is intrinsically a motor system, and the sensory order by which we are acquainted with external objects as well as ourselves, the higher mental processes which construct our common sense and scientific knowledge, indeed everything mental, is a product of what are, correctly interpreted, constructive motor skills. (1977, p. 272)

Going beyond the cybernetic *feedback* mechanisms emphasized by earlier information-processing models, constructivist models add the complementary influence of *feedforward* mechanisms that serve to prepare the organism for some selective subset of possible experiences.

---

and psychotherapy, of course, George Kelly's *The Psychology of Personal Constructs* (1955) was a pioneering effort, to be complemented by a range of later constructivist accounts of adaptation, development, and psychological services. (For developments related to Kelly and "personal construct psychology," see the *International Journal of Personal Construct Psychology*, as well as Adams-Webber 1981; Bannister 1975; Button 1985; Epting 1984; Fransella 1972; Landfield 1971; Landfield and Leitner 1980; Leitner 1987; Mancuso and Adams-Webber 1982; Neimeyer and Neimeyer 1987; and Wilkinson 1981.) R. A. Neimeyer's (1985) history of personal construct psychology is also a valuable resource. For constructivist approaches outside the tradition established by Kelly and his followers, see Bruner 1986; Delmonte 1989; Gonçalves 1989a, 1989b; Guidano 1984, 1987, 1990; Guidano and Liotti 1983; Ivey 1986; Ivey and Gonçalves 1988; Joyce Moniz 1985, 1988, 1989; Kegan 1982; Keeney 1983; Mahoney 1988a, 1988b; Mahoney and Gabriel 1987; Mahoney and Lyddon 1988; Maturana and Varela 1987; Reda 1986; Segal 1986; Varela 1979; von Foerster 1984; von Glaserfeld 1979, 1984, 1989; and Watzlawick 1984.

The neural schematics of human vision illustrate the extensive influence of feedforward activity (see figure 5.1). (Other discussions of feedforward mechanisms can be found in Coren 1986; Eccles 1977; Houk and Lehman 1987; Pribram 1971; Varela and Singer 1987; and Weimer 1977. For a very different meaning of "feedforward," see Gardner and Gardner 1988.) On the assumption that visual experience is highly correlated with neurochemical activity in the visual cortex, only about 20 percent of that activity can be attributed to impulses from the retina. The lateral geniculate nucleus (LGN) serves as the primary relay center within the thalamus for neural connections to and from the visual cortex. As shown in the figure, impulses from the retina can influence—but do not specify— activity in the visual cortex. On the average, as much as 80 percent of what we "see" may be a tacit construction "fed forward" from the superior colliculus, the hypothalamus, the reticular formation, and the visual cortex itself. This is, moreover, but one illustration: "a similar diagram (with other names, of course) could be made for any other center of the central nervous system" (Maturana and Varela 1987, p. 162).

Our nervous systems—in complex interdependence with the other bodily systems—are highly recursive and continuously active (appendix D). Research in neuroscience makes it clear that it is patently incorrect to think of the brain and nervous system as being passively at rest until or unless they are stimulated. Continuous "oscillating" activity can be found at all levels, from individual cells to large aggregates. As shown in the example of human vision, a stimulus does not cause neurochemical activity but, rather, "joins" the ongoing activity continuously being generated within the system. Moreover, the greatest proportion of that endless activity is self-referential (recursive). Numerically speaking, there are 10 motor (efferent) neurons for every sensory (afferent) receptor; and for every motor neuron, there are 10,000 interneurons (neurons that connect only with other neurons). If we accept the traditional notion that one's sensory receptors constitute one's contact with the outside world, we are forced to conclude that one is much more extensively connected

Figure 5.1   The Neural Schematics of Human Vision

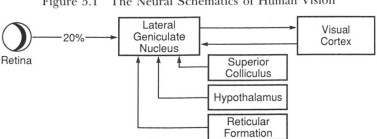

SOURCE: Adapted from Varela (1987). © 1989 M. J. Mahoney

with oneself than with the external environment (at a ratio of 100,000 to 1).

Constructive processes in perception and cognition are easy to illustrate and are particularly apparent in situations involving ambiguity or incompleteness. Thus, for example, in figure 5.2 it is easy to "see" a square even though none is there. And depending on how one "looks at" (perceptually constructs) the matrix of shaded rectangles in figure 5.3, it may appear to be a loosely patterned collection of rectangles, a vague outline of a human head, or a remarkable likeness of a well-known historical figure.

A Preview of Practical Relevance

Feedforward mechanisms in perception are but one illustration of a whole family of constructive processes in thought, memory, and the various other "faculties" of mind and consciousness. They are, however, important in that they emphasize the extent to which much of what we experience throughout the days of our lives are the changing states of our own structure, not the raw forces of the external world. In making such a statement, however, I collude in the dualism between reality and personal experience; and I intend instead to emphasize the other side of that duality—that is, the personal side of experiencing reality. The single most practical implication of motor metatheory and the concept of feedforward mechanisms is that we are active participants in the construction and

Figure 5.2   An Example of Perceptual Construction

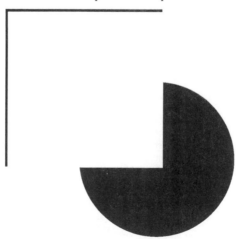

Figure 5.3 Shaded Rectangles Afford the Perception of a Familiar Face

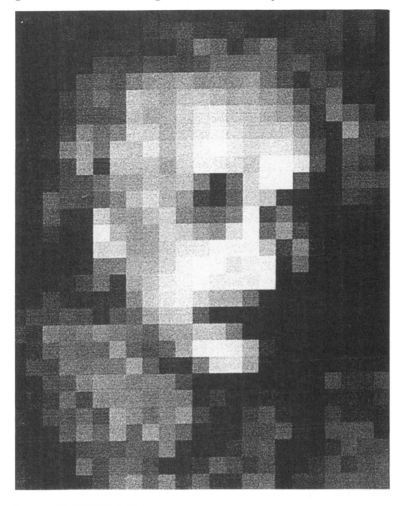

SOURCE: © 1989 M. J. Mahoney
NOTE: Computer photograph courtesy of Barry S. Isenstein

experience of the whole range of human thought, feeling, and action. As active participants, we are also "responsible" (accountable) for our experience and expression of that range of activities. Finally, the metaphor of activity implies a capacity for movement and, hence, those forms of change that are more frequently occasioned by mobility than by immobility.

Moment to moment and cell for cell, the constructivists maintain that we are actively self-perpetuating processes that reflect a dynamic polarity between structural stasis and change. Moreover, at both literal and meta-phoric levels, the concept of feedforward mechanisms suggests that the experience of novelty is, indeed, a novelty. To the extent that feedforward processes dominate in our experience, there is a correspondingly diminished likelihood of novelty, surprise, or anything resembling learning or knowing. If we perfectly "anticipate" our ever-unfolding future, the systems achieving that fit remain virtually unchallenged and unchanged. It is only when they are violated that feedforward processes—and the implicit "personal life theory" from which they emanate—may undergo change.

I dwell here on the concept of feedforward mechanisms and proactive knowing because of their important implications for the psychological practitioner. In my opinion, *an understanding of feedforward mechanisms is important to optimal life counseling, particularly when that understanding includes some lessons about how to "work with" such mechanisms in psychotherapy.* The essential challenge in change—the existential heart of learning, if you will—is the experience of novelty. As the pioneering educator John Dewey noted early in this century, learning requires novelty (McDermott, 1981). Without novelty—that is, without a difference that makes a difference—the individual projects past and familiar personal life theories onto each arriving moment and, not surprisingly, life flows on as usual. Novelty entails challenge, but not all novelties or challenges are necessarily good for the developing individual. Rates, ranges, and rhythms of learning are highly individualized. The facilitation and pacing of individually appropriate developmental challenges are therefore fundamental to all educational and therapeutic enterprises.

THE PRIMACY OF THE ABSTRACT

The second major feature of psychological constructivism is the assertion that learning and knowing necessarily involve predominantly tacit (beyond awareness) processes that constrain (but do not specify) the contents of conscious experience. This is, of course, an assertion of structure akin to that suggested by Noam Chomsky (1957): a "transformational lexicon/grammar of experience" in which "surface structure" particulars—the momentary content of experience—is determined by a more basic, "deep structure" level of processes that work to create order, relatedness, and meaning in experience. Ironically, one of the best illustrations of this assertion comes from a perceptual phenomenon, and the strongest formal "proof" of an abstract order is also the most rigorous application of empiricism to itself. The perceptual phenomenon also has some historical interest.

On 24 May 1832, the Swiss naturalist L. A. Necker wrote a letter to a colleague about his puzzlement over sudden changes in the apparent position of a crystal he had been observing with a microscope. The rhomboid crystal he was trying to draw was like the one shown in figure 5.4. Necker discovered that this change could be voluntarily influenced by a selective focus of attention (Necker 1832; see also Gregory 1987; Romanyshyn 1981). Another way of increasing the likelihood of a shift in the "perspective" of the cube is to blink one's eyes. The Necker cube can be a useful ally in illustrating (to clients, students, and colleagues) that a change in perspective does not always presume or entail a change in physical stimulus (or situation). By focusing on corner A versus corner X, for example, one can influence the apparent three-dimensional perspective of the figure.

Although Necker did not go on to make conceptual contributions to constructivist theory, his famous cube has been a popular exemplar of (1) structural ambiguity, (2) the impossibility of "seeing" more than one perspective at a time, and (3) the active involvement of the perceiver in perceptual processes. The Necker cube remains perhaps the single most

Figure 5.4   The Necker Cube

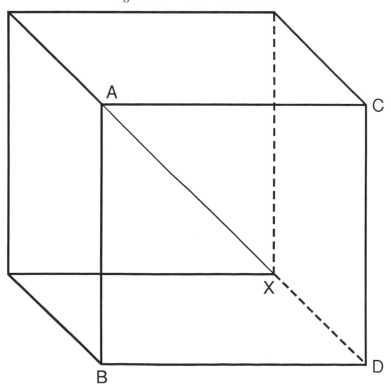

SOURCE: © 1989 M. J. Mahoney

popular visual example of ambiguity, and one of the clearest experiential illustrations of the primacy of central ordering processes in the resolution of perceptual ambiguity. Given the extent to which we continue to rely upon perceptual (and particularly visual) metaphors in our analyses of knowing in general, such an exemplar is particularly important.

Deep and Surface Structures

There are, of course, many other illustrations of how the meaning of an ambiguous figure may change. The perceptual paradoxes skillfully portrayed by the Dutch artist M. C. Escher offer some of the most entertaining examples. But ambiguity can also exist at the level of formal symbolic processes—language and mathematics, for example. Consider the statement "Visiting relatives can be fun." Its meaning is structurally ambiguous, and yet it is clear that it is a meaningful statement. Such ambiguities abound in everyday narrative, not to mention the languages of science and clinical services. They are resolved, in the vast majority of cases, tacitly—without our explicit awareness.

The formal proof of an abstract order was offered by Hayek in a rigorous self-application of empiricism. If, as empiricism argues, all knowledge is a deliverance of sensory experience, then the determinants of that experience are worthy of our interest and analysis. What Hayek demonstrated was that the contents of that experience are necessarily created through fundamental figure/ground classification processes operative at levels far removed from the "experience of the experience":

The contention which I want to expound and defend here is that . . . all the conscious experience that we regard as relatively concrete and primary, in particular all sensations, perceptions, and images, are the product of a superimposition of many "classifications" of the events perceived. . . . What I contend, in short, is that the mind must be capable of performing abstract operations in order to be able to perceive particulars, and that this capacity appears long before we can speak of a conscious awareness of particulars. . . . When we want to explain what makes us tick, we must start with the abstract relations governing the order which, as a whole, gives particulars their distinct place. (1978, pp. 36–37)

According to Hayek, the very sensations that the logical empiricist had hoped would serve as the basis of knowing are themselves the products of more basic self-organizing ("classification") processes. Said another way, perceptions and all manner of other cognitive activities often reflect more about their owner than they do about the events in the physical world that may have occasioned them:

This implies that the richness of the sensory world in which we live, and which defies exhaustive analysis by our mind, is not the starting point from which the mind derives abstractions, but the product of a great range of abstractions which the mind must possess in order to be capable of experiencing that richness of the particular. (1978, p. 44)

The writings of Michael Polanyi have also been influential in encouraging the acknowledgment of abstract processes in human knowing. In his discussions of personal knowledge and "the tacit dimension," for example, Polanyi demonstrated that "tacit knowing is more fundamental than explicit knowing: *we can know more than we can tell and we can tell nothing without relying on our awareness of things we may not be able to tell"* (1958, p. x). All skilled performances are inherently tacit, for example, and our attempts to describe or explain them are notoriously unsuccessful. One can recognize a human face, tie a shoe, or ride a bicycle with considerably greater ease than one can explain how to achieve any of these performances. Indeed, one of the characteristics of skill development is this "tacitization" process, which may spring from the tendency of our nervous systems to "automate" a skill efficiently as soon as possible. Having had ample access to their own experiences of tacitization, however, many behavioral scientists still adamantly avoid the tacit dimension in their theory and research—though even conscious mental processes and consciousness have been (regrettably) unpopular topics for most twentieth-century experimental psychologists (Hilgard 1977, 1987; Klinger 1971; Pope and Singer 1978; Singer 1974; Singer and Pope 1978).

Unconscious or Superconscious?

As strongly as they have fought the use of references to consciousness, advocates of the sensory metatheory of mind have shown an even stronger aversion to the concept of unconsciousness. Although ideas about unconscious processes had been expressed long before Freud, only recently has the term *unconscious* begun to be liberated from exclusively psychoanalytic connotations.* As Weimer (1987) has noted, for

*For an overview of both historical and contemporary ideas on the concept of unconscious mental processes, see Archard 1984; Bowers 1987; Bowers and Meichenbaum 1984; Coan 1987a; Ellenberger 1970; Hilgard 1977, 1987; Holender 1986, 1987; Jaynes 1976; Kihlstrom 1987; Klein 1977; Lazarus 1987; Libet 1985; Miller 1983; Nalimov 1982; Nisbett and Wilson 1977; Polanyi 1951, 1958, 1966; Reiser 1984; Shevrin and Dickman 1980; Stern 1983, 1987; Wachtel 1987; Weiner 1975; and White 1988. Recent studies of self-deception, subliminal perception, and the emotional aspects of knowing are also worth noting: Balay and Shevrin 1988; Goleman 1985; Gonçalves and Ivey 1987; Groeger 1986; Hardaway 1990; Izard, Kagan, and Zajonc 1984; Jacoby and Kelley 1987; Jacoby and Whitehouse 1989; Jacoby, Woloshyn, and Kelley 1989; Kemp-Wheeler and Hill 1988; Lombardi, Higgins, & Bargh 1987; Robles, et al. 1987; Safran and Greenberg 1987; and Van Den Bergh and Eelen 1984.

In a bit of self-disclosure about my own changing relations with the word *unconscious* and its meanings, let me say that having been originally schooled as a behaviorist, I resisted the idea of unconscious processes when I first encountered it in the writings of Hayek, Polanyi, sensationalists, the paradox of an "unsensed sense" is as foreign as the idea of an "imageless thought." For this reason, those sensationalists who have acknowledged unconscious processes have generally done so only reluctantly, and most have quickly relegated them to the domain of sub-cortical processes, an inescapable aspect of our animal heritage. This distinction between higher and lower centers is itself a legacy of ideas in neuroscience (appendix D), and one that misrepresents the operational structure of the nervous system. It is now widely acknowledged that tacit ordering processes are involved in all aspects of our lives and in all parts of our brain and body.

The tacit rules of order described by Hayek are different from *the* unconscious depicted by Freud, however. Hayek's realm of the abstract is no seething caldron of repressed impulses and unresolved conflicts, and is not described as necessarily lower than the processes considered conscious. Although Hayek, like Freud, refers to tacit (unconscious) processes as "primary," it is clear that the former is suggesting a distinctly different conceptualization:

It is generally taken for granted that in some sense conscious experience constitutes the "highest" level in the hierarchy of mental events, and that what is not conscious has remained "sub-conscious" because it has not yet risen to that level. There can of course be no doubt that many neural processes through which stimuli evoke actions do not become conscious because they proceed on literally too low a level of the central nervous system. But this is no justification for assuming that all the neural events determining action to which no distinct conscious experience corresponds are in this sense sub-conscious. If my conception is correct that abstract rules of which we are not aware determine the sensory (and other) "qualities" which we consciously experience, this would mean that of much that happens in our mind we are not aware, not because it proceeds at too low a level but because it proceeds at too high a level. It would seem more appropriate to call such processes not "sub-conscious" but "super-conscious," because they govern the conscious processes without appearing in them. (1978, p. 45)

Hayek also questioned whether the central task of psychoanalytic therapy—that is, the successful achievement of insight through making the unconscious (tacit) conscious (explicit)—is always a good or beneficial undertaking.

---

and Weimer. It was an unsavory "foreign obstacle" in an otherwise exciting literature. The more I read, reflected, and experienced, though, the more apparent and inescapable became the conclusion that the formative level of abstract ordering processes is primary in all living systems. Without them, there can be no distinct phenomena to constitute the particulars of experience; "higher-order" processes are undeniably responsible for "edging" out the figures from the grounds in the changing flow of conscious awareness.

The Essential Negatives of Abstract Orders

As if it were not enough to invoke the pervasive operation of processes well beyond our awareness, an additional insight into those abstract ordering rules is that they are fundamentally negative; indeed, Weimer (1982b) refers to them as "contexts of constraint." At the individual and collective level, of course, it is easy to illustrate how prohibitory rules may be particularly important because of their special relationships with the maintenance of life and the social order (upon which lives may depend). Culturally transmitted prohibitions about actions have substantial survival value for both the individual and society. At a metaphorical level, it is easy to appreciate, for example, that the basic message conveyed by pain is "no, do not do that (again)." A negative rule does not specify what to do; it indicates only what not to do, but that prohibition may be of critical importance.

A somewhat related issue has to do with the differential power of positively specified (prescriptive) versus negatively rendered (proscriptive) rules for action. Negative rules seem to specify "less," and yet convey substantially "more" relevant information than do explicit prescriptions. In teaching a child the essence of ethical action, for example, there are an infinite number of positive examples, unlimited possible ways of acting ethically. Rather than trying to enumerate such a list, however, it is much more efficient (for both parent and child) to convey a few general prohibitions (such as, do not hurt anyone, do not steal, do not lie). It is not coincidental, then, that religious and societal rules are predominantly negative ("thou shalt not . . ." and "the state shall not . . .").

As Hayek and Weimer have both discussed this feature extensively, I will not further belabor it. For those interested in the psychological significance of negatives, however, I also recommend excursions into both philosophy and rhetoric (Bachelard 1968; Burke 1962, 1965, 1966; Cassirer 1944, 1955a, 1955b, 1957; Gregg 1978; Osborn 1972). And for those who simply want to know what this means for everyday life, Hayek offers a fitting capsulization:

Since our whole life consists in facing ever new and unforeseeable circumstances, we cannot make it orderly by deciding in advance all the particular actions we shall take. The only manner in which we can in fact give our lives some order is to adopt certain abstract rules or principles for guidance, and then strictly adhere to the rules we have adopted in dealing with the new situations as they arise. Our actions form a coherent and rational pattern, not because they have been decided upon as part of a single plan thought out beforehand, but because in each successive decision we limit our range of choice by the same abstract rules. (1967, p. 90)

He argues that, in complex systems like ourselves, there is little that can be done in the way of accurately anticipating and predicting specific particulars. Hayek contends that it is the *explanation of the principle* (rather than the particular) that is most appropriate and promising as a goal in the social and behavioral sciences (1952a, 1964, 1967, 1978). This last point bears on our methodologies for studying human change and its facilitation as well as on our theoretical conceptions regarding the complexity of our subject matter. Methodologically, constructive metatheory is consistent with recent moves toward the more "ecological" or "ethnographic" methodologies that have abandoned naïve objectivism without retreating to total subjectivism (Barrom, Shadish, and Montgomery 1988; Bryk and Raudenbush 1988; Cook and Campbell 1979; Dar 1987; Hedges 1987; Hill 1982; Keeley, Shemberg, and Zaynor 1988; Krenz and Sax 1986; Neimeyer and Resnikoff 1982; Shadish 1986; Wachter 1988).

These methods entail not only serious reconsideration of qualitative research, but also recognition that human subjects and human experimenters jointly participate in the activities of research. "We may think of the distance between the psychologist and the subject as diminishing, as the psychologist loses loftiness and as the human beings who comprise the subject matter of the field are considered once again to be as truly human as those who inquire about them" (Scheibe 1988, p. 66). Moreover, many modern constructivists are also actively interested and/or involved in studies of self-organizing complexity (appendix E), as well as evolutionary and developmental processes (chapters 6–7). In this sense, then, constructive metatheory also exhibits an extensive engagement with some of today's leading developments in the sciences of complexity, theoretical biology, and evolutionary epistemology.

RADICAL AND CRITICAL CONSTRUCTIVISMS

Although the conceptual differentiation within the modern constructivist movement may seem subtle, it is, I believe, significant. The third defining feature of psychological constructivism—self-organizing development (see page 95)—highlights this differentiation within modern constructivism.

In discussing this hypothesized distinction, I am reminded of an epigram that cautions about all such dichotomies: "There are two kinds of people in the world: those who believe that there are two kinds of people, and those who do not."* We construct our distinctions as well as our perceptions. With this in mind, let me suggest that there are two impor-

---

*I want to attribute this pithy little koan to the philosopher C. West Churchman, and I have a trace memory of having first encountered it in Ian Mitroff's classic study, *The Subjective Side of Science* (1974), but I have been unable to identify its exact location.

tant variants of modern psychological constructivism that differentiate themselves on their stance regarding idealism and realism. *Radical constructivism* is on the idealist end of the spectrum and has been differentially endorsed and expressed by Heinz von Foerster, Ernst von Glaserfeld, Humberto Maturana, Francisco Varela, and Paul Watzlawick. This perspective is most elegantly expressed in theory and research on *autopoiesis* (self-organizing systems). (See appendix C for a brief overview of the radical constructivism of Maturana and Varela.)

In its most extreme expressions, radical constructivism comes close to the classical position of ontological idealism, arguing that there is no (even hypothetical) reality beyond our personal experience. Von Glaserfeld has stated this position most clearly:

Radical constructivism, thus, is *radical* because it breaks with convention and develops a theory of knowledge in which knowledge does not reflect an "objective" ontological reality, but exclusively an order and organization of a world constituted by our experience. The radical constructivist has relinquished "metaphysical realism" once and for all. (1984, p. 24)

A similarly strong statement was made by Watzlawick in the epilogue to his edited volume, *The Invented Reality* (1984). In considering what life might be like for the person who "managed to accept reality fully and totally as his or her own construction," Watzlawick concluded that this achievement would entail increased tolerance for differences of perspective, an increased sense of responsibility, and "total *freedom*. Whoever is conscious of being the architect of his or her own reality would be equally aware of the ever-present possibility of constructing it differently" (pp. 326–27). But to assert that reality is "fully and totally" constructed by the individual, and that he or she has "total freedom" to reconstruct that manufactured reality, is equivalent to embracing *solipsism*, the doctrine that the individual human mind has no grounds for believing in the existence of anything but itself. Radical constructivists deny this equivalence, however, and appeal to the "implicate order" and "participatory reality" of the physicists David Bohm and John Archibald Wheeler (see Bohm 1980; Wheeler 1982; Weimer 1982*b*).

Critical constructivists, on the other hand, do not deny the existence and influence of an unknowable but inescapable real world. They are, instead, critical or hypothetical realists, admitting that the universe is populated with entities we call "objects" but denying that we can ever "directly" know them. Representatives of modern critical constructivism include Guidano, Hayek, Kelly, myself, Piaget, and Weimer. For critical constructivists, the individual is not a self-sufficient, sole producer of his or her own experience. Rather, the individual is conceived as a "co-creator" or "co-constructor" of personal realities, with the prefix *co-* emphasizing an interactive interdependence with their social and physical environments.

Critical constructivists believe that some form of critical or hypothetical realism is required on a number of philosophical grounds (Agnew and Brown 1989*a*, 1989*b*; Campbell 1974*a*, 1987; Fuller 1988; Gholson et al. 1989; Leplin 1984; Mahoney 1989*e*; Popper 1972*a*, 1983; Radnitzky and Bartley 1987; Rorty 1979; Weimer 1979, 1982*b*).

One compelling argument for some form of realism invokes the selection processes acknowledged by evolutionary studies. Without such selection, there could be no learning. Although our knowledge of the world is (and always will be) inherently fallible and imperfect, its unknown and unknowable *degree of validity* (that is, correspondence with reality) is less pertinent here than its adaptive viability. After those bruising months of early "toddling" in each of our lives, most of us somehow learn to navigate around and through the (apparent) walls and furniture of our local, daily worlds. Such learning could not occur without the "winnowing" (selective abandonment) of nonviable activity patterns. We must therefore infer a "beyond-our-constructions" world that imposes constraints on what will and will not "work" in this part of the universe. These constraints do not determine (or "instructively inform") the contents of our constructions, but do constitute "real" boundaries on their viability. The negative constraints of selection indicate that—although we may indeed be imprisoned in our individual patterns of ordering our experience—we should not be so foolish as to deny a world beyond our direct perceptual access. To do so—and to act in strict accordance with such a denial (which no living idealists or radical constructivists have done)— could be literally life threatening. (Another argument for realism—or against solipsism—is offered by Weimer [personal communication]: it is easier to read a book than it is to write one. This would not be the case if we were the sole architects of our experience.) Assuming I have not miscontrued their writings, my hunch is that those individuals who endorse a "radical" form of constructivism would agree on this point.

To summarize, the distinction between radical and critical constructivisms may turn out to be important. I believe that more time must pass before we can evaluate their respective contributions, and am also well aware that my own inclination toward critical constructivism reflects undeniable biases in my interpretation of the matter.

COMPLEXITY AND SELF-CONSTRUCTION:
A RECONNAISSANCE

It is time to pull these strands together and explore their potential implications for how helping professionals construe human change processes, particularly those involved in learning, adaptation, and psychological development. Constructivists have shown that our position as observer and knower must always be taken into account, and that doing so is not a simple matter. We are, in fact, both subject and object of our own personal knowing, and aware of only a few of the processes that underlie our efforts. The tacit rules by which we live (eat, breathe, intuit)—in other words, the scaffolding of personal realities—limit what we do and do not know and what we can and cannot experience. To complicate matters, both sides of the great divide between organism and environment are now known to be open and dynamic. To the best of our current knowledge, the dynamics involved in complex systems suggest that tensions are fundamental to the creation and maintenance of the order we experience and describe as "real" and "me/mine." In other words, existence as we know it is an ongoing pattern of recursive activity. The order inherent in form, living and otherwise, requires the operation of dynamic self-stabilizing processes.

For those of us alive to the excitement of ideas, some of the proposals of constructive metatheory are music to make us dance. My claim is not that this perspective has "sewn up" the challenge of understanding ourselves and our worlds, but only that it has shown us some different ways of questioning our prior knowledge about all three domains (understanding, worlds, and ourselves). Scientific breakthroughs, after all, are seldom just "correct answers" to specific burning questions; they are more often invitations to change the nature and qualities of the questions being asked.

Constructive Metatheory: Problems and Promise

It should come as no surprise that my overall evaluation of constructive metatheory is positive. Although it is comprised of necessarily fallible conjectures, its proponents are at least admittedly aware of that necessity. Moreover, as a perspective in theoretical psychology that has embraced the nonjustificational viewpoint of modern epistemology (chapter 2), it invites rather than avoids its own criticism, revision, and potential development. For inveterate conceptual pilgrims like myself, this explicit openness is a welcome assurance of future movement and the freedom it requires. Moreover, despite the apparent novelty of some of its assertions, constructive metatheory incorporates aspects of the wisdom embedded in many major theoretical perspectives in psychology. Psychoanalysts, behaviorists, cognitivists, existentialists, and humanists can all find many threads of their respective traditions in the conceptual tapestry woven by psychological constructivism. While this was not an explicit intention of constructivist theorists, it reflects their openness to valuable contributions from a diversity of sources. Given this conceptual richness and diversity, constructive metatheory may be a particularly promising candidate for the continuing exploration of "integrations" and convergence among the major psychological theories.

My enthusiasm for psychological constructivism is, however, not unbridled; I am also concerned about its potential problems. Some of those problems apply differentially to specific theories and models. George Kelly's (1955) theory of personal constructs, for example, has been criticized for its failure to deal with emotional and developmental processes, as well as for its relative disuse of standardized psychometric measures and its sole reliance on what some would call "qualitative" and "personological" research methods. While Kelly may not have waxed eloquent on developmental and emotional processes, his successors have; and the "personological" flavor of their assessment methods should count as an asset rather than a liability in understanding the uniqueness of individuals (Allport 1942; Bühler 1935; Carlson 1971; DeWaele and Harré 1979; Frenkel 1936; Jacob 1987; Murray 1938; Olney 1972; Snyder and Fromkin 1980; Spengemann 1980; White 1963). Likewise, recent attempts to elaborate constructivist approaches to counseling and psychotherapy have met with some resistance among orthodox behaviorists (Erwin 1988; Eysenck 1988; Rachlin 1988; Staats 1988). I shall not here belabor the specifics of their arguments, but will note that they often reflect a continuing reluctance to tolerate (or acknowledge) some of the ambiguities necessitated by human complexity. Of greater importance to my evaluation are the more general arguments that sweep across the basic assertions of constructive metatheory. At this level there are only a few criticisms in print; their sparsity may reflect the relatively recent interest in constructivist approaches. The problems I discuss here are therefore necessarily conjectural.

Foremost among the potential problems of constructivism is, in my opinion, its relative embeddedness in abstractions unfamiliar to many modern psychologists. Such abstractness is probably unavoidable given the complexity of the phenomena to be addressed, not to mention the explicit acknowledgment of the limitations of explicitness (that is, the primacy of abstract or tacit processes). I agree with Maturana, Varela, and others that the life sciences in general are in sore need of concepts and a language that can more adequately address the dynamics of development and the complexities of lifelong becoming. Be that as it may, the invention of new terms (like *autopoiesis*) may create new obstacles in the process of overcoming old ones. Unlike the phenomena they are used to describe, our symbols for communication are seldom as fluid or as flexible. They assist us in ordering our experience, of course, but do so in a manner that necessarily violates the dynamic and ineffable complexities of that experience.

A second potential problem has to do with the distinction between radical and critical constructivism. As I have already elaborated, those versions of psychological constructivism that focus almost exclusively on the autonomy of the individual and his or her unlimited freedom to (re)construct personal experiences may, in fact, constitute a disservice to the living systems they purport to serve. The important concept of organizational closure, for example, should not overshadow the complementary concepts of openness and reciprocal exchange. Intentionally or otherwise, those proponents of radical constructivism who preach an "all in your head" sermon to therapists and clients are, in my opinion, flirting with the edges of professional irresponsibility. The parameters responsible for the pains of starvation, rape, and oppression are not confined to the nervous systems of their victims.

This same point has been made with regard to the assumption of rationalist supremacy in some forms of cognitive psychotherapy (Mahoney, Lyddon, and Alford 1989). When the Roman slave Epictetus (A.D. 60–138) wrote his famous manual on how to be happy as a slave, he did not consider the possibility of social action against the practice of slavery. Happiness was to be achieved not by changing the world, but only by changing one's view of that world. Regrettably, this is the same message conveyed by representatives of radical constructivism who promise to change objective reality with "just" our minds (see figure 5.5). Much more than its radical counterpart, critical constructivism embraces the complex and reciprocal dynamics of changes in ourselves and our worlds. In addition, the critical approach is a more likely candidate for transcending the vicious cycling of unilinear person/reality constructions that Buss (1978) has noted in past psychological revolutions.

Finally, I am concerned that constructive metatheory may fail to earn the explorations it deserves because of its emphatic assertions about the limitations and uncertainties of our epistemic endeavors. In philosophy of science, for example, constructivist perspectives have survived not because they have been enthusiastically embraced, but because their detractors have been unable to refute them. A dogmatic faith in the possibilities of certainty, objectivity, and Laplacean determinism is still dominant in the libraries and laboratories of science, and challenges to those possibilities have not been warmly received. Humans, including scientists, do not generally exhibit an alacrity for conceptual transformations that take them "too far, too fast" beyond the comforts of the realities with which they are familiar. Notwithstanding the recent rise in the popularity of constructivist approaches to life counseling, such resistance is also apparent in that domain.

This last concern is particularly relevant to the area of practice, where constructivist psychotherapies generally take a more teleonomic (self-directional) than teleological stance. Rationalist interventionism prevails as the major strategy of praxis in psychological services. With the important exceptions of some humanistic and client-centered therapies (which are always directive, no matter how subtly), most modern psychotherapy is practiced as a "corrective" intervention guided by teleological theories about human nature and lifespan development. Although their contents may vary, each of these theories harbors cultural and technical supersti-

Figure 5.5   A Portrayal of the Potential Power of Constructivism

SOURCE: Reproduced by permission from *The Family Therapy Networker*, September/October 1988

tions about why people suffer and what to do about it. I use the term *superstitions* here in the sense employed by Hayek:

An age of superstitions is a time when people imagine that they know more than they do. In this sense the twentieth century was certainly an outstanding age of superstition, and the cause of this is an overestimation of what science has achieved—not in the field of comparatively simple phenomena, where it has, of course, been extraordinarily successful, but in the field of complex phenomena, where the application of the techniques which prove so helpful with essentially simple phenomena has proved to be very misleading. (1979, p. 176)

Whether the goal of therapy is to foster insight and "release" from culturally imposed inhibitions or to modify "maladaptive" behavior through environmental engineering, it is assumed that the modern therapist can be relied upon to orchestrate a rational "solution." That solution often involves reducing the "burdens" of civilization and its contingencies and shaping patterns of experience that are more pleasant or adaptive—as deemed by the therapist and/or social community (Burrell 1987; Campbell 1975; Foucault 1965; Halleck 1971; London 1964, 1969; Szasz 1970).

Needless to say, I concur with the assertion that social and cultural phenomena cannot be ignored or reduced to the dimensions of a billiard table without rendering a serious disservice to both the client and the culture. But we have thus far made little progress in understanding "the attunement of humanity to its environment, and as a result psychology is in danger of contributing to the breakdown of modern society rather than the evolution of it" (Weimer, 1982b, p. 279). When Donald Campbell (1975) elaborated this same concern, however, in his presidential address to the American Psychological Association, his warnings were met with forty pages of mostly critical reaction (in the May 1976 issue of the *American Psychologist*). Psychologists are human, too, and therefore fallible, opinionated, and frequently resistant to change. This, then, is my final concern: that the revisions constructive metatheory would require in the domain of psychological services may involve more of a conceptual/practical perturbation than many practitioners and policy makers are now willing to endure. Above and beyond what this would mean for psychological constructivism as a viewpoint, I am concerned about what it would mean for our clients and our cultures.

As therapists and as planetary citizens, we bear a privileged responsibility to both:

We must learn to evolve within the framework of spontaneously developed features, the exact nature of which we may never know or anticipate completely. Therapy cannot go against the grain of those spontaneous factors on pain of disrupting the client's adjustment in directions that the therapist will likely never have considered, nor be able to cope with. (Weimer 1982b, p. 280)

The approach to therapy outlined in this book is an attempt to illustrate how psychological services *can* be rendered in a manner that is respectful of the complex reciprocity between individuals and their social contexts. It is in terms of that complexity and reciprocity that, in my opinion, constructive metatheory has already made significant contributions to our understanding of human change processes.

6

Evolution and Human Development

The scientific method is, after all, only the evolutionary process grown self-conscious.
—George Herbert Mead

Our quest for basic principles and processes of human change is nowhere more apparent than in the life science studies of beginnings and begettings: the emergence of life as we know it on this planet and the evolution of that life form we find most fascinating, *homo sapiens.* The study of our development as a species is relevant to the study of our development as individuals. Who and what we are, as well as what we may and may not become, are limited by factors that have been shaping life forms for millions of years.

THE EVOLUTION OF EVOLUTIONARY THEORY

The history of humanity involves much more than fossilized bone fragments and the remains of ancient cultures. Concurrent with the evolution of our bodies and cultures has been the evolution of our ideas, our conjectures about who and why we are, where we have come from, and how most wisely to approach our future. Just as Copernicus was not the first person to suggest a heliocentric (sun-centered) planetary system nor Freud the discoverer of the unconscious, so it was that Charles Darwin did not invent the idea of evolution. Although his work was undoubtedly pivotal in advancing modern evolutionary theory, Darwin's ideas had been tossing around for many centuries before he formalized their presentation and offered evidence of their accuracy.

Early Evolutionary Thought

In the early Asian writings of Confucius, the world was said to have begun from a simple, single source and to have slowly developed through gradual unfolding and branching. The early Taoists believed that *parinama* ("evolution") involved the emergence of new properties in nature due to the disturbance of a prior equilibrium. Since nature was said to be unitary, the novelty of these emergent features was thought to be illusory in that they had to have been implicit in nature from the beginning (Boorstin 1983; Bowler 1988, 1989; Bronowski 1973; Callebaut and Pinxten 1987; Depew and Weber 1985; Eiseley 1958; Goudge 1974; Gould 1977a, 1977b, 1980a; Hayek 1944, 1948, 1964, 1978; Hull 1985; Kauffman 1985; Levins and Lewontin 1985; Mayr 1982, 1988; Polanyi 1958; Richards 1987; Ruse 1986; Schilcher and Tennant, 1984; Shapere 1974; Sober 1984).

Prior to the works of Plato and Aristotle, evolutionary thinking was common in pre-Socratic Greece. Anaximander believed that the first humans originally developed inside a fishlike creature and later migrated to the dry land. Anaximenes thought that plants, animals, and humans appeared on the planet in that order, each reflecting the generative power of nature *(physis)* and resulting from the interaction of the sun's warmth and the earth's moist elements. Democritus contended that the first humans had been solitary, asocial, and unskilled until the demands of survival forced them to band together. He thus introduced the important notion that language and culture became both a product and a process in the unfolding.

These familiar ideas were soon buried, however, under the weight of Platonic and Aristotelian thinking. Plato believed that the real world was a realm of perfect and unchanging forms that could only be apprehended by thought, not by the senses. Like the many philosophers he was to influence in the centuries to come, Plato considered reality singular, external, and stable. So also did Aristotle. Although he is sometimes credited with having anticipated the essence of evolutionary theory, Aristotle was not an evolutionist. The confusion may stem from the fact that he developed an elaborate classification system for differentiating "kinds" of things and even went so far as to state that "nature passes from lifeless objects to animals in an unbroken sequence" (Goudge 1974, p. 175). This statement is somewhat misleading, however, in that Aristotle was talking about the gradations of existence rather than about a historical "passage" from one life form to another. He did not think it possible that one "kind" of animal could slowly change into another, or that the

Great Chain of Being could have emerged out of simple beginnings. For him as for Plato, reality was eternal and unchanging.

These fixed ideas about unchanging forms were to suppress the development of evolutionary thinking for nearly two thousand years. Sporadic attempts to revive a naturalistic analysis of life's origins were undertaken by such writers as Lucretius, Cicero, and Horace, but their words fell on ears effectively deafened by the dogma of Christianity. As the Christian religion gained power throughout Europe, the doctrine of one-shot creationism was force-fed to students; any talk of gradual emergence was deemed heresy. Conceptual Inquisitions continued until after the Renaissance, when philosophy and the nascent sciences of geology and paleontology reopened the issue. Kant, Laplace, and even Descartes had speculated on the origins of the universe and our solar system, while the geological studies of Charles Lyell had revealed the earth's long and changing physical history. Darwin's dominance in the history of evolutionary thinking should not, therefore, overshadow the substantial efforts of such predecessors, contemporaries, and successors as John Ray, Carolus Linnaeus, Georges-Louis Leclerc (the Comte de Buffon), Edward Tyson, Erasmus Darwin (Charles's grandfather), Pierre-Jean Cabanis, Jean-Baptiste de Lamarck, Georges Cuvier, Thomas Henry Huxley, Herbert Spencer, James Mark Baldwin, and Ernst Haeckel (Bowler 1988, 1989; Eiseley 1958; Goudge 1974; Gruber 1985a, 1985b; Richards 1987).

Darwin's Debt to the Scottish Moralists

As we have seen in chapter 5 (see also appendix E), ideas about the spontaneous emergence of a complex order like that exhibited in biological evolution had begun to appear early in the eighteenth century. The most influential of these ideas emanated from Bernard Mandeville and David Hume and were expressed in the context of the "economic social philosophy" elaborated by the Scottish moral philosophers. Between 1705 and 1728, Mandeville published several versions of a book originally titled *The Grumbling Hive, or Knaves Turned Honest* and later changed to *The Fable of the Bees, or Private Vices and Public Benefits*. It triggered widespread outrage over its assertion that "private vices" often result in unintended "public benefits," and that the worst sins and sinners may still do something for the common good (Gould 1982; Hamowy 1987; Hayek 1979; Richards 1987; Schweber 1980; Sober 1984). This controversial volume became one of the most widely read documents of the time; the more it was attacked as evil and outrageous, the more it was read—especially by the young. Even after half a century, Samuel Johnson is said to have remarked that every young man of the times had obtained a copy of *The Fable of the Bees* "in the mistaken belief that it was a wicked book" (Hayek 1979, p. 252). Following its scathing denouncement by one of his professors, for example, the young Adam Smith quickly turned to reading it. It remains the cornerstone of Smith's (1776) argument for economic liberty in *The Wealth of Nations.*

The main link between Mandeville and Smith was a young man whose thoughts on evolution were inspired by the former and adopted by the latter. David Hume was, in Hayek's words, "perhaps the greatest of all modern students of mind and society" (1978, p. 264), and his critical rationalism bore the clear stamp of Mandeville's revolutionary ideas. Hume's classic contributions on human nature and human understanding, for example, would echo Mandeville's recognition of the narrow bounds of human knowledge and the fundamentally emotional and self-referential aspects of all human action. Vico's *Scienza Nuova* (1725) appeared at about the same time, emphasizing the social contexts of human emergence; this idea and those of Mandeville would later converge in the influential thinking of J. G. Herder. Hume built upon this insight and, of course, added his own far-ranging elaborations which would significantly influence the writings of Adam Smith and his successors.

These writings on the spontaneous emergence of complex orders reflected the central theme of evolutionary theory (appendix E). There were thus a host of "Darwinians before Darwin," and David Hume was probably the most influential of that group. The point is that Darwin and the other evolutionary theorists owe an intellectual debt to Hume and his colleagues. As the Scots had pointed out, the division of labor in society amounts to a widely distributed division of knowledge, and the great advantage of the social (and "market") order is that it capitalizes on that distribution. The abstract rules governing that order are connected only by means, not by ends—a point that allows infinite freedom within the limits of social sanction. Individuals acting only out of self-interest can therefore contribute to the preservation and refinement of a viable social order. Introduced by Mandeville in his "wicked" little book, this idea is still difficult to grasp. Nevertheless, as Hayek and Weimer have forcefully argued, it lies at the heart of our revered concepts of liberty, freedom, individual rights, and social responsibilities.

Darwin's Evolution

In his autobiography, Darwin (1969) recalls having been influenced by his reading of T. R. Malthus's *Essay on Population* (1798/1926) which highlighted the "struggle for existence." Malthus argued that a population that expands beyond its own food supply will eventually be cut back by increasing illnesses and deaths due to malnutrition and starvation. Darwin had already encountered the concept of "struggle" in the geological writings of his friend Lyell, but he actually inverted the insight of Malthus in his evolutionary theory. Where Malthus had interpreted his insight as one that outlined a *stabilizing* factor in population density, Darwin was struck by its capacity ultimately to "select" (by preservation) "favorable variations" within a population. "What was for Malthus a process of destruction and stasis became for Darwin an instrument of improvement and change" (Sober 1984, p. 16). In adopting this idea, Darwin had also begun to realize that the "struggle for existence" was not just between predator and prey but also *within* species as individuals competed for limited resources and advantages.

At the same time, a young naturalist named Alfred Russel Wallace (1864) had also recognized the concept of natural selection in Malthus's book.* Bedridden with a fever in 1858, he had re-read Malthus's little book and later reported that "it suddenly flashed upon me that this self-acting process would necessarily *improve the race,* because in every generation the inferior would inevitably be killed off and the superior would remain—that is, *the fittest would survive*" (cited in Boorstin 1983, p. 474). In the next forty-eight hours Wallace wrote a paper on natural selection and sent it to Darwin, asking that—if Darwin thought well of it—he should forward it to Charles Lyell to be read before the Linnean Society in London. Darwin was shaken by the paper because it was a "scoop": Wallace's little paper captured the essence of the work that Darwin had been "sitting on" for many years.

What followed was one of the finer moments in the history of science. The scrupulous Darwin did, indeed, forward Wallace's paper to his good friend Lyell, who then orchestrated an arrangement that gave both Darwin and Wallace credit for their work. In the papers read before the Linnean Society on 1 July 1858, Darwin and Wallace were described as "two indefatigable naturalists [who had], independently and unknown to one another, conceived the same very ingenious theory to account for the appearance and perpetuation of varieties and of specific forms on our

---

*Although their reading of Malthus may have helped crystallize their ideas, however, both Darwin and Wallace were well read in literatures far beyond natural science, and modern scholars now question whether Malthus deserved such unanimous credit. Darwin, for example, had steeped himself in the writings of Adam Smith and the Scottish economists, all of whom emphasized the earlier insights of Mandeville and Hume (Hamowy 1987). Moreover, as noted in Howard Gruber's (1974) scholarly biography, Darwin's personal notebook revealed that he had begun reading Hume's *Inquiry Concerning Human Understanding* in August 1838, a month before his Malthusian inspiration. As Robert J. Richards also documents, Hume's psychology had been endorsed by Erasmus Darwin and Hume was also Charles Darwin's "then favorite philosophical author" (1987, p. 109). Like the life forms he hoped to understand, Darwin's ideas varied over time and were selectively winnowed by his observations, reasoning, and exchanges with colleagues. Had it been otherwise—and had Malthus's book on population been a sufficient catalyst—it would be difficult to understand why it took more than twenty years for Darwin to put his theory into print. Even then his thinking continued to evolve, and when he turned to more complex issues his writing continued to reflect the legacy of the Scottish moralists.

Besides their published works, I am indebted to both Hayek and Weimer for illuminating conversations on this topic. I also appreciate Weimer's generosity in sharing chapters of an unfinished book on *Rational Constructivism, Scientism, and The Study of Man and Society.*

planet, [and who] may both fairly claim the merit of being original thinkers in this important line of inquiry" (cited in Boorstin 1983, p. 465).
Darwin's *On The Origin of Species* was written in eight months and published the next year (1859). Although they diverged in their later opinions, Wallace was generous in referring to their conceptual product as
"Darwinian" theory.

The "abuses of reason" in reactions to and elaborations of evolutionary thinking have been considerable. T. H. Huxley wrote that Darwin's
book "was badly received by the generation to which it was first addressed, and the outpouring of angry nonsense to which it gave rise is
sad to think upon." With commendable perspective, Huxley added that
"the present generation will probably behave just as badly if another
Darwin should arise and inflict upon them what the generality of mankind
most hate—the necessity of revising their convictions" (cited in Boorstin
1983, p. 476). His prediction was apt, as is illustrated by many modern
evolutionists themselves.

SELECTED ISSUES IN EVOLUTION

Little imagination is required to recognize the relevance of evolutionary
thinking for our understanding of human development both individually
and collectively (Bateson 1985; Butterworth, Rutkowska, and Scaife
1985; Gruber 1985*a*, 1985*b*; Lerner 1984; Mischel 1971; Oyama 1985;
Raff and Raff 1987; Sameroff 1983). At the same time, however, it is
noteworthy that so many divergent interpretations have been drawn from
the same conceptual corpus. This may be due, in part, to (1) the theoretical diversity within the evolutionary paradigm itself, (2) the fact that
evolutionary perspectives continue to evolve, and (3) the pervasive operation of emotional (and other psychological) processes in our inferences.
The major schools of thought in modern psychology can trace important
aspects of their development to the fertile soils of evolutionary theory.
This is a telling comment. How is it possible that such diverse perspectives could have emerged from the same metatheory? The answer, I
believe, involves an appreciation both of the inherent generativity of the
concept of *development* (Collins 1982; Harris 1957), as well as of the
resourcefulness of psychological theorists in adapting evolutionary theory to their conceptual needs. In this last sentence, for example, I have
inverted the usual meaning of *adapting,* using it to refer to the creative
activity of theorists rather than to reactive conformity. Such semantic
dexterity is made possible by the inherent ambiguities and creative potential of our symbolic processes. In this section I shall outline and briefly
annotate some of the concepts and issues that have contributed to diverse
interpretations of evolutionary theory. My hope is that this discussion will
help to identify some of the more common misconceptions about evolu-

tion, as well as to highlight issues that remain at the forefront of contemporary research in this area. Readers interested in the big picture of biological evolution will find an outline and resources in appendix F.

The Nature of Adaptation and Selection

Two of the most frequently abused concepts in evolutionary theory are those of *adaptation* and *selection* (Buss 1988; Dupre 1987; Gould 1980*a*, 1980*b*, 1982; Gould and Lewontin 1979; Kauffman 1985; Laszlo 1987; Lewontin 1978; Sober 1984; Stebbins and Ayala 1981; Vermeij 1987). The first term is derived from the Latin verb *adaptare*, which means "to alter so as to make fit." Its essence is "to change," with the implicit rider that such change is guided by the need to conform, comply, accommodate, or fit. *Selection*, on the other hand, comes from the Latin *seligere*, meaning "to choose." Both terms can be used with very different meanings. In the preceding paragraph, for example, I suggested that psychologists have changed ("adapted") evolutionary theory to meet their own conceptual needs. A different meaning is implied, however, when one asserts that a living system is "well adapted" to its environment. In some interpretations of the latter statement, the sense is that the organism has found (and now occupies) its *econiche*—that is, a viable or "proper" place in the ecosystem. Thus, the concepts of adaptation and selection are necessarily entangled in assumptions about the relationships between organisms and their environments—the famous nature/nurture controversy.

Consider, for example, the following definitions of *adaptation* offered by a modern resource book:

(i) *evolutionary adaptation,* which concerns the ways in which species adjust genetically to changed environmental conditions in the very long term; (ii) *physiological adaptation,* which has to do with the physiological processes involved in adjustment by the individual to climatic changes and changes in food quality, etc.; (iii) *sensory adaptation,* by which the sense organs adjust to the changes in the strength of the particular stimulation which they are designed to detect; and (iv) *adaptation by learning,* which is a process by which animals are able to adjust to a wide variety of different types of environmental change. (McFarland 1987, p. 3)

The emphasis in all four proposed definitions is on changes in the environment leading to changes in the organism. As we shall see, such a one-sided portrayal is considered increasingly less tenable by modern evolutionary specialists.

Throughout his career Darwin maintained that the two main goals of his work were to demonstrate that evolution had, in fact, occurred (which was contrary to the earlier notion that species had been separate from the outset); and to show that natural selection had been the chief agent of that change. The principle of natural selection was to become the essence of Darwinian theory. Two of its corollaries have become important for modern considerations. First, Darwin favored the doctrine of *gradualism:* that is, that evolutionary change is a gradual process of small genetic variations (or mutations) that are preserved and propagated by their relative advantages in the struggle for existence. The doctrine of gradualism implies that evolutionary change has been a slow, smooth, and continuous process. A second and related corrolary was the doctrine of *adaptationism:* that is, that later generations are better adapted to their environments because the more "favorable" variations of their ancestors had been incorporated into their genetic makeup:

More recent forms must, on my theory, be higher than the more ancient; for each new species is formed by having had some advantage in the struggle for life over other and preceding forms. . . . I do not doubt that this process of improvement has affected in a marked and sensible manner the organisation of the more recent and victorious forms of life; but I can see no way of testing this sort of progress. (Darwin 1859, pp. 336–37)

The doctrines of adaptationism and gradualism were adopted as valid when evolutionary studies showed a burst of popularity during and after the 1950s. The perspective termed the *modern synthesis,* or *neo-Darwinism,* has basically endorsed the doctrines of gradualism and adaptationism. The writings of Theodosius Dobzhansky and Ernst Mayr were instrumental in that synthesis, which essentially merged Mendelian genetics with Darwinian ideas and integrated diverse specializations in biological science around a Darwinian core.

The Limits of Adaptationism. Without belaboring the technicalities, recent research and developments within evolutionary biology have challenged the doctrines of adaptationism and gradualism. Some of these developments have emerged from studies of the "level" at which selection operates—from the "microevolution" of the so-called selfish gene (Dawkins 1976) to the "macroevolution" of entire species. "Progress" in adaptation is difficult to measure (as Darwin noted) in part because adaptation itself is difficult to define. Among other things, (1) adaptation is always relative to the (environmental) context of the the adapting organism and to the conceptual perspective of the labeling observer; (2) the current and apparent utility of a bodily structure or behavior permits no logical inferences about its origin; (3) many apparent adaptations were by-products of other changes or may have served different original functions; and (4) genetic changes have often been maladaptive in the sense

that their functional specialization left later generations less capable of
changing their activities when their environments changed.

The adaptationist doctrine also presumes a strict, reductionistic determinism in which changes in the organism are "caused" or "driven" by
its environment. The inadequacy of this view is aptly captured by a metaphor borrowed from Francis Galton. In strict selectionism the organism
is portrayed as if it were literally a smooth sphere, such as a billiard ball,
whose changing positions and directions are totally determined by the
environmental forces impinging upon it. But Galton suggested that it is
more accurate to think of the organism as a polyhedron—that is, a sphe-
roid with many "facets" on its surface which reflect its internal structure
and history. The organism does not, therefore, roll smoothly (or in a
straight line) with the punches of its environment; rather, it responds to
those punches in a manner that reflects its own complex makeup:

The facets are constraints exerted by the developmental integration of organisms
themselves. Change cannot occur in all directions, or with any increment; the
organism is not a metaphorical sphere. When the polyhedron tumbles, selection
may usually be the propelling force. But if adjacent facets are few in number and
wide in spacing, then we cannot identify selection as the only, or even the primary
control upon evolution. For selection is channeled by the form of the polyhedron
it pushes, and these constraints may exert a more powerful influence than the
external push itself. This is the legitimate sense of a much maligned claim that
"internal factors" are important in evolution. . . . Organisms are not billiard balls,
struck in deterministic fashion by the cue of natural selection, and rolling to
optimal positions on life's table. They influence their own destiny in interesting,
complex, and comprehensible ways. We must put this concept of organism back
into evolutionary biology. (Gould 1980a, p. 129)

It is, in fact, at this juncture that studies of spontaneous self-organization
have merged with those of evolutionary biology in re-asserting the importance of the organism in its own determination. Richard Levins and
Richard Lewontin have called this merger "constructivism" because it
emphasizes the fact that the organism continuously "participates in its
own construction" (1985, p. 105). (I shall return to that concept in my
discussion of the "active organism.")

The rejection of adaptationism should not, however, be viewed as a
denial of the power of environmental constraints. Of all the species
known to have graced our planet, for example, over 99 percent are now
extinct. We are in the upper 1 percentile just by being here. That consolation loses some of its assurance, however, when one realizes that "being
here" does not necessarily mean that we are "better adapted" than our
extinct compatriots. The much-despised cockroach, for example, is also
an occupant of that lone centile and—although it has changed much less
than we have—may yet demonstrate its greater survival abilities in the
regrettably real prospect of nuclear war.

The Decline of Gradualism. Adherence to the doctrine of gradualism has also declined in the last few decades, but not without resistance or protest. Drawing on the extant data from genetics, embryology, and taxonomy, for example, Richard Goldschmidt (1933) suggested that speciation might be caused by sudden and substantial leaps in genetic makeup. In his view, mutants producing monstrosities could permit "a small rate change in early embryonic processes to produce a large effect embodying considerable parts of the organism" (1940, p. 891). Goldschmidt coined the term *hopeful monsters** to express the unconventional idea that such mechanisms may have played an important role in macroevolution. His scientific colleagues were not ready to consider such a possibility, however, and Goldschmidt was publicly ridiculed for suggesting it. The extensive "gaps" in the fossil record were, according to these experts, an artifact of sampling. It was thought that, in the long run, paleobiology and archeology would fill in those gaps and show Darwin to have been correct. Moreover, Darwin himself had left little room for misinterpretation of his conviction: "If it could be demonstrated that any complex organ existed, which could not possibly have been formed by numerous, successive, slight modifications, my theory would absolutely break down" (1859, p. 189). He was convinced that gradualism applied to changes at all levels, from cells and organs to entire species. Contemporary theory and research have vindicated Goldschmidt, however; and the theory of *punctuated equilibria* has become widely accepted. Formalized by Stephen Jay Gould and Niles Eldredge (1972, 1977), the theory maintains that abrupt changes are evident at a number of levels—from the emergence of specialized organs to the appearance of new species (Eldredge and Tattersall 1982; Gould 1977*a*, 1977*b*, 1980*a*, 1980*b*, 1982, 1989; Kauffman 1985; Lewin 1988*c*). Such a perspective is called "saltationist" because it involves sudden "jumps" (saltations). What were once thought to be gaps in the fossil record are now viewed as dramatic leaps. According to the "new" theory, species change very little after they have emerged.

As Goldschmidt had anticipated, the leaps themselves appear to be related to slight differences in developmental pace and timing, which become powerful parameters in the dynamic tension between variation and fixation at the chromosomal level. Ironically, it has been the greatest relative slowing of some changes—such as physical maturation—that has afforded the widest range of *plasticity* ("change ability") in life forms. We humans, for example, exhibit the greatest known "slowing" or retardation of our biological development. Relative to other flora and fauna, we have specialized in remaining less specialized—an achievement called *neoteny* or *neotenization.* The similarities in form of the adult and infant

*Hopeful Monster is also the name of the publisher of Francisco Varela's (1986) little book on the recent conceptual leap in the cognitive sciences.

human are substantially greater than are those in the adult and newborn forms of any other earthly organisms. This dramatic slowing of our development has made us significantly more vulnerable (especially early in life) and, at the same time, substantially more versatile in the face of a complex and changing environment (see appendix F).

   The Nature of Selection.   Now there is no debate about whether selection occurs, but only about the nature of selection processes and the operation of other variables (many of them "organismic") in the overall orchestration of change and stabilization. The doctrine of gradualism, for example, claims that selection operates only at microscopic levels and therefore produces slow and gradual changes. Darwin's friend T. H. Huxley had tried to dissuade him of the gradualist doctrine, arguing that it was an "unnecessary difficulty"; but Darwin believed that any notion of discontinuities would open the conceptual door to "supernatural" processes. The theory of punctuated equilibria does not argue that Darwin or the neo-Darwinian "modern synthesis" were incorrect, so much as that they were incomplete. Moreover, the core of the contrast between these perspectives has far-reaching implications for our ideas about change itself:

In the largest sense, this debate is but one small aspect of a broader discussion about the nature of change: Is our world . . . primarily one of constant change (with structure as a mere incarnation of the moment), or is structure primary and constraining, with change as a "difficult" phenomenon, usually accomplished rapidly when a stable structure is stressed beyond its buffering capacity to resist and absorb? It would be hard to deny that the Darwinian tradition, including the modern synthesis, favored the first view while "punctuationalist" thought in general, including such aspects of classical morphology as D'Arcy Thompson's (1942) theory of form, prefers the second. (Gould 1982, p. 383)

Though I will later discuss the punctuationalist perspective in relation to theories of human psychological development (chapters 7–9), note here the close reiteration of a familiar theme: that is, that the essence of change is a saltational (nonlinear) "cycle of disorganization and reorganization" (Carson 1975, p. 88).

Active and Passive Darwinism

The concept of *plasticity* or mutability is inherent in any theory of change, human or otherwise. At its core is the issue of how much change is possible—a question psychological theories have answered very differently (chapters 1, 3). In evolutionary theory, variation is a prerequisite for the operation of selection processes. As we have seen, however, traditional renditions of that theory have mistakenly assumed both that all such variation is random and microscopic, and that selection processes operate in only one direction—that is, from the environment to the organism. The philosopher Karl R. Popper has termed this perspective *passive Darwinism* because it assumes that a "hostile environment" is the ultimate shaper of organisms and their behavior. In contrast to this one-sided portrayal is the viewpoint of *active Darwinism,* which argues that even the earliest life forms on earth were already "active explorers, actively and curiously searching for new environments . . . or, sometimes, merely for slightly modified ways of living, for slightly new ways of behaving, and especially for trial behavior" (Popper 1982*b,* p. 39). In other words, organisms do quite a bit of selecting themselves. With even the most primitive forms of action and locomotion, the organism exerts its own pressures on the selection pressures that affect it: it selects and influences its own habitat and participates in an ongoing reciprocity with its world (Bandura 1978, 1986; Endler and Magnusson 1976; Epstein and Erskine 1983; Lerner and Busch-Rossnagel 1981; Magnusson and Allen 1983; Mahoney and Thoresen 1974; Thoresen and Mahoney 1974).

This assertion can be illustrated at a number of levels. Consider, for example, recent insights about the relationships between vision, movement, and life support. In 1974, Donald T. Campbell offered a fascinating conjecture about how the emergence of vision might have come about as an "opportunistic exploitation of a coincidence." That coincidence was the fact that transparency is almost perfectly correlated with penetrability: that is, movement is possible only in "clear" mediums (such as air and water) and generally impossible in opaque ones. Exceptions to that coincidence are rare (such as fog and clear glass), and Campbell reasoned that vision was therefore selected as "a wonderful substitute for blind exploration" (1987, [1974*a*], p. 48). This intriguing analysis has recently been revised and refined, however, by the discovery of yet another coincidence. As shown in figure 6.1, the evolutionary emergence of vision made only a tiny portion of the electromagnetic spectrum perceptually accessible to sighted organisms. Why such a small slice? The answer appears to involve an even more peculiar coincidence, recognized by Günter Wächtershäuser:

For the most part, oxygenic photosynthesis uses only those segments of the electromagnetic spectrum which are now used for visible light. That is, there is a close overlap between those wavelengths employed for photosynthesis and those now used for vision. . . . Radiation in other ranges would, in general, be either non-nourishing or poisonous. Hence only that narrow non-lethal segment now used for vision would qualify as a viable and exploitable source, through photosynthesis, for nourishment.

For the early photosynthesizers, a new, secondary, problem now emerged—yet one that was to be crucial to the development of vision from photosynthesis.

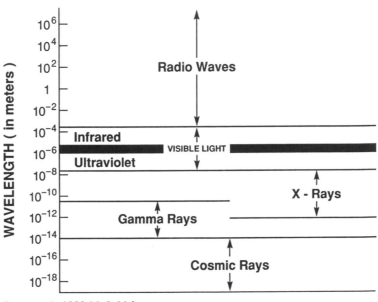

Figure 6.1   The Spectrum of Electromagnetic Radiation

SOURCE: © 1989 M. J. Mahoney

Lighting conditions fluctuate locally. How was the organism to locate and remain in a place of optimum radiation? The solution was to adapt the already developed apparatus for photosynthesis—for feeding from light—to the new, additional function of detecting light in order to control movement: i.e., *photocontrolled locomotion.* It is now that vision begins, gradually and primitively, to be developed, and it is also now that the association between light and movement becomes crucial. (Bartley 1987*d,* pp. 27–30)

In other words, photosensitivity and vision did not emerge *after* the evolution of movement, but rather along with it. Locomotor abilities emerged out of the efforts of early life forms to maintain and expand their access to the life-supporting (nutritional) resources of light. Their active quest for light was, however, a search not for information (in the modern sense), but for food. In the time span of biological evolution, it was probably much later before Campbell's coincidence came into play and vision took on some of the functions it now serves.

As Wächtershäuser notes, his and Campbell's analyses are complementary rather than conflicting, and there is, literally, much more to vision than meets the eye. Grant (1963) also notes that the leap from anaerobic (non-oxygenating) to aerobic metabolism not only was a major step in self-organizing efficiency, but also reflected one of those synergistic processes wherein life forms transformed the environment to which they were adapting. By giving off oxygen as a by-product, photosynthesis "created an atmosphere which made the development of respiration possible" (p. 64).

Early life forms thus exploited the vision-photosynthesis coincidence and poured oxygen into the atmosphere; later life forms realized a "windfall profit," so to speak, and developed respiration and the refined visual capacities we associate with anticipatory movements. What is particularly important about these developments is their illustration of the fundamentally active generation of sensory capacities. The neuron reflects that same legacy in its own evolution (see appendix F). Theories of passive perception are therefore untenable:

Perception is not a process of passive acquisition of information from the environment by an apparatus which itself is the result of passive adaptation to this same environment. It is rather a process of active foraging within the environment by means of an apparatus which in its major characteristics is shaped by the organism's own foraging activities. As Popper would have it: organisms by being active seekers are the active makers of their senses. (Wächtershäuser 1987, p. 138)

Activity lies not only at the heart of knowing, but also at the heart of much of life itself: "We are largely active makers of ourselves" (Popper 1982b, p. 45). This emphasis on the "active organism" was also a major thrust of Charles Sherrington's (1906, 1940) important contributions in neuroscience (appendix D). Moreover, the power of active knowing is essentially grounded in *praxis*—that is, in the embodied and ongoing behavior of being.

The Myth of Cerebral Primacy

Another doctrine that deserves reappraisal is *cerebral primacy,* which maintains that the brain is and has been the most important organ in human development. (The process of *encephalization* ["headification"] is discussed in appendix F.) What began with a slight swelling of the anterior end of the embryonic neural tube has culminated in the rather large heads we now balance atop our upright trunks. The disproportionately large heads (and brains) of humans have long been a source of (unwarranted) pride to their owners. As documented by Harry Jerison (1973, 1976, 1979), there is, in fact, a modest relationship between brain size (relative to body weight) and general intelligence. But relative size loses its predictive power at the level of the higher primates. The Cro-Magnons, for example, had larger brains than we do; they are now extinct. Finally, some of the (misguided) impetus for a brain-centered view of evolution may have stemmed from the popularity of Haeckel's famous Law of Recapitulation, which mistakenly argued that organisms, in their individual development, pass through the same stages as did their species in its evolution (see appendix F). This doctrine, accepted by Theodore Meynert and his student Sigmund Freud, also encouraged the belief that "higher" life forms should credit their heads (and particularly their intellect) for their "higher" status.

Although contrary evidence was available in the 1920s, the doctrine of cerebral primacy remained popular until the late 1970s. Elementary textbooks glibly explained that mammalian and primate evolution reflected a clear and common pattern: that is, that the brain first enlarges or is refined, and then its increased power to command life support creates opportunities for the body to be modified. As Gould (1980b) has noted, even the experts have had difficulty moving away from a cerebral (brain-centered) model of human evolution. Early writers on the topic maintained that increases in brain size either preceded or functionally over-shadowed all major changes in the human body. In the theoretically crucial case of our shift from a four-legged to a two-legged posture, for example, they thought that this development had occurred gradually and was less significant than the later expansion of the human neocortex.

But the "sudden" enlargement of our brains is now known to have followed rather than preceded *bipedalism* (two-leggedness), thanks to a very important "little old lady" by the name of Lucy. Discovered in 1974 by Donald C. Johanson, Lucy's three-million-year-old skeleton was 40 percent intact, and her pelvis was complete enough to end debates about her walking capacities. Lucy was not only a master of upright posture, but she was also probably fleet of foot. The evidence again points to complex, dynamic reciprocities between brain and body as well as between organism and environment. The "received view" in modern expressions of evolutionary biology now acknowledges that body and brain co-evolved; each contributed changes that altered their relations and, in doing so, they altered their opportunities for still further development (Lovejoy 1988).

The doctrine of cerebral primacy has served as a context for much of the research and writing in the life sciences during the last century. This fact may explain why it also shares features with perspectives that I call "rational supremacy" and "neurophilia." *Rational supremacy* is the assertion that lies at the core of rationalist cognitive therapies. It is straightforward, albeit mistaken, in its contentions that: (1) thinking and reasoning can and should control or guide one's life; (2) irrational thought is dysfunctional; (3) psychological disorders are the expression, among other things, of irrational or unreasonable beliefs and images; and (4) effective therapy requires the identification and "correction" (for example, by rote substitution or reasoned argument) of irrational beliefs. Not surprisingly, rationalist and constructivist cognitive therapies endorse very different approaches to life counseling (Mahoney and Lyddon 1988).

Neurophilia is an exclusive preoccupation with the nervous system as the

most likely "mother lode" in refining our understanding of human behavior and experience. Many, but not all, neurophiles are also reductionists: they intend to account for the warp and woof of our lives without
resource to anything beyond biopsychology and neuroscience (appendix
D). This is not the place to launch into a critique of reductionism, which
(along with dualism) has been one of the greatest obstacles to progress
in scientific psychology (Hilgard 1987). Suffice it to say that research in
both biological and cultural evolution (which have important differences
[see pages 121–23] have now made it clear that "bottom-up" analyses
simply cannot offer an adequate account of complex self-organizing phenomena. As Hayek (1978), Polanyi (1958), and Weimer (1987) have
shown, the qualitatively different properties of "emergent" phenomena
cannot be reduced to the properties of the levels that generated them.
As important as it is to integrate the knowledge of psychobiology and
neuroscience into psychological theories and models, it would be a grave
mistake to presume that such knowledge will be sufficient to account for
the full range of dynamics and complexities of lives in process.

Emergence: Mind, Morals, and Culture

This last point leads toward a family of issues that have puzzled and
plagued evolutionary scientists for a long time. Were Darwin still alive,
he would most likely be appalled at the abuses of his conceptual system.
As noted by Loren Eiseley (1958), even within his lifetime Darwin had
been forced to deal with a number of distortions perpetrated by certain
religious sects and political ideologies. An inversion of Haeckel's erro-
neous Law of Recapitulation, for example, invited some fundamentalist
clergy to argue that "primitives" and "savages" were not the surviving
vestiges of early human forms, but rather "degenerate" peoples who
demonstrated the Biblical fall from grace. The proponents of this view
were called "degenerationists" because they were convinced that humans
had not arisen from savagery, but rather had degenerated to it. These
"savages"—who were predominantly non-Caucasian—were described as
incapable of becoming civilized. To put it bluntly, all manner of racist and
sexist prejudices were reasserted in the wake of evolutionary thought,
even though many of those same prejudices were contradicted by the
evidence (Gould 1981).

There were, of course, a number of individuals who were commendably outspoken in defense of human rights. In 1514, for example, Bar-
tolomé de Las Casas had challenged the practice of slavery and argued
that the most "uncivilized" were still fundamentally human (Boorstin
1983); and ten years after the publication of Darwin's *Origin,* John Stuart
Mill (1869) attacked *The Subjection of Women.* Moreover, Wallace's differences with Darwin skirted the edges of some of these issues. In his eight

years of travel through the Malay archipelago, Wallace—in contrast to Darwin—had become fascinated with the similarities (rather than differences) evident in humans and their communities. In 1855, Wallace wrote to a friend, "The more I see of uncivilized people, the better I think of human nature"; and in 1873 he challenged interpretations of natural selection that diminished the intellect and morality of prehistoric humans (cited in Eiseley 1958, p. 303). Wallace was also impressed with the transformation of those selection processes by the emergence of the hominid brain. Although his views may have encouraged the aforementioned errors of cerebral primacy, they were also timely conjectures on the biological significance of the mind. Darwin's eventual break with Wallace came, in fact, in response to the latter's contention that the principle of selection could not by itself account for the complexity and capacities of the human brain.

We are today still so close to some of the issues involved here that it is only reasonable to expect ourselves to remain somewhat "unreasonable" in their analysis. The origins, abilities, and destiny of the human mind have evoked more wholesale speculation than almost any other topic in the history of ideas. Most pertinent here are those perspectives that have outlined the extremes of deterministic simplicity and co-determinate complexity. It is also here, again, that the insights of the Scottish moral philosophers—well articulated in the recent writings of Campbell, Hayek, and Weimer—become obviously important. Consider, by way of synopsis, Campbell's (1974b) lucid comments on diverse opinions about reductionism in the philosophy of biology. Beginning with the acknowledgment that Darwinian theory has been thoroughly reductionist, Campbell goes on to elaborate four principles entailed in the hierarchical organization of biological systems:

1. **All higher-level processes** are constrained by lower-level laws (including those of subatomic physics);

2. The **self-ordering** (teleonomic) achievements of higher levels depend on lower-level mechanisms and processes;

3. The **principle of emergence**: living systems encounter selective systems that cannot be described by the laws of physics and chemistry (past, present, or future);

4. The **principle of downward causation**: all lower-level processes in a hierarchical system are constrained by the laws of the higher levels that have emerged from them.

The first two principles are familiar to most reductionists, while the last two acknowledge the warrant for some (though not all) of the central assertions of the vitalists, the humanists, and the psychological constructivists. Integrating the social sentiments of Dobzhansky's *Biology of Ultimate Concern* (1967) and the generativity emergent in Polanyi's *Tacit Dimension* (1966) and *Personal Knowledge* (1958), Campbell concludes with an "attitude of awe of superior unknown powers; for certainly we do not yet know much about the selective system that shaped civilized social man" (1974*b*, p. 184).

Illustrations of emergence and downward causation are plentiful at all levels of biological evolution, but they are most extensive (and perhaps least appreciated) in the domain of human social developments. It is, in fact, in this domain that the insufficiency of biological reductionism is most apparent. *Emergence* comes from the Latin verb *emergere* ("to come out of"), and one of its uses was to signal a decisive point or stage in development or change (also called a "crisis" or "emergency"). The emergence of nuclear power in this century, for example, has resulted in the "emergency" inherent in the ever-present possibility of self-annihilation. Or, the emergence of vicarious learning processes, language, and symbols resulted in the (unanticipated) power of modern media. The products and by-products of technology are filled with illustrations of the reciprocal interaction of "higher-" and "lower-order" processes. Campbell's choice of the term *downward* was to emphasize that underappreciated direction of influence.

Campbell's four principles reflect a theme we have already encountered in the cognitive sciences: that is, the complementary operation of "top-down" and "bottom-up" processes in self-organization. Campbell's inclusion of the "top-down" component without denial of its "bottom-up" incarnation stands in contrast to the extreme claims of both reductionists and rationalists. Contrary to the assertions of Edward O. Wilson's (1975) "sociobiology" and Albert Ellis's (1962, 1985*a*) "rational-emotive theory," for example, human values are not and cannot be the simple products of genetics and rational thought. Echoing the sentiments of Wallace a century earlier, Hayek (1979) noted that it is patently false to assume that the evolution of culture has occurred in that last 1 percent of human tenure on the planet. In contrast to Wallace, however, Hayek pointed out that culture was not (and is not) a product of the human mind. Rather, *"mind and culture developed concurrently and not successively"* (p. 156). As David Hume and his compatriots had realized long before Darwin had himself become bipedal, the evolution of society, language, morals, laws, and economy is the result of individual human actions in continuous interface with dynamic selection processes.

Division of labor is a good example (and it is not confined to humans). The apparent survival value of division of labor stems from its affordance of mutual adjustments of activities among individuals who do not know one another. It is most elaborate in humans, where it has resulted in a veritable transformation of the living order. This was the transition from face-to-face social interaction to what Popper and Hayek have appropriately called "the abstract society":

The great change which produced an order of society which became increasingly incomprehensible to man, and for the preservation of which he had to submit to

learnt rules which were often contrary to his innate instincts, was the transition
from the face-to-face society, or at least groups of known and recognizable members, to the open abstract society that was no longer held together by common
concrete ends but only by the obedience to the same abstract rules. What man
probably found most difficult to comprehend was that the only common values
of an open and free society were not concrete objects to be achieved, but only
those common abstract rules of conduct that secured the constant maintenance
of an equally abstract order which merely assured to the individual better prospects of achieving . . . individual ends. (Hayek 1979, p. 164)

The abstract society is not, however, to be confused with a totally impersonal one. As I shall discuss in chapters 7 to 9, our psychological needs
for one another—for authentic, caring human contact—have never been
so apparent or so urgent.

Our understanding of the selection processes that operate in social
systems is limited, as Campbell noted; but it is clear that our ability to
constrain our actions via abstract rules (tacit "traditions") has been significant. Hayek points out, however, that tradition is not unchanging, and
that cultural selection creates but is not "guided" by reason. All progress
is therefore based on tradition, just as all revolution is against a prevailing
order. While there is always room for the improvement of a self-organizing system, "we cannot redesign but only further evolve what we do not
fully comprehend" (Hayek 1979, p. 167). For those of us who presume
to console and counsel on the complexities of a life in process, what is
particularly relevant in all of this is its appreciation for the background
out of which individual and collective development emerge. The sources
of human values lie in a dynamic and individualized coalition of (1)
genetic or biological inheritance; (2) socially transmitted rules (most of
which are tacit and prohibitive); and, finally, (3) only "a thin layer of rules
[that were] deliberately adopted or modified to serve known purposes"
(p. 160).

Among other things, we practitioners would do well to appreciate the
embedded wisdom in cultural traditions and the necessity of constraints
in the protection of individual freedoms. Contrary to the teachings of
Freud, Rousseau, and Marx, the inhibitions imposed by civilized life are
not "evils" or "burdens" to be lightly discarded in the nurturance of the
person. Indeed, one of the regrettable abuses of psychiatry and psychological services has been their frequent attempt to eradicate the concepts
of good and evil and to transcend the moral sense of right and wrong.
Moreover, we are in danger of undermining the social fabric that has
made our civilization possible when we violate the rights and responsibilities of the individuals who comprise that fabric. Many of those violations
of human rights have been condoned by the allegedly rational (and,
hence, justified) policies of so-called progressive societies. I thus concur
with Gandhi's reported response to the question "What do you think of

Western civilization?" After a brief pause, he is said to have responded, "It seems like a good idea." To believe that we can deftly engineer personal and collective development is the ultimate expression of rationalist hubris:

Though [spontaneous evolution] clearly produces . . . much that we did not foresee and do not like when we see it, it does bring . . . new possibilities [which] always also bring a new discipline. . . . Unfortunately, progress cannot be dosed. . . . All we can do is to create conditions favourable to it and then hope for the best. It may be stimulated or damped by policy, but nobody can predict the precise effects of such measures; to pretend to know the desirable direction of progress seems to me to be the extreme of hubris. Guided progress would not be progress. . . . To confine evolution to what we can foresee would be to stop progress. (Hayek 1979, pp. 168–69)

Rationally planned evolution is not evolution; we should not confuse teleological (goal-directed) engineering with teleonomic (spontaneously self-organizing) activity. The idea that we can confidently lift ourselves up by our own "bootstraps" and achieve "progress, intelligently planned" is one of our most costly illusions. Thus, Skinner's *Walden Two* (1948) and all other versions of planned utopias may be fascinating as fantasies but dangerous as blueprints. If we ever mistakenly move *beyond* the freedom and dignity that lie at the heart of our moral codes (Skinner 1971), we will have indeed fulfilled the dire predictions of the degenerationists.

EVOLUTIONARY EPISTEMOLOGY (E²)

Evolutionary epistemology, or E², is the study of evolving knowledge and knowing systems. Like the theory of biological evolution, E² is indebted to the eighteenth-century Scottish social philosophers for their insights into the emergence of cultural evolution. Except for the works of Herbert Spencer and James Mark Baldwin at the turn of the present century, however, little had been written about the relationships between evolutionary theory and epistemology until relatively recently. Soon after the explorations of Spencer and Baldwin, for example, E² and its "natural selection epistemology" dropped out of sight until its recent conceptual revival. The individuals most responsible for that revival have been Karl R. Popper and Donald T. Campbell, two of the most influential participants in twentieth-century epistemology. E² was first formalized by Campbell (1974a) in a classic paper of that title. Campbell argued that, at minimum, E² proposes an approach to the study of knowing that is compatible with the fact that humans are the products of both biological and social evolution. Moreover, a cardinal assertion of E² is that "evolution—even in its biological aspects—is a knowledge process" (Campbell

1974a/1987, p. 47). With systematic clarity, Campbell went on to formal-
ize the basic assertions of E² in the language of systems, science, and
epistemology:

1. A blind-variation-and-selective-retention process is fundamental to all inductive achievements, to all genuine increases in knowledge, to all increases of
fit of system to environment. [By "blind," Campbell means that "variations are
produced without prior knowledge of which ones, if any, will furnish a select-
worthy encounter" (1974a/1987, pp. 56–57).]
2. In such a process there are three essentials: (*a*) Mechanisms for introducing
variation; (*b*) Consistent selection processes; and (*c*) Mechanisms for preserving
and/or propagating the selected variations. Note that in general the preservation
and generation mechanisms are inherently at odds, and each must be compromised.
3. Many processes which shortcut a more full blind-variation-and-selective-
retention process are in themselves inductive achievements, containing wisdom
about the environment achieved originally by blind variation and selective-
retention.
4. In addition, such shortcut processes contain in their own operation a blind-
variation-and-selective-retention process at some level, substituting for overt
locomotor exploration or the life-and-death winnowing of organic evolution.
(1974a/1987, p. 56; see also Campbell 1959, 1960)

These principles are an attempt to describe the processes that integrate
life and death with knowing. What emerges from the combined writings
of Popper, Campbell, and their proliferating compatriots is a comprehensive metatheory of sentient (experiential) and sapient (epistemic) development.*

In his famous essay "Of Clouds and Clocks," Popper also places variation and selection processes at the core of all knowing:

My theory . . . consists in a certain *view of evolution* as a growing hierarchical system
of plastic controls, and of a certain *view of organisms* as incorporating . . . this
growing hierarchical system of plastic controls. . . .
    Error-elimination may proceed either by the complete elimination of unsuc-
cessful forms . . . or by the (tentative) evolution of controls which modify or
suppress unsuccessful organs, or forms of behavior, or hypotheses. . . .
    Our schema allows for the development of error-eliminating controls (warning
organs like the eye; feed-back mechanisms); that is, controls which can eliminate
errors without killing the organism; and it makes it possible, ultimately, for our
hypotheses to die in our stead. (1972b [1966], pp. 23–25)

*It is ironic that Popper, an ardent critic of psychology and "psychologizing," has helped
accelerate the acknowledgment that, as Weimer (1979) puts it, "psychology is essential to
epistemology." Having openly stated his intent to "bypass psychology" in linking the mind
to natural science, Popper viewed his theory as a biological philosophy. As (conceptual)
evolution would have it, however, both biology and philosophy have recently found themselves dealing with decidedly psychological issues.

Noteworthy here are Popper's emphases on the primary role of epistemically "negative" information—his famous fondness for the demonstrable powers of falsification and disconfirmation—and his assertion that the "higher" mental skills of humans essentially "internalize" the selection pressures of the neighboring world.

Advocates of E² are generally what Campbell has called "critical hypothetical realists." Unlike their idealist and radical constructivist counterparts, Campbell and Popper do not doubt the material existence of what A. N. Whitehead (1957) called "furniture in the universe." Indeed, it is our endless "bumps" up against the furniture of our local universe that comprise the "errors" that can potentially teach us about our own structural limits and our relationships with our world. We venture bold questions; nature's most life-relevant answers come in the form of no's, whether whispered or thundered. This reflects, again, the essential negativity of abstract rules (chapter 5). Pain conveys more urgent (life-relevant) information than does pleasure, for example, and disconfirmed expectations offer more logical information than do confirmed ones. A mistaken conjecture—in the lessons it may render when it fails—teaches more than its more successful (and less potentially informative) counterpart. Moreover, negation and denial lie at the heart of the distinction processes that permeate all descriptive knowledge.

E² lies at the heart of modern critical epistemology which, in turn, represents the long-awaited triumph of skeptical criticism over the authority-based illusions of *justificationism*. William W. Bartley, a major figure in this revolution, has made it clear that E² argues for the analysis of rationality as fallible viability, thereby avoiding the mistakes of perspectives that presume themselves to be amply or specially authorized, "validated," or unequivocally justified:

The highest creative thought, like animal adaptation, is the product of blind variation and selective retention. Growth of knowledge is achieved through variation and selective retention—or, to use Popper's phrase, through conjecture and refutation. Science is, on this account, *utterly unjustified and unjustifiable*. It is a shot in the dark, a bold guess going far beyond all evidence. The question of its justification is irrelevant. . . . The issue, rather, is of the viability of the mutation— or of the new theory. This question is resolved through exposing it to the pressures of natural selection—or attempted criticism and refutation. Survival in this process does not justify the survivor either: a species that survived for thousands of years may nonetheless become extinct. A theory that survived for generations may eventually be refuted—as was Newton's. There is *no* justification—*ever*. The process that began with unjustified variations ends in unjustified survivors. (1987*d*, p. 24)

Bartley goes on to challenge the arrogance of logical empiricism and its faith in sense perceptions as the building blocks and foundational authorities of a theory of knowledge. First-person experience is not authoritative in the objectivist sense of guaranteeing knowledge. Experience "winnows" our conjectures in valuable ways, of course, but it is also limited by boundaries that reflect the current epistemic range of the individual.

In my opinion, evolutionary epistemology is one of the most exciting research themes in the life sciences and philosophy.* Some of the most fascinating conjectures in philosophy and the sciences of complexity, for example, are being spawned by a generation of evolutionary epistemologists (for example, Burrell 1987; Cairns, Gariépy, and Hood 1990; Callebaut and Pinxten 1987; Emery and Csikszentmihalyi 1981; Granit 1977, 1982; Greenberg and Tobach 1990; Guidano 1987, 1990; Hull 1988; Jantsch 1980, 1981; Jantsch and Waddington 1976; McGuire and Essock-Vitale 1982; McGuire, Essock-Vitale, and Polsky 1981; Ruse 1986; Salthe 1985; Schilcher and Tennant 1984; Weimer 1987; Willmuth 1986). Moreover, they have helped to illustrate the promise of an essentially *developmental* view of life and knowing. As we shall see, such a view has become an imperative for the theoretical psychology that underlies psychological services.

CONCLUSION

Like Copernicus's unsettling truth that the ground beneath us is moving, the insights of evolutionary studies have challenged some cherished beliefs about our unique and changeless character, not to mention about the capacities of our reason. These studies have also revealed that, beneath the surface order of our lives, there teems ceaseless and complex activity. Variation is pervasive, and yet order emerges. The fundamental characteristics of evolving, self-organizing systems reflect an inherent participation in their own development. According to Erich Janstch and Conrad H. Waddington (1976), for example, those characteristics include the following:

1. A state of dynamic nonequilibrium (both within the system and between it and its environment).
2. The complementarity (mutual determination) of the system's structures and functions.
3. The complementary operation of deterministic and indeterminate (random/chance) processes.
4. The capacity to undergo qualitative changes between dynamically stable states or "regions."

*E^2 is *not* sociobiology, the extreme version of a genetic approach to human nature popularized by E. O. Wilson (1975). For recent discussions of sociobiology and its strong claims about the genetic bases of human experience, see Buckley and Jones 1979; Kitcher 1985, 1987; Ruse 1986; and Vining 1986.

5. Autocatalysis (self-precipitation) "drives" the system through an ordered succession of such changes.
6. The system's resilience is inversely related to its stability.
7. In the long run, flexibility is favored over (is more viable than) rigidity.
8. Exploratory, experimental, and variational processes are apparent at many levels.
9. Adaptations between the system and its environment are reciprocal; in humans, social and symbolic influences outweigh genetic ones.
10. Heterogeneity (variation) becomes symbiotic (mutually advantageous) to coordinating systems.
11. A "healthy" (viable) system both seeks and resists qualitative change; resilience implies the capacity for flexible transformation.
12. The openness inherent in evolving systems requires their imperfection, perennial uncertainty, and a strength or "courage" that helps them transcend these existential contingencies.

These paraphrasings of mine capture the essential features of dynamic balance, active variability, and "fluidity in transformation" that Jantsch and Waddington emphasize. Besides emphasizing the change capacities of living systems, these characteristics hint at implications for psychological services. There is, for example, a recommendation that working with, rather than against, systemic perturbations may be ultimately more conducive to survival (both individual and collective): "Going *with* the fluctuations also seems to become the best way of 'defusing' them when they tend to get so big as to threaten the long-term viability of an evolving system—as they certainly do in today's highly metastable (resilient) society, which has itself prepared the means for its own extinction" (Jantsch and Waddington 1976, p. 7).

Perhaps the most important contributions of evolutionary studies to our understanding and facilitation of human change processes lie in their acknowledgment of the dynamics and complexity of life in development. Disequilibrium (disorder) is often associated with change, for example; and it is the living system's capacities to negotiate episodes of such "imbalance" that constitute its self-organizing "resilience." In our small corner of the universe, activity (even when "blind") and explorations of the unknown play a central role in the survival and differentiation of life forms. There are lessons here for psychotherapy, if only in the reminder that our (often-stressful) encounters with the new and the unknown are the "growing edges" of development itself. Likewise, despite the confident claims of rational planners, those encounters and their sequelae cannot be predicted or controlled with even modest degrees of certainty. Confronting this existential insight can be a productive challenge for client and counselor alike.

Finally, evolutionary studies emphasize that surviving and thriving involve interdependencies between the living system and its changing media. We are, in other words, the products, producers, and processes of variation, selection, and retention—all at the same time, and all still in progress. As unfinished sculptures and sculptors, then, our form and function both stabilize and change, and our lives exhibit both common and unique patterns of ongoing construction. It is to those patterns and constructions that I now turn.

7

▲▼▲▼▲▼▲▼▲▼▲▼▲▼▲▼▲▼▲▼▲

Human Psychological Development

The hand that rocks the cradle rules the world. —William R. Wallace

The concepts of change, evolution, and development are similar, and it should not be surprising that studies in "human development" and "developmental psychology" share a legacy with evolutionary studies (Bonner 1982; Charlesworth 1986; Collins 1982; Harris 1957; Kauffman 1985; Marx 1988; Raff and Raff 1987; Sameroff 1983; Snyder 1988). Even though those concepts have a lengthy and multicultural history, however, much of their current fascination has grown out of the activities of the last two centuries. Somewhat ironically, it has taken research psychologists a long time to make psychological development—both early and lifespan—a central priority for study. Though possible reasons for this tardiness of interest are suggested by histories of developmental inquiry and analyses of the relationships between evolutionary and developmental studies, I shall defer their discussion to other sources (Butterworth, Rutkowska, and Scaife 1985; Chamberlain 1911; Hilgard 1987). I shall not, however, defer a strong affirmation of the timeliness and importance of developmental studies for all the sciences and humanities, especially for psychology, education, and health science services. Indeed, a significant element of the third axial shift I discussed in chapter 2 has been the shift toward a deeper acknowledgment of developmental processes in what had been assumed to be a simple and stable physical world. Lyell, Darwin, Einstein, and Freud were the leading figures in challenging old myths about *terra firma,* the origins and plasticities of life forms, the relativities of space and time, and the illusions of rationalist accounts of human life.

In Ilya Prigogine's influential *From Being to Becoming: Time and Complexity in the Physical Sciences,* this ongoing shift has been described as a "subtle revolution":

> Since the beginning of Western science, we have believed in the "simplicity" of the microscopic—molecules, atoms, elementary particles. . . . This conception—historically one of the driving forces of Western science—can hardly be maintained today. . . . If there is simplicity somewhere in physics and chemistry, it is not in the microscopic models. It lies more in idealized macroscopic representations. (1980, p. xiii)

He goes on to link the concepts of complexity and time in his theory of *dissipative structures* (appendix C), which has direct relevance for our understanding of the concept of development and the dynamics of its processes (Brent 1978, 1984; Ford 1987; Guidano 1987; Jantsch 1980, 1981; Kelso and Schoner 1988; Thelen 1988, 1989a, 1989b, in press; Ulanowics, 1989).

Acknowledgments of time, process, complexity, and development have been expressed in a wide variety of modern perspectives: autopoietic, constructivist, dynamic, dialectical, evolutionary, hermeneutic, holistic, self-organizing, systems, process-oriented, and so on. Contributions from adherents of these perspectives have been the driving force of the third axial shift. In essence, they have all recognized the illusions of rationalist objectivism and begun to explore the alternative complexities of active and interactive open systems. As most parents, educators, and mental health professionals would probably attest, an understanding and harvest of those complexities is itself a formidable challenge.

DEVELOPMENTS IN IDEAS ABOUT DEVELOPMENT

Needless to say, it is beyond the scope of this chapter to attempt a comprehensive overview of developmental psychology; excellent introductions and scholarly analyses are readily available (Breger 1974; Eisenberg 1987; Gibson 1988; Hetherington, Lerner, and Perlmutter 1988; Klein 1987; Magnusson 1987; Oates and Sheldon 1988; Osofsky 1987; Rheingold 1985; Sroufe and Cooper 1988). It is, nevertheless, pertinent to summarize selected developments within that field that have bearing on our conceptualizations of the individual "in process" and on our practices in professional life counseling. To place these developments in both historical and conceptual context, let me therefore pay some brief respects to the history of ideas about children, growth, and lifespan development.

Scattered across the centuries there have been important affirmations of the value of the child and the importance of childhood experiences. In *The Republic,* for example, Plato (in the character of Socrates) states that "the beginning is the most important part of any work, especially in the case of a young and tender thing; for that is the time at which the character is being formed and the desired impression is more readily taken." Regrettably, the same wise man said that children's first lessons should be as "spectators of war" (377 BC/1907, p. 194). Acknowledgments of the importance of early experience have been expressed over the years by many other writers: "The childhood shows the man, as morning shows the day" (John Milton); "Tis education forms the common mind: Just as the twig is bent the tree's inclined" (Alexander Pope); and, perhaps most famous, "The child is father of the man" (William Wordsworth). (For modern debates on the significance of childhood and the power of early [versus later or ongoing] experience, see this chapter and Clarke and Clarke 1976; Kagan 1988; Lerner and Busch-Rossnagel 1981; and Wachs and Gruen 1982.) Despite these affirmations, however, work on the care and education of children remained relatively undeveloped until the last two centuries. Following the Renaissance, children's needs began to become an issue of fundamental social concern thanks to the humanizing, "organic" recommendations of Jean Jacques Rousseau in the eighteenth century and of Robert Owen, Friedrich Froebel and Elizabeth Peabody in the nineteenth. Although as early as 1531 a law had been passed in the Netherlands requiring schooling (or trade apprenticeship) for all children, it was a century before such laws became common.

Concepts of development, growth, and education were significantly influenced both by their heritage in evolutionary studies and by the pressing need for practical information about the care and teaching of infants and children. Chamberlain (1911) lists Dietrich Tiedeman as the "father of child psychology," primarily because Tiedeman's 1787 biography of an infant predated Charles Darwin's (1877) by almost a century. Other historians have emphasized the contributions of Maria Montessori, Wilhelm Preyer, and Millicent Shinn. In the United States, G. Stanley Hall was the undisputed pioneer of the "child study movement," having formed the National Association for the Study of Childhood in 1893, just one year after having founded the American Psychological Association.

Hall's work in the child development movement was diverse, but he is perhaps best remembered for two things: his popularization of the concept of *adolescence,* and his attempt to popularize the (misguided) "recapitulation" theory of human development. Prior to the first achievement, the assumption that children were "miniature adults" was not uncommon, and there was relatively little appreciation of children's psychological transitions and developmental processes. In his fascinating review of extant views on stages in the human lifespan, Chamberlain (1911) mentions other developmentalists who were employing the transitional concept of *adolescence* either before or at the same time as Hall—for example, Clouston, Gulick, and Lacassagne. (Chamberlain quotes Pythagoras as having classified persons "80 years and over" as "dead" [1911, p. 66]—perhaps an error in translation.) The importance of experiences in adolescence for later psychological development is now extensively documented, especially in the domain of identity ("self") development (chapter 9). Concisely, recent research on identity and moral development—some of it inspired by feminist theorists in those areas—has offered novel insights into the paradox that "self," which is more flexible in adolescence than in later periods, is experienced primarily with/through "others," and vice versa (Byrne and Shavelson 1986; Chandler 1987; Golombek et al. 1989; Marsh and O'Neill 1984; Moore 1987; O'Mahony 1984, 1986; Petersen and Hamburg 1986). Besides the prevalent insensitivity to children's developmental needs, there was embarrassingly little acknowledgment of their basic human rights. Laws prohibiting cruelty to animals were generally in effect many years—and sometimes centuries—before the establishment of child welfare legislation and child protective agencies.

Hall's second achievement was short-lived but significant, and also served to deepen the general appreciation of children's different status. Even before Darwin's 1859 volume and the ill-fated recapitulation theory proposed by Ernst Haeckel (appendix F), there had been a growing sentiment for at least the toleration of more immaturity on the part of young children. This sentiment was influenced by the popularity of Rousseau's (1762) *Emile* and the later popularity of evolutionary accounts of play and pretend as contexts for the development of adult civility (Bretherton 1984b; Bruner, Jolly, and Sylva 1976; Fein 1981; Mahoney 1989b; Richards 1987; Siviy and Panksepp 1987; Winnicott 1971). Rousseau had argued that children's "natural inclinations" and interests should be tolerated and encouraged, and Hall was instrumental in integrating that philosophy with Haeckel's notion that each child repeats the history of the species in his or her individual development.

Paralleling these achievements by Hall were those of John Fiske, a nineteenth-century American historian and philosopher who did much to popularize evolutionary thinking. In his *Outlines of Cosmic Philosophy,* published in 1874, Fiske was "the first to indicate [the] true significance of the prolongation of human infancy in the evolution of humanity" (Chamberlain 1911, p. 2). Although his insight lies at the core of modern appreciations of the importance of early experience and parenting, its social and familial implications are still less than optimally reflected in our educational and child-care policies (Bowlby 1988; Gould 1977a, 1977b, 1980a, 1980b, 1982; Lerner 1984; Scarr, Phillips, and McCartney 1990; Winnicott 1965; Yogman and Brazelton 1986). The modern debate, at least in psychology, seems to have shifted from whether early experience is developmentally significant to such issues as how significant, how early, and with what implications for the qualities and trajectories of individual lives. The consistency debate in personality theory, for example, does not deny patterns and continuities in individual lives; instead, the basic arguments are over the sources, structures, dynamics, and pliability of those patterns.

STAGES AND STRUCTURES, SYSTEMS AND PROCESSES

One of the most important developments in development has been the conceptual shift from stages and structures to systems and processes. To appreciate that shift, one must realize that science did not recognize process dynamics until the twentieth century, and that prevailing views of change had been confined to physical enlargement (hypertrophy), duplication (as in mass production), and other metaphors of alterations in matter over space/time. As I discussed in chapter 2, the classical view was closer to rationalist objectivism than to critical constructivism. The assumption had been that of a single, stable, external world capable of being described with simple, timeless, mathematical precision. Other than "natural disasters" and "supernatural interventions," such a world could be changed only by simple, discrete, fully determined forces. The challenge—at least for those bold enough to muddle in the affairs of life—was to identify and, if possible, harness those forces—preferably to one's own and the world's best interests.

For the vast portion of written history, the majority of our human peers lived their lives at the *relative* mercy (rather than mastery) of their environments, in large part because they believed (and therefore felt and acted) as if the forces shaping their lives were external to them and beyond their influence. They overlooked much that was there, often did more damage than good to themselves, and suffered unnecessarily. On the other hand, of course, our forebears were also persistent and resourceful survivors, and although "active agent" theories of human nature may be somewhat recent, the activity of those agents is not. Moreover, lest our modern times seem relatively less pervaded by illusions, one need only note the sizable market for modern belief systems (religious and otherwise) that simply (and often irresponsibly) invert the balance of power in promising complete personal sovereignty over the forces that shape our lives (Buss 1978; Conway and Siegelman 1978; Duke and Johnson 1989; Hersh 1980). The truth, or what may serve as a wisp of its shadow, probably lies in the serpentine dance of these two extremes.

The Stages and Structures of Life

The earliest theories of development were little more than elaborations of enlargement, cycle, and horizontal stage theories, with successive changes being literally chained to chronological time (figure 7.1). The essence of such theories was that development involves a fixed sequence, a pattern determined by the laws of nature. This monotonous and powerless state of affairs was moderated by associationist and vertical stage theories, which became particularly popular after the Renaissance. More recent theoretical developments have been in the direction of complexity and differentiation. Consider, for example, some of the theories of lifespan development that have drawn and maintained the attention of developmental researchers and professional life counselors (table 7.1). In none of these is the progression from one state to another considered to be an automatic unfolding. The individual has re-entered the drama of development as an active agent, however cast and constrained. That agent and his or her activity are central emphases in modern developmental research.

Also noteworthy is the modern consensus that both continuities and discontinuities are evident in human psychological development. There are, for example, periods of relatively rapid and dramatic change, most notably in childhood. When 2.5-year-old children were asked to find a toy that had been hidden in a room, and were given a "big hint" by being shown a replica of the toy and its hiding place in a miniature room, they were unable to make the symbolic transfer from model to reality (DeLoache 1987). Although they could later find the miniature toy in the room replica (original location), they were unable to use that information to guide their search in the actual room (an analogous location). For children three years of age, however, the miniature model was an effective aid in their search (figure 7.2). The processes that underlie such developments remain a central focus of developmental researchers. Although Piaget's works are still dominant influences, their limitations have begun to encourage novel conjectures about knowledge development (Baillargeon 1987; Carey 1985a, 1985b; Furth 1987; Gelman and Baillargeon 1983; Mandler 1988; Pascual-Leone 1987).

Consider, for example, the work of William F. Brewer and his colleagues on the nature of knowledge restructuring in psychological development (Brewer and Nakamura 1984; Vosniadou and Brewer 1987). Drawing on work in several different areas, they have suggested that there are two basic forms of knowledge restructuring: "weak" and "radical." The former involves relatively minor adjustments in domain-specific knowledge, while radical restructuring entails dramatic shifts in core constructs and their relations. The two types of restructuring may overlap, but they appear to involve different mechanisms, and only radical

Figure 7.1   Common Metaphors of Development

TERM	REPRESENTATION		REMARKS
	time 1	time 2	
Expansion, Hypertrophy			Development is equated with hypertrophy (enlargement). The shedding of former exoskeletons (molting) offers some metaphors.
Association, Contiguity, Conditioning	a ⟶ b c ⟶ d	a or c ⟶ b or d	Emphasis is on linear chaining, with cohesion supplied by temporal continuity and/or contingent reward or punishment.
Horizontal Stage	1 ⟶ 2	1 ⇢ 2 ⟶ 3	Development is a sequential pattern of "passages" through universal life periods.
Cycle			Emphasis is on two-dimensional repetition of an identical physical pattern. Examples: Sisyphus, Vico's cycles of history.
Static Balance, Homeostatic			This is classical homeostasis: all development is return to or maintenance of a set point or narrow range of balance.
Vertical Stage	2 1	3 2 1	Development is an ascension or qualitative improvement in a valued dimension; it can be "blocked" at any point.
Vertical Spiral			Adds a third dimension to cycle theories and confronts the paradox of simultaneous novelty and familiarity.
Dynamic Balance, Consistency			Development involves a dynamic, ongoing process of balancing and re-balancing in response to endless "perturbations".
Differentiation, Self-Organizing, Constructivist, Evolutionary			Development involves a progressive move from simple and undifferentiated forms to complexly ordered ones.
Transformation, Metamorphic, Revolutionary			An organically-based stage theory empasizing dramatic metamorphosis via transient regression and vulnerability.

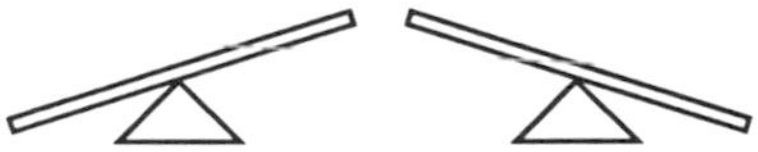

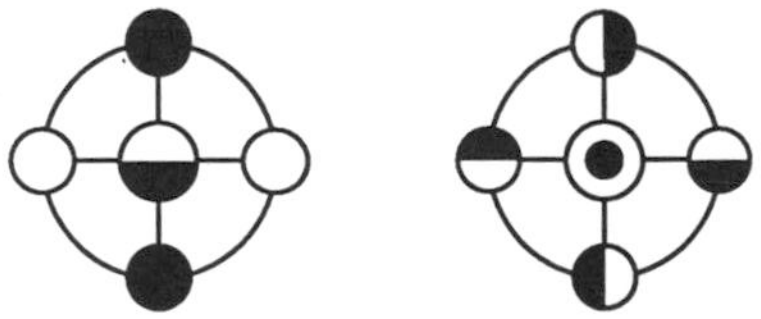

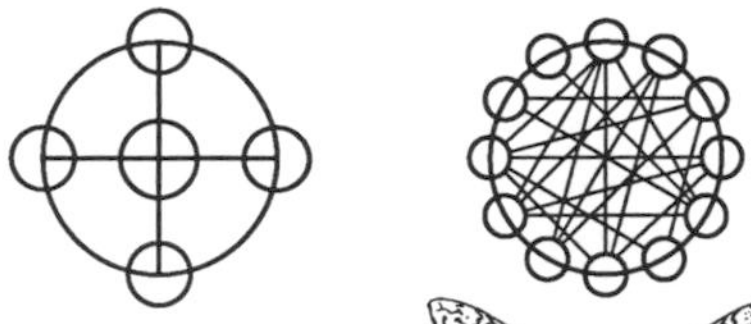

SOURCE: © 1989 M. J. Mahoney

Table 7.1   Basic Stages in Human Psychological Development

Theorist	Stages (in developmental order)
Aurobindo*/Wilber*	1 Sensori-motor · 2 Bio-emotional · 3 Representational · 4 Rule/Role · 5 Reflective · 6 Integrative · 7 Transpersonal · 8 Intuitive · 9 Transcendent · 10 Spiritual
Erikson*	1 Trust vs. Mistrust · 2 Autonomy vs. Shame, Doubt · 3 Initiative vs. Guilt · 4 Industry vs. Inferiority · 5 Identity vs. Diffusion · 6 Intimacy vs. Isolation · 7 Generativity vs. Stagnation · 8 Integrity vs. Despair, Disgust
Freud	1 Oral · 2 Anal · 3 Phallic · 4 Latency · 5 Genital
Guidano	1 Selfhood · 2 Attachment · 3 Emotionality · 4 Abstraction, Identification, Differentiation · 5 Autonomy · 6 Identity Dynamics
Kegan*	1 Incorporative · 2 Impulsive · 3 Imperial · 4 Interpersonal · 5 Institutional · 6 Interindividual
Kohlberg*	1 Preconventional (Instructional Hedonism) · 2 Conventional (Rule Conformity) · 3 Postconventional (Human Rights, Personal Conscience)
Loevinger*	1 Impulsive · 2 Self-Protective · 3 Conformist · 4 Self-Aware · 5 Conscientious · 6 Individualistic · 7 Autonomous · 8 Integrated
Maslow*	1 Physiological · 2 Safety · 3 Love and Belongingness · 4 Self-Esteem · 5 Self-Actualization · 6 Self-Transcendence (Knowledge, Aesthetics, Spirituality)
Patanjali* (Vedic Yoga)	1 Physical Needs · 2 Power · 3 Emotionality · 4 Love, Agape · 5 Rationality, Communication · 6 Intuition · 7 Spirituality
Perry*	1 Power · 2 Basic Dualities · 3 Multiplicities · 4 Relativisms · 5 Commitments
Piaget	1 Sensorimotor · 2 Preoperational · 3 Concrete Operational · 4 Formal Operational

AGE (in years) †

Age scale: 0 1 2 3 4 5 6 8 10 12 14 16 18 20 30 40 50 60 70

* Did not link stages to specific ages.

† Note changes in scale at ages six and twenty.

© 1989 M. J. Mahoney

Figure 7.2   Age Differences in Children's Cognitive Abilities

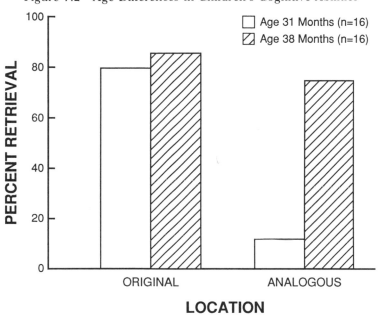

SOURCE: redrawn from DeLoache (1987)

restructuring "can account for the emergence of new theories or new paradigms" (Vosniadou and Brewer 1987, p. 55).

The shifts that occur in a child's knowledge show some parallels to shifts in the history of ideas (chapter 2). The radical restructuring of human knowledge caused by the Copernican revolution in astronomy has some parallels with children's developing knowledge of astronomy (see figure 7.3). It is tempting to infer that children's knowledge development in this area may pass through the same stages as our scientific theories (a conceptual version of recapitulation theory!). More pertinent (and probably more warranted), however, is the realization that educators, parents, scientists, and psychotherapists might all be well served by a better understanding of the role of prior ("old") knowledge in learning:

A major result of recent work in cognitive science has been an awareness of the importance of old knowledge in the acquisition of new knowledge. . . . Clearly to the degree possible, it is preferable to elaborate old schemata and to relate incoming information to what is already known. However, the use of existing knowledge to support new knowledge appears to operate differently in the case of weak restructuring than it does in the case of radical restructuring.

. . . It is not clear, however, what role prior knowledge plays in radical restructuring. . . . The debate on the role of prior knowledge in radical restructuring raises important questions about both the content and the methods of instruc-

Figure 7.3   The Development of Children's Knowledge of Our Solar System

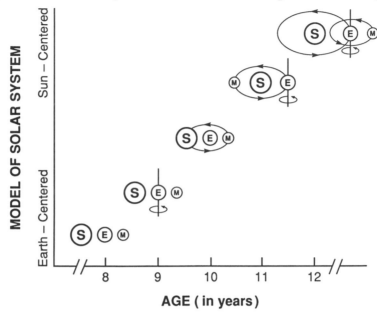

SOURCE: Redrawn from the data of Smith, Lynch, and Reesink (1987). © 1989 M. J.
Mahoney

tion. . . . How much of the child's prior knowledge should the instructor rely
upon? It may be preferable to try to identify only those aspects of the existing
knowledge that are compatible with the new theory and use this information in
the acquisition process. Alternatively, it may be better to present children with
a completely new theory, ignoring what they already know. (Vosniadou and
Brewer 1987, pp. 55–56)

The relevance of these questions for psychotherapy practice needs little
elaboration.

Modern syntheses of contributions from cognitive, developmental, and
systems sciences have begun to suggest that the processes of change that
comprise knowledge restructuring reflect dynamic tensions and opponent processes (Weimer 1987). In the language of autopoiesis (appendix
C), the self-organizing system seeks a "moving balance" between familiarity ("confirmation") and novelty (figure 7.4). Each individual is always
doing his or her momentary, contextual "best" to maintain a dynamic
balance between the familiarity of "experience as usual" and the novelty
that results when anticipatory (feedforward) mechanisms are challenged,
if not thwarted, in his or her ongoing constructions of personal order.

Figure 7.4 The Dynamic Balance between Novelty and Familiarity (Confirmation) in Developmental Challenges

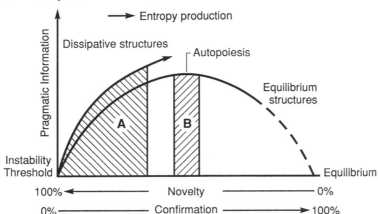

SOURCE: Redrawn with permission from Erich Jantsch, *The Self-Organizing Universe.* © 1980, Pergamon Press.

Living systems exhibit new forms of development when their efforts at adaptation occasionally fall out of step with their changing world and, after a period of relative disorganization and distress, emerge with a more viable pattern of interaction (Dewey 1934; Kelso and Schoner 1988; Nelson and Nelson 1978; Thelen 1988, 1989a, 1989b, in press). In his integration of the affective and cognitive constructs of Piaget and Freud, psychologist Hans Furth reminds us that learning and knowing are active attempts to serve dual functions: the conservation of biological integrity and the expansion of the assimilable environment. Indeed, he adds that "the developmental sequence of conservation, expansion, disturbance, compensation, reconstruction, conservation is valid for all areas and at all stages of development" (1987, p. 78). If this is the case, the simplified prototype of development would be something like that depicted in figure 7.5, with transient "deconstructions" or episodes of relative disorganization preceding (and perhaps affording) saltatory "leaps" toward greater complexity and differentiation. Lest that figure render too optimistic a view of knowledge development, we should remember that "an organism with schemes that no longer expand will in the long run die" (p. 79). In the long run, of course, even the most expansive and resilient of "schemes" cannot avert that result.

It is also important that emotionality and the "moving balance" (equilibration) versions of modern systems theories have assigned roles of special significance to the interdependent processes of changing and maintaining patterns of activity. The measurement and portrayal of those processes has itself invited new challenges in both theory and methodology. Not coincidentally, they are the same challenges faced by researchers

Figure 7.5 An Illustration of the Dynamics of Systemic Order and Disorder in Periods of Development

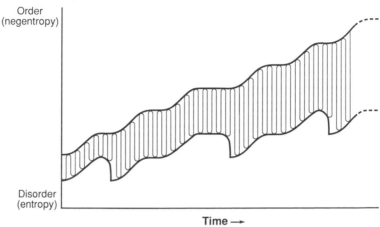

SOURCE: © 1989 M. J. Mahoney

studying complex phenomena and self-organizing living systems (appendices C and E).

The Development of Process

The general shift of interest within and beyond stage theories and toward the more complex dynamics of process theories has been accompanied by a reappraisal of the relationship between structure and function, with contemporary opinion acknowledging that these dimensions are inseparable. One consequence of that acknowledgment has been a decline in the popularity of static ("architectural") views of psychological or personality structure and an increasing appreciation that such structures are actively maintained and elaborated. There has also been considerable effort to incorporate aspects of selected stage theories (table 7.1) into conceptually larger perspectives that respect system dynamics and the fundamental "process nature" of experience itself, including those patterns we call development (Brainerd 1978; Fischer and Silvern 1985; Ford 1987; Furth 1987; Guidano 1987; Kegan 1982; Pascual-Leone 1984, 1987; Thelen 1988, 1989a, 1989b, in press). Stage theories persist, of course, and some of their advocates still maintain that failures and deficiencies in earlier life stages can lead to irreversible "foreclosures" and constraints on adult identity and personality. Besides the psychodynamic self psychologies (chapter 9) see, for example, the extensive work on ego identity status stemming from Marcia's (1966) efforts to operationalize

Erik Erikson's (1968) theory of lifespan identity development (Adams, Markstrom and Abraham, 1987; Côté and Levine 1988a, 1988b, 1988c; Kroger and Haslett 1988; Larkin 1987; Orlofsky and Frank 1986).

To their credit, many modern psychodynamic self psychologies also illustrate ongoing efforts to integrate stages and structures with system dynamics. Indeed, the concept of process has become central to ongoing attempts to understand "sensitive periods," plasticity, continuity, vulnerability, and resilience in development (Bornstein 1989; Bornstein and Sigman 1986).

To translate all of this into less technical terms, the question of process is multiple: *What* changes when a person (or an organism) changes? *How* does that change take place (that is, how initiated, organized, and executed)? And, ultimately, *what should one do* (or not do) with an understanding of such processes? The answers to such questions are still sketchy, but they are (I believe) beginning to suggest some welcome contours for our ever-human (and therefore occasionally clumsy) efforts at helping. The acknowledgment of process as primary in human experience is significant in itself, a step that requires a fundamental acknowledgment of time and the lifespan dynamics of "temporal becoming." It is a step heralded by increasing numbers of psychotherapy researchers, and one that was made long ago in the phenomenological, "experiential," and existential-humanist movements (Bugental 1978, 1987; Chessick 1986; Daldrup et al. 1988; Gadamer 1975; Greenberg and Pinsoff 1986; Guidano 1987, 1990; Mahrer 1985; Rice and Greenberg 1984). That acknowledgment is increasingly apparent today in the contributions of constructivists, interactionists, and complex systems specialists.

The most conservative answer to the question of process might be abstention: that is, that we don't know, and that developmental processes remain a mystery to life scientists. The boldest responses have taken the form of specific models and theories encompassing all lifespans of all individuals, past, present, and future. Somewhere beyond these extremes, in their dialectic, lies the possibility that the abstainer and the advocate contribute to a common emergence—that is, the clarification of significant dimensions in the concept of development. When mechanical models were popular, for example, mechanical metaphors were prevalent. The models proposed by Freud and Piaget invited an appreciation of depth and dynamics in change processes and were complementary in significant respects (Furth 1987). Freud's was basically a "dynamic equilibration" and horizontal stage theory, and Piaget's equilibration processes were the driving force beneath a vertical stage theory of development. There are scholars, I am sure, who would challenge my horizontal-versus-vertical portrayals of Freud and Piaget, respectively, and I concede that the caricatures I have drawn are simplifications. For the moment, however, the point is that both were pioneers in focusing our attention on development and the child, and that both appealed to

active organismic processes in the negotiation of life's challenges and
opportunities.

THE ISSUE OF HUMAN PLASTICITY

As I remarked in the opening chapter, one of the central issues in all
theories of human development—including all theories of personality,
psychopathology, psychotherapy, learning, and adaptation—is the question of limits and possibilities for human change. Among known life
forms, humans are readily distinguishable—even remarkable—in their
flexibility and resourcefulness in the complex reciprocities of adaptation
(chapter 6, appendix F). As much as evolutionary studies have emphasized the unusual resilience, mutability, and resourcefulness of humans,
they have also reflected the risks, vulnerabilities, and coexistence of
human resistance to change. As we have already seen, the issue of possible change has been embedded in a number of philosophical and conceptual debates. Beyond the polarities of Parmenides and Heraclitus, the
physical and life sciences have struggled with this question in one form
or another since their beginnings.

Most recently, the issue of plasticity has been debated in dialogues
about "cross-situational consistency" versus "situational specificity" in
human behavior, the relative importance of character "traits" versus
psychological "skills," and the "continuity" versus "discontinuity" of
learning and development (Bandura 1986; Baumrind 1989; Block 1971;
Bowers 1973; Cantor and Mischel 1977; Clarke and Clarke 1976; Costa
and McCrae 1988a, 1988b; Digman 1989; Endler and Magnusson 1976;
Epstein 1973, 1979, 1980; Kagan 1984; Lerner 1984; McCrae and Costa
1987, 1989; Mischel 1973, 1979; Radke-Yarrow 1989; Sroufe and Jacobvitz 1989; Wachs and Gruen 1982; Woodruff-Pak 1989). The new view,
however, is that organisms—and especially we humans—are both vulnerable and resilient, and that the extremes of human plasticity are most
apparent at the extremes of human interaction.

The Effects of Neglect, Abuse, and Rejection

The extremes of human interaction cover a wide expanse and are associated with strong, bipolar emotions (chapter 8). At one extreme is love
(in all its forms), and at the other revulsion, often expressed violently
(Clark and Reis 1988; Dubé and Hébert, 1988; Hofer 1984; Levy and
Davis 1988; Pistole 1989; Shaver and Hazan 1988; Waring et al. 1980).
Though I shall have much to say about love and human caring in the
chapters that follow, at the moment let me look at human interactions at

the other end of that spectrum. Rescued from scientific rhetoric, one fact now stands clear, naked, and ugly to all the world:

1. The physical, emotional, and psychosocial neglect, abuse, and rejection of human beings is potentially hazardous to their health and well-being.

2. The risks of such hazards are substantially amplified when experiences of neglect, abuse, or rejection occur *(a)* very early, *(b)* repeatedly, *(c)* with emotional intensity, and *(d)* with experienced reference to the capacities or appraisal of the self.

Though some experts would, of course, object to such strong wording, the essence of the message has never been so thoroughly acknowledged (Besharov 1989; Daro 1988; Kazdin 1989; Sroufe and Rutter 1984).

The earliest clinical and scientific evidence for these assertions came from observations and studies of the ill effects of institutional care on children's—and especially infants'—development. Pioneering figures here included Lauretta Bender, John Bowlby, Dorothy Burlingham, Anna Freud, William Goldfarb, David Levy, and René Spitz. The "failure to thrive" of these children was attributed to "anaclitic depression" by psychoanalytic specialists, but Bowlby and his colleague Mary Ainsworth were among a group who would blaze new paths in the study of infant-mother relations and later psychological development (chapter 8).

The research literatures on the incidence, forms, and effects of parental neglect and abuse are now gigantic and growing (Aber and Allen 1987; Dubé and Hébert 1988; Egeland 1988; Evoy 1981; Hart and Brassard 1987; Kilgore 1988; Nurius, Lovell, and Edgar 1988; Rieder and Cicchetti 1989). Moreover, the evidence is now considerable that these dysfunctional patterns of parent-child interaction are (1) frequently related to patterns of emotional distress, self-abuse, and psychopathology in the family, and (2) often perpetuated across generations and through spouse selection ("assortative mating") (Goldstein 1988; Gottman and Katz 1989; Gottman and Krokoff 1989; Kazdin 1989; Kerr and Bowen 1988; Kilpatrick 1975; Merikangas et al. 1988; Sroufe and Rutter 1984; West and Prinz 1987; Yogman and Brazelton 1986). Although it may sound oversimplifying, Virginia Satir (1972) captured much of the essence of such dysfunctional families in summarizing their three most common and absolute injunctions (to the child and to one another): DON'T TRUST, DON'T FEEL, and DON'T TALK ABOUT IT.

The effects of neglect and abuse—particularly physical and sexual—are now documented well beyond what should be needed for immediate actions in the forms of education, prevention, detection, and treatment. As yet less acknowledged are the incidence and effects of psychological maltreatment in the subtler forms of emotional rejection and disempowerment (Hart and Brassard 1987). In his volume on the psychological consequences of parental rejection, for example, John Joseph Evoy argued that such rejection is "a deeply destructive human experience"

(1981, p. 53) shared by many people in today's culture. Though the consequences of perceived parental rejection are complexly individualized, Evoy summarized some of their main features:

- "deeply damaged self-esteem," with feelings of self-rejection and even self-hate;
- "convictions of personal worthlessness" which are very resistant to challenge or change;
- feelings that their worthlessness is "transparent" to other people;
- a desperate longing to be loved co-existent with the simultaneous conviction that they are unlovable;
- feelings of aloneness and not belonging;
- fears of mental illness;
- chronic anxiety and vigilance about being rejected again;
- chronic problems with intimacy, usually related to the rejected person's inability to genuinely "give" or "receive" love;
- chronic (though often stifled) feelings of anger, resentment, guilt, hostility, and depression; and
- in some, a feeling that "something inside them had died" (p. 70).

Needless to say, these are experience patterns frequently encountered in psychotherapy. They reflect the painful but powerful "personal realities" through which the rejected person organizes his or her life. I shall discuss those realities and their embeddedness in emotional and identity development in much greater detail (chapters 8 and 9).

Psychological Resilience

The concepts of psychological *vulnerability* and *resilience* have become increasingly popular as studies in developmental psychopathology have begun to focus on the range of individual responses to adverse experience. According to Garmezy and Masten, vulnerability refers to "the *susceptibility or predisposition of an individual to negative outcomes*" (1986, p. 509). The emphasis here is on the individual being unusually likely to developing and/or remaining mired in personal problems (in whatever forms). *Resilience* has been variously defined but generally refers to an individual's capacities (1) to endure, survive ("effectively cope with"), and master severe challenges (as from privation, pain, and abuse) and (2) to maintain (and sometimes enhance) the quality of one's psychological integration in the process. The growing acknowledgment of psychological resilience has helped refine the quality of questions being asked about human psychological vulnerability (Aber and Allen 1987; Baltes, Featherman, and Lerner 1987; Belsky and Nezworski 1987; Cytryn et al. 1986;

Field, McCabe, and Schneiderman 1988; Goldstein 1988; Hart and Brassard 1987; Hetherington 1989; Kazdin 1989; Lewis et al. 1988; Quay and Werry 1986; Rutter 1987; Sroufe and Rutter 1984; Werner 1986; West and Prinz 1987).

The significance of individual differences in vulnerability and resilience can be portrayed in a number of ways. Clinically, the psychologically vulnerable individual is more likely to be repeatedly in and out of treatment (figure 7.6), especially when one's life circumstances remain stressful and one has few sources of emotional support. In contrast, the resilient person is more likely to be able to use professional treatment as an opportunity to improve his or her coping skills so that later adjustment is moderately, and sometimes dramatically, increased. Moreover, individual responses to similar events may exhibit different patterns in vulnerable and resilient persons. Figure 7.7, for example, depicts two hypothetical individuals experiencing the same external stressors and entering into a professional counseling relationship. Note that the responses of the more vulnerable individual are more extreme and their range is confined relative to the wider span of possibilities that might be explored by the more resilient person.

But what distinguishes the resilient child (and adult) from his or her siblings? Why do some children who are statistically at risk emerge healthy and, in some cases, even hardier than some of their well-parented peers? Historically, this question first emerged in the study of familial patterns and schizophrenia, but it has now infiltrated the entire field of developmental studies. Under such labels as *coping, hardiness, invulnerabil-*

Figure 7.6   Selected Hypothetical Patterns of Psychological Development

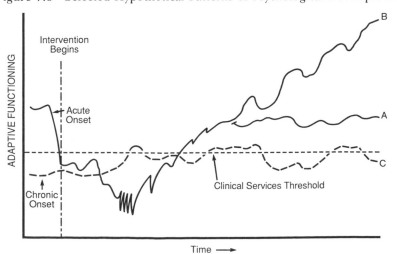

SOURCE: © 1989 M. J. Mahoney

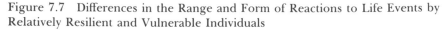

Figure 7.7   Differences in the Range and Form of Reactions to Life Events by Relatively Resilient and Vulnerable Individuals

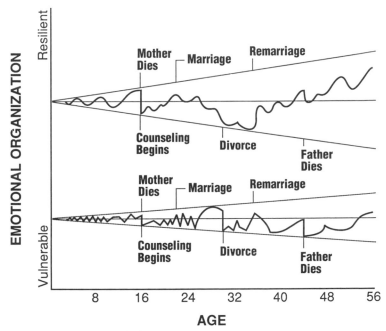

ity, and *the survivor personality,* the resilient human has now become a bona-fide scientific phenomenon and one worthy of research (Allred and Smith 1989; Anthony and Cohler 1987; Antonovsky 1979; Band and Weisz 1988; Block and Block 1980; Dienstbier 1989; Emery and Csikszentmihalyi 1981; Ford and Thompson 1985; Garmezy and Masten 1986; Garmezy and Rutter 1983; Hetherington 1989; Kobasa, Maddi, and Kahn 1982; Kobasa et al. 1985; Lerner and Busch-Rossnagel 1981; O'Grady and Metz 1987; Perloff 1983; Vitaliano et al. 1987; Wilson, Harel, and Kahana 1988).

Various theories have been proposed to account for the differential protection or "buffering" from certain forms of stimulation, such buffering being an important part of psychological resilience (see figure 7.8 for a neodynamic illustration). Although our understanding of psychological resilience is still preliminary, some patterns are noteworthy in their possible implications for parenting, education, and the mental health professions. Allowing a wide margin for individual differences, resilient and "hardy" individuals have frequently exhibited one or more of the following characteristics:

Figure 7.8   A Neodynamic Portrayal of "The Human Buffering System"

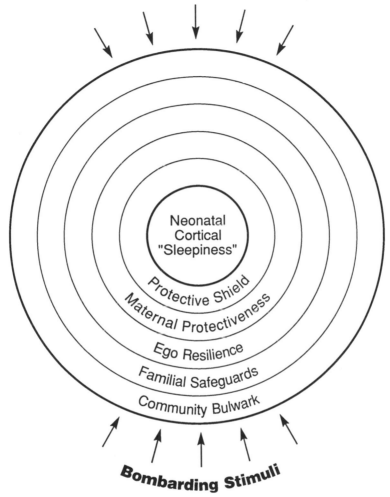

Neonatal
Cortical
"Sleepiness"

Protective Shield

Maternal Protectiveness

Ego Resilience

Familial Safeguards

Community Bulwark

Bombarding Stimuli

SOURCE: Redrawn from Anthony (1987)

1. Early awareness that his or her parents (and possibly other family members) were not functioning well.
2. Identification and frequent use of alternate persons as sources of security, nurturance, and developmental identification (in some instances, these surrogates were characters in novels or totally fictional fantasies).
3. Early identification and refinement of a special talent (academic, artistic, athletic) that opened new developmental paths and social networks.

4. High motivation to develop, often expressed in unusual tenacity and intensity of activity.
5. A tendency to experience frustrations and even trauma as challenges and opportunities for development.

Results from studies of health, happiness, and well-being suggest that some aspects of resilience are similar to those associated with "optimal experience" and life satisfaction: namely, a sense of "meaning," "purpose," or "coherence," and a perceived network of caring others—both of which encourage hope, coping, and personal engagement (Antonovsky 1979; Argyle 1987; Aron and Aron 1987; Beiser 1974; Burt 1984; Campbell et al. 1989; Cohen and Wills 1985; Csikszentmihalyi and Csikszentmihalyi 1988; Frankl 1959, 1978, 1985; Friedman and Booth-Kewley 1987; House, Landis, and Umberson 1988; Kreppner and Lerner, in press; Nowack, 1989; Thompson 1989; Walsh and Shapiro, 1983; Warr 1978). Not surprisingly, there are also apparent relations among patterns of emotional experience, capacities for intimacy, and identity development (see Chamberlaine et al. 1989; Pistole 1989; Waring and Chelune 1983; Young 1988).

ACTIVITY AND INTERACTION IN DEVELOPMENT

Another significant trend in developmental studies has involved increasing acknowledgments of preparedness, activity, human interaction, and some forms of complex cognitive development at early ages (Baillargeon 1987; Cohen 1979; Epstein 1987; Fischer 1980; Gibson 1987, 1988; Hale and Lewis 1979; Keil 1981; Kuhl and Meltzoff 1982; Mandler 1988; Meltzoff and Moore 1977, 1983; Palermo, in press; Sroufe 1979; Waggoner and Palermo 1989). The ideas that a newborn is a *tabula rasa,* and that he or she spends months in "cortical sleepiness" (Anthony 1987), are no longer tenable in light of modern studies. Research on infants, for example, has shown that they are much more skilled in perception and memory than previously believed. They are active and selective in their attention, they are quickly attuned to the sounds and smells of their primary caregiver, and they develop expectancies and rudimentary concepts long before they have taken their first steps or uttered their first words. These developments are not exclusively cognitive, however; in fact, most of them emerge in the context of behavioral activity, emotional experiences, and communicative exchanges (Bornstein 1985, 1988; Comparetti 1981; Fogel and Thelen 1987; Greenspan and Greenspan 1985; Hartup 1989; Meltzoff 1985a, 1985b; Smith and Pederson 1988; Stern 1985; Trevarthen 1982).

Some studies of fetal and infant development have also challenged the sharpness of traditional distinctions between organism and environment, not to mention "innate" versus "acquired" (learned) activity patterns (Bronson 1982; Easter, Barald, and Carlson 1987; Krasnegor et al. 1987; Meaney et al. 1988; Pick 1988; Schanberg and Field 1987; Smotherman and Robinson 1990; Thatcher, Walker, and Giudice 1987; Uttal and Perlmutter 1989). The work on fetal activity *in utero* by A. Milani Comparetti (1981) and colleagues is particularly intriguing. Prior to their studies, it was assumed that there was no meaningful pattern to fetal activity (other than speculations about the influence of the mother's diet). The occasional kicks, punches, and shifts in position of the fetus were interpreted as a nuisance or "noise" in the overall process of gestation. However, Comparetti's research showed that there are clear patterns that emerge in the womb, especially after the seventh week following fertilization. This is about the time that the fetus has grown to sufficient mass (weight) as to be no longer suspended in amniotic fluid and, therefore, occasionally "bottoms out" or touches the sides of the uterus. Observing the fetus with an echoscope (sonagraphy), the researchers were impressed with the *continuity* of motor activity (with only short rest periods) and the *richness of movement patterns* in the fetus. Movement patterns at twenty weeks of gestation, for example, appeared "similar to the mature repertoire of the basic motor patterns described . . . in adult athletes" (p. 184).

Comparetti and his colleagues also found that these unborn athletes were actively involved in determining the time and phasing of their own births (in collaboration with their mothers, of course). There was, in other words, an intimate *reciprocity* between mother and fetus throughout the pregnancy, and particularly around labor and the birthing process. "This awareness of fetal collaboration in labor allows us to consider that a disorder of delivery may be due to failure by either party—the mother or the fetus" (1981, p. 188). An unexpected catastrophe added still more information about such reciprocity. In the midst of one of their studies, there was a major earthquake in northern Italy, imposing considerable stress on everyone (including the pregnant women) in that region. Prior research had shown that extreme physical or emotional stresses on pregnant mothers are associated with an interesting pattern in the fetus. After an initial phase of increased activity, the fetus becomes virtually motionless and, if it survives, shows a regression in motor activity. This pattern was observed after the earthquake, with some fetuses remaining inactive for as long as two months. Moreover, follow-up observations over the next two years suggested that—relative to children born to mothers outside the earthquake region—the fetally stressed children were less behaviorally interactive with their physical and social worlds (including their mothers).* Such early experiences may therefore play an important part

*I am indebted to Dr. Mario A. Reda of the University of Cagliari for this information. Regrettably, Dr. Comparetti died before the project was completed; and, to my knowledge, the follow-up results have not yet been published.

in an individual's developing sense of self, world, and his or her interactions.

Other work on early human interaction and its impact on the developing child has also challenged the myth of the "empty, inert infant." As Daniel N. Stern (1985) and others have documented, the experiential world of the infant is highly interpersonal and much more interactive than previously believed (Bornstein 1985, 1988; Fogel and Thelen 1987; Hartup 1989; Klein 1987; Lewis and Rosenblum 1974; Magnusson 1987; Meltzoff 1985a, 1985b; Smith and Pederson 1988; Smotherman and Robinson 1990; Trevarthen 1982; Wahler and Dumas 1989). Long before they develop words and language, children learn to communicate and to infer messages from the people around them. When their efforts and inferences are ignored or thwarted, however, they respond accordingly. The majority of these early interactions are related to emotions, emotional development, and the quality of the alliance between the child and the primary caretaker.

EMOTIONAL DEVELOPMENT AND ATTACHMENT

Until relatively recently, studies of the developing infant and child were generally focused on separate domains: perceptual development, cognitive development, motor skill development, language development, and so on. Reflecting the third axial shift in the history of ideas, however, modern research is exploring the complex interdependence of these domains and the development of the individual as a whole organism. This emphasis is particularly evident in two overlapping areas that have unquestionable relevance for counseling and psychotherapy: emotionality and affectional bonding. As the latter is inherently emotion-based, I shall briefly review it here and leave to chapter 8 contemporary work on emotionality and human change, owing to its importance and complexity. From a developmental perspective, both topics are inseparable from the domain of identity and "selfhood" development (see chapter 9).

The Development of Affect

There is no doubt that infants and young children experience emotions, but there is less consensus as to how those experiences contribute to individual functioning and development. Figure 7.9 shows a simplified portrayal of current views, the so-called positive and negative emotions emerging initially from undifferentiated activity and sensitivity. In line with Heinz Werner's (1948) "ontogenetic principle," affective development is thus portrayed as proceeding "from a state of relative globality and lack of differentiation to a state of increasing differentiation, articula-

Figure 7.9 The Differentiation of Human Emotions

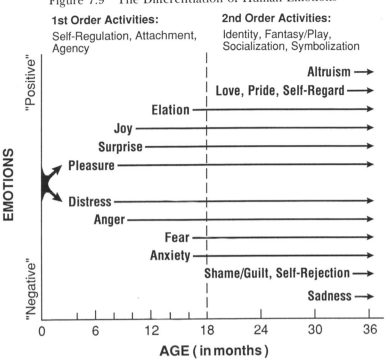

SOURCE: © 1989 M. J. Mahoney. Integrated from Bridges (1932), Emde (1984), and Sroufe (1984).

tion, and hierarchic integration" (1957, p. 126). Anger appears before fear and anxiety, and sadness is generally observed only after considerable development in identity, socialization, and symbolic processes. Emotions play a key role in the child's organization of his or her experience and are probably "the principle organizing factors in consciousness" (Izard 1978, p. 391).

Though the biological bases of emotionality are important (see chapter 8), more pertinent here is the recent evidence that the emotions experienced and expressed by both infant and caregiver may be related to brain opioids. Studies by Jaak Panksepp, Tiffany Field, and others have shown that social attachments and the distress of separation or loss may be mediated by the activity of endorphins and other brain opioids (Field and Reite 1985; Kraemer 1985; Panksepp 1986; Panksepp, Siviy, and Normansell 1985; Sahley and Panksepp 1987). Panksepp and his colleagues summarize that work by stating, "It is presently certain that brain opioids are powerful influences in controlling the activity of social affect circuitry in the brain. Endogenous opioids can inhibit separation distress circuits in all mammalian and avian species that have been studied" (1985, p. 38). The pain of separation or loss is only one aspect of this phenomenon, however, and those same brain chemicals may be involved in many of the pleasures experienced when emotionally bonded humans (at any age) are "attuned," "entrained," or otherwise "resonant" with one another (Field and Reite 1985; Stern 1985). The point here is not that parental or romantic love can be "reduced" to brain chemistry, but rather that the individual is a coherent whole embedded in human relationships. For those who need a "biological basis" for the power of emotionality and relationships, this research may be particularly interesting (see also chapter 8 and appendix D). At any rate, it reminds us that body, brain, and the behaviors that relate them to their environments comprise a complex and dynamic unity.

An apt illustration of this point is provided by recent refinements in our understanding of children's fears and their development. Two of the most extensively studied fears in infants are of separation from the primary caregiver ("separation anxiety") and of unfamiliar persons ("stranger anxiety"). Both appear at about the same ages (roughly five to eight months), and there has been some research linking that timing to the infant's development of a stable schema for the caregiver's face. A third fear is exhibited during or soon after these two, and is one most parents are glad to see—namely, the fear of heights. Until recently it was assumed that fear of heights was related to perceptual and cognitive developments; this was, at least, the interpretation offered by Gibson and Walk (1960) in their classic studies of the "visual cliff." The visual cliff is a physical arrangement in which clear Plexiglas is placed over an elevated floor which abruptly drops off to a lower elevation. The "cliff" is this apparent drop-off; the Plexiglas is to ensure that the child cannot actually fall over the cliff.

Researchers have studied infants' reactions to the cliff, and particularly their apparent discomfort at being asked to crawl, walk, or be placed on its "far side" (Campos et al. 1978). It is now apparent that a strictly ethological or perceptual interpretation is inadequate to account for the range of infants' reactions. To begin with, depth perception and fear of heights precede (rather than follow) skilled locomotion in many infants. Moreover, recent studies have shown that infants' reactions to the experiment are modulated by nonverbal communication with their mothers. If the mother shows signs of concern when the infant nears the cliff, he or she generally backs away and remains on the shallow ("safe") side. When the mother's face expresses calm or encouragement, however, the infant is much more likely to explore the edge and risk crossing over the cliff (Campos et al. 1983; Lewis 1987; Tronick 1989). The point, again, is that multiple systems are operating interdependently, and that infant-caregiver communication is a powerful factor in the child's early forays into the world.

Attachment Theory

As we have seen, the human fetus and infant are both active and interactive. The most important interactions between young children and their caregivers are emotional and communicative. But there is much more to the story than just this. While they are acting and interacting, children are also developing. For the first eighteen months or so, their activities are focused on self-regulation, emotional attachment, and their own agency or competence. These activities are supplemented over the next year and a half with emphases on identity development, fantasy, play, socialization, and symbolic processes (figure 7.9). During those first three years—and in the primary context of their human relationships—the child develops a sense of his or her body, self-worth, and competence. Those human relationships and their vital importance to the developing individual have been emphasized by numerous writers. If I could recommend only one resource on the relevance of this fact for psychotherapy, however, it would be John Bowlby's *A Secure Base* (1988) or his classic pair of 1976 lectures, "The Making and Breaking of Affectional Bonds" (the latter are reprinted in his 1979 book of that title).

Attachment theory and its relevance for both developmental psychopathology and psychotherapy have become major themes of research over the last quarter-century. Although the theory has been most extensively elaborated by Bowlby (1969, 1973, 1980), he has acknowledged the important contributions of such colleagues as Mary D. S. Ainsworth, Inge Bretherton, Tiffany Field, Harry F. Harlow, Robert A. Hinde, Mary Main, L. Alan Sroufe, Colwyn Trevarthen, Everett Waters, and many others, including their students. The range and relevance of contributions from this approach have been substantial.* Although Bowlby notes important differences between the ethology-based conceptual framework of attachment theory and the psychodynamic theories of Sigmund Freud, Adolf Meyer, Melanie Klein, Heinz Kohut, Margaret Mahler, and D. W. Winnicott (chapter 9), he has also acknowledged important parallels between the two traditions.

The central assertions of attachment theory are straightforward:

1. At all ages, human beings exhibit their greatest happiness and well-being when they are confident that there are one or more trusted persons within their psychological proximity who will come to their aid should

---

*See Ainsworth 1979, 1985*a*, 1985*b*, 1989; Belsky and Nezworski 1987; Bretherton 1985; Bretherton and Waters 1985; Cassidy 1986; Cicchetti 1987; Field 1987; Field et al. 1988; Ford and Thompson 1985; Goldberg 1988; Grossmann and Grossmann 1990; Guidano 1987, 1990; Guidano and Liotti 1983; Hazan and Shaver 1987, 1989; Hetherington 1989; Liotti 1984, 1987; O'Connor, Sigman, and Brill 1987; Parkes and Stevenson-Hinde 1982; Paterson and Moran 1988; Pistole 1989; Reda 1986; Rutter 1971, 1981; Sroufe 1979, 1984, 1987; Sroufe and Cooper 1988; Sroufe and Waters 1976; and West, Sheldon, and Reiffer 1989.

difficulties arise. This trusted and available "attachment figure" can be construed as providing a secure base from which his or her companion can operate.

2. Although it is not confined to infancy or childhood, the need for a secure personal base in the form of an attachment figure is most evident and urgent during these early developmental eras.

3. The primary biological function of intimate emotional bonds is to provide such secure bases in and from which the individuals involved can explore and elaborate their "working models" of self and intimate other, as well as the world they occupy.

4. Lifespan personality development involves the ongoing construction and reconstruction of these working models, reflecting a dynamic and generative tension between continuity (familiarity) and change (novelty).

5. A healthily functioning adult is not "compulsively self-reliant" and maximally autonomous; he or she is, instead, capable of trusting and relying on others, as well as providing a secure base for companions.

6. Private (and predominantly unconscious) models of self, others, and the world become increasingly firm (resistant to change) with the confirmation of experience, and such confirmation tends to accelerate as the infant, child, adolescent, and adult become more active and effective participants in selecting and creating their own environments.

7. The primary responsibilities of the psychotherapist are to provide a secure base that is safe, emotionally supportive, and respectful of the client's current experience. The main task of therapy is exploration, with the intent to understand and appraise old, unconscious stereotypes of self and world and to experiment with feeling, thinking, and acting in novel ways.*

Note the resonances here with the constructivist perspective (chapter 5), the evolutionary and ethological approaches (chapter 6), the caring-based and relationship-oriented moral development highlighted by women's studies (for example, Gilligan 1982; Kegan 1982), and the emphasis on dynamic systems of personal meanings (what I have termed "personal realities") embedded in and interactive with human relationships. At the conceptual level, part of the appeal of attachment theory is its compatibility with aspects of several major schools of thought (psychodynamic, behavioral, experiential, cognitive, family systems, and so on). Moreover, the extensive evidence generated in its explorations and refinements have been impressive in their corroboration of its viability and promise.

*Points 1, 2, and 5 are paraphrasings from Bowlby 1979, pp. 103–5. Points 3 and 4 are based on Bowlby 1988, p. 120, and Sroufe 1987, p. 22. Point 6 is drawn from Bowlby 1988, p. 130, and Sroufe 1987, pp. 22–23. Point 7 is paraphrased from Bowlby 1988, pp. 138–39.

Early laboratory research on attachment patterns and the experienced security of personal bases were inspired by Ainsworth's "strange situation" methodology. This procedure involves bringing infants and mothers into an experimental room and then observing (and sometimes physiologically monitoring) the infant's responses to a series of incremental challenges (encountering a stranger, being left alone, and so on), with the sequence culminating in reunion with the mother. It is in this last phase (reunion) that different patterns of infant-mother attachment are most evident. Ainsworth (1979) and her colleagues have described three general patterns:

A. **Anxious avoidant,** in which the infant shows conspicuous avoidance of and inattention to the mother when she returns (even though telemetric heart-rate recordings often reveal that the infant is experiencing considerable emotional distress); if picked up by the mother, the infant does not cling and usually avoids eye contact or interaction.

B. **Securely attached,** in which the infant immediately seeks contact with the mother and maintains proximity to her, sometimes exhibiting emotional release through brief "protest" or crying; the infant is capable of being comforted, however, and clings securely if picked up; after emotional processing, he or she is likely to become rapidly reorganized and display an interest in play.

C. **Anxious resistant,** in which the infant displays anger and ambivalence at the mother's return, alternating between seeking and resisting contact; if picked up, he or she soon wants to be released; when released, he or she soon signals a desire to be picked up; the infant is not readily comforted.

Sroufe capsulized these differences by saying:

the securely attached infant can stay organized in the face of stress, directly expresses affect, and may smoothly regain equilibrium given support from trusted persons. The ambivalent/resistant infant has a low threshold for threat, becomes quickly disorganized, and cannot readily regain equilibrium. The avoidant infant has already learned to guard against strong affect, expresses affect indirectly, and avoids contact when it is most needed. (1984, p. 119)

For a preview of what these differences may mean in a lifespan perspective, see figure 7.7 (page 145) and substitute the labels *securely attached* for *resilient* and *insecurely attached* for *vulnerable.* Subsequent research has suggested that these attachment patterns are associated with different trajectories of later psychosocial development, with insecure relationships more frequently linked with subsequent problems in emotional adjustment.

A fourth category, also classified as insecurely attached, has recently been suggested by Mary Main and her colleagues. It is called "D" for "disorganized and disoriented" (Carlson et al. 1989; Main and Cassidy 1988; Main and Solomon 1986). In this attachment pattern, upon reunion the

child seems to attempt to control or direct the parent's attention and behavior and assumes a role that is usually considered more appropriate for a parent with reference to a child. There are two subgroups: controlling-punitive . . . [in which] the child acts to humiliate, embarrass, or reject the parent . . . [and] . . . controlling-overbright/caregiving . . . [in which] the child may be solicitous and protective toward the parent . . . in a manner suggesting that the parent is dependent on the child. (Main and Cassidy 1988, pp. 418–19)

The parallels between this pattern and "the adult child" of abuse, neglect, and rejection are particularly noteworthy (Ainsworth 1985a, 1985b; Melges and Swartz 1989).

It is important to remember that *the attachment relationship is a relationship,* and that both parties make their own contributions to it. Indeed, as I shall elaborate in my discussion of psychotherapy, changes in those contributions are often associated with developmental changes in one or both participants. Self-evaluations emerge on both sides, even when one member of the dyad is relatively new to the world. The studies of interaction and reciprocity discussed earlier underline the importance of remembering that, in human relationships, the differential size, knowledge, and power of the parent relative to the infant do not negate the fact that both persons participate in creating, maintaining, and changing the "affectional bond" that attaches them. In discussing "attachments beyond infancy," Ainsworth has defined such a bond as

a relatively long-enduring tie in which the partner is important as a unique individual and is interchangeable with none other. In an affectional bond, there is a desire to maintain closeness to the partner. In older children and adults, that closeness may to some extent be sustained over time and distance and during absences, but nevertheless there is at least an intermittent desire to reestablish proximity and interaction, and pleasure—often joy—upon reunion. Inexplicable separation tends to cause distress, and permanent loss would cause grief. (1989, p. 711)

Commendably, Bowlby and his colleagues have been careful to avoid pejorative labels that denigrate either member of a pair or imply negative judgments about their patterns of coping (for example, insisting on the use of "anxious attachment" rather than "dependency").

I shall not here belabor the evidence bearing on attachment theory. The resources cited earlier offer ample documentation that this is a powerful conceptual framework, and that its implications for theory, research, and practice warrant exploration. As Bowlby and others have emphasized, this theory and its empirical evaluation are themselves in their early stages. Longitudinal studies where early attachment was observed are now in their second decade of follow-up assessments. However, self-report measures and standardized interviews of past and present relationships (with parents and intimate others) have shown considerable promise as tools in assessing adult relationship patterns and their relationship to self-reports regarding emotional attachments (Armsden 1986; Armsden and Greenberg 1986; Frank, Avery, and Laman 1988; Hazan and Shaver 1987, 1989; Levy and Davis 1988; Main and Goldwyn, in press; Pistole 1989). Over all, the combination of laboratory, longitudinal, and self-report studies suggest that, relative to their insecurely attached peers, children, adolescents, and adults who feel secure in their intimate relationships:

1. Exhibit earlier greater flexibility and resilience in their engagements with their worlds
2. Exhibit and experience themselves as more competent in a variety of realms
3. Are more likely to engage in exploratory behavior and to remain behaviorally organized in the face of novelty and stress
4. Are more sought out and popular among their peers
5. Report higher self-esteem
6. Are more capable of establishing and maintaining secure and satisfying relationships with others
7. Are at less risk of developing major psychological disorders
8. Are more likely to express their feelings directly, to seek comfort when they are distressed, and to offer comfort to their distressed companions.

A partial illustration of some of these differences was offered in Rathunde's (1988) four-year study of 193 adolescents and their experiences at home and in school. He used a measure of parenting practices to classify family contexts as either "developmentally attuned" or "permissive/authoritarian." In contrast to the latter extremes, a developmentally attuned family context was defined as one in which trust and nurturance were strong and the child was provided with choices, encouraged to explore and develop a sense of mastery, and challenges were paced and altered so as to be neither boring nor overwhelming. Figures 7.10 and 7.11 show the differences in adolescents' reported qualities of experience in different realms.

Current estimates of attachment patterns among parents and children in the United States are that approximately 60 percent can be characterized as secure, with the other 40 percent being anxious avoidant (25%) or anxious resistant (15%) (Hazan and Shaver 1989). The "disorganized/disoriented" classification was proposed only recently and is therefore

Figure 7.10   Quality of School Life for Children from Different Family Contexts

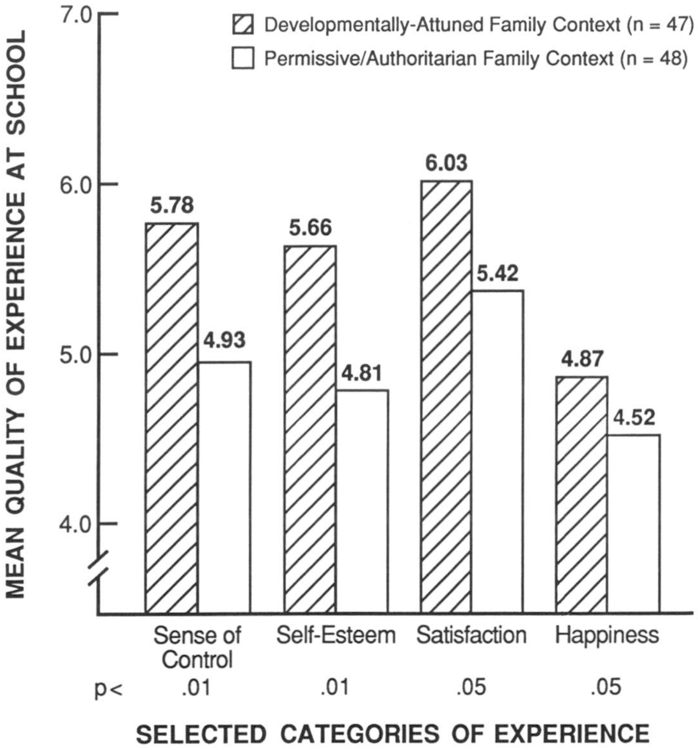

MEAN QUALITY OF EXPERIENCE AT SCHOOL

Developmentally-Attuned Family Context (n = 47)
Permissive/Authoritarian Family Context (n = 48)

	Sense of Control	Self-Esteem	Satisfaction	Happiness
Developmentally-Attuned	5.78	5.66	6.03	4.87
Permissive/Authoritarian	4.93	4.81	5.42	4.52
p<	.01	.01	.05	.05

SELECTED CATEGORIES OF EXPERIENCE

SOURCE: Redrawn from the data of Rathunde (1988)

not included in these estimates. There is also evidence that adult life styles and relationship patterns may reflect the original attachment pattern, and that there may be intergenerational continuity in the propagation of these interaction patterns.

This last point brings us back again to the issue of plasticity and the ability of the adolescent or adult to develop new patterns of experiencing self and others. Bowlby is careful to distinguish attachment theory from "stage" and "critical period" perspectives that doom ("fixate") an individual to a developmental limit determined in early life. At the same time, however, he acknowledges that one's "working models" generally become progressively more firm with age and (self-confirming) experience. Thus, a delicate balance is suggested between continuity and possibilities for change, and between past experiences and present or future vulnerabilities:

Inner working models are constructed over time and are continually elaborated and, at times, fundamentally changed. At the same time, inner working models

Figure 7.11   Quality of Home Life for Children from Different Family Contexts

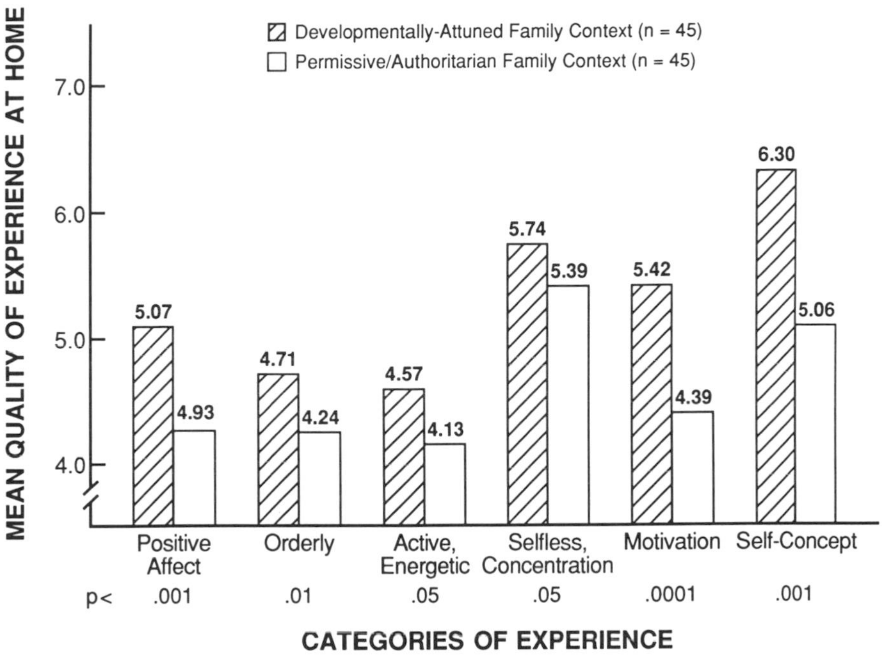

Developmentally-Attuned Family Context (n = 45)
Permissive/Authoritarian Family Context (n = 45)

MEAN QUALITY OF EXPERIENCE AT HOME

Category	Developmentally-Attuned	Permissive/Authoritarian	p<
Positive Affect	5.07	4.93	.001
Orderly	4.71	4.24	.01
Active, Energetic	4.57	4.13	.05
Selfless, Concentration	5.74	5.39	.05
Motivation	5.42	4.39	.0001
Self-Concept	6.30	5.06	.001

CATEGORIES OF EXPERIENCE

SOURCE: Redrawn from the data of Rathunde (1988)

become somewhat firm even in early childhood, and such beginning models influence both the child's experiences and how these experiences are processed. Thus, there is a great deal of force on the side of basic continuity—that is, continuity in terms of the core features of one's representations of self, others, and relationships. Moreover, even when fundamental change occurs, it is presumed that early experience retains influence. This may take the form of a tendency to resume the previous pattern in the face of loss or other serious stress, or it may take the form of issues which remain salient or challenging for the individual. (Sroufe 1987, p. 24)

In his portrayal of psychotherapy, Bowlby appeals to the "strong inclination" of the human psyche to heal itself, and depicts the therapist's job as one of co-creating optimal conditions for such "self-healing" (1988, p. 152).

As Sroufe (1987) has noted, however, attachment theory does not contend that prior working models are erased when dramatic psychological change has taken place. Rather, these models are said to have been transformed. As I described it to one client, "it is not as if you trade in an "old self" for a "new self" so much as that the new one respects and incorporates its predecessor." Under conditions of stress, old patterns (and prior working models) are frequent phenomena. Rather than viewing these episodes as setbacks, regressions, or relapses, however, I believe it is more accurate and therapeutic to respect them as intermittent expressions of previous scaffoldings for ordering experience. The fact that they remain "in reserve" is a reflection of the undeniable "historicity" of our efforts to cope.

Another point with clear clinical relevance is the apparent frequency with which psychologically vulnerable (and resilient) individuals develop strong attachments to pets, particularly dogs. To my knowledge, the frequency, intensity, and role of human-animal attachments has received relatively little research attention. (There is a relatively small and recent literature on the use of pets in treating problems of loneliness and inactivity, particularly in elderly clients, but there has been little work to date on the role of human-animal attachments in the early and lifespan coping patterns of individuals whose human relationships have been dysfunctional or unsatisfying.) The point here is that an unusually strong attachment to a pet should not be automatically viewed (by the therapist) as eccentric or inappropriate; that attachment may well have served the individual to salvage and enjoy his or her own capacities to give and receive in a caring relationship.

Let me close here with a reiteration of attachment theory's fundamental emphasis on the role of emotions, with particular focus on social communication and self-organization. As Bowlby (1988) has noted in his discussion of the therapeutic relationship.

There are . . . no more important communications between one human being and another than those expressed emotionally, and no information more vital for constructing and reconstructing working models of self and other than information about how each feels towards the other. . . . Small wonder therefore, if . . . during the course of psychotherapy and restructuring [of] working models, it is the emotional communications between a patient and . . . therapist that play the crucial part. (1988, pp. 156–57)

Those emotions and emotional communications will be my next focus in the study of human change processes.

8

Emotional Processes and Human Experience

The ruling passion, be it what it will, the ruling passion conquers reason still.
—Alexander Pope

Some of the most exciting developments in our understanding of human experience have been in the areas of emotionality, identity, and the complexities of psychological development. Moreover, the complexities of the infinitely unique "self," or "personal identity," that emerges in the process of lifespan development are among the most formidable and promising challenges facing both scientific and service psychology in the twenty-first century. We have made some important beginnings, to be sure (see chapter 9), but our generous "misunderstandings of the self" (Raimy 1975) are clearly among the most worthy of our attention in refining future theories and therapies. Because of the extensive interdependence of the processes underlying human emotionality and personal (self) development over a lifespan, my narrative on those processes will not be neatly linear. What I hope to show, however, is that clear implications for training and practice emerge from the expanse of work surveyed. Those implications reflect important contributions from diverse theoretical perspectives and, at the same time, suggest new possibilities for developing an integrative, transtheoretical approach to counseling and psychotherapy.

The relevance of emotionality, development, and identity for psychotherapy requires little elaboration. Emotions involve the pulses, passions, and tensions that "change" as a life moves toward, away from, and around the never-ending challenges of the unfolding moment. Develop-

ment is the wayward path of that movement, visible only historically as
the embodied and, hence, emotional explorations that constitute a life
course. Feeling literally illuminates and energizes activity. As Luigi Pirandello put it poetically in somber notes:

[We humans] are born to a sorry privilege, that of *feeling* ourselves to be alive,
with the resultant great illusion: that is, to take as an external reality what is in
fact an internal feeling of ours for life, and is changeable and varied, according
to the times, our situation and our luck.

   This feeling about life . . . [is] exactly like a lantern which makes us see ourselves
scattered over the earth, and makes us perceive good and evil; a lantern which
projects all around us a more or less extensive circle of light, beyond which lies
the blank shadow, a fearful shadow, which would not exist if the lantern was not
lit in us, but which we must unfortunately believe to be real, as long as the lantern
is alight within us. When at the end it is snuffed out, perpetual night will greet
us after the misty daylight of our illusion, or rather, we will be left to the mercy
of Being, which will only have shattered the vain forms of our reasoning. (1987
[1904], p. 159)

Emotionality is fundamental to beliefs and behavior.

THE EMOTIONAL BASES OF PERSONAL REALITIES

If we now reflect on some of the convergences among the cognitive,
evolutionary, and developmental sciences, one clear implication is that
knowing, feeling, and action are inseparable expressions of the same
system, and that their trajectories over time reflect the dynamics of developmental self-organization. What is particularly exciting about this
assertion is that it integrates some of the disparate specializations of
the sciences and humanities into a fundamental dialectic. That is, rationalists and empiricists—not to mention cognitivists, behaviorists,
and humanists—can see the vestiges of their respective traditions in
the acknowledgment that the living system actively "feels" and "ex-
plores" its worlds, somehow in that process developing and differentiating in patterns we describe as "adaptation," "learning," and "development." The separation between knowledge and existential
phenomena, itself a forced distinction with centuries of inertia, is no
longer tenable. This is, in fact, one of the modern manifestations of
the third axial shift (chapter 2), and one reflected in the resurgent
popularity of phenomenological, "qualitative," and hermeneutic approaches in a variety of sciences and humanities (Davidson 1988; Madison 1988; Messer, Sass, and Woolfolk 1988).

Personal Realities and Emotional Experience

This acknowledgment has particular relevance for our understanding of one another, and therefore for our efforts to help. As I indicated in chapter 2, our tacit theories of self and world—what I have termed "personal realities"—lie at the heart of all of our experience. To reiterate briefly, the range and qualities of our personal experience are inseparable from our individual attempts to "know" ourselves and one another as well as our worlds and the directions of our development. These felt and lived realities are uniquely individualized. They are, in fact, so familiar to us—and we are so thoroughly engaged in enacting them—that we rarely realize the extent to which they permeate our lives. We may sense them now and then, but they are most influential when they are least obvious. More often than not, our appreciation for their role comes in the midst of surprise, crisis, and the struggle to regain self-organization.

It is important to remember that personal realities are not explicit beliefs or verbalizable assumptions (even though important aspects of their organization can sometimes be crudely expressed in words). Nor are they unchanging, even though their experiential inertia is formidable. Despite the fact that psychological change is often considered more difficult and emotionally stressful than is psychological continuity, the latter can also be demanding. It is not easy, for example, to maintain a coherent sense of identity, self-worth, or competence in the face of multiple and chronic challenges to old patterns. From a systems perspective, personal "problems" often reflect the failure of old activity patterns in the face of new challenges, and the discrepancy is experienced emotionally.

Feelings must not, however, be equated with problems. Emotions are not the problems; our estranged relationships with our emotionality (and that of our companions) are more fundamentally problematic than the emotions themselves (appendix G). Regrettably, many modern societies stigmatize intense emotions as "uncivilized" or dangerous, and their educational practices discourage the experience and expression of affect (particularly negative affect: anger, anxiety, and sadness). These practices reflect a trenchant denial of human embodiment, the powers of life "passions," and continuing homage to the illusions of the intellect. The alternatives to these practices are not, however, confined to their extreme opposites. We need not revive the illusion of "noble savagery" or condone irresponsible actions in the context of intense affect. We can feel intensely and still act responsibly.

The important point here is that our clients and children are unlikely to develop healthy and satisfying relationships with themselves and their bodies unless they come to acknowledge, respect, and explore the range and power of their feelings. Similarly, for us to be optimally helpful as both parents and professional helpers, we must do more than talk about the wisdom of experiencing and expressing what we feel in socially responsible and self-caring ways. We must, recursively, *feel* our way toward that wisdom and those ways, and we must "make peace with our own process" in the process.

A second point of emphasis is that personal meanings rarely change without emotional involvement. As we saw in chapters 4 and 5, psychological change involves changes in the tacit personal "contracts" that constitute meanings. Those changes are frequently associated with intense affect, and many contemporary theorists argue for a dynamic interdependence. At the professional and practical level, the fact that emotionality is central to psychological services means that the latter are necessarily imbued with issues of (e)valuation and ethical complexities. Professional helpers offer optimal services, I believe, when they are aware of such issues and appreciate the operation of emotional processes in each individual's attempts to elaborate and order his or her life. In this regard, the most important domains of human understanding and professional assistance lie not so much in the *contents* of personal realities as in their ongoing *processes*.

Core Ordering Processes

The central assertion here is that we do, indeed, construct and reconstruct what Bowlby has termed "working models" of ourselves and our circumstances. To emphasize the *processes* rather than the *products* of those ongoing constructions, however, I have here used the term *personal realities* to describe this dynamic system of meaning-making activities, and I describe those activities as "core-ordering processes."* Since such processes are deep-structural and tacit (chapter 5), of course, attempts to "portray" them are necessarily limited in what they can convey. Nevertheless, figure 8.1 offers a tolerable (over)simplification. Four "core" and actively interdependent processing "themes" are proposed: (1) valence or value, (2) reality or meaning, (3) personal identity, and (4) power or control. From the perspective being developed here, these four themes

---

*Similar concepts can be found in Alfred Adler (see Adler 1988; Ansbacher and Ansbacher 1956; Beck 1967; Bruner 1986; Carlsen 1988; Dinkmeyer, Dinkmeyer, and Sperry 1987; Frank 1961, 1985; Frankl 1978; Holton 1986; Kuhn 1962; Pepper 1942; Reinelt, Otalora, and Kappus 1984; and Schutz and Luckmann 1973).

For recent theory and research related to personal realities, see Andrews 1989; Beck, Brown, and Steer 1989; Caspi, Bem, and Elder 1988; Deutsch et al. 1988; Dollinger 1986; Epstein and Erskine 1983; Foa, Steketee, and Rothbaum 1989; Hermans 1989; Hersh 1980; Higgins 1987; Klinger 1977; Lerner and Busch-Rossnagel 1981; McWhinney 1984; Mayerson and Rhodewalt 1988; Melzack 1989; Miall 1989; Miller 1988; Safran et al. 1986; Sass 1988a, 1988b; Snyder and Higgins 1988; Sternberg 1988; Strickland 1989; Taylor and Brown 1988; Unger, Draper, and Pendergrass 1986; Weinstein 1989.

Figure 8.1   A Hypothetical Portrayal of Core Ordering Processes in Human
Experience

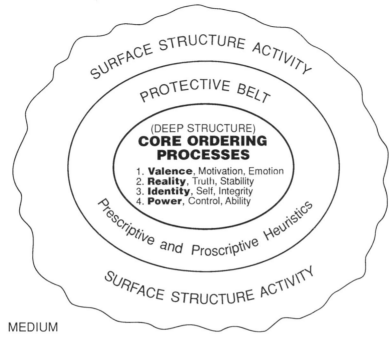

SURFACE STRUCTURE ACTIVITY

PROTECTIVE BELT

(DEEP STRUCTURE)
**CORE ORDERING
PROCESSES**

1. **Valence**, Motivation, Emotion
2. **Reality**, Truth, Stability
3. **Identity**, Self, Integrity
4. **Power**, Control, Ability

Prescriptive and Proscriptive Heuristics

SURFACE STRUCTURE ACTIVITY

MEDIUM

SOURCE: This figure draws on Guidano (1984), Lakatos (1970), and Mahoney (1974, 1976, 1980*b*). © 1989 M. J. Mahoney

lie at the core of every person's lifelong efforts to organize and reorganize
their experience.

The "protective belt" that metaphorically surrounds these core processes is comprised of positive ("prescriptive") and negative ("proscriptive") "heuristics," the "do" and "don't" rules for action, which are
themselves enacted in "surface structure" exchanges with the world.
When I discuss the phenomena of "resistance" and "relapse" in psychotherapy (chapter 12), these heuristics and their self-protective functions
will be further elaborated. For the moment, my focus is on the core
ordering processes that define and constrain both the quality and the
contents of our moment-to-moment experience.

Although there are many mundane ways of illustrating how our personal realities and their generators (our core ordering processes) influence the quality of our daily lives, those most interesting to the researcher
and psychotherapist are connected with the experience patterns associated with the major psychological disorders. I have sketched such an
illustration in table 8.1, elaborating the matrix of core themes, or realms,

with the experience patterns now thought to characterize the various disorders.* For the sake of contrast, I have also ventured some descriptions from the "optimal experience patterns" depicted by recent research on health and well-being (Aldwin et al. 1989; Argyle 1987; Aron and Aron 1987; Beiser 1974; Csikszentmihalyi and Csikszentmihalyi 1988; Diener 1984; McLennan, Gotts, and Omodei 1988; Warr 1978; Willits and Crider 1988). The accuracy of particular depictions is less important here than is the viability of our attempts to conceptualize patterns of experience as uniquely individualized expressions of core ordering processes. When it comes to change and its facilitation, an understanding of and deep respect for such processes requires little defense. Since human knowing is active, embodied, and fundamentally emotional, an understanding of emotional processes is central to our efforts to parent, educate, and professionally counsel. Such an understanding begins with the history of ideas about feelings (also conceivable as the history of feelings about ideas—Appendix G).

*For representative recent work on experience patterns in anxiety disorders, see Barlow 1988; Chambless and Gracely 1989; Craske and Barlow 1988; Fisher and Wilson 1985; Lucock and Salkovskis 1988; MacLeod and Mathews 1988; Maddux, Norton, and Leary 1988; Öhman 1986; Williams, Kinney, and Falbo 1989; and Yee and Miller 1988. It is particularly important to note that although such patterns may be importantly related to "residual (unconscious) arousal" (Cacioppo et al. 1987) and attentional processes, they cannot be reduced to mere physiological "arousal" (Dienstbier 1989; Mahoney and Meyers 1989; Neiss 1988).

Guidano (1987), Heimberg et al. (1989), and Kendall and Watson (1989) discuss some of the parallels between anxiety and depression. For representative recent work on the latter, see Beck et al. 1988; Carlson and Kashani 1988; Cicchetti and Schneider-Rosen 1986; Derry and Kuiper 1981; Emde, Harmon, and Good 1986; Hammen (1988); Hawkins et al. 1988; Izard and Schwartz 1986; Kashani and Sherman 1988; Klein et al. 1988; Kuhl 1987; Kuhl and Helle 1986; Kuiper and Derry 1982; Pilkonis, in press; Pinkley et al. 1988; Rutter 1986; and Zuroff and Mongrain 1987.

For discussions of the phenomenology of the eating disorders (anorexia, bulimia, and obesity), see Garner and Garfinkel 1985; Guidano 1987, 1990; Guidano and Liotti 1983; Hornyak and Baker 1989; Humphrey 1986; Johnson and Holloway 1988; and Strauss and Ryan 1987. The extent to which such patterns are influenced by cultural and gender stereotypes is discussed by Chernin 1985; Hutchinson 1985; and Orbach 1978, 1982. The experience and personal meanings associated with alcohol abuse and drug addiction are discussed by Connors and Maisto 1988; Critchlow 1986; Harlow, Newcomb, and Bentler 1986; Hutzell and Peterson 1986; Leigh 1989; Mann, Sher, and Chassin 1987; Marlatt and Gordon 1985; Newcomb and Harlow 1986; Peele 1985; Vaillant 1983; and Zinberg 1984.

The experiences of guilt, embarrassment, and shame are addressed by Kaufman 1989 and Klass, in press, and Harriet G. Lerner (1985) offers an insightful commentary on anger patterns in intimate relationships. The relationship between "negative affect" and what has been called "neurosis" and "emotional disorder" is elaborated in Averill 1988; Dienstbier 1989; Kopp 1989; Kuipers and Bebbington 1988; Morrison, Bellack, & Bashore 1988; Panksepp and Clynes 1988; Watson and Clark 1984; and Watson and Pennebaker 1989. Studies of moods, their cycles, and their assessment include Berner 1988; Boyle 1989; Larsen 1987; Lorr, Shi, and Youniss 1989; McFarlane, Martin, and Williams 1988; Mayer 1985, 1986; Mayer and Bremer 1985; Mayer and Gaschke 1988; Mayer, Mamberg, and Volanth 1988; Mayer and Salovey 1988; Meyer and Shack 1989; Thayer 1989; Tuckman 1988; Watson 1988; Watson and Tellegen 1985; Zevon and Tellegen 1982.

Table 8.1 Common Experience Patterns in Psychological Disorders

Realm	Anxiety	Depression	Eating and Substance	Borderline and Identity	Psychoses	"Optimal"
Affect	Frequent worry and anger about past and potential pain, fear, or other distress and generally associated with apprehensions about one's capacities to handle same. Frequent actions include active avoidance.	Sadness, listlessness, anger, and fear are often followed by apathy, withdrawal, and the erosion of former satisfactions and pleasures. Life is a heavy burden.	Reduced impulse control and a tendency to rely on external factors to help regulate emotional organization lead to wide swings of mood and perception. Control is sought and lost in absolutes and extremes.	Among the hallmarks of the borderline pattern are frequent, sudden, and intense shifts in affective organization and psychological stability. Impulsive, dependent feelings of urgency are common.	Confusion, fear, anger, and apathy or hopelessness are common. Affect is often inappropriate to social context. The common belief that psychotics do not feel is a cruel myth.	Developmental challenges are encountered with emotional flexibility. After trauma, there is relatively quick recovery of emotional balance and self-organized activity.

Table 8.1 (Continued)

Realm	Anxiety	Depression	Eating and Substance	Borderline and Identity	Psychoses	"Optimal"
Meaning	Uncertainties and inconsistencies are associated with patterns of worry, apprehension, and vigilance; life is an endless and tense struggle to avoid pain.	The certainties of life are negative—including the world, the future, and the self (see below). Life is hopeless; self is helpless/bad/guilty; pain is inevitable.	Life is alternately very orderly and out of control according to fluctuating degrees of balance in controlling or being controlled by a substance or activity.	Life's order and personal meanings may exhibit dramatic reversals depending on vicissitudes of self-appraisal and prevailing (in)consistencies in social relations.	Impairments in active ordering and meaning-making skills can vary tremendously and limit a person's experiential capacities. At the same time, the personal realities frequently created by psychotic persons deserve our respect and close study.	Meaningful order and relatedness of realms may enhance the sense of coherence, purpose, and active participation in an ongoing life.

Table 8.1   (Continued)

Realm	Anxiety	Depression	Eating and Substance	Borderline and Identity	Psychoses	"Optimal"
Power	Intense preoccupation with power and control; frequent sense of vulnerability; fears of inadequacy, inferiority, and/or rejection.	The primary source of hopelessness is the sense of being overpowered. When resilient agency is not developed, apathy and despair are the frequent effects.	As in anxiety patterns, power and control are central themes of developmental challenge. Life is organized around control. It gets disorganized when deviations that threaten systemic balance exceed personal capacities.	Power is also important to persons whose sense of self, stability, and lovability becomes a lifelong and painful struggle. The need for power and control here, however, is to help stabilize, make meaningful, and achieve a sense of personal identity.	The full human range of possibilities is probably represented—from the most grandiose and delusional to the most meek, helpless, and vegetative. Relationships among agency, identity, and emotionality are apparently different from normal.	Power and personal agency are important expressions of many other factors: individuality, freedom, responsibility, and viability. The power here sought is in the process rather than the product.

Table 8.1 (Continued)

Realm	Anxiety	Depression	Eating and Substance	Borderline and Identity	Psychoses	"Optimal"
Self	Self is generally experienced as both subject and object, and also as inadequate and vulnerable to many demands; efforts to develop self-control or other powers are common.	Self is experienced as an object—often an object of pity, contempt, and anger. In untreated chronic isolation, the sense of selfhood recedes with a progressive disengagement from life itself.	Self is multiple, with two to three predominant forms: (1) in control, (2) out of control, and (3) witnessing. Alterations covary with changes in other realms, and progressive development is associated with identity development.	The search for and stability of the self are enduring life themes, with frequent rejection of a succession of selves and a corresponding sense of core instability in experiencing.	Early psychodynamic theory asserted that lack of ego strength prevented any significant self-system development. Modern theories continue to view psychoses as serious impairments of identity development.	The self is experienced as an active, absorbed, subjective "I," usually unaware of itself due to its "dereflection" and temporary suspensions of self-conscious-ness in its full engagement with some activity.

HUMAN EMOTIONS: THEORIES AND ISSUES

Although emotionality has, until recently, received less systematic attention from psychologists than either behavior or cognition, this neglect has been only relative. The literature on emotion is extensive, and attempts to be comprehensive or integrative can themselves be emotionally overwhelming. This was, at least, William James's reaction after having reviewed the literature as it existed a century ago:

> as far as "scientific psychology" of the emotions goes, I may have been surfeited by too much reading of classic works on the subject, but I should as lief read verbal descriptions of the shapes of rocks on a New Hampshire farm as toil through them again. They give one nowhere a central point of view, or a deductive or generative principle. ([1890] vol. II, p. 448)

After a century there is still no central point of view, but there have been some significant advances in theory and research. Even using conservative estimates, for example, there are now dozens of distinguishable theories of emotionality, hundreds of volumes devoted to that topic, and tens of thousands of articles dealing with various aspects of human affect. This chapter is focused on the key questions and apparent directions of recent theory and research on human affect as they bear on human change and its facilitation.*

The Nature of Emotions

The growing consensus about the importance of emotional processes in human experience and psychological development has also highlighted some basic questions about what emotions are, what functions they serve, and how they interact with other phenomena. At the present time, at least seven broad clusterings of theories are possible (see table 8.2). Such groupings must be viewed as hypothetical, however, given the extent to which modern theorists tend toward integrative, multidimensional perspectives. Although differential emphasis may be placed on one aspect, for example, most theories of emotion acknowledge the following components as fundamental to the nature of human emotionality: (1) biological processes, especially those related to neurochemical and endocrine functions; (2) communicative expression, with emphasis on emotional

---

*Valuable resources that overview issues in theory and research include Izard, Kagan, and Zajonc 1984; Plutchik and Kellerman 1980; and Scherer and Ekman 1984. Modern expressions of the reconceptualization of emotion are illustrated by Bar-Levav 1988; Campos, Campos, and Barrett 1989; Carver and Scheier 1990; Frank 1988; Kopp 1989; Maturana 1989b; and Sroufe 1984. Greenberg and Safran's (1987, 1989) work on emotion in psychotherapy offers a valuable summary and integration with explicit emphasis on implications for theory, research, and practice.

Table 8.2   The Major Theorists on Emotion

Psychodynamic	Physiological
Sigmund Freud	William James
Carl Jung	Carl Lange
Wilhelm Reich	Walter B. Cannon
D. Rapaport	Philip Bard
Melanie Klein	William McDougall
Otto Kernberg	John B. Watson
Merton Gill	Harry F. Harlow
Robert Holt	J. W. Papez
H. Dahl	John I. Lacey
	Jaak Panksepp

Activation/Arousal/Motivation	Evolutionary
Duncan B. Lindsley	Charles Darwin
D. Bindra	Herbert Spencer
P. T. Young	Robert Plutchik
Elizabeth Duffy	Silvan S. Tomkins
Magda B. Arnold	Carroll E. Izard
Stanley Rachman	Paul Ekman
	I. Eibl-Eibesfeldt

Cognitive	Social Constructionist
Albert Bandura	David Hume
Aaron T. Beck	Adam Smith
Albert Ellis	Adam Ferguson
Jerome Kagan	James R. Averill
Richard S. Lazarus	John M. Broughton
George Mandler	Joseph J. Campos
Karl H. Pribram	Robert N. Emde
Stanley Schachter	Leslie Greenspan
Peter J. Lang	Rom Harre
Howard Leventhal	Theodore R. Sarbin
	Colwyn Trevarthen
	Daniel Stern
	Michael Lewis

Organizational/Adaptive
Jean Piaget
René Spitz
R. W. Leeper
John Bowlby

Table 8.2   *(Continued)*

Organizational/Adaptive
Mary S. Ainsworth
L. Alan Sroufe
Leslie S. Greenberg
Jeremy D. Safran
Hans G. Furth
Gary E. Schwartz

behavior; (3) cognitive processes, including basic attentional, perceptual, and evaluative operations; (4) subjective experience, emphasizing the phenomenology of feeling; and (5) motivational components that include intentions, directions, and differential readiness toward various classes of activity. These components are often difficult to sharply distinguish, however; and researchers have come to acknowledge that *desynchrony* (limited temporal coordination) among them is common (Lang 1979; Rachman 1980). In other words, it is not unusual for "head and heart" to be "out of synch," and for changes at one level (such as physiological) to be only remotely or complexly related to changes at another (such as cognitive or behavioral).

Attempts to specify the most basic human emotions have resulted in some consensus (see table 8.3), but it would be misleading to suggest that such consensus is universal. Over five hundred different emotional terms and concepts have been identified (Averill 1975; Davitz 1969; de Rivera

Table 8.3   Renditions of Basic Human Emotions

Psychoevolutionary Theory (Plutchik)	*Amplification Theory (Tomkins)*	*Differential Emotions Theory (Izard)*
Fear	Fear	Fear
Anger	Anger	Anger
Joy	Joy	Joy
Sadness	Distress	Sadness
Acceptance		
Disgust	Disgust	Disgust
Anticipation	Interest	Interest
Surprise	Surprise	Surprise
	Contempt	Contempt
	Shame	Shame/shyness

1977). Subtleties of emotional experience are culturally influenced and individually expressed. Those subtleties become particularly important in psychotherapy, where communication may be enhanced or impaired depending on the degree of shared sensitivity to their personal and cultural meanings (Heath, Neimeyer, and Pedersen 1988; Matsumoto et al. 1988; Oler 1989; Russell 1983; Sogon and Masutani 1989).

Distinguishing Cognition and Affect

The impossibility of segregating emotional processes from those involved in thinking and action has been recently highlighted by attempts to do just that—for example, in debates about the relative primacy of cognition versus affect in human experience.* These debates have underlined the ambiguity of pivotal distinctions in traditional analyses of our own activity. Is the preliminary "appraisal" of a stimulus fundamentally cognitive, for example, or affective? It depends on what one means by those terms, of course. Since all responses of an organism are technically mediated by receptor-effector coalitions, at what point does one draw the line between these two realms? Likewise, given the evidence that the human brain utilizes feed*forward* as well as feed*back* processes in its complex operations, what sense does it make to call one direction of influence primary over the other?

Prior to the resurgence of constructivist theory in cognitive science and psychotherapy, however, the assumption was that cognitive processes precede and overpower their affective counterparts. The holistic or interactionist perspective advocated here does not, however, consider any of the "prime mover" arguments to be adequate—as is particularly apparent in the realm of cognitive-emotional interdependence. The extant evidence points to emotional processes as playing a central role in virtually all activities of the individual. The whole human system is permeated with the valent properties most primitively (and powerfully) associated with affectivity. Recall that, at the biological level, what we now classify as emotional activity first appeared more than 165 million years ago with the emergence of the earliest mammals (appendix F). The *paleomammalian* ("old mammal's") brain marked a new level of brain organization emerging out of and in service to the relatively primitive life-support capacities of the older *reptilian complex,* which was itself little more than a crude amplification of the ancient vertebrate brain stem. For the most part, this second brain is what we now call the *limbic system*—the subcortical archi-

---

*See Izard, Kagan, and Zajonc 1984; Lazarus 1982, 1984; Parrot and Sabini 1989; and Zajonc 1980, 1984. Interestingly, Piaget has been faulted for emphasizing cognitive processes and neglecting emotional ones. Although he clearly devoted more attention to the former, a close reading of his views on affect makes it clear that he was not a "rational supremacist" (see Brown and Weiss 1987; Furth 1987; and Piaget 1981).

tecture of our most important approach/avoidance and "emotional" behavior patterns (appendix D). Besides introducing dramatic increases in behavioral plasticity, the emergence of the mammalian limbic brain also brought three new aspects of body-brain and organism-environment relationships: (1) rudimentary and yet powerful capacities for learning and memory—a primitive, "gut-level" kind of knowing; (2) neurological systems that simultaneously monitored and adjusted both internal (bodily) and external (behavioral) realms (affording, among other things, homeostasis); and (3) the first appearance of interpersonal attachment—emotional relationships—expressed initially in the form of devoted caretaking behaviors toward offspring.

When the neocortex of primates and their legacy, the hominids, first appeared some 115 million years later, it again emerged out of and in service to the limbic brain which spawned it. All of which is to say, among other things, that our arrogant left hemispheres would have us believe that our rationality has somehow transcended its own evolutionary heritage in the "lower" brains. While it is true that the limbic system is partially independent of the neocortex in its functioning, this apparent separation is misleading. Feeling is not exclusively limbic, and knowing is not exclusively neocortical. Besides the important interactions between these subbrains via the frontal and prefrontal areas, much, if not most, of our "higher" mental functioning is itself steeped in the patterns and preferences of our "feeling brains." This applies to all levels of that functioning—from base perception to abstract reasoning. Contemporary research in sensation and perception has amply corroborated Sir Charles Sherrington's insight that all perception is based in feelings and felt contrasts (Callaway and Thompson 1953; Sherwood et al. 1988).

Arousal and Motivation

Etymologically, the term *emotion* derives from the Latin *e movere*—literally, "to move" or to bring movement out. Even though psychological theories of motivation rarely acknowledge their interdependence with the study of emotion, their organizing concept is of similar heritage: *motivate* literally means "to move." The relationship between emotionality and adaptive or maladaptive movement is also documented extensively throughout the literatures of experimental psychology, psychopathology, and psychotherapy. Over a wide range of particulars, organisms are depicted as if they were either pushed or pulled by their needs, drives, and dispositions to seek or avoid the poles proposed by the theory of choice. Without the hypothesized tension created by polarized concepts or operations, little action and, hence, little learning is expected. Ever moving between the stick and the carrot, the organism is in a perpetual cycle of losing and regaining some form of emotional/motivational equilibrium.

Earlier analyses of human motivation were dominated by "push/pull" and "dispositional" explanations that amounted to hedonic set-point theories (see Mauro 1988).

THE FUNCTIONS OF EMOTIONS

Until recently, the study and understanding of emotionality were impaired by old stereotypes that viewed affect—particularly negative affect—as an obstacle and a liability in terms of human development. Those stereotypes can be briefly summarized:

1. Emotions in general have been segregated from the "higher" mental functions and relegated to "lower" and "more animal/less human" realms of functioning.
2. Emotions have been characterized as volatile forces that motivate and/or "move" the individual to act in irrational and potentially destructive ways.
3. Emotions have been rendered as one of the "prime movers" in the interactions of thought and action.
4. With rare exceptions, intense emotionality has been assumed to have a disorganizing influence on adaptation and purposive behavior.
5. The "negative" emotions of anger, anxiety, and depression have been characterized as particularly dangerous and, hence, undesirable or intolerable.
6. The vast majority of professional efforts to deal with acute and chronic patterns of intense emotionality have sought to discharge, eliminate, regulate/control, or—at the very least—understand (and thereby somehow transcend) such patterns.

Recent studies have challenged these myths, however, but it may be many years before their conceptual inertia has dissipated.

Contemporary studies offer a different rendition of the roles played by emotion in virtually all realms of human experience. Those roles include the following.

1. Emotional processes are pervasively involved in directing attention, and the "negative" emotions may be particularly powerful in this respect (Carver and Scheier 1990; Cornsweet 1969; Ingram 1990a, 1990b; Izard, Kagan, and Zajonc 1984; Larsen and Cowan 1988; Mandler 1975, 1984; Scherer 1984; Watts 1989; Wegner and Giuliano 1980; Yee and Miller 1988).
2. Emotions are pervasively involved in acts of perception and perceptual biases, as well as in learning and memory; much of that involvement

is at a tacit (unconscious) level (Baron and Moore 1987; Bower 1981; Bower and Cohen 1982; Clark 1986; Davis and Schwartz 1987; Dixon 1981; Greenberg and Safran 1987; Hansen and Hansen 1988; Isen and Daubman 1984; Kim and Baron 1988; Pennebaker and Beall 1986; Simon 1986; Van den Bergh and Eelen 1984; Yee and Miller 1988). For discussions of emotional self-awareness, the "feeling of knowing," and the development of "metaknowledge" about affect, see Bloom and Capatides 1987; Butterfield, Nelson, and Peck 1988; Lewis et al. 1989; Lewis, Sullivan, and Vasen 1987; Shaver et al. 1987; Welwood 1979).

3. Emotional development and cognitive development are integrally related, from infancy to death (Averill 1986; Bloom and Capatides 1987; Lewis, Sullivan, and Vasen 1987; Malatesta and Izard 1984; Maturana 1989; Rodrigue, Olson, and Markley 1987; Shaver et al. 1987).

4. The negative emotions are generally associated with reduced curiosity and exploratory behavior, as well as with impaired performance (Lane and Schwartz 1987; Maddi, Hoover, and Kobasa 1982).

5. Through their neurophysiological and biochemical foundations, emotional processes are inherently related to other psychological phenomena relevant to the individual's health and well-being (as in stress patterns, hormonal activity, and immune system functioning) (Aron and Aron 1987; Beiser 1974; Blanchard and Blanchard 1988; Diener 1984; Ketterer 1987; Kravitz 1988; Lacey 1959; LeDoux 1986; Lyddon 1987; Panksepp 1982; Salovey and Birnbaum 1989; Solomon 1987; Su, London, and Jaffe 1988; Walsh and Shapiro 1983; Warr 1978).

6. The expressive behavioral or motoric aspects of emotions play an integral role in their experience and in interpersonal communication, especially in the strong affective bonding that characterizes parent-child and all subsequent intimate relationships (Breger 1974; Campos, Campos, and Barrett 1989; Eisenberg et al. 1988; Greenspan and Greenspan 1985; Klein 1987; Parkes and Stevenson-Hinde 1982; Segal and Yahraes 1978; Stern 1985; Termine and Izard 1988; Yogman and Brazelton 1986; Zajonc and Markus 1984). For work on facial patterns and emotional communication, see Adelmann and Zajonc 1989; Cacioppo et al. 1988; Ekman 1972; Ekman and Friesen 1971; Feinberg et al. 1986; Fox and Davidson 1988; Fridlund, in press; Lewis, Sullivan, and Vasen 1987; Riccelli et al. 1989; Scherer and Ekman 1984; Valentine 1988; Zajonc, Murphy, & Inglehart 1989).

7. The experiential aspects of emotionality are important elements in the development of an individual's sense of self and in his or her psychological change (Guidano 1987, 1990; Linville 1985, 1987; Lyman and Waters 1986; Miall 1986).

8. Significant psychological change is frequently associated with episodes of emotional intensity, variability, and distress (Frank 1973; Frank et al. 1978; Greenberg and Safran 1987, 1989; Mahoney et al. 1989; Purzner 1988; Rice and Greenberg 1984).

Whether all of these can be considered functions is, of course, dependent upon the criteria one uses for such classifications. As developments in theoretical psychology and evolutionary studies have begun to show, however, the distinctions made between structure and function may ultimately be, as A. D. Ritchie once said, "at bottom merely a question of what changes slower or faster" (cited in Sherrington 1940, p. 109).

Within and beyond the preceding assertions about the possible functions of emotions have been two families of assumptions that have more to do with emphasis than with absolute judgment. The *functional, organizational,* and *evolutionary* theories of emotion have emphasized the fundamentally "positive" or "valuable" role of affect in the viable adaptation and progressive development of the individual. By way of contrast, *dysfunctional, disorganizational,* and *maladaptive/pathological* theories have emphasized the dangers inherent in the unbridled or amplified expression of emotions. As we shall see, these differing families of theories suggest very different approaches to the conceptualization and treatment of various patterns of emotional experience.

Even more pertinent for our purposes, however, are some of the practical implications of the foregoing generalizations. Conceptually, we have just begun to emerge from an era in which emotions were extensively neglected and, when acknowledged, were regarded as unwelcome vestiges of our animal legacy. Intense affects were viewed as disorganizing influences on adaptation, impediments to rationality, and dangerous forces in the conduct of our everyday lives. The socially defined negative emotions of anger, anxiety, and depression have figured prominently in our models of mental health and mental illness, and our psychotherapies have been dominated by the assumption that these emotions are potentially dangerous and dysfunctional. Let me therefore turn to a consideration of emotionality from the perspective of psychotherapy.

EMOTIONS AND PSYCHOTHERAPY

There is a certain irony in the fact that psychotherapy was first dubbed the "talking cure" when its most dramatic feature was not talking per se but what that talking evoked: the intense emotional reliving and "discharge" of earlier trauma. Adding to that irony is the fact that most modern psychotherapy is, indeed, conducted by two or more "talking heads" (with only occasional references to the bodies beneath them). This relative imbalance may, in fact, be partly responsible for the recent growth of experiential, evocative, and "body therapies." Although the claims of exclusively "somatic" therapists may warrant moderation, there is increasing acknowledgment that comprehensive psychological services include a focus on experiences and practices related to human embodiment (Mahoney 1990a). Studies of "bodymind" integrations (with no separating hyphen) have also helped to illuminate the roles of emotionality in psychological change.

All major theories of psychotherapy have recognized the central importance of emotional patterns in motivating people to seek some form of help, and implicitly or explicitly acknowledged that episodes of intense affect are common during the "improvement" or "cure" process. This point is illustrated in one of the surveys introduced in chapter 1 (Mahoney et al. 1989). U.S. clinical psychologists reported general agreement that personal psychological development often involves episodes of anxiety, depression, and excitement (figure 8.2, 8.3, and 8.4). Most respondents also agreed that feelings generally change more slowly than do thoughts (figure 8.5). There was modest consensus that some in-

Figure 8.2   U.S. Clinical Psychologists' Acknowledgment That Psychological Development Involves Anxiety

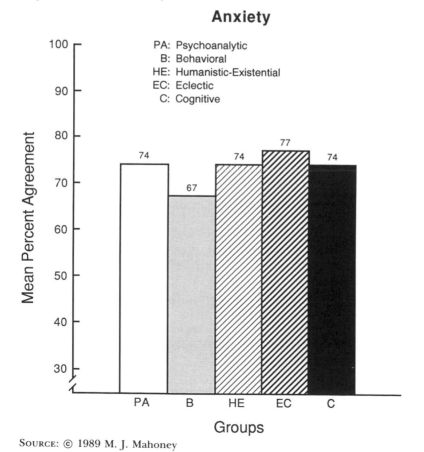

SOURCE: © 1989 M. J. Mahoney

Figure 8.3   U.S. Clinical Psychologists' Acknowledgment That Psychological Development Involves Depression

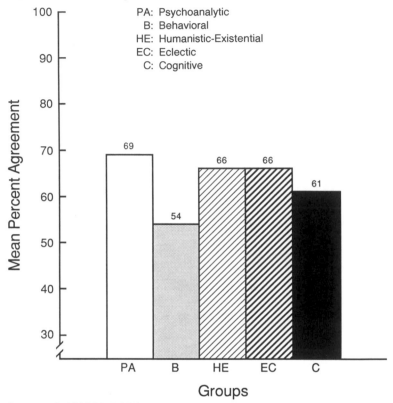

SOURCE: © 1989 M. J. Mahoney

dividuals experience "feeling out of control" (figure 8.6) and episodes of "sensed unreality" (figure 8.7) during their psychological development. As noted earlier, behaviorists depicted personal change as less difficult than did nonbehaviorists (see figure 1.4), but this was only true for behaviorists who had not been in therapy themselves. Respondents from all theoretical orientations agreed that, in optimal practice, the psychotherapist should help the client clarify thoughts and feelings, but behavioral respondents were less inclined to encourage emotional expression (Figure 8.8).

Two points are being developed here. First, significant and enduring personal change is not the easy, overnight, painless endeavor some marketing firms have successfully sold. Second, those approaches to therapy that appreciate these difficulties and respect the emotional intensities that may accompany them are, relative to their counterparts, more likely to

Figure 8.4   U.S. Clinical Psychologists' Acknowledgment That Psychological Development Involves Excitement or Joy

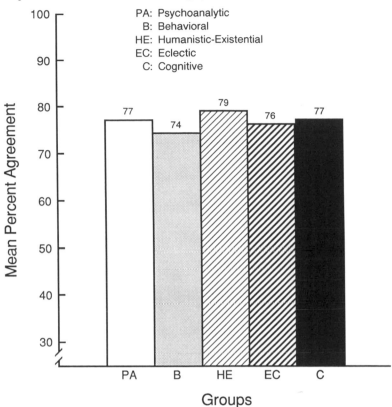

SOURCE: © 1989 M. J. Mahoney

accept and encourage the kinds of experiences that seem to be important to psychological development. Those therapists who disregard or de-emphasize emotional experience, who underestimate the difficulties of significant personal change, or who are themselves emotionally detached, overcontrolled, or undeveloped are less likely to foster or appreciate the importance of first-person experience in lifespan development (see chapters 10–13).

An interesting corollary finding from the previous study is worth mentioning. Half of the psychologists were asked to depict their clients' experiences of personal development and half were asked to respond according to their own experiences of development. There were significant (p < .01) differences on 60 percent of the items, with clinicians depicting their own development as less difficult or distressing than that attributed to psychotherapy clients. Relative to the latter, therapists de-

Figure 8.5   U.S. Clinical Psychologists' Acknowledgment That Feelings Change
More Slowly Than Do Thoughts

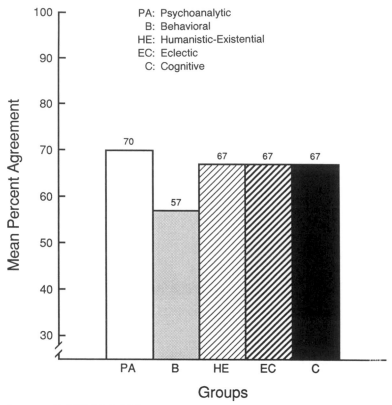

SOURCE: © 1989 M. J. Mahoney

scribed themselves as less resistant to change, more consistent in their
progress, and less likely to feel out of control or unreal (figures 8.9, 8.10,
8.11, 8.12). These therapist-client differences were again attenuated in
therapists who reported having been in personal therapy. Other research
has also suggested that personal therapy may help to refine a therapist's
self-awareness and interpersonal nurturance (MacDevitt 1987; McNair
and Lorr 1964; Norcross, Strausser-Kirtland, and Missar 1988; Peebles
1980; Strupp 1955; Sundland and Barker 1967; Wogan and Norcross
1985). The existing research does not, however, suggest that the personal life of the psychotherapist is always less difficult or distressing than
that of other human beings, including one's own clients. Psychotherapists
do appear to treat and experience their own problems differently than
those of their clients, but there is increasing acknowledgment that professional helping is an extremely demanding endeavor and involves both

Figure 8.6   U.S. Clinical Psychologists' Acknowledgment That Psychological Development Involves Episodes of Feeling Out of Control

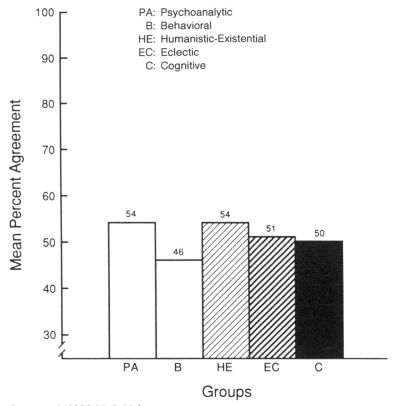

SOURCE: © 1989 M. J. Mahoney

costs and benefits for its practitioners (Guy 1987; Kilburg, Nathan, and Thoreson 1986; Norcross and Prochaska 1986a, 1986b; Prochaska and Norcross 1983a; Scott and Hawk 1986).

Emotionality and Change

The relationships between emotionality and cognitive-behavioral plasticity have long been recognized and exploited in the ancient arts of "persuasion and healing," and Dr. Jerome D. Frank's work (1973) of that title remains a classic statement on the emotional and interpersonal contexts of effective psychotherapy. Frank and his colleagues have also conducted some of the most interesting research on the parameters relating emotionality and change. In one set of studies, for example, they examined

Figure 8.7   U.S. Clinical Psychologists' Acknowledgment That Psychological Development Involves Episodes of Sensed Unreality

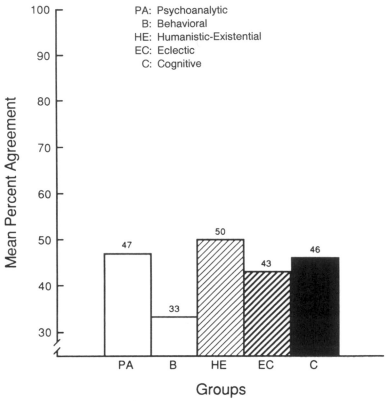

SOURCE: © 1989 M. J. Mahoney

the effects of artificially induced arousal on attitude change (Hoehn-Saric 1978). Using actual psychotherapy clients as their volunteers, they compared changes in sessions where clients had inhaled ether (which causes cognitive confusion), adrenalin (which involves less cognitive impairment), or a placebo (aromatic water). Regardless of whether they knew what was causing their arousal, clients changed more during ether sessions than adrenalin sessions, but—and this is important—that change was delayed in appearance and individually variable. Nevertheless, these findings suggest that the cognitive disorganization associated with central nervous system depressants may encourage at least short-lived episodes of emotional lability (which is, of course, the source of both the promise and the danger of such drugs).

These findings and other research studies have emphasized an important point about the relationship between emotional arousal and psycho-

Figure 8.8   U.S. Clinical Psychologists' Acknowledgment That Emotional Expression is Encouraged in Optimal Psychotherapy

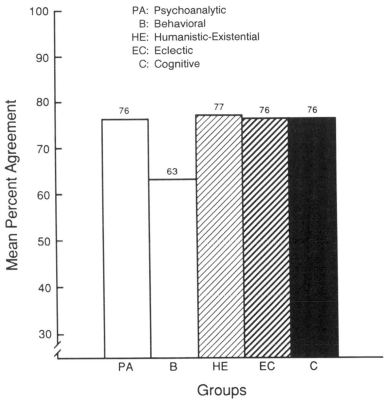

SOURCE: © 1989 M. J. Mahoney

logical change. As Leslie Greenberg and Jeremy Safran (1987, 1989) have aptly noted, the processes of therapeutic change are closely linked to affective experience but not adequately captured by simple catharsis hypotheses. Thus, although evocative and expressive techniques (such as pillow pounding and screaming) may have short-term effects on some measures of tension and distress, they are generally insufficient in facilitating significant and enduring psychological change. Instead, it appears that the experience and expression of intense emotionality in psychotherapy is most likely to facilitate change when (1) the affect involved has been previously avoided, unconscious, or conflict-laden; (2) the individual experiences that affect as personally meaningful; and (3) episodes of emotional intensity are later "harvested" by reviewing and restructuring the memories, beliefs, or self-appraisals they involve. The word *later* in this last point emphasizes the importance of a therapist's timing. In the midst

Figure 8.9   U.S. Clinical Psychologists' Estimates of Their Own and Their Clients' Resistance to Change

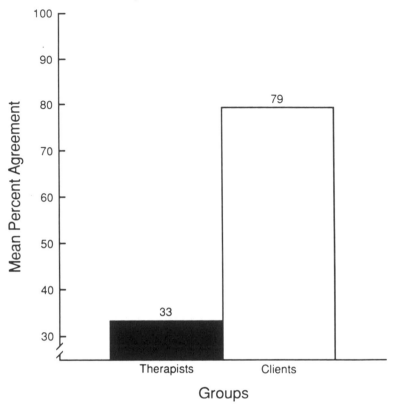

SOURCE: © 1989 M. J. Mahoney

of intense affect, most clients are not receptive to interpretations and are more likely to want assurances, empathic responding, and basic human compassion. It is afterward, when they may feel exhausted from their emotional experience, that clients are more likely to want help in "processing" their experience and exploring its implications for their life patterns (Clarke 1989; Kraemer and Hastrup 1988; Labott and Martin 1987, 1988; Pennebaker and Beall 1986).

Greenberg and Safran summarize their view on the importance of timing and respect for individual differences by noting that

although accessing previously unacknowledged emotions is therapeutic for some in-session states, for others the completion of emotional expression is important, and for still others a process of emotional restructuring is warranted. Hence, there is no single change process involving emotion in psychotherapy, but, rather,

Figure 8.10   U.S. Clinical Psychologists' Estimates of Their Own and Their Clients' Experience of Inconsistent Developmental Progress

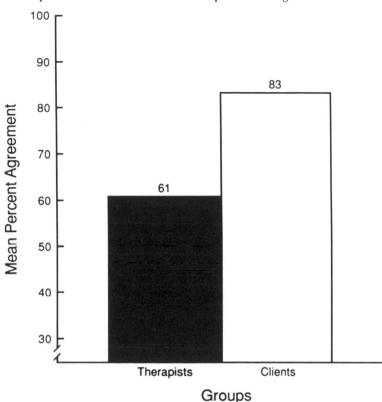

SOURCE: © 1989 M. J. Mahoney

a number of different processes. Regardless of the specific affective process involved in a particular change context, however, we argue that the evocation of emotional material in an immediately felt manner is prerequisite to the change of certain memory structures that are involved in the generation of emotional experience. (1987, p. viii)

Some of Greenberg's creative studies of the "two-chair" technique in gestalt therapy have corroborated these assertions and lent further clarification to the processes of emotional restructuring. Client self-reports, observer ratings, and voice quality analyses suggest that, when the psychotherapy client "dialogues" with "parts of his or her self," the conflicts that emerge show some consistent patterns of "give and take" before "resolution" and restructuring are achieved. As has been documented in more recent studies of "good sessions" and "good moments" in psychotherapy, those patterns emphasize the importance of the therapist's un-

Figure 8.11   U.S. Clinical Psychologists' Estimates of Their Own and Their Clients' Experience of Episodes of Feeling Out of Control

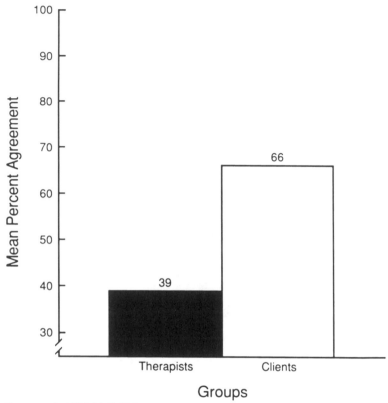

SOURCE: © 1989 M. J. Mahoney

derstanding, compassion, and counsel in optimal helping (chapters 10 to 13). In the context of a good working alliance, such experiences can lead to greater experiential freedom, increased self-awareness, and significant changes in self-appraisal.

Major Treatment Strategies

There can be little doubt that emotionality has played a central role in the conceptualization and practice of psychotherapy. In the emergence of psychological services over the last century, emotional processes have clearly remained a primary realm of emphasis for most, if not all, of the more than four hundred distinguishable forms of modern psychotherapy. The centrality of the affective realm may stem from multiple sources,

Figure 8.12   U.S. Clinical Psychologists' Estimates of Their Own and Their Clients' Experience of Episodes of Sensed Unreality

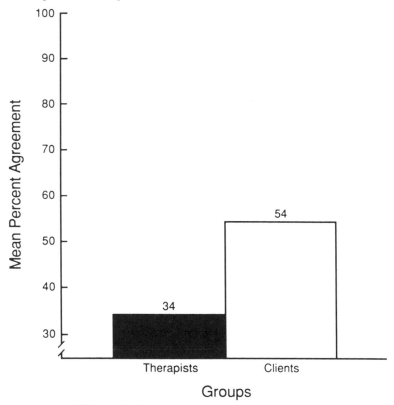

SOURCE: © 1989 M. J. Mahoney

including the fact that the pain of emotional distress and its associated disorganization of daily functioning are among the most common reasons for entering psychotherapy. Likewise, the process of changing, whether inside or outside psychotherapy, tends to be stressful and pervasively emotional. Theory and practice in psychotherapy have, until recently, reflected three fundamental methods of dealing with emotionality: discharge, insight, and control (see table 8.4).

Discharge Therapies.   The method of *discharge* or *catharsis* is one in which the individual is encouraged to experience intense affect in the interest of dissipating it. A wide range of hypotheses and theories have been offered in defense of this method (Blanck and Blanck 1974, 1979; Jackins 1965; Janov 1970; Keleman 1979; Mahrer 1978; Nichols and Zax 1977; Purzner 1988; Scheff 1979; Stampfl and Levis 1967). These defenses range from storage metaphors, in which emotions are depicted as "pent up" and potentially toxic, to drive theory and conditioning interpretations, wherein emotional responses or associations are said to be weakened via repetition to the point of extinction or exhaustion. Across these diverse theoretical rationales, cathartic methods frequently focus on the imaginal reliving of a prior trauma or a feared experience. The archetype of this approach, of course, is the case of Anna O.; and the "talking cure" pioneered by Joseph Breuer in her treatment significantly influenced the young Sigmund Freud.

Other therapeutic approaches have also, of course, emphasized the role of emotional discharge in psychological change. Wilhelm Reich's (1942, 1949) system of therapy was one of many "body therapies" that have emphasized the restoration of "psychological balance" by encouraging the full experience and expression of intense affects. Various forms of existential, humanistic, and gestalt therapies have also endorsed the use of techniques to facilitate such experiences (Daldrup et al. 1988; Gendlin 1962, 1978; Perls 1969; Perls, Hefferline, and Goodman 1951; Polster and Polster 1973). "Perls himself, however, de-emphasized the importance of emotional discharge in therapy, and derided what he called Freud's 'excremental theory' of emotions" (Greenberg and Safran 1987, p. 68). The effectiveness and sufficiency of simple discharge techniques have been questioned and qualified by research on change processes in psychotherapy.

Insight Therapies. The second major method of negotiating intense or distressful emotions in psychotherapy has been that of *insight,* generally associated with the development of some form of rational understanding of the affective pattern in question. Insight was combined with abreactive and cathartic methods by Freud and his followers, but it is clear that psychodynamic approaches are no longer the only or major users of insight-facilitating methods in psychotherapy. The cognitive therapies, for example, and some versions of behavioral, existential, and humanistic therapies often employ strategies designed to "make sense of" or otherwise explain and understand a client's emotional experiences (see Bugental 1978; Herink 1980; Wachtel 1987). There are, to be sure, different kinds of insight—the most popular probably being (1) *developmental,* which focuses on the etiology of a current problem; (2) *functional,* which focuses on the antecedents and consequences of an emotional experience; and (3) *experiential,* a hybrid form that seems to parallel Bertrand Russell's (1945) description of "knowledge by acquaintance" (as contrasted with the more intellectual category of "knowledge by description"). With the exception of experiential insight, the other forms are decidedly in the tradition of rationalism and rational supremacy discussed earlier.

Table 8.4   Views of Emotion in Different Metatheories

Theory	View of Emotions	'Pathology'	Treatment Plan
Psychodynamic	Emotions are expressions of the "spillover" of excessive psychic energy, which often take the form of neurotic symptoms, denied impulses, and defense mechanisms.	Disease and dysfunction are the result of "strangulated" affect, disowned impulses, and inadequate discharge of psychic energy.	Emphasis is on facilitating *insight* into psychic conflicts and disclaimed impulses to action. Insight and "corrective emotional experiences" (including *discharge*) emerge from the *transference* relationship and therapist-guided interpretations.
Behavioral	Emotions are conditioned responses that can themselves serve as discriminative stimuli for other responses. They often have an undesirable disorganizing effect on skilled behavior.	Maladaptive patterns of emotional behavior are the result of skill deficiencies and/or pathogenic conditioning histories.	Emphasis is generally on "counter-conditioning" undesired emotional responses, with desensitization, extinction (in-vivo exposure), massed practice ("implosion" or "flooding") techniques most often aimed at *eliminating* or *controlling* such responses.

Control and Elimination Therapies.   The third basic method of negotiating intense emotionality is that of straightforward *control,* with the general intent of regulating untoward affect, usually in the direction of restored equilibrium or social desirability. In one sense, of course, cathartic and insight methods also seek to control emotional experiences and expressions, but their means are much less direct than what are here termed

Table 8.4   *(Continued)*

Theory	*View of Emotions*	*'Pathology'*	*Treatment Plan*
Humanistic	Emotions constitute value experiences that guide the person's sensing, acting, and reflecting. Feelings "fuel" both action and awareness, both of which are dynamic processes.	Dysfunctions develop when emotions are denied, suppressed, or interrupted (and left "unfinished").	Emphasis is on facilitating *self-awareness* and experiential, emotional, and *expressive freedom* and spontaneity. Feelings receive primary focus as valuable guides to personal activity.
Cognitive	*Rationalist:* Emotions are the products of thoughts and images, as well as interpretations of perceptions.	Negative emotions are the result of negative, irrational, and incorrect patterns of thinking.	Emphasis is on *eliminating, controlling,* or *replacing* intense negative affect by identifying and altering irrational thought patterns (via disputation and/or rehearsal of alternate thoughts).

controlling methods. The latter may range from medical management—including chemotherapy and psychosurgery—to biofeedback and behavior modification. With diverse rationales, the fundamental strategy of emotional control methods is to intervene upon a pattern of emotional experience (whether chronic or acute) and somehow to regulate its parameters (frequency, intensity, duration, and so on) by voluntary means. The more severe the emotional pattern and the more it appears to jeopardize personal or social functioning, the more likely it is that the controlling intervention will itself be severe.

The effectiveness of these three general strategies for helping individuals to negotiate their experiences of emotional distress is difficult to estimate given the current research evidence and the failure of researchers to isolate these strategies from other aspects of therapeutic practice. Theoretically, at least, one can conceive of the possibility that—for some individuals, at some points in psychotherapy—experiencing, expressing, understanding, and controlling various emotions may be important. At

Table 8.4   (Continued)

Theory	View of Emotions	'Pathology'	Treatment Plan
Cognitive	*Constructivist:* Emotions are primitive and powerful knowing processes that reflect individual patterns of organization and disorganization in experience.	Dysfunctional and distressing patterns of emotional experience reflect the individual's imperfect attempts to adapt and develop. Some emotional disorganization reflects stages in overall systemic reorganization.	Emphasis is on the *experience* and appropriate *expression* of emotions, as well as on the *exploration* of their development, functions (past and present), and possible roles in emerging life developments. Within the limits and flexibility of each individual, periods of emotional disorganization may afford and reflect opportunities for change.

the same time, however, it is less likely that the same strategy is always appropriate for each client at every point in his or her psychological development. Moreover, these three therapeutic strategies may convey implicit messages about the alleged danger and undesirability of intense emotions (especially "negative" ones), and those messages may actually impede a client's progress in integrating emotional experiences with changing patterns of activity and self-construal. Let me therefore conclude this section with a brief consideration of alternate approaches to emotional processes in psychotherapy.

Developmental and Constructivist Approaches

The perspectives previously discussed in the contexts of constructive metatheory (chapter 5), evolution (chapter 6), and emotional development (chapter 7) converge on a less judgmental approach to affectivity and its adaptive functions in the organization of personal experience. Rather than viewing intense emotions as impediments to development or targets for modification, a developmental or constructivist perspective considers emotions to be primitively powerful *knowing* processes that are integral to the lifespan self-organization of the individual. From this view, emotions are still associated with episodes of discomfort and disorganization, but the latter are seen as (1) natural expressions of an individual's current personal realities, and (2) necessary (and often facilitating) elements in the reorganization of that person's tacit assumptions about self and world. Indeed, such a perspective suggests that clients should be encouraged to examine their awareness of and reactions to their own feelings, as well as to appreciate that episodes of distress—even though painful—may be necessary elements in the unfolding of their individual development.

This portrayal exhibits some parallels to the concepts of punctuated equilibrium in evolutionary theory and of radical restructuring processes in complex, open systems. John Dewey aptly described the dynamics of such development in two passages:

Life itself consists of phases in which the organism falls out of step with the march of surrounding things and then recovers unison with it—either through effort or by some happy chance. And, in a growing life, the recovery is never mere return to a prior state, for it is enriched by the state of disparity and resistance through which it has successfully passed. If the gap between organism and environment is too wide, the creature dies. If its activity is not enhanced by the temporary alienation, it merely subsists. Life grows when a temporary falling out is a transition to a more extensive balance of the energies of the organism with those of the conditions under which it lives.

. . . The live being recurrently loses and reestablishes equilibrium with his surroundings. The moment of passage from disturbance into harmony is that of intensest life. (1981[1934], pp. 535, 538)

A recurrent problem in psychotherapy, of course, is the failure of the individual to negotiate those transitions successfully.

Emotional processes reflect the individual's trial-and-error attempts to negotiate the endless and unpredictable challenges that emerge in his or her life path. When those challenges do not exceed one's current coping capacities, they are "assimilated" and life moves onward toward the unknowns of tomorrow. (The next problem, or challenge, is, of course, "always in the mail.") When a challenge is excessive, a "crisis" may be experienced and affective intensity is common. This is often the point at which an individual will seek professional help. The point I am emphasizing here is that episodes of intense emotional "disorder" are often natural expressions of a human system's attempts to restructure itself in a viable manner. Systemic disorganization appears to be an important ante-cedent to reorganization. Such reorganization is not automatic, pleasant, or quickly achieved, and herein lie some of the most challenging ques-tions facing modern psychotherapy researchers. How can the helping professional facilitate such reorganization and assist the client in nego-tiating that process? I shall return to this important question in my discus-sions of the experience of change and principles of optimal psychother-apy (chapters 10–13). For the moment, it is enough to say that clients and therapists alike might be less frightened by and impatient with the pain and perseverance of emotional struggles if such "fallings out" were viewed as natural expressions of an open, developing system in search of a more "extensive balance" with its world.

Although it may sound strange to question how it feels to feel, the nuances of individual emotional experience make it clear that universal patterns of emotional experience and expression coexist with virtually infinite diversity and unmistakable individuality. Cycles of moods and emotional expressions are in constant, dynamic flow, and it is now appar-ent that different combinations of emotions can be experienced simulta-neously (Ellsworth and Smith 1988; Harter and Buddin 1987; Larsen 1987; Lyman and Waters 1986; McFarlane, Martin, and Williams 1988; Mayer and Bremer 1985; Mayer and Gaschke 1988; Mayer, Mamberg and Volanth 1988; Mayer and Salovey 1988; Tuckman 1988; Watson 1988; Watson and Tellegen 1985; White and Younger 1988; Zevon and Telle-gen 1982). These cycles are familiar to most people and are probably not unrelated to other expressions of cycles or rhythmic patterns in a wide range of human experiences (see appendix D; Gilbert 1989; Klinger 1971, 1977; Mauro 1988; Pope 1985; Pope and Singer 1978; Singer 1966; Singer and Pope 1978).

The point here is that people are "feeling" most (if not all) of the time, and that it is the quality, intensity, and perseverance of their feeling patterns that are most likely to move them toward seeking professional help. In addition to those individuals whose primary complaint is their pain or exhaustion, however, there are those who are distressed by their *inabilities to feel*. Sometimes it is a wide-ranging and virtually continuous "detachment" or disengagement from their bodies, their companions, and so on. In others, it is a pattern of "emotional withdrawal" (sometimes described as "numbing" or "tuning out"), especially during episodes of threat or stress. Still others describe themselves as being on emotional "roller coasters," with "good" and "bad" feelings changing abruptly. Finally, in posttraumatic stress disorder, it is common for episodes of complete "denial," "forgetting," and emotional distancing to be punc-tuated with painfully real "relivings," dreams, or rememberings of earlier trauma.

Researchers investigating emotional processes in psychotherapy have begun to acknowledge that individuals vary considerably in their capacities to experience different feelings. More often than not, those who are skilled at "not feeling" have survived traumas or training that somehow taught the adaptive value of emotional detachment. Indeed, those skills appear to be related to personal identity (chapter 9) and individual experiences of psychological change (chapter 12). We need further clinical research on patterns of personal phenomenology, the experience and expression of affect (including detachment skills), and the dynamics of emotional development (such as differentiation), both inside and outside the therapeutic hour. As Greenberg and Safran aptly note, "it is not a matter of how much or how often affective expression occurs in therapy that is important to change. . . . Rather, the . . . context or meaning of the affective expression is of crucial importance" (1987, p. 102). This point is worth bearing in mind as we next address the individuality of life experience patterns.

CONCLUSION

This chapter and appendix G document the longstanding and pervasive acknowledgment of affective processes in human self-organization, personal realities, and the continuities and changes that characterize each individual life. Our label of *Homo sapiens* is both too much and not enough. We are both men and women, and less knowledgeable than we usually realize. Our lives are not adequately described as a sequence of either thoughts or actions without these activities being extensively interwoven with life-seeking passions. In the metaphorical shadows of our precellular ancestors, we, too, seek the nurturance and affirmation of light (chapter 6, appendix F) and seem to literally "feel our way" through the ambiguities and novel experiences that afford changes in our self-world constructions. As both Bowlby (1988) and Pirandello have poignantly conveyed, it is our feelings and their patterns—our "secure bases" of continuity and our bold ventures into novelty—that illuminate and constrain (without specifying) the particulars of our lives. Although it has become increasingly difficult to deny the significance of emotional processes for human change, many questions remain unanswered (not to mention crudely formulated). My goal in this chapter has been to emphasize the centrality of continuing studies of emotionality to future refinements in our understanding and practice of psychotherapy.

9

The Self in Process

Wherever we may be at the present time in the evolution toward more authentic theories of self (and toward a more coherent understanding of our own selves), we are currently at an exciting but not comfortable point. —Frank Johnson

The cognitive, developmental, and emotional (r)evolution(s) have redirected mainstream experimental psychology back "inside" the organism; and the "modern synthesis" in psychology is, in part, an attempt to integrate and transcend inside/outside and mind/body dualisms. What cognitive and life scientists found when they looked inside the most "promising primates," however, was much more than they had anticipated. The recent and ongoing (re)discoveries of emotionality, unconscious processes, and personal meanings are cases in point. But perhaps the single most important (re)discovery of twentieth-century psychology has been that of the self, which has (again) become a cardinal concept after a moratorium that lasted over half a century. As Louis A. Sass quipped, "The 'self,' once banished by mainstream psychology to the cloudland of unobservable and irrelevant abstractions, seems to have returned with a vengeance" (1988a, p. 551). Whether it is a vengeful return or simply the persistence of a centuries-old mystery, however, self studies are now center stage in psychological laboratories and clinics around the planet. This resurgence has harvested widely from the social and behavioral sciences, of course; but much of its impetus has also been drawn from clinical practice, developmental studies, and the pervasive influence of the arts and humanities (Allport 1955; Cernic and Longmire 1987; Gergen 1971; Glasser 1972; Glover 1988; Heelàs and Lock 1981;

Johnson 1985; Kreilkamp 1976; Lifton 1976; Lukes 1974; Mikhailov 1976; Morris 1972; Moustakis 1956; Perry 1975; Sampson 1985, 1988; Sanford 1966; Stern 1987; Yardley and Honess 1987; Young-Eisendrath and Hall 1987).

THE VICISSITUDES OF THE SELF

As John Broughton points out in his discussion of the "ideology" of the self, "Anyone approaching a psychology of 'the self' with some serious-ness immediately encounters a perplexing multitude of issues" (1986, p. 130). Besides the existence of several hundred words and terms that are synonymous with or integrally related to the self, the use of hyphenated terms that are self-focused, ego-related, or person-centered has acceler-ated at a rate that has begun to alarm lexicographers and library scien-tists. To complicate matters further, some scholars have introduced new words (such as *autopoiesis, proprium,* and *selfhood*) in efforts to avoid the connotations of earlier terms.

Needless to say, I shall not here attempt to resolve these terminological complexities or to cover the vast sweep of literatures (past and present) devoted to this most perplexing and personal of topics. Comprehensive reviews and scholarly discussions have already addressed such technicali-ties (Baumeister 1987; Broughton 1986; Johnson 1985; Lapsley and Power 1987; Lukes 1974; Sass 1988a). Rather, my focus shall be on recent insights, developments, and trends in both theories and therapies of self, which attempt to integrate theory, research, and practice.

The Emergence of Individuality and Consciousness

My discussion of personal identity and the psychology of self picks up on the themes and issues introduced in the first chapter. It is, in fact, the "self consciousness" (*sans* hyphen) of modern life that forces an awareness of the inescapable synergy of self and system. This conceptual integration presupposes, of course, a prior separation of these elements. As recent studies attest, our awareness and affirmation of the self have emerged concurrently with our beginning appreciations of consciousness itself (Coan 1987a; Jaynes 1976; Neumann 1954; Popper and Eccles 1977). That is, *consciousness* and *self consciousness* are significantly related, even when the former intentionally aims at "selfless" awareness (Walsh and Vaughan 1980; Wilber 1981; Wilber, Engler, and Brown 1986). It is perhaps not surprising, then, that the origins of ideas about individuality and personal experience lie in the spiritual traditions of virtually all cultures. The "soul" or "spirit" of each person became his or her sacred expression of a unified existence, and it was the "stirrings" in individual souls that bade them seek the Light and Words of their holy writings. Later, their personal "conscience" and subjective experiences of the sacred would be recognized as valid causes of individual differences (in belief and practice), which laid the foundations for cultures more tolerant and appreciative of human diversity.

The evidence is now substantial that "person variables," "human factors," and self-referencing processes pervade all human experience. Recall, for example, that the most frequently occurring character in all REM dreams is the self, who is reported (though not always "seen") in 95 percent of such dreams. Moreover, the vast majority of our dreams are narrative in structure: that is, they tell a story. These stories, which we experience at least five times per night, are probably related to patterning and repatterning processes in our lives. Also noteworthy is the fact that sleep-onset disturbances ("insomnia") appear to be related to individual capacities to relinquish control and self-reference: "Relinquishing voluntary control over the flow of one's conscious thought seems to be a necessary condition of sleep induction. . . . You have . . . to let your mind lose *you* and find some other focus for its waning attention." (Foulkes 1985, p. 67). In any case, they illustrate the infinite individuality (and hence diversity) expressed in self-narratives, both in and out of sleep and dream processes.

Individualism and Human Rights

As previewed in chapter 7, theories of individual psychological development have been regarded as theories of personality; and the development of identity and "moral sentiments" (both social and spiritual) are common elements of developmental "progress" as depicted by modern theories (table 7.1, page 150). In their five-volume *A History of Private Life,* Philippe Ariès and Georges Duby document the slow emergence of privacy, private life, and the individual as a unique phenomenon from pagan to present times (1987, 1988, 1989, 1990, in press). In his discussion of the possibilities and experience of solitude between the eleventh and thirteenth centuries, for example, Duby remarks, "In feudal residences there was no room for individual solitude, except perhaps in the moment of death" (1988, p. 509). Beginning late in the twelfth century, however, there were increasing signs of a desire for freedom and autonomy. At the same time that people were venturing forth in greater numbers, Christian interpretations of their holy scripture began to emphasize active service and self-transformation over the more routinized expressions of full-time rituals and prayer. The times were ripe for the (re-)emergence of humanism, and there were many signs that individuality and its expression were being transformed into valued responsibilities. Indeed, the history of common law and the concept of liberty reflect increasing recognition, affirmation, and protection of individual human rights and freedoms. *Individualism* came to mean very different things, however, ranging from (1) a resurrection of the "egoism of Epicurus and the Stoics" (Lukes 1974, p. 594; see also Wallach and Wallach 1983) and (2) the biological and genetic uniqueness of living systems to (3) the fundamentally recursive and self-descriptive aspects of self-reflection (Brent 1984; Jantsch 1980; Medawar 1981; Pattee 1977; Weimer 1987) and (4) an appreciation for individual differences and their diverse expressions.

It was not until the Renaissance and the Enlightenment that the idea of a person as a "unique life process" began to flourish. That idea is still, by no means, universal, and its message is complexly dynamic. An acknowledgment of the individual within the social system (and vice versa) is, in fact, just now beginning to bridge that gap between individual and family therapies (Allen 1988; Nichols 1987). By the end of the eighteenth century, however, individualism had come to be scorned as an obstacle to progress and a symptom of rampant egoism. French thinkers of the time were particularly acidic in their critiques, warning that individualism was inimical to liberty, and that it would result in the withdrawal of citizens from public life and one another, and thus in the erosion of the social order. In Germany, however, the romantic ideal that glorified personal uniqueness, originality, and self-development was also gaining ground. Meanwhile, in North America, Ralph Waldo Emerson and Walt Whitman were singing the praises of self-reliance and independence. As we saw in chapter 1, these different interpretations and evaluations of individualism persist today. Since the many forms of both individualism and collectivism, as well as the perennial tension between them, are beyond the scope of this book, I defer their discussion to other sources (Bellah et al. 1985; Doepke 1989; Hayek 1978; Lasch 1979; Sampson 1985, 1988; Seligman 1989; Yankelovich 1981) and will instead examine some recent developments in our understanding of the self and its role in lifespan psychological development.

THE NATURE OF THE SELF

Now that the self has (re)gained the interest and respect of psychological researchers and practitioners, some challenging issues have emerged as central to our understanding of its operations. One of these issues is how we conceptualize the self, and another is the related issue of how we go about measuring changes and continuities in the self over time. Definitions and methodologies abound, of course, and there are wide-ranging differences in their assumptions about the nature of the self and its psychological operations (Baumeister 1987; Broughton 1986; Cushman 1990; Doi 1985; Epstein 1973; Guidano 1987, 1990; Harré 1984; Harter 1983; Rosenberg 1979; Rosenberg 1988; Silverman 1987; Yardley and

Honess 1987; Young-Eisendrath and Hall 1987). Without belaboring that range and those differences here, it is important to note that the meaning of *self* varies with cultures, ages, and ideologies. In contrast to the "self-contained" or "body-bound" notions of self popular in Western cultures, for example, the terms for *self* or *person* in many Asian languages include references to the social or family system in which a person is embedded. Moreover, research on self-attributes and their desirabilty suggest that cultural experiences and gender-role stereotyping often exert a significant influence (Anderson and Zinsser 1988; Belenky et al. 1986; Chodorow 1989; Cota and Fekken 1988; Cousins 1989; Gilligan 1982; Hughes and Demo 1989; James 1989; Josselson 1987; Klein and Erickson 1987; Marsella, DeVos, and Hsu 1985; McNamara and Richard 1989; Moore 1968; Roland 1988; Sampson 1988; Schweder and LeVine 1984; Triandis 1989; White and Kirkpatrick 1985). Thus, the experience of self is multiply determined and highly individualized.

Self as Object

More than any other writers on the topic, David Hume, John Locke, and Thomas Hobbes established a narrow empirical net around the concept of self. They argued that it was no more than the accumulation and association of experiences. When Hume's introspective search for his own "self" revealed nothing that did not ultimately relate to specific experiences, he concluded that there was no self to be experienced. His and others' mistake in this domain was to neglect the process of searching itself, which many modern theories (including constructivist and humanist) now acknowledge as a uniquely individual life-ordering process. As noted in chapter 5, Hayek has demonstrated "the primacy of the abstract" in human experience; the research reviewed in this chapter emphasizes that the central—though hardly unified—"core ordering processes" of human experience include those imperfectly described by the self and its activities.

When experimental psychology established itself as a separate discipline from philosophy, the self immediately became an issue of theoretical controversy. Its first real champions were William James and his student Mary Whiton Calkins. Although many of his efforts would be ignored for half a century, William James pioneered some early distinctions regarding the self and its relations to the ongoing stream of personal consciousness. In volume I of his 1890 *Principles,* for example, he distinguished four constituents of the Self (a term he capitalized): (1) the material Self, which included the body, the family, and personal properties; (2) the social Self, which is comprised of interpersonal sentiments; (3) the spiritual Self, which is comprised of psychic faculties, dispositions, and an "inner" or subjective sense of being; and (4) the pure Ego, which was said to be the inner principle of personal unity. Among other things, James anticipated the vast multiplicity of social selves now acknowledged, having stated that "a man has as many social selves as there are individuals who recognize him" (p. 294). Rivalry and conflict among these different selves was said to be common. James also maintained that this complex of selves is based in *felt* experience, and that the two primary "self-feelings" were self-complacency and self-dissatisfaction. He also maintained that certain action patterns are prompted by the Self, especially self-preservation and self-seeking or self-loving.

James's chapter on "the consciousness of self" was to become an influential classic for later generations of psychologists. His most famous distinction in this realm, however, may have been that between "self as subject" or "knower," which he termed the "I," and "self as object" or "known," which he called the "Me." As Susan Harter (1983) pointed out in her scholarly review of "developmental perspectives on the self-system," the vast majority of research in self psychology has been—until relatively recently—disproportionately focused on the object ("Me") rather than the subject ("I") in that dichotomy. "The self as subject, process—as active agent—has received far less attention, particularly from a developmental perspective" (Harter 1983, p. 277). At least some of this relative imbalance may relate to the dominance of extreme objectivism in psychology. Fortunately, shifts in research emphases have recently begun to redress that imbalance, as I shall discuss.

After James, his student Mary Whiton Calkins was a formidable champion of the self. Titchener argued that the concept of self should be left out of psychology because it would bring in the realm of meaning, which (he believed) lay beyond the purview of psychology as a descriptive science. Calkins "stuck to her guns," according to Hilgard (1987, p. 506), and became the first to use the term *self psychology* to designate this important realm of research (Calkins 1915, 1916, 1919, 1927). She was honored for her contributions by being elected the first woman president of the American Psychological Association in 1905. Unfortunately, the groundwork she and William James had laid would be almost lost under the sweep of behaviorism and the rational objectivism of early experimental psychology.

Self as Illusion

The oldest recognized perspective on self actually preceded that developed by Hume, Locke, and the British empiricists by more than two thousand years. This is the view primarily associated with Buddhism, in which the self or ego is viewed as one of many illusions created by the mind. In their 1980 invitation to move "beyond ego" and on to "transpersonal" dimensions, for example, Roger Walsh and Frances Vaughan begin with the Buddha's famous statement: "We are what we think. All that we are arises with our thoughts. With our thoughts we make the world" (cited in Walsh and Vaughan 1980, p. 15). This statement is reminiscent of constructive metatheory (chapter 5). Although there are important parallels between Buddhist psychology and constructivism, there are also important differences. Modern constructivists have not, for example, adopted the Buddha's Four Noble Truths or Eightfold Path as central to their theory, research, and practice, although modern Buddhists would probably have little reluctance in endorsing the constructivist principles of active knowing, the structural primacy of (tacit) abstraction, and the dynamics of self-organizing development (Mosig 1989).

The "self as illusion" perspective has become increasingly popular in American and European quarters over the last few decades, in part because of the popularization of Asian philosophies and their teachings. Some of the most influential works in this popularization process have been by Ram Dass (1970, 1971, 1978), J. Krishnamurti (1964), Stephen Levine (1979), Tarthang Tulku (1977), and Alan Watts (1966). With regard to my discussion of the nature of self, perhaps the single most valuable recent work on "contemplative" perspectives is that edited by Ken Wilber, Jack Engler, and Daniel Brown (1986). Wilber is one of the foremost spokespersons for modern transpersonal psychology, and both Engler and Brown have been key figures in attempting to bridge some of the cultural and communicative gaps between Western and Eastern views of health and human development. In looking at similarities and differences between Buddhist psychology and psychoanalytic object relations theory, for example, Engler has noted that "the fate of the self is *the* central clinical issue in both psychologies" (1986, p. 22). How that self and its fate are to be understood and "worked with" in psychotherapy are approached somewhat differently, however.

The "Looking Glass" Self

At the turn of the present century, a handful of social scientists had already noted the importance of social interaction in adaptation and survival, and it was from their efforts that the perspective known as *symbolic interactionism* later developed. James Mark Baldwin, George Herbert Mead, and Charles Horton Cooley were the principal figures in developing the idea of the "looking glass self," which maintained that the self is a product of imitation, internalization, and inferences prompted by (what we believe are) other people's perceptions and evaluations of us. It should be remembered that these conjectures were coming out of an intellectual context that had embraced evolutionary theory and the ethological role of the "group" (community, tribe) in defining the lives of its constituents.

Although Cooley and Mead are more generally associated with symbolic interactionism and the "social mirror" that generates self, Baldwin actually went much further than either of his colleagues in outlining specific stages of self and knowledge development (Broughton 1986). Among other things, he recognized that the twentieth-century resurgence of self psychology was historically related to the rejection and transcendence of Cartesian dualism. Although his resolution of that dualism was itself naïvely rationalistic, it was a pioneering statement about boundaries, dialectical tensions, and recursive epistemology. Also, these early assertions about interpersonal and vicarious processes in human learning and socialization were to serve as the foundations for social learning theory and its contributions to self psychology (Bandura 1977, 1986).

But there was and is much more to "personal being" and "selfhood" than was suggested by symbolic interactionism. According to John M. Broughton (1986) and other critics, this approach has tended (1) to lose sight of the individual "I" in experience; (2) to confound perceptions and communications of self with its actual, unfolding existence; and (3) to obscure the role of both contexts and histories in the structuring of personal experience. According to such criticisms, symbolic interactionism can account only for "internalized conventionality" but not for the active and generative uniqueness of the self. Nevertheless, the philosopher Rom Harré opens the tenth and final chapter of his treatise on *Personal Being* by acknowledging that, in a way, "the first nine chapters draw out in detail the original insight of G. H. Mead, that the self owes its form and perhaps its very existence to the circumambient social order" (1984, p. 256). This is a core assertion of the "social constructivist" (sometimes called "social constructionist") approach to human experience in general and to personal identity in particular (Broughton 1986; Harré 1984).

Self as Social Persona

The acknowledgement that social environments are the primary contexts for identity development is a major stride for mainstream psychology. It was assisted, of course, by studies in the present century that have looked more closely at the development of self-awareness and self-knowledge in children (Lewis and Brooks-Gunn 1979). Also of importance was the recognition that human adolescence is frequently a period punctuated by formative experiences for identity and self-esteem (Erikson 1950, 1959, 1968; Guidano 1987, 1990; Smollar and Youniss 1989). What is most significant about the studies of self-awareness in animals and human infants is the consistency with which impairments in early socialization are linked with delayed and diluted self-awareness, not to mention frequent emotional distress and behavioral dysfunction. Monkeys or apes who are reared in complete isolation fail to recognize themselves in a mirror, for example, and experience considerable (though not immutable) difficulty in relating to peers if they are later introduced into their lives. Even if they are raised in the presence of animals from other species, this effect is not eliminated. The most warranted conclusion from this research is similar to one reached at a recent conference on the possibility of programming self-awareness ("consciousness") into modern supercomputers. A necessary prerequisite for such consciousness, it seems, is for two systems of the same type to interact. The development of symbolic self-knowledge—the kind involved in self-awareness and other self-relationships—requires interaction with "others" of the same systemic "family."

The acknowledgment of our social embeddedness has been an important step for scientific and therapeutic psychology (and especially, of course, for those varieties that have heretofore neglected or diminished the importance of human relations in psychological development). Contributions from social psychology have been significant in deepening our understanding of the complex interface of personal identity and social influence processes (Buss 1980; Deci 1980; Goleman 1985; Sanford 1966; Sherif and Cantril 1947; Snyder 1987; Wegner and Vallacher 1980). Some assertions about the powers of society have been extreme, however, when the "inner citadel" of the self has been negated in deference to social influence processes (Christman 1988). Such extreme views portray the self as an infinitely mercurial mask or character repertoire which is altered to fit different social forums. This is, in essence, the "presentation of self in everyday life" that Erving Goffman (1959) has described; and it presumes that "impression management" is the sole or central concern of all social beings. The emphasis here is on representations of self that are influenced by their social contexts, as well as on self- and person-perception as they are moderated by the individual's awareness of and sensitivity to the appraisals of others. Among other things, these portrayals have been criticized for ignoring or diminishing issues of authenticity and the frequent differences between personal and collective experience.

Self as Defensive Center

In Western quarters, the most popular view of the self among mental health professionals over the last half century has been that linked with early Freudian concepts and the "ego psychology" and "object relations" theories that have emerged in post-Freudian theorizing. Because of their important influence on other approaches in self psychology, these contributions warrant thoughtful consideration.

First, it is important to remember that Freud had abandoned the use of hypnosis in the treatment of his early clients when he realized that this technique circumvented the phenomenon of resistance. In 1914 he made his famous dictum that the pyschoanalytic approach was defined by two central acknowledgments: of resistance and of transference mechanisms.

Freud came to believe that the real work of psychological change lay in the realm of resistance to change; and that the latter was "energized" by various "defenses of the ego" (the defense mechanisms). His 1914 essay "On Narcissism" addressed the wide variations in persons' self-esteem and the apparent limits of where and how "psychic energy" and attention could be distributed. He asserted that our limited amounts of that energy ("libido") can be invested primarily in ourselves ("ego cathexis") or in others ("object love"). His term for the ego (das Ich) had several meanings (including the Self and "I"), and his translators have not always agreed on what he meant by the term in different contexts. What is noteworthy about this assertion was Freud's assumption that self-interest and caring for others are inversely related (a prejudice, in my opinion, that underlies many modern criticisms of self-focus—see chapter 1). Freud believed that people who were unusually preoccupied with themselves would have little psychic energy available to invest in important human relationships, including the "transference" that constituted the primary vehicle of change in psychoanalytic therapy. From 1914 until the present, a large portion of psychodynamic therapists have accepted this assumption, with the result that "narcissism" is still a stigmatizing label with pessimistic overtones about the possibility of psychological change. Recent departures from this tradition (such as Fromm 1956) have signaled new directions for theories and therapies of identity development.

It was in his 1923 monograph on *The Ego and the Id* that Freud first elaborated his famous three-component model of the structure of the mind. In doing so, he added the superego as a witnessing and evaluating component comprised of the conscience and "ego-ideal." The *id* (*das es;* literally, "the it") was a term that Freud borrowed from Georg Groddeck (1923), who had, in turn, borrowed it from Nietzsche (Tuttman 1988; Tuttman, Kaye, and Zimmerman 1981). With his reformulated model, Freud had placed the ego (or self) at the center of the system as a coordinator of conflicting impulses (from the atavistic id below and the socialized superego above) as well as the demands of the immediate world outside. Although critics of psychoanalysis (including myself) have faulted Freud for some of his biases and assumptions in the development of that theory, he deserves credit for having attempted to integrate the simultaneous and complex dynamics of existential/biological and social/moral influences in the primary context of the self. He viewed resistance and the defense mechanisms as serving to protect the self from being overwhelmed by impulses and conflicts (most of which, he believed, were not conscious). Although one can point to important differences between Freud's views and those of some contemporary constructivist and developmental theorists, there are also important parallels and promising lines of shared emphasis.

I have used the terms *self* and *ego* interchangably in the foregoing discussion, although some modern theorists prefer to differentiate them. As Jane Loevinger (1987) has aptly noted, the disagreements among modern Freudians in the realm of self or ego psychology are substantial (DeAngelis 1987; Kugler 1987; Levine and Kravis 1987; Pine 1989; Redfearn 1987; Straker 1987; Young-Eisendrath and Hall 1987). This may be due in part to the diversity of contributions that followed in the wake of Freud's early work. Heinz Hartmann's *Ego Psychology and the Problem of Adaptation* appeared in 1939, and Anna Freud published her *The Ego and the Mechanisms of Defense* in 1946. In the meantime, of course, Alfred Adler, Erich Fromm, Karen Horney, and Carl Jung (among others) had split with Freud over a variety of issues relating to the self, basic human nature, and the value of social sensitivity. It is therefore not surprising that their contributions were permeated with analyses of the self and its development relative to the family, society, and intimate love (Adler 1979; Fromm 1941, 1956; Horney 1945; Jung 1957).* The works of Erik H. Erikson (1950, 1959), Otto Kernberg (1967, 1968, 1975, 1976), Melanie Klein (1932), Heinz Kohut (1966, 1971, 1977), Jane Loevinger (1976), Margaret Mahler (1968, 1972; Mahler, Pine, and Bergman 1975), and James Masterson (1981, 1988) have also been central to the development of modern psychodynamic theories and therapies of the self. (For an example of more eclectic studies of self-knowledge development, see Pipp, Fischer, and Jennings 1987.)

Though it is beyond the scope of the present discussion to attempt an in-depth comparison of modern psychodynamic self psychologies, we should recognize that their contributions have been important in shaping the questions that now face self theorists. Heinz Hartmann's attempts to systematize psychoanalytic theory also helped to clarify its central focus: the individual life process that is "selectively lived" by the self. Hartmann, with the help of Gordon Allport, Anna Freud, Kurt Lewin, Gardner Murphy, and David Rapaport, was a significant pioneer in the modern convergence on the self from diverse theoretical directions. In particular, he challenged Freud's view of the ego as "a structure ontogenetically younger than the id" (Arieti 1967, p. 13), and argued that the id and ego originated simultaneously. This was, of course, a major shift toward the empowerment of the self system and a relative de-emphasis on the strictly biological dominance of the id.

---

*Pioneering work on the social psychology of "ego involvement" was also published at midcentury (for example, Sherif and Cantril 1947). I had the honor of knowing Muzafer and Carolyn Sherif at the Pennsylvania State University; some preliminary work together on the psychology of self change was abandoned after Carolyn's tragic death.

The tacit cognitive psychology that has imbued much of psychoanalytic theory has also been informative, and represents a creative mixture of both mechanistic and organic metaphors of the individual. Consider, as a brief illustration, the fascinating work of Margaret Mahler and her colleagues on the psychosocial process of "individuation." Mahler's work has played a central role in the elaboration and refinement of what is called *object relations theory,* and it has been in the development of this theory that Freud, Piaget, and others have been interpreted as convergent (Broughton 1986; Furth 1987; Kegan 1982; Mahler 1968, 1972; Mahler, Pine, and Bergman 1975). Although a literal interpretation of its title might suggest that this is a theory about people's relations to objects, the derivation of the title suggests a provocatively different meaning. To begin with, the term *object* is based in the root *ject,* which means "to throw"—an action, and one whose motion is fundamentally "outward." The prefix *ob* emphasizes throwing that is "from" or "away from."* From the context of a developmental epistemology, then, object relations theory has to do with "our relations to that which some motion has made separate or distinct from us, our relations to that which has been thrown from us, or the experience of this throwing itself" (Kegan 1982, p. 76). According to Robert Kegan and others, modern object relations theory views activity and process as fundamental to individuation, and the latter is now recognized as an evolution of activities and experiences that express personal meanings and their relations.

Like Piaget, Freud had recognized that human adaptation involves extensive efforts to organize experience. Informally stated, the organism's ability to prepare for action sequences requires some consistency or stability in both the organism's world and in its abilities to organize its own activities. Freud focused on the concepts of cathexis and fixation; Heinz Hartmann and Anna Freud later developed the idea of *object constancy* (which was, in turn, parallel to what Piaget meant by *conservation skills*). Adding to this convergence, the philosopher Ernst Cassirer (1944, 1955a, 1955b, 1957) later demonstrated that much of this world- and self-ordering activity is eventually achieved through language, whose primary function is "symbol fixing." It was not until the work of Mahler and her colleagues, however, that an elaborate description of possible developmental phases in this phenomenon were suggested.

It is with Mahler's work, for example, that we begin to recognize that *individuation*—the process of becoming a unique and distinct living system—is both theoretically and experientially inseparable from *separation*—the process of distinguishing and distancing that system from rules, roles, and relationships that constrain its independent identity. According to Mahler, separation-individuation is the fundamental process

---

*It was Duns Scotus (chapter 2) who, in 1309, first used *ojectivus* to depict subject-free knowing; this notion later became the hallmark (and eventual nemesis) of *objectivism.*

through which both object constancy (an orderly world) and coherent selfhood are developed. This process is itself comprised of four main phases (each with subphases) that unfold between five months and three years of age (table 9.1). Over all, much of that process is stimulated by separations from and interactions with the mother; and Bowlby (1988) acknowledges that there are important parallels between aspects of Mahler's views and attachment theory.

Because Mahler's work and object relations theory have played important roles in framing psychodynamic formulations of the so-called narcissistic and borderline personalities, they have been a significant force in shaping some psychotherapies of the self. Rather than develop an elaborate evaluation of these approaches here, I shall defer most of my commentary for my discussion of therapeutic interventions. For the time being, however, three criticisms of Mahler's work bear remembering: (1) it focuses almost exclusively on the mother's role as an emotional object in the young child's life, with relatively less discussion of the child's active and interactive contributions to his or her own sense of self; (2) it generally fails to discuss the wide range of individual differences in the pacing

Table 9.1   Mahler's Phases of Individuation

1. *Autistic Phase* (0–1 month)
   Primitive undifferentiated and poorly organized efforts to self-regulate and satisfy biological needs.

2. *Symbiotic Phase* (1–5 months)
   Continuing fusion with the mother and lack of differentiation between inside and outside and I/not-I; "omnipotence" is prevalent.

3. *Differentiation Phase* (5–9 months)
   This marks a sensoriphysical "hatching" process in which the infant begins to experience his or her body as separate from that of the mother.

4. *Practicing Phase* (9–15 months)
   Although psychological self and non-self remain substantially fused, the toddler is "grandiose," exhilarated with personal abilities and achievements, and fundamentally "narcissistic."

5. *Rapprochement Phase* (15–24 months)
   A crucial step for later development, this represents the "psychological birth" of the individual, which is accomplished by an emotionally felt separation from the mother and a loss of grandiosity and omnipotence; pronounced feelings of anxiety and vulnerability are negotiated to the extent that child and mother remain attuned and responsive despite their separateness.

6. *Consolidation Phase* (24–36 months)
   "Emotional object constancy" is achieved via integrative and relatively stable representations of self and mother; good and bad aspects of both are consolidated, as are other partial representations of each.

and resolution of the developmental phases described; and (3) by modern standards at least, it fails to discuss the possibly powerful differences of same-gender (daughter-mother) and opposite-gender (son-mother) separations, not to mention the possible importance of male presence and participation in the child's early life (Chodorow 1978; Dinnerstein 1976; Hamilton 1989; Harter 1983; W. I. Thompson 1981).

Self as Agent, Theory, Process, and Project

The final major grouping of theories about the nature of the self views the self as a predominantly tacit, process-based, and fully embodied working theory of itself and the world. The term *theory,* as used here, does not imply an explicitly articulated set of beliefs, however, so much as an abstract and open set of organizing principles. This perspective, which has become increasingly popular over the last decade, is represented in the diverse writings of a number of contemporary workers. A partial list would include Albert Bandura (1977, 1986), Michael Berzonsky (1989), John Bowlby (1988), O. G. Brim (1976), Seymour Epstein (1973), Oscar Gonçalves (1989a, 1989b), Anthony Greenwald (1980), Vittorio Guidano (1987, 1990), Rom Harré (1984), Susan Harter (1983), Hubert Hermans (1987), Allen Ivey (1986), Robert Kegan (1982), George Kelly (1955), myself (1990b), Hazel Markus and Paula Nurius (1986), Mayte Miró (1989), Morris Rosenberg (1979), and E. E. Sampson (1985). There are, of course, important differences in the contentions of the various theorists, and there are many more self-as-theorist proponents than I can adequately represent here. The essence of this perspective is that the self is a complex and dynamic metaphor for the unique and spontaneous self-organizing processes that *are* each person in his or her step-by-step, moment-to-moment becoming. In this view, *who* and *how* one becomes are expressions of deeply ingrained patterns of activity that are fundamentally emotional and minimally explicit. The conceptual underpinnings and practical implications of this perspective permeate this book.

DISORDERS OF THE SELF

An important trend in the history of classifications and theories of human psychopathology has been the increasing recognition that the "disorders of the self" are widely distributed across virtually all other categories of human distress and dysfunction (Fontana et al. 1989; Gara, Rosenberg, and Mueller 1989; Guidano 1987, 1990; Hartman and Blankstein 1986; Ingram 1990a, 1990b; Krueger 1989; Pelham

and Swann 1989; Robey, Cohen, and Gara 1989). This insight is recent, as is the formal recognition of the experience patterns labeled
narcissism, borderline, and *multiple personality.* In their discussion of the
evolution of diagnostic categories called *personality disorders,* for example, Blashfield and McElroy (1989) showed that the four versions of
the *Diagnostic and Statistical Manual* (DSM) of the American Psychiatric
Association have evidenced dramatic and discontinuous shifts in the
categorization of psychological dysfunctions between 1952 and 1987.
The final line of their historical account is telling: "Borderline and narcissistic are concepts that were introduced in the DSM-III and had no
clear historical roots in the earlier editions" (1989, p. 131). While they
may have been ignored in those editions, however, these concepts had
begun to influence psychological theories and therapies long before
1952.

Early Onset Identity Disorders

In one recent twist of psychiatric classification, for example, separate
categories have been created for "gender identity disorders" and "identity disorders originating in infancy, childhood, or adolescence." The
latter are described as patterns of "severe subjective distress" related to
"uncertainties" about identity issues. To earn an official diagnosis, an
identity disorder must (1) persist for more than three months; (2) be
serious enough to impair an individual's social, academic, or occupational functioning; and (3) not be serious enough to qualify as a "borderline" personality. Uncertainties and distress about three or more of the
following "identity issues" are also required: patterns of friendship, sexual orientation, religion, career, morals, group loyalties, and long-range
goals.

    A separate disorder marked by early developmental onset is called
"reactive attachment disorder of infancy or early childhood." Reflecting
the increasing recognition of the significance of human attachment in
psychological functioning, this classification pertains to individuals who
have exhibited "markedly disturbed social relatedness" before the age of
five. These disturbances in human relationships may be expressed in lack
of interest in social interaction or in "indiscriminate sociability." They
are also associated with grossly obvious inadequacies of child care, such
as extreme neglect, abuse (physical, emotional, and sexual), and instability or inconsistency in caregivers (or their caregiving). Interestingly, there
is no discussion in DSM-IIIR of the relationship between early onset
identity disorders and attachment disorders. As discussed in the context
of attachment theory (chapter 7), however, such a relationship is readily
apparent.

Body Image and Embodied Self Disorders

Scattered across several groupings within the DSM-IIIR are disorders in which the individual exhibits distressing and dysfunctional relationships with his or her own body. In "body dysmorphic disorder," for example, the individual is preoccupied with imagined defects in his or her physical appearance. (The American Psychiatric Association has yet to acknowledge the relationship among psychological patterns involving violations of the body—as in sexual trauma—unusual bodily experiences, and "depersonalization" [Cash and Pruzinsky 1990; Gara, Rosenberg, and Mueller 1989; Krueger 1989; Mellor 1988; and Young 1988].) More extreme and dysfunctional preoccupations with bodily functioning are exhibited in "hypochondriasis" and "somatization disorder," both of which involve a chronically negative appraisal of the body and its viability. Individuals who struggle with eating disorders—particularly anorexia and bulimia— also report poor relationships with their bodies and bodily functions. Not surprisingly, these same individuals appear to be more vulnerable to struggles in respect to other issues of identity, human intimacy, and control (especially of impulses). Although patterns of distress in respect to embodiment and eating are not invariably associated with borderline psychological functioning, these classifications share important themes and issues (Armstrong and Roth 1989; Pope and Hudson 1989; Zanarini, Gunderson, and Frankenburg 1989).

Fascinating data on the embodiment of self and its psychological burdens and blessings come from recent breakthroughs in the understanding of the *phantom limb phenomenon* (Melzack 1989). Universally, about 95 percent of individuals who suffer the amputation or loss of a limb report still feeling that limb as "really there" (often for years), and many suffer chronic pain in the lost body part. The source of that pain is clearly not "peripheral" or "afferent" (sensory), but rather central and "efferent" (motor). There is also evidence that children born with partial or missing limbs still vividly feel and act as though these appendages were full and functional. It is as though their "body sense" were still intact, and researchers now believe that there are instructive parallels between some of the mysteries in immunology (where literal rejection of the "not-self" is a central puzzle) and those mysteries that characterize disorders of felt embodiment. The results of experimental surgery on newborn monkeys, for example, have corroborated the hypothesis that the phantom limb experience is generated by constructive processes in the developing body-brain system. Even when the sensory nerves from their forelimbs (arms) were completely severed and they were blinded by having their eyelids sutured together, young monkeys learned to walk, grasp objects, and make precise hand-to-mouth movements.

According to Melzack, such studies suggest the activity of a "body-self neuromatrix," which is experienced as a unifying point of orientation in the world. Cyclical feedforward and feedback dynamics are also implicated, resulting in "a creative, constructive process in which meaning, structure and pattern are imposed on inputs" (1989, p. 12). In body image and body experience disorders, those meanings, structures, and patterns may be particularly difficult to change for at least two reasons. First, as we have already seen, major psychological changes are often associated with intense emotionality and the bodily experiences that reflect them. When the experience of that body (and some of those emotions) constitutes the problem, however, there are added complexities. Second (and relatedly), many individuals who suffer from such disorders develop skills in "numbing out" and in either ignoring or denying bodily signals. In my opinion, it is in the treatment of body image and body experience disorders that it may be particularly wise to supplement traditional ("talking heads") psychotherapies with aspects of the somatic or "body therapies" (Mahoney 1990a).

Borderline Personality Disorder

There is no better way to introduce the intensity with which the *borderline* personality is currently debated than by quoting the pithy opening to Martin Leichtman's insightful history of that concept:

Unless God speaks to one directly about the definition of borderline personality disorders, it is probably foolhardy to venture into the area at this time. To be sure, God has apparently spoken to some about the matter, but, as is his wont, he has done so in differing and, at times, contradictory ways. As a result, to grapple with the borderline concept is to wander onto a battlefield littered with the remains of earlier definitions, fought over by bitterly contending factions, and shelled by other factions who would obliterate the concept altogether in the conviction that it is the devil's handiwork or, at the least, a holdover from pagan times. Nor can refuge be found behind either old or new DSM-III definitions. If one thing is certain, it is that those definitions are not the work of God, but of a committee. (1989, p. 229)

Amen. Table 9.2 summarizes the six most influential renditions of the borderline personality in the past half century.* Amidst descriptions of the borderline person as "stably unstable," the concept itself has exhibited considerable diversity.

Two themes that have survived these various renditions are note-

*See American Psychiatric Association 1987; Goldstein 1989; Grinker, Werble, and Drye 1968; Gunderson 1984; Kernberg 1967, 1975; Knight 1953; Links, Steiner, and Mitton 1989; Mann et al. 1988; Melges and Swartz 1989; Shapiro 1989; Snyder, Pitts, and Pokorny 1986; Stone 1986; Trull, Widiger, and Guthrie 1990; and Zanarini, Gunderson, and Frankenburg 1989.

Table 9.2   Selected Renditions of the Borderline Personality

Stern (1938)	Knight (1953)	Kernberg (1967)
Narcissism	Impaired secondary-process thinking	Poor impulse control
Inferiority feelings		Poor anxiety tolerance
Rigidity		Primary-process thinking
Hypersensitivity	Poor integration	
Masochism	Impaired environmental adaptation	Primitive projections
Poor resiliency		Excessive denial
Negative response to therapy	Unstable object relations	Pronounced "splitting"
"Deep organic" anxiety	Impairments in realistic planning	Pathological object relations
Poor reality testing	Weak defenses against unconscious impulses	Extreme idealization
		Feelings of omnipotence and devaluation
		Excessive and unrealistic fantasy
		Instability of experience

Grinker, Werble, and Drye (1968)	Gunderson (1984)	American Psychiatric Association (1987)
Defective affectionate relations	Intense and unstable human relationships	Affective instability
Impaired self-identity	Unstable sense of self	Intense, uncontrolled anger
Prevalent anger	Impulsivity	Poor impulse control
Depressive loneliness	Manipulative suicide attempts	Chronic feelings of emptiness or boredom
	Negative affect	Physically self-damaging acts or gestures
	Poor achievement	Severe and persistent identity disturbances
	"Ego-dystonic" psychotic experiences	Intense and unstable relationships
		Intense fears of abandonment
		Recurrent accidents or fights

worthy: the concept of a continuum—a symbolically connective "border-land"—between neurosis and psychosis; and the centrality and insepara-bility of affect, identity, and intimacy in the structuring (ordering) and destructuring (disordering) of human experience. Although I cannot here do justice to the significance of those themes, it is clear that they lie at the heart of theoretical ferment in developmental psychopathology and psychotherapy. In the evolution of psychodynamic conceptualizations, for example, these themes permeate the contributions of Anna Freud, Heinz Hartmann, Karen Horney, Otto Kernberg, Melanie Klein, Heinz Kohut, Margaret Mahler, James F. Masterson, D. W. Winnicott, and many others. While its critics may be correct in asserting that the diagnostic label of borderline may have become a "wastebasket term" reflecting the limited understanding of the profession, it is a term and idea not likely to be discarded in the near future. Indeed, continuing debates about its manifestation in individual lives show signs of shedding important light on our basic assumptions about self development and its vicissitudes. Interestingly, the same two themes that have survived the evolutionary "rapids" of the borderline concept have also emerged in recent understandings of multiple personality disorder.

Histrionic Personality and Narcissism

Two other patterns of disorders of the self are *histrionic personality disorder* and *narcissistic personality disorder.* The histrionic individual is said to be in constant need of praise, approval, or attention. He or she may be self-centered, preoccupied with appearance, and emotionally shallow. This last feature is sometimes expressed via the inappropriate timing and exaggeration of emotional displays and sexual flirtation. Even though it is separately categorized, narcissism and the narcissistic personality have gained prominence through the writings of some of the same authors who have shaped modern concepts of the borderline individual (Akhtar 1989; Cooper 1989; Glassman 1988; Goldberg 1989; Kernberg 1989*a*, 1989*b;* Masterson and Klein 1988; Plakun 1989; Ronningstam and Gunderson 1989; Stone 1986; Straker 1987; Young-Eisendrath and Hall 1987). The narcissistic personality exhibits many parallels: lack of empathy, intolerance of criticism, exploitation of others, a sense of entitlement, constant attention and approval needs, and frequent feelings of envy. Noteworthy here is the paradoxical convergence on narcissism as a "pathology" of the individual and of contemporary society (chapter 1). Intentionally or inadvertently, psychopathologists and psychotherapists have fueled the rhetoric of those who would pit the self against its social systems in an impossible conflict (rather than a complementary coalition).

The modern lack of compassion for Narcissus is noteworthy, as are the animosity and insults directed toward those who exhibit this pattern. In both technical and trade writings, for example, Narcissus is commonly portrayed as a vain and conceited young man capable of loving only himself. Homer and Ovid recorded very different versions of this myth, however; and interpretations of the story have rendered "a bewildering variety of meanings" (Seznec 1974, p. 288). Besides the popular version that depicts him as captivated by his own reflection in a pool, Narcissus was also described (by Ovid) as a ghost looking for itself in the river of death, and (by Hesiod) as a grief-stricken youth longing for the image of his beloved, dead twin sister (Durant and Durant 1935–75; Zimmerman 1964). According to Hamilton (1940), Narcissus' self-preoccupation was inflicted by Nemesis (the goddess of righteous anger) in response to the prayers of a woman whom he had rejected. Her prayer was not, however, that he suffer, but that he learn to love himself. It is prophetic that the maiden who remained in love with Narcissus for life was Echo, who could do nothing but repeat what had been said to her.* The point is that our value judgments necessarily influence the labels we apply to ourselves and others.

Multiple Personality Disorder

The phenomenon of *multiple personality* (MPD) is diagnostically categorized as a "hysterical neurosis" (dissociative disorder). To qualify for this diagnosis, an individual must exhibit two or more distinct personalities or "personality states" that each show consistent patterns of experience, with two or more of these personalities alternating in their "full control" of the person's activity. The concept of *dissociation* was introduced by Pierre Janet in 1889 to describe a mechanism in which a thought or pattern of thought could be split off from the primary personality and eventually develop some form of autonomy (Ellenberger 1970; Price 1987). More than anyone else, however, it was Morton Prince (1906), founder of the *Journal of Abnormal Psychology,* who laid the early foundations for the study of dissociation and multiple personality. Ironically, such study was slow to develop despite the considerable publicity given to a few isolated cases. Prior to the popular reception of the book and movie titled *Sybil,* the most famous case of MPD was reported in Thigpen and Cleckly's *The Three Faces of Eve* (1957). (For a fascinating update on Eve's own experience of her therapy and the publicity accorded the book and movie, see Sizemore 1989.)

Prior to 1980, multiple personality was thought to be a rare and mysterious psychological malady; since then it has been recognized as not so rare and much less mysterious. The work of Colin A. Ross and his colleagues has been particularly valuable in both demystifying and documenting the incidence of multiple personality disorder (C.A. Ross 1989; Ross, Norton, and Wozney 1989; Ross et al. 1989). Prior to 1980, only two hundred cases of this disorder had been reported in the world litera-

*Ironically, Echo is also the name of the first love of another tragic figure, Buddy Holly, whose music continues to haunt and inspire modern seekers of "true love ways" (Goldrosen and Beecher 1987).

ture. Since the "official" recognition of MPD, however, an estimated six thousand cases have been diagnosed in North America alone. Besides suggesting that MPD is hardly rare, studies of some of these cases have offered the following insights about this pattern:

1. Persons exhibiting MPD are predominantly female (88%).

2. The majority (80%) of MPD individuals report having been extensively abused (sexually and/or physically) as children.

3. In most cases of MPD, there are not just 2 or 3 personalities: the average is 16 with a median of 8 to 9.

4. The most common "alter" personalities are those of (a) a child (86%), (b) an older or younger person (84%), (c) a protector (84%), and (d) a persecutor (84%).

5. Multiple somatic complaints are common (especially sexual indifference, nausea or digestive difficulties, amnesia, dizziness, palpitations, orthopedic pain, menstrual problems, and blurred vision).

6. Persons exhibiting MPD have often been in the health care system for years before receiving an MPD diagnosis (the most common prior diagnoses have been affective disorders, personality disorders, anxiety disorders, and schizophrenia).

7. Persons struggling with MPD are highly suicidal (over 70% attempt to kill themselves; at least 2% succeed).

Needless to say, our understanding of MPD has come a long way in the last decade, although, of course, we have a long way to go.

Beyond the preceding clarifications about MPD, two points bear emphasis here. The first is that the extreme "splitting" involved in dissociation appears to be a common response to early physical and sexual abuse, and the second is that multiplicity and dream-state dissociation are common phenomena (Foulkes 1985; Gabel 1989). In contrast to the pathological connotations associated with such splitting, however, it now appears that it reflects the young child's best efforts to survive cruel violations of both body and being. Without their awareness, these children have managed to hold onto life by creating alternate personalities that assume self-protective functions (for example, as the "real" victims of the torture, as protectors of other parts or expressions of the child, and so on). Even though this may turn out to be a costly strategy in the long run, it was the best they could come up with at the time, and served to help them through unimaginable pain in their early development. Having counseled several persons exhibiting MPD, I can attest to that pain.

To emphasize the healthy functions of splitting, consider the case of Patricia F., a woman who was referred to me for depression and problems in self-esteem. A bright and lively person of thirty-eight, Patricia had struggled with feelings of inferiority and personal disability for more than twenty years. A psychiatric nurse by profession, she was concerned that the "chronicity" of her personal problems might be a sign of "deep-seated pathology." After several early sessions of getting acquainted and building a working alliance, I asked Patricia if she would like to explore the technique of *streaming,* a modified free association technique in which the individual is invited to report verbally the spontaneous contents of his or her stream of consciousness (see chapter 11; Mahoney 1983). The two most important differences between streaming and free association are that the former respects and emphasizes clients' needs and rights to protect and pace their own privacy (that is, they are not required always to report all conscious contents); and interpretations are generated primarily by the client rather than the therapist, with an emphasis on personal (rather than universal or presumed) meanings. Patricia assented, and over the next few sessions we devoted time to her immediate thoughts, images, and feelings as they emerged in the context of that technique. A recurrent scene in her reports referred to a time when she was eighteen to twenty-four months old. Patricia remembered being in her crib and crying for what seemed like hours (she spontaneously massaged her abdomen, recalling that her "tummy" was sore from crying so long and hard).

Patricia's recollection was that she was frightened and lonely. The only light in her room came from under and outside the bedroom door. In three separate sessions, she exhibited ambivalence when that scene emerged in her streaming: she alternated between anxious crying, "Someone's coming! Someone's coming!" and plaintive requests, "Mommy . . . Daddy . . . please come here . . . *please. . . .*" Finally, in her sixth session of streaming, she reported that scene again and, in a crescendo of crying, suddenly jumped to her feet and began pacing around the room. She reported that, in her imagery, the door had suddenly opened and her childhood bedroom had been filled with light. What had terrified her, she said, was that she had suddenly found herself watching the scene from somewhere "up in the corner of the ceiling." That is, her toddler "body was still in the crib," but she wasn't "in her body." Patricia paced nervously around the room and was inconsolable, pulling on her hair and screaming "This is terrible, Mike! I must be going crazy! I don't believe in that out-of-body shit. I'm just decompensating. . . . Oh, God! . . . Am I splitting apart? I can't stand it! I don't want to be schizophrenic!"

I postponed my next session in order to remain with Patricia and help her assimilate her experience. I tried, unsuccessfully, to Socratically encourage her to explore other interpretations of her vignette. She seemed locked onto the dire conclusion that it could mean nothing other than a degenerative move into psychosis. When she remained disconsolate and anxious after a second hour, I deviated from my usual strategy in processing stream-of-consciousness work and offered the following interpretation as a possibility.

"Patricia, I am concerned about your distress and the difficulties you are having in considering any other possible meanings for your experience. This is just a hunch and I could, of course, be wrong—you need to check this out with your own feelings—but my sense is that there was something very healthy and self-protective about the split in your imagery."

She stopped pacing and stood facing me. How, she asked, could splitting be anything but pathological? I continued, "Well, . . . my sense is that something very painful might have happened to you after that door opened [she sat down, incredulous but intent on my every word], . . . and perhaps some part of you did not want to go through that pain again. . . ." My voice trailed off, and Patricia said that she did not understand. I asked whether she could recall any later incidents in her life when she had been in an accident or gone into shock because of a physical trauma. She related an incident in which she had suffered a broken leg in an automobile accident. When I asked her to describe how she had felt, her voice reflected a sharp increase in anxiety: there were obvious parallels (for example, she had felt "detached" from her body while they had waited for the ambulance).

Patricia stood up nervously, walked around the room once, and then sat back down. Her anxiety spilled over into anger: "Mike, don't play games with me! What are you driving at? What does it mean?" It was not a time for me to be nondirective. I said, "Patricia, I am not trying to play games. I know you are hurting and frightened, and perhaps even angry. My point is that I do not want you to go home thinking that the only possible meaning of all this is that you are going crazy. You could be [she looked into my eyes], . . . but I don't think so. I think you experienced something called 'witnessing,' which is a common and healthy response when things get too intense or painful. [She began grooming her hair with one hand.] I don't claim to know what all of this means—we have some important work ahead of us—but I wanted you to know that what you experienced today could have been not only self-protective but also a major step forward in understanding and resolving some of your problems."

Patricia wasn't convinced. We agreed to meet again the next day, and it was several weeks before she recalled that her father had, in fact, opened her bedroom door and brutally beaten her for having cried so long. During a holiday visit, her mother confirmed the memory and confessed that it had not been an isolated incident. Although she was relieved to learn that her memory had not been a confabulation, it took Patricia several months to process the emotional significance of that discovery.

We still have much to learn about splitting, witnessing, and the complexities of "multiplicity" in personality development. I believe, however, that an important first step lies in destigmatizing (or "*de*pathologizing") a natural and life-seeking reaction to unnatural and life-threatening circumstances.

A second and related point worth emphasizing here is that "we are all covert multiples" (Price 1987, p. 387): that is, the human personality is complexly faceted and decidedly multiple in its range of experiences and expressions (Assagioli 1973; Elster 1985; Gabel 1989; Hilgard 1977; Linville 1985, 1987; Markus and Nurius 1986; Rosenberg and Gara 1985; Stone and Winkelman 1985). This is hardly news to those who have enjoyed the world literatures of the last few centuries. Jorge Luis Borges (1964), for example, has written about such multiplicities in his own works (for example, "Borges and I") and in those of Shakespeare ("Everything and Nothing"). The most recognized master of multiplicity in twentieth-century literature, however, is likely to be the Portuguese genius, Fernando Pessoa (1974), whose works are still being discovered more than half a century after his death in 1935. A quiet clerk, Pessoa made a modest living translating business letters into English and French. Beneath his quietness, however, he lived many lives; three "heteronyms" emerged from within him and wrote large quantities of poetry, each in a unique style. These poems and Pessoa's painful emotional oscillations are captivating in their expressions of inner experience and the postmodern search for something beyond subjectivism and objectivism. Even beyond their artistic power, however, Pessoa's works may be valuable guides in future studies of multiplicity. Those visiting Lisbon can still share a symbolic glass of port with this quiet, bespectacled multiperson, who sits patiently in bronze just outside the Brasileira bar.

Multiplicity per se has never been the core of the problem. Lewis Thomas put it succinctly:

It would embarrass me to be told that more than a single self is a kind of disease. I've had, in my time, more than I could possibly count or keep track of. The great difference, which keeps me feeling normal, is that mine (ours) have turned up one after the other, on an orderly schedule. . . . It is the simultaneity of their appearance that is the real problem, and I should think psychiatry would do better by simply persuading them to queue up and wait their turn, as happens in the normal rest of us. (1974, p. 42)

There is much more to MPD than "taking turns," of course, but Thomas's point is important. There is nothing inherently bad or diseased about the multiplicity of personal experience; it is the relative order and "friendly relations" among our many "possible selves" that may be most important. Like the concept of the borderline personality, that of the "multiple" must acknowledge a continuum of dynamics and complexities whose evaluation as good or bad (healthy or diseased) must ultimately confront the interrelatedness of self-care and social responsibility.

PSYCHOTHERAPIES OF THE SELF

As psychology and psychotherapy have entered the second century of their own identity development, some interesting insights have emerged. One of those insights is that *all psychotherapies are psychotherapies of the self.* They always have been, even when their theorists and practitioners have sometimes ignored or denied the importance of the self. By necessity, all psychological services are experienced uniquely by individual service seekers. Thus, psychotherapy has always been modulated through self systems (both clients' and therapists'). The self has always been in the system, but it has only recently recognized its own pervasive roles in the structuring of its own experience. The person in *person*ality, the victim/survivor in psychopathology, and the self in virtually all theories of consciousness are still only crudely understood. Even within the limits of that understanding, however, it is now apparent that the psychological processes underlying personality, adaptive functioning, and lifespan development reflect a teleonomic and only partially aware agent, a self-moving continuity permeated with feeling and ever engaged in action, and a dynamic capacity for reflectivity (reflexivity) that creates *jectives* (thrown separations, as in sub*jectivity* and ob*jectivity,* intro*jectivity* and pro*jectivity,* and de*jection* and re*jection*).

The self has become "common grounds" for dialogues among advocates of very different theories and therapies. It is as if a "meta-perspective" has emerged which allows glimpses of the importance of different (and often tacit) perspectives in shaping the contours of perception. A fitting visual metaphor is inspired by the logotherapist Viktor E. Frankl and shown in Figure 9.1. Reminiscent of Plato's metaphor of the caves (chapter 2), imagine that all personal experience is, at best, a dynamic stream of shadows whose illumination comes from the lanterns of emotion (Pirandello, chapter 8). If this is true, what we each "see" (experience) will be dramatically different depending on our position relative to the source of the light. Figure 9.1 offers some simple but extreme illustrations. Note that this figure is forced to resort to the static "symbol fixing" that the philosopher Ernst Cassirer has emphasized. Even though our felt experience of the shadows in everyday life is dynamic and temporal, our symbolic representation of distinctions and patterns in those experiences hinges on central or core organizing stabilities. In figure 9.1 the cone, the cube, and the sphere—which might well represent the primitive and perfect "universal forms" of Plato, Aristotle, and (dynamically) Kant— must be freeze-framed in two-dimensional contrasts. Even so, the point is that the contrasts and forms of what we experience are significantly related to our infinitely unique individual perspectives.

Over the past few decades there has been growing acknowledgment

Figure 9.1   An Illustration of Different Views Depending on Vantage Points

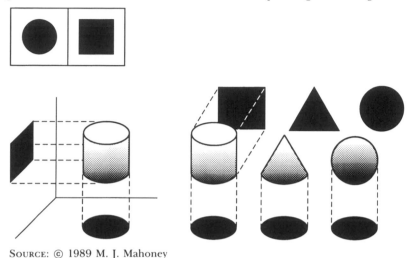

Source: © 1989 M. J. Mahoney

that the quality of personal experience and changes in the patterns of that experience are fundamentally expressed in *individual* activities. To reiterate, all psychological changes involve changes in personal meanings, and the emphasis here is on the very personal part of those meanings and changes. Born of and constrained by its social and intimate contexts, the self system is now being recognized as a powerful moderator of all aspects of learning and development. This core insight, which deserves more elaboration than I can here offer, is why self psychology may be the single most important (r)evolution in recent theoretical psychology. But that insight has also spawned a variety of expressions and practices. Not surprisingly, the psychotherapies of the self have reflected a variety of theories about the nature of the self and the nature of self disorders.

Psychotherapies of Self Deficiency and Ego Defense

Although the works of William James and Mary Whiton Calkins preceded Freud's ventures into the ego defense mechanisms, Freud and his conceptual heirs were pioneers in the psychotherapy of the self. With rare exceptions, that psychotherapy has been based in a "deficiency and defense" metatheory of human nature and psychological functioning. In essence, that metatheory contends that psychological distress and dysfunction are the result (and ongoing expression) of (1) structural deficiencies (or weaknesses) in personality (with emphasis on the ego or self); and (2) an imbalancing prevalence of psychological "defense mechanisms" that suppress experience patterns (especially those involving identity, emotional [motivational] intensity, and potentially dangerous impulses to action).

Although it could be illustrated in half a dozen different expressions, the centrality of deficiency/defense assumptions is particularly apparent in the self psychology of the late Heinz Kohut. For Kohut, the nucleus of psychopathology lay in structural defects and deficiencies in the self. Defensive and compensatory processes were said to drive and lead the person in two directions: the guilt-ridden pursuit of pleasure; and the "tragic" (albeit creative) attempt to move "beyond the pleasure principle" and to manifest the patterns of a core or "nuclear" self. A "tension arc" is said to connect these bipolar aspects of the self, with the person being "driven" by pleasure-seeking ambitions and simultaneously "led" by their ideals. Kohut was respectful of his psychoanalytic heritage even though he was eager to differentiate his theory from that of Freud. He made a point not to affirm Freud's famous dictum, for example, that the analytic approach is defined by an acknowledgment of resistance and transference. Like Freud, however, Kohut was resistant to the idea that his own self or personality entered into his psychological services: "I have not been able to find indubitable evidence of the influence my own personality may have had on an analysand's available choices" (1977, p. 263). Likewise, although he wrote from a more explicitly "self-healing" perspective than Freud and relied less on conflict resolution as the mechanism of change, Kohut's approach was still decidedly "corrective," and he shared a fundamental pessimism about the possibility of fully transcending or transforming self-defects.

Modern psychotherapies of the self are still prevalently psychodynamic, and most psychodynamic therapies continue to express an allegiance to the deficiency and defense metatheory. Freud was not particularly optimistic about the potential power of such therapies, but, then again, neither was he keen on singing the praises of human nature or human potential. As Ernest Becker put it powerfully in *The Denial of Death* (1973), Freud believed in the necessity of illusions and the inevitability of neurosis. Such are the consequences of the unmanageable conflicts that confront every conscious existence. The resolution of conflict, the discharge of affect, and the reinvestment (shift) of psychic energy are the metaphors that permeate psychodynamic formulations of human change processes. Because those processes are themselves embedded in repetitive patterns of human relating, it is in the context of their relationship to the psychotherapist that clients "relive," "rework," and resolve their personal history and current experience of conflicts.

Conceptual rivalries among modern psychodynamic theorists and practitioners have centered on (1) fundamental assumptions about the plasticity of the self, (2) the relative strength of tendencies toward progressive versus regressive development, and (3) optimal therapeutic conditions—especially the nature and development of the "working alliance" and "transference/countertransference" relationships (Levine and Kravis 1987; Pine 1989; Young-Eisendrath and Hall 1987). The followers of Alfred Adler, Karen Horney, Otto Kernberg, Heinz Kohut, and James F. Masterson, for example, are at odds with one another about the nature of structural deficiencies and the centrality of conflict in explaining individual differences in identity development and psychological functioning. As we saw in earlier discussions, these differences have reflected important differentiations in theories of the self and the understanding of its disorders. In his proposed distinction between "real" and "false selves," for example, Masterson (1988) epitomizes some of these differences by portraying the former as almost ideally healthy and the latter as pathologically defended.*

The Behavioral Self-Control Therapies

As has been documented elsewhere, the concept of and clinical demand for practical suggestions about "self-control" were major factors influencing the development of clinical behavior therapy, cognitive behavior modification, and the cognitive psychotherapies (Bandura 1969, 1977, 1986; Mahoney 1974, 1990*b;* Mahoney and Arnkoff 1978; Meichenbaum 1977). Briefly stated, after the publication of Joseph Wolpe's (1958) volume, clinical behavior therapy accelerated its movement in the direction of outpatient services. One of the first practical issues that had to be addressed, however, was that clients had to be enlisted as "engineers" of their own contingencies in their everyday environments. To their credit, behavior therapists realized that some of the most important changes in a client's life would take place outside the official fifty-minute hour. These therapists began encouraging their clients to learn behavior principles and to engineer the stimuli and contingencies in their lives according to their desires for changing behaviors. Meanwhile, people like Lloyd Homme and Joseph Cautela were sneaking thoughts and other cognitive events into the behavioral purview by conceptualizing them as "coverants" (covert operants) and "covertly conditioned" (mediational) responses. These early insights and explorations on the part of clinical behavior therapists served a valuable role in shaping modern theory and research on the phenomenon of self-control.

*The *real self* is said to be (1) capable of deeply experiencing a wide range of feelings; (2) expectant of "appropriate entitlements"; (3) assertive and capable of self-activation; (4) high in self-esteem; (5) self-comforting; (6) capable of commitments; (7) creative; (8) capable of intimacy; (9) able to be alone; and (10) confident of its own continuity (Masterson 1988, pp. 42–46). The *false self* is said to be opposite on all of these because its primary purpose is not adaptation but defense: "In other words, the false self does not set out to master reality but to avoid painful feelings, a goal it achieves at the cost of mastering reality" (p. 23). Note the hint of objectivism in this contrast.

As self-control became a more common and valued focus of both research and practice, however, it began to blend into areas generally associated with the cognitive sciences. Clinical behavior therapists, for example, recognized that it was important for clients to "rehearse" or "practice" their developing skills in contexts and roles similar to those that prevail at the edges of current performance. Since it was often impractical or impossible to simulate *in vivo* more than a small fraction of real-life challenges, behavior therapists began to rely more and more on simulating them in imagination and "associating" them with different imaginary consequences. It was here, in the practical contexts of human services, that "cognitive clinical" approaches made some of their most important contributions.

Although early behavior therapists were insistent on labeling everything they did as "behavioral" (as, of course, it was), their increasing reliance on imagery and other private events brought them into increasing contact with the very domain that John B. Watson and B. F. Skinner had stridently disempowered. Moreover, as emotion theorists and experiential psychotherapists would later point out (chapter 8), psychoanalysts and behaviorists may have offered different rationales and diverse rituals for their counsel, but both ended up converging on the power of "corrective emotional experiences" in the service of adaptation. On important dimensions, then, behavioral, experiential, psychoanalytic, and cognitive viewpoints have each offered valuable contributions to an integrative understanding of the (un)changing self.

In its most orthodox forms, of course, applied behaviorism has not acknowledged the concept of the self, let alone its lifespan processes. And, even in the more liberal forms of clinical behavior therapy, the self has remained an object of control much more than a subjective experiential process—as is also true of some of the cognitive therapies.

Cognitive and Developmental Self Therapies

It is more than coincidence that the modern cognitive psychotherapies have also converged on the primacy of the self and the power of emotions. The different theories and techniques associated with those therapies have also reflected a range of assumptions about what the self is and how it is involved in therapeutic considerations. Although there are other dimensions on which they could be grouped and contrasted, I believe that the different emphases and actions of rationalist and constructivist approaches are particularly noteworthy. For reasons (and feelings) already discussed, rationalist psychotherapists (be they cognitive, behavioral, or otherwise) tend to operate from an authority-based (justificational) perspective (chapter 2). Such a perspective essentially "authorizes" or "justifies" their practices, which tend to be ("rationally") "interventional" (corrective, instrumental, manipulative, therapeutic). More often than not, psychotherapies based in a rationalist-interventionist tradition are also teleological (goal-directed), ahistorical, and homeostatic (that is, they pursue a return to a static, rather than dynamic, equilibrium).

My opinions and evaluations of the rationalist and constructivist contrast have already been elaborated. If I am to be identified with reference points in that contrast, I prefer those that do not presume to base in or build from unquestioned authorities (be they reason, research, or revealed truths). With the evolutionary epistemologists, I prefer to place my fallible faiths in the questing and questioning processes that constitute all exploratory behavior. Such a perspective does not presume to "justify" its principles or practices in dogma, even though it respects the probability that wisdom is embedded in tradition. In my understanding of them, evolutionary, constructivist, and developmental perspectives welcome the dynamically (im)balancing activities that challenge their differentiation and development. Such views also lean toward the empowerment of the organism in its exchanges with its mediums, and I endorse that inclination when it remains at the self-examining ("critical") rather than self-sufficing ("radical") end of the power curve (chapter 5). In contrast to its more rationalist counterparts, such an approach is teleonomic (directed, but not by a single, explicit goal), thoroughly historical and socioculturally sensitive, and homeorhetic (developmental: dynamically self-organizing).

Needless to say, rationalist and constructivist psychotherapies also differ in their practical strategies (table 9.3). While the former tend to be corrective in emphasis, the latter are more cautious about prescribing simple solutions to life problems—as is particularly the case when issues of the self are involved. Briefly stated, rationalist psychotherapies generally emphasize the ("rational") control of self by means of ritualized techniques. Intense and undesired emotions are often assumed to constitute the client's problem(s), and the modification and manipulation of those emotions is a central goal in psychotherapy. This is to be contrasted with the constructivist acknowledgment of lifelong self ("organizing") processes, which are fundamentally embodied and experiential. From the constructivist perspective, intense emotions are powerful allies in and expressions of the individual's past and unfolding development.

Because later discussions include illustrations of some techniques employed by constructivist psychotherapists (see chapters 11, 12), I shall defer further elaboration until then. Suffice it to say here that, in my opinion, much of the promise of the modern constructivist movement lies in its willingness to address—both theoretically and in lived-life pragmatics—the complexities and constraints as well as the possibilities and sanctities of the human self in process. It will be here, I believe, in exploring

Table 9.3 Differences Between Rationalist and Constructivist Cognitive Psychotherapies

| Philosophical and Theoretical Differences | | | Practical Differences | | |
Issue or Area	Rationalist View	Constructivist View	Issue or Theme	Rationalist View	Constructivist View
Ontology (the nature of reality)	Realism-reality is singular, stable, and external.	Relativism-realities are individual and collective constructions of order in experience.	Intervention emphasis	(a) ahistorical (b) problem-focused (c) control-focused (d) teleological	(a) historical (b) process-focused (c) development-focused (d) telenomic
Epistemology (theories of knowing)	Rationalism-knowledge is authorized as valid by logic or reason; reality is revealed via the senses.	Constructivism-knowing is behavioral and emotional as well as cognitive; the validity of knowledge is less important than its viability; sensation is proactive.	Conceptualization of problems	Problems are deficits, dysfunctions, or their emotional correlates; they should be redressed, controlled, or eliminated.	Problems are current and recurrent discrepancies between challenges and capacities; they reflect limits in current affordances and should not be mistaken for their abstract ordering processes.

Table 9.3   (Continued)

| Philosophical and Theoretical Differences | | | Practical Differences | | |
Issue or Area	Rationalist View	Constructivist View	Issue or Theme	Rationalist View	Constructivist View
Causal processes (theories of causality or change)	Associationism—learning and change are linear chains of discrete causes and effects.	Structural differentiation—learning and development involve refinements and transformations of self-organizing processes.			
Basic functions of human nervous system	To control and direct action and feeling via valid mental representations.	To order and organize experience via viable self-organizing processes.	Conceptualization of affect	Affect, especially intense and negative, is the problem; irrational and unrealistic cognitions are its cause.	Affect expresses a primitive and powerful form of knowing; emotional experience, expression, and exploration should be encouraged.

Table 9.3 (Continued)

Issue or Area	Philosophical and Theoretical Differences		Issue or Theme	Practical Differences	
	Rationalist View	Constructivist View		Rationalist View	Constructivist View
Nature of representation	Representations are accurate copies that correspond to the "real" world.	Representations are predominantly tacit, dynamic constructions of order that constrain but do not specify plans of action.	Resistance	Resistance reflects (a) lack of motivation, (b) ambivalence, or (c) motivated avoidance. Resistance is an impediment to therapeutic change and must be "overcome."	Resistance reflects natural self-protective processes that guard systemic integrity and resist rapid or substantial "core" change. Resistance should be worked with rather than against.
Body-brain relationship	Cerebral primacy: the brain leads, and the body follows.	Somatopsychic unity: body and brain are inseparable and interdependent.	Relapse and regression	These phenomena reflect failures in maintenance and generalization which should be avoided and minimized.	These phenomena reflect limits in current capacities or cycles (or spirals) in psychological development; they involve important opportunities for learning.

Table 9.3   (Continued)

	Philosophical and Theoretical Differences			Practical Differences	
Issue or Area	Rationalist View	Constructivist View	Issue or Theme	Rationalist View	Constructivist View
Cognition-behavior-affect relationship	Rational supremacy: "higher" intellectual processes can and should direct feelings and actions.	Holism: thought, feeling, and action are structurally and functionally inseparable.	Insight and metacognition	Insight into irrational and unrealistic beliefs is necessary and (almost) sufficient for therapeutic change.	Insight may help to transform personal meanings and scaffold change, but emotional and behavioral enactments are also very important.
Nature of emotionality	Emotions as problems: negative and intense affects are to be controlled or eliminated.	Emotions as primitive, powerful knowing processes: disorder and affective intensity are natural elements of development.	The therapeutic relationship	The therapeutic relationship entails technical instruction and guidance.	The therapeutic relationship entails a safe, caring, and intense context in and from which the client can explore and develop different relationships with self and world.

the dance of personal and collective (and, importantly, intersubjective) processes, that we are most likely to refine the tone of our questions.

Transpersonal Therapies of the Self

As I have said, most modern transpersonal approaches reflect a strong commitment to or legacy from Buddhist philosophy. One of the primary goals of psychotherapy based in Buddhist doctrine is to move beyond and transcend those stages of human development that are preoccupied with identity or ego. According to the transpersonal perspective developed by Roger Walsh, Frances Vaughan, and their colleague Ken Wilber, for example, the path toward personal development is the same as that involved in spiritual enlightenment: it is "the path of no self." The individual is encouraged to "disidentify" from both external and internal views of self, including all roles, activities, possessions, achievements, and relationships. Such detachment or transcendence involves a kind of "ego death." When this is successfully achieved, the individual is said to be less interested in their "personal melodrama," and his or her identity is expanded to encompass "the I that is We" (Moss 1981).

Jack Engler was the first to note an apparent cross-cultural paradox in Buddhist and psychoanalytic views. He noted, for example, that Buddhist psychology has generally viewed the self or ego as an obstacle to personal development, whereas psychoanalytic writers have considered the deficiencies or conflicts of the ego as their primary therapeutic focus. The lack of a sense of self is considered a serious psychological disorder by psychoanalysts, while "the deepest psychopathological problem from the Buddhist perspective is the *presence* of a self and the feeling of selfhood" (1986, p. 24). As a result, Buddhist (and transpersonal) counselors attempt to foster transcendence of ego issues, while their psychoanalytic colleagues have sought to strengthen the ego. These appear to be opposite strategies, with one group aiming at experiences of "no self" and the other intent on elaborating and stabilizing experiences of a coherent self. While there are, indeed, differences between the two approaches, there are also important areas of convergence.

This last point is illustrated in reports by Engler, Daniel Brown, and others regarding the frequency with which persons struggling with "borderline personality disorder," for example, often arrive at Buddhist workshops and retreats with the illusion that they have already attained considerable enlightenment. The experience of "no self" is common among these persons, and they may be understandably drawn to workshops that encourage it. However, as Engler and others have emphasized, the experience of a stable sense of self is a precondition for transcending that experience and achieving a genuine (and healthy) experience of no self. To put it tersely, *"you have to be somebody before you can be nobody"* (Engler

1986, p. 24). Thus, the two approaches are described as complementary rather than in conflict. The borderline individual is said to require first the conditions and experiences that will help one strengthen and organize one's experience of self. Only when this is achieved (usually after considerable time and effort) is the individual ready to explore the disidentification processes fostered in Buddhist and transpersonal psychologies.

CONCLUSIONS

It is in discussions of identity and selfhood that we at last find ourselves close to home—though still moving, of course. The reason is that all experience ultimately springs from the realm of the self (as in the metaphor of *home*), and that here its possibilities and limitations are determined. It is here that we finally come to realize that all *"living systems contain their own descriptions"* (Pattee 1977, p. 259), and that those descriptions are always in the process of being regenerated and revised. This lifelong activity and reflexivity generate what Vittorio Guidano has aptly termed a *Complexity of the Self* (1987). We have, I believe, just begun to risk imagining some of the dynamics and complexities that both stabilize and destabilize lives in process.

As I have emphasized in the preceding chapters, there is a distinctly personal and emotionally embodied core to human experience. That experience is a dynamic mixture of reflective and unreflective activity, with the behavior of the individual integrally related to his or her "working models" (current personal realities) of self and world. The *élan vital* ("life force") the vitalists proposed is a powerful organic metaphor that captures important aspects of the oscillating "opponent processes" in our spontaneous self-organization. But even more significant is our dawning realization that the self and system are not only interactive and co-constructive but also developmentally dynamic, especially with regard to the changing shape and substance of their boundaries. At the psychological level, the lifelong becoming of a human self is complexly interpersonal and intrapersonal.

One's identity development is not only inseparable from one's past and present human intimacies but, moreover, inseparable from all of those "related" lives that participate in the lives that most significantly influence our own. Hence, we cannot help but be affected at some levels by the births, deaths, marriages, illnesses, triumphs, and ambiguities in the lives of extended families, friends, and other life cohorts. The existential bell does, indeed, toll for thee, me, and the collective we. And, while we may be "all one" in this inescapable connection, we are also "al'one" (alone) in the individuality of our phenomenal lives. More than in any other area of recent scientific and scholarly focus, the roaming realm of the self has shown itself to be connected with the history of ideas (and the idea of histories), human embodiment, emotional experience, phenomenology, the dialectics of human interaction, and the eternal confluence of epistemology (how we know), ontology (what we try to know), and individual "intersubjectivity" (the uniquely personal and yet pervasively interpersonal human knower and knowing processes). At least part of what seems to be unfolding in this, the third axial shift, is a shift from identifying exclusively with emotions (as in the ages of Anxiety, Anger, or Despair) to a more extensive and developmental identification with the dynamics of self and system. We can hope, of course, that an Age of Peace and Self/Planet Responsibility will be among the benefits of that shift.

Our long journey through the history of ideas, experimental psychology, cognitive science, and the nuances of a developmental and co-constructive "evolutionary epistemology"—this undeniably challenging journey has finally brought us back upon ourselves. "We have met the enemy," Walt Kelly said, "and they is us." The question is whether they/we can also be allies, and what the the implied fighting is all about. It is in the conjoint dynamics of individual patterns of psychological stabilization and destabilization processes that one can discern important lessons from diverse theoretical perspectives. The genius of both Freud and Piaget, for example, was reflected in (1) their recognition of the relations between structure and function; (2) their acknowledgment that, as Pierre Janet had proposed, dissociation and emotional defense play important roles in adaptation (Piaget discussed such detachment as "decentering"); and (3) their assertion that proactive processes are biased in the direction of maintenance rather than change of the system (that is, the priority of "fixation," resistance, and "assimilation" over chaotic instability and runaway "accommodation"). The quest for a comprehensive theory of identity development has, of course, become a central preoccupation of theorists and therapists of the last few decades.

As earlier discussions have illustrated, each self is a unique epistemic ("knowing") and experiential process, most saliently exhibited in individual patterns of affect, meaning construction, and action. Like Pirandello's lantern of feeling, self-related emotionality lights a path of embodied experience, the vast majority of which is unreflective and therefore outside of awareness. This is the *Lebenswelt* that Husserl emphasized: "the immediate flow of unreflective life, . . . the world as we actually live it" (Madison 1988, p. 44). Like a spontaneous projector of different light forms and frequencies, such a self process formidably constrains and construes the reflections of its own castings. It is an ever-present but invisible navigator or sculptor in a lifelong journey or project. As such, it is seen mostly in its own wake or works, or in its rare glimpses of its own imaginative powers.

As Freud realized, what may first develop as self-defensive patterns sometimes become self-handicapping or self-destructive in the context of later life circumstances. He leaned toward a self-effacing view of human nature, however, and left it to the humanists and self/ego theorists (especially Adler, Fromm, and Horney and their modern inheritors) to develop more balanced views of self-protection and self-elaboration in the dynamics of ongoing adaptation.

III

PSYCHOTHERAPY:
PRINCIPLES,
TECHNIQUES, AND
EXPERIENCES

10

✠✠✠✠✠✠✠✠✠✠✠✠✠

Principles of Developmental Psychotherapy

Two strangers meet by prearrangement; their purpose, to wrestle with life itself; their goal, to win from deadness more life for one of them; their risk, that one or both of them will find life filled with pain and anxiety for some period of time; their certainty, that if they persist in good faith with their struggle both will be changed in some measure.

—James F. T. Bugental

With this chapter I begin the transition from theory and research to practice. It will be here that we harvest some of the most important practical lessons from my earlier surveys of the history of ideas, the cognitive sciences, evolutionary studies, complex phenomena, human lifespan development, emotionality, and psychology of the self. Contributions to our understanding of human change processes from each of these areas can now be interwoven with existing theory and research in psychotherapy. Although I shall not here attempt to review or critique the extensive literatures dealing with psychotherapy process and outcome, I will, in presenting some working principles of human development and human helping, draw extensively from the writings of psychotherapy researchers, theorists, and practitioners. As will be apparent, I strongly believe that all three of these groups embody important parts of the other two. My primary goal in this chapter is to suggest a working conceptual system—a metatheoretical base—for construing and enacting the practice of psychotherapy. In doing so, of course, I cannot help but impose my own constructions and values on that system. The leap from theory and research to training and practice is always more than a matter of linear or logical translation (and vice versa). Fortunately valuable examples of versatile bridges are already available.*

First, some prefatory comments on the nature of theory, the complexities of eclecticism, and the dangers of technolatry. As to the nature of theory, I simply note that explanation is a complex concept requiring much more than the description of patterns. I shall defer on the technicalities involved and simply state that what is presented here is neither a formal, explanatory theory nor an explicit physical model of human change processes. It is a system of conjectures toward "working principles" that may merit use in our continuing efforts to develop such theories and models. As Hayek, Weimer, and others have made very clear, our best investments of hope and activity with regard to theoretical (and, I believe, therapeutic) psychology lie in the domain of general principles rather than in the prediction and attempted control of any given particulars (Hayek 1952a, 1952b; 1964, 1978; Weimer 1979, 1980, 1987). What this means for the practice of psychotherapy is that we can hope for and contribute to an ongoing refinement of general principles that bear on the delivery of optimal professional services, but we should not expect (or, I believe, desire) an explicit "operating manual" that dictates correct conduct for all clients, under any circumstances, and at every point in time.

This moves us closer to the complexities of eclecticism and the dangers of *technolatry* (technique worship). In the tradition of Cicero, its Roman founder (chapter 2), eclecticism is an "instantiation" of a fundamental evolutionary mechanism: diversify and select. Cicero chose not to join any single "school of thought" but, instead, to study them all and select the "best features" of each. As we saw in chapter 1, eclecticism is now the most popular label used by U.S. psychologists to describe their theoretical orientation. Not surprisingly, there is considerable diversity among the eclectics themselves (Jensen, Bergin, and Greaves 1990). Some prefer the connotations of the term *integration* over those of *eclecticism*, since the latter has sometimes been used to imply being unprincipled or lacking commitment. Moreover, there has been debate about "types" of eclecticism, with *technical eclecticism* sometimes connoting an expedient borrowing of techniques rather than a coherent integration of theoretical assumptions. With Stanley B. Messer (1986), C. H. Patterson (1989), and others, I do not believe in the possibility of purely "atheoreti-

---

*Some of my favorite bridges have been engineered by Frank 1973, 1987; Friedman 1988; Garfield and Bergin 1978, 1986; Greenberg and Safran 1987, 1989; Kiesler 1966, 1973; Lazarus and Davison 1971; Rice and Greenberg 1984; and Strupp 1986, 1989.

For discussions of the valuable traffic across such bridges, see Barrom, Shadish, and Montgomery 1988; Cohen, Sargent, and Sechrest 1986; Conway 1988; Gaston and Marmar 1989; Hoshmand 1989; Jacob 1987; Keeley, Shemberg, and Zaynor 1988; Martin 1989; Morrow-Bradley and Elliott 1986; Phillips 1989; Shemberg, Keeley, and Blum 1989; Stricker and Keisner 1985; and Zeig 1987.

cal" practice. No matter how diversified and flexible the practitioner may be, he or she cannot help but operate out of assumptions about human nature and the nature of psychological change processes. Our selections (of clients, techniques, and theories) are neither random nor irrelevant, and we are wise to examine the patterns and preferences in our ongoing choices.

Finally, let me be clear that I am not against technique; I am against technolatry. Since the next chapter is almost exclusively devoted to discussions of techniques and exercises that may be useful in the practice of psychotherapy, I am hardly a "radical non-interventionist." Techniques are meaningful rituals of communication, human relatedness, awareness, and self-influence. In psychotherapy and personal development projects, they are the enactments of life seeking life. My aversion, if such it be, is to the mistaken empowerment of the technique rather than to its enactor(s). This point will be elaborated in chapter 11, but is included here to register caution about interpreting what follows as the "right," "best," "correct," or "only" ways to conceptualize and attempt to facilitate human development. Although I will draw from my clients' and my own experiences as illustrations, I shall not present detailed "case histories" and elaborate descriptions of practical exercises. Those are more appropriate for another project.

My discussion continues now with a brief acknowledgment of tacit assumptions and then a review of the three basic questions introduced at the beginning of the book. This will be followed by working descriptions of some general principles of human development and human helping. Selected exercises for assessing and facilitating psychological development will be presented in chapter 11. Chapter 12 will focus on the *personal* experience of change and what it may teach us about our understandings and services as mental health practitioners. Finally, chapter 13 will conclude this narrative with a return to the point from which I began in chapter 1: the realm of the self, this time with special emphasis on the self of the professional helper.

TACIT ASSUMPTIONS ABOUT HUMAN NATURE

All theories of human change contain implicit assumptions about human nature. These conceptual stowaways are our "hidden human images" (Friedman 1967, 1974). They are not images in the sense of clear and explicit depictions, however. Rather, they are tacit and generative rules for *constructuring* our experiences and embodying our trial-and-error efforts at surviving and becoming. Reflecting our deepest hopes and fears about ourselves, humanity, and the human condition, these implicit images constitute the hidden ground in which literature, philosophy, psychotherapy, religion, and social thought all meet. The human image might well be called the matrix from which each of these fields emerges, which they continue to embody within them, and which continues to bind them together in essential ways. (Friedman 1974, p. 10)

The importance of these tacit rules for our understanding and facilitation of human development is not difficult to imagine, although I suspect that we have yet to appreciate fully their extent and power in our lives and in our professional counsel. They constrain not only our sense of *who* and *how* we are, but also our aspirations and apprehensions about future possibilities—who and how we can (and cannot) be.

The relative validity of our diverse human images is less pertinent here than is the recognition that our tacit assumptions about human nature unquestionably influence how we view and serve individuals who seek psychological services. Table 10.1, for example, summarizes some of the differences and similarities among modern metatheories with regard to their views of human nature and other concepts related to human change processes. Needless to say, studies of what we mean by "human nature" are themselves in their infancy, and we have only begun to appreciate the fact that our would-be facts in this realm are themselves necessary arte-facts of our questions and methods of inquiry (Ford 1987; Gilbert 1989; Stevenson 1981). Scholarly documentation of the influence of gender-role biases, historical contexts, and cultural traditions is now extensive. Thus, the relativity of our understanding and the diversity of our questions, methods, and views should be kept in mind as we return to the three basic questions that underlie all psychological services.

RECASTING SOME BASIC QUESTIONS

Recall the assumptions on which all psychological and educational services rest: (1) that humans can, in fact, change; (2) that humans can help other humans change; and (3) that some forms of helping are more effective than others in encouraging or facilitating that change. These seemingly simple assumptions have spawned vast literatures in counseling, education, psychiatry, psychology, and social work. Although this book has been organized around the questioning of those assumptions, it has also invited a deeper appreciation of the complexities invoked by those simple-sounding questions. Based on the literatures surveyed in the preceding chapters and the existing research on psychotherapy process and outcome, I propose that each of those questions can be responsibly answered in the affirmative, but that each affirmation requires some qualifications.

Table 10.1 Theoretical Views on Selected Issues in Psychological Change

		Human Nature	Plasticity	Power	Self	Adaptation	Change Process
Psychoanalytic	Orthodox	Fundamentally negative; dominated by biological impulses (e.g., sex and aggression).	Very limited after sixth year.	Psychic determinism makes the individual primarily an effect, rather than a cause, in development.	Equated with "ego," the "reality" checker that coordinates id and superego.	The progressive domination of ego (and superego) over id.	Emotionally charged "reliving" and "undoing" combine with insight in the social context of transference.
	Neodynamic	Neutral to positive; self and social needs can transcend biological.	Limited but not insignificant.	A sense of power can develop if needs for other people are balanced with needs for separation and individuation.	The separate-but-related individual 'self' is the central point of differentiation from orthodox psycho-analysis.	The ongoing dynamic balance of self-system integrity and social sensitivity/responsibility.	"Corrective emotional experiences" override deficient or dysfunctional lessons about the integrity of self and social system.

Table 10.1 　(Continued)

		Human Nature	Plasticity	Power	Self	Adaptation	Change Process
Behavioral	Radical	Neutral to negative; human nature *is* biological conditionability.	Virtually unlimited and lifelong.	All power for change rests in power to change environmental contingencies.	A mentalistic concept devoid of meaning.	Behavioral conformity to environmental contingencies.	Conditioning (classical and operant).
	Liberal	Neutral to positive; human nature is not a central topic.	Considerable, but sometimes limited by genetic variables and learning history.	Variable, depending on individual's skills in "behavioral self-management."	A problematic domain in which the subject and object of "behavior technology" are the same.	Compliance with environmental and "self-regulated" contingencies.	Conditioning, with "covert" or private events involved in chained associations.
Humanistic	Naturalist	Neutral to positive; emphasizes the "natural science" analysis of human characteristics.	Considerable, with emphasis on social, symbolic, and scientific teachings.	Considerable, usually via rational reflection and social reform.	An important domain dictated by the social context of human development.	The balancing of individual and collective needs.	Reason (scientific) combined with social influence.
	Spiritualist	Positive, with some varieties linking human nature with godliness.	Virtually infinite; perhaps immortal.	Extensive, although many individuals fail to appreciate or exercise their own potential.	An important domain, with "local self" reflecting a universal "larger Self."	The integration of individual and collective expressions of Being.	Spiritual experiences "awaken" the individual to greater meanings and potentials.

Table 10.1   *(Continued)*

		Human Nature	Plasticity	Power	Self	Adaptation	Change Process
Cognitive	Rationalist	Neutral to positive; intellect and reason elevate humanity over other life forms.	Virtually infinite within the limits of reason.	Extensive, via "rational restructuring" of personal meanings.	An important domain of reflective "self-talk."	Rational compliance with existing rules for survival.	Rational restructuring.
	Constructivist	Neutral to positive; emphasis is on lifelong *activity*.	Considerable, but with individual limits.	Considerable within the contexts that constrain individual development.	An essential domain of development that constrains all others.	The ongoing coordination of individual activity with changing opportunities and constraints.	"Deep structure" differentiation results from trial and error efforts to maintain or regain dynamic equilibrium.

Can Humans Change?

Yes, humans can change, *but* there are also constraints on human plasticity, and we are just beginning to appreciate the nature of some of those constraints. Indeed, as we saw in chapter 2, the history of human ideas is itself a history of change, with contrasts and differentiations emerging out of revered traditions in our questioning processes. It is not just ideas that have changed over the centuries. The people expressing those ideas have also been changing, and many of their ideas have reflected the ongoing openness of humanity at both personal and collective (intersubjective) levels. Various ideological "movements" of the past and present century leave little doubt that individuals and communities can and do exhibit remarkable capacities for action, organization, resilience, and creativity: witness, for example, the movements variously labeled "human rights," "women's," "peace," "freedom," "ecology," and "health." With the emphasis on physical activity in the last, we are currently living in what future writers may well describe as the "movement movement," perhaps an appropriate label for an age when change has come to be recognized as the rule as much as the exception.

From the material presented in chapters 1 and 3, it is also clear that psychologists are among those humans most clearly exhibiting the capacity to change. Besides the dynamics of shifting theoretical allegiances, psychologists' changes have included a deepening appreciation for the difficulties and complexities of change itself. Our changing views of human learning and knowing reflect shifts in our "human images," suggesting that simple, mechanical, and explicit (computational) metaphors have become less interesting than their complex, organic, and abstract alternatives.

It was, in fact, in the literatures of constructivism, evolution, and human development (chapters 5-7) that the significance of some of these shifts began to exhibit their potential relevance for psychotherapy theory and practice.

Yet another qualified affirmation of the human capacity for change is rendered in current studies of human development. Psychological plasticity is particularly apparent in infancy, childhood, and adolescence, but it is also unmistakably exhibited by many individuals at much later stages of the life cycle. The traditional dichotomies and debates continue, of course. Averaging across large samples, basic personality patterns have been described as relatively stable across the lifespan (Costa and McCrae 1988a, 1988b). At the same time, however, there is evidence to suggest that some "elders" are still learning and developing well into their eighth and ninth decades. Even though early experiences may render a person vulnerable to or constrained by some life patterns, the capacity to change remains considerable. The life stories of those we now label "resilient," "hardy," and "survivors" have offered inspiring illustrations of this point. Change may not be easy, but its presumed impossibility has been repeatedly disconfirmed.

Finally, the literatures on emotionality and selfhood complement each other in highlighting the pain, possibility, and complexity of significant psychological change (chapters 8 and 9). Studies of human affect and mood, for example, indicate that personal experience is commonly cyclical or rhythmic, and that some kinds of change are associated with relatively intense episodes of emotionality (Apter 1982; Gilbert 1989). It is not coincidental that the modern resurgence of interest in affect has coincided with the (re)discovery of the self. In their valuable analysis of emotional processes in psychotherapy, Greenberg and Safran underscore this parallel: "Emotional experience is integrally linked with personal identity" (1987, p. 167). Changes and continuities in the one are inseparable from changes and continuities in the other. Although we are not the only animals who feel, we are apparently unique in our development of a self-awareness of such feeling. That awareness and that self are a matter more of our "hearts" than of our "heads," but there are promising signs that these domains are becoming significantly less segregated.

As we saw in chapter 9, our perennial debates about human plasticity *are* our debates about human possibility and the malleability of the core ordering processes that characterize a psychological self. The question Can humans change? is ultimately personal and interpersonal: Can you/I/we change? Modern experts render remarkably similar responses to that question (Mahoney and Craine 1988). They agree, for example, that effecting changes in the self is more difficult than it is easy, with psychodynamic and behavioral respondents endorsing the most extreme positions on this issue (figure 10.1). Across theoretical orientations, psychotherapists and psychotherapy researchers also agreed that core dimensions (what I have termed "core ordering processes") are at least moderately difficult to change (figure 10.2). Although they agreed that effecting changes in each of these dimensions was more ethical than not, respondents believed that interventions in the realm of a person's values were generally more ethical than those focused on their sense of self (81.6 percent versus 57.1 percent agreement, respectively).

The question of human plasticity is thus an invitation to further questions and to reappraisals of our basic assumptions about human nature and lifespan psychological development. Bluntly, we are learning that psychological change is neither simple nor easy and yet that it is pervasive and relentless. Humans can and do change in significant ways; they also exhibit important psychological continuities. Moreover, individuals often struggle with the tensions they experience between these simplifying extremes of conceptual reference. Of central importance to psychotherapy practitioners is the realization that the processes underlying human psychological change are nonlinear and complex, thereby preventing

Figure 10.1   Perceived Difficulty of Self System Change by Representatives of Different Theoretical Orientations

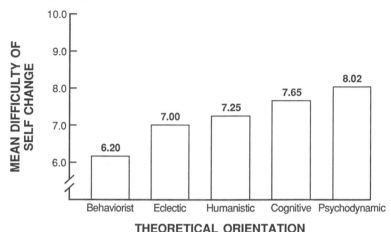

SOURCE: © 1989 M. J. Mahoney

perfect predictions of what will happen to the particulars of any given individual's life. This point is worth remembering as we counsel those we serve. We should be cautious, then, in what we claim to know "for sure" and what we "guarantee" to provide. We should also strive to maintain a balanced awareness of both the problems and the promise of exploring and establishing new experience patterns. As we move toward embracing both the complexities and the possibilities for human psychological change, let us hope that we also move toward more peaceful, self-caring, and socially responsible patterns of participation in the overlapping lives of our selves and our global community.

The issue of human plasticity is clearly complex. It touches upon the puzzles of "intractable" psychological dysfunctions and the "hard work miracles" wrought by individuals who manage to turn tragedy and trauma into triumphs of the spirit. Nor are possibilities for change simply abstract issues to be debated in the arid and lofty climates of disembodied intellectuals. The issue is a real one, and it is faced daily by those who struggle with the limits of their own powers over the patterns of experience that determine their quality of life. This point was powerfully conveyed in an exchange I had with a psychotherapy client almost a decade ago. Karen Z. had sought my services in the hope that she could obtain some relief from chronic and intense depression. In the course of our work together, she reluctantly "discovered" that she had been sexually abused by her father and several of his friends in a series of cruel episodes in her childhood. After months of denial, Karen confronted her mother and family physician: both confirmed that the abuse had occurred. The

Figure 10.2   Transtheoretical Estimates of the Relative Difficulty of Changes in Core Ordering Processes

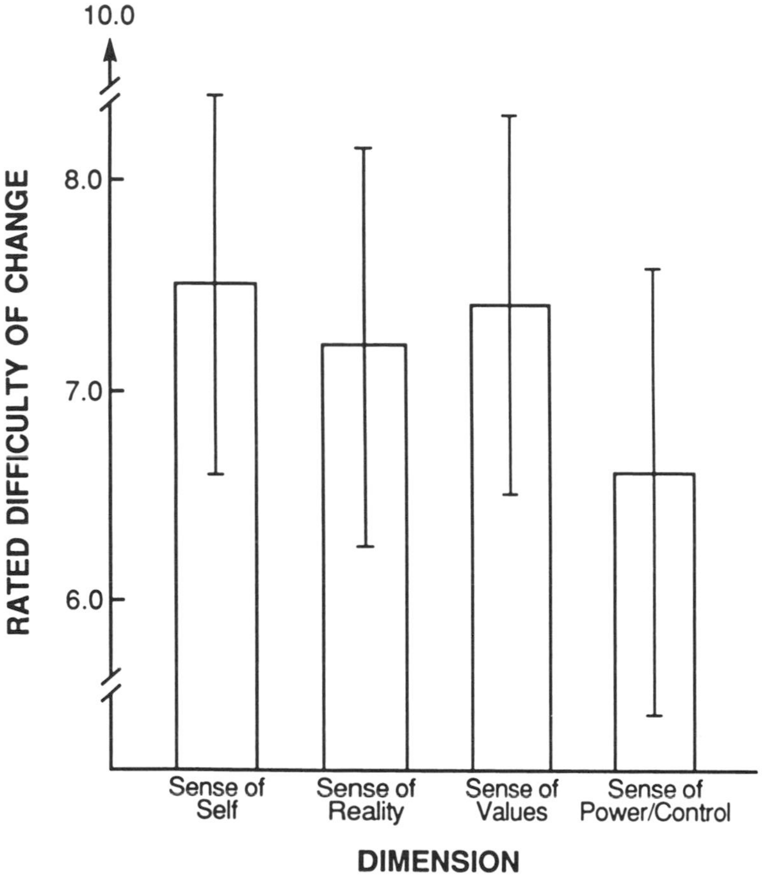

SOURCE: © 1989 M. J. Mahoney

incidents had never before been acknowledged or reported, her father had never been confronted, and she had received no psychological treat- ment—only stitches and tranquilizers.

As these facts began to register with her, Karen struggled to stay "emotionally alive" and to salvage some sense of sanity in the wake of such cruelty, denial, and neglect of her psychological needs. She also began to realize why her marital relationship had long felt painful and hopeless. She had not been able to tolerate even being touched by her husband; their only child had been conceived after he had forced their last intercourse (twelve years earlier). When she informed her husband of her discovery about having been abused as a child, his response was

"So what? That was years ago." She did not try to discuss it with him any further.

Then came a "moment of truth": Karen resolved to honestly assess the damages to her life and to choose how to invest her future energies. Determined to "know where she stood," Karen opened our next session with a direct question: "Mike, how much can I change? I mean, can I change enough to ever have a normal, happy sex life? If my Daddy . . . [she began to cry] . . . if the person who was supposed to keep me safe and protect me did just the opposite . . . so cruelly, and so early . . . [she wiped her eyes and cleared her throat] . . . well, I just want to know what I can hope for. You tell me to be gentle and self-caring with myself. Now tell me straight: would it be better for me to give up on ever having a happy sex life or is it possible to recover from that kind of thing?"

I can still hear her voice and see the intensity in her eyes, and re-member the shadows of guilt I felt as I retreated toward an "aca-demic" (rather than a "therapeutic") response. "Well," I began, "there *are* some experts who would say that you were violated so early and so cruelly that the scars will always be there . . . [she wiped her eyes again] . . . and that you might be better off accepting that." Her head dropped, and she brushed away another tear. "But then again," I added, "there are others who would say that we should never underes-timate the strength and resilience of the human spirit. Some might even say that . . . well, *if* you were able to trust again and to risk shar-ing yourself so intimately with someone, that your happiness in sexual intimacy might be far greater than can be imagined by people who were never abused." She slowly lifted her head, looked into my eyes, and asked, "And which group are *you* in?" I could not evade her di-rectness, and could feel my own heart pounding as I responded. "Karen," I said, "I may be wrong . . . and I could be doing you a disservice to say this . . . but I agree with the second group . . . I believe that many people are stronger and more resilient than we real-ize, and I will not foreclose on the capacities of the human spirit." She smiled nervously and said, "I thought so."

I continued working with Karen for three more years, applying the principles and techniques outlined in this and the next chapter. She traveled a long distance psychologically, filing for divorce, launching a career at midlife, and beginning to explore new social groups and friendships. Karen still drops me a card every year at the holidays. In one of our last contacts—five years since our work together—she in-cluded a little note that simply read, "Remember that question I once asked you about how much I could change? Well, thanks for being honest with me . . . and for believing in the human spirit. You were right!"

Can Humans Help Humans Change?

Yes, humans can help humans change, *but* they can also hinder such change. Even at its best, professional help is limited. Some of those limits are related to the psychological functioning of the human helper (chapter 13), and some lie in the realm of the client and the contexts of his or her living. It is important that we realize that licensed professional helpers with the best of intentions can, at times, act and interact in ways that exacerbate their clients' difficulties. Although negative treatment effects appear to be much less frequent than positive, they are hardly insignificant. The most extensive and striking examples of negative human interaction, however, occur regrettably in the realm of parenting. Neglect, abuse, and rejection are three patterns known to jeopardize the developing child's quality of life. Combined with the positive contributions of attentive nurturance, encouragement, and love, however, the range of parent-child and child-other relationships is remarkable. It is in this realm that the potential impact of humans on one another is unmistakably reflected in the breadth and depth of both their joy and their suffering.

The impact of humans upon humans is, epistemologically, one of the most fascinating and frightening facts of the social and behavioral sciences. That impact is fundamentally related to at least three things: human emotionality, self-reflection, and the use of symbols. Personal values and human relations are permeated with affect, which is the heart of psychological "movement" (motivation and learning). The human role in human change is writ large in the archives of virtually every literature, universally. There are, for example, countless illustrations of how the ideas and teachings of individuals have dramatically influenced later views of humans and their worlds (chapters 2–5). Evolutionary studies (chapter 6) have also emphasized that cultural and "human influence processes" have been much more important than genetics in shaping the problems and promises of the modern individual. These studies have taught us that the human mind is unmistakably interpersonal. The "abstract society" is hardly impersonal: it emphasizes our essential connectedness to one another and, simultaneously, the ultimate recursiveness (reflexivity) of our understanding and activities. When supplemented with the insights derived from studies of human psychological development (chapter 7), two clear statements emerge: emotionally charged human relationships constitute the most powerful contexts in which significant psychological change is facilitated, neglected, or hampered; and relationships with self—which are forged and revised in interpersonal relationships—are central to the quality of an individual's life experience. Together, these assertions reflect the complex and generative reciprocity of self and social system. Out of respect for that complexity and reciprocity, professional services must consistently honor both the individual in the system and the system in the individual.

Humans can and do both help and hinder one another in their efforts to change. On the negative side of this generalization, the incidence and painful consequences of abuse, neglect, and rejection have never been so painfully apparent. On the positive side, it is also evident that intimate human relationships can offer an empowering "secure base" in and from which participants may explore and develop. The more pressing question, then, is not *whether* we can help one another in our respective life navigations, but whether we can learn to more deeply appreciate and develop the kinds and qualities of relationships conducive to such helping. It is clear, for example, that affectively "intimate" relationships are the most powerful in their influence on individual development (chapter 8). Our relatively few "close" relationships (including those with our selves) are the crucibles within which we forge our developing senses of self, world, and their dynamics.

This point was elaborated in my discussion of the fact that human psychological change is integrally related to self-system issues, and that human relatedness plays an important role in self-system development. *Intimacy* (from the Latin *intimare,* meaning "inmost" or "deepest") is not just sexual; it characterizes a wide range of human interactions. These are the relationships that most powerfully (dis)allow and (en/dis)courage changes and stabilizations in self experience and expression. Given the power of these intimate exchanges, it is important to acknowledge the contributions of all parties involved (that is, parent *and* child, therapist *and* client, teacher *and* student). It is, in fact, for this reason that the study and care of the helping professional is such an important priority in our developing understanding of mental health services (chapter 13).

Studies of the psychotherapist's contribution to the therapeutic experience have begun to make it clear that the magnitude of that contribution is exceeded only by that attributable to the client (Bergin and Lambert 1978; Beutler, Crago, and Arizmendi 1986; Garfield 1986; Lafferty, Beutler, and Crago 1989; Lambert 1989; Luborsky et al. 1986; McConnaughy 1987). After their extensive review of the existing literature over a decade ago, Allen Bergin and Michael Lambert concluded that "the largest variation in therapy is accounted for by preexisting client factors, such as motivation. . . . Therapist personal factors account for the second largest proportion of change, with technique variables coming in a distant third" (1978, p. 180). In Lambert's more recent (1989) review of research on this question, even more striking results were obtained. In four major research projects at the University of Pittsburgh, Johns Hopkins University, the Veterans Administration in Pennsylvania, and McGill University, for example, the therapeutic impact attributable to the psychotherapist was eight times greater than that associated with treatment techniques.

The "person" of the therapist, and the "therapeutic alliances" she or he is capable of encouraging and co-creating, are much more central to the quality and effectiveness of professional services than are the specific techniques, explicit interpretations, and theoretical scaffoldings for structuring and enacting the experience of psychotherapy (Claiborn 1982; Eaton, Abeles, and Gutfreund 1988; Horvath and Greenberg 1989; Levy 1963; Linehan 1988; Messer 1988; Natsoulas 1988; Spiegel and Hill 1989; Strupp 1986; Tichenor and Hill 1989; Winstead et al. 1988). The bottom line here is that humans can, indeed, help other humans change. It is the *quality* of their (our) relationships with other humans that most powerfully influences the quality of lives and the pace and direction of developments within them.

Are Some Forms of Helping Better Than Others?

Yes, some forms of helping are better than others, *but* our understanding of those forms, their differences, and their effects is still rudimentary. Despite the ceaseless attacks on psychotherapy (some of which have made important points about that endeavor), it seems increasingly clear that professional psychological services can, indeed, help; and that their helpfulness in reducing various patterns of dysfunction and distress is, on the average, at least moderately better than that of "no treatment." (This conservative accounting does not include the inestimable value of human care, compassion, and companionship during the struggles of personal development.)*

There are many levels at which we may respond to the question regarding "better" forms of helping. To begin with, the question itself invokes a series of unknowns that have to do with what "kinds" of change are really better, for whom, and under what circumstances. Neither we nor our clients are seeking just *any* change. We are particularly interested in fostering change "for the better" and, in the realm of prevention, in minimizing or avoiding change "for the worse." But how are we to know what changes to pursue and whether a given change is really for the better or worse? On what basis do we claim confidence in that knowledge and, pragmatically, what does it mean in terms of our efforts to help? If some forms of helping are better than others, what are they? How and why do they help? How are they best practiced and trained? Under what circumstances are they more and less helpful? These are questions that must be examined continuously by practitioners and researchers alike. Such questions also move us much closer to the challenges inherent in "knowing

*For recent reviews and discussions of this complex issue, see Barker, Funk, and Houston 1988; Elkin et al. 1988*a*, 1988*b;* Garfield and Bergin 1986; Goldfried, Greenberg, and Marmar 1990; Hollon and Flick 1988; Luborsky et al. 1988; Luborsky et al. 1986, 1988; Orlinsky and Howard 1986, 1987; Patterson, 1984; Ryle 1984; Sandell 1987; and Stiles, Shapiro, and Elliott 1986.

how" (to practice, train, supervise) versus "knowing that" (as in knowing that those who "know how" offer better help).

Better is thus an oversimplifying term for a complex set of considerations. Be this as it may, I believe that there is warrant for a qualified yes to the third basic question. Some forms of helping are, indeed, better than others. In terms of individual psychological development, for example, the "best" forms of helping come early in the lifespan. The parent who offers a secure emotional base for the developing child is a powerful and positive influence in that child's later developmental trajectory (Bowlby 1988). Affectionate and responsible parenting contributes immensely to the life quality of the individual and is a key element in the prevention of psychological disorders and dysfunctions. Within the specialized realm of psychotherapy, the facilitation of psychological development is significantly influenced by the "person" (personality, personal development) of the therapist and the quality of the relationship he or she can co-create with clients (Lambert 1989). As I elaborate in the next section, the optimal therapeutic relationship is secure, developmentally flexible, and fundamentally caring. Such a relationship is also sensitively attuned to the individual(s) being served; it is one in which each person's experiences and developmental dynamics are respected.

BASIC PRINCIPLES OF HUMAN PSYCHOLOGICAL CHANGE

Since all theories are "born refuted" (Weimer 1979)—that is, in the presence of evidence and reason that contradict them—the task of the practitioner is neither to avoid theory (which is impossible) nor to identify the "one true system" that can prescribe or guide his or her activities in helping. Rather, the most important task in this realm is to choose a "conceptual base camp" from which to operate while one continues the explorations that constitute "The Work" of learning to comfort and to facilitate development. Such a base camp must, I believe, be pliable, portable, and itself capable of development, so that one's deep-felt commitments can be anchored in its abstractions while, simultaneously, one's unfinished lessons can be pursued within its moving expanse. This is a tall order, to be sure, and entails the dynamic complementarity of stability and change that has permeated this book.

In the pages that follow I shall outline, as best I can, the base camp from which I now operate in my clinical work. I do not claim it to be true, valid, or better than its alternatives. It has been helpful to me and, I believe, to those who have most powerfully influenced its development (my clients). A large part of its utility, I believe, stems from its inherently developmental nature. This being the case, I shall be both surprised and disappointed if the following system of principles does not develop in unforeseen ways in the future.

My narrative is organized around two related themes which are summarized as general principles of human psychological development (see pages 268–69) and general principles of human helping (see pages 270–71). As we saw in my earlier discussion of human images, our assumptions and assertions about human nature and psychological development are necessarily reflected in how we approach and "conduct" psychotherapy. This being the case, it behooves us to examine closely both the former and the latter. Each of the principles suggested here has been touched upon (at least once) in the literatures already surveyed. I do not presume to demonstrate the validity of any of them, although I have confidence in the viability of most. As will be apparent, my attempts at describing some working principles reflect important contributions from evolutionary studies, cognitive science, experimental and developmental psychology, psychoanalytic, existential, behavioral, and humanistic perspectives, and studies of psychotherapy process and outcome.

Needless to say, these assertions reflect condensations and extrapolations from a wide expanse of theory and research. I shall not presume to compare this attempt at the specification of general principles with other valuable efforts in this domain (for example, Bandura 1986; Ford 1987; Furth 1987; Gilbert 1989; Kegan 1982; Orlinsky and Howard 1987; Thelen 1988). The commonalities shared with these other perspectives easily prevail over the differences, and a more practical question is how those principles are illustrated in the enactment of psychotherapy. Practical guidelines for helping should reflect an understanding of basic developmental processes. In a technical sense, one might expect that some of the most important guidelines for practice would be more proscriptive than prescriptive (Burrell 1987). In the domain of professional ethics this is, in fact, the case: most of our rules for ethical conduct are stated as prohibitions and cautions rather than as positive directives (Everstine et al. 1980; Keith-Spiegel and Koocher 1985; Miller and Thelen 1987; Pope, Tabachnick, and Keith-Speigel 1988). There are, however, many other abstract rules for optimal practice which can be positively expressed (see pages 270–71).

As here conceived, the optimal therapeutic relationship creates a special and intimate human context—a context in and from which the client can safely experiment with and explore familiar and novel ways of experiencing self, world (especially the interpersonal), and possible relationships. Such experiments and explorations—which are individualized to match the client's current competencies and experiential horizons—are constrained only by the requirements that they be self-caring and socially responsible.

In the most helpful enactments of psychotherapy, moreover, the helping professional recognizes and respects (1) the power of affective processes in (mis)directing attention and action, (2) the role of episodic "disorder" or "disorganization" in the genesis of new developments, and

GENERAL PRINCIPLES OF HUMAN DEVELOPMENT

1. Human experience is a lifespan unfolding of epistemological (knowing) processes; humans are active, feeling, embodied theories.
2. Humans experience themselves and their worlds via primarily tacit *core ordering processes* that construct and maintain such ongoing stabilities as phenomenological reality and personal identity.
3. Personal meanings are participatory relationships expressed in patterned activities (cognition, affect, physiology, and behavior).
4. All psychological change involves changes in personal meanings (regardless of how these are brought about).
5. Human psychological development reflects the pervasive and lifelong operation of basic self-organizing processes.
6. Human self-organizing processes are functionally structured so that the center of the living system—its core ordering processes—are given special protection against changing; that protection is most apparent when demands for change are extensive and urgent ("too much, too quickly").
7. Psychologically, there are at least four core ordering processes: *(a)* reality (the organization and relatedness of experience), *(b)* identity, *(c)* value (valence), and *(d)* power (control).
8. Core ordering processes are most formatively influenced by early, repeated, and intense emotional experiences, especially those involving pain and intimate human relationships.
9. Human relationships that involve strong (positive or negative) emotional bonds offer the most powerful contexts for both functional and dysfunctional psychological development.
10. An individual's relationships with self are the most powerful determinants of his or her quality of life and resilience under stress. Importantly, self-relationships are inseparable from social and symbolic relationships; self and system are integral, as are identity and intimacy.
11. A professional helping relationship can offer a valuable interpersonal base in and from which service seekers can explore and experiment with their personal realities.
12. The intimacy afforded by a professional helping relationship is generally more accessible, secure, and facilitative to the person served when the professional helper is more, rather than less, self-aware, self-accepting, and self-caring.

13. Positive or progressive psychological development, which must be individually defined, is facilitated by the presence of safe, stable, and caring others who accept and encourage experiential explorations.

14. Resistance to change is common (even when the change is desired) and reflects basic self-protective processes that influence the pacing and direction of change.

15. Although (over)simplifying, general patterns of personal experience can be described as lifelong spirals with recurrent phases:

   a. A state of dynamic balance which perpetuates itself as long as possible under the prevailing "seas" of perturbation, until

   b. a challenging episode emerges (usually in the form of a crisis or novelty). If the challenge is accommodated, life "returns" to (a new) dynamic balance; if not

   c. Cycles of system-wide disorder and disequilibrium emerge; these cycles are often experienced as distressing and disorganizing.

   d. Individuals usually attempt to regain their psychological balance via familiar activities used to cope with previous life challenges.

   e. When old solutions are unsuccessful and systemic disorder continues or grows, increased variability in all forms of experience are common (for example, sleep, eating, affect, intimacy, thought patterns).

   f. Within this variability, individuals often report "real-time" phenomenological patterns called *oscillations,* which are cycles of "expansions" (openings, "accommodations") and "contractions" (closings, "assimilations") along the dimensions of core ordering processes.

   g. Although emergent patterns are unique, there are three broad clusters: (1) deterioration or decompensation; (2) compromised balance (a pattern in which life order is at least marginally restored, but at high and often rising costs to the individual); and (3) differentiation, in which new and often more complex core ordering processes emerge out of persistent trial-and-error risk taking, creative skill developments, and chance events.

GENERAL PRINCIPLES OF HUMAN HELPING

1. Human helping is an abstractly principled interpersonal process that is highly individualized and infinitely unique.
2. Although neither sufficient nor necessary, a helper's capacity to experience, accept, and understand an individual's phenomenology is facilitative of the helping process.
3. The helping process reflects the dynamics of experiential reorganization in the conjoint contexts of *(a)* a secure and caring *relationship, (b)* a tacit or explicit *rationale* for possibility or progress, and *(c)* active engagement in *rituals* that involve personal meanings and strong emotions.
4. Three abstract rules offer general guidance in helping: *(a)* tend first to safety and urgency issues, *(b)* gentle and consistent nurturance are preferable to their contrasts, and *(c)* be patient: the optimal pace of change is determined by the core ordering processes of the person being served.
5. The helping process can be facilitated by real and symbolic modeling of psychological resilience, health, and well-being.
6. Optimal helping encourages the experience and responsible expression of all emotions.
7. It is generally more helpful to work with, rather than against, resistance and other self-protective processes.
8. Optimal helping respects the power and diversity of cultural, gender-related, and individualizing experiences.
9. The responsible helper is generally more, rather than less, conscious and accepting of his or her own humanness.
10. Optimal helping respects and involves the biological embodiment of the individual.
11. Optimal helping respects the social and interpersonal embeddedness of the individual.
12. Optimal helping encourages the empowerment of the individual as the primary agent of choice and action in his or her own life.
13. Optimal helping respects the power and diversity with which individuals may experience and express religious and spiritual issues.
14. Optimal helpers are capable of inviting and co-maintaining a nonsexual intimate relationship with those they serve, a relationship in which the helpers' emotional needs are subservient.
15. Optimal helping often involves the encouragement of human compassion, forgiveness, and love, each directed at both others and self.

16. Optimal helping encourages self-caring and social responsibility.
17. Within the constraints of law and ethics, optimal helping respects and protects individual rights to privacy.
18. The optimal helper is willing to seek and accept help from others.
19. Optimal helping respects the power and resilience of the human spirit.
20. Optimal helping respects each person's ultimate right and responsibility to make his or her own life choices whenever possible.

© 1989 M. J. Mahoney

(3) the role that his or her relationship with emotionality may play in influencing clients' relationships with their own affective processes. In the course and wake of successful psychotherapy, clients often report greater comfort with those processes and their expression. This increased comfort is sometimes expressed in amplifications of both awareness of and capacities for emotional "absorption," as well as a differentiation of affective experience so that new feelings or new mixtures of feelings emerge.

Those qualities of personhood and relatedness that characterize successful psychotherapists are a central topic of modern theory and research (Lambert 1989). There is now little doubt that some therapists are significantly more helpful than others across diversities of clients and psychological problems. The classic illustration here might well be the naturalistic comparison of "supershrink" and "pseudoshrink" reported by Ricks (1974). Two therapists saw adolescent clients with comparable problems involving intolerable anxiety and feelings of isolation, unreality, and vulnerability. Analyses of individual sessions and case notes revealed that therapist A was more patient with his clients, particularly those who had been diagnosed as most "disturbed." While developing a strong and affectionate bond with them, he was attentive to their needs for everyday problem solving and openly encouraged their gradual development of autonomy. He was empathic with their anxieties and struggles, about which he was reassuring, and he was careful not to rush into "deep material" before his clients were ready to do so.

Therapist B, on the other hand, spent less time with his most distressed clients and often rushed them toward intense confrontations with their deepest fears and concerns. When those confrontations resulted in the intensification of their distress and exacerbations of their problems, therapist B frequently withdrew from them emotionally and reported difficulties in relating to them during sessions. His case notes suggested that he was frightened by their experiences and the degree of their "pathology." He described them with terms like "ominous" and "hopeless," and even told some clients that he believed their "spirit had been broken." Did the different persons and human relatedness of therapists A and B make any difference in the lives of their young clients? Long-term follow-up evaluations revealed a striking statistic: the likelihood of clients having deteriorated into schizophrenia in their adult life was different by a ratio of more than 3 to 1 depending on which therapist they had seen. While 27 percent of therapist A's clients were eventually diagnosed as schizophrenic, that diagnosis was later applied to 84 percent of those adolescents treated by therapist B. This retrospective study was not methodologically pure, of course (as none are), but its findings are undeniably provocative. The research literature devoted to this topic has also lent ample corroboration for the assertion that some forms of helping are, indeed, better than others; and that these forms are more closely allied with the person and abstract "style" of the psychotherapist than they are with theoretical orientations or specific techniques. What is particularly interesting about that literature is its recent recognition that the person and style of the therapist are complexly related to the therapist's apparent (1) psychological development, (2) views of human nature, and (3) epistemological preferences (Chessick 1986; Coan 1987*b;* Conway 1989; Gilligan 1982; Halleck 1971; Hill et al. 1988; J.A. Johnson et al. 1988; Keinan, Almagor, and Ben-Porath 1989; Krasner and Houts 1984; Larson 1980; McGovern, Newman, and Kopta 1986; Mahoney et al. 1989; Norcross and Prochaska 1983; Plous and Zimbardo 1986; Wogan and Norcross 1985).

HELPING METAPHORS

The elaboration of general principles may be helpful in our efforts to refine our professional services, but we should also remember that those services will also reflect many ordering processes that are beyond our capacities to verbalize. The primacy of the abstract is everpresent in our lives (as well as in the lives of those we counsel). There is, however, an important "middle ground" between our explicit rules of conduct and our tacit experiential processes. Although cognitive scientists have only recently begun to document and "authorize" the power of metaphors in knowing, that power has been 'known' and exercised by poets, playwrights, and psychotherapists for some time now. Our theories of change—which *are* our theories of personality, psychopathology, lifespan development, identity, and systems—are most powerfully captured in the generativities and multiplicities that are afforded by metaphors.* Indeed, it has been from the realms of metaphor that some of the newest "horizons" in theoretical and therapeutic psychology have emerged. It is also from here that we may begin to more deeply appreciate the ever-fresh lessons of mythology, rhetoric, and religious symbolism. The history of ideas (chapter 2) and the history of feelings (appendix G) unmistakably converge in the metaphorical concepts and practices of modern psychotherapy. We are well advised to explore and experience the power of metaphors in each of these realms, and to recognize that such explorations necessarily entail a never-ending process.

Among the most popular metaphors for scaffolding the experience of psychotherapy have been those that involve transitions and travel. Freud, for example, suggested the analogy that the psychotherapist serves as a "midwife to the soul." Another example is offered by the frequency with which metaphors of travel and journeying are employed in popular and professional portrayals of psychotherapy (witness the service-oriented journal titled *Pilgrimage*). The journey or pilgrimage metaphor is particularly apt, I believe, because it echoes well with the reported experiences of many psychotherapy clients. On a journey, for example, there are issues of paths, modes and abilities for movement, pacing, pauses, obstacles, challenges, choice points, destinations (near and far), directions, companions, encounters and dialogues with companions, guides, and other travelers, and so on. This metaphor also encourages an attribution of the power for movement to the client (although the professional helper may offer to "carry some of the load" temporarily). The journey metaphor also lends itself well to the inevitable separation process at the conclusion of treatment: after walking together through the time and terrain of experience, therapist and client part ways and continue on separate paths.

An illustration of a client's resonance with metaphors of travel came from my final session with Patricia F., the psychiatric nurse who had been frightened by her own "witnessing processes" in a stream-of-consciousness exercise (see pages 232–33). Like many other psychotherapists, I use symbolic rituals of separation to facilitate the "matriculation" from psychotherapy to life-after-psychotherapy. One of those rituals is the request that the client write or record a brief synopsis of his or her experience of our work together. Those synopses have taught me many lessons about that work. Consider the following crystal offered by Patricia:

*For recent discussions of the power of metaphor in learning and psychotherapy, see Angus and Rennie 1988; Canda 1988; Cox and Theilgaard 1987; d'Aquili, Laughlin, and McManus 1979; Engel 1988; Evans 1988; Gonçalves 1989a; 1989b; Gorelick 1989; Hamburg 1988; Johnson 1987; Katz et al. 1988; Kopp 1972, 1976; Lakoff 1987; Lakoff and Johnson 1980; MacDonald et al. 1989; Muran and DiGiuseppe 1990; Orlinsky 1989; and Trick and Katz 1986. For recent analyses of metaphor in cognitive psychology, see Glucksberg 1989 and Glucksberg and Keysar 1990.

I didn't want to do this exercise. I sat down several times to start it, but nothing came except tears and I had to stop because I was crying. It is still hard for me to believe that we won't see one another every Tuesday morning.

Anyway, the only thing I could come up with to summarize my experience of psychotherapy is an image that came to me while I was crying. I was a little girl, maybe four or five years old, and you were my father. You were teaching me how to ride a bicycle without training wheels. I had long pants on and a long sleeve shirt, and we were on the playground behind my old school. It must have been a weekend, because there were no other people there. You began by putting one hand next to mine on the handlebars and the other on the bicycle seat. As I tried to keep my feet on the pedals and get them going in smooth cycles, you ran along with me, just fast enough to help me balance, but not so fast that I was too scared.

After a while, you relaxed your grip on the handlebars and just touched them lightly with your finger. When you took your hand off, I screamed, "No! No! Not yet!" and the front wheel began to wobble sideways. You grabbed hold again and helped me straighten it out. I think you said something reassuring, but I don't know what it was. I also think that you smiled at me, but I wasn't looking at your face.

It seemed a long time before you took your hand all the way off the handlebars, and I kept looking over to see that it was still there to help me if I needed it. You were always there, running along with me and saying nice things that I can't remember. My next "scare" was when I realized that you had begun to relax your grip on the bicycle seat. I didn't know you had done that until I wobbled so badly that I almost fell. You caught me around the waist and the bicycle just leaned to the side, rolling along underneath us at a very silly angle. I think I laughed or you laughed, but now I am crying.

Sometime later you let go of the seat entirely. I think I said, "I can't do it!" and you said I could. "You can steer for yourself," you said, "and you can keep your balance." "But I will fall!" I said, and I did. This time you didn't catch me, and I hit the pavement with my shoulder. You were right there, lifting the bike off me and picking me up. You held me and you let me cry. You helped me learn that the hurt goes away. Then you said, "Let's try again." I did. I kept falling, of course, and you kept picking me up.

Somewhere in all that you started dropping back. I was making bigger and bigger circles around the playground, and you were slowing to a walk around the center. Even though you were more distant, your voice stayed close to me. I was so excited about my own power to move that I began to get up from my falls and back on my bike before you could reach me. Later you just walked slowly around the middle and smiled encouragement at me. Sometimes you said, "Don't watch me. Watch where you're going."

That is how it felt. I will always remember your voice and your smile. Thank you for being so patient with me. Thank you for teaching me to keep trying.

In this marvelously developmental image there is a multiplex metaphor of movement, balance, direction, affection, patience, empowerment, and much, much more.

Another example of a developmental metaphor for psychological change is that of *transformation,* or *metamorphosis.* In this metaphor the change (transition) process is often symbolized by the physical metamorphosis of a caterpillar into a butterfly (chapter 7 and figure 7.1, page 149). Several years ago I was working with a client who was virtually obsessed with that metaphor. He was also painfully impatient to make the transition from the "worm" he had been to the "wings" that he so desperately desired. He longed for the day that he would awaken to find that he had "shed" his old self and finally emerged in a new form of being. From then on, he thought, he would be free of his past and his life would be blissful. Then one day he arrived for a session in an unusually relaxed mood. When I commented on his apparent peace with himself, he related a brief story he had just heard from a friend who had just returned from a workshop where the transformation metaphor had been discussed. The workshop leader had talked about early scientists' attempts artificially to accelerate the rate of metamorphosis. When one researcher discovered a way substantially to reduce the duration of the pupal (cocoon) stage, it was considered a major breakthrough. He had found that slowly and slightly raising the temperature surrounding the transforming organisms accelerated their metabolic rates so that they emerged from their cocoons in much less time than usual. The discovery had been heralded for several months, as a bona-fide miracle of science, but its promise was soon shown to be premature. Other investigators were able to replicate the original findings, but they noticed something that had been overlooked by the pioneering scientist. Although the experimental organisms spent less time in the pupal stage, they emerged with a common defect: their wings had not fully developed, and they were incapable of flying. With that concluding statement, my client sighed deeply and said, "I guess I'll just have to learn patience."

These two illustrations from psychotherapy clients also suggest that different metaphors may serve individuals differently, so that an important practical question is not which metaphor is best (for all clients, always) but, rather, which families of metaphors are more useful to whom, for what purposes, and so on. This implies that there is merit in knowing a range of possible metaphors and in being sufficiently flexible and perceptive that one can encourage reliance on multiple metaphors according to the client's current phenomenology and primary concerns. As those concerns and experience patterns change, new and different metaphors may become more appropriate and helpful (Hatcher, Huebner, and Zakin 1986).

DEVELOPMENTAL PSYCHOTHERAPY

I shall not further belabor the tentativeness of the foregoing principles or their relationship to other efforts at theoretical integration. The parallels between some of the aforementioned principles and those discussed by John Bowlby (1979) should also be apparent. Before moving on to selected techniques for encouraging psychological development, however, it might be helpful to suggest a general outline for the application of these principles in the service of individual clients. The temporal scaffolding for developmental psychotherapy outlined in table 10.2, though succinct and tersely stated, covers the basics as I currently understand them.

Intake and Early Assessment

The initial contact with a client is intended to afford a global first impression of his or her immediate needs (especially those that may require special attention because they involve possible injury of self or others). Beyond direct questions about this realm, diagnostic classifications may also be helpful in assessing risk of suicide. Individuals diagnosed as severely depressed or borderline, for example, are often at greater risk of self-injury. There is also recent evidence suggesting that persons suffering from panic and multiple personality disorders may be at much higher risk than was previously realized (Markowitz et al. 1989; Ross 1989). Intake interviews also help to assess clients' presenting concerns, their expectations regarding psychotherapy, and the compatibility of each of these with the psychotherapist's competence, style, and capacity to establish a caring bond with a particular person. One's personal values are extremely important here (Jordan and Meara 1990; Keith-Spiegel and Koocher 1985; London 1964; Norcross and Wogan 1987). It is difficult to be optimally helpful to clients, for example, if one does not like them, cannot relate to their concerns, or harbors negative feelings about some aspect of their self-presentation. Although these impediments may be related to an infinite number of possible particulars, some of those most commonly reported in psychotherapy supervision include the therapist's having negative associations with the client's interpersonal style, religious preference, gender-role compliance and sexual preference, and the severity or specifics of his or her presenting concerns.* Referral is the appropriate course of action when a therapist feels that he or she might experience devaluative feelings toward a prospective client.

When there is compatibility between prospective client and psychotherapist, a written therapeutic contract is recommended, and the client

*Illustrations and discussions of value judgments in these domains are particularly apparent in addressing clients' religious beliefs (Bergin and Jensen 1990; Meyer 1988; Shafranske and Malony 1990), gender-related issues and feminism (Beutler, Crago, and Arizmendi 1986; Brown 1990; Good, Dell, and Mintz 1989; Johnson and Stone 1989; Jones, Krupnick, and Kerig 1987; Lerner 1989; Loring and Powell 1988; Lyons 1983; Mednick 1989; Sapadin 1988; Strouse 1974; Worell 1988), the elderly client (Whitbourne 1989), and homosexual clients (Edelwich and Brodsky 1982).

Table 10.2   A Temporal Scaffolding for Developmental Psychotherapy

Interval or Stage	General Focus and Realms of Activity
Intake	1. Identification of primary and other presenting concerns/problems 2. Risk and urgency appraisal 3. Basics about current life situation (e.g., significant others, employment, health, and brief medical history) 4. Brief life history and basics about family of origin 5. Initial assessment of therapeutic "fit" (compatability, mutual regard, relevant professional expertise, and so on); referral if appropriate 6. Assessment of client expectations for psychotherapy (e.g., prior therapy experience, goals, fears, etc.) 7. Initial global appraisal and, when appropriate, assurances (e.g., warrant for hope, wisdom of having sought help) 8. Agreement on a "therapeutic contract" (e.g., goals, roles, the process of active inquiry and exploration, and agreement to review progress and reappraise goals at specified interval) 9. Review of client rights and therapist responsibilities; signing of informed consent
Assessment	1. Basic psychometrics of choice, with special attention to core issues (identity, reality, power, and values) 2. Basic health assessment (including diet, sleep, exercise, chemical use/abuse, and medical history) 3. Self-system assessment and appraisal of current developmental level
Leveling	1. Discussion of possible choices of focus; selection of a domain of present focus (specific problem[s], recurrent patterns, coping skills, or experience-generating processes) 2. Agreement on a general preliminary strategy for addressing that level
Early work	1. Deepening development of working alliance (via authentic caring, affirmation, and encouragement) 2. Active behavioral homework exercises; encouragement of self-exploratory activities (if appropriate, initiation of personal journal work, life-review project, meditation, and/or physical activity) 3. More detailed exploration of current life situation and primary and secondary concerns 4. More intensive and extensive exploration of life history, family of origin, and identity development

Table 10.2   *(Continued)*

Interval or Stage	*General Focus and Realms of Activity*
Intermediate work	1. Except in cases of borderline functioning, extreme emotional instability, or where acute self-focus might be risky, introduction of exercises aimed at amplifying *(a)* self-awareness, and *(b)* positive self-relationships (e.g., stream of consciousness work, mirror time, dream and fantasy work, and so on) 2. In-session exercises emphasizing exploration, novelty, and empowerment (e.g., dialectical dialogues, psychodrama) 3. Homework assignments aimed at self-caring rituals, internalization/exploration of novel "real world" adaptations, and emotional/conceptual/behavioral edging 4. If appropriate, encourage involvement of willing family members and significant others; involve co-therapists and other relevant professionals as needed 5. Acknowledgment of, respect for, and work *with* (rather than against) resistance 6. Emphasis on pacing and respect for cycles of progress and regress

Review and choice	1. Review of general goals
	2. Review of work to date
	3. Global appraisal of progress
	4. Assess client satisfaction and motivation for or merit of continued therapy
	   a. if agreement is to discontinue, proceed to stages below
	   b. if agreement is to continue, return to "leveling" stage and proceed with selective adaptations and elaborations of exploratory exercises

Assessment	1. Repeated as outlined above with additions or deletions suggested by work to date

should be asked to sign an appropriate form reflecting his or her "informed consent" (for example, Handelsman and Galvin 1988; Handelsman et al. 1986; Talbert and Pipes 1987). The choice of instruments for psychometric assessment should also be sensitive to the culture, gender, and personal characteristics of the client (Beutler 1989; Brown 1990; Mancuso and Shaw 1988; Robins 1988). When the client is taking prescription medications (whether psychotropic or not), an appropriate reference source (such as the *Physicians' Desk Reference*) should be consulted for information about possible side effects and contraindications (Meyer

Table 10.2 *(Continued)*

Interval or Stage	General Focus and Realms of Activity
Exit	1. Assess client attributions of responsibility for progress and sensed autonomy; if disempowering beliefs are expressed, suggest a graduated schedule of separation
	2. Affirm client's uniqueness and strengths as an individual
	3. Affirm client's past pursuit of personal development (intent, effort, activity)
	4. Encourage future openness to professional counsel
	5. Discuss possible expressions and experiences of the separation process
	6. Develop an individualized separation ritual which includes a symbolic exchange and an explicit farewell
	7. If appropriate, encourage follow-up contacts at graduated intervals

and Fink 1989). Finally, client and therapist should be in agreement about the level or focus of their initial work together.

The Level of Therapeutic Focus

Leveling is itself a complex phenomenon reflecting a choice made by every psychotherapy client: the choice of where and how to focus his or her attention and energies in the therapeutic work. There are theoretical differences as to whether that choice lies solely in the domain of the client (Messer 1986), of course; and there are complexities involved in deciding what constitute different domains. James Bugental (1978) has offered a valuable discussion of this choice based on Abraham Maslow's analysis of the kinds of motivation that bring an individual into professional counseling. A person presenting with complaints of painful anxiety, depression, and relationship difficulties, for example, might be multiply motivated to seek different benefits from psychotherapy. Should one focus first or foremost on one's affective malaise, daily functioning, self-understanding, or perception of and participation in a primary relationship? What personal variables and social contexts bear on a treatment of choice (Beutler 1989)? The choice of treatment focus remains a controversial one for modern psychotherapies, in part because it reflects a choice among different assumptions about human experience and psychological development. With the decline of prime-mover (first-cause) arguments in psychology (chapter 3), there has been a corresponding retreat from strong claims about the "only" or "most important" targets of therapeutic focus.

This is not the place to belabor such long-standing conflicts as those expressed in debates about whether symptoms (or behaviors) are the "problems" (versus expressions of more "deep-seated" causes of such problems). The point worth emphasizing, however, is that each client who seeks our services is likely to have a unique constellation of primary, secondary, and tertiary concerns. I also believe that clients have a right (indeed, responsibility) to express their preferences in terms of which concerns are most important to them at that time and what their hopes and expectations are regarding the services they will receive. Not everyone needs or wants the same thing, all the time. Some individuals want reassurance and encouragement. Some want assessments, diagnoses, or explicit training in coping skills. Most seek some form of self-understanding (chapter 12), and many are interested in self-exploration. The point is that these are all legitimate and understandable desires. In my opinion, a responsible psychotherapist respects those desires, is flexible enough to deal with a wide range of them and to adjust his or her services to each client's current concerns, and is professional enough to refer clients elsewhere when referral is in their best interest.

The responsible practice of psychotherapy involves a respect for each individual and the full range of an individual's requests for help or guidance. Not all such requests can (or should) be met, of course, but all deserve acknowledgment. Deserving of even more than acknowledgment, however, is a choice faced by many clients—namely, the choice between *first-order* and *second-order* focus. This is an artificial distinction, to be sure, but it is more complex than simply "surface" and "depth." As Gregory Bateson (1972) presented it, first-order change is a relatively minor modification of the parts of a system. More often than not, such modifications are goal-directed (teleological) and instrumental in emphasis. Second-order change involves a transformation of the entire system, structurally and functionally. There is more ambiguity and risk in this latter form, of course, but it is also capable of affording greater variation and complexity in development.

The dilemma here can be cast in a caricature that fits many psychotherapy clients. The individual has a long history of life concerns, distress, and dysfunction that seem to cluster and intermingle. They frequently report feeling lonely, self-critical, and confused. A succession of self-improvement projects, self-help groups, and counselors may have been of valuable (and variable) assistance at different points in their lives, but the individual continues to struggle with daily experiences that are painful or unsatisfying. When I am working with such an individual, I try to be sensitive to his or her current level of stress, coping capacities, and any known-to-be imminent life challenges. (There are, of course, always others that are imminent but unknown.) Sometimes, I believe, I serve them best by helping them focus on the problem solving required by the concrete demands of everyday life. With varying degrees, others may want reassurance or affirmation; and most seek to improve their "understanding" (of themselves, life, and other unfathomables). When I encounter veteran "pilgrims" who have found little relief from a variety of solutions, I am even more intent than usual on what they say and how they feel about choosing a level for our work.

As will be illustrated in the next two chapters, a client's choice to explore "depth work" is, fundamentally, a choice to risk the subtlety and power of his or her own experiencing—what existential and phenomenological specialists have long noted as the individually unique essence of lifelong human endeavor. Whether enacted as a leaning or a leap, it entails a movement of more than attention into the processes of living. Herein is embodied the drama of core ordering processes under self-review. An alliterative triad is helpful in thinking about the issue of levels of work in psychotherapy: the three P's of problem, pattern, and process (table 10.2). (Although they are described somewhat differently by Bowlby [1979], these same levels are central to the sequencing of services he outlines.) Problems are felt discrepancies between the way things are and the way one wants them to be: they are the literal and figurative aches and pains of a life in process. Rare is the psychotherapy client who does not report problems (or who does not devote substantial time and energy to problem resolution). Patterns are regularities or recurrent themes in problems. This week's "crisis" for a client may be an intense argument with a spouse. If problems with intimacy, anger, and relationships have been recurrent themes in his or her life, however, then a pattern is discernible. Most clients are aware of at least some patterns in their episodes of distress and dysfunction. The *process level* is the most difficult to describe, partly because it invokes a greater degree of both abstraction and experiential absorption. This is the level of core ordering processes, the domain of tacit rules that generate and constrain the particulars of problems and patterns. Some psychotherapy clients are immediately drawn toward this realm; others approach it only after having been initially preoccupied with problems or patterns; and still others never exhibit much interest in "the deep stuff," as one client put it.

I do not recommend one level over another and can, in fact, cite examples from my own practice and supervision that illustrate the frequent futility of attempting to push or pull a client "up" or "down" a level in his or her own "best interest." One thing that has become increasingly clear to me over the years, however, is that clients should be informed that work at the process level (1) is fundamentally experiential; (2) often leads to insights, understandings, and life choices that are unforeseeable and irreversible; and (3) offers no guarantees about what it may lead to in later psychological development. As Robert Frost put it so elegantly in the poem "Escapist—Never," it may well entail an endless "chain of longing" in which the seekers seek seekers and "life is a pursuit of a pursuit forever." This is not always the case, of course, but it is a possibility, and one (I believe) clients should be informed about in considering a choice of process-level depth work. In my experience, such work entails "openings" and "ongoingness" much more often than "closures" and "completions." These are important considerations.

Although rarely stated, my affinity and affection for process work should also be apparent. It has certainly permeated my own personal and professional development over the last quarter-century. Nor should it be surprising that the bulk of my current commitments in the areas of professional workshops and private practice are focused on process levels, with special attention to the unique burdens and blessings of mental health practitioners (chapter 13). Thus, although I maintain that work at the level of specific problems and circumscribed patterns are equally legitimate foci for treatment, my personal preferences lie in the domain of lifespan developmental processes.

Early and Intermediate Work

As the therapeutic relationship develops and there is further clarification of the client's concerns, responsible self-exploratory activities can be prescribed. Some of these may be intended to clarify feeling patterns in everyday activities, and others may be designed to refine basic coping and problem solving skills. Although it varies with individual clients and their circumstances, the rationale that I most commonly offer to clients is that these self-exploratory exercises may (1) help me to understand them better, (2) help them better understand themselves, and (3) encourage them to explore more meaningful, satisfying, "effective," or health-engendering patterns of activity and experience. When appropriate, many of these exercises can be begun within the therapeutic session and then later relegated to "homework" (Shelton and Ackerman 1974). For some clients and exercises, compliance with homework assignments may be facilitated by the use of a written (rather than verbal) prescription (Cox, Tisdelle, and Culbert 1988).

Not surprisingly, it is in the context of early and intermediate work that clients most often report "oscillations" in their phenomenology and "resistance" (chapter 12). It is also in these phases that the psychological development of the individual client may be facilitated by inviting the participation of significant others and, if couples or family therapy is feasible, the introduction of co-therapists (Allen 1988; Hoffman 1981; Kerr and Bowen 1988; Nichols 1987). Because each of these components may amplify the client's distress and tax his or her resources, it is particularly important for the psychotherapist to be psychologically present, patient, and as encouraging as possible throughout this period.

The Time It Takes to Change

It is often in the pursuit of intermediate work that an important (and recurrent) generalization about human development is encountered: namely, *significant psychological change is rarely easy or rapid.* There may be important exceptions to this generalization, but it is nonetheless warranted. This is not to say, however, that invaluable services cannot be offered on a short-term (time-limited) basis or even in a single consultation. I spent only two hours with Milton Erickson and yet it was a pivotal experience in my life (Mahoney and Eiseman 1989). Nevertheless, as the originator of the "lifestyle" concept (Alfred Adler) knew well, important changes in individual "styles" of living a life are seldom wrought in a weekend. When an individual is struggling to differentiate core ordering processes—the embodied and experiential dimensions of "meaning," "selfhood," "power," and values—dramatic changes tend to unfold along a timeline measured minimally in months and more often in years.

This is a controversial point—conceptually, empirically, economically, and ethically. Critics of long-term, depth psychotherapy have labeled it "interminable," with the occasional insinuation that its length is dictated more by theoretical biases and psychotherapists' financial desires than by the best interests of their clients. I am sure that such biases and interests have, in fact, exerted influences that have not been beneficial to some of the individuals being served. At the same time, however, I believe that the current swing of the pendulum toward the extremes of brief and "strategic" psychotherapy raises another set of complex and value-laden issues. Briefly put, the amount of psychotherapy (however it may be quantified) is nowhere near as important as its quality. No matter how it is financed, one does not ensure better quality by demanding or discouraging either briefer or more extensive engagements in service.

The issue here is not whether time-limited counseling "works." Brief psychotherapy can be very helpful, particularly when it is focused on a specific problem (Garfield 1989; Mandel 1981). Nor am I opposed to the strategic use of paradox or other "uncommon" methods in psychological services. Responsibly practiced, such techniques may be very beneficial to some individuals (Ascher 1989; DeBord 1989; Dowd and Milne 1986; Hill 1987; Hunsley 1988; Rossi 1973; Shoham-Salomon, Avner, and Neeman 1989). As a reader of Adler, Bateson, and Reusch, a friend and colleague of Viktor Frankl, and a former client of Milton Erickson, however, "I fear that little of their systemic wisdom is being expressed in some of their contemporary translations" (Mahoney 1986*b*, p. 289). The point here is that neither time in treatment nor strategic technique is the key concern in optimal psychotherapy. Many individuals report their greatest psychological changes months and even years after the termination of their treatment (Frank et al. 1978; Reynolds 1980), and most attribute their progress to the quality of their relationship with their therapist (Elliott and James 1989). Likewise, the continuing growth of psychological self-help groups and the welcome infusion of health psychology in both private and public sectors speak candidly to the "ongoingness" of adjustment and the quest toward well-being (Jacobs and Goodman 1989; Krantz, Grunberg, and Baum 1985; Matarazzo et al. 1984; Taylor 1990). Coping and problem-solving skills can result in enduring changes in life quality, as can chance encounters with the world (Bandura 1982).

At some level of analysis, of course, space and time are dynamically inseparable. This is also true of treatment focus (level) and developmental process. When that focus is directed "inwardly" and core ordering processes are explored, the potential ramifications for the person's life are on another magnitude of order. This point bears particular emphasis since the therapeutic techniques to be reviewed next are predominantly experiential and self-exploratory in focus.

Review, Choice, and Exit

At predetermined points in time, it is helpful for both therapist and client to review progress to date and to assess the client's motivation for (and likely benefit from) continued therapy. In my experience, this is most often the point at which clients who have previously focused on problem or pattern levels may now consider the risks and potential of experiential process work. It is important that that choice be adequately discussed, and that the client reflect upon it before making a decision. In other words, the choice should not be made in the first session of review. Also important here is an emphasis on the client's acknowledging that the choice is ultimately his or her own. Even though one may request the therapist's opinion on the matter, I believe that the latter should be withheld until the client has indicated his or her own preference. An important exception to this is if the therapist feels that it would not be in the client's best interest to pursue "depth work" at that point in time (in which case one should, of course, be discouraged from doing so).

When the client decides that it is time to discontinue regular treatment, attributions and expectations about their experience and their future deserve special attention (see table 10.2). The separation process after intensive psychotherapy can be one of the most powerful (and, hence, potentially helpful or harmful) elements in the entire project (chapter 11). This is particularly the case when a strong emotional bond has been established and/or separations have previously been difficult experiences for the client. An individualized separation ritual may be helpful in explicitly marking and expressing the client's choice to withdraw from the helping relationship and to move on with his or her life. Among other things, the client should be commended for his or her efforts toward personal development and encouraged to remain open to and engaged in continuing development and to future professional services if they would be helpful.

11

𝕬𝕬𝕬𝕬𝕬𝕬𝕬𝕬𝕬𝕬𝕬

Selected Techniques for Encouraging Psychological Development

Theory has worth as preparation only; the critical struggle lies in the Act.
—Nikos Kazantzakis

Having already noted my concerns about technolatry and the possible tyranny of technique (Mahoney 1986*a*), I shall not belabor this point beyond a brief capsule summary. The remainder of this chapter will then be devoted to selected techniques for encouraging psychological development. The modifier *selected* is important here: I do not use all exercises with every client, and I do not consider any of them essential to the quality of professional services I provide. Moreover, each exercise is structured in a way that makes it individualized. I encourage such individualization. In practice, each of these techniques is explored only as it is deemed appropriate for a given client and only after sufficient trust and caring have developed in our relationship so as to afford a feeling of safety in experiential explorations. Finally, my rationale for each exercise is the same: I want to better understand what it is like to be the person I am serving—that is, to experience the self (selves), world(s), and emotions that characterize his or her life. In doing so, I also hope to assist the client in exploring and developing new and more satisfying understandings and enactments of that experience.

TECHNIQUES AS THERAPEUTIC RITUALS

Knowing that change is possible is not the same as *knowing how* to facilitate it. We yearn to learn technique because we desire the power of enacted knowledge, which is the heart of *praxis* ("doing," the existential basis of "Being"). What is sometimes overlooked, however, is that "technique" is not a special subset of isolated skills or mechanical movements so much as a term for the practice and performance of an art (*techne* [Greek] means "art"; *performare* [Latin] means "to give form"). To the extent that it is "applied science" (in the best sense of both terms), then, psychotherapy is undeniably an art form (Bugental 1987; Chessick 1986; Grusky 1987). And, as science educators have begun to acknowledge, learning to do "good science" requires more than textbook examples and didactic instruction. It requires the actual "doing" (praxis), preferably in the context of a talented mentor. In other words, "knowledge by description" must be supplemented with "knowledge by acquaintance," much of which will remain tacit (Kuhn 1977). This is also true in the practice of psychotherapy, where experiential apprenticeship, professional modeling, and quality supervision are of fundamental importance (chapter 13, appendix H).

Among mental health practitioners, the popularity of simple and straightforward prescriptions for practice should not be surprising. Responsible and facilitative life counseling is a complex and potentially draining endeavor. Navigational aids and conceptual systems that help guide our actions are warmly welcomed. What I am driving at here, however, is the danger of granting techniques more credit than they deserve. Notwithstanding the many problems in conceptualizing and measuring the effects of psychotherapy, the existing literature is consistent in its suggestions that therapeutic techniques and theoretical orientations are much less powerful predictors of change than are client and therapist characteristics (in that order) combined with the quality of the human relationship that they develop. Indeed, Hans Strupp asserts that "techniques *per se* are inert unless they form an integral part of the therapist as a person" (1978, p. 314). This does not mean, however, that techniques are unimportant or optional in either therapy or clinical research. We are *always* practicing via technique, usually with little "awareness" of how we are doing what we are doing. "Listening," for example, is conceptualized and practiced quite differently by psychotherapists (witness Freud's [1963] endorsement of "evenly hovering attention," Rogers's [1957] "reflective listening," and Reik's [1949] "listening with the third ear"). The same diversity could be illustrated in the techniques of questioning, interpretation and simply "being psychologically present" to a client.

Techniques are ritualized methods of human relatedness and communication. They are, if you will, stylized languages for expressing and exploring the ongoing narrative of a life in process: "continarration" (James Joyce, 1980 [1939], p. 205). But it is important not to confuse the medium of the language with the messages it may bear. In other words, there is more to the message than the medium. If we learn to think of different techniques as "languages" (many of which are nonverbal), we can begin to appreciate some of the points being made in dialectical psychology and hermeneutics.

To summarize, we can profitably *use* special techniques, but we should be cautious about empowering any tool to the point that it subjugates rather than serves its user (Barrett 1967). Our learning to be helpful can be aided by *practicing* the operations specified in various treatment manuals. We are sadly mistaken, however, if we embrace the illusions that "eye contact" is equivalent to human contact, that "taking turns talking" is the same as genuine dialogue, and that strictly following a prescriptive manual absolves us of the responsibility of making (thoroughly fallible) decisions of our own in the context of individually unique circumstances and choice points. Techniques and the personal meanings they invoke are always embedded in human relationships—a point to bear in mind as I discuss selected rituals for the encouragement of psychological development.

Among the valuable contributions of Jerome D. Frank (1973, 1985, 1987) to our understanding of the basic ingredients in psychotherapy has been his elucidation of what I call "the three R's of helping": a role-defined *relationship*, a *rationale* or metaphor for the change process, and experiential *rituals* for effecting change. My focus here is on this last component. A "rite" or "ritual" (from the Latin *ritus* and *ritualis*) is a prescribed form of activity that is set apart from others because of its special significance. Traditionally, that significance has been associated with spiritual or religious meanings, and many rituals are undertaken in solemn and sacred ceremonies (both private and public). In the wake of cross-cultural studies in anthropology, psychology, and sociology, however, we have come to recognize rituals as universal phenomena that express and serve a variety of human needs (Canda 1988; Cheal 1987, 1988*a*, 1988*b*, 1988*c;* d'Aquili, Laughlin, and McManus 1979; Hope 1988; Rando 1985; Rosenthal and Marshall 1988; van der Hart 1981). Not surprisingly, the literatures on ritual overlap extensively with those on consciousness, healing, health, metaphor, and relationships (interpersonal, intrapersonal, and spiritual).

The point toward which I am driving here is that rituals play an important role in human helping. They are embodied enactments that serve special functions in human psychological experience and development. Those functions are almost as diverse as the rituals themselves and their performers: the pursuit of meaning, hope, power, relief, confession, forgiveness, sacrifice, appeasement, celebration, encouragement, and nurturance (to name a few). According to Murry Hope (1988), there are numerous ways to classify rituals and a wide variety of intentions in their practice. His list includes rites of ancestral remembrance, social transition (initiation, farewell, and welcome), self-exploration, purification, thanksgiving, and protection. All forms of psychotherapy involve rituals; and—

although they may be described and rationalized quite differently—there is considerable overlap in their form across theoretical orientations (Frank 1973; Goldfried 1982; Norcross 1986, 1987; Omer and London 1988; Prochaska 1984; Wogan and Norcross 1985).

The techniques discussed below are illustrations of exercises that may be helpful with some clients in encouraging psychological development. In lieu of a more extensive elaboration of how, where, and when they "fit" into a developmental approach to individual psychotherapy, I defer to the temporal scaffolding outlined in table 10.2 and discussions in chapters 10, 12, and 13.

THERAPEUTIC WRITING

The use of writing as an element in therapy and personal development has long been recognized, but it remains less extensively studied than many other techniques (Brand 1980; Brand and Leckie 1988; Hettich 1990; White and Epston 1990). The vast majority of these applications involve narrative writing, correspondence, personal journal ("diary") work, and autobiographical "life review" projects.

Correspondence and Narrative Writing

In the course of psychotherapy, it is not unusual for a client to report feeling distress over unresolved conflicts or "unfinished" emotional processes (Greenberg and Safran 1987). Some of these feelings may be related to childhood experiences, and many are associated with human relationships. In encouraging clients to experience and express those feelings, a number of techniques may be helpful. One example suggested by Sheldon Kopp (1972) is the "unsent letter." The client is instructed to write a candid letter to the individual(s) with whom he or she feels "unfinished." Since the letter will not be sent, the client is encouraged to express the full range and intensity of his or her feelings without concern for their impact on the other person(s). This is often an emotionally intense undertaking. Once it is completed, the client is next asked to write two more unsent letters.

The first is to be a letter from the person the client has just written, and the latter is asked to write it as if he or she were that person and had just received the original (unsent) letter from them. For many individuals, this return letter will reflect anger and defensiveness on the part of the other person. After this is completed, the client is asked to write a final letter from that person, this time rendering it as the client hopes it could be (for example, apologetic, grateful, affectionate). Although all three letters may be difficult projects for some clients, this third one is often particularly challenging. I have seen individuals totally "block" at this point, unable to imagine their imaginary corespondent as capable of the desired compassion or insight. When I am working with an individual who reports unresolved anger toward parents, for example, I often encourage him or her to imagine those parents writing back about their own childhood, their feelings and frustrations with their own parents, and so on.

Besides correspondence (both hypothetical and real), some clients report deriving substantial benefits from writing poetry, short stories, and informal musings. The range and functions of such writings are discussed by Michael White and David Epston (1990), and illustrations are offered in the *Journal of Poetry Therapy* (published by Human Sciences Press for the National Association for Poetry Therapy; see also the journals *Pilgrimage* and *The Arts in Psychotherapy*).

The Personal Development Journal

One of the most common techniques for encouraging self-exploration is the use of a private diary as a medium in and through which to examine private life. A good example is Hugh Prather's *Notes to Myself* (1970), in which he reflects:

I just don't believe that most people are living the smooth, controlled, trouble-free existence that their careful countenances and bland words suggest. Today never hands me the same thing twice and I believe that for most everyone else life is also a mixture of unsolved problems, ambiguous victories and vague defeats—with very few moments of clear peace. I never do seem to quite get on top of it. My struggle with today is worthwhile, but it is a struggle nonetheless and one I will never finish. (P. 25)

"Private writing" may contribute in important ways to understanding and facilitating individual change processes. Clients may exhibit a wide range of reactions to the suggestion or assignment to begin keeping a diary. When there is general resistance to the idea of refining self-awareness (versus this particular method of approaching it), this may be important to explore.

Those who do keep some form of journal or diary also exhibit a remarkable range of styles in expressing their self-study. In my own clinical experience, I have found that some clients prefer more structure than others in their initial writing assignments. There are, of course, well-developed programs for "intensive journal work," and there are guides to different styles of diary keeping (for example, Progoff 1975, 1980; Rainer 1978). The research literature on this topic is now becoming more robust (Brand 1980; Brand and Leckie 1988; Hettich 1990; Houlding and

Holland 1988; Judge 1988; McAdams et al. 1988; Powell and Brand 1987; Stewart, Franz, and Layton 1988; White 1981; White and Atkinson 1980; Wrightsman 1981). The format I currently use with clients involves separate categories for entries: current events, memories, a structured "life review project" (see pages 292–94), dreams and fantasies, and reflective "notes to myself." For some individuals (particularly at later stages in their writing) I also encourage a "dual entry" format to encourage reflection and perspective taking. This involves their usual style of writing (as in the preceding categories) plus an additional running commentary (usually to the side or in the margins) which is entered later, after reading and reflecting upon their primary entries. I believe that the multiplicities of dialogue and perspective taking afforded by such personal writings deserve a much deeper appreciation in our search for helpful methods of counsel.

When, in writing this chapter, I reviewed boxes full of my clients' personal journals (and my own journaling in response to them), I was struck by the extent to which my clients' journaling processes—above and beyond the structure and content of their private bookkeeping—have taught me invaluable lessons about the endurance, resilience, and complexity of human change processes. In sharing their lives so openly with me, and in risking to trust the dynamics of their own development, these individuals have helped deepen my appreciation that it is the lessons and challenges of professional practice that should most powerfully guide research and theory. An illustration comes from the personal journal of Olive W., an agoraphobic woman whose crystalline descriptions of her own development were invaluable in my own developing ideas about resistance and rhythms in human change processes (chapter 12). Olive's fear of experiencing panic attacks eventually dissipated to the point that she became more and more willing to risk venturing out of her house by herself. Her progress was hardly linear, however, and she experienced "waves" of both terror and excitement in her preliminary excursions. One diary entry was particularly vivid in its portrayal of her experience of what I have come to call developmental "expansions" and "contractions" (chapter 12):

Last night I dreamt that I lived in a large fortress in the desert. I was alone there except for an old priest; I think he was you. Every morning he sat in a small chapel and prayed. Sometimes I prayed, too, and sometimes I entered the confessional. He was always in the priest's chamber in the confessional (and, somehow, in the dream, I didn't question how he could be two places at once).

At some point I began leaving the fortress during the day and going for short walks in the desert. They were scary at first, but later I began to find things that fascinated me. Mostly wildflowers and smooth stones and animal tracks. I returned to the fortress every night before dark. But then my trips outside got longer and longer until one day I wasn't sure whether I could make it back before dark.

Suddenly I was on the edge of a bottomless abyss. It was like pictures I've seen of the Grand Canyon, except that it was all dark at the bottom. In fact, there was no bottom. I knew that if I fell I would never hit anything. I would just fall forever. I was paralyzed with terror. I didn't want to fall into the abyss, but I couldn't get home before dark. I woke up crying, and I heard you say, "Olive, be gentle with yourself and trust. . . ." You said something else, too. I think it was about my being able to move in more than two directions, but, by then, I was too awake to remember it.

Besides helping therapists to understand the phenomenology of individual clients' experiences, personal journals (and the process of writing them) may be valuable aids in helping individuals gain perspective on their past and present life. The scaffolding and rescaffolding of one's experiential patterns and personal meanings is often facilitated in the process. Writing and journal keeping are not invariably appreciated (or performed) by clients, however; and therapists are wise to respect individual differences in responsiveness to such techniques.

The Life Review Project

The *life review project* is often addressed via a journal, but it can also be approached as a separate exercise. As the literature on this topic attests, there is no single or standard format.* The central concern, however, is that the individual reflect on his or her life and, in so doing, strive to develop a better understanding of who and how he or she has been, is now, and might become. Some of the most useful literature on life review is in the area of aging and geriatric psychology, where there is evidence that "successful aging" is associated with integrative reflections (Birren and Hateley 1985; Birren and Hedlund 1987; Lewis and Butler 1974; Wong 1989). Indeed, "obsessive reminiscence" appears to be related to less satisfying experiences in later life, while the meaning making afforded by creating a coherent "life story" seems to contribute to well-being.

In psychotherapy and professional workshops, I use a format for life review that goes as follows. The individual is asked to begin by labeling a card or sheet of paper with each year since the year before his or her

*Life review and "psychobiography" represent overlapping literatures. The classics here include the works of Charlotte Bühler (1935), Else Frenkel (1936), Henry A. Murray (1938), and Gordon Allport (1942). Contemporary expressions are diverse: Butler 1963, 1980–81; Lieberman and Falk 1971; LoGerfo 1980–81; McAdams 1988; Malde 1988; Reynolds 1980; Tarman 1988, and Williams and Scott 1988. Family of origin work and "genogram" techniques are discussed by Beck and Munson 1988; Friedman, Rohrbaugh, and Krakauer 1988; and Kerr and Bowen 1988. For illustrations of recent work on autobiographical memory in cognitive and developmental psychology, see Brewer 1986; DeWaele and Harré 1979; Johnson 1988; M.K. Johnson et al. 1988; Olney 1972; Ross 1989; Rubin 1986; and Spengemann 1980.

birth. (My rationale for using the year *before* birth as a temporal marker is that it invites an awareness of intergenerational influences and the family circumstances into which one was born). The initial assignment is to begin making entries on each card (that is, events, memories, or associations with that year). Those entries need not be explicit memories; they can be feeling tones, song titles, world events, the recollections of others, and so on. Moreover, there is no requirement that the life review be conducted in strict chronological sequence, or that entries be confined to "facts." Vague impressions, trace memories, and hunches are welcomed, and the individual is encouraged to "skip around" and make entries as they come to awareness. (Some people like to note the date of their entries and later examine patterns in their recall.)

Additional pages (cards) for a given year are added as space requires. Photographs, report cards, and other mementos can also be attached. In the context of this exercise, individuals are encouraged to consult whatever sources seem appropriate (scrapbooks, contacts with family and friends, and so on). Needless to say, this "personal research" often evokes strong emotions in itself. When the individual feels that he or she has arrived at a "first draft" or "initial sketch," I ask the client to bring the material to the session. (Individuals vary, of course, in how long this takes, how much they collect, and how ready they feel to call such a collection a coherent first effort; all of these are potential grist for hermeneutic mills.) Within the constraints of the available space, I then ask clients to "lay out their life" (usually on the floor). If they request instructions about how to do that, I encourage them to use whatever structure or format appeals to them. (The variance here is again impressive; although many people use linear, left-right matrices, others develop personally meaningful clusters, spirals, and other configurations.) Once their "life" is laid out, I ask them to "walk through it" (physically, if possible, but at least metaphorically), beginning wherever they want, and pausing and reflecting wherever they choose.

The research phase of the life review project is often emotionally challenging for individuals: in recalling and recording their developmental histories, they frequently encounter personal memories and life episodes that are still difficult to acknowledge. The later review phase (literally, a review of the review) can also be challenging and potentially heuristic. Because of my constructivist leanings, I try to avoid being cast in the role of the expert interpreter at this (or any other) stage. Instead, I encourage individuals to share their own emerging (and sometimes changeable) impressions of their life history. Helpful queries here are: What is your attention drawn to? What do you sense (see, feel) right now? What patterns are apparent to you? What were your most important choices? and What does it mean for you? It is also sometimes helpful to ask about important calendar dates and associations with months or seasons, many of which involve "anniversaries" of significant life events.

STREAM OF CONSCIOUSNESS

My clients' journals and life review projects have helped alert me to how much does not get said or shared, even in the "best" of our fifty-minute hours. When we meet once per week, our time together represents less than half of 1 percent of their "time in the trenches of life," as one client put it. In my attempts to better understand the complexities and ongoing movements of their lives, I have also reviewed the possible contributions of other forms of assessment. My early professional training included a heavy dose of skepticism about the merits of psychometrics, and I continue to be concerned about the abuses of diagnostic classification. Even though I remain more skeptical and cautious in these domains than many of my colleagues, however, I have also become more open to the potential contributions of psychological assessment.*

One of the primary purposes of assessment is to refine our understanding of the felt experience of the person being served. In the mid-1970s, I began exploring assessment methods that were less focused on symptomatic snapshots and more attuned to *in vivo* samples. In retrospect, this was a major event in my professional development. Where I had previously instructed clients as to what to look for and what to change (for example, their beliefs and self-statements), I was now inviting them simply to examine themselves and their lives—in session and otherwise. This amounted to a shift toward experiential focus and exercises in imagery and meditation.

There are, of course, a wide range of experiential techniques, particularly if one includes those associated with fantasy exercises, spontaneous imagery, and the contemplative exercises of various spiritual traditions.† The varieties of meditation, for example, are often clustered according to their strategic use of attention. Some prescribe a *fixed focus* of attention (for example, a mantra, a sound, or a point of light), while others prescribe a *flexible focus* (for example, the changing contents and perspectives of awareness [Goleman 1977]). The latter strategy is sometimes termed "mindful" meditation. Between these extremes are *guided focus* practices,

---

*Regrettably, much of the clinical assessment literature focuses almost exclusively on technicalities of measurement theory (for example, reliability and validity) rather than on balancing such issues with practical contributions to the understanding of client and therapist. For representative discussions of this and related topics, see Corcoran and Fischer 1987; Kendall and Hollon 1981; Kuykendall, Keating, and Wagaman 1988; Mahoney 1988d; Mehrabian and Russell 1974; Merluzzi, Glass, and Genest 1981; Piotrowski and Keller 1984; Safran et al. 1986; Schacht 1985; Shaw 1980; Turk and Salovey 1988; and Zautra, Guarnaccia, and Reich 1988.

†Craven 1989; Daldrup et al. 1988; Foulkes and Fleisher 1975; Gendlin 1962; Ketterer 1985; Klinger 1971, 1977; May, Angel, and Ellenberger 1958; Natsoulas 1988, 1989b; Pope and Singer 1978; Singer 1974; and Singer and Pope 1978. For discussions of fantasy and pretend as developmental processes, see also Bretherton and Beeghly 1982; Eckler and Weininger 1989; Flavell, Flavell, and Green 1987; Leslie 1987; Watkins 1986; and Wellman and Estes 1986.

in which the target of attention is shifted as part of the unfolding structure of the exercise. The Japanese psychotherapies (particularly Naikan, but also Morita) reflect a guided focus format [Reynolds 1980]. They allow the client's attention to shift in its focus, but place categorical constraints on general topics and periods of emphasis.

As previewed in chapter 9, stream of consciousness is an exercise in which the client is invited to attend to and, as best one can, report ongoing thoughts, sensations, images, memories, and feelings. It is a technique that falls into the flexible focus (mindful) class of meditative exercises, and bears resemblances to at least three procedures in early psychology: the "imageless thought" methodology of Charlotte Külpe (1909) and Oswald Bühler (1935) (in the Wurzburg school), the technique of "active imagination" employed by Carl Jung (1960–1979), and the "free association" technique developed by Sigmund Freud (Kris 1982). The latter is probably best known, and it is important to note two significant differences between psychoanalytic free association and "streaming." First, the person's privacy needs are honored in stream-of-consciousness reporting; and, second, therapist interpretations of the reported "stream" are not considered the primary or ultimate authority on their meaning (Mahoney 1983). In other words, clients are not asked to report everything that enters their awareness (as in free association), and are encouraged to respect the ebb and flow of their ability and willingness to share the contents of their immediate experience.

The intent here is to encourage a sense of safety and trust as well as to acknowledge the client's self-protective tendencies (chapter 12). I inform people that they may recall or experience things in the context of streaming that they may not want to share (or to share immediately). By inviting them to be aware of these experiences, I hope to deepen their awareness of their own processes of selecting and configuring the contents that they are sharing from their private life. In my opinion, the "censoring" and "defense" mechanisms involved are fundamentally self-protective; besides recognizing their operation, I invite clients to appreciate their self-caring intentions.

The second difference between free association and streaming is that the interpretation of reported contents is less central to the latter than is the process of focusing inward and respectfully "witnessing." As a constructivist, I do not ascribe to a universal theory of meaning, and I do not presume to know what any given particular of consciousness may mean to another individual. Interpretation is important and potentially powerful in the (re)scaffolding of experience, but there is no single or certain source of "true" (valid) interpretation. In this sense, at least, Freud was clearly hermeneutic in his practice, but not hermeneutic enough by today's standards. When clients ask me what their stream (or some of its contents) really "means" about them, I ask them to take (and, with rare exceptions) keep the lead in interpreting it: What do you think?

How do you interpret it? What does it remind you of? What are you feeling now as you reflect on it? I believe that the meaning of a person's reported stream is most (albeit imperfectly) understandable from the context of that person's own orderings or meanings (rather than mine or those of anyone else). I am more interested in the style and emotional tone of their search for meanings rather than in the explicit contents or expressions of the meanings themselves.

As with other techniques (be they intended for assessment or intervention), I recommend that psychotherapists first explore this exercise with themselves before using it with clients. For those practitioners who doubt the existence of resistance (chapter 12), I recommend both streaming and mirror time (see pages 301–8). Because it provides a record for later review, a tape recorder is helpful for both a therapist's self-explorations and later applications with clients. For a variety of possible reasons, streaming can be a challenging and emotionally intense undertaking. More than any other technique I have used, it has facilitated the recall of experiences that were painful and formative in clients' earlier development but which had come to be denied, distorted, or "forgotten." As Bowlby and others have documented, such self-defensive processes are much more common than we may yet realize (Bowlby 1979, 1985; Evoy 1981). I therefore caution against the use of this technique (1) in early sessions of psychotherapy or when only a few sessions remain before termination, (2) in the absence of a strong "working alliance," (3) without the client's having chosen to work at the level of experiential processes, (4) immediately post-trauma, (5) late in a session (that is, without allowing time for sufficient processing of the experience), and (6) with individuals who are currently struggling to develop, recover, or maintain an integrated sense of self or reality (see chapter 9; Baumeister 1990; Bentall 1990; Cassano et al. 1989). Stream-of-consciousness reporting can be a powerful and unsettling experience (for both client and therapist) and should be approached with all due respect. For many individuals, it is difficult enough simply to "look inward," let alone to put words on their experience and to then share those words with another person. To illustrate, consider two clinical vignettes and an anecdote from a professional conference.

The first illustration comes from my work with Karen Z., the woman who asked me where I stood on the issue of human plasticity (pages 259–65). Streaming was introduced only after we had met for almost twenty sessions and established a good working relationship. With the aforementioned reassurances about her privacy, I invited Karen to relax and, when she felt ready, to focus her attention inward and to share what she could of her experience. Like many other clients, she was slow to get started, and I employed one of several priming strategies (Mahoney 1983). After her fourth session of streaming, she began to move more quickly and deeply into a spontaneous flow of reporting, and her reports began to reflect both wide-ranging and recurrent themes. In her fifth session, she began to experience unexpected stomach cramps and asked if she could lie on the floor. I suggested that she might want to abandon the streaming exercise and simply relax. She insisted that it felt like "good pain" and lay down on her side. Within minutes, she began crying in a childlike voice and talking as if her parents were present. (In witnessing Karen's report, I recall feeling initially frightened by her intensity and obvious pain.) She began wringing her hands together as if she were wiping them, and sobbing, "I'm a bad girl. . . . I know I'm a bad girl. . . . I'm all yucky."

Karen spent almost twenty minutes on the floor, much of it in a fetal position and sobbing. Fortunately, my next hour was unscheduled, and we had time to begin processing her experience. Karen had no idea what it meant, but she reported feeling that it was "frighteningly important." She asked if she could stream again in our next session. I tentatively agreed but encouraged her to review her decision when the time came. She arrived for that session in a state of anxious arousal and insisted that she "had to stream immediately." I invited her to relax first and to "get a reading" on whether it was self-caring for her to stream again. She stated that it was and, after several minutes of silence, spontaneously returned to her position on the floor. Karen cried again intermittently for ten minutes and repeated some of the same phrases and gestures exhibited in her earlier session. I then invited her to return her attention to her bodily sensations, her location, and my voice. She slowly regained composure and returned to a sitting position. This time her imagery had taken her somewhat "further" and she was puzzled by a smell she could not identify.

It was not until the next session that Karen thought she could identify that smell. She said, "It doesn't make sense, Mike. It's something I never smelled until I was married." The smell, she said, was semen. I was as unprepared for that revelation as was Karen. She was frightened and confused, twice commenting that she was "just making it all up" and that this was "all pretend." I encouraged her to temporarily relax her concerns about whether it was "real" and what it "meant," and to instead focus on what she was feeling in the exercise. Karen struggled to make sense of her experience and eventually phoned her mother and related her distress. Her mother cried and reluctantly confessed that Karen had, in fact, been sexually molested by her father on more than one occasion. He was usually intoxicated, she said, and in several of these episodes had invited two or three of his "drinking buddies" to join him. When she had attempted to stop them, Karen's mother had been threatened with being beaten. She told Karen that she had "prayed that it had all been forgotten." In disbelief, Karen obtained copies of her childhood medical records and discovered that she had twice required sutures (at ages seven and nine) to repair vaginal tears. As mentioned earlier, we ended up working together for more than three years in attempting to repair the damage wrought by her cruel abuse.

Another woman, Dolly T., was also unprepared for what she discovered in the process of streaming. A forty-six-year-old music teacher, she had originally presented with the complaint of chronic grieving over the death of her cat more than a year earlier. During our intake interviews, she reported having lived a happy and relatively uneventful life as the only child of a minister and a pharmacist. Her father had died when Dolly was thirty-five, and she had continued to live with her mother until her death several months before that of the cat. Dolly was cheerful and verbal during each of our sessions, her only complaint being that she awakened every night at 3 A.M., trembling and crying over the absence of her cat. In a review of her progress during our ninth session, Dolly said that she wanted to try "some of those exploration exercises" that I had mentioned during intake. We began with journal work and the life review project. The latter revealed something suggestive: Dolly could not reveal many details of her life between the ages of six and seventeen.

Over the next several months, I introduced the technique of streaming. Dolly enjoyed it at first and was playful in her reporting (humming songs, chuckling at her shifts in attention, and using the exercise to pose abstract questions about life). During her fifth session of streaming, she reported the "intrusion" of puzzling images: unidentifiable shadows cast on a wall by candlelight, a mountain stream with "bloody rocks," and "hot sparks" up and down her spine. Over the next few sessions, the shadows reappeared in her report, and she identified the wall as that of her childhood bedroom. At several points in her self-report, she spontaneously rubbed her wrists and wiped perspiration from her forehead. She appeared to be hyperventilating, and I reminded her to breathe deeply and take her time. She reported feeling bewildered by the contents of her streaming and wondered "who was directing this show."

Soon thereafter, she reported "entering streams spontaneously" while she was at home. A distressing scene kept recurring: she and her mother were standing at the front door of their house. The scene was slowly elaborated over several weeks of streaming: her mother seemed upset; her mother was upset with her father; she and her mother were wearing coats; there was a suitcase on the floor; they were leaving for a trip without her father. Over the next few weeks, Dolly reported feeling unusually tired and anxious. She could not recall having taken any trip with her mother and said that she had never witnessed an argument between her parents. To investigate the matter, she phoned her only living relative, an older cousin. He was mysteriously evasive when she asked him questions about her parents and her childhood. During a later phone conversation, however, he admitted that her father (his uncle) had been considered "a bit strange" by other family members. Within hours of that conversation, Dolly entered a prolonged state of emotional crisis.

Her journal entries became progressively more disorganized and she reverted to printing and childlike sentences. During a spontaneous session of streaming at home, Dolly recalled an early incident in her life. The description of it in her journal was painfully vivid. She was six years old and, against her parents' advice, had gone by herself to her father's church on a Saturday afternoon. Two young men who were riding by on bicycles saw her, stopped, and chased her. They carried her into the basement of the empty church where they gagged her, tied her hands, raped her repeatedly, and then fled. Dolly lost consciousness several times in the ensuing hours and remembered wishing that she were dead. Her hold on life (or its hold on her) was strong, however, and she spent hours on the floor mesmerized by the bright rays of sunlight that came through a nearby window. Just before sunset she managed to free her wrists, but she remained in the church until after dark. Later she made her way to a "secret hideout" under some shrubbery near their house. Her father found her there late that night and carried her to her room. After carefully removing her bloody dress, he told her that she was now "ruined for life," and that he had to punish her. He then raped her himself.

Needless to say, Dolly's story was one of the most painful I have ever heard. During a later phone conversation, her cousin reluctantly disclosed that Dolly's father was thought to have been a member of a Satanic cult. In her words, "his daytimes had been spent in the service of God, but after dark he was the Devil's handyman." Dolly's 3 A.M. "night terrors" began to make some sense to her: that was apparently the time when her father had regularly visited her bedroom. As a teenager she had apparently been impregnated by him twice. The first child was aborted by a veterinarian, but Dolly had hemorrhaged badly and had required hospitalization. Her medical records listed the cause of her uterine bleeding as "self-inflicted injury." Her second baby, a boy, was carried full term and delivered by her mother. Within hours of his birth, however, the cruelty forced upon mother and child was truly heinous: Dolly was forced to drown her newborn son in a nearby river as part of a sacrificial ceremony orchestrated by her father. The baby's desperate cries for life eventually dissipated, but the sounds and sights of that profane torture became later material in Dolly's recurrent "night terrors."

Over the next eighteen months Dolly struggled valiantly to maintain her psychological stability and to survive recurring waves of despair. She felt intermittently suicidal, and I obtained a written contract from her promising that she would not attempt to hurt herself without first meeting with me. Dolly also knew and accepted the fact that she might need to be hospitalized if the risk of self-injury so warranted. In my prior clinical experience, I had never seen anyone struggle so long with such intense anguish. Finally, at the end of a session of almost continuous crying, I tried to say something that would be encouraging. "Dolly," I said, "I wish I could take your pain away, but I can't. For what it is worth, though, I do think that the worst is over. You survived many cruel violations of your mind and body as a child, and you have now confronted those memories as an adult. It will take time for all the wounds to heal, but I do believe that you are past the worst of it. . . ."

My voice trailed off because of the look on her face—a tired sadness etched with skepticism. Dolly replied, "Thank you, Mike. I know you are trying to help, and I appreciate that. But . . . well, . . . you have been on target before, but this time I think you are wrong." When she left that day, I made an entry in my own journal about how utterly hopeless she seemed to feel, and how difficult it was for me to feel so limited in what I could offer. Several weeks later, however, another piece of the puzzle explained her intuition about my being wrong. Dolly recalled having found a strategy to avoid her father's late-night visits. At the age of fourteen, she began leaving her bedroom at midnight and going to her mother's private bedroom. Her mother said that she understood, and invited Dolly to sleep there with her. In the course of their first night in bed together, however, Dolly's mother insisted that they play a "touching game" that culminated in Dolly's being asked to fondle her mother's genitals. Although it was less violent than her father's method, it was still intrusive, abusive, and demeaning. When she told me about this incident, I realized that she had been right in reading her own intuitive awareness of more to come: the worst had not, in fact, been over.

Over the course of yet another year in therapy, Dolly made significant strides in moving beyond her early traumas and in accepting her self as a valuable—and, indeed, "strong-spirited"—person. She read extensively on religion and spirituality, and her journal expanded into a number of art projects and new hobbies (pottery, flower arranging, and watercolors). Our work together was cut short by my relocation to another part of the country, but Dolly continued her treatment with another therapist. I last heard from her a few months ago—almost six years since our last session—and she reported "finally feeling free" and that she had found "great strength in her faith." Dolly is the only person I have counseled who was sexually abused by both parents. Besides teaching me so much about human resilience, I also learned to be much more cautious about telling anyone that "the worst is over."

My final anecdote comes from a professional conference in Brussels, Belgium. I was describing the stream-of-consciousness technique to an audience of psychotherapists, most of whom were behaviorists. Before I had reached the point of sharing illustrations from the experiences of my clients, a young woman in the audience stood up and screamed, "You ought to be ashamed of yourself. What you are doing is unethical!" I paused and then asked her to help me understand her charge. She said, "My God, man! You are asking people to look inside themselves!" I said,

"That is right. I *am* asking people to look inside themselves. But can you tell me why that is unethical?" She was shaking with anger: "Don't you see? There is no telling what they might find. . . ." As her voice trailed off, I invited her to continue by simply saying, "And . . ." "And," she went on, *"we have not been trained to deal with it!"* I told her that I thought her reaction reflected well on her strong feelings about ethical practice, and agreed with her observation that many training programs do not adequately prepare psychotherapists to deal with some of the unknowns of our own and our clients' private lives. Needless to say, I think that they should.

MIRROR TIME

In retrospect, I am surprised that my earliest work in self studies did not include more "reflection," especially in the realm of visual perception. The possibilities of a mirror give it special significance as a tool in self studies. It took a pivotal coincidence with two clients to open my eyes to the potential power of mirrors as aids in the encouragement of psychological development. I was seeing Adam K. for a variety of problems that included anxiety, bulimia, depression, and obsessive-compulsive patterns. Adam was quite proud of his "untreatability by some of the best therapists in the country." As will be elaborated in chapter 12, Adam was also a classic example of resistance as an identity-related phenomenon. We were nearing the end of his life review project and close to our twentieth session when a serendipitous event altered the course of our later work together. Adam's next session was scheduled two hours after my regular appointment with Gary G., a thirteen-year-old who had been court-referred after his mother had had him arrested for possession of marijuana. Gary was angry, scared, and quiet. Despite the circumstances, we were able to develop some rapport, and I invited him to take his time and to share only what he felt ready to share about what he was feeling. To my surprise, Gary's first sharing was a gift: a small mirror he had won as a prize at a local carnival over the weekend. Across the top it read "Harley Davidson Motorcycles." I was touched and, after thanking him, I put it up on my favorite bookcase. We had a good session, and I filled much of the following hour writing notes about this welcome development in our work.

Then the doorbell rang; it was Adam arriving for his session. As we greeted each other and found our chairs, Adam began an energetic ventilation of his anger and anxiety over a new crisis in his life. The specifics changed from week to week, but the pattern was consistent: Adam lived from one crisis to the next, and preferred to spend much of our time together ventilating his anger and, as he put it, "wailing at his

Wall." In this session he began with a fast-paced narration about an interaction at work that he feared might have made him look "weird" to his peers. But Adam was clearly distracted, as was reflected in recurrent lapses in his story and inconsistent eye contact with me. After a few minutes, he stopped and pointed to my newly acquired mirror. "Excuse me, Mike, . . . but was that mirror there last week?" "No," I said. "Well, . . . umm . . . if you wouldn't mind moving it . . . uh . . . I keep catching glimpses of myself in it and I lose track of what I was saying." Reaching for both the moment and the mirror, I said, "Sure," and placed the mirror on my desk, directly in front of Adam. He was out of his chair in seconds, pacing the room and half laughing. "Oh, no! You don't want to see me in front of a mirror!" "I don't?" "Oh, no-o-o! You wouldn't want to see that!" "It's beginning to sound more and more interesting."

I put the mirror face down on my desk and assured Adam that it was not a "requirement," but an "invitation," and that I would respect his right to choose whether or when he was ready. Over our next four sessions, Adam related that he spent hours per day in agony before the mirror in his apartment. He picked at his skin and fussed with his hair, and sometimes he obsessed about the places between and behind his teeth that he couldn't see. He concluded with the statement that he did not feel ready to "do mirrors." I thanked him for his candor and assured him that he need not ever do mirror time in our work together. Two months later, in the trough of a depressive cycle, Adam brought up the topic of the mirror again. By then I had begun experimenting with mirror-based reflective exercises, using myself and some willing colleagues as volunteers. There was now a full-length mirror on the back of my office door. I told Adam that I would be willing to lead him through an exploration of "mirror work"; and, after some brief instructions in relaxation and intention-setting, we both stood up solemnly and walked toward the large mirror. I stood to the side, out of the range of its reflection, and leaned against a bookcase. Adam looked like someone on his way to a formidable challenge. When he was finally about a meter away from the mirror, he stopped and kept his head down. He posture reminded me of a nine-year-old facing a dive off a 10-meter platform. After a few lingering moments, Adam made his "dive" by looking up and confronting his image in the mirror. His breathing accelerated, and his first words were "heart rush."

After more than a minute of silent gazing, Adam's breathing slowed, and I asked him what he was feeling. His face suddenly broke into a grin, and he said, "That guy in the mirror doesn't look as fucked up as I feel." He chuckled, and I failed to stifle an incredulous "What?" "Yep," he continued, "he looks more real than me." I stood there silent and mesmerized. "In fact," Adam said, "I wouldn't mind *being him!*" That was the beginning of a whole new path in our work together. It also encouraged me to consider introducing some other clients to the technique of mirror time.*

Studies of direct attention to the self through a mirror have been remarkably sparse. There are, to be sure, some valuable investigations of the development of self-consciousness in which mirror self-recognition is used as the prototype. As noted in chapter 9, that research suggests that early attachment and social relations are critical variables in healthy identity development (Gallup 1977, 1982, 1985; Lewis and Brooks-Gunn 1979; Loveland 1986; Morin and Deblois 1989; Priel and Schonen 1986). Apes raised in isolation or with members of other species exhibit profound problems in later socialization and apparent difficulties in recognizing their own mirrored image.

Although Lacan (1977, 1978) discussed the mirror stage in psychological development, I know of no references to his use of the mirror as a tool in psychotherapy. Other psychodynamic writers have used mirrors in assessment and treatment, however, and have acknowledged its significance to the developing individual (Elkisch 1957; Frenkel 1963, 1980). Occasional references to the uses of mirrors can also be found in some writings on gestalt psychotherapy, self-awareness, body image, and certain forms of meditation (Gardner et al. 1989; Goleman 1977; Hatfield and Sprecher 1986). Fascinating discussions of the powers attributed to mirrors at different times and by different cultures are offered by Benjamin Goldberg (1985) and George MacDonald and his colleagues (1989).

---

*In the present century, it is worth noting the frequency with which the mirror has been used as a metaphor for important processes in psychological development. In self psychology and many psychodynamic perspectives, for example, "mirroring" refers to some of the interpersonal processes between parent and child or therapist and client, with the former serving as a metaphoric reflector of the latter's psychological projections (chapter 9). More than those of any other writer, the works of Jacques Lacan (1977, 1978) have encouraged a greater appreciation for the significance of the mirror in human psychological development. Lacan postulated a period of infancy (between six and twelve months) which he called the "mirror stage" because it is when, in spontaneously recognizing the baby in the mirror as "me," there begins an experiential split between the subject and the other. Lacan's work has also been at the forefront of the modern shift in depth psychology from biological metaphors to constructivist and narrative-based alternatives (Davis 1966; Kugler 1987). Lacan's preoccupation was with the "birth of subjectivity" in the individual and its relation to the centrality of narrative in human development. The mirror offers an "unreal" reflection of self in which imagination and perception are fused. It is perhaps not surprising, then, that mirrors of one form or another have been used in a variety of approaches to personality and developmental processes.

There is, for example, considerable reference to "self-perception" and the "looking glass self" in research on social cognition, social comparison, and self-monitoring (Buss 1980; Carver and Scheier 1978; Duval and Wicklund 1972; Kleinke 1978; Suls and Greenwald 1983; Wegner and Vallacher 1980). Interestingly, in most of this work, mirrors are used only rarely and, even then, only indirectly. A prototypical experiment, for example, involves student volunteers filling out a questionnaire in the absence or presence of a mirror. In some studies, the mirror's presence is unexplained; in others, it is said to be merely coincidental (for example, it is there for temporary storage). This somewhat oblique approach to the dimension of self-awareness is itself an interesting phenomenon in psychological research.

Over the last few years, my colleagues and I have begun to explore those powers with both clinical and experimental populations.

Beyond a pool of fascinating case examples, our current data sets consist of three laboratory studies. The first involved volunteers who were outpatients in individual psychotherapy (Blanco et al. 1986). Four clinical groups were comprised of persons suffering from phobic disorders ($N = 16$), unipolar depression ($N = 12$), obsessive-compulsive disorders ($N = 13$), and eating disorders ($N = 19$). For comparison purposes, a group of twenty-three nonclinical volunteers also underwent an identical "mirror time" procedure, which consisted of a five-minute resting baseline and 15 minutes of looking into a mirror while responding to basic questions about their feelings and self-perception. Four measures of physiological activity were obtained throughout both phases: heart rate, skin conductance (gsr), muscle tension (emg), and peripheral skin temperature. As shown in figure 11.1, there was considerable group variability in these dimensions of activity during both baseline and experimental phases.

Of particular interest were some apparent "patterns of patterns" within various groups. From a complex developmental systems approach, novel stimuli and challenging tasks may cause at least momentary disorganization and reduced coherence among interrelated subsystems. Under most circumstances and for relatively normal individuals, for example, heart rate is positively correlated with skin conductance and muscle tension, and negatively (inversely) related to skin temperature. Using the degree of positive or negative correlation between selected pairs of these physiological responses, one can look for temporal patterns of systemic (in)coherence—episodes of "deregulation" that may reflect the system's organizational dynamics (appendix E). Figure 11.2, for example, suggests different patterns of dynamics in the cardiac and muscular responses of individuals in some groups. Normal subjects exhibited the expected strong positive correlation between these measures during baseline. With the introduction of the mirror, however, they showed a significant decline in physiological coherence followed by a gradual recovery over the next 15 minutes. Individuals labeled depressive showed minimal physiological coherence throughout both phases of the study; their slight reactivity to the experimental phase is noteworthy. Persons seeking psychotherapy for phobia (most were agoraphobic) showed a distinctly different pattern, however. They exhibited a strong *inverse* relationship during baseline and a sharp change toward increased physiological coherence when the mirror was introduced. This change in the coordination of the two systems was variable and began to dissipate over the 15-minute experimental period.

A somewhat similar pattern was found when the ongoing correlation between muscle tension and skin conductance was examined (figure 11.3). Normal subjects again "decompensated" briefly at the beginning

Figure 11.1   Physiological Measures during Resting Baseline and Mirror Exposure

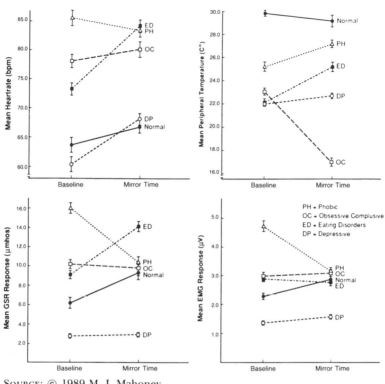

SOURCE: © 1989 M. J. Mahoney

of the experimental phase, but quickly regained their former physiological "balance." Depressive subjects also showed their earlier pattern of weak and relatively unresponsive physiological coordination. In this particular comparison, phobic subjects showed their most dramatic inversion of the pattern exhibited by normals. Under the minimal stress of a resting baseline, phobic subjects appeared to be apprehensive and maximally disorganized. When the novel challenge of mirror time arrived, however, they quickly organized themselves (at least as reflected by these two measures) to a degree indistinguishable from that of their nonclinical peers.

These interpretations are, of course, open to interpretation, and there have not been any reported independent attempts to replicate these procedures or findings. At present they pose only interesting questions.

Also interesting was the extreme variability in physiological coherence exhibited by eating-disordered and obsessive-compulsive clients. Their physiological responses to the presence of a mirror were much less con-

Figure 11.2 Physiological Concordance between Peripheral Muscle Tension (EMG) and Galvanic Skin Response (GSR)

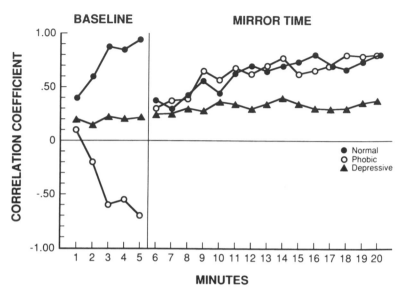

SOURCE: © 1989 M. J. Mahoney

Figure 11.3 Physiological Concordance between Peripheral Muscle Tension (EMG) and Heart Rate

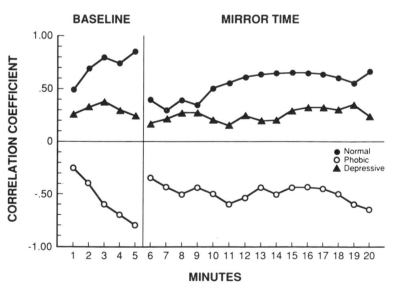

SOURCE: © 1989 M. J. Mahoney

sistent than those seen in the depressed, phobic, and normal groups. In two laboratory studies with nonclinical volunteers, individual differences were again noteworthy. Among other things, the nonclinical studies offered an important lesson about control groups. After a resting baseline, experimental subjects looked at their own mirror images and were asked to describe what they liked or disliked about their face, body, personality, and self. Control subjects looked at slides of human faces and rated their attraction to each. Physiological responses were highly variable in all groups, including the control (Gabriel 1990; Mahoney, Craine, and Gabriel, 1987). It is possible that the evaluative component and the vicarious human eye contact (Kleinke 1986) may have influenced the responding of some control subjects. Whatever the explanation, the striking range and variability of subjects' responsivity suggest that mirror exercises may be promising procedures for studying individual differences in psychological organization and development.

Practical considerations in the uses of mirror time in psychotherapy deserve a volume of their own. Suffice it here to say that many of the same qualifications and cautions that apply to stream-of-consciousness work also apply to work with mirrors. I recommend that practitioners experiment with themselves first, using an audio or video recorder for later review. I recommend use of a full-length mirror and a standing position (to maximize range of movement and perspective), but I have also witnessed productive sessions from seated reflections in a hand-held mirror. A brief (5-minute) relaxing meditation is often helpful prior to an interval of 5 to 15 minutes of mirrored self-reflection. Needless to say, individuals suffering from eating and body image disorders may find this procedure particularly stressful (chapter 9).

Many clients will use the mirror as a medium for initiating or continuing dialogues (with therapist, self, or other characters, real and imaginary). I encourage such dialogues, especially when they move beyond intellectual exchanges. Some individuals will experience strong reactions to eye contact with themselves, and many report a "felt difference" depending on which of their eyes they focus upon. In their homework assignments, I have also had clients report that differences in illumination may help (or hinder) some aspects of mirror work, and the privacy of their home has allowed many to explore their perceptions of and feelings about their nude body.

Some clients have found it helpful to listen to guiding questions or general instructions for structuring their experience of mirror time, particularly when they are just beginning this type of exercise. I have offered such instructions and questions during in-session exercises and then provided them with an audiotape of examples. These questions and instructions have included the following: "Gently observe what you notice first as you look in the mirror. Witness what you are thinking and feeling. Look into your own eyes. What do you see? How have you changed or remained the same since you were a child? Are there any differences between the person you see in the mirror and the person you feel yourself to be? What do you (dis)like about yourself? What does this remind you of? Close your eyes for a few seconds and take a deep, relaxing breath. Set your intentions to be self-aware and self-caring. Before you reopen your eyes, invite yourself to also open to the possibility of seeing or feeling yourself in a new or different way."

The strategy of opening and closing the eyes (or of shifting focus from one eye to the other) can evoke significant reactions in some clients. This is also true of the strategy of asking them to exaggerate facial expressions reflecting strong emotions (and of giving voice to such feelings). Spontaneous dialogues between subselves are not uncommon and are often initially expressed as dichotomies (for instance, good and bad selves, strong and weak selves, critical and nurturant selves, and so on). The *hakomi* therapist Ron Kurtz (1986) refers to them as the "family of self." (In the modern Hopi language, *hakomi* means both "who you are" and "who are you?"; in its ancient use, the term meant "how do you stand in relation to these many realms?") For a psychotherapist, this is where experience with emotionally intense self-dialogues can be particularly reassuring and facilitative (see Greenberg and Safran 1987; Stone and Winkelman 1985). I pay particularly close attention to the emergence of new and potentially integrative characters in these dialogues. To facilitate movement beyond a painful "stalemate" in some "wars between the selves," I have on occasion encouraged clients to invite comments from a wise or caring companion (either imaginary or based on such real-life characters as a grandparent, childhood friend, or counselor).

As with other self-exploratory techniques, I recommend that time be reserved later in the session for discussion of the client's experience of mirror time. Even though it is relatively simple, straightforward, and similar to the everyday "mirror checks" many people have performed since childhood (with varying degrees of awareness), this exercise should not be taken lightly. In the absence of a familiar task structure (such as personal hygiene or cosmetic preparations), the mirror can be a powerful instrument of self-confrontation. Since some clients report that mirror-time exercises have influenced the quality and focus of their subsequent everyday glimpses in mirrors (and many other reflecting surfaces), I also recommend homework assignments that involve the client's generation of encouraging and self-caring messages in these spontaneous encounters with self.

OTHER IMPORTANT TECHNIQUES

Needless to say, there are many techniques that can facilitate self-exploration and psychological development. In this final section, my intention is simply to highlight a few techniques whose potential contributions to mental health services have yet to be adequately explored or appreciated.

Embodiment Exercises

Among the techniques and domains of consideration that have been most consistently neglected by psychotherapy researchers are those that involve human embodiment. In the wake of the disembodying effects of Cartesian dualism (chapter 2) and rationalist discourse, it is perhaps not surprising that today's "talking cures" are portrayed as if they transpired between "talking heads." Those heads may complain about the bodies beneath them, but it has only been recently that embodiment and embodied activities have begun to receive more serious attention as important issues in life counseling. From the history of ideas to current horizons in the understanding of cognition, complexity, and lifespan development, much human mentation has entailed denials of and diversions from the biological embodiment of core ordering processes (Becker 1973; Berman 1989; Duby 1988; Feher, Naddaff, and Tazi 1989; Starr 1982). Ironically, the metaphors employed to express much of that mentation have themselves been permeated with body-based experience (Johnson 1987; Lakoff and Johnson 1980). Both the metaphors and the bodies have been abused, however, which is among the reasons that feminist contributions figure importantly in our future refinement of mental health services (Anderson and Zinsser 1988; Belenky et al. 1986; Chernin 1985; Dinnerstein 1976; Freedman 1988; Gilligan 1982; Hsu 1989; Hutchinson 1985; Lerner 1985; Orbach 1978, 1982).

My purpose here is not to review the many approaches to human embodiment expressed in the literatures of sensory awareness, somatics, dance, movement meditation, massage, and exercise. Descriptions and evaluative reviews are readily available.* My intent here, rather, is to underline three considerations that are relevant to the practice of developmental psychotherapy: (1) bodily experiences (and changes therein) are central to the experience of psychological change; (2) the treatment of the human body has been traditionally considered the primary (if not exclusive) domain of medicine; and (3) professionals who serve others via direct contact with or counsel regarding their bodies should be vigilant in the precautions and judgments they exercise. Given the literatures

---

*See American Academy of Physical Education 1984; Berger and Owen 1988; Bliss 1985; Cash and Pruzinsky 1990; Crews and Landers 1987; Dosamantes-Alperson and Merrill 1980; Feder and Feder 1981; Feiss 1979; Frick 1982; Hill 1978; Hornyak and Baker 1989; Keleman 1979; Matarazzo et al. 1984; Minton 1989; Mitchell 1987; Montagu 1978; Morgan 1985*b*, 1985*c;* Pattison 1973; Simons et al. 1985; Tucker 1983*a*, 1983*b;* Whitcher and Fisher 1979; and Willison and Masson 1986.

surveyed in the second part of this book, the first point needs little elaboration.

The second point is a reference to the regrettable "turf battle" that continues to characterize relations between psychiatry and psychology (Buie 1989; Wright and Spielberger 1989), as well as between "mainstream" (allopathic) medicine and its alternatives (Weil 1983); I shall not engage in that battle here. The professions involved face ever more complex issues as body, brain, and psyche come to be recognized as inseparable domains. Although some of the arguments have invoked ethics and the "best interests" of the client as the primary issue, historical patterns suggest that less noble motivations are also likely to be operative (Boorstin 1983; Starr 1982; Weil 1983). This is not to deny that ethical issues are involved, but only to suggest that these are not the only domain of conflict.

The third point also invokes ethical complexities. There are many signs that body-focused forms of intervention are becoming more popular and, in some quarters, "standard practice" as part of psychotherapy. This development raises important issues about the ethics of "therapeutic touch" and "physical psychotherapies" (Goodman and Teicher 1988; Holub and Lee 1990; Jansen and Barron 1988; Kilburg 1988; Willis 1987). Most psychotherapists have not been trained in "somatic intervention techniques," and there are ambiguities as to standards for professional competence in their use (King 1989). In instructing a client to sit or walk with an awareness of his or her physical center of gravity, for example, need we require the psychotherapist to be "board certified" in kinesiology? I think not. Is it appropriate for a psychotherapist to encourage clients to explore and experience such activities as dance, aerobics, recreational sports, massage, or movement meditation? I believe that it can be. Given the evidence that physical activities may make important contributions to the developmental progress of many psychotherapy clients, to ignore these domains would itself reflect questionable judgment on the part of the practitioner. Recent surveys suggest that the recommendation of physical activity as an adjunct to psychotherapy is now common practice regardless of the therapist's theoretical orientation (Mahoney et al. 1989).

But there is an important caveat here. Touch is an extremely powerful form of human interaction (Montagu 1978). Recall that human skin shares a special "ancestral" relationship with the brain and nervous system: they originate from the same layer of tissue in the earliest stages of fetal development. Later, touch becomes a powerful means of communication: its absence or presence and its various qualities can dramatically influence the development and health of newborns. Adult humans also express strong desires to touch and be touched, often in certain ways, by selected others, and only under specified conditions. The "laying on of hands" is a venerable tradition in the multicultural history of healing, and metaphors of touch continue to permeate our narratives about human attributes and interpersonal relations.

The point is that touch has a special significance in the realm of mental health services. The psychotherapist has a privileged role in an emotionally intimate but nonsexual relationship with his or her clients. To add the sensual properties of extensive physical touching to that intimacy is, I believe, to risk damaging both the quality of the relationship and the well-being of the client. This is because some forms of touching may make it more difficult (or impossible) for therapist and client to honor the roles and boundaries essential to a professional helping relationship. The kinds of touching that are potentially dangerous, in my opinion, include those that are painful, intrusive, potentially seductive, or physically intimate—including (but not confined to) sexual contact (Akamatsu 1988; Brown 1988; Committee on Women in Psychology 1989; Edelwich and Brodsky 1982; Pope 1987, 1988; Pope, Keith-Spiegel, and Tabachnick 1986).

I am not, however, advocating extreme distance, nor do I believe that a rigid and absolute avoidance of all physical contact is likely to be in the best interests of all clients. Appropriately timed hugs, hand holding, and other physical expressions of assurance and affection can be valuable and beneficial experiences for many psychotherapy clients. The point here is one of caution. Hugs and embraces mean different things to different people at different times; the practitioner will do well to remember this. Needless to say, I do not believe that a psychotherapist should offer both mental health services and massage to the same client (even if the practitioner is competent and "certified" in both). When there is reason to believe that a client might benefit from "therapeutic touch," a responsible option is to refer them to a competent specialist in that area. In this regard, competence includes the provision that the somatic treatment be nonsexual, and that the practitioner not attempt to practice psychotherapy in the context of their "bodywork." There are many qualified and competent somatic therapists with whom psychotherapists can effectively collaborate in serving the needs of individual clients. As future practitioners move toward such collaborations, we may hope to see a more adequate and beneficial treatment of the whole client.

Art, Music, and Bibliotherapies

There is little debate about the fact that music, art, and literature can make important contributions to the quality of a person's life. Beyond the sheer aesthetics of these domains, they often invite both familiar and novel experiences that may help "stabilize" or "inspire." Regrettably, however, inclusion of the arts in psychotherapy remains less common than might be expected on the basis of this knowledge. In contrast to the gargantuan literatures on other aspects of professional helping, there are relatively few books and journals devoted to this topic (for example, Cunningham and Sterling 1988; Feder and Feder 1981; Gfeller 1988; Miller and Schyb 1989; Stratton and Zalanowski 1989). A somewhat more substantial literature exists on bibliotherapy, which has become an element of standard practice in modern psychotherapy (Fuhriman, Barlow, and Wanlass 1989; Giblin, 1989; Scogin, Jamison, and Gochneaur 1989; Starker 1988a, 1988b). The main controversy here is whether self-help manuals have themselves been adequately evaluated prior to their marketing and whether their effects are comparable to those of in-person psychotherapy (Forest 1987, 1988; Lubusko and Forest 1989; Rosen 1987; Saper and Forest 1987). The bottom line, of course, is, Do they help? and, if so, Which are most helpful for what and whom?

Those questions remain unanswered, although Starker (1988a, 1988b) reports the titles of the books most frequently recommended to clients by their physicians and psychotherapists. Their popularity need not correlate with their helpfulness, of course, and the issue of *individual* needs remains an important consideration here. I find it interesting, for example, that the debate over prescriptive bibliotherapy has focused almost exclusively on the shaky credentials of many "self-help" guides rather than on the possible values of reading classics in poetry, drama, fiction, and so on. For what it is worth, I do recommend some books, some music, and various forms of art (appreciation and practice) for some clients. More often than not, however, my recommendation takes the form of an open-ended homework assignment in which the client is asked to experiment in or explore these realms. For example, I may suggest that the client bring me examples of favorite books, paintings, or music, or I may ask the client to visit a museum, bookstore, or music store and simply "browse" with an openness to feeling drawn toward (or repulsed by) any of the offerings. The results have often been both unexpected and positive.

Psychodrama and Role Playing

Having already stated my inclination toward experiental process work, it should come as no surprise that I employ role playing and psychodrama techniques with many clients. My enactments of psychodrama are not as extensive as those of some of my colleagues, but I value the contributions these exercises can make to a client's experiential repertoire (as well as our relationship). Thanks to Vittorio Guidano, I am also fascinated by Georges Polti's (1921) analysis of thirty-six dramatic situations and the emotions to which they may be related. Due to space limitations, I shall only acknowledge (and not review) the existing theory and research on these methods (Abele 1989; Blatner 1989; Franz 1989 [1940]; Fryrear and Stephens 1988; Hudgins and Kiesler 1987; Joyce-Moniz 1989; Kipper 1989; Moreno 1946, 1959, 1962; Skafte 1987). I shall not, however, resist quoting some pertinent material from Kenneth Burke's *The Philosophy of Literary Form.* In the context of discussing issues of identity and relationships with authority, Burke recommends that both of these concepts, along with that of human relations in general, *"should be analyzed with respect to the leads discovered by a study of drama"* (1973, p. 310). Reminiscent of my earlier discussions of the contractual theory of meaning (chapter 4) and the participatory nature of knowing (chapter 5), Burke concludes with a fascinating point about conflict resolution:

The difference between the symbolic drama and the drama of living is a difference between imaginary obstacles and real obstacles. . . . Much "symbolic action" in works of art deals with conflicts within the communicative or superstructural realm. . . . Hence, to some degree, solution of conflict must always be done purely in the symbolic realm (by "transcendence") if it is to be done at all. (P. 312)

There are multiple meanings of *transcendence,* of course, but the chase after these should not divert one's attention from the point he is making about symbolic action. The psychological affordances of dramatization have thus far been only barely glimpsed.

Spontaneous role playing and dramatization within sessions can be helpful in a number of ways. Besides "rehearsals" for real-life challenges, such exercises may help an individual move beyond chronic constraints on their own experience. This is, I believe, where the "philosophy of as if" of Hans Vaihinger (1924 [1911]) blends with the power of "possible selves" (chapter 9). The experience of possibility is often facilitated by "pretending," where the shackles of an assumed order are temporarily relaxed. Nor is it surprising that many clients experience major strides in their own development as initially "unreal," "incredible," and (for some) "untrustworthy" (chapter 12). As Adler, Kelly, Moreno, and others have realized, inviting an individual to act temporarily "as if" he or she (or one's circumstances) were different can be a powerful catalyst in the differentiation of both that person's experience and those circumstances.

Inner Companion Exercises

The study of "private dialogue" in modern psychology is often equated with the study of self-regulatory speech and the "self-statements" that have become central to concepts and techniques in the cognitive psychotherapies (for example, Beck 1976; Ellis 1962; Meichenbaum 1977; Vygotsky 1962, 1978; Zivin 1979). These studies have offered valuable contributions to our understanding, among which the most important may be that most humans "talk to themselves" (as well as to other real and imaginary beings). These are what Colman McCarthy calls "our inner companions," the characters who accompany us on our lifelong journeys and participate, through private dialogue, in our triumphs and tragedies and everything in between. They reflect our "interior lives—an intimacy of the spirit—and (a) trusting that what results is not an invasion of our privacy but an expression of our awareness" (1975, pp. 18–19).

In the context of our discussions and as part of their journal exercises, I sometimes ask my clients to list and describe their "inner companions." "With whom do you talk, inside yourself, when you are carrying on the business of living your life? Do you talk to some more than others? How have they changed over the years? How do your moods or feelings influence your choice of a conversation partner?" With questions like these in mind, clients have returned with wide-ranging reports: themselves (with many subparts), their mother, father, lover, close friend, me (or another counselor), heroes and heroines, former teachers, imaginary friends, and so on. Many also reported talking frequently to religious figures (saints, gods, spirits of nature [Heery 1989]). I have also asked individuals to record and share with me their monologues, dialogues, and prayers. Those sharings have often taught me a lot about their hopes and fears, as well as their trust, faith, and commitment to these powerful imaginary companions.

The words of Kenneth Burke (1973) are again apropos: "It is of great importance to study the various strategies of 'prayer' by which men seek to solve their conflicts, since such material should give us needed insight into the processes of prayer ("symbolic action," "linguistic action," "implicit commands to audience and self") in its many secular aspects, not generally considered 'prayer' at all" (1973, pp. 312–13). The most important question in terms of psychotherapy may not be "who or what do they pray to" so much as "what and how do they express what they are feeling and seeking?"

Identity Clarifications and the Personal Epilogue

There are a number of exercises that may help an individual clarify his or her current sense of personal identity. One of my favorites is a sentence-completion task that I learned in a workshop with James Bugental. The client is provided with a writing instrument and eight blank sheets of paper and instructed that he or she will be given the beginning of a sentence. The task is to complete that sentence eight times (once on each sheet) with the first completions that come to mind. The only constraint placed on the completions is that they should not be temporary states (such as moods or transient sensations). The client is then given the beginning of the sentence: "I am. . . ." When one has completed that sentence eight times, one is then asked to sort one's responses as follows.

"Imagine now that you are facing your own imminent death. Your energies are drained and you are tired. Imagine that holding on to each facet of your identity requires some energy, and that you must begin letting go of some of them. Look back through your eight statements and separate them into three groups: (1) those aspects of your identity that you would let go of first, (2) those that you would hold onto with your dying breath, and (3) those about which you cannot decide. Be aware of your own thoughts and feelings as you do this."

Many people will complete that sentence with their name, occupation, personality attributes, roles in relationships, and so on. Being asked to reflect on which of those facets of identity are most central to them can be challenging. Likewise, being asked to imagine one's imminent death is not a welcome exercise for most people and, like the personal epilogue, it is contraindicated in individuals who are at risk for suicide. I have modified the sentence-completion exercise with some individuals and adapted it toward the clarification of core ordering processes. In this adaptation, the individual is given twenty-four sentence beginnings that are generated by crossing the dimensions of time (past, present, future), affirmation and denial, and the four themes of core order (identity, reality, power, and value) (table 11.1). One is asked to complete each sentence with the first response that comes to mind and to skip around and enter one's completions in whatever sequence they emerge. In this adaptation, I delete the "near death" sorting task and focus instead on the client's phenomenology during the task and the sequence of his or her completions. Obviously many other adaptations are possible, and I recommend personalizing the exercise to fit the needs of individual clients.

An exercise that is appropriate only for selected individuals is called the *personal epilogue.* It involves the preparation of materials and ceremonies appropriate for the recognition of the person's death. Obviously, *this is not a technique to be employed with individuals who are feeling suicidal, unstable, or emotionally vulnerable;* it can, in fact, evoke or temporarily amplify such feelings. The writing of "obituaries" and epitaphs has been used in some forms of psychotherapy, particularly with elderly and terminally ill cli-

Table 11.1   Selected Sentence Beginnings

I was	I am	I will be
I was able to	I am able to	I will be able to
I liked	I like	I will like
I believed	I believe	I will believe
I was not	I am not	I will not be
I was not able to	I am not able to	I will not be able to
I did not believe	I do not believe	I will not believe

ents, but there is little research literature on the potential impact of such techniques. When it is used with good clinical judgment and close professional supervision, however, the personal epilogue can constitute a powerful exercise in personal development. In my experience, it is important to emphasize that the epilogue is always a tentative "makeshift" arrangement which is to be periodically reviewed and revised throughout one's remaining life. In other words, it should not be presented as if it were a final statement or reflection, but always as a "semifinal" specification of desires which are recorded, in part, to convey personal feelings and wishes "in the event of 'untimely' death."

Needless to say, the personal epilogue is not an exercise to be suggested or undertaken lightly. I again recommend that psychotherapists contemplating its use first experiment by undertaking it themselves and then employ it in individual cases only after careful reflection or consultation. Some individuals will use the epilogue exercise as an opportunity to put their personal "papers" in order. Some will make elaborate preparations for a funeral ceremony, specifying music to be played, symbolic rituals of transfer (as of personal objects), and passages to be read (such as favorite pieces of literature or religious scripture). Other individuals will write or (audiovisually) record their own messages for their family and friends. Importantly, this exercise will often evoke present-life actions on the part of the performer. Things that the individual may have long intended to do or say may suddenly get done or said, often with intense emotions and consequences that cannot be fully anticipated. Many of these actions will be in the realm of intimate relationships (past and present) and relationships with self.

Resolution and Completion Rituals

The last set of exercises to be discussed here are focused on "unfinished business" and their resolution. (For other resources on this topic, I recommend Canada, 1988; Hope 1988; van der Hart 1981; and van der Hart and Ebbers 1981.) Psychological processes of completion or resolution are often facilitated by being translated into symbolic actions. I generally encourage clients to think of explicit, embodied rituals they can perform to symbolize and give form to their intentions. One man who had chronically grieved over a past romance developed an elaborate ceremony in which he separated himself from his lover by tearing apart photographs of them together and throwing her portions into a fireplace. Another woman who had never forgiven her father for his emotional distance visited his grave, vented her anger verbally, and then (unexpectedly) cried for the first time in years and told him how much she missed him.

An older woman who was tired of being "leaned on" as the "strong one" by her family and friends developed a fitting ritual to "lighten her load." She filled her daughter's old Girl Scout backpack with heavy rocks, each one representing the demands placed upon her by a different individual. Each afternoon she put the backpack on and walked more than a mile to a "special place" she had found where she could be alone. Day by day, one by one, she removed a rock, spoke out loud about her unwillingness to "carry" that person's demands any longer, and threw it as far as she could. When the backpack was finally empty, she converted it to another use: it was now to carry little treats for herself, books, and "treasures" that she found on her daily walks.

I have also encouraged some clients to embark on physical life review "pilgrimages." It can vary according to the person and his or her circumstances, of course, but the general idea is to set aside the time and resources to physically retrace one's life up to the present (Lewis and Butler 1974). This entails a return to the place of one's birth, visiting former houses, schools, playgrounds, cemeteries, and so on. For some individuals, this journey may be most productive if it includes opportunities to talk with family and friends, particularly those who were significant figures in their earlier development. I recommend the use of a journal, camera, and tape recorder for collecting impressions of the experience.

Separation Rituals and Psychotherapy Termination

Needless to say, the range of possible rituals is as infinite as the uniqueness of the individuals who perform them. I continue to be impressed with that range as well as with the power of enactment in facilitating developmental transitions. One of the most important of those transitions is *termination,* the "exiting" or separation process at the completion of psychotherapy. This constitutes the formal "breaking of an affectional bond" (Bowlby 1979), and it deserves thoughtful consideration, open discussion, and the authentic expression of feelings. Milton Erickson used to say that "my voice will go with you," and he was right, but it is much more than one's voice. Moreover, clients' voices and stories remain with their therapists, which is why the lives of the latter are often so full, rich, and sometimes exhausting (chapter 13).

One need not be psychoanalytic to acknowledge that psychotherapists and clients alike develop strong attachments to one another (Edelson 1963). One of the unique challenges facing the professional helper is an acceptance of that fact and a continuing commitment to set and protect the many kinds of boundaries (physical, temporal, and emotional) necessary for optimal service to clients. When that service is finished and the participants prepare to take their separate paths, the "leavetaking" may be one of the most important events in the experience (for both of them). At its best, it entails a powerful episode for both therapist and client:

If this process can develop in an undisturbed way a surprisingly uniform experience dominates the very last period of the treatment. The patient feels that he is going through a kind of re-birth into a new life, that he has arrived at the end of a dark tunnel, that he sees light again after a long journey, that he has been given a new life, he experiences a sense of great freedom as if a heavy burden had dropped from him, etc. It is a deeply moving experience; the general atmosphere is of taking leave forever of something very dear, very precious—with all the corresponding grief and mourning—but this sincere and deeply felt grief is mitigated by the feeling of security, originating from the newly-won possibilities for real happiness. Usually the patient leaves after the last session happy but with tears in his eyes, and—I think I may admit—the analyst is in a very similar mood. (Balint 1950, p. 197)

This rendition reflects considerably more warmth than Freud's famous essay "Analysis Terminable and Interminable" (1953–1966) [1937] where there is relatively little mention of the human relationship being severed.

Bowlby (1979) recommends that interruptions during the course of treatment (due to holidays, canceled sessions, and so on) may provide important opportunities for both therapist and client to observe the latter's construction of and response to the separation. This, in turn, may encourage deeper self-awareness and explorations of how and why such responses might have developed. As Marshall Edelson aptly notes, the problem of termination is not merely one of determining when or how to "end" therapy, but rather how to orchestrate a separation "so that what has been happening keeps on 'going' inside the patient" (1963, p. 14). Indeed, the choice of *when* and *where* to stop is always a personal choice between the parties involved. Since the work of psychotherapy, like that of psychological development in general, often reflects a "spiraling" of movement over personal issues (Bowlby 1979, p. 154), there are numerous opportunities for enacting this choice. When practiced from a developmental perspective, it is also important to note that termination is never necessarily "terminal." That is, in having helped develop a secure base for the client's developmental explorations, the psychotherapist does not insist that that base can never again be visited (whether for occasional "check-ins" or for a new series of services). Circumstances permitting, the developmental therapist will metaphorically "reserve a space" in his or her "base camp" for occasional visits or the return of the client (even if only for reaffirmation and, if necessary, referral).

A related point here is that some clients report distress over feeling pressured toward the separation—as if they were supposed to have "all of their issues" resolved and to feel fully autonomous by a certain hour on a certain day. This is clearly at odds with the philosophy espoused in this book (as well as in attachment theory), and it is one of the reasons that I recommend consideration of graduated separation processes for many clients (table 10.2, page 272). Nor should either therapist or client feel compelled to deny or suppress their feelings about the upcoming separation: if ever there were a time to encourage authentic experiencing and expression of feelings, it is during this "axial turn" in the relationship between counselor and client.

In preparing for the separation process, it is important to emphasize to clients that they have been the primary agent of change in their own life, and that changes will continue long after psychotherapy has ended. For some individuals, it is also wise to prepare them for the possible emotional "oscillations" they may feel after termination (particularly in terms of sadness and anger). I believe that separation rituals are particularly important in marking the transition to separate paths, and I recommend a symbolic exchange and an explicit "farewell" in the process. The exchange may be a written note expressing one's reflections on the work together and an affirmation of the individual. Since I always request that clients write a brief summary of their experience in psychotherapy, I have received some touching treasures over the years.

CONCLUSION

The difficulties of everyday praxis are fundamentally existential and epistemological. In presuming to offer counsel on life and its living, the psychotherapist should be deeply aware of his or her inescapable responsibilities in posing, making, and dis/en-couraging choices of action the results of which cannot be confidently known beforehand. Choices must be made, however, despite the absence of certain and complete knowledge. Procrastination and refusals to take action are no less choices than are impulsive decisions and "blind" activity. Moreover, even though many clients do not want to hear about the unsure footing beneath their own or their counselor's knowledge, it is ethically imperative that they embrace as much responsibility as possible for the choices that will affect their future life quality. At these choice points, I find welcome consolation in some sage advice offered by Fitz-James Stephen in 1874:

What do you think of yourself? What do you think of the world? . . . These are questions with which all must deal as it seems good to them. They are riddles of the Sphinx, and in some way or other we must deal with them. . . . In all important transactions of life we have to take a leap in the dark. . . . If we decide to leave the riddles unanswered, that is a choice; if we waver in our answer, that, too, is a choice: but whatever choice we make, we make it at our peril. . . . We stand on a mountain pass in the midst of whirling snow and blinding mist, through which we get glimpses now and then of paths which may be deceptive. If we stand still we shall be frozen to death. If we take the wrong road we shall be dashed to pieces. We do not certainly know whether there is any right one. What must we do? "Be strong and of a good courage." Act for the best, hope for the best, and

take what comes. . . . If death ends all, we cannot meet death better. (Cited in
James 1956 [1896], pp. 30–31)

This means, of course, that psychological services based in modern understandings of science do not (and, indeed, cannot) offer guarantees and
glib solutions.

   Existential risk lies at the heart of human knowing. It is not coincidence
that the major works in evolutionary epistemology reflect some of the
same insights as those in existential philosophy. It is in our endless
encounters with the unknown that we struggle to "wrestle more life from
deadness" and more meaning from the chaos in and out of which our
lives emerge. In the concluding chapter of this book, I shall return to that
insight and some of its implications for the care and nurturance of professional helpers.

12

▲▼▲▼▲▼▲▼▲▼▲▼▲▼▲

The Personal Experience of Change

During the twenty months in which I experienced psychotherapy, perhaps one of the major constants was surprise. . . . This voyage of discovery was the most incredible I've ever known.
—Roger Walsh

The human experience of psychological change is fundamentally the same whether inside or outside psychotherapy. Whatever its contexts, we now know that change is highly individualized and unlikely to be adequately conveyed by any single or simple listing of stages or clusters of focus. To speak of the "experience of change" is a complex task made more difficult by the fact that our language tends to make nouns out of verbs and separate words out of inseparable feelings. Woven and rewoven by the enchanted looms of self, the unfinished web of "felt experience" connects all varieties of empiricist, experiential, and phenomenological points of view.

To create a context for this discussion of our understandings of human change, let me begin by recalling that our understandings are themselves exhibiting considerable change (chapter 2). The first and second axial periods encouraged opposite emphases in some of the classic tensions in human ideas. It is not coincidental that the modern (or postmodern) shift (still in process) represents a complex differentiation of views on such classic dualities as reason and experience, physical and mental, and self and system. Nor is it coincidental that phenomenology and hermeneutics—the study of experience and the study of meanings—are now at the forefront of late twentieth-century thought. Indeed, human lives are

changing more rapidly than ever before and the quest to understand
change has never been more intense.

There is today as well a wealth of written material devoted to the power
and privacy of felt experience. A small but significant slice of that writing
deals with the experience and process of psychotherapy. Although my
remarks in this chapter draw upon both of these literatures, I do not
intend to make an exhaustive catalogue of their methods and findings but
will defer to other sources.* My purpose in this chapter is to highlight
those dimensions and patterns of change that have greatest practical
relevance for psychotherapy. These issues cluster into four basic domains: the personal organization of experience, resistance to change,
oscillative processes in change, and changing relationships with self and
others.

THE PERSONAL ORGANIZATION OF EXPERIENCE

The experience of change—particularly the experience of change associated with psychotherapy—is sometimes described differently by its
owners than by professional "change agents." Indeed, psychotherapists'
perceptions of change and the strategies for effecting it are often different
from those of their clients (Mahoney et al. 1989; Norcross and Prochaska
1986a, 1986b; Prochaska and Norcross 1983b). The fact that psychotherapists view their own psychological development as less difficult and
emotionally turbulent than that attributed to psychotherapy clients is a
case in point (chapter 8). Since severe psychological distress is likely to
impair the quality of a psychotherapist's professional services, we might
welcome   the   possibility   that   these   reported   differences   in
phenomenology are not illusory. But—as the literature on the personal
life of the psychotherapist reveals (chapter 13)—the responsibilities and
(di)stress experienced by mental health professionals are unique and
undeniably challenging. Moreover, extant surveys suggest that psychotherapists may be particularly vulnerable to neglecting, minimizing, and
postponing their own self-care needs.

There is another facet to this issue, however, which again bears lessons
about the complexities of psychological balance and developmental
movement. Psychotherapists' capacities to help appear to be related to
their own abilities both to emphatically "relate to" their clients' distress
and yet, both simultaneously and intermittently, to remain sufficiently

*See resources on constructivism, emotionality, hermeneutics, and phenomenology in
chapters 2, 3, 5, and 8. For a range of views on the experience and process of psychotherapy,
see Brewin 1989; Bugental 1978, 1987; Canda 1988; Claiborn 1982; Frank 1973, 1985;
Friedman 1988; Gendlin 1962; Glass and Arnkoff 1988; Greenberg and Pinsof 1986; Kiesler
1973; Levy 1963; Mahrer et al. 1989; Orlinsky and Howard 1975; Rice and Greenberg 1984;
Varghese 1988; and Walsh 1976.

"distant" from (or "transcendent" of) those pains and struggles so that they can facilitate their expression and, when appropriate, their rescaffolding. There are both parallels and differences here between the roles of the psychotherapist and of the medical emergency professional. In both roles, professionals cannot be optimally efficient in providing services if they are terrified or emotionally traumatized by the pain or trauma of those they serve. The analogy is limited, however, in its application to the mental health professional: that is, to be optimally helpful, psychotherapists must also be able to phenomenologically approximate and be emotionally present to the experiences of those they serve. I shall return to this challenging paradox in the final chapter.

The issue of similarities and differences in psychotherapists' and clients' experiences of change also encourages reflection on the role of "jects" and "jectives" in our thought. Recall from chapter 9 that *jectives* are "thrown" separations—the literal boundaries of being and becoming—that lie at the heart of human selfhood and consciousness. Ironically, it is in the constructive activity of such "edging" that human knowing processes create their own subtle barriers and limitations. It is no coincidence, then, that our age marks the "twilight" of both subjectivity and objectivity—the decline of absolute jectives—and the dawn of an age when identities are dynamic and the ultimate metaphors for power invariably invoke process (Dahlmary 1981; Gonçalves 1989*a*, 1989*b*; Guidano 1990; Harré 1984; Kegan 1982; Madison 1988). This transition, which I have called the third axial shift (chapter 2), reflects an increasing acknowledgment of relativities and the complex interdependence of knower, known, and knowing.

The central point here is that the experience of change cannot be separated from the "experience of experience," if you will; studies of phenomenology must therefore remain a central focus of our understanding. From my previous discussions, it is also apparent that all such experience is necessarily embodied, individualized, contextualized (especially culturally and socially), and constructive. Adding to this complexity is the fact that the identifiable *contents* of experience are themselves generated and constrained by abstract *processes* well beyond our explicit awareness. In other words, all experience of change must be contrasted or "edged" in order to be experienced at all (at least in popular meanings of conscious "experience"). Emotionally meaningful "figures and grounds" are continually being created. Hence, *the experience of change is relative to each individual and cannot be separated from the predominantly tacit and personalized experience of stasis.* It is here, again, that core ordering processes (chapter 8) figure prominently. Attempts at broad generalizations may offer helpful reference points from which to begin explorations, but they cannot help but bias the latter.

It is possible, for example, to render capsule descriptions of the general experience patterns associated with psychological disorders and hypothetically "optimal" well-being (see table 8.1). All such renderings, however, necessarily invoke the perennial and productive tension between understanding individual particulars and transpersonal generalizations. This is, indeed, the heart of the issue regarding "idiographic" and "nomothetic" research methods (Allport 1937, 1961; Stern 1911; Windelband 1894), as well as of debates about subjectivity and objectivity in science (Scheffler 1967). As Hubert Hermans reminds us, this was one of the classic teachings of Socrates: "The relationship between the general and the particular is a fundamental property of all scientific thought" (1988, p. 786). Try as some may to segregate them, the realms of public and private are interdependent, and the challenges facing science and service are not orthogonal.

Of all of the lessons that have been learned about the nature, nurture, and development of human experience, the most important has perhaps been that which has focused on the central paradox of reflective inquiry: namely, that no two persons or lives are ever identical, and yet abstract principles can capture some of their commonalities. "The particular eternally underlies the general; the general eternally has to comply with the particular" (Goethe, in Hermans 1988, p. 785). As the developing science of psychology continues to enrich its valuable connections with human and social services, one of its basic assertions must be that individual differences ("person variables") are prevalent and powerful in the organization and development of human lives. Needless to say, I believe that the growing acknowledgment of the person in psychology and epistemology represents a welcome and promising developmental challenge.

RESISTANCE TO CHANGE

Even though resistance was one of two defining characteristics of psychoanalysis for Sigmund Freud (the other being transference), studies of the phenomenon of resistance are relatively recent. In 1904, Freud explained his abandonment of "suggestion" (hypnosis) by saying that "it does not permit us . . . to recognize the resistance with which the patient clings to his disease and thus even fights against his own recovery; yet it is this phenomenon of resistance which alone makes it possible to comprehend his behavior in daily life" (1963 [1904], p. 67). The idea of resistance did not, however, originate with Freud; it emerged on many earlier fronts and in the context of great strides in physical science, biology, and medicine (where it took on both different and similar meanings). Only later did the concept of psychological resistance become an item of interest and an issue of debate among advocates of different approaches to psychotherapy.

The most divergent views on the topic have typically been expressed by psychoanalysts and behaviorists (Wachtel 1982), although the existence of psychological resistance has been less controversial than its interpretation. In the national survey of U.S. clinical psychologists reported in chapter 1, for example, behavioral respondents were almost equivocal in their reactions to the statement that "personal psychological development involves episodes of reluctance or resistance to change" (Mahoney et al. 1989, p. 254). Their average strength of agreement with this statement was 59 percent. Not surprisingly, psychodynamic respondents showed a substantially stronger acknowledgment of resistance (74%), as was also true of representatives of humanistic-existential, eclectic, and cognitive perspectives (70%, 70%, and 69%, respectively; figure 12.1). Though there are no comparable data from earlier surveys, there are many signs that the concept of resistance has recently become more generally acceptable (indeed, welcome) in psychology (Baumeister and Scher 1988; Bernstein et al. 1989; Dubs 1987; Lewis and Evans 1986;

Figure 12.1 U.S. Clinical Psychologists' Acknowledgment of Resistance to Change

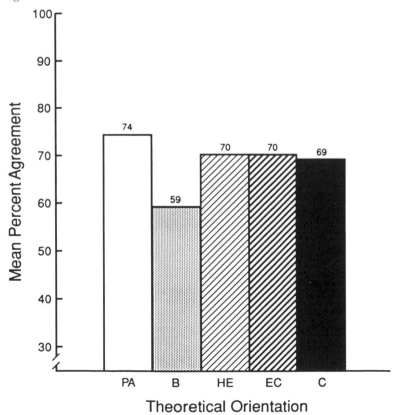

SOURCE: © 1989 M. J. Mahoney

Otani 1989; Snyder 1988; Wachtel 1982). Beyond the different meanings of the term in fields other than psychology, important differences have developed in the meanings of resistance for psychological theories. Current theories of resistance include (1) motivated avoidance, (2) motivational deficit, (3) ambivalent choice, (4) reactance, and (5) self-protection.

Motivated Avoidance

Freud's concept of resistance was much more than a cornerstone to his theories of personality and motivation, of course, but it was a major impetus to a whole family of theories emphasizing the "motivated avoidance" aspects of adaptation and consciousness. Freud believed that repressed instinctual impulses fueled such avoidance, and that the psychotherapy client had to "live through" or "work through" discoveries of those impulses. This is essentially the same assumption and therapeutic strategy elaborated by Freda Fromm-Reichmann (1950) and other later practitioners of psychoanalysis. Particularly important is Freud's portrayal of the human drama as one of inescapable conflict, much of it camouflaged and well beyond our capacities of awareness. Moreover, as reflected in the earlier quote, there was a self-defeating tone to Freud's depiction of pained humans "clinging" to their "diseases." Given such a view of humanity and motivational dynamics, it is not surprising that psychotherapies faithful to this orthodoxy have come to be viewed as less hopeful than some of their modern alternatives. When awareness of self is cast as both the enemy and the ally, a plot for conflict has already been implied. Such conflict is recognized in other theories of resistance, of course, but it is described and explained in different terms.

Motivational Deficit

Although they have rarely been recognized as theories of resistance, many expressions of classical learning theory invoked metaphors of "habit strengths" and "drives" that afforded related ideas (including those of deficit or insufficiency). Indeed, many of the most enduring criticisms of "drive theory" have focused on its reification of motivational constructs (Bandura 1969, 1986; Hilgard 1987; Sahakian 1976). Early explanations of lack of learning (and failures to change) as being due to insufficient drive and inadequate reinforcement were soon recognized as illogical (tautologous) when the criteria defining learning and motivation were the same. Such explanations have yet to run their course, however, as is evidenced in their continuing use by some modern behaviorists. Although other influences were involved, the emergence of "two-factor" learning theories and distinctions between stimulus-response (S-R) and radical behaviorisms were accelerated by acknowledgments that resistance (and failure) to change could not be adequately understood as simple deficiencies in motivation (Mowrer 1960*a*, 1960*b;* Rachlin 1988).

Ambivalent Choice

The third distinguishable perspective on resistance exhibits important parallels with the first two. Like motivational deficit theories, it is less commonly acknowledged than its psychodynamic counterparts, but it has received increasing recognition in the last two decades. In theories of behavioral self-control and "behavioral choice theory," resistance to change and apparent violations of E. L. Thorndike's Law of Effect are often attributed to the ambivalence of choice. Technically, this has been termed the *reversing consequence gradient,* which is illustrated in figure 12.2. From such perspectives, it is not mere coincidence that voluntary behaviors known to be difficult to change are commonly associated with different varieties of immediate and delayed consequences. The immediate effects of poor impulse control, for example, are often pleasant even though transitory (as in eating, smoking, and substance abuse). Their negative consequences are much more delayed. Conversely, the immediate consequences of persistent or hard work may be neutral or negative, but their ultimate effects can be highly positive (as in bookkeeping, exercise, and studying).

Figure 12.2   The Reversing Consequence Gradient

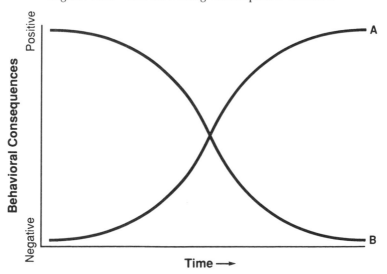

SOURCE: © 1989 M. J. Mahoney

Beyond their apparent face validity, such theories have an appeal that reaches toward complexity: they acknowledge choices and dualities of valence. In doing so, ambivalence theories incorporate an awareness of time and a recognition of the agency of the organism missing in the first two theoretical clusters. Also important are their acknowledgments of "rule-governed" behavior and the operation of both symbolic and self-regulative processes in adaptation. Needless to say, these are welcome acknowledgments.

Reactance

The fourth major grouping of theories of resistance might be termed *reactance* after Jack Brehm's (1966) theory of that title. Although expressions of this perspective are still primarily confined to social psychology (for example, Deci 1980; Wicklund 1974), there is a parallel literature on *counter-control* in the areas of delinquency and antisocial personality disorders. Technically, reactance theory maintains that

> when a person believes himself free to engage in a given behavior, he will experience psychological reactance if that freedom is eliminated or threatened with elimination. Psychological reactance is defined as a motivational state directed toward the re-establishment of the threatened or eliminated freedom, and it should manifest itself in increased desire to engage in the relevant behavior. . . . Basically, the magnitude of reactance is a direct function of (1) the importance of the freedom which is eliminated or threatened, and (2) the proportion of free behaviors eliminated or threatened. (Brehm 1966, pp. 15–16).

Although the "directness" of the proposed functions remains to be demonstrated, there is now a substantial literature documenting that changes in perceived freedoms—in both choices and responsibilities—can be powerful influences in human behavior (Bandura 1986; Perlmuter and Monty 1979; Taylor and Brown 1988; Thompson 1981; Wicklund 1974). Relative to its conceptual predecessors, reactance theory offers the welcome addition of an explicit emphasis on phenomenology (personal perceptions) and the centrality of the dimension of freedom (and hence power) in the living of human lives. In studies of both prosocial and antisocial behavior, these emphases have also invited a deeper appreciation of the bonds between self and social systems.

Self-Protection

The fifth and final cluster of theories about resistance is here termed *self-protective* because of their relative emphasis on the "natural" and (potentially) healthy functions served by activities that may resist, decelerate, or otherwise impede psychological change. There are both obvious parallels between such theories and those in the other four groupings, and also important differences. The primary distinguishing characteristic of the self-protective metatheory of resistance is its emphasis on individuals' healthy caution about embarking upon or embracing experiences that challenge their integrity, coherence, or (felt) viability as a living system. Self-protective theories have only recently been so labeled, even though elements of their philosophy have been expressed in a number of approaches over the years. Their most explicit discussions are offered in the writings of humanist, existential, and constructivist psychotherapists (Bugental 1978, 1987; Bugental and Bugental 1984; Guidano 1987, 1990; Liotti 1987; Mahoney 1988a, 1988b, 1988c; Mahoney and Lyddon 1988).

There is some warrant for the assertion that psychodynamic formulations of resistance have also appealed to self-protective functions (as in the operation of defense mechanisms). Moreover, the psychodynamic view of the self as a defensive center (chapter 9) clearly invokes associations with self-defense. The parallels between psychoanalytic and self-protective theories are circumscribed, however, in that the latter convey a much more positive and proactive portrayal of resistance. As we have seen, Freud's view of resistance was inherently conflictual and connoted a self-defeating dynamic. In large part, the resistance he wrote about was a resistance to consciousness and self-knowledge. Self-protective theories are more similar to modern complex systems formulations in that they acknowledge "essential tensions" in development without berating the processes involved, whether they serve conservative (stasis-preserving) or "revolutionary" (change-producing) functions (Jantsch 1980; Kuhn 1977).

This differentiation is an important one. What is complicating, however, is that self-protective theorists generally concur that resistance processes operate at a tacit (unconscious) level of awareness. For Freud, this absence of awareness was part of the "pathology" of the individual; and—although "making the unconscious conscious" did not eradicate that pathology—the development of "insight" (particularly into one's resistance) was thought to be a pivotal process in at least understanding one's unfortunate plight. Self-protective theorists, on the other hand, tend to view the tacitness of resistance processes as neither pathological nor particularly uncommon. Among constructivists, for example, the primacy of abstract ordering processes in experience implies that explicit awareness will always lag far behind the individual's self-organizing dynamics. The contrast between Freud's model of heavily defended (un)-consciousness and Hayek's metaphor of "superconscious" edging processes is pertinent here (chapter 5). Thus, while constructive psychotherapists may encourage their clients in exercises that help to "make the tacit explicit" (Guidano 1987, 1990), they conceptualize the functions of "explication" and interpretation (hermeneutics) in a different manner than do their psychodynamic colleagues.

To summarize, self-protective theories appeal to the generalization that all living systems exhibit "resistance to change" in that the preservation of basic life-support functions is a powerful priority: that is, the maintenance of systemic (or organismic) integrity is a fundamental imperative. In respect to the diversities of biological evolution, it is therefore not coincidental that those organisms who have hearts, central nervous systems, and lungs also evidence structural features that serve to protect these subsystems (such as bony encasements, redundant "circuitry," and so on). In those complex systems (like ourselves) that have evolved symbolic capacities, the metaphor is further complicated by a recursiveness that is hierarchical (appendices C,D,E). To the limited extent that we can express them (chapter 10), the core ordering processes of humans are more than biological. They involve, for example, the continuity or orderliness of experience (that is, reality, meaning), the preservation of a phenomenological sense of self (identity), the perpetuation of enacted values or valences (most apparent in emotional experience), and the maintenance of some sense of power (agency, control). From such a perspective, resistance to change is not an expression of pathology but, rather, a reflection of basic self-organizing processes operating in the service of the individual's phenomenological needs to feel safe, secure, and viable.

Two brief stories of psychotherapy clients may help illustrate the relationship between resistance and core ordering processes. Olive W. was thirty-three years old and had always lived with her parents. She first contacted me by phone and requested treatment for her agoraphobia (see pages 291–92). She reported that she had not left her house without accompaniment for over three years. For two of those years, her only trips out had been to see a therapist who described herself as psychoanalytic. According to Olive, her previous therapist had often let her sit silently for the entire session. When Olive had once exploded in anger over what she perceived as the therapist's indifference, she was told that her problem was her fear of men and sex. As an intended antidote to that fear, Olive had been encouraged to "visit the singles bars and get laid."

Our work together was initially focused on helping her take the risk of making solo excursions outside her house. A major event in her progress came when she was able to drive her car alone for a distance of ten miles, phoning me from designated checkpoints. She then drove to my office. I naïvely expected her to be jubilant over her hard-won freedom. Instead, she was terrified: "Mike, I'm so scared . . . and I feel so ashamed." She continued, "I know that I should feel great about this—Good God, how I have longed to be free again! . . . But this progress, this change—it's all so frightening and I'm scared that if I keep improving, I may overcome my agoraphobia but . . . well, what if I lose 'me' in the process?"

Another client I was seeing at the time also taught me about the powerful relationship between identity and resistance. Adam K., who was instrumental in stimulating my work on mirror time, was a struggling law student of thirty-four when I first met him. As his eighth therapist in twenty-two years, I was not surprised by the range of challenges he brought to therapy. Adam had been bulimic and depressed for ten years and had struggled with anxiety, self-contempt, and obsessive-compulsive rituals since early childhood. I had been recommended to him by his psychiatrist, who had described him as "impossible: the epitome of the difficult client." Adam arrived late for our first session and spent the first twenty minutes angrily attacking me and the profession of psychotherapy. "What are you going to say to me that is any different from all the other shrinks?" Trying to sidestep his onslaught, I asked what he was ready to hear. "Oh, that's cute!" he barked back. "Are you a gestalt therapist or a transactional analyst?"

I danced around verbally for a few more minutes, hoping that he would finish ventilating and that we could then move on to form an alliance. When he proudly announced that none of his previous therapists had been able to make a dent in his depression, I took the lead. "Adam, what would it take for you *not* to be depressed?" He seemed intrigued by my question and commented that no one had asked him that before. I waited through a lengthy silence as he reflected. Finally, he looked at me with a sheepish grin and said, "I know this doesn't make any sense, but it's the only thing I can think of. For me not to be depressed, I would have to be a different person."

In terms of the experience of change, self-protective theories encourage both psychotherapists and clients to recognize that psychological change is seldom simple, easy, or entirely pleasant. The more that change is central to a person's experience of self and world, the more likely is one to encounter emotional complexities and ambivalence about its undertaking or progress. Consistent with the literatures on affect, health, and stress, this perspective acknowledges that all change involves challenges (even when that change is perceived as intentionally self-produced and/or desired). From the vantage point of psychotherapeutic strategy, self-protective theories of resistance encourage patience, compassion, and a healthy respect for individual differences in the pacing of change. In contrast to alternative views, for example, resistance is not seen as the enemy and something to be overcome in the process of development. Instead, ambivalent feelings about change are considered normal and common; activities that functionally postpone choices or divert linear progress are not viewed as pathological (even though they may be frustrating or puzzling). To the extent that such activities express self-caring and self-protective functions, they are viewed as powerful allies to be worked with rather than against in the course of professional services. From such a perspective, all acts of dishonesty and diversion are considered to serve (phenomenologically defined) self-protective functions. Even suicidal ideation may express such functions. The phenomenological intent in suicidal thoughts, for example, is often to "terminate" the feeling of extreme pain and anguish. This *intent* is healthy and self-caring; it is the drastic decision to engage in life-terminating *behavior* that is potentially tragic. Helping individuals to differentiate their self-caring intentions from self-destructive actions can be an important element in assimilating and moving beyond suicidal crises and the "micro-suicides" of self-abuse.

I do not mean that the psychotherapist who endorses a self-protective theory of resistance must be unconditionally patient or accepting (neither of which is humanly possible). As the literatures on psychotherapy process have begun to clarify, there are times for effort and surrender, just as there are times for patience, reflection, and constructive confrontation. Knowing when those times are "now" is a perennial challenge for the practitioner. Our quest for general principles will never yield prescriptive rules for deciding which posture is clearly best for which individual(s) at any given point in his or her life. Among the most burdensome responsibilities of the mental health professional are these existential "judgment calls," when the professional service provider must make decisions about the safety and well-being of other lives.

OSCILLATIVE DYNAMICS IN THE PROCESS OF CHANGE

The word *oscillate* comes from the Latin *oscillare,* which means "to swing" or "vibrate," especially between two points. It does not translate to simple ideas of change or variance, and yet it speaks to many themes in the history of ideas, feelings, and actions. The "life rhythms" acknowledged by Herbert Spencer (1897 [1855]) and John Dewey (1934), Thomas Kuhn's (1977) "essential tensions," and Walter Weimer's (1987) "rhythmic opponent processes" are examples. The literatures of virtually all fields are permeated with the play of tensions and the inseparabilities of dynamics, drama, and development. Nor is it coincidental that major theories of learning, personality, psychopathology, and psychotherapy all assume the operation of generative conflicts in the phenomena they study. Of more central significance here is the fact that the experience of change is commonly recognized to involve conflicts, tensions, and (in one form or another) resistance. I do not claim to understand much more than the foregoing acknowledgment. Indeed, for me, some of the most intriguing puzzles about human change processes have to do with the dynamic nature of development. It is for this reason that I believe that some of our greatest strides in understanding and facilitating human changes will come from studies of oscillative processes in human self-organization.

Expansions and Contractions

There have, of course, been many previous acknowledgments of oscilla-tive tensions in experience: the yin and yang (Tao) of Asian philosophy; the dialectics of Zeno, Socrates, Plato, Hegel and Marx; the historical cycles of Giambattista Vico and the developmental spirals of T. S. Eliot; the dynamic conflict between instinct and social influence of Sigmund Freud; the moving toward and against of Karen Horney; the "escape from freedom" of Eric Fromm; the "loosening and tightening" of George Kelly's constructs; and the boundary conflicts of modern self psycholo-gies (to name a few). Despite the extensiveness of their acknowledgment, however, their renderings and interpretations have been legion. Having already qualified my claim to understanding these phenomena, I here share some observations and conjectures based on my experiences as psychotherapist and researcher.

An important point here is that I do not believe that individuals diag-nosed as borderline are the only ones who experience fluctuations in major psychological dimensions (identity, affect, attachment, and percep-tions of reality and self-efficacy). Although such fluctuations may be more pronounced or disorganizing in some lives, dynamic variations are perva-sive in all human experience. The theoretical reasons for this are spread across the disciplines I have tried to span in the preceding chapters. The practical point is that lives change from moment to moment; although our clients seek (as we do) to find and move in certain stabilizing patterns and currents, that search and that movement lead us inevitably through rapids and reverses. "The way home," as one client put it, "is not sim-ple."

Over the course of my work as a psychotherapist, I have found myself relying more and more on a metaphor that developed (for me) in the mid-1970s. The experiences and reports of several clients contributed to that development. In the course of counseling Karen Z., for example, I began to explore the phenomenology of oscillation in the dynamics of her development. Karen, the thirty-eight-year-old woman whose stream-of-consciousness reporting I previously discussed (see pages 295–97), and I worked together for over three years and corresponded at intervals for another six. One of the fascinating aspects of her reported experience during that period was the intermittent alternation of very stressful epi-sodes and relatively "good times." She described the former at their worst, as "tunnels." "They come in when I'm in trouble," she said. "They keep me away from things and they won't let anything in . . . just enough to function" (Mahoney 1985c, p. 34). As we saw earlier, in the context of her stream-of-consciousness work, Karen exhibited bodily contrac-tions. For her, "good times" were initially experienced only "at a safe distance," and a "good morning" was one when she did not wake up crying. Toward the end of (and especially after) her work in therapy, periods of feeling good became both more common and less minimal in their character.

I began to listen for oscillative themes in other clients' reports and had little difficulty recognizing them. Reminiscent of the oscillative dynamics of open, developing systems (chapters 6–8), my clients reported considerable variability in many different domains of their lives (for example, sleep cycles, digestive patterns, sexual interest, somatic sensations, relative energy level, and so on). Patricia F., the psychiatric nurse who had been frightened by her experience of "splitting" or "witnessing" (see pages 232–33), used the terms *expansion* and *contraction* in her personal journal:

An expansion is when I feel safe, at least for the moment. That is when I hear the birds singing or notice the sky. For a moment, at least, I am not in immediate danger of dying, or I forget about it, or something. And I am like a child—discovering, enjoying, and allowing myself to play.

According to Patricia, such moments were rare relative to her contractions: "When I am in a contraction, I am holding on tight and trying to just make it through the next moment. Survive . . . that is all I am trying to do . . . and when the contractions are bad, I am sure that I will fail. I feel terrified and hopeless." Other clients used similar terms. In episodes of contraction, they reported feeling "loosely wrapped" and in danger of "falling to pieces" or "coming apart." Each expression conveyed a felt threat to their coherence or integrity. Expansions, on the other hand, were described with terms that reflected feeling relatively "together," "centered," and "in balance." Consistent with research on affect and development, such periods of expansion were also associated with greater playfulness and increased exploratory activity (Gibson 1988; Maddi, Hoover, and Kobasa 1982; Rodrigue, Olson, and Markley 1987). Such explorations can, of course, lead to the "chance encounters" that often influence life paths in unanticipated ways (Bandura 1982).

Simplifying as it must be, figure 12.3 depicts a hypothetical grid in which the the extremes of expansion and contraction are contrasted with the extremes of activity and passivity. In this connection, the studies of emotionality in chapter 8 reveal some important themes. Activity and passivity are primary dimensions of human experience, and it is no accident that human conflicts cluster around issues of power, possibility, morality, and personal rights. Time and space prevent me from indulging here in conjectures on the promise and problems of this (or any other) two-dimensional map for what Humberto Maturana (1988) has aptly termed the "multiversal" territory of lived experience. Nevertheless, such a grid may be of use in future views and practices of psychotherapy. Nontechnical discussions of oscillative processes in development may help to "naturalize" the change experience for both counselors and clients. Many of my own clients have found it reassuring to learn that waves and cycles are common aspects of everyday experience, and that sudden changes in phenomenology are not necessarily dangerous or deviant.

In her diary entries (see pages 291–92), Olive W. made frequent references to "waves of contraction" in the course of her development. For Olive, the contraction was both literal and metaphoric: she experienced tension headaches, muscle tremors, spastic colitis, and difficulty in breathing, as well as apprehension, generalized anxiety, and crippling panic:

> *"How to explain the fear beyond fear, the*
> *Sadness that seems to have no end, the*
> *Waves that keep coming and coming, and—*
> *Who knows their origin, where they began, or*
> *Where they are going, or*
> *Why they are. . . .*
> *Of waking at 3 A.M., surrounded by darkness, by silence, sure that*
> *Only you—and you, alone,*
> *Are at that moment conscious and feeling.*

Figure 12.3   A Two-Dimensional Portrayal of Active and Passive Expansion and Contraction Experiences

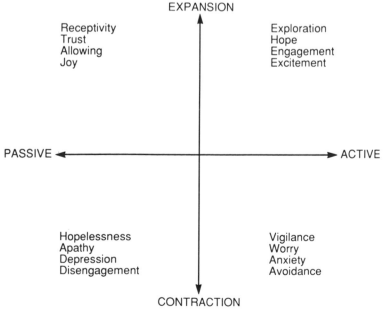

SOURCE: © 1989 M. J. Mahoney

Fortunately, these "dark nights of the soul" were not endless, and Olive eventually moved on to more hopeful and satisfying times.

Adam K. also contributed to my understanding of oscillative processes in personal development. Although Adam's sense of identity had become attached to his always having a problem (he shuddered at the thought of "not having a problem to organize my life around"), at the same time he repeatedly complained about always feeling "in crisis" and at the "bad end" of the spectrum. In one session he remarked that other people's lives seemed to at least show movement, and that his co-workers seemed to have "swings" of "good moods" as well as bad: "It's like there is a pendulum that swings from good to bad, and somehow my pendulum is always on the bad side." When I remarked that cycles and movements are part of being alive, he was not consoled. Commenting on what he wanted from me, he half jokingly asked, "Mike, couldn't you do something to get me over on the 'good' side and then nail me there?" Struck by the multiple possibilities in that metaphor, I gave him the homework assignment of spending several minutes each day watching the pendulum clock at his office.

Several months later, Adam left an insightful message on my phone-answering machine:

This is just an inspiration. For weeks now I have sat in the chair across from the clock and tried to figure out how I could stay on the good side without stopping the movement. It reminded me of something Ram Dass once said about people who use drugs: they don't want to "get high," they want to "be high." Today as I got up to return to work I walked past the clock and shot it an angry glance. It still had me puzzled. Then I suddenly realized that my attention had always been focused on the bottom of the damn thing—the big chrome circle that moves through the full arc. I stopped in my tracks, took a step backward, and peered through the glass. There, at the top of the pendulum, was something I had never before noticed, even though it was obvious. The damn thing pivots on a well-oiled joint. When I put my face against the glass and looked down the thing, I realized something. I can't keep my moods from moving, but if I move my attention up higher on the shaft I don't have to be swinging at either extreme (chuckle, chuckle). Now don't go getting Freudian on me, but I also thought that I might try sliding down every once in a while on the "good" side and enjoying myself, and then scrambling back up to the top when it swings toward the "bad." Mull that over, my dear shrink.

When Adam's life began to "get better," no one was more surprised than he. I can still vividly recall the session in which he described his first conscious experience of expansion. Even though his life situation was hectic and stressful, he was bothered by the fact that he was coping remarkably well. After a session in which I had suggested that his malaise over doing so well was itself understandable and healthy, he had a power-ful experience while walking down the hallway to his apartment. "I had lived there for six years," he said later, "and I knew that hallway blind. But that night . . . well, it was as if it were all new to me and it felt as if, for the first time, I was a *real* person walking down it. It seemed unusually bright, and I noticed colors in the carpet and details in the wallpaper that I had never seen before. There were also sounds and smells I had never noticed before. It was all so strange and unsettling. . . . What was so very familiar to me was suddenly very different. I felt frightened and excited at the same time. I remember turning the key in my door and fully expecting to find a whole different world inside."

Selected Clinical Considerations

I conclude this discussion of oscillative processes in development with three brief practical comments. First, remember the phenomenon of mood-related state dependency in learning and memory (chapters 4 and 8). Clients' recall and reports of their experiences may be significantly influenced by "where they are" in their metaphorical pendulum ride. I have had the repeated experience, for example, of clients in the midst of a painful contraction not being able to recall that they reported or enjoyed a period of expansion just days or weeks earlier. Rather than attempt to convince them that my memory was more accurate than theirs, I have generally found it more useful to help them label their "down" episode as a contraction and to reassure them that it is part of the nature of a contraction for them to feel absorbed in their pain and momentarily unable to recall *or anticipate* their life ever being different. (The same principle applies to the recall and expectations of the psychotherapist.)

Second, the dimensions of possible oscillations are only crudely captured by figure 12.3. Many individuals experience "swings" in the clarity of their identity, for example, and report feeling variations in their "being themselves." One client was particularly frustrated with his unending search to "find himself." In my experience, that search is a lifespan project; and, more often than not, individuals "carve away" the "not me" episodes or action patterns from the self-seeking processes that continue. With sensitivity to the risks and distress of severely dysfunctional oscillations in felt identity (chapter 9), I try to reassure individuals that these variations are a normal aspect of psychological development. With similar qualifications and a sensitivity to possible delusional and hallucinatory episodes, I also reassure clients about oscillations in what may feel real to them from time to time. Episodes of developmental progress, for example, are often described with terms like "pretend," "unreal," and "incredible," particularly when the episodes are dramatic or occur after a period of prolonged struggle or stasis. A useful analogy here is that children (and other creative people) often engage in pretend and fantasy play in their (unconscious) preparations for new roles and realities. In its original Latin meaning, *pretend* (from *praetendere*) implies not deception so much as a "stretching forth" or a preparatory inclination. "Let it be 'pretend' for a while," can be a reassuring maxim; pretend is often the precursor of possibility.

Finally, oscillations bear rich opportunities for developmental explorations. Even in the midst of agonizing contractions, for example, a client can be encouraged to experiment with responsible ways to express his or her pain and with capacities to self-comfort. As the literatures on emotionality attest, it is in the crucibles of personally meaningful intense affect that patterns of experiencing may be most powerfully rescaffolded. Ira Progoff has aptly described the phenomenology of acute contraction:

The movement downward into the valley of our emotions is like a chaotic retreat while it is taking place. The structure that had previously given us support is now breaking apart. . . . Now, as it is breaking apart, everything within us is segmented. This is the source of the confusion, of the panic, and of the outcry. (1980, p. 50)

Progoff believes that individuals move through cycles of difficulty, despair, deterioration, and then integration. That integration, he believes, is most apparent "where the confusion and the life-disorganization is at its fullest . . . in the depths of the darkest moment" (pp. 47–48).

Many individuals who seek professional services report a history of detachment from or denial of their feelings, and are often frightened by the intensity of their affect (positive and negative) and their changing relations with that domain. Among other things, this is why it is particularly important that psychotherapists be aware of their own feelings, fears, and expectations about their sequelae. From a developmental perspective, the object of psychotherapy is not to eliminate or dampen experiential oscillations, but to encourage a healthy respect for their role in the dynamics of personal psychological change. Likewise, this is why symptomatic relief is not the sole or most important focus of optimal psychotherapy (chapter 13). The effectiveness of psychotherapy cannot (or, more accurately, should not) be equated with emotional equilibration. As in both childbirth and dying, the comforting presence and caring of a significant other may make other life transitions less frightening and painful.

CHANGING RELATIONSHIPS

To reiterate, all experience—including the experience of change—is recursive or self-referential. This is the essence of the principle that all significant psychological change involves changes in personal meanings; and, furthermore, that all such changes involve different relationships among the core ordering processes. These changing relationships are an inevitable correlate of the structural reorganization that is inherent to the dynamics of development in living systems. Our understanding of those dynamics is still rudimentary, however; and our efforts to learn more are hampered, in part, by the inadequacies of languages and the historical momentum of misguiding ideas.

Since meanings are inseparable from ordering relations (chapters 4–5), any discussion of changes in meanings must also address changing relationships. In colloquial English, the term *relationship* usually refers to a human connection, but the potential uses of the term are far broader. In the context of my present discussion, for example, a psychotherapy client may experience change in a number of relationships ("contracted meanings"): their relationship to their own feelings, to the ambiguities in their lives, to the boundaries (edges) between the familiar and novel, and so on. In such developments, personal meanings change (such as the meaning(s) of anxiety, control, depression, friendship, intimacy, life, and so on). Moreover, as these meaningful relationships change, so does the individual's attention to and activity within them. In the remainder of this section, I shall attempt to illustrate some of these changes.

SHIFTS IN ATTENTION, CHANGES OF MEANING

What changes when a person changes? Patterns of thought, feeling, and behavior may change, or course; but there is a web of relatedness among these (and other) dimensions that also changes in the process. When Adam K. began to experience changes in his well-entrenched nightly rituals of bingeing and purging, for example, it was not the simple result of some strategic intervention on his part or mine. Indeed, the "critical incident" that appeared to have inaugurated that change was something neither of us had anticipated. Our therapeutic focus had been on his depression and self-rejection. Then one morning before dawn my phone rang.

"Mike, this is Adam. Did I wake you up?"

I mumbled, "No, no, it's okay." He was eager to tell me something.

"Guess what? [He didn't wait for my guess.] Last night I didn't binge or purge!"

I managed a profound "What?"

"For the first time in ten years, I went to bed without stuffing myself and vomiting!"

My head was beginning to clear, and I sat up in bed. "I want to hear about it, Adam."

"Well, I went to this party at Bill's house and I met a woman . . . and, uh [I could hear his smile on the other end of the phone] . . . well, she asked me to drive her home and, uh . . . well, I'm just now getting back to my apartment. I've got to see you some time today."

When he arrived at my office that afternoon, Adam was really charged. "Mike, you've got to do something with my bulimia, . . . surgically remove it, . . . hypnotize me. . . . I don't care what, it just has to be gone from my life." I motioned for him to sit down, but he wanted to pace. "This woman called me today—she wants to have dinner tonight! She likes me, Mike! This could be a real chance at a relationship with a woman!" He sat down. "But she wouldn't want to have anything to do with me if she knew what I do in the kitchen and bathroom every night. That's why you've got to remove my bulimia—today!" He stood up and began pacing again.

Meanwhile, I was trying to buy time in order to reflect on the magnitude of these new developments in Adam's life. I was worried about his desperate sense of urgency. He interrupted my reflections: "So what can you do?" Then, with a rare twinkle in his eye: "Got any magic you've been holding out on me?" We both smiled.

"Adam, slow down a second. I want to process all of this."

"I don't have time to slow down," he tossed back. "I need quick results or I am going to blow my chance."

For some reason I found myself slipping into the "dense" character style of the television detective Colombo (Peter Falk). "Well, let me see if I've got this straight now. You have binged and purged every single night for the last ten years. ["Yes, yes," he acknowledged impatiently.] And your previous attempts to break out of your bulimic pattern have all failed—medication, behavior modification, Jungian analysis . . ."

"YES, damn it! They got worse! You know all that already." His pacing was now so fast that I could feel air currents when he passed close by my chair.

"And last night you met a woman whom you spent the night with and——"

He cut me off and stood before me, yelling with clenched fists. "God damn it, Mike! What are you driving at! You *know* all that!"

"I'm sorry, Adam," I said, "I'm not trying to be coy. It's just that your eating and purging have been around a long time, and they haven't responded well to direct efforts to eliminate them." Adam sat down slowly and voiced a lingering "Yeahhh. . . ." "Well, I could be wrong—and you will have to be the judge of that—but it just seems to me that rushing in and demanding a drastic overhaul might be an insult to your system." He managed a muffled "What?" "Look, Adam, I don't think either of us fully understand what bingeing and purging have meant to you, but my hunch is that they were the best coping strategies you could find during some earlier periods in your life. They gave you comfort—or control—or something else you needed then. [He nodded gently.] Now they are seriously risking your health, and we both want to reduce them. But I just wonder whether we should use a Sherman tank approach. Given that their first sign of changing has emerged spontaneously, I worry that rushing in and pushing against them might do more harm than good."

Adam was silent for several minutes, sitting slumped in the chair. "I was afraid you were going to say something like that." We spent the rest of that session and several others dealing with his apprehensions about how intimate to be with his new companion, Heather. As their relationship continued, Adam became much more efficient and moderate in the execution of his rituals. He began to digest food he had never absorbed before. When he risked telling Heather that he did have "some issues" around food, she expressed concern about his health and then disclosed that she struggled with social anxieties. The dreaded rejection was transformed into affirmation.

Over the next few months, Adam reported some fascinating things about his food-related rituals. They became not only briefer but also "less interesting." Even though they continued for some time later, they lost much of their original salience for Adam. "It's like they are still around, but they aren't center stage in my life any more. They don't have the same role or something, like their meaning or function has changed." It has now been over six years since our last session, but I have heard from Adam at least once a year. He reports that he is still "vulnerable" to bingeing when he is very stressed, and that he went through a period of psychological dependence on prescription medication. His life has stabilized considerably (his most recent call was to invite me to his wedding), although he still struggles with episodes of depression and, in his words, "a few dear compulsions."

Needless to say, case histories never *demonstrate* anything unequivocally (but the same is true of the grandest and most rigorous experimental studies [Weimer 1979]). They can, however, *illustrate* and invite reflection. I believe that Adam's experience illustrates at least four points that have important practical implications: even when they improve, personal problems are rarely eliminated (completely eradicated); the life events responsible for initiating changes are multiple, and many lie outside the realm of professional interventions; changes in life quality involve changes in attention as well as in affective meaning and action; and life changes that may have been encouraged or initiated in the context of treatment are often amplified long after psychotherapy has ended. We should not be surprised, then, that clients' focal concerns often change in the course of treatment (Hatcher, Huebner, and Zakin 1986).

Changing Relations with Self

The most common concerns presented by clients in psychotherapy cluster into four broad categories: intimacy, empowerment, openness to human relationships, and guilt and self-forgiveness (Elliott and James 1989). These concerns are also, of course, expressed in patterns of affective engagement with self and world. It should not be surprising, then, that the dimensions of change most often reported by clients during and after therapy also reflect the centrality of such concerns. The most common such dimensions have been self-understanding (often termed "insight"), affective expression, increasing assumption of responsibility, feeling personally understood by the therapist, and feeling encouraged. Besides reporting more hope, psychotherapy clients also commonly state their their relationships with others have improved, and that they have experienced increases in their self-esteem and in their sense of personal agency or power. Self-efficacy, hope, and self-forgiveness are therefore important considerations in our conceptualization of psychological services (Bandura 1977, 1986; Beavers and Kaslow 1981; Fitzgibbons 1986; Frank 1985; Hillman 1965; Hope 1987; Pingleton 1989; Richards 1988).

The literatures on health, self, psychological dysfunctions, and psychotherapy process all point to the centrality of relationships with self in quality of life and possibilities for psychological development (Elliott and James 1989; Hartman and Blankstein 1986; Levy and Farber 1986; Miller and Thayer 1988; Suls and Fletcher 1985). Our recognition of the centrality of relationships with self, however, does not reduce the complexity of those relationships. As noted in chapter 9, the number of concepts with a *self-* prefix is itself dizzying. In addition, there are considerable disagreements among psychologists regarding the nature and effects of attention to the self.* In studies of clients' experiences in psychotherapy, however, the most common client intention is "understanding self and problems" (Elliott and James 1989, p. 450). Changing relationships with self are closely associated with progress in psychotherapy. The most commonly reported dimensions in which those changes take place are: (1) openness versus closure (as to novel experience, intense affect, or awareness); (2) activity versus passivity with regard to self; and (3) self-acceptance versus self-rejection. Each deserves at least brief comment.

Openness to Experience. Openness versus closure to experience has already been emphasized in my earlier discussion of expansions and contractions in the process of change. It is important to reiterate here that this issue of possibility lies at the heart of all debate about human plasticity. Our popular modern concepts of vulnerability and resilience (chapter 7), for example, are permeated with connotations of possibility and power. I want to emphasize here that clients' oscillations often relate their openness and closure to their experience of and with their psychothera-

---

*Baldwin and Holmes 1987; Briggs and Cheek 1988; Burnkrant and Page 1984; Buss 1980; Byrne 1988; Exner 1973; Fenigstein, Scheier, and Buss 1975; Gergen 1965; Gibbons et al. 1985; Greenberg and Pyszczynski 1986; Ingram 1990a, 1990b; Neisser 1988; Piliavin and Charing 1988; Rhodewalt and Agustsdottir 1986; Rogers, Kuiper, and Kirker 1977; Strauman and Higgins 1987; Swann and Read 1981a, 1981b; Tellegen and Atkinson 1974; Wegner and Giuliano 1980; and Wysocki, Chemers, and Rhodewalt 1987.

pist. Regardless of the theoretical orientation or methods of the therapist, clients report a common emphasis on the felt presence or absence of a caring emotional bond. For most clients, the availability of such a bond is related to issues of trust, respect, and balance of power. The point is that an individual's openness and closure are not fixed channels of experience, but dynamic developmental processes that have individualized rhythms and intensities. Optimal therapeutic practice cannot, therefore, consist of encouraging only one direction of healthy development. Openness and closure (or, more accurately, opening and closing) are more than interesting metaphors for developmental processes. As with all other expressions of life metabolism, it is the coordination of these processes that constitutes an ever-present challenge.

Personal Agency.   Activity versus passivity in relation to the self is also a dimension that has received considerable attention in self-efficacy theory and constructivist approaches to psychotherapy. As with openness and closure, neither pole is adequately rendered as good or bad; activity and passivity are relative and complementary. While some life circumstances may respond well to extra effort, others may be more satisfyingly altered by acceptance and surrender. It is in this regard, at least, that we are wise to seek a viable balance between "learned helplessness" and what Fogle (1978) has termed "learned restlessness."

Self-Valuation.   Finally, the evaluative and thoroughly emotional posture of acceptance versus rejection of the self should be acknowledged as a common dimension of human concern. This is not to presume the adequacy of current concepts or measures of self-appraisal or self-esteem (chapter 9). Refinements in those concepts and measures will figure importantly in the future contributions of psychology to life quality issues and human rights. What should not be overlooked in the quest for such refinements, however, is the centrality of self-valuation in human health and well-being. Rejection is not confined to interpersonal relations; neglect, rejection, and abuse can all be intrapersonal. It is, indeed, when these patterns become "internalized" and "identified with" that they become most powerful and tenacious in their influences on a life. This being the case, it becomes all the more important for the psychotherapist to be sensitive to the complexities and dynamics of self-relationships (in clients, of course, but also in themselves).

Intimacy and the Therapeutic Relationship

As mentioned earlier, clients most commonly report their experience of the therapeutic relationship in terms of the quality of their emotional bond with the therapist. This bond appears to provide the "secure base" described by Bowlby (1988), even when this is not an explicit intent of either participant. Trust, respect, and the balance of power in the relationship are central to evaluations of its quality. Moreover, studies of the effects of psychotherapy have begun to suggest consistently that the person and personality of the psychotherapist are second only to those of the client in accounting for different patterns of psychological change.

I am making two points here. First, psychotherapy is a special form of human relationship, and the quality of that relationship appears to be a significant factor in influencing the lives of its participants. Second, unique demands are placed upon the psychotherapist, as I shall elaborate in the next chapter.

Finally, it is important to reiterate that the secure base provided by optimal psychotherapy is a base and not a permanent home. For better and for worse, and in unpredictable ways, psychotherapy clients will interact differently with intimate others both during and after their experiences in psychotherapy. The intimate others in their lives will also contribute in important ways to clients' developmental options and experiences, particularly to their self-relationships. As we saw in chapter 9, *what is happening in any individual life is necessarily inseparable from what is happening in the lives with which that life is intimately involved, and vice versa.* The psychotherapist, as one of those intimate others, enters a complex multiversal system of human relatedness. By encouraging and modeling explorations in the realm of human and self-relatedness, the therapeutic relationship and the therapist will exert their own unpredictable influences on the lives of those most intimately involved with the client (Brody and Farber 1989). Likewise, important developments in practitioners' lives will have an impact on their psychological presence to and practice with their clients, just as events in the lives of clients (and their intimates) will contribute in both subtle and profound ways to the private life of the psychotherapist (chapter 13).

CONCLUSION

The simple-sounding assertion I made at the start of this chapter—that change is only change relative to what remains familiar—contains provocative complexities. What is familiar is itself dynamic and relative. It does not remain unchanged in a passive sense but is, rather, actively regenerated, again and again, like a mobile base camp. Its familiarity derives not from its being timelessly static or unchanging, but from its being *familia* to us—that is, "home," "intimate," and "close." Since families (familiarities) are also dynamic and developmental, the experience of change is necessarily a complex phenomenon. I wish I could find words and phrases that could simplify that complexity without insulting it, but I cannot. One metaphor I have found helpful here, however, is that of *celeration* (both *ac-* and *de-*). It is a concept that helped to revolutionize both science and mathematics because it introduced the notion of *second-order change:* that is, the rate of change of a changing variable (Cohen 1980; Kuhn 1970a, 1977; Olby et al. 1990). Although we must go beyond simplistic notions of rates and variables, the concept of celeration may at least help us to remember the relativities involved in our experience and its vicissitudes.

13

The Person and Experience of the Psychotherapist

A psychotherapist had best recognize that the profession will continually press on her or him to change and evolve.
—James F. T. Bugental

Consistent with the metaphor of developmental spirals, this final chapter brings me back to where I started, but at a different level of analysis. I return now to the realm of the individual and focus on the psychotherapist. My intention is to highlight the person of the helping professional and to emphasize the importance of "person variables" in our conceptualization of both service and servant.

Those who offer comfort and counsel on the living of individual lives are often some of the most influential "agents" in those lives. As noted in chapters 10 and 11, the amount of variance in clients' responses to psychotherapy that can be attributed to "therapist variables" is second only to that attributable to "client variables" (Bergin and Lambert 1978). The quality of their relationship—and the potential power of their "working alliance" (Greenberg and Pinsof 1986)—is a superadditive interaction of the human beings literally interacting. In a series of independently conducted studies, a variety of outcome measures have indicated that the "person" of the therapist is at least eight times more influential than his or her theoretical orientation and/or use of specific therapeutic techniques. Michael Lambert's (1989) valuable summary of that research merits paraphrasing here:

Existing research on psychotherapy indicates that (1) the individual psychotherapist is a significant factor in the process and outcome of professional services; (2)

his or her impact can be both positive and negative, a fact that merits substantial care in selection, training, and clinical referrals; (3) therapist effects are apparent across a wide range of client diagnoses, severities of clients' psychological dysfunctions, levels of therapist experience, and therapists' theoretical orientations; (4) therapist effects remain significant even in those studies where therapists have been meticulously selected, trained, supervised, and monitored to minimize differences among therapists and their practices; and (5) this phenomenon is sufficiently robust to be apparent across a wide range of research methods and process and outcome measures.

Although these findings were contrary to the expectations of most psychotherapy researchers of the last quarter-century, they are entirely consistent with both classic and modern analyses of "persuasion and healing" (Frank 1987). In his treatise on rhetoric, for example, Aristotle left little doubt about the relative powers of *logos* (logic), *pathos* (emotion), and *ethos* (personal character) in persuasive communication: "Character *(ethos)* is the most potent of all the means of persuasion" (cited in Glaser 1980, p. 316).

The central point here is clear: the person who is the professional influences the person who is the client. Equally clear and also central to the theme of this chapter is the inverse of that statement: clients also influence their therapists. Reflecting some of the complexity and reciprocity I have described in previous chapters, the processes and experiences of serving as a professional life counselor are themselves significant influences in the life of the psychotherapist. Like their clients, psychotherapists change in complex ways and as a result of challenges and choices they have not anticipated. Except for those clients who are themselves mental health practitioners, however, the changes that emerge in the lives of psychotherapists are probably more complex in that they reflect an experiential involvement with the private struggles and developments of many other individuals.

Although the literature on the person and experience of the psychotherapist is relatively less extensive than that devoted to other topics in the social sciences, it is neither small nor insignificant. As in previous chapters, my intent here is to highlight relevant works and to offer integrative summaries of their potential implications for practice. More elaborate discussions (as well as a valuable diversity of interpretations) are available in the original resources.* My discussion is organized around four broad themes: (1) the multiple motives for and meanings of becoming and being a psychotherapist; (2) the responsibilities and risks of being a mental health practitioner; (3) the privileges and enrichments of life

---

*In particular, I recommend Barron 1978; Beutler, Crago, and Arizmendi 1986; Bugental 1978, 1987; Dent 1978; Dryden and Spurling 1989; Farber 1983a, 1983b, 1983c, 1985, 1989; Frank 1973, 1985; Goldberg 1986; Gurman and Razin 1977; Guy 1987; Henry, Sims, and Spray 1973; Kottler 1986; Kottler and Blau 1989; Norcross and Guy 1989; and Orlinsky and Howard 1977.

counseling; and (4) the importance of taking care of the "serving self." I will then conclude both chapter and book with remarks on the implications of all of this (including the previous chapters) for graduate training, psychotherapy supervision, the working alliance of scientific research and professional services, and the lifespan care and development of the mental health practitioner.

THE MULTIPLE MOTIVES AND MEANINGS OF HELPING

The motives for becoming and being a psychotherapist are themselves complex, and broad generalizations should again be grounded in the person and life circumstances of the individual practitioner. Despite a diversity of motives, however, it is clear that increasing numbers of the U.S. population have been drawn toward careers as professional helpers. According to estimates based on U.S. statistics (Goldberg 1986), for example, there are over 100,000 mental health practitioners in that country alone (31,000 psychiatric social workers, 29,000 psychiatrists, 26,000 clinical psychologists, 10,000 counseling psychologists, and 10,000 psychiatric nurses). While the United States can claim one of the highest ratios of mental health practitioners to its citizenry, it is worth noting that this ratio is hardly generous: for every such practitioner, there are at least 235,000 U.S. citizens (and 30 percent to 70 percent of those citizens may require psychological services in the course of an eighty-year lifespan [Sartorius, Nielsen, and Stromgren 1989]).

According to the self-reports of practitioners, the motives for choosing a career in mental health range from financial and pragmatic issues to philosophical and humanitarian concerns. Many practitioners report that they enjoy the relative independence and range of choices made available to them, for example, and the challenges inherent in the profession are frequently described as motivating. The prestige and social recognition associated with performing psychological services are potentially motivating for some individuals, and the financial rewards of practice (particularly when it is "independent") are also commonly noted.

Although little literature has been devoted to the topic, it appears that some of the motives for career choice are related to practitioners' images of the psychotherapy process. David Orlinsky (1989) has described four of the most common such images. In the first, psychotherapy is considered a "treatment," and the professional may be influenced by motives commonly represented in the medical professions (such as the identification and reduction of pathologies, the restoration of health). Some researchers have, in fact, blamed excessive reliance on this image for the use of inappropriate methods and concepts in the study of psychotherapy process and outcome (Stiles and Shapiro 1989).

A second basic image of psychotherapy portrays it as a form of education and relies extensively on metaphors of learning, guidance, and counseling. The common assumption here is that personal problems are the result of inadequate or inappropriate learning experiences. If this assumption is granted, the motives of the psychotherapist may be more like those of the teacher than the physician, and the client may be treated more like a pupil than a patient. Basic skills training, educational problem solving, and goal-oriented instructional packages are also more likely to be employed.

Orlinsky's third image is of psychotherapy as a "correctional" or "reform" process, which he maintains is put forth as an unflattering view by critics of mental health practices. The motivating dimensions of this image are confined to practitioners' desires for power, authority, and the capacity to manipulate clients' freedoms in accordance with their individual compliance to such authority. Let us hope that this is a rare source of motivation for one's choosing to become a psychotherapist.

The fourth image of psychotherapy appeals to its parallels with religious activities and the individual's search for spiritual development and transpersonal purpose or meaning. As I noted earlier in respect to therapeutic rituals (chapter 11), that search may include acts of confession, attonement, forgiveness, private dialogue (prayer), and an infinite range of ceremonies. The role of the psychotherapist in such endeavors is that of the "secular priest(ess)" or "lay ministry" in that one often offers interpretations of personal struggles, suggests activities appropriate to spiritual development, and encourages a deepening faith in the process and outcome of such engagements (Frank 1973, 1987; Frankl 1959; Friedman 1988). Needless to say, practitioners who view psychotherapy from this perspective may trace some of their career motivations to philosophical, spiritual, and humanitarian concerns. As Orlinsky (1989) and others have noted, the metaphors afforded by these four images of psychotherapy are often intermingled in integrative and generic models.

Psychological motives for wanting to become and be a psychotherapist have also been suggested, ranging from desires for power and "safe" (time-limited, nonsexual) intimacy to personal fulfillment and self-understanding (Guy 1987). As I shall discuss later, emotional growth and personal satisfaction are frequently reported benefits of practicing psychotherapy, with many practitioners stating that their professional experiences have effected positive changes in their own lives (such as increased reflectivity, assertiveness, self-assurance, and interpersonal sensitivity). Unfortunately, however, the possibility that mental health practitioners may be serving some of their own psychological needs in the process of serving those of others has also invited a judgmental dichotomy about the person of the professional. At the one extreme, he or she is portrayed as an eccentric, if not severely disturbed, individual who preys upon the ignorance, fear, and psychological vulnerabilities of others. At the opposite extreme, the psychotherapist is characterized as a paragon of human development: perfectly mature, vibrantly healthy, heroic, wise, saintly, and virtually superhuman.

The Wounded Healer Metaphor

Some of the more complex and controversial motives for becoming a psychotherapist include those in which the practitioner uses the role of a helping professional to serve his or her own personal needs. Sometimes those needs are compatible with the professional role and the "best interests" of clients, as when a therapist finds personal fulfillment in facilitating the development and well-being of other persons. But there are also potentially dysfunctional motives for counseling others, such as when the practitioner uses professional practice as a means of reducing his or her own loneliness or sense of vulnerability. This is an important consideration since a substantial proportion of mental health professionals report that their motives for career choice include desires for self-understanding, "self-healing," and the resolution of personal problems or existential issues (Goldberg 1986; Guy 1987). Often referred to as the *wounded healer* phenomenon, this remains an important priority for future studies of psychotherapy and the person of the psychotherapist (Henry, 1966; Rippere and Williams 1985).

Among the many interesting facets of the wounded healer metaphor is its source: namely, the oral and written histories of healing and healers. Over the millennia and across diverse cultures, there has been a relatively robust finding that those individuals who are "chosen," "self-selected," and revered for their alleged therapeutic powers also have themselves struggled with and survived the forces believed to be responsible for illness or psychological suffering. Histories of psychological services document the fact that modern psychotherapeutic services emerged out of cultural traditions involving mythology, mysticism, magic, religion, and medicine (for example, Alexander and Selesnick 1966; Bromberg 1959; Canda 1988; Ehrenwald 1976; Ellenberger 1970; Frank 1973). Prior to the relatively recent marriage of medicine and modern science, for example, the identified healers in many cultures were individuals whose knowledge of health and the "forces" involved in *therapeia* (Greek for "healing" or "curing") had been gained through personal suffering and/or apprenticeship with another healer. Shaman, sorcerer, magician, witch, and witchdoctor were more than social roles: they were highly honored persons within their communities. One did not choose the profession so much as one was chosen for it by means of visions, revelations, and formidable (and frequently dangerous) developmental challenges (often involving core ordering processes).

Historically, individuals identified as professional healers were typically conceptualized and approached as if they were magical mediums

and Hermes in the flesh. In virtually all versions of the healer's development, there are pivotal and/or recurring episodes of severe existential
circumstances and choices. The healer must repeatedly face danger, pain,
and death, for example; and his or her identity must be at least periodically associated with the abstract Greater Forces necessary to survive and
succeed in the face of life challenges. It is, indeed, the fact that the healer
has faced and survived these encounters that makes him or her potentially
more qualified to counsel others on their own struggles. As James Guy
put it, "the 'wound' of personal distress may itself render the therapist
more empathic, sensitive, and effective in treating the psychic pain of
others" (1987, p. 15). In many cultures, of course, the "wounds" of the
healer are considered sources and symbols of their power. Psychological
wounds may also create the potential for powerful communication in that
they may serve "the drive to connect" and "the dream of a common
language" (Rich 1978, p. 7).

The question is, of course, complex. The psychotherapist who has
never struggled with intense feelings of vulnerability or existential
predicaments may have difficulty understanding (let alone feeling empathic toward) a client for whom these are overwhelming concerns. At the
other extreme, the severely distressed practitioner who harbors little
hope for happiness or well-being in his or her own life is unlikely to be
encouraging of such hopes in the lives he or she counsels. But how are
we to know when a psychotherapist's form or intensity of personal distress is likely to interfere with responsible and effective functioning as a
helping professional? This is a pressing question with obvious implications for the quality of mental health services; the only answer afforded
by existing research is that we simply do not know (Deutsch 1985; Gurman 1973; Guy 1987; Whitfield 1980).

The Guru Metaphor and Related Illusions

The wounded healer metaphor has been occasionally abused by critics of
psychotherapy, whose frequent message is that psychotherapists are "just
as crazy" as their clients, or that psychological services are either ineffec-
tive or ill advised. I do not question that many psychotherapists have
suffered and continue to suffer with significant personal issues, nor do I
deny that the available evidence suggests that some psychotherapists may
actually do harm to their clients. Even though "negative effects" appear
to be rare exceptions to a more positive rule, their undeniable existence
demands intense and continuing scrutiny. But studies of the "average"
effect of psychotherapy by the "average" psychotherapist with the "average" client are likely to tell us little about the complex range of persons
and developmental dynamics involved.

The wounded healer metaphor offers a case in point. The qualifier *wounded* is most likely a reference not only to the healer's personal history of struggle, but also to her or his current status of continuing vulnerability (from the Latin *vulnare,* "to wound"). In this rendition, the "wound" is not a historical experience but a present theme in the functioning of the healer. Consider, for example, the extreme contrast to the wounded healer metaphor: namely, that of the *perfect practitioner,* often characterized as a *guru.* In this use, "perfect" refers not only to the most appropriate and effective enactments of counsel but also to personal embodiments of psychological and (if possible) physical well-being. The absolutely perfect practitioner is, of course, a misguided and misguiding illusion, but it still operates in the tacit life ordering that goes on in psychotherapists' lives. The (illogical) inferential leap here is from wounded healer to paragon of well-being (Coan 1977, 1979). Such a leap can lead to excessively stringent personal standards, and practitioners are wise to monitor the criteria they impose in their personal self-evaluations. The psychotherapist who believes (and feels) that he or she should be totally free of personal problems and always perfect in practice may fail to learn from his or her mistakes and inadvertently collude in his or her own distress and burnout (Kottler and Blau 1989).

For example, several years ago I was invited to speak at a foreign university on the occasion of its four hundredth anniversary. I had not anticipated the elaborate ceremonies that were to surround my talk, which was introduced by a high-ranking government official and delivered in a gigantic theater filled with more than two thousand people. I felt painfully nervous, to say the least, but managed to render my presentation, which was warmly received. One of my concluding remarks had to do with the human side of the professional helper and with our need to reappraise traditional assumptions that optimal psychotherapy is best rendered by paragons of psychological adjustment. Having begun my research career with studies on self-control, anxiety management, and coping skills, I noted that my audiences were sometimes surprised to learn that I was shy and sometimes felt nervous in public presentations. My point was that I, like all humans (be they therapists, clients, or others), struggle with the themes and edges of my own psychological development, and that our understanding and facilitation of development would be better served by more open acknowledgments of such feelings and struggles.

As I was being ushered down from the stage, I was informed that Professor A, one of the most influential living psychologists in the world, had requested a private meeting with me in his office. I was escorted to a room that resembled a library more than an office, where I waited nervously for the professor to arrive. In a few moments he came in, followed by an entourage of admirers and attendants—all of whom he soon dismissed so that we could speak privately. I remember wondering how old he was; his writings had been among the classics my college professors had studied in their early training.

The professor motioned for me to sit down and offered generous compliments on the talk I had just given. I thanked him and said what an honor it was to meet him. He then walked around his desk and leaned backward against it, looking down into my eyes. "You said in your talk that you sometimes feel shy and nervous about speaking in public." I said, "Yes." "But you are very good at it. I did not notice your anxiety." I smiled and thanked him for the compliment and then said, "Well, I may look calm from the outside, but I struggle with strong feelings inside." He looked surprised and began to pour us each a small glass of cognac. "Then your anxiety is relatively mild?" he asked. "No, sir," I said, "not at all. Sometimes I feel absolutely terrified." I will never forget his stare; it was as if he could not believe what he was hearing. For what seemed like the better part of a minute, he stood silently gazing into my eyes, not once blinking. "Forgive me for my persistence," he said, handing me the glass of cognac. "I do not mean to challenge the honesty of your statement. . . . It just surprises me so." I sipped my cognac slowly and then said, "Still, it is true." He looked away for several moments and then walked over and sat next to me, knee to knee.

What followed was one of my most unforgettable experiences. With a chilling tone of solemnity in his voice, the professor swore me to secrecy regarding what he was about to say. I assented. Then, haltingly and with frequent pauses to wipe tears from his eyes, he related how agonizing had been his own struggle with public-speaking anxiety. Over the many years of his exceptional career, he had managed to avoid doing more than two dozen public lectures, and had declined many opportunities for travel because of their speaking requirements. Now, at the age of eighty-three and in the twilight of both his life and his career, many colleagues and friends were intent on his being honored at banquets and award ceremonies that required acceptance speeches. He said that he felt like a fool and a failure in not being able to accept their invitations and in not being willing to tell them why. My talk earlier that evening and my admission of my own struggles in that domain had made his dilemma all the more poignant for him. After talking for almost three hours about how and when and where we felt our respective inhibitions, we concluded our evening with the agreement that shyness was not a sin and that we would each remember our conversation and imagine one another's supportive presence in our future audiences. He died less than a year later, but not before accepting some of those longstanding invitations. My bet is that his final acceptance speeches were more meaningful to him than the many decades of scholarship for which he was being honored.

All of which is to say that mental health specialists need not (and, indeed, should not) labor under the illusion that they must be (or must appear to be) paragons of socially defined adjustment. We best serve our profession and our clients, I believe, when we make our best efforts to be honest with ourselves, to be aware of our own experience, and to be open to exploring its meanings and values. We also need to acknowledge that our own struggles can sometimes impair our services, and that even the most kindhearted and well intentioned of us can at times say and do things that are harmful to clients. It is for this reason, in part, that the wise and responsible practitioner is always engaged in the lifelong project of personal development. That project should include work that allows the psychotherapist to share intimately with trusted colleagues and professional mentors. As I shall further elaborate, I also believe it is important that these confidants be "more" than friends or lovers: they should themselves be responsible professionals who can be candid in encouraging our processes of discernment and in confronting us with their perceptions of our phenomenological blind spots and biases.

Besides imposing unrealistic expectations about the private life and personal functioning of the therapist, the guru metaphor may also encourage clients to disempower themselves by relying too heavily on the advice of their counselor and not taking responsibility for their own life choices. Sheldom Kopp put it succinctly:

So often intent on learning the rules of the game of life, the patient/pilgrim often tries hard to get the guru/therapist to instruct him. He is sure that there must be more to life than he has been able to establish, some hidden order to be discovered that will provide the key to happiness, to perfection, to a problem-free life. The therapist seems to know what he is doing. Surely he has discovered and mastered the rules of the game. The patient cannot believe that the therapist has only learned to play "the game of no game" . . . [and] that the only rules that the therapist follows and teaches are meta-rules, rules about rules. (1972, p. 120)

A common illusion in guru-seeking clients seems to be the belief that some day they will wake up and have their life "figured out," "put together," or otherwise "fixed" once and for all. From that point on, they assume, their life will be "smooth sailing." While this illusion may offer temporary comfort in moments of distress, it flies in the face of the fact that the next problem is always in the mail. As Kopp aptly notes, if the client is to live his or her own life, he or she must again and again "trade the illusion of certainty for the holy insecurity of never knowing for sure what it's all about" (p. 121). It was in this same existential and Socratic spirit that Richard Bach suggested that a special handbook for masters—a manual for "advanced souls"—would almost surely end with seven prophetic words: "Everything in this book may be wrong" (1977, p. 181). The moral, it would seem, is that the answers are not to be found in any book or authority, but rather that they must be endlessly pursued and construed by the pilgrim in process.

The Role of Caring in Professional Helping

Although some definitions of psychotherapy (or specific approaches to it) have emphasized the role of "positive regard" and affection in the helping relationship, this facet has only recently begun to emerge as a scientifically respectable focus of research. With the accumulating evidence on the "working (or therapeutic) alliance" and the personal contributions of the individual psychotherapist, for example, there has come an increasing acknowledgment of the affective life of the counselor and, in particular, his or her capacity to invite and co-maintain a highly specialized human relationship involving mutual trust and genuine caring (Bowlby 1979, 1988; Elliott and James 1989; Greenberg and Pinsof 1986; Greenberg and Safran 1987). The experience and expression of that caring are, of course, unique to the persons involved, but the centrality of caring has never been more widely recognized. This being the case, two points are worthy of brief comment.

First, current knowledge suggests that a psychotherapist is more likely to be able to experience and share genuine caring with his or her clients to the extent that she or he has experienced (and continues to experience) being cared for by others. In other words, some patterns of past and present life experiences may make it relatively more difficult for some individuals to assume (and optimally enact) the role of professional caregiver. Victims of severe and chronic neglect, abuse, and rejection, for example, may face substantial challenges in just learning to trust and to know and love themselves without the added responsibilities of encouraging and facilitating these developments in others (Evoy 1981). As Erich Fromm (1956) noted in contrasting his views of self-love with those of Freud and the pathologists of narcissism, predominant or excessive self-focus is an expression not of "too much" but of "too little" self-love. Without the capacity for self-love, there is limited ability authentically to love or to care about another person.

This point has particular relevance for the mental health practitioner in that it emphasizes the importance of self-awareness and self-care in protecting and refining the quality not only of the practitioner's life but also of his or her services. Regrettably, some practitioners appear to derive satisfaction from what Fromm has termed *neurotic unselfishness*, an attribute they often regard with pride as if it were a redeeming character trait. According to Fromm, such individuals may go to great lengths to live a lifestyle of constant self-sacrifice and extensive public (or client) service, taking great personal pride in their (public) humility, in living their life "entirely for others," and in not wanting much of anything for themselves. Indeed, these individuals are said to exhibit a pattern remarkably similar to that described by Bowlby (1979) as *compulsive self-reliance* in that they experience great difficulty requesting or accepting help from others. It should not be surprising, then, that these same individuals are said to be frequently troubled by depression, fatigue, problems in intimate relationships, dissatisfactions with their work, and a chronic sense of anger or hostility which may be related to feeling inadequately appreciated. Bowlby states that "to do this work well requires of the therapist not only a good grasp of principles but also a capacity for empathy and for tolerating intense and painful emotion. Those with a strongly organized tendency towards compulsive self-reliance are ill-suited to undertake it and are well advised not to" (1979, p. 154).

The second point is that caring is not a commodity but a process and, in particular, a process involving a developing relationship. As Milton Mayeroff put it, "Through caring for certain others, by serving them through caring, a (person) lives the meaning of his (or her) own life" (1971, p. 2). According to Mayeroff, the basic pattern of caring involves experiencing the cared-for person as an extension of one's self as well as a separate and developing life process. Such caring entails a respectful knowledge of the other, a sensitivity to the rhythms in his or her development (and in one's relatedness to the person), a patience with the pacing of his or her development, a commitment to mutual honesty and trust, a humility that reflects openness to learning, and a deep sense of possibility, hope, and the courage required to risk excursions into the unknown. Fundamental to all these features, of course, is the deepfelt desire and commitment to help the other person develop in ways that he or she experiences as satisfying and self-actualizing. Serving as an instrumental facilitator of such development can be one of the richest rewards of a career in psychotherapy.

THE STRESSES OF BEING A PSYCHOTHERAPIST

Every profession or career affects physically and psychologically those who practice it. The effects of serving as a mental health professional are particularly apparent, and although some of these effects are positive, others are decidedly negative. Even using conservative estimates of psychological dysfunction and distress, "the total incidence of therapist impairment begins to seem substantial" (Guy 1987, pp. 207–8). In two surveys of psychiatrists, for example, over 90 percent felt that they suffered special emotional problems resulting from their role as a psychotherapist, 73 percent reported having experienced moderate to incapacitating anxiety in their first years of practice, and 58 percent reported having experienced serious depression (Guy 1987; Guy and Liaboe 1986). Likewise, in a survey of 264 psychotherapists, Deutsch (1985) found that significant personal problems were frequently reported, with the most common being relationship difficulties (82%), depression (57%), substance abuse (11%), and suicide attempts (2%). Early studies of suicide rates among psychiatrists suggested figures four to five times greater than those reported for the general population, but other investigations showed little or no difference in the suicide rates of these groups (Guy 1987). The scant research thus far reported on suicide among psychologists suggests that males in this profession may exhibit a slightly lower rate of suicide, while female psychologists may commit suicide at a rate nearly three times greater than national norms (Steppacher and Mausner 1973). A difference of comparable magnitude has been reported for male and female physicians. The reasons for this differential risk between the genders remain unknown; it may be that female health professionals are under greater stress due to gender role stereotypes involving expectations that they be the "primary nurturer," unconditionally compassionate, or unrealistically self-sacrificing.

The sources and effects of psychological impairment and possible methods of prevention and resolution must be considered a high priority for future research, services, and policies in the profession (Guy, Poelstra, and Stark 1989; Kilburg, Nathan, and Thoreson 1986; Laliotis and Grayson 1985; Lester 1989; Parker 1983; Payne and Firth-Cozens 1987; Rippere and Williams 1985; Scott and Hawk 1986). As I mentioned earlier in respect to the wounded healer metaphor (Henry 1966), some psychotherapists may enter the profession with (and, indeed, because of) pre-existing personal problems. Others may develop such problems for reasons unrelated to their practice as a psychotherapist. Although the available evidence is still too sparse to permit quantitative statements about proportions, it seems increasingly clear that the practice of psychotherapy is a significant factor in the development and exacerbation of many psychotherapists' personal distress and dysfunction. One cannot participate in a therapeutic role and bear witness to the narratives of many human lives without being profoundly influenced in the process. Mental health practitioners often go to their graves with painful memories of their clients' vivid accounts of tragedy, neglect, abuse, injustice, anguish, and cruelty. Just as Milton Erickson could assure a departing client that "my voice will go with you" (Rosen 1982), the practitioner can be equally assured that aspects of clients' life experiences will remain (and "go with") him or her. As Chessick put it, psychotherapists often take their clients' "anguish to bed with them at night and grieve about it in their dreams; it remains like a gnawing theme in the back of their minds" (1978, p. 5).

This being the case, it should not be surprising that psychotherapists exhibit special vulnerabilities to work-related stress, "burnout," and episodes of career dissatisfaction. The most common sources of stress reported by psychotherapists are presented in table 13.1. In the survey conducted by Hellman and his colleagues (1987), "the work" inherent in psychotherapy was also reported to be a source of stress (that is, developing and maintaining a therapeutic alliance, personal depletion from being

Table 13.1   Common Sources of Stress
among Psychotherapists

1. *Working Conditions*

Isolation

Excessive workload

Excessive proportion of difficult
clients

Time pressures

Organizational politics

Professional conflicts

Excessive paperwork

Economic uncertainty

Inactivity

2. *Personal Issues*

Physical exhaustion

Emotional depletion

Felt responsibility for clients'
well-being

Low self-esteem

Spillover of work into private life

Relationship difficulties

Doubts about efficacy of therapy

Emotional self-control

Inevitable loss of clients
(termination)

Circumstantial stresses (e.g., change
of residence, family events)

3. *Client Behaviors*

Suicidal statements or attempts

Aggressive or hostile behavior

Intense anxiety

Premature termination

Depression, despair

Impulsive acts

Intense dependency

Phoning therapist at home

Paranoia

Psychopathic behavior

Seductive behavior

Schizoid detachment

Unexpected social encounters

Erratic fee payment

Missed sessions

Late arrivals

Reluctance to leave at end of
session

Resistance

Condensed from Farber (1983c, 1989), Farber and Heifetz (1981), Guy (1987), Hellman,
Morrison, and Abramowitz (1987), Norcross and Guy (1989), Smith (1980), and Whitfield
(1980).

emotionally engaged in clients' struggles, and such mundane mechanical
hassles as scheduling). Older therapists reported experiencing less distress from these sources than did their younger colleagues, and those
with moderate caseloads reported less stress and professional doubts
than did psychotherapists with either light or heavy caseloads. In other
research, however, the actual number of "cases" being seen was less
predictive of therapists' distress than was their perception of that "load"
and their satisfaction with it (Raquepaw and Miller 1989).

Also not surprising is the finding that psychotherapists' experiences of personal distress, when intense or chronic, may impair therapeutic effectiveness (Beutler, Crago, and Arizmendi 1986). One recent survey indicated that three out of four psychotherapists report having experienced "personal distress" in the preceding three years (Guy, Poelstra, and Stark 1989). Of these, 37 percent believed that their distress had reduced the quality of their services to clients; 5 percent reported that it had resulted in their rendering "inadequate treatment." The majority reported doing something to reduce their distress, with personal therapy (27%), reducing their work load (17%), and family therapy (11%) being the most common responses. It should be reiterated here that the therapist's capacity to become emotionally involved is an important element in one's capacity to both care and help. Ironically, more effective therapists may be more vulnerable to the stresses of their work than their less engaged and less helpful colleagues. The former also appear to be more capable of maintaining high-quality caring in the presence of their own "bad moods" (Gurman 1973), and experienced clinicians report increased resilience in the face of work stress. The point is that personal distress is common among psychotherapists and may jeopardize the quality of their services.

Suicide, negative affect, and resistance to change emerge as the main clusters of client behaviors that psychotherapists experience as distressing (table 13.1). All three are common elements in the lifespan experience of the practitioner. As training requirements reflect, for example, it is highly likely that student therapists will have encountered at least one (and sometimes many) suicidal crises before they earn a license to practice. Virtually every practitioner is intermittently involved with clients' struggles with literal life-and-death matters. Almost 1 out of every 4 U.S. psychotherapists experience the death by suicide of a client, and they often react with acute emotional distress similar to that experienced after the loss of a parent (Chemtob et al. 1988).

Burnout is now a popular term for patterns of exhaustion, depersonalization, and reduced self-efficacy associated with chronically excessive work demands (Kahill 1988). Responses to such demands are always individualized, of course, but they often include somatic problems, withdrawal, substance abuse, and complex mixtures of negative attitudes toward self, life, and the worth or meaning of one's work (table 13.2). At some point in their career, most psychotherapists will be personally familiar with the symptoms of burnout. To lend some encouraging ballast to this portrayal, however, let me note that most are likely to take steps to deal with their personal distress. Personal therapy and self-care regimens are their most common choices and constitute my next major topic. Before making that transition, however, the positive side of being a psychotherapist merits at least passing acknowledgment. Most psychotherapists are "moderately to very satisfied" with their life's work, and many

Table 13.2   Common Symptoms of Professional
Burnout

1. *Physical*
   Exhaustion or chronic fatigue
   Headaches
   Increased vulnerability to colds and flu
   Sleep disturbances
   Back pain
   Gastrointestinal problems
2. *Behavioral*
   Increased alcohol use
   Increased caffeine and nicotine consumption
   Increased drug use (licit and illicit)
   Increased absenteeism and social withdrawal
   Overeating
3. *Emotional and Psychological*
   Reduced sense of self-efficacy
   Negative attitudes about self, clients, work, and life
   Reduced professional commitment
   Increased irritability, anger, and hostility
   Depression
   Anxiety
   Emotional distancing and depersonalization

Condensed and adapted from Kahill (1988).

report personal psychological benefits (Guy 1987; Norcross, Strausser-Kirtland and Missar 1988; Thoreson, Miller, and Krauskopf 1989). I shall return to these benefits in my later discussion of the privileges of the profession.

TAKING CARE OF THE SERVING SELF

Since a psychotherapist's quality of life may both positively and negatively influence the quality of his or her professional services, it is somewhat puzzling that the care and well-being of practitioners and other health service professionals has only recently become a topic of widespread interest (Kilburg, Nathan, and Thoreson 1986; Payne and Firth-Cozens 1987; Scott and Hawk 1986). Indeed, it has become increasingly apparent that future refinements in the training of psychotherapists should include explicit recommendations regarding health behavior and psychological self-care (Guy 1987).

Personal Therapy for Psychotherapists

In two famous essays, Sigmund Freud (1953–1966) [1937] referred to psychoanalysis as an "impossible profession" practiced by a "poor wretch" whose work was both "terminable and interminable." Asking himself the rhetorical question where and how that "wretch" might acquire the ideal qualifications for his or her work, Freud responded that it begins in self-analysis. To this day, the "training analysis" remains an important requirement in orthodox psychoanalytic apprenticeships, and ongoing (lifespan) excursions into personal treatment remain most extensively pursued by practitioners who describe themselves as psychoanalytic or psychodynamic in orientation. Current estimates suggest that between 70 percent and 80 percent of clinical practitioners seek personal therapy at some point in their lives; few studies have focused on the personal treatment experiences of therapists. As Norcross, Strausser, and Faltus put it, "The silence is deafening" (1988, p. 53).

At least some of the sounds in that silence have, however, been provocative.* Over all, female psychotherapists and those endorsing an "insight-oriented" approach appear to be more likely to seek personal therapy than their male and less insight-oriented counterparts, with relationship conflicts, depression, and anxiety being their most frequent presenting concerns. Practitioners from psychodynamic, eclectic, existential, and humanistic orientations are more likely to seek personal therapy than are their cognitive and behavioral colleagues. Psychologists appear to seek help from psychiatrists about as often as from other psychologists (35% and 36% of the time, respectively), while psychiatrists exhibit a 10:1 ratio of preferring to be treated by another psychiatrist rather than by a psychologist. This ratio may reflect a confounding variable, however, since psychodynamic perspectives are currently more popular in psychiatry than in psychology, and that—nine times out of ten—psychoanalysts seek treatment from other psychoanalysts.

Behaviorists have shown the lowest rates of seeking treatment at all; and, when they do, they are much less likely than their nonbehavioral peers to seek services from a professional who shares their own theoretical orientation. In one recent survey by Norcross, Strausser, and Faltus (1988), those behavior therapists who had been in personal therapy chose to see another behavior therapist only 6 percent of the time; the rate at which therapists of other orientations chose a personal therapist of their same orientation was three to fifteen times greater than this. The same

*See, for example, Buckley, Karasu, and Charles 1981; Deutsch 1985; Fleischer and Wissler 1985; Freudenberger and Robbins 1979; Garfield and Bergin 1971; Garfield and Kurtz 1976b; Greenberg and Staller 1981; Guy and Liaboe 1986; MacDevitt 1987; Norcross and Prochaska 1986a, 1986b; Norcross, Strausser, and Faultus 1988; Norcross, Strausser-Kirtland, and Missar 1988; Prochaska and Norcross 1983b; Strupp 1955; and Wampler and Strupp 1976.

survey suggested that women therapists seeking personal treatment exhibited more of a preference for women therapists as their own clinical experience increased; male therapists chose to see male therapists more than 80 percent of the time. Consistent with the results of an earlier study by Grunebaum (1983), the characteristics psychotherapists value most in finding a therapist for themselves include competence, experience, warmth and caring, openness, flexibility, and a special personal relationship. The alleviation of symptoms or problems is often rated as a less significant priority by therapists in treatment than is their feeling understood, cared about, and encouraged to explore and expand their own self-understanding (Buckley, Karasu, and Charles 1981; MacDevitt 1987; Wogan and Norcross 1985).

Debates continue, of course, about the magnitude of the effects of personal therapy on therapists' professional functioning. The existing research remains scant and sometimes difficult to interpret, but there is a perceptible trend toward acknowledging replicable positive treatment effects for therapists (primarily in the realms of self-awareness, self-esteem, appreciation for the powerful role of the therapeutic relationship, and increases in the reported use of nurturance, self-disclosure, and experiential techniques in their work with their own clients). There is also a discernible trend toward a stronger endorsement of the values of personal therapy. In a survey reported by MacDevitt (1987), for example, 100 percent of those therapists who had experienced at least one session of personal treatment reported it to be of some personal value, and 82 percent rated it between "very valuable" and "absolutely essential." Likewise, over 90 percent of the psychologists, psychiatrists, and clinical social workers surveyed by Norcross, Strausser-Kirtland, and Missar (1988) reported improvements in their cognitive, behavioral, and emotional functioning as a result of personal therapy.

But there is another side to this issue. The practicing psychotherapist bears a responsibility to seek help for his or her personal "impairment" or dysfunction so as to be sure of providing clients the highest possible quality of professional services. But what about the person of the psychotherapist? What about his or her pain and well-being as a legitimate (and commendable) motive for help seeking? Even though eight out of ten practitioners do enter personal therapy, do they do so often enough and with results that are reflected in their health, life satisfaction, and well-being? Apparently not. The statistics for psychotherapists having *ever* been in personal therapy may be misleading. To begin with, the majority of personal treatment experiences occur as part of a therapist's professional training. The possible need for or benefits of personal therapy do not, however, end with the granting of a degree or license. Regrettably, those individuals who did not experience personal therapy during training are also much less likely to seek personal treatment at later points in their careers (Guy, Stark, and Poelstra 1988). Even more distressing are findings that suggest that many psychotherapists are least likely to seek personal therapy when they are most distressed (Deutsch 1985; Guy, Stark, and Poelstra 1988; Norcross and Prochaska 1986a, 1986b). Less than half of those therapists reporting significant depression have sought personal treatment, for example. Likewise, current estimates suggest that personal therapy is sought by only one out of every four therapists with an acknowledged substance abuse problem and only one out of every three therapists who have attempted suicide. If personal therapy for the psychotherapist is rated so valuable, why is it so "underutilized," particularly when it might be most needed?

The reasons for this pattern are probably multiple. Elaborating on a list suggested by Guy (1987), I have come up with these likely candidates: (1) feelings of embarrassment or humiliation about being identified as a psychotherapy patient or client; (2) reluctance to assume what some consider a dependent role; (3) boundary issues and dual-role complexities created by wanting a trusted friend or colleague to be one's therapist; (4) concerns about confidentiality; (5) mistaken beliefs that a prior episode of personal therapy (most often completed during early training) should have been "enough" and that seeking additional treatment would reflect badly on either oneself or the previous therapist; (6) doubts about either the effectiveness of therapy (in general) or one's personal capacity to derive benefits from it; (7) negative experiences in previous personal therapy; (8) difficulties in finding a trustworthy and accessible professional who can deal with the complexities of being a "therapist's therapist"; (9) reluctance to undertake the emotional and financial commitments involved; and (10) the tendency of many psychotherapists to treat their own psychological and health needs as secondary to those of their clients and families. What is particularly ironic (and, indeed, distressing) about the phenomenon of underutilization of psychotherapy by psychotherapists is its implicitly negative commentary on the stigma or risks associated with seeking mental health services. Why should the layperson respect or seek such services if its own practitioners are reluctant to do so? The public image of psychotherapy (and of the psychotherapist) will be slow to change until the sources of underutilization are addressed. A high priority for future research should be the clarification and amelioration of factors that contribute to practitioners' reluctance to seek personal therapy (appendix H).

As I now move toward the more general issue of self-care among mental health professionals, several points bear reiteration. Personal therapy for psychotherapists can be recommended as an activity that may help protect the quality of professional services to clients. But that is not its only function or possible benefit. From a developmental perspective, personal therapy can also be an important expression of self-caring—a willingness to prioritize one's self and its embodiment as a worthy life-span project and to act on a commitment to seeking and protecting one's own safety, health, and well-being. As many professionals (including myself) have testified, it can also be a preciously humanizing and self-nurturing experience (Bugental 1978, 1987; Guy 1987; Mahoney and Eiseman 1989). Being the seeker of help may not always be easy for the helping professional, but it is often a powerful reminder of the fact that helping and seeking help are universal human expressions. Each seeker and helper form a bond and forge a dialogue that is unique to the individuals involved. Although the contingencies of existence are not overcome, the mysteries of life not solved, and the intermittent pains of being conscious not eliminated, there is, at its best, something that borders on the sacred in the sharing and caring exchanged in the process of wise life counsel. Moreover, there are infinities of potential lessons in self-awareness and self-definition (for example, regarding what is and is not shared, how much caring is risked, and the experience of eventual separation and divergent life paths). The point is that personal therapy is hardly a "cure" for the range and complexity of problems encountered in lifespan development (many of which are intensified by being a psychotherapist). It can be, however, a valuable crucible for forging ever deeper commitments to the life of the self involved and the value of serving other lives in process.

Enactive Self-Care

There are, of course, many ways of being self-caring; personal therapy is not the only option (although practitioners are wise to examine differences in what they prescribe for themselves and their clients [Norcross and Prochaska 1986a, 1986b]). Given some of the special stresses of psychotherapy, it is particularly important that the practitioner develop and maintain patterns of self-care appropriate to the demands of his or her work. To reduce some of the distress associated with the isolation and emotional demands of psychotherapy, for example, increased interaction with colleagues and collaborative "peer supervision" are recommended. Practitioners are also wise to monitor their "felt" caseload and to make appropriate adjustments (as in quantity or severity). The diversification of one's clinical duties can also be helpful when one has the option of combining direct client services with supervision, teaching, consultation, administration, research, and writing.

The degrees of freedom available to different practitioners vary considerably, of course, and many potentially stressful factors may not be readily controlled. This being the case, it is important that the psychotherapist remain vigilantly sensitive to his or her own physical, emotional, and psychospiritual needs. In my own work with practitioners, both individually and in workshops, I emphasize that these three realms are interdependent.

Physical Needs. With a few important exceptions, the physical needs of the psychotherapist are not much different from those of other human beings. The exceptions have to do with the levels of stress to which the therapist may be subjected and the relative physical inactivity required by most forms of modern psychotherapy. Given these factors, the practitioner is wise to maintain patterns of physical activity, rest, and recreation that are conducive to maximizing his or her health and resistance to stress-related illnesses. (This recommendation assumes that health is personally valued, of course; for a discussion of the ethical issues involved in presuming or prescribing health as a value, see Ugland 1989.) Ideal patterns of healthy behavior are outlined in the generalizations of modern health psychology (American Academy of Physical Education 1984; Matarazzo et al. 1984; Taylor 1990), but the need to individualize such patterns is everpresent. Sleep needs vary considerably, for example, and yet insufficient (or unsatisfying) rest is a common factor in burnout. Regular physical activity (preferably both aerobic and anaerobic) is probably more important than many psychotherapists have realized: the evidence is now clear that reactions to a variety of stressors may be influenced by cardiovascular fitness, and that exercise, self-esteem, and mood are integrally related (for example, Crews and Landers 1987; Morgan 1985*b*, 1985*c;* Sonstroem and Morgan 1989).

Activities that accentuate and affirm one's embodiment are also to be recommended (stretching, dance, massage, and movement meditations). In between client sessions, for example, I suggest that practitioners devote a few valuable minutes to gentle range-of-movement stretching (with particular emphasis on the lower back [see B. Anderson 1980]), self-massage (especially of the facial muscles, neck, and shoulders), and walking (stationary, if necessary; the point is to gently stimulate circulation via large muscle activity). Stress-reducing exercises can also be valuable between sessions and after completing a day's schedule of clinical responsibilities. With the intention of minimizing the spillover of stress from session to session and from work to home, I recommend that practitioners engage in brief "entry" and "exit" meditations aimed at focusing one's attentions on individual clients and then "letting go" of one's professional "load" when making the transition to family life or nonprofessional activities. Even though some relaxation exercises require considerable time (at least in the early stages of skill development), the psychotherapist should recognize that significant benefits can be derived from just a few minutes of concentrated attention. This same statement applies to some of the therapeutic exercises discussed in chapter 11. The psychological distress associated with a difficult session and/or a difficult day can be substantially reduced by a few moments of self-nurturing mirror time, for example, or a personal journal entry that expresses self-compassion or humor.

Also important to recognize are the potential benefits of recreational endeavors—hobbies, music, art, and play, particularly when pursued for their inherent enjoyment (rather than competitively or for social approval). Besides their being fun, such activities also help to teach the ability to "flow" with a task and to allow oneself to become optimally absorbed in its process (Csikszentmihalyi 1975; Csikszentmihalyi and Csikszentmihalyi 1988; Jerome 1980). Play and play therapy are not just for children; they are important elements of healthy adult development and relationship enhancement (for an array of practical options, see Center for Applied Psychology 1990). Related to this, I recommend that practitioners place a high priority on purely recreational vacations (preferably several brief ones per year plus one or more lengthy retreats from all professional responsibilities).

Emotional Needs.   Taking care of one's emotional needs must also be individualized. It is also here where personal therapy may constitute a worthwhile consideration. The demands of psychotherapy are diverse, and clients' intense emotional experiences are common sources of stress for the practitioner (table 13.1). Moreover, the structure of the therapeutic relationship and the dynamics of psychological development are such that the therapist must often modulate his or her emotional expressions in deference to the immediate needs and best interests of the client. In some practitioners, a double-edged skill develops—namely, the ability to "withdraw," "distance," or "control" emotional reactions. This skill is potentially valuable when used appropriately to "dance" with the dynamics of a client's development (for example, to conserve the therapist's energies for continuing work, to protect professional role boundaries, or to avoid "startle reactions" and impulsive judgments that might hinder a client's emotional processing).

The same skill can be used inappropriately, however, to create or maintain a "detachment" from the client's emotional experiences. Such detachment is, in fact, a likely factor in therapeutic failures where "the common denominator is . . . the hesitation of the therapist to invest as fully, to be as truly present, as the client needs" (Bugental 1988, p. 534). There is also some evidence to suggest that this double-edged skill may be a contributing factor to the personal relationship difficulties often reported by psychotherapists. In Barry Farber's (1989) study of "psychological-mindedness," for example, individuals who scored high on this dimension did not exhibit deficits in emotional responsiveness but did show clear signs of being less overtly expressive of their feelings. This inhibited style of expression was interpreted as possibly contributing to perceptions of such individuals as "withholding" their feelings. Likewise, in his excellent discussion in *The Personal Life of the Psychotherapist,* James Guy (1987) appends a noteworthy subtitle: "The Impact of Clinical Practice on the Therapist's Intimate Relationships and Emotional Well-Being."

Statistically, however, psychotherapists do not report significantly higher frequencies of relationship difficulties than the general population, and many practitioners and their spouses have noted that—after some frequently destabilizing episodes in the early stages of training and practice—positive benefits to the relationship could be credited to one (or both) partner(s) being a psychotherapist. The sources of relationship conflict among psychotherapists and their spouses (who are often, and increasingly, also psychotherapists) seem to center around emotional depletion, resentment over clients' needs taking priority over family plans, and the complexities of work schedules (such as "jokes about the need to make an appointment in order to get the attention of the therapist mate" [Guy 1987, p. 113]).

Beyond recreational activities and personal therapy, the emotional needs of the psychotherapist are most likely to be met (to whatever degree) by that individual's intimate others: lover/spouse, family, and close friends. The evidence is clear that those practitioners who are supported by and supportive of their intimate relationships also tend to be more satisfied with their work and report less emotional distress (for example, Izraeli 1988; Thoreson, Miller, and Krauskopf 1989). Recall from chapter 9 that it is also in the context of intimate relationships that self-relationships are most powerfully formed and changed. This point again emphasizes the importance and complex interconnectivity of human attachments in lifespan development and its counsel. Clients are often "working" on past and present aspects of their own emotional attachments in the context of the therapeutic relationship (itself a specially structured attachment). Psychotherapists, meanwhile, are operating out of their own self systems and the secure bases in and from which those systems are nurtured. Furthermore, the significant others who participate in the therapist's personal life are themselves being influenced by other attachments, past and present, as well as by their spouse's work as a therapist (Farber 1989). It is within this complex web of emotional ties that the practitioner is most likely to seek the satisfaction of his or her own emotional needs. When those needs are satisfactorily met, the work of rendering quality professional services can be much easier; when they are not, both the therapist and his or her clients may suffer.

Psychospiritual Needs.   The third and final category of interdependent needs spans a range from conceptual material and technical information to more abstract desires to understand the "meaning of life," "the worth of the work," and the limits and possibilities of human experience. A psychotherapist's needs to learn about theoretical and technical developments are often served by books, journals, workshops, professional conferences, and conversations with colleagues. In the experience of many "therapist's therapists" (including myself), however, it is the needs at the more abstract and spiritual end of this spectrum that are less adequately addressed by traditional professional resources. Regrettably, it is also at this end of the spectrum where mainstream scientific psychology has been most delinquent in its efforts and offerings. The word *spiritual* has long been regarded as anathema to science, perhaps because of its historical associations with *religion* and the continuing battles over the boundaries between the "natural" and the "supernatural." Although it was briefly addressed in earlier discussions of the ongoing conflict between advocates of "natural (science) humanism" and "spiritual humanism," this point bears brief elaboration here.

First, the meanings and perceived importance of religion and spirituality to psychotherapy have begun to change over the last few decades. In a national survey of mental health professionals, for example, Bergin and Jensen (1990) reported that 77 percent of the respondents said that they tried to live their lives in accordance with their religious beliefs. Even though only 44 percent acknowledged active participation in an organized religion, 68 percent reported that they were seeking "a spiritual understanding of the universe and one's place in it" (1990, p. 6). Likewise, in another recent survey, Shafranske and Malony (1990) reported that 65 percent of U.S. clinical psychologists acknowledged that spirituality was personally relevant to them, and 54 percent reported that it had emerged out of their sense of personal identity. Although the participants generally agreed that it was inappropriate for a psychotherapist to read scriptures or pray with a client, 91 percent reported inquiring about the religious backgrounds of their clients, and only 15 percent believed that religious or spiritual issues were beyond the scope of psychology. Although psychologists viewed religious and spiritual issues as relevant to clinical practice, most had received limited exposure to this topic in their professional training.

Second, among the many personal and public meanings of *spirituality* are those that focus on its Latin origin (*spiritus*, "breath"), which share the common themes of (1) life (or the principle of life), (2) lively (vigorous, energetic), and (3) an identifying character, mood, or quality (as in "the spirit of science").

The third and final caveat here is that confrontations with the relentless contingencies of existence often force a dialogue with (or denial of) issues of spirituality and faith. Indeed, the most viable modern theory of knowing—William Bartley's "comprehensively critical rationalism" (1984, [1962] chapter 2)—acknowledges that all claims to knowledge must ultimately make a "leap of faith" and "retreat to a commitment" that cannot itself be rationally defended (Mahoney 1976; Weimer 1979). The issue, then, is clearly not a simple contest between pure or scientific reason and blind or unquestioning faith. But these are technicalities, of course, and they may be less interesting than are the more practical issues surrounding psychotherapists' needs to at least make peace with spirituality (whether their own or their clients').

Rare is the psychotherapist who has not spent hours with human beings who were struggling with the anguish of tragedy, trauma, or death. John W. lost his two children in an auto accident caused by a drunk driver; his dreams and his waking moments are filled with their plaintive cries of "Daddy, please don't let me die!" Marilyn P., an emotionally reserved psychotherapist, is suffering with her mother's slow and painful death from cancer. Both have been lifelong atheists, but Marilyn now feels angry and cheated. A young couple come in with a severely handicapped newborn; they want to know how to cope with their mixture of feelings. A minister with thirty-five years of experience in the pulpit complains that he has lost his feeling of faith; he says he has also lost his identity, and wants to commit suicide. The phone rings on a lazy Sunday afternoon; a former client is in the intensive care unit of a local hospital and has asked that the therapist be with her while she dies. And on and on. Coping skills may be valuable in dealing with such difficult challenges, but personal hardiness and health are also significantly influenced by more abstract issues of life meaning and purpose (Antonovsky 1987; Campbell et al. 1989; Nagy and Nix 1989; Nowack 1989; Wong 1989).

Whether they are called spiritual or not, I believe that psychotherapists are wise to acknowledge and affirm their own needs for abstract scaffoldings for the many mysteries and miseries of life they have and will encounter. One cannot counsel others through tragedies and "dark nights of the soul" without repeatedly confronting issues of life and death, meaning, purpose, personal identity and (in)significance, and the fundamental "aloneness" (a contraction of "all one"-ness) with which these issues must be ultimately met. There are, to my knowledge, no books that can lay such issues to rest, once and for all, for either therapist or client, but many offer some valuable companionship in their exploration.*

To conclude this lengthy discussion of the importance of taking care of the caring self, I offer two sets of questions and practical reflections I have found useful in my work with psychotherapists. The first is a list of questions relating to self-care (table 13.3), which I recommend be read slowly, periodically reviewed, and shared with colleagues. The second is more of a reflective "desiderata" for practitioners (table 13.4).

THE CHALLENGING PRIVILEGE OF HELPING

Protecting and promoting one's own health, happiness, and overall well-being is, however, only one part of the picture, in that the practice of psychotherapy is also a frequent source of developmental challenges and

*Becker 1973; Bettleheim 1960; Bugental 1981, 1987; Dass and Gorman 1985; Durant and Durant 1970, 1935–75; Fox 1979; Friedman 1967; Kazantzakis 1960 [1927]; Klemke 1981; Tillich 1952; and Watson 1979.

Table 13.3   Self-Care: Some Reflective Questions

1. How happy are you most of the time?
2. How do you feel about yourself?
3. Who and what do you love?
4. How healthy do you feel right now?
5. Do you seek and accept help or comfort from others?
6. How do you feel about your work?
7. Is your rest usually adequate and satisfying?
8. Do you often feel loved and appreciated?
9. What are your fears?
10. What gives meaning or purpose to your life?
11. Do you forgive yourself?
12. What are your hopes?
13. Do you often feel lonely?
14. What do you treasure as joys and enjoyments?
15. What *don't* you talk about with anyone?
16. What do you feel when you look at yourself in a mirror?
17. What could you *do* to be more self-caring?
18. With whom can you talk about your inner life?
19. Do you laugh and cry?
20. How honest are you with yourself?
21. What forms of music and movement do you enjoy?
22. What are your spiritual needs and comforts?
23. If you could change three things in your life, what would they be?

©1989 Michael J. Mahoney

both rewarding and inspiring experiences. The fact of the matter is that most psychotherapists are not burned out and, in fact, are very happy in both their work and their interpersonal relations (Guy 1987; Thoreson, Miller, and Krauskopf 1989). They derive their greatest satisfaction not from income or status but from helping people change, from developing deeper understandings about human nature, and from experiencing both intimacy and involvement in the process.

Accelerated Psychological Development

Above and beyond their relative health and life satisfaction, the psychological development of mental health practitioners is often substantially accelerated (which can, of course, be a source of stress). Technically stated, "the practice of psychotherapy has been found to promote signif-

Table 13.4   Reflections on Therapeutic Practice

1. Prepare for each session in private reflection. No matter how briefly, always take time to center your attention on the individual(s) you are about to serve.

2. Cultivate your commitment to helping; respect and honor the privilege of your profession.

3. Appreciate the complexity and uniqueness of each life you counsel.

4. Accept the fact that your understanding is limited; give yourself permission not to know.

5. When you get lost in a session and don't know what to say or do, take a moment to recenter in your intentions to help.

6. Trust in your clients' capacities to endure and harvest their individual struggles.

7. As much as possible, be emotionally present to their suffering; feel *with* them.

8. Recognize that you cannot take away anyone's pain (although you may often wish that you could).

9. If you are frightened by intense feelings (theirs or yours), remember to breathe and, if appropriate, express what you are feeling.

10. Offer comfort and encouragement as you can.

11. Foster faith in the possibilities and process of personal development.

12. In the dynamic dance of a client in process, learn both to lead and to follow.

13. Whenever possible, let the client do most of the work.

14. Honor a client's pacing and encourage his or her empowerment, especially in the process of your parting.

15. Cultivate your faith in yourself as a person and in the value of your services as a professional.

16. Be gentle with yourself; be patient with your own process.

17. Pace yourself: honor your limits and back off when you need to.

18. Establish personally meaningful routines of self-care.

19. Protect your private life.

20. Cherish your friendships and intimate relations.

21. Rest, play (repeat often).

22. Be willing to ask for and accept comfort, help, and counsel.

23. Keep the Faith (however you experience it) and share it when you can.

icant personal growth in the practicing psychotherapist" (Guy 1987, p. 243). Clients and clinical activities cause changes in the practitioner that range from theoretical to phenomenological. Relative to their less experienced peers, for example, more experienced therapists tend to be more active in sessions, less distressed by clients' emotional experiences, and more skilled at relying on abstract knowledge to guide their interactions with clients (Beutler, Crago, and Arizmendi 1986; Martin et al. 1989). Although less experienced (and younger) practitioners are often perceived to be less mature, they also devote more attention to the details of their clients' lives and offer more individual counsel than their senior and veteran peers.

At the conceptual level, there is also evidence that practicing psychotherapy and experiencing it as a client are both associated with changes in attitudes about human change. When experienced psychotherapists were asked to report their present and past beliefs about human development and optimal psychotherapy, for example, there was substantial evidence of change (Mahoney and Craine 1988). Looking at the absolute magnitude of change in their beliefs (regardless of the direction of the change), the two best predictors were measures of time and experience in the roles of both therapist and client (figure 13.1). Across orientations and levels of experience, there were also some fascinating patterns in their changing beliefs about the relative importance of different factors in successful psychotherapy. As shown in figure 13.2, the greatest changes involved increased appreciations for the therapeutic relationship, the therapist's personality, and the client's social support system,

Figure 13.1   Total Belief Changes Over the Course of a Professional Career as Related to Levels and Types of Experiences

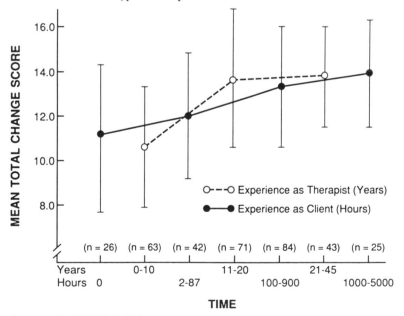

Source: © 1989 M. J. Mahoney

Figure 13.2   Relative Changes in Psychotherapists' Rated Importance of Factors
in Successful Psychotherapy Over the Course of Their Professional Careers

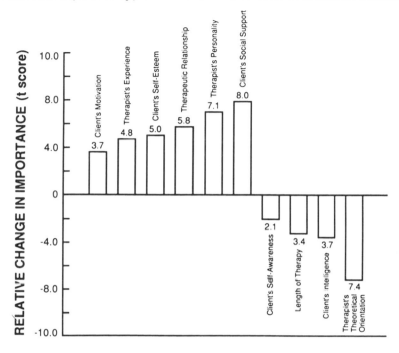

FACTORS IN SUCCESSFUL PSYCHOTHERAPY

Source: © 1989 M. J. Mahoney

with the most striking change in the other direction being a substantial
decline in the perceived importance of the therapist's theoretical orientation.

At the more personal level, reported changes in psychotherapists have
included increases in self-awareness, assertiveness, self-esteem, sensitivity, reflectiveness, emotional resilience, openness, and spirituality. Bugental again offers a crystalline "insider's view":

I am not the person who began to practice counseling or psychotherapy more
than 30 years ago. . . . And the changes in me are not solely those worked by time,
education, and the life circumstances shared by most of my generation. A powerful force affecting me has been my participation in so many lives.
    . . . My life as a psychotherapist has been . . . the source of anguish, pain, and
anxiety—sometimes in the work itself, but more frequently within myself and with
those important in my life. . . . Similarly that work and those relationships have
directly and indirectly brought to me and those in my life joy, excitement, and
a sense of participation in truly vital experiences. (1978, pp. 149–50)

It is in that participation that the seeds of systemic perturbation and development are most furtively sown.

The Privilege of Participation

That participation is also a privilege known intimately by psychotherapists. Being a psychotherapist means, in part, "having a window on the human soul" and having "privileged seats at the enthralling pageant of human life" (Bugental 1978, pp. 149–50). It is hardly a spectator activity, however; and it is in the process of human engagement that its challenges and privileges are most apparent. Besides witnessing the courage and resourcefulness of their clients, psychotherapists serve as temporary but invaluable sources of security, comfort, and encouragement. Consider the following remarks of a young therapist in training:

I love the electricity of a person in process—the alternating currents of fear and confidence, joy and pain, action and rest. I feel inspired by their risking engagement with the unknowns of their own unfolding life, and I derive some of my deepest satisfactions from feeling like I have been instrumental in that process. It feels like I am genuinely serving somebody: not only each of them as individuals, but also something greater . . . something precious . . . maybe the human spirit.

Comparable testimonials to the privilege of the profession are also ubiquitous in the writings of senior practitioners (see the special issue of *Pilgrimage* 14 [5 (1988)], and especially Lamper 1988).

Contrary to Alexander Pope's famous assurance, hope does *not* spring "eternal in the human breast." Rather, it must be vigilantly nurtured through an active—enactive—faith in the possibilities and preciousness of human life in process. If nothing else, our vast literatures and laboratories have taught us that the meaning of life does not lie comfortably nestled within any single theory, model, or scripture. The lesson, it seems, is that such meaning must be endlessly and individually re-created in our lived-life struggles and triumphs.

Like those they intend to serve, scientists and practitioners alike are wise to recognize both the limits and the potential of their understanding. Those of us who seek to understand, comfort, and counsel human lives in progress must therefore be vigilant in the responsible nurturance of our own hopes as well as in learning the lessons of our fears and failures. Our counsel must also be more than rational or strategic rhetoric; rather, our "reason must be guided by an informed heart" (Bettleheim 1960, p. viii). To most valuably serve those who seek our counsel, we must also invite and affirm their "courage to be" (Tillich 1952). Without such courage there will be diminished engagement and exploration, which constitute the experiential pulse of a human life. The courage to be is not synonymous with the courage to change, however; sometimes it is even more frightening and difficult to accept what is unchanging or unchangeable. Indeed, we are wise to recognize that the processes of human psychological development may be best served (or least violated) when the quest for change is appreciated in a context broad enough to include and respect change-resisting continuities. Change is not always in the best interests of the individual, and continuity constitutes the fabric of coherence in all lives.

Thus, there are both responsibilities and privileges involved in serving as a psychotherapist: there are burdens, to be sure, but also unmistakable blessings. The latter, though more difficult to put into words, are no less precious for that fact.

Epilogue

As I move toward closure of this book, it should be apparent that its narrative journey has been more than a simple accounting of the scientific foundations of psychotherapy. One of its central messages has, in fact, been the inescapability of complexity and interpretation in human knowing, and hence the pervasiveness of personal meanings in all attempts to share or apply such knowledge. This message is experientially emphasized by the fact that no two readings of this book will ever be quite the same (whether performed by the same reader or not). You, the reader, are always "in the text," and your reading is not a mechanical processing of information but an organic participatory relationship that changes with the dynamics of your own unfolding experience (including the acts of reading and rereading). Moreover, your understanding of what you have read must necessarily be limited by the contexts or "horizons" of your own experience. This is also true, by the way, of my understanding of what I have written. Such are the "postmodern" lessons of the history of ideas, evolutionary epistemology, and hermeneutics.

Appropriately, I found inspiration for the closing words to this ten-year project in a discussion of the "philosophic centrality" of human imagination, the power of metaphor, and the role of interpretation in opening up new worlds and new perspectives. On the final page of his tribute to the tradition of Hermes, G. B. Madison (1988) cited Paul Ricoeur's (1981) reference to the "half-open door" between metaphor and imagination. In rereading it, I realized that it is in the traffic through that door that we most deeply sense the realm of possibility: possible selves and possible worlds. It is in our endless search for new meanings amid old truths that we approach the ageless mystery and dynamic union of individual being and lifelong becoming. Here walks the changer and the changed, a moving continuity of process. Like Madison, I therefore yield the last words of this work to the poet, the undisputed master of possibility and process: "Poetry is the breath and finer spirit of all knowledge; it is the impassioned expression which is in the countenance of science" (Wordsworth, *Lyrical Ballads*, preface to 2d ed.).

Appendix

A. ATTENTION AND PERCEPTION

There is little debate among cognitive scientists that humans both do perceive and are selective in what they attend to among the changing arrays of possible perceptions. What is controversial is the adequate modeling and explanation of such phenomena. Researchers following the objectivist and realist traditions tend to emphasize the invariant structures of the world and their reflection in our perceptual processes. Workers more aligned with the idealist and constructivist traditions, however, tend to emphasize the extent to which our attention and perceptions are influenced by organismic variables. Indeed, I do not think it would be far from the mark to say that the major debate in contemporary theories of perception is yet another expression of the longstanding conflict between realists and idealists. The relevance of that debate for clinical issues and psychotherapy is also readily documented (for example, Bentall 1990; Ben-Zeev 1988; Watts 1989).

Let me begin by calling attention to the phenomenon of attention—a phenomenon that has long been acknowledged and yet that remains only crudely understood.*

*Recommended general resources on this topic include Anderson 1985; Hillyard 1985; Hirst 1986; Hochberg 1979; LeDoux and Hirst 1986; Norman 1969; Parasuraman and Davies 1984; Posner 1982; Posner and Marin 1985; and Posner and Snyder 1975. For specific theories and models that have been influential in this area, see Broadbent 1954, 1958; Cherry 1953; Deutsch and Deutsch 1963; Kahneman 1973; Kahneman and Treisman

Attention and the Dynamics of Figure-Ground

Although it was dealt with at length by William James in his 1890 *Principles of Psychology,* the concept and study of attention soon receded against the background of Titchener's sensationalist research program and was virtually ignored by behaviorism. As a research topic, attention remained generally unattended until the cognitive revolution at midcentury, with the pioneering work of people like E. Colin Cherry, Donald Broadbent, and Ann Treisman. These early theories of attention appealed to metaphors of "filtering" and "funneling" to explain how it is that humans "select" and attend to certain aspects of the available stimulus array while disregarding the remainder. The models these researchers proposed have not, for the most part, illuminated the phenomenon under study, other than to emphasize and creatively illustrate how selective and dynamic attention may be.

The study of attention has, however, undergone some recent changes that may offer new metaphors and models. Ironically, some early studies of the electrophysiology of attention were going on concurrently with those being conducted by cognitive psychologists with virtually no net impact on one another. The investigations of the Russian physiologist E. M. Sokolov (1963) are a case in point. His studies of the "orienting reflex" would later become appreciated for having helped to pioneer more recent studies on the role of physiological habituation in attention and perception. Traditionally, habituation has been regarded as the gradual loss of "interest in" or responsivity to an unchanging stimulus. It was thought to be the result of physiological *fatigue:* that is, the depletion of local neurochemicals relevant to an organism's perception of a stimulus. But the fatigue explanation of habituation was soon recognized to be false: if there is any slight change in the stimulus or its background, for example, the organism quickly re-orients toward it (thereby showing that its preceding lack of interest in the stimulus was not due to physiological fatigue).

The many studies devoted to attentional processes have been generally interested in clarifying the mechanisms by which attention is said to shift, as well as in the phenomenon of *selective attention*—the processes that permit a perceptual "figure" to be carved out of its background. Until recently, information-processing models assumed that selective attention served (1) to focus an organism's perceptual processing on the stimuli most relevant to its current adaptational demands, and (2) to efficiently minimize its engagement with irrelevant stimuli by suppressing or ignoring their presence. This assumption was effectively demolished by Mi-

---

1984; Marcel 1983*a*, 1983*b;* Pomerantz and Pristach 1989; Treisman 1969; Treisman and Gelade 1980; Treisman and Paterson 1984; and Wickens 1980, 1984.

chael P. Wapner, whom Bernard Baars (1986) has termed an influential "scientific isolate" in the cognitive revolution. Wapner noted that all the funnel and filter theories of attention are based on a contradiction: namely, the assertion that an organism can be insensitive to something it is (perceptually) rejecting or excluding:

The idea of a system "rejecting while being insensitive" is a contradiction. And, in fact, it's the central contradiction in the concept of "attention as a filtering mechanism." . . . Filtering is based on the idea that the system must save information-processing capacity for other things, so somehow the system doesn't deal with everything, although it still has to process the stuff before it knows what to reject. That's a paradox, and a contradiction. I think it's the result of a central misunderstanding of how the thing works. (In Baars 1986, p. 319)

Wapner goes on to discuss neural habituation and suggests that it cannot be explained as inhibition. To inhibit requires work, so that if attention were to "filter out" by means of inhibition, it would not be saving resources.

What Wapner offers as an alternative is a perspective that "allows the organism not only to 'attend' to something, but simultaneously to monitor what it's not attending to" (Baars 1986, p. 320). In other words, he argues that attention and perception are "relational," with "figure" and "ground" changing over time. Contrary to the views proposed by James J. Gibson (see pages 381–85), Wapner contends that there is inherent ambiguity in virtually all experience (including perception), and that the organism "abstracts" objects from of a background that it creates. If something unexpected changes in that background, habituation will cease and the organism will re-orient, now attending to the former background as "figure" and relegating the former figure to momentary background. These assertions are generally congruent with ones I discuss in chapter 5, particularly in terms of the need for a dynamic, dialectical view of subject-object relations and the fundamentally hermeneutic nature of all perception.

Wapner's perspective might be called "transactional" given its emphasis on the dynamics of attention and perception. He also emphasizes the role of tacit expectations in all experience (especially perception) and notes that emotionality and motivation are inherently involved in such experience. Thus, he says, "*emotion is fundamentally the experience of violation of context and the reorganization to a new context. That is, an emotional experience is fundamentally a transition*" (Baars 1986, p. 334). Perception is therefore an emotional event, particularly when novel experiences are encountered. This acknowledgment of the importance of emotion and motivation in cognition has been regrettably rare in the field. With some important recent exceptions, cognitive scientists have generally ignored this domain (Bower 1981; Bower and Cohen 1982; Davis and

Schwartz 1987; Gilligan and Bower 1983, 1984; Hamilton, Bower, and Frijda 1988; Izard, Kagan, and Zajonc 1984; Johnson and Magaro 1987; Singer and Salovey 1988). Also of interest is Fair's (1988) contention that the reticular, limbic, and "mesolimbic" systems in the brain—the latter two pervasively emotional (see chapter 8)—may coordinate so as to "steer" attentional processes. (For a sampling of works specifically devoted to the study of cognitive-emotional relations, see de Sousa 1987; Greenberg and Safran 1987; Mandler 1975, 1984; Piaget 1981; and Simon 1986.) Hans Furth's (1987) essay on Freud and Piaget, aptly titled *Knowledge As Desire,* is a stimulating treatise on the inseparability of cognition and affect. Whatever else it may or may not be, all knowing (learning, memory, and so on) is fundamentally evaluative and therefore emotional.

For illustrations of the everyday complexity of attentional processes and some exceptional abilities in this domain, I recommend perusal of the literatures in exercise and sport psychology. In the phenomenon of *flow,* for example, experienced athletes frequently report a fascinating state of body/brain integration in which highly skilled actions are almost automatically performed while the individual "witnesses" them (Csikszentmihalyi 1975; Csikszentmihalyi and Csikszentmihalyi 1988; Jerome 1980; Mahoney 1989*b*). Reports of the phenomenon suggest parallels with Hilgard's (1977) studies of the "hidden observer" in hypnosis. In studies of world-class long-distance runners, for example, William P. Morgan and his colleagues (Morgan 1985*a*, 1985*b*, 1985*c;* Morgan and Pollock 1977) have noted that different attentional strategies are often used to deal with the "wall" of pain frequently encountered in the final stages of a race. Many marathon runners utilize a "dissociative" attentional strategy in which they try to ignore their pain via distractive mental activities (such as arithmetic problems, detailed reminiscences of their childhood, recall of favorite music, and so on). The most skilled runners, however—the "élite" marathoners—have all abandoned such strategies in their running and developed ways of "tuning in" to their bodily feedback without experiencing it as painful. Among other things, this finding suggests that Wapner's ideas may be on target, and that personal meanings enter into real-world attentional and perceptual processes. (For research relating personal meaning to pain perception and attentional processes, see Thompson 1981 and Turk, Meichenbaum, and Genest 1983.)

James J. Gibson and "Direct" Perception

Although the realist-idealist debate does appear in some work on attention, it is much more apparent in the study of perception, where both perspectives remain fashionably modern. The most influential realist in recent cognitive science has been James J. Gibson, a conceptual renegade who rejected the bulk of what was mainstream in the information-processing research of his time. A specialist in perception and vision, Gibson rejected the very concepts of "information processing" and "mental representation" and challenged the artificiality of studies involving the tachistoscope and contrived ambiguity. In his major publications (1950, 1966, 1979), Gibson argued that "perception is direct, requiring no inferential steps and no processing of information" (Neisser 1981, p. 214), a radically different assertion, of course, than those being made by cognitive scientists during those decades. Gibson's major works were *The Perception of the Visual World* (1950), *The Senses Considered as Perceptual Systems* (1966), and *The Ecological Approach to Visual Perception* (1979). Besides the autobiographies of Gibson and his colleague-wife Eleanor J. Gibson, (1987), see also Lombardo's (1987) description of the development of the Gibsonian approach.

Early in life Gibson was impressed with the human capacity to perceive stabilities in a world that was often moving. As an eight-year-old accompanying his father to work, for example, he already "knew what the world looked like from a railroad train and how it seemed to flow inward when seen from the rear platform and expand outward when seen from the locomotive" (cited in Neisser, 1981, p. 214). It was much later, of course, before Gibson developed the central idea in his lifelong work—namely, the idea that perception requires invariance. That is, to "see" an object and experience it as stable and unchanging despite its or one's own movement (such movement altering the array of light arriving at the retina), it is necessary to assume the existence of *invariances*, or stable characteristics. His critics and later cognitive scientists admitted that such invariances are important, and argued that they were actively created by the perceiver as a means of ordering perceptual experience. Gibson disagreed. He chose to focus not on the perceiver or the nervous system, but on the environment as their source. Gibson thus argued that there are existentially real "invariances" (stabilities) in the physical world that "afford" (allow) the organism to perceive that world directly and accurately:

When the senses are considered as perceptual systems, all theories of perception become at one stroke unnecessary. It is no longer a question of how the mind operates on the deliverances of sense, or how past experience can organize the data, or even how the brain can process the inputs of the nerves, but simply how information is picked up. This stimulus information is available in the everyday environment. (1966, p. 319)

Gibson believed that the invariant information in the "perceptual array" offered by the environment was so rich and precise, in fact, that ambiguity, illusion, and error were "all but impossible" (Neisser 1981, p. 215).

Gibson's views came to be called "ecological" because of their relative emphasis on the environment and the virtually perfect perceptual "fit" between organism and environment. Despite their unorthodox reincarnation of a perspective closely akin to the philosophical doctrine of *naïve realism* (also called "The Doctrine of Immaculate Perception" [Mahoney 1974]), the approach developed by Gibson became popular and gained the support of several other influential cognitive scientists. In reviewing his last book soon after Gibson's death, for example, Frank Restle termed him a "seer" and "our one original, irreplaceable creative genius" (1980, p. 291). Likewise, Ulric Neisser has acknowledged that working with Gibson during the last years of his life had a profound impact on his own views of cognition. In writing Gibson's obituary, Neisser described him as "a hardheaded scientist who increasingly appeared also as a seer, that is, a man with a special relation to the truth" (1981, p. 214). Also in 1987, Neisser conceded that he had switched from constructivism to Gibsonian realism, an outlook that flavors two volumes he edited (Neisser 1987*b;* and Neisser and Winograd 1988). Neisser's most recent work is certainly "ecological" in the sense of being more aligned with the study of perception and cognition relevant to real-life experiences, and there are signs that he has adopted Gibson's unwavering belief in the "directness" of our perception. There can also be little doubt that Gibson's work—which was influenced during his life by his wife, Eleanor J. Gibson (1987, 1988)— remains a vigorous element in modern studies of perception (Epstein 1987; Mace 1974, 1977; Natsoulas 1989*a;* Pinker 1984; Rock 1974, 1983; Shaw, Turvey, and Mace 1982; Turvey and Shaw 1979).

Another influential realist in the study of perception and cognitive processes has been Roger N. Shepard (1975). Probably best known for his early work on the rotation of mental images, Shepard has lent considerable support to the idea that human mental representations and their structures are directly related to the structures of the real world. He has proposed, for example, that "human and animal reactions are guided by abstract general principles that reflect the invariant properties of the world in which we have evolved," (1987*a,* p. 252) and that the principles of mind are based in the abiding regularities of the external world. Taking these assertions a step further, Shepard has argued that psychological science—in particular, perceptual psychology—may now be ready to declare some "universal laws" similar to those offered by Isaac Newton in the seventeenth century. One candidate, Shepard suggests, is a "universal law of (stimulus) generalization":

A psychological space is established for any set of stimuli by determining metric distances between the stimuli such that the probability that a response learned to any stimulus will generalize to any other is an invariant monotonic function of the distance between them. . . . These empirical regularities are mathematically derivable from universal principles of natural kinds and probabilistic geometry that may, through evolutionary internalization, tend to govern the behaviors of all sentient organisms. (1987b, p. 1317)

In essence, Shepard is arguing that our evolutionary heritage may include the "internalization" of the structural properties of physical reality, rendering us capable of accurately perceiving the environment that has selected us.

Despite the generous enthusiasm for Gibson's work on the part of some cognitive psychologists, critiques have been plentiful; and in 1990, the "Gibsonian movement" appeared to be recruiting fewer adherents than in years past (Boring 1952a, 1952b; Boynton 1974; Hochberg 1979, 1981; Kitcher 1988; Marr 1982; Pribram 1977; Weimer and Palermo 1982). The criticisms leveled at Gibson's theory have included the facts that he minimized the role of learning in perception and was apparently unimpressed with the pervasiveness of ambiguity and illusion in everyday experience. His theory therefore fails to account for illusions, minimizes the importance of ambiguity, and does not deal with the well-documented aspects of perceptual organization emphasized by gestalt studies. Moreover, his emphasis on the environment rather than the organism has led some observers to consider him a behaviorist (which he was not), and his outright rejection of cognitive processes made his theory totally untenable for some cognitive scientists.

For my own part, though I agree with the bulk of those criticisms, I believe that James J. Gibson contributed one of the most important insights in modern studies of perception. That insight was not, however, the assertion of "ecological optics," environmental invariants, or direct perception. It was, instead, the assertion that *the organism is an active, exploratory agent and therefore an important participant in all perception.* Gibson believed that the most important parts of our visual system are our legs, because they permit the exploration of affordances and invariances in what reaches our retinas. He said it in a number of different ways, but they all boiled down to the fact that, in all perception, a centrally important component is the organism's use of its own movement (as of eyes, head, and body) and the "subjective feelings" they produce: "Proprioception or self-sensitivity is seen to be an overall function, common to all systems, not a special sense," and "the activity of orienting and that of exploring and selecting—the commonsense faculty of attending" is an important component in perception (1966, p. 320). (See also Powers 1973, for another expression of this insight in the language of information systems; Merleau-Ponty 1962 offers a rendition from the perspective of phenomenology.) This may be what Shaw and Pittenger meant when they paraphrased Gibson as saying, *"The act of picking up perceptual information is the act of experiencing it"* (1977, p. 111). As Piaget (1926) had already pointed out, we do not sit back and passively register the worlds we encounter. Rather, we actively seek them out, act upon and interact with them and, in so doing, gain multisensory experiences and, in Russell's famous distinction, a "knowledge by acquaintance" rather than simply a knowledge "by description" (1945).

Thus, attention and perception remain a perplexing paradox for scientists who are still operating out of traditional, information-processing models of cognition. Despite Gibson's appeal to the common-sense notion of direct perception and despite the many elegant efforts of computer programmers to simulate attentional processes, progress in our understanding has been minimal. Moreover, the most exciting developments in these areas have suggested alternative assumptions and invited the consideration of processes not usually acknowledged, let alone closely examined, by cognitive scientists. From a clinical standpoint, it should be clear that attentional (and "intentional") processes play a critically significant role in both the maintenance and change of personal meanings. The fact that personal meanings and perception are inseparable can also be readily illustrated. In the daily drama of the divorce court, for example, when a "love relationship" has ended, the individuals involved often report radically altered perceptions of their former partner. Although these shifts in perception usually unfold over long periods of time, they can also be abrupt and unsettling.

B. CONNECTIONISM

Although it is hailed as having emerged in the last decade, connectionism reflects an influential legacy from classical associationism and its varied expressions earlier this century. It is not coincidental, for example, that the learning theorist E. L. Thorndike (1898) also called his approach "connectionism" at the turn of the century. Although the modern revival of connectionism in the cognitive sciences arose out of the associationist tradition, it was also fueled and formed by the frustrations and perseverance of cognitive scientists. Those most intent on modeling the mind by computer were and are a hearty and energetic lot. However, the continuing failure of linear, logical computational programs adequately to simulate human performance proved to be a growth-generating experience for many workers in this area.

The History of Connectionism

Historical accounts of modern connectionism are still rare (Atlan 1986; Stengers 1985). However, from a variety of sources describing different aspects of that history, it is possible to piece together a sketch of some of the pioneers and markers in its emergence (Bechtel 1988; Broadbent 1985; Fahlman and Hinton 1987; Feldman and Ballard 1982; Fodor and Pylyshyn 1988; Hillis 1985; McClelland and Rumelhart 1985; Massaro 1988; Minsky and Papert 1988; Pagels 1988; Pinker and Mehler 1988; Pylyshyn 1980; Schneider 1987; Smolensky 1988). For illustrations of the significant collaboration between "computational neuroscience" and connectionist models, see Churchland 1986; Gluck and Rumelhart 1990; Malsburg and Bienenstock 1986; Segal 1988; and Sejnowski, Koch, and Churchland 1988. I also recommend Winograd's (1980) description of how his conceptualizations of language comprehension changed in the process of his connectionist explorations. Finally, see table 4.1 (pages 74–75) to view the markers in connectionist history in the context of other events in the cognitive sciences.

In 1943, two foundational papers were published. Warren McCulloch and Walter Pitts published their "Logical Calculus of the Ideas Immanent in Nervous Activity." It was the one of the first and most influential discussions of what they termed "neuro-logical networks," drawing together machinery and logic as a possible means of modeling brain functioning. In that same year, Norbert Wiener and his colleagues published a seminal paper on the "cybernetic" modeling of purposive behavior. They helped plant the idea that negative feedback loops could be used in mechanical systems to provide a self-corrective method of targeting a specified path of activity. Such ideas were cast on the fertile fields that would spawn artificial intelligence and several other expressions of modern cognitive science. In 1948, at the famous Hixon Symposium on "Cerebral Mechanisms in Behavior," Wiener joined McCulloch, John von Neumann, and others in discussing the relationship between brains and computers. At about the same time, Newell, Shaw, and Simon demonstrated that a computer could prove some of the theorems of Whitehead and Russell's *Principia Mathematica* (1913).

The origins of connectionism therefore lie in the earliest expressions of what is now called "computational neuroscience." Donald O. Hebb described a formal theory of neural connectivities—expecially "cell assemblies"—in his 1949 *The Organization of Behavior.* By 1951, Marvin Minsky had built a mechanized learning system called "Snark," which

had three hundred tubes and a lot of motors. It needed some automatic electric clutches, which we maintained ourselves. The memory of the machine was stored in the positions of its control knobs, 40 of them, and when the machine was learning, it used the clutches to adjust its own knobs. We used a surplus gyropilot from a B24 bomber to move the clutches. (Cited in Pagels 1988, p. 119)

Such crude and creative beginnings have ushered in our modern supercomputers.

The serial computers came next and, ironically, signaled a period of relative dormancy in connectionist attempts to model neural networks. The next major event in connectionist history was the work of Frank Rosenblatt on neuronlike learning systems that he called "perceptrons." In his 1962 *Principles of Neurodynamics,* Rosenblatt described perceptrons as networks "designed to permit the study of lawful relationships between the organization of a nerve net, the organization of its environment, and the 'psychological' performances of which it is capable" (Pagels, 1988, p. 122). Rosenblatt simulated perceptrons on the serial computers then available, but apparently alienated some colleagues in artificial intelligence by making enthusiastic claims about the capacities of his brainchild, a child he considered superior to the computers on which he simulated it.

Minsky, who was one of Rosenblatt's high school classmates, joined efforts with Seymour Papert in what many observers considered the annihilation of the perceptron idea. In their 1969 *Perceptrons,* they used rigorous mathematical analyses to demonstrate the formal and (they thought) formidable limitations of Rosenblatt's brainchild. According to Pagels, Rosenblatt thereafter died in a boating accident "that may have been a suicide" (1988, p. 122). Research on perceptrons also died, or was significantly absent, for almost a decade. Ironically, both Minsky and Papert would later develop a deeper appreciation for Rosenblatt's work, and each would write their own version of a "society of mind" theory in which brains are portrayed as complexes of many different kinds of interacting mechanisms (Minsky 1987; Papert 1982).

Connectionist research resurfaced in the late 1970s and showed significant acceleration through the 1980s. An important element in this resurgence was the development of innovative programming strategies called *massively distributed parallel processing,* a phenomenon made possible only by modern supercomputers. The term was shortened to *parallel distributed processing,* now frequently abbreviated to *PDP.* Instrumental in the development of PDP have been David Rumelhart, James McClelland, Geoffrey Hinton, and their PDP Research Group centered at the Institute for Cognitive Science at the University of California, San Diego. Other important contributors to PDP research and what came to be called the "connectionist movement" have been J. A. Anderson, M. A. Arbib, D. H. Ballard, J. A. Feldman, T. Kohonen, and R. A. Ratcliff. The umbrella term *connectionism* has been used to acknowledge the fact that there was (and is) a "new look" in the efforts of computer scientists and artificial intelligence (AI) experts to model human learning and perceptual/conceptual processes. There seems to be relatively general consensus that connectionism has, indeed, been a novel approach to the study of cognition. But enthusiasm has recently mingled with criticism and challenge, and there are indications that connectionism may ultimately serve as a bridge toward even more complex and lifelike models of perception, learning, memory, and the integration of brain and body.

The Problems and Promise of Connectionism

Along with the enthusiasm it has engendered, connectionism has also evoked strong criticism. Thus, for example, Paul Smolensky has asserted that "the connectionist approach will contribute significant, long-lasting ideas to the rather impoverished theoretical repertoire of cognitive science," that "it will heal a deep and ancient rift in the science and philosophy of mind," and that it is likely that "connectionist models will offer the most significant progress of the past several millenia on the mind/body problem" (1988, pp. 2–3). Those are promises of considerable proportions. In the same article, however, Smolensky also acknowledged that "it is far from clear that connectionist models offer a sound basis for modeling human cognitive performance." Indeed, he has noted that it is "far from clear" whether these models "can contribute to the study of human competence," whether they "offer a sound basis for modeling neural computation," and whether they have "adequate computational power to perform high-level cognitive tasks" (p. 2).

As critics of the connectionist movement have pointed out, the problems and limitations inherent in this perspective may be considerable (for example, Casey and Moran 1989; McGuinness 1989; Reilly 1989). A balanced evaluation of the merits and liabilities of connectionism must also acknowledge, however, important differences among the various expressions of that approach. The connectionism that Smolensky outlines, for example, makes room for "subsymbolic processes"; while the connectionist account of memory offered by McClelland and Rumelhart reflects an adherence to more traditional computational and representational models. There is, then, no unified theory of connectionism; there are, instead, multiple connectionist models.

To their credit, connectionist models have gone beyond the limiting confines of earlier serial-processing models of cognition. In doing so, they have encouraged cognitive scientists to think about human knowing in terms of widely distributed informational processes. Also to their credit is the fact that the pioneers and proponents of connectionism have maintained that neuroscience offers metaphors for modeling the mind that are more relevant and productive than are the machine/bit/chip metaphors of computer technology. Connectionist models have, however, failed (1) to offer a coherent or comprehensive theory of cognition, (2) to liberate themselves from computational and representational metaphors for knowing, and (3) to faithfully reflect some aspects of neural architecture and functioning. These are, of course, judgments that reflect alternative assumptions about adequate theories and models of mind. (For a discussion of the conceptual differences between theories and models, see Weimer 1979.) According to their harshest critics, connectionist models have remained steeped in reductionist associationism, computational rationalism, and a form of functionalism relatively insensitive to the structural dynamics of living systems. In the theoretical realm, contributions from connectionism have been rare. The novel offerings of connectionist models have been primarily descriptive and programmatic rather than explanatory and formally theoretical.

Different models have expressed varying endorsements of representational metaphors, but virtually all contemporary forms of connectionism remain thoroughly computational in emphasis. In other words, the quantifiable "habit strength" of connections has continued to serve as a root metaphor for their conceptualizations. And if there is any doubt that the computational spirit is alive and well and still very optimistic, contemporary expressions are legion (Boden 1981; Globus 1989; Haugeland 1985; Jackendoff 1987; Pagels 1988; Sejnowski, Koch, and Churchland 1988; Waldrop 1988b). To their credit, some recent explorations have tried to simulate the coalitional (decentralized) control structures inspired by the early work of Adam Smith (for example, Waldrop 1989). Although some of the proposed computations have been commendably inspired by studies in neuroscience, the majority have failed to incorporate even basic knowledge about neurons and neural networks. Consider, for example, the reactions of a noted neurobiologist to the connectionist models of McClelland, Rumelhart, and the PDP Research Group:

Non-neurophysiologists should be aware that several of the central assumptions of these models could turn out be be dead ends for neural network research. In particular, there is emphasis in these models on the linear addition or subtraction of the "weights" of synaptic inputs that converge onto each neuron. However, we have known for decades that synaptic weights for biological neurons do not summate in the linear fashion one uses when adding resistances "in series." Instead, they summate as conductances connected in parallel. This is formalized in the Goldman equation or the parallel battery equation, well known to neurophysiologists but unfortunately neglected by many computer modelers. . . . It will be ironic if research on parallel processing is slowed down because of the use of serial summation of synaptic weights instead of the more powerful parallel summation. (Segal 1988, p. 1107)

The "new look" in the neurobiology of learning and memory—probably best exemplified by Gerald Edelman's (1987) theory of "neuronal group selection"—does, in fact, incorporate the biological nonlinearities associated with parallel (rather than serial) summation (appendix D).

In conclusion, the problems and promise of connectionism are difficult to evaluate at the present time. In their critical analysis, Jerry Fodor and Zenon Pylyshyn propose that connectionist models "may provide an account of the neural (or 'abstract neurological') structures in which Classical cognitive architecture is implemented," but that "mind/brain architecture is not Connectionist at the cognitive level" (1988, p. 3). The distinction here is not simply between reductionistic "neurologizing" and abstract conceptualization, but does invoke the importance of distinguishing levels and domains of analysis. Even at multiple levels, however, it is worth noting the final paragraph of Minsky and Papert's updated epilogue to their 1969 demolition of perceptrons:

How much, then, can we expect from connectionist systems? Much more than the above remarks might suggest, since reflective thought is the lesser part of what our minds do. Most probably, we think, the human brain is, in the main, composed of large numbers of relatively small distributed systems, arranged by embryology into a complex society that is controlled in part (but only in part) by serial, symbolic systems that are later added. But the subsymbolic systems that do most of the work from underneath must, by their very character, block all the other parts of the brain from knowing much about how they work. And this, itself, could help explain how people do so many things yet have such incomplete ideas of how those things are actually done. (1988, p. 280)

C. AUTOPOIESIS: THE SELF-ORGANIZATION OF LIVING SYSTEMS

The contributions of Humberto Maturana and his student/colleague Francisco Varela to the sciences of complexity have only recently begun to be appreciated, but they have already influenced the thinking and research of many other scientists (see chapter 5 and appendix E; Szentágothai and Érdi 1989). One way of introducing their work is to relate it to other studies in *natural epistemology*—that is, the "necessary unity of mind and nature" Gregory Bateson (1979) wrote about. Toward the end of his life, Bateson was asked who else was carrying forward the study of *"Creatura,"* the world of the living. He is said to have replied that "the center for this study is now in Santiago, Chile, under a man named Maturana" (cited in Dell 1985, p. 5). As it turned out, there were and are important differences in the systems developed by Maturana and Bateson.

Maturana began his career as an experimental neurophysiologist working in collaboration with Warren S. McCulloch and Walter H. Pitts, and interacting with the constructivist Heinz von Foerster at the Biological Computer Laboratory at the University of Illinois. McCulloch was himself an important contributor to what he called "experimental epistemology" and the modeling of "natural" knowing systems. Their early work together on the anatomy and physiology of vision is often cited as evidence for specific "feature detectors" in the visual cortex, but it was actually an elegant demonstration of how neural systems create the "contents" of experience by means of "contrast enhancement" and "opponent processes." Years later, reflecting on this early research, Maturana recalled that it had helped him realize that the central purpose of his work was not to map the perceived world onto the nervous system but, rather, to understand how that system participated in the generation of its own experiences (McCulloch 1965; Maturana 1977; Winograd and Flores 1986). It turns out that all biological systems exhibit dynamic and complementary "opponent processes." Although this fact had long been recognized in some domains (such as vision and motivation), the operation of opponent processes is now acknowledged in virtually all major theories of motivation and personality (compare Beuter et al. 1989; Mahoney 1985c; Solomon and Corbit 1974; Weimer 1987).

In 1970 and 1975, Maturana published articles on the neurophysiology of cognition and the "organization of the living" in which he outlined a novel approach he and Varela would elaborate in the years that followed. They coined the term *autopoiesis* (literally, "self-creation" or "self-production") to describe their work on the self-organizing properties of all living and knowing systems, which they consider to be identical (Maturana 1970, 1975, 1977, 1978, 1980, 1987, 1988, 1989; Maturana and Varela 1980, 1987; Varela 1979, 1984, 1987; Varela, Maturana, and Uribe 1974). Arciero (1989) has pointed out, however, that *autopraxis* might be a more appropriate term in that it emphasizes the (ever-)present participle process or activity of "self-doing" rather than the product of that activity:

An autopoietic system is organized (defined as a unity) as a network of processes of production (transformation and destruction) of components that produces the components that: (1) through their interactions and transformations continuously regenerate and realize the network of processes (relations) that produced them; and (2) constitute it . . . as a concrete unity in the space in which they exist by specifying the topological domain of its realization as such a network. (Varela 1979, p. 13)

In Maturana and Varela's approach, learning is defined as changes in an organism's behavior congruent with the changing relations between the organism and its "medium" (a term they prefer over *environment*). More precisely, Maturana and Varela assert that the interactions of living systems with their medium are "structure-determined," meaning that changes in either are "triggered" (as contrasted with "produced") by their interaction. Thus, learning does not consist of being "instructed" by external agents or environments. Maturana and Varela have also asserted that learning cannot consist of the "pick-up" of prepackaged information from outside the living system, nor can it be understood as the acquisition of internalized "representations" of its medium. The changes exhibited by an organism in the course of its "structural coupling" with its medium reflect the organization and structure of the organism. They do not offer information about the medium itself.

Structure Determination

Autopoietic systems are "structure-determined" in the sense that the changes they can undergo are determined by their organization and structure. It is important to emphasize, however, that *structure* and *organization* are not considered synonymous by Maturana and Varela. *Organization* (from the Greek *organon,* meaning "instrument") refers to "the relations between components that define and specify a system as a composite unity of a particular class, and determine its properties as such a unity." *Structure* (from the Latin *struere,* "to build"), on the other hand, "refers to the actual components and to the actual relations that these must satisfy in their participation in the constitution of a given composite unity" (Maturana 1980, p. 32). In other words, *organization* refers to the abstract relations that *define* a given individual or system as being itself and an instance of a class, while *structure* refers to the actual (concrete) particulars that comprise that individual or system at any given point in time. The extent to which you are still the "same person" that you were as a child, for example, is a measure of the extent to which your organization has remained invariant. Meanwhile, however, your structure has changed continuously (the cells comprising you have been extensively repaired and/or replaced through metabolic processes). As one walks (or breathes), for example, bodily structure changes (the relations of components to one another) while systemic organization remains invariant. This means, of course, that what the organism can experience is necessarily limited by its structure, which is itself but a passing form of its organization. As Maturana put it, "What I am saying is that to a structure-determined system, nothing can happen which is not determined by it—by how it is made, its structure" (1987, p. 74).

The ongoing structural changes (and exchanges) that living systems undergo are the result of "perturbations," which can arise from interactions with their medium or, recursively, with themselves. These perturbations "trigger" structural changes in the organism but do not automatically convey information about the nature or properties of the perturbing entity. They are not, in other words, "instructive" in the traditional sense of that term. Perturbations do not "cause" changes in the organism by putting something into it (like "information"); they simply trigger changes of state that are structure-determined by the organism. From this perspective, "information" is not something transferred or processed. Instead, "information" is literally translated from its Latin origin: *in formare,* "that which is formed from within." Among other things, structure determination implies that objective knowledge is impossible to achieve and, moreover, that all knowledge about another living system must necessarily reflect the structure of the observing/knowing system. Structure determination emphasizes that our "personal realities" are, in fact, inaccessible to others, and that we should remember that our under-standing of other people (and our shared worlds) is inevitably influenced by our own organization.

Organizational Closure and Self-Reference

Maturana and Varela assert that the organization of living systems is operationally closed—a view that has significant implications about the range of possible changes within such systems. Organizational closure is not thermodynamic closure: that is, it does not deny the fact that the system is "open" to exchanges of matter/energy with its medium. Living systems are "structurally coupled" to the mediums in which they exist. Technically, structural coupling refers to "a history of recurrent interactions leading to the structural congruence between two (or more) systems" (Maturana and Varela 1987, p. 75). Although the organization of the system cannot change without its either disintegrating or changing its identity, its structure can and does change. In this *structural plasticity,* any structural changes that are triggered by structural coupling may themselves beget (and constrain) further structural changes.

Organizational closure refers to the fact that the defining feature of any unity—in this case, a living system—is its capacity to maintain its integrity. Maturana and Varela emphasize that we are fundamentally biological organisms—we are living systems—and, as such, the "bottom line" in our adaptation is to maintain our status as such—that is, to stay alive. For these researchers, all living systems are, by definition, "adapted" (or, better yet, "adapting"), and there are no "degrees" of adaptation. Adaptation requires structural changes in a living unity that are congruent with the changes in its medium; if it cannot or does not make those changes, it disintegrates (dies). Structure-determined systems are also necessarily "perfect" in the sense that they cannot but be "true to" their structure: that is, they always behave in accord with it. Such concepts as *control* and *purpose* are therefore deemed meaningless except as expressions of an observing system trying to understand another system. Because they are structure-determined and organizationally closed, living systems are said to be "autonomous" in the sense that they survive, prosper, or perish under the "self-law" of their own makeup. We again encounter the phe-nomenon of reflexity or recursiveness.

An important implication of this approach—and one that converges with that of other approaches to complexity—is that all living systems are necessarily self-referential. As Edgar Morin put it, "the living being, from the bacterium to homo sapiens, obeys a particular logic according to which the individual, though ephemeral, singular, and marginal, consid-ers itself the center of the world" (cited in Guidano 1987, p. 3). The implications of this point for human psychological services are far-reaching, as Guidano has aptly noted:

The essential feature of this perspective considers the self-organizing ability of a human knowing system as a basic evolutionary constraint that, through the maturational ascension of higher cognitive abilities, progressively structures a full sense of self-identity with inherent feelings of uniqueness and historical continuity. The availability of this stable and structured self-identity permits continuous and coherent self-perception and self-evaluation in the face of temporal becoming and mutable reality. For this reason, the maintenance of one's perceived identity becomes as important as life itself; without it the individual would be incapable of proper functioning and would lose, at the same time, the very sense of reality. (1987, p. 3)

(For technical discussions of recursiveness, self-referentiality, and identity in biology and complex systems, see Hull 1978; Medawar 1981; Morin 1981; Pattee 1977; and Salthe 1989.) We are the way we are because our history of interactions with our worlds is not a "past" history at all, but rather an everpresent, forward-leaning "preparedness" to perpetuate ourselves.

Finally, and with important implications, Maturana and Varela have emphasized the difference between what the living system is doing and what it may appear to be doing from the perspective of an observer. The observer may infer, for example, that an organism is demonstrating "learning" when it improves its ability to handle its environment. From the standpoint of the living system, however, what has occurred has been only an ontogenic structural drift with conservation of its organization (and, therefore, adaptation).

To put it another way, "everything said is said by an observer," which is to say that the subject-object relationship is again a necessary consideration in our attempts to understand the self-organization of life, and the perspective of the observer is neither passive nor detached. This is where language assumes a crucial role in human affairs, since humans interact so extensively via symbols (you and I are structurally coupling right now). According to Maturana (1977), we humans live in a "multiverse" rather than a "universe"; we each bring forth our unique experiences of reality, and these multiple realities that we create are all equally legitimate when their individual structural sources are taken into account. This is, of course, yet another reflection of the importance of hermeneutics to contemporary science (Goguen and Varela 1979; Locker and Coulter 1977; Madison 1988; Maturana 1987, 1988; Maturana and Varela 1987; Pattee 1977, 1978, 1979; Varela 1987; Wachterhauser 1986).

Radical Constructivism Revisited

To comment on the full sweep of autopoietic theory, I shall begin with Paul Dell's evaluation, appropriately couched in the terminology and recursiveness of the theory itself:

With full awareness of his inability as an observer to avoid illusion or to operate outside of language, Maturana has proceeded to set forth a generative hypothesis: we are structure-determined autopoietic unities who operate in structural coupling with our medium. . . . Without escaping his constitutively limited standpoint as a human observer, he has delineated a generative mechanism which has enormous explanatory power and, yet, is fully congruent with his constitutively limited standpoint as a human observer. (1985, p. 17)

Dell enthusiastically endorsed that hypothesis and mechanism, and concluded that, with Bateson, Maturana has offered a sound "ontological biology" on which to found the social and behavioral sciences. Dell also concluded that the principle of structure determination is capable of explaining the nature of social systems, the nature of language and its emergence, and the nature of observers and language-based constructions of reality.

I concur with the assertion that Bateson, Maturana, and Varela have made important contributions to our understanding of living systems and the knowing inherent in their living. I do not, however, believe that autopoietic theory (or any other theory, for that matter) has explained the nature of language, social systems, or epistemic observation. My own current evaluation of autopoiesis would instead emphasize its valuable contributions in the following areas: (1) the fundamental significance of systemic integrity, coherence, or organization in the basic survival of living systems; (2) the recursive (or self-referential) nature of all adaptation and knowing; (3) the importance of plasticity in learning; (4) the whole-being embodiment of knowing (which challenges traditional dualisms between mind and brain, brain and body, and so on); (5) the rejection of rationalist objectivism; (6) the rejection of representationism in theories of cognition; (7) the emphasis on language (and symbols) as an important medium of human interaction; and (8) the recognition that our traditional distinctions between subject and object (observing and observed systems) are in sore need of conceptual reappraisal. This last point is still being elaborated by Maturana and Varela (Maturana 1988, 1989; Varela 1984).

Since I agree with each of the foregoing assertions, I look forward to the future contributions of autopoietic theory and research. My primary reservation about the autopoietic perspective has to do with its relative failure to address the complexities of an organism's interactions with its "medium." Beyond the heuristic abstractions of "structure determination," "organizational closure," and "structural coupling," what is it that determines an organism's adaptations to/of its environment? What are the parameters of "congruence" between the structures of a living system and its medium? Why are some systems capable of much wider ranges of self-restructuring than others, and what are the explicit implications for parenting, education, and psychological services?

Another way of expressing this reservation is to say that, in my fallible understanding of it, current autopoietic theory pays too little attention to the world in which the living system lives, not to mention to the mentation involved and the processes by which that system learns, changes, or develops. Although I concur with Maturana and Varela that we can never directly or objectively know the world that constitutes our medium—that is, we can never directly reach "cosmic bedrock"—this limitation should not prevent us from acknowledging the existence and influence of that realm. As many cognitive therapists have learned over the last two decades, psychotherapy clients can be urged to "restructure" their perceptions and beliefs about self and world, but the self-perpetuating aspects of that self and the everyday constraints imposed by that world are not always conducive to that undertaking.

D. DEVELOPMENTS IN PSYCHOBIOLOGY AND BRAIN SCIENCE

With the important exception of those clinical researchers and practitioners who have focused on psychiatry, neurological impairments, and biological aspects of adaptation, psychobiological considerations have not been popular or prominent topics in theories of human change and psychotherapy. The reasons for this neglect are probably multiple, and lie well beyond the scope of this appendix. My intent here is briefly to document the relevance of such considerations for theory, research, and practice.

Historical Contexts

In table A.1, the extensiveness of my condensation of the major events in the history of psychobiology and brain science may give some idea of the professional energy devoted to this topic over the centuries (with clear acceleration over the last five). The significance of the brain in human behavior has been recognized for at least five millennia, and head and heart were contrasting choices of emphasis in early theories of human thought, feeling, and activity. The conceptual separations of mind and body likewise appeared relatively early, as did the still prevalent

Table A.1   Selected Events in the History of Psychobiology and Brain
Science

3000 B.C.	Imhotep	first recorded reference to the brain (the Edwin Smith papyrus)
850 B.C.	Homer and others	endorsed *cardiocentric theory* (heart as the seat of intelligence), an idea long popular in Egypt and parts of Asia
500 B.C.	Alcmaeon	endorsed *cephalocentric theory* (brain as the central organ of intelligence)
400 B.C.	Hippocrates	extension of cephalocentric theory; brain viewed as central to pain, pleasure, and perception
350 B.C.	Plato	asserted that the soul, located in the head, was responsible for reason; the heart was said to receive input from the senses and to "execute" reason; emotion and desire were attributed to the liver and loins (see chapters 2 and 8; appendix G)
330 B.C.	Aristotle	defense of cardiocentric theory; outlined principles of association (contiguity, similarity, and contrast)
280 B.C.	Erasistratos, Herophilos	first recorded dissections of the human brain; Herophilos distinguished sensory and motor nerves; Erasistratos related human cortical convolutions to greater intelligence
170 B.C.	Galen	first *in vivo* and intrusive brain function experiments; concept of *psychic pneuma;* proposed a centralist model of brain and spine organization but de-emphasized neocortex; his views would dominate for almost seventeen centuries
A.D. 1504	da Vinci	first wax castes of ventricles
1527	Paracelsus	challenged the prevailing views of Galen and Hippocrates; argued that diseases are caused by agents external to the body; recommended herbs and minerals as possible curative agents
1543	Vesalius	first detailed drawings of convolutions in brain cortex; founder of modern neuroanatomy
1628	W. Harvey	described blood circulation

Table A.1   *(Continued)*

1650	Descartes	mechanistic (reflex) theory of mind and movement; reassertion of Platonic mind-body dualism; homunculus theory of mind
1651	Hobbes	based all ideation in sensation; emphasized principle of association
1672	T. Willis	distinction of white and gray matter in the brain
1685	M. Malpighi	first studies of brain surface via microscope
1690	Locke	based all knowledge in experience (sensory or reflective); "tablula rasa" at birth; distinguished primary and secondary qualities in perception
1718	van Leeuwenhoek	first observation of nerve "vessels" via microscope
1745	de La Mettrie	refinement of Descartes's mechanical theory of mind and movement
1749	Hartley	proposed vibratory actions within nervous system as mechanisms of learning (association)
1762	Baader	established *decussation* (right/left crossover) of nerve pathways
1779	Mesmer	published theory of "animal magnetism" and pioneered aspects of modern hypnotherapy; encouraged a resonance/dissonance metaphor of nervous functioning
1780	de Condillac	published first diagram of "reflex action"
1791	Galvani	first experiments on "animal electricity"
1800	Bichat	proposed the operation of a "vital force" in maintenance and self-organization of life; founded "vitalism"
1803	de Biran	introduced concept of "feeling of effort" and challenged mind-body dualism; emphasized the centrality of voluntary and intentional acts in the study of brain function
1810	Gall	introduced *phrenology,* a popular expression of efforts to localize brain functions

Table A.1   *(Continued)*

1811	Bell	elaborated the principle of differentiation between sensory and motor nerves (first noted by Herophilos); made important observations on reflex action
1822	Magendie	experimental demonstration of the polarity of the spinal roots, encouraging the polarization of sensory and motor functions
1822	Flourens	demonstrated separate sensory and motor functions in cortex; anticipated important aspects of "equipotentiality" (Lashley)
1825	Bouillaud	founding of neuropsychology
1829	Weber	showed that sensation is relative to *change* in stimulation (rather than to absolute intensity); concept of threshhold; pioneered studies of muscle sensation
1834	Mueller	theory of "specific energies of nerves"; encouraged search for specialization and localization of function
1838	Matteucci	founding of electrophysiology
1839	T. Schwann	proposed that cells are the basic units of the nervous system (in contrast to the "reticular network")
1843	J. S. Mill	proposed *mental chemistry* as a nonmechanical metaphor for the processes operative in the generation of complex ideas
1848	DuBois-Reymond	reported preliminary studies leading to the discovery of the nerve action potential
1849	Helmholtz	first measurement of nerve impulse speed; pioneering work in optics and acoustics
1855	Spencer	his *Principles of Psychology* laid the foundations for evolutionary epistemology
1855	Bain	proposed that the brain is capable of spontaneous activity
1856	Bernard	description of neural networks
1859	Darwin	his *Origin of the Species* encouraged developmental perspectives on nervous systems

Table A.1   *(Continued)*

1860	Fechner	in *Elements of Psychophysics,* proposed a methodology for the study of mind-body relations
1861	de Broca	demonstration of localization of function in the brain
1863	Sechenov	published *Reflexes of the Brain* and discovered the phenomenon of inhibition in the central nervous system
1865	Deiters	first accurate drawings of a nerve cell; distinguished axons from dendrites
1869	Galton	published *Hereditary Genius,* emphasizing genetic factors and individual differences
1870	Fritsch and Hitzig	experimental demonstration of an "excitable" region of the (motor) cortex
1873	Wundt	*Principles of Physiological Psychology* helped launch experimental psychology; used introspection as method; emphasized "creative synthesis" in all perception
1875	Caton	first measurement of electrical activity in the cortex via the "evoked potential"
1878	Bernard	theory of brain-regulated homeostasis (a self-sustained "milieu interieur")
1885	Golgi	beginnings of nerve histology
1885	Ebbinghaus	first quantitative studies of memory (his own)
1886	Cattell	first studies of span of attention and free association
1888	Fere	showed that skin's electrical resistance (gsr) was related to emotional responding
1890	Horsley	beginnings of neurosurgery
1890	James	offered influential theories of emotion, attention, perception, consciousness, and will
1890	Jackson	founding of what was to become modern neurology
1891	Waldeyer	first use of the term *neuron*
1895	Freud	proposed two types of neurons *(phi* and *psi)* specialized for external and internal worlds, respectively

Table A.1   *(Continued)*

1896	Dewey	challenged the concept of the reflex arc as oversimplifying; emphasized holistic adaptation
1897	Sherrington	theory of synaptic function; discovery of proprioception and reciprocal inhibition; motor theory of neural integration
1900	Ramón y Cajal	first observation of the nerve synapse, demonstrating that neurons are independent cells (contrary to network theory); launched the neuron doctrine
1900	Pavlov	pioneering work on the "conditioning" of reflexes
1902	Franz	published first studies of the effects of frontal lobe removal
1904	Elliott	discovery of neurotransmitters
1909	Brodmann	early efforts in meticulous cortical mapping
1909	Cushing	reported first studies of cortical stimulation in conscious subjects
1921	Richter	pioneered studies of rhythms in bodily systems
1929	Berger	founding of encephalography
1929	Dale	identified acetylcholine and "cholinergic" nerves
1929	Cassirer	proposed theory of "symbolic consciousness" as alternative to sensory-associationist accounts of thought
1929	Lashley	showed that removal of large sections of the rat's cerebral cortex had little impact on performance; doctrine of *equipotentiality*
1930	von Holst	theory of nervous oscillators recast neurons as spontaneous pattern generators rather than passive conduits of electricity
1930	Eccles	demonstrated central inhibition of reflexes

Table A.1   *(Continued)*

1932	Hinsey and Harris	foundation of neuroendocrinology and the study of brain-pituitary-endocrine interactions; marked the end of the electrical "dry model" of brain function and the beginnings of the "wet look"
1936	J. Z. Young	used giant squid axon to study nerve activity
1936	Moniz	pioneered surgical procedure of prefrontal lobotomy
1936	LeGros Clark	outlined hypothalamic connections in human brain
1937	Papez	identified the lymbic system as the substrate of emotionality
1937	Penfield	refined cortical mappings via electrical stimulation and authored theory of memory permanence
1937	W. B. Cannon	pioneered work on the "wisdom of the body," especially the sympathetic nervous system
1947	Granit	pioneered work on the activity of single cells in the retina
1949	Hebb	dynamic, holistic theory of brain function emphasizing cell assemblies and "reverberating circuits"; suggested synaptic modification in learning
1949	Moruzzi and Magoun	identified the reticular activating system as a dynamic regulator of some body-brain relations
1949	von Békesy	discovered standing wave patterns in cochlea; founded neuroanatomy of audition
1949	MacLean	introduced triune model of the human brain (chapter 6)
1950	Sperry and von Holst	revived theory of efference (motor metatheory) by demonstrating central system dominance over peripheral activity in fish and insects
1952	Hayek	in *The Sensory Order*, proposed that the nervous system orders its experience actively (motorically), and that abstract processes are involved in all perception, action, and learning

Table A.1   *(Continued)*

1959	Held	reafferentation experiments demonstrated that perception is actively constructive and that human plasticity is considerable
1958	Eccles	pioneering work on plasticity and organization of cortex
1959	Mountcastle	experimental demonstration of the "vertical" organization of the cerebral cortex
1966	Gibson	portrayal of the senses as motoric perceptual systems
1968	Sperry	demonstrated differences between the two cortical hemispheres in specializations and functions
1973	Powers	in the efferent (motoric) tradition, suggested that "behavior is the control of perception," encouraging a dynamic, systems view
1975	Hughes and Kosterlitz	discovery of endogenous opiates in the brain, a major event in the development of hormonal theories of brain/behavior regulation
1978	Edelman	theory of neuron group selection ("neural Darwinism") in which the nervous system actively generates and selects among its own self-organizing processes

Primary sources: Adelman (1987), Boorstin (1983), Breasted (1930), Changeaux (1985), Elsberg (1945), Gross (1987), and Hearst (1979).

dichotomies between sensory and motor functions. Although Descartes's mechanistic theory of mind and movement was a dominant influence on later thinking, vitalistic and self-organizational concepts have been voiced for almost two centuries.

It appears that the history of psychobiology reflects several interesting cycles (or spirals) of emphasis. The most noteworthy include:

1. The shift toward increasing "localization"—as from brain to brain area to "reticular networks" to individual neurons to synapses to transmitter substances and specific chemicals, followed by the (relatively recent) return to networks, systems, and holistic notions of body-brain relations.

2. The shift from hydraulic metaphors of internal dynamics (such as

the four counterbalancing "humours," which were popular even before Galen and Hippocrates) to mechanical and then electrical metaphors, followed by the return (particularly since 1975) to the "wet look" and the hormonal theory of behavioral and neural regulation.

3. The shift from the centrality of the heart and "gut level" (in Homer, Plato, and Aristotle) to cephalocentric (brain-centered) theory (also reflected in the doctrine of cerebral primacy [see appendices F and G]), followed by the gradual re-empowerment of affect (as by James, Freud, Sherrington, and MacLean).

4. The shift away from ideas and abstractions as sources of activity or direction (as in Plato and Aristotle) and the move toward biochemical polarities, followed by the recent resurgence of constructivist interest in the power and guidance of abstract processes (as in Cassirer and Hayek).

5. The shift from proactive and participatory models of perception and experience (as in Buddhist doctrines) toward relatively reactive (reflexive) and sensory (input-focused) models, followed by the re-assertion of participatory and motor (activity-focused) models in the last two centuries (as by Sherrington, Hayek, Held, and Gibson).

The implications of these conceptual spirals appear to be tied to recent developments that have contributed to the growing interest in this area.

Recent Developments

Content analyses of publications over the last century reflect the fact that psychobiological thinking has become increasingly popular and that its terminology and focus have also changed. "Evolutionary" and "genetic" concepts dominated in the first half of this century, for example; and "biological" and "brain" references then became increasingly popular in the second half (Ellis, Miller, and Widmayer 1988). This popularity has been encouraged by some of the leading theorists and researchers in the field, many of whom have suggested that recent developments in our understanding of psychobiology represent conceptual revolutions in our thinking about cognition, consciousness, and a variety of other human experiences (Eccles 1977; Popper and Eccles 1977; Pribram 1971, 1977, 1986, 1990; Sperry 1988). Central to these assertions have been a host of assumptions about the relationships among physiological signals and psychological experiences (Cacioppo and Tassinary 1990).

The increasing popularity of psychobiological concepts and theories can also be traced to a number of developments in psychology, psychiatry, health science (including medicine), and the rapidly developing specialty known as "cognitive neuroscience." The latter discipline emerged out of the interface of cybernetics, computer science, and the cognitive sciences (for example, McCulloch 1965; McCulloch and Pitts 1943; its origins are discussed in chapter 4 and appendix B). Modern expressions are dominated by research on "neural networks," with a central controversy being whether computational algorithms can adequately "reduce" psychological phenomena to physiological processes (Churchland and Sejnowski 1988; Coles 1989; Eimas and Galaburda 1989; Hatfield 1988; LeDoux and Hirst 1986). Counterbalancing the expressions of reductionism are theories and research emphasizing the evolutionary, emergent, self-organizing, and abstract properties of neural systems (Glezer, Jacobs, and Morgane 1988; Sarnat and Netsky 1981).

Efforts in cognitive neuroscience have also resonated with continuing attempts to offer biologically based theories of perception, learning, and memory (for example, Black et al. 1987; Changeaux and Konishi 1987; Kohonen 1984; Lisberger 1988; McGaugh 1990; Wise and Desimone 1988). By and large, these efforts have reflected the valuable legacy of D. O. Hebb's (1949) learning theory, particularly the plasticity of synaptic connections and the dynamics of "reverberating circuits" in the nervous system (Brown et al. 1988; Érdi and Szentágothai 1985; Kolb 1989; Malsburg and Bienenstock 1986; Purves 1988; Segal 1988). Interestingly, it was also Hebb (1975) who once estimated the "half life" of knowledge in psychology as approximately five years and recommended that graduate students learn general concepts rather than memorize specific facts (Mahoney 1976). Consistent with the assertions of Hayek (1952b) and the constructivists (chapter 5), this also appears to be a strategy reflected in the "higher" brain functions (Wise 1987).

Two other sources of encouragement for the growing popularity of psychobiological emphases have been of immense practical relevance. Techniques for "imaging" brain structures and functions have been revolutionized in the last decade, and continue to reflect refinements and breakthroughs (Andreasen 1988; Hibbard et al. 1987; John et al. 1988). The impact of these refinements on working hypotheses and theories of brain function and dysfunction has been truly phenomenal. Also influential has been the emergence and proliferation of the field called *psychoneuroimmunology*, an interdisciplinary specialization that studies the interdependence of psychological factors and the functioning of the endocrine, nervous, and immune systems (Solomon 1987; Su, London, and Jaffe 1988). Although simple relationships have been elusive, complex ones have been identified and well replicated. It is clear, for example, that in many individuals negative affect and low levels of perceived self-efficacy tend to reduce resistance to disease.

Bodybrain Dynamics in Self-Organizing Development

Taken together, the recent developments in psychobiology reflect a convergence and conceptual integration remarkably resonant with the emphases of evolutionary epistemology and constructivist metatheory. When the "dry look" of the electrical metaphor for brain function began to give way to the "wet look" of hormonal regulation, for example, Richard Bergland left little room for ambiguity in his assertion that the brain is, in essence, a gland, and that all of its activities involve hormones:

The new paradigm views the brain as a complex whole, an organ that does not stand apart from the rest of the body. . . . We now have no choice: we must acknowledge the unity of the brain and the body, admit that brain hormones are really body hormones and recognize that hormonal therapies aimed at making the brain whole again must replace reductionistic therapies aimed at bridling its electrical currents. (1985, p. 82)

As radical as it may sound, this is a view that has gained considerable support in the last fifteen years.

Likewise with the increasing acceptance of the idea that body and brain are integrated subsystems that both drive and reflect the dynamics of self-organizing development. Even if we focus only on the brain, the motor metatheory is clearly more adequate than its sensory counterpart (Weimer 1977). Spontaneous self-organizing activity is ubiquitous, driven by "oscillators" and oscillating subsystems that generate incomprehensible degrees of diversity in activity patterns (Bienenstock 1985; Changeaux 1985; Gilbert 1989; Jeannerod 1985; Schöner and Kelso 1988; Traub, Miles, and Wong 1989). These oscillations and this activity and diversity now appear to be fundamental to the full range of psychological experiences: attention, sensation, perception, learning, memory, concept development, and so on.

The implications of this last point have only recently been integrated into a formal theory, but it is a theory that is at the forefront of current psychobiological thinking. Gerald M. Edelman's (1987) theory of *neuronal group selection,* for example, is a creative application of evolutionary concepts to neural functioning. Edelman has suggested that the brain—like the evolutionary processes that afforded its development—relies extensively on selection as its primary strategy of self-organization. It is not neurons, however, so much as synapses that are selectively eliminated in individual development (for example, an eight-month-old human infant has twice as many cortical synapses as an adolescent). Through its own active generation and selective elimination (and, hence, retention) of different "neural connectivities," lifelong "epigenetic" processes create (and re-create) relations among populations of cells.

Finally, at the level of processes and phenomena more familiar to the psychotherapist, Edelman's theory implies that, to some extent,

every perception [may be] considered to be an act of creation and every memory an act of imagination. The individualistic flavor and the extraordinary richness of selective repertoires suggest that, in each brain, epigenetic elements play major and unpredictable roles. Categorical genetic determinism has no place in such systems; neither has instructionist empiricism. Instead, genetic and developmental factors interact to yield systems of remarkable complexity capable of an equally remarkable degree of freedom. The constraints placed on this freedom . . . do not seem as impressive as the unending ability of . . . the brain to confront novelty, to generalize upon it, and to adapt in unforeseen fashions. (1987, p. 329)

This modern expression of the generativity, dynamics, and complexity of the human nervous system is reminiscent of Sherrington's apt metaphor that the brain operates like "an enchanted loom where millions of flashing shuttles weave a dissolving pattern though never an abiding one; a shifting harmony of subpatterns" (1940, p. 184).

Conclusion

The point of all this is neither to reduce human change processes to biochemical patterns nor to "neurologize" about key concepts in psychotherapy—quite the contrary. There are already too many instances of perpetuated misinformation about brain and behavior. The often-cited statement that humans use less than 10 percent of their brain potential is one example (most modern experts agree that this assertion is meaningless given our current ignorance about the concepts of brain "use" and "potential"). Another is the widespread "false certainty" about the number of neurons in the human brain. Soper and Rosenthal (1988) examined thirty-one introductory psychology texts and found that their estimates ranged from ten billion to one trillion; fewer than one third of the authors cited a source for their statement, and only one concluded that we do not really know.

The point is that brain and body are integrated systems and are, moreover, embedded in and interactive with social systems that influence their functioning (McGuire and Troisi 1987). Just as the body (and bodily experience) are unmistakably "in the mind" (Johnson 1987), the body is also "in" the brain, and vice versa. (I shall here resist discussion of the important differences between the concepts of *mind* and *brain* [see Popper and Eccles 1977; Pribram 1986; Sperry 1988].) The experience and implications of our biological embodiment should not be overshadowed by our interest in our own encephalization. To neglect that embodiment is to risk "cephalocaudal inversion: a rare disorder which enables the afflicted person to sit on his/her own shoulders" (Mahoney 1980*c*, p. 511). With the help of continuing work in clinical health psychology and behavioral medicine, we can hope that past and present turf battles between psychology and medicine will be replaced in the near future by collaborative alliances that recognize and encourage the health-seeking holism of active, developing selves in complex and dynamic systems.

E. THE SCIENCES OF COMPLEXITY

Western philosophy and science have traditionally glorified order and denigrated disorder. Our notions of reality, rationality, and meaning have assumed and sought to reveal a "natural" and universal order, the ultimate and absolute rules of Truth and existence. It is not coincidental, then, that violations of the prevailing order have usually been cast in negative terms. The diseases and "pathologies" of the brain and body, for example, are commonly called "disorders," and civil "unrest" has been stigmatized as a threat to social and moral order. Science has been enshrined as the search for universal regularities, and deviations from the "received view" of order (that is, currently consensual reality) have rarely been welcomed. Indeed, in the context of human societies, individuals or groups who have challenged the "natural" or "revealed" order of things have been branded as evil, "possessed," subversive, "demented," unhealthy, and generally undesirable (Berger 1967; Berger and Luckman 1966; Foucault 1965, 1970; Goffman 1963; Gove 1982; Jones et al. 1984; Scheff 1975; Szasz 1970).

We humans are developmentally "open" systems, however, and everything we now know about knowing indicates that we are particularly bent upon and adept at "ordering" our lives and the worlds through which we live them. Studies of comparative psychology and developmental processes in scientific thought suggest that humans are unique in their development of capacities to stabilize, "fix," or otherwise abstract structural properties (their own and that of their worldly neighborhoods [Holton 1986; Szamosi 1986]). The frenzied search for a "grand unifying theory" in physics is a relevant illustration. It is also an ironic one because the intensity of that search has contributed to the conceptual revolution reflected in the decline of rationalist objectivism. In physics, a grand unifying theory (GUT) would explain the relations of the four known forces in our universe: gravitational, electromagnetic, and weak and strong nuclear. (For a survey of past and present efforts to pull it all together, see Bohm 1980; Boslough 1985; Briggs and Peat 1984; Gutting 1980; Hawking 1988; Holton 1986; Pagels 1988; Radnitzky 1987b; Rorty 1979; Waldrop 1988a; and Weisskopf 1979.)

Historical Antecedents of the Sciences of Complexity

A central aspect of the third axial shift has been its so-called deconstruction of classical rationalism, objectivism, and the linear determinism that had dominated philosophy and science since their respective origins. The emergence of the critical and "postcritical" philosophies inaugurated some of the ideas that would lead to the study of complex phenomena in the present century. Although I have dated the inception of the third

axial period at approximately 1900 (chapter 2), there were clearly important precedents to the developments that marked that turning point. The
contributions of David Hume, Immanuel Kant, and the Scottish "moral
philosophers" are among the most important of those precedents.
Weimer (1982) has documented the conceptual bankruptcy of eighteenth-century rationalism demonstrated by Hume and later elaborated
by Kant, Hayek, and Popper. In showing that no act of inductive inference
can be logically "justified," Hume laid the groundwork for the later
demolition of all justificational (authority-based) epistemologies. A skeptical empiricist himself, Hume demoted "scientific method" to "mere
animal belief" and, along with all other forms of induction, reclassified
it as *psycho*logical rather than logical (Hayek 1944, 1948, 1952*a*, 1952*b*,
1964, 1967, 1973, 1978, 1979, 1982; Weimer 1979, 1982*a*, 1982*b*, 1987).

Hume paved the way for later criticisms of rationalist interventionism
and was an important contributor to pre-Darwinian evolutionary
thought. "By stressing the limits of explicit rationality; the unavailability
of conclusive method in knowledge acquisition; and the psychological
basis of knowledge, inference, and expectation, Hume was able to account for the appearance of rational social phenomena by emphasizing
the notions of the evolution of social systems over time and the spontaneous formation of an order" (Weimer 1982*b*, p. 259). As Hayek has noted,
Mandeville and Hume showed that the sense of justice in society "was not
originally implanted in man's mind but had, like that mind itself, grown
in a process of gradual evolution which at least in principle we might learn
to understand" (1978, p. 265). In other words, our moral and social rules
are not the products of conscious or explicit rational planning. Society
and its complex dynamics are instead what Adam Ferguson (1767) described as *the result of human action but not of human design.*

The Perils of Rationalist Interventionism

Rationalist interventionism is the practice of trying to manipulate, control, or otherwise intervene in the ongoing dynamics of an open system.
As noted in chapter 4, however, it is simply ludicrous to assert that any
given individual (or group of "experts" or executives, for that matter) can
(a) have access to, (2) adequately comprehend, and (3) accurately infer
the future implications of the vast and ever-changing information distributed throughout a complex order. This is, nevertheless, the assumption of those who purport rationally to plan and strategically to control
aspects of that order (economically and otherwise), and it lies at the heart
of utopian philosophies and rationalist interventionism:

That we should not be able fully to shape human affairs according to our wishes
went against the grain of generations which believed that by the full use of his

reason man could make himself fully master of his fate. It seems, however, that this desire to make everything subject to rational control, far from achieving the maximal use of reason, is rather an abuse of reason based on a misconception of its powers, and in the end leads to a destruction of that free interplay of many minds on which the growth of reason nourishes itself. True rational insight seems indeed to indicate that one of its most important uses is the recognition of the proper limits of rational control. (Hayek 1967, p. 93)

The perspective championed by Hayek in the Humean tradition is one that has sweeping implications for psychotherapy. I endorse Hayek's perspective and suggest that it recommends a therapeutic "style" that is flexible, open, and individually empowering without being preoccupied with controlling, corrective, and directive techniques.

The point being made here relates not only to the limits of explicit rationality but also to the wisdom of teleological thinking. *Teleology* (from the Greek *telos,* "end," and *logos,* "order") refers to "final causes" or to directionality defined by a specific goal or end-state. The concept has a rich history in theology. In theology the teleological argument—also known as the "argument from design"—served as a major rationalization for the existence of God until it was logically demolished by Hume and, inadvertently, by Kant (see Hick 1964; Hume 1947 [1779]; Kant 1929 [1781]; Kaufmann 1958, 1959, 1961; and Matson 1965). The underlying assumption of teleology is that all order requires or implies intentional or purposeful design. But the complexities of social and economic life posed significant problems for that assumption, and additional challenges were provided by later evolutionary studies and the maturation of the biological sciences. According to Atlan (1987), it was not, however, until the 1950s that an alternate term was developed to describe spontaneously emerging orders.

Teleonomy is now used differently by various writers, but I use it here to refer to directionality without a final goal. Since *nomos* means "law" in Greek, the two terms are semantically—or, more accurately, etymologically—indistinguishable, but I know of no other single term that might convey what is central here: that is, the self-organizing emergence of directionality. The most kindred term is perhaps Waddington's *homeorhesis* (1940). The two best examples of teleonomy are perhaps biological evolution and human personality development. There is an apparent directionality to both (at least in historical hindsight), and yet neither can be said to be seeking a specific final form or destination. The distinction between teleological and teleonomic systems is important since very different principles apply in their operation. Hayek (1952*b*, 1964, 1967, 1973, 1978) develops this same distinction in terms of rationally planned and spontaneously emergent orders. He terms the former a *taxis* and the latter a *cosmos.* I have chosen not to use his terminology here only because it is probably even less familiar to most readers than the terms I have employed. For a readable discussion of Hayek's concepts, Weimer (1982*b*) is the best available secondary source. Burrell's (1987) analysis elaborates the relevance of Hayek's thinking for the conceptualization and practice of psychotherapy.

A teleological system, for example, is developmentally constrained by its "singleminded" aim at a specific end-state, a concrete and literal spatiotemporal "destination." It is an operationally "closed" system whose movements through space and time are not open to renegotiation. It is literally "bound and determined" by its operational logic.

A teleonomic system is one that reflects self-organizing directionality. The emphasis is shifted from destination to general direction, and the latter is neither narrow nor simple. In a living system, for example, the directions and forms of development are infinite in their diversity and yet undeniably bounded. The "contexts of constraint" (limits) of spontaneously self-organizing systems are their operational and experiential boundaries, so to speak, which vary in and across systems. Some of these boundaries are the phenomenological limits that psychotherapy clients often describe. As I illustrated at the conclusion of this book, there are important differences between psychological services that are based in rationalist interventionism and those associated with a respect for teleonomic, self-organizing processes.

Chaos and the Study of Dynamic Systems

The foregoing developments in philosophy laid the groundwork for ideas that are central to modern analyses of dynamic, complex systems. The most recent illustrations of those ideas have come from the relatively new field of study called "chaos." As James Gleick put it, "Where chaos begins, classical science stops. For as long as the world has had physicists inquiring into the laws of nature, it has suffered a special ignorance about disorder. . . . The irregular side of nature, the discontinuous and erratic side—these have been puzzles to science, or worse, monstrosities" (1987, p. 3). Gleick's book is probably the best nontechnical overview of this area, but Pagels (1988) also offers an introduction and Hofstadter's (1985) *Metamagical Themas* contains some enjoyable essays on the topic. Although they often wax technical, I also recommend some of the original classics in nonlinear dynamics and catastrophe theory (Lorenz 1963; Mandelbrot 1977; Maruyama 1963, 1977; Monod 1971; Sparrow 1982; Thom 1975; Woodcock and Davis 1978; Yorke and Li 1975; and Zeeman 1976, 1977). (For synopses of current applications, see Ornstein 1989 and Pool 1989*a*.)

The study of "dynamic systems" became increasingly popular in the 1970s, and a veritable revolution in both method and theory resulted in more and more conferences, books, and journals devoted to the study of physical change processes and what some have termed "the science of becoming" (as contrasted with the earlier preoccupation with fixed states of being). Some proponents of this new perspective claim that twentieth-century science will be remembered for three things: relativity, quantum mechanics, and chaos. "Relativity eliminated the Newtonian illusion of absolute space and time; quantum theory eliminated the Newtonian dream of a controllable measurement process; and chaos eliminates the Laplacian fantasy of deterministic probability" (Gleick 1987, p. 6). As Karl Popper (1972*b*) noted in his brilliant essay on the differences between clouds and clocks as determined systems, there is substantially less predictability in the behavior of complex, open systems than in simple, closed ones. Meteorologists must deal with that complexity in their weather predictions, and it is not coincidental that some of the major figures in the field of chaos have struggled with the dynamics of weather, fluid turbulence, and living systems. In such dynamic systems, there is a sensitivity to tiny differences in the value of early "input" variables which may dramatically alter the course of later developments. This "sensitive dependence on initial conditions" is termed "the Butterfly Effect" in meteorology, based on the half-facetious notion that the air turbulence created by a butterfly's wings somewhere over the Mediterranean today may influence the development of a hurricane off the coast of North America next month. As far-fetched as that metaphor may seem, it captures the essence of the principle.

Historically, the pioneers in the study of system dynamics are few. Jules Henri Poincaré was a key figure in the earliest attempts to develop a science of dynamic systems and to apply the methods of algebraic topology to their study. He was the last great mathematician to argue in favor of using geometrical concepts to improve studies of physical systems in movement. His mathematical style was more intuitive than rigorous, and yet he was among the first to understand the possibility of studying the process dynamics of complex systems. After Poincaré's death in 1912, the algebraic topology he founded continued to thrive, but interest in the study of dynamic systems declined. A partial exception to that decline was the work of D'Arcy Wentworth Thompson, whose 1917 *On Growth and Form* is still considered a classic. Thompson had catalogued a wide range of natural forms and noted that their undeniable similarities might imply a similarity in their morphogenetic (form-generating) processes. He showed, for example, that similarities in the skulls of different species became apparent when they were graphed on a rectilinear grid so that differences in size were taken into account.

Poincaré and Thompson were unique in their foresights, however, and it was not until the middle and latter half of the present century that their contributions were to become more generally appreciated. One of the first scientists to extend their works was C. H. Waddington, the evolutionary biologist. In the 1930s, Waddington and his colleagues studied morphogenesis via the embryonic development of ancient ammonites (spiral-shelled sea animals similar to the chambered nautilus). These studies convinced Waddington that the concept of homeostasis (steady-state maintenance) developed in the nineteenth century by Claude Bernard had to be supplemented with a new concept, which he termed "homeorhesis." *Homeorhesis* (which means "same path" in Greek) refers to processes of biological development that pursue a stable (invariant) course of change or development. Again, the shift in emphasis was from (teleological) destinations (in this case, the static equilibrium of "steady states") to more general directions (developmental paths). In terms and concepts reminiscent of Alfred North Whitehead's "process philosophy," Waddington argued for the importance of studying the changes observed in living systems throughout the course of their development. In significant respects, the writings of Whitehead and Waddington on "epigenetic processes" in development would prepare their respective fields (philosophy and biology) for their later encounters with the ideas developed by Ilya Prigogine and his colleagues (see below and Hartshorne and Peden 1981; Waddington 1940, 1968–72).

As to the recent explosion of interest in the study of complexity, a few individuals and events offer a sketch of significant developments. Edward Lorenz was a meteorologist at MIT in 1963 when he made the first major breakthrough in the study of complex system dynamics. Lorenz developed differential equations to deal with how three interacting variables might change over time, and how their relationships might be relevant to the prediction of weather. What Lorenz encountered was, much to his own surprise, that slight changes in the initial conditions of systems resulted in dramatic differences in their ultimate form and function. Lorenz's work led him to discover the phenomena now called *strange attractors,* in which the "temporal becoming" of a system demonstrates recursive or self-referential processes. Later, Benoit Mandelbrot and his "fractal geometry" elegantly demonstrated how seemingly simple recursiveness can account for some of the infinite complexities encountered in phenomena ranging from the snowflake to continental shorelines (Mandelbrot 1977).

Studies of fluid dynamics and turbulence have converged upon some fascinating complexities in ostensibly simple phenomena and, conversely, the emergence of some simple rules that can describe dynamic regularities in nonlinear phenomena. What scientists had formerly ignored as "random" or "chance" noise in the universal order has become an increasingly popular topic of study. The idea of "error variance," for example, was itself an error. The variance, diversity, and mutability of complex phenomena have now been recognized as a leading area of scientific inquiry. The patterned dynamics of the water stream as it is parted by your toothbrush are both simple and complex; we are beginning to appreciate the complementarity of those concepts. The particulars of specifics are no more predictable than they were a century ago, but some fascinating patterns and processes have recently been suggested.

There have been many significant contributions to the study of nonlinear dynamics since the publication of the Lorenz equations, and the range of their expressions is itself testimony to the robustness of complexity as a research direction. In the tradition of Poincaré, for example, E. Christopher Zeeman (1976, 1977) and René Thom (1975) have shown the relevance of topological models of sudden change in their writings on *catastrophe theory*. There were some sparks of enthusiasm over their ideas in the late 1970s, especially when some of the fundamental forms of catastrophe were expressed in terms familiar to behavioral scientists. But those sparks did not develop into a flame, and future historians may well wonder whether the meager appreciation of catastrophe theory was due, in part, to its unfortunate choice of sociobiology as a "running mate" when the latter was just about to be rejected for its extremism by mainstream science (Kitcher 1985, 1987).

Studies in medical physiology have also brought some of these phenomena closer to home for psychologists by illustrating how our "brains make chaos in order to make sense of the world" (from Skarda and Freeman 1987, p. 161; see also Babloyantz, Salazar, and Nicolis 1985; and Pool 1989*b*). There is now little doubt that we experience and express opponent processes at numerous levels, and "mistakes" in our self-referential biology lie at the heart of both cancer and the dreadful diseases of "immune deficiency." As research in the field of psychoneuroimmunology has shown, the moving balance that constitutes health is fundamentally related to our relations with ourselves. The ongoing and coordinating activities of the human body and nervous system, for example, reflect both rhythms and "dysrhythms," and recent advances in the study of several "disorders" suggest that slight differences in integrative, self-organizing capacities may result in both acute and chronic patterns of human suffering (Antonovsky 1979; Aschoff 1981; Healy and Williams 1988; Larsen 1987; Luce 1971; McGuire and Troisi 1987; Watson and Tellegen 1985; Weil 1983; Zevon and Tellegen 1982). The point is that models embracing complex nonlinear dynamics have begun to demonstrate their superiority over traditional and simplistic accounts of our experience. "Disorder" is not an aberration but a necessary aspect of the essential tensions that characterize self-organizing, living systems.

Order out of Chaos

Another area of research that has made contributions to our conceptualization and study of complex phenomena has been in *nonequilibrium thermodynamics,* a specialization that bridges chemistry and physics. Until recently, the "laws" of thermodynamics were thought to be so well demonstrated that they were beyond revision. Perhaps the most famous such law was that announced by Rudolph Clausius in 1850 and termed the "second law of thermodynamics," also known as the "law of entropy." *Entropy* is the amount of disorder in a system at a given point in time; negative entropy, called *negentropy,* refers to the amount of order in a system. Briefly stated, the law of entropy asserts that all physical processes in the universe contribute to an inevitable increase in entropy (disorder), the ultimate consequence being that the universe is gradually moving toward a random (disorganized) distribution of its total mass and energy. Illustrations of this principle in elementary science classes have shown how drops of ink in a liquid solution will tend to distribute themselves evenly throughout the solution. This random distribution is said to reflect a static equilibrium, in which the drops have reached a resting state of total, random disorder. The implications of the law of entropy were not optimistic: in its portrayal, the future holds only an ultimate and inevitable degeneration of existing structures.

The Self-Replicating Hypercycle. But the law of entropy was at odds with more than human hopes. Biology and the young life sciences were full of counterexamples to degeneration and disorganization. Evolutionary perspectives showed that, at least in living systems, there was a clear and forceful trend toward self-organization and structural complexity. By and large, life exhibits relentless differentiation and ordering rather than degeneration. This apparent paradox went formally unresolved for more than a century, although it continually reared its dual heads in nineteenth- and twentieth-century debates over physical determinism and the "tough-" and "tender-mindedness" of "hard science" and the humanities (Eiseley 1958; Fiske and Schweder 1986; Hook 1958; Kimble 1984; Monod 1971; Richards 1987; Snow 1964). However, with progress in theoretical and evolutionary biology and thermodynamics, the paradox has now been scaled to proportions that resolve the apparent contradiction. Some of these contributions came from the evolutionary biologist C. H. Waddington and later from the works of Manfred Eigen. Eigen formulated a principle of natural self-organization based on "the self-reproducing catalytic hypercycle," now known simply as the *hypercycle.* In essence, the chemical activity described by the hypercycle is recursive and "auto-catalytic" (self-precipitating), so that two or more molecular systems (as of proteins and nucleotides) interact in such a way that by-products of their interaction actually serve to stabilize and perpetuate their pattern of interaction (see figure A.1). In biological systems a hypercycle is the most basic and primitive form of symbiosis, and it is likely that the self-reproducing hypercycle played an important role in precellular, cellular, and systemic evolution (see appendix F; Eigen 1971; Eigen and Schuster 1979; Eigen and Winkler 1981; Jantsch 1980).

Figure A.1   The Self-Reproducing Hypercycle

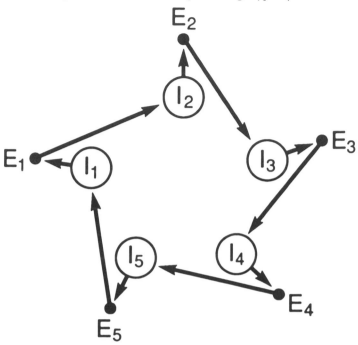

SOURCE: © 1989 M. J. Mahoney

Dissipative Structures. In chemistry, the major breakthrough in the study of self-organizing complexity is associated with the work of Ilya Prigogine and his colleagues on what they call "dissipative structures." Until the work of Prigogine, the non-equilibrium that was pervasively encountered in the study of thermodynamic systems was believed to be an uninteresting and temporary disturbance of the true (static) equilibrium predicted by the law of entropy. But, like his colleagues studying turbulence and chaos, Prigogine believed that the wellsprings of order lay somewhere in the dynamics of disorder. He struggled to develop a theory that could explain how a relatively simple system, like that depicted in figure A.2, could "lawfully" become one as complex as that in figure A.3. After thirty years of work, he eventually demonstrated just that. In 1977, Prigogine was awarded the Nobel prize in chemistry for his *theory of dissipative structures* and its revolutionary reframing of the second law of thermodynamics (Prigogine 1980; Prigogine and Stengers 1984; for more comprehensive discussions of Prigogine's work and its implications, see Jantsch 1980, 1981; Jantsch and Waddington 1976; and Zeleny 1980).

Figure A.2   The Structure of a Chemical System before Transformation

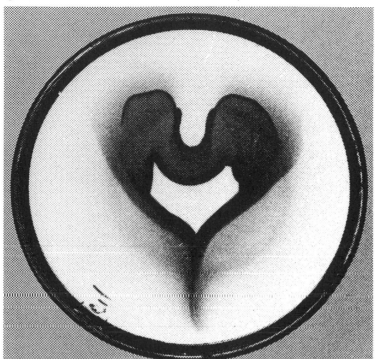

SOURCE: Photograph courtesy of Fritz Goro.

Briefly stated, Prigogine's work showed that the law of entropy applies only to thermodynamically isolated systems, and the universe itself is the only such system now known (other than those "artificially isolated" systems created in scientific laboratories). In a thermodynamically *isolated* system, neither matter nor energy can leave or enter. A thermodynamically *open* system, on the other hand, allows for the exchange of both matter and energy with its environment. Finally, a thermodynamically *closed* system can accommodate gains and losses of energy, but not of mass (Brent 1978). In open systems, both living and nonliving, the second law must be revised to account for the spontaneous emergence of structures that are self-perpetuating and relatively stable over time. Prigogine was able to show that this remarkable accomplishment is achieved only under conditions that are far from equilibrium. In such systems, *coherence*, or structural integrity, is achieved by means of *dissipative structures*, so-called because they literally dissipate (scatter or "dump") their internally generated entropy (disorder) into their surrounding environment and simultaneously drain that environment of its assimilable negentropy (order).

Transcending the assumptions of Newton and Clausius, Prigogine

Figure A.3   The Structure of a Chemical System after Transformation

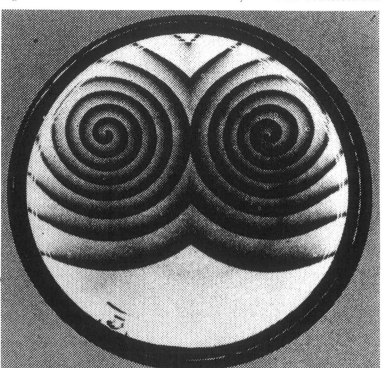

Source: Photograph courtesy of Fritz Goro.

demonstrated that order emerges from chaos via nonlinear dynamics. And, no matter how stable they are, dynamic systems are always undergoing *perturbations* (literally, "agitations" or "deviations") that reflect the complex interplay of their internal self-organizing activities and their ongoing exchanges with their local environments. So long as these perturbations do not exceed the "balancing" capacities of the system, it moves onward (through space and time) at the same average level of organizational complexity that would have been predicted by the second law of thermodynamics. But the perturbations can get out of hand as a result of both outside and inside dynamics. If the perturbations exceed a certain threshhold (the *bifurcation point*), a whole new level of principles is required to account for the processes that emerge. Prigogine subsumes this shift to a new level under the general principle of *order through fluctuations* because it involves a literal transformation of the system's organization brought about by the amplification and dynamic stabilization of some of its fluctuations. Those familiar with classical cybernetics may recognize that these dramatic shifts reflect the runaway operation of "deviation-amplifying" (positive feedback) processes, in contrast to the "deviation-dampening" (negative feedback) processes that maintain a fixed equilibrium (Maruyama 1963, 1977).

Readers familiar with Herbart's or Piaget's theories of "equilibration" may sense parallels in Prigogine's ideas. Living systems like ourselves exist as dynamic tensions of equilibrating ("balancing" or "ordering") and disequilibrating ("unbalancing" or "disordering") processes. We survive by transforming the high energy of disequilibrium into structures that serve our self-organization. Beyond our achievement of basic survival, however, we "develop" by undergoing changes in our organizational make-up. When the perturbations challenging an open system exceed that system's current assimilative capacities, whole-system fluctuations are amplified. It is here, within the context of our episodes of "disorder," that reorganization emerges:

What occurs . . . is that the macroscopic process of perturbation itself becomes a "giant" fluctuation which takes on steady state characteristics of its own. The properties of these macroscopic processes as a result become supraordinate to, rather than merely statistically derivative from, the "random" perturbations of its constituent elements at the microscopic level. The system as a whole thus shifts to a new, higher order, more complex structural form whose parts are governed by a new set of functional properties and characterized by a new set of statistical parameters. The age-old problem of "emergence" is thus given a specific place within this general theoretical approach. (Brent 1978, p. 380)

The new dynamic equilibrium that emerges is not a return to some prior (homeostatic) set point, however. Rather, it is an irreversible leap in the structural identity of the system. If and when such restructuring occurs, the more complex system that emerges is capable of assimilating perturbations like the ones that initiated its transformation (as well as others not yet encountered). The emergence of a more viable organization is not, however, an inevitable outcome of runaway fluctuations: some systems will settle into a less viable structure and suffer the consequences. In other words, the dynamics of disorder create opportunities for reorganization, but do not create or guide a system in its structural metamorphosis. Some systems will lack the capacities, resources, or good fortune to sustain a successful transformation, in which case they will struggle (chronically) and/or degenerate in the process.

Research in neuroscience has already demonstrated the relevance of Prigogine's work for our understanding of the organizational dynamics of the central nervous system (see appendix D) and there is increasing acknowledgment of its implications for our conceptualization of human psychological development and psychological services (Bienenstock 1985; Bienenstock, Soulie, and Weisbuch 1986; Brent 1978, 1984; Dell 1982a, 1982b; Dell and Goolishian 1981; Ford 1987; Szentágothai and Érdi 1989). Suffice it to say here that this is not, in my opinion, just another (misguided) attempt by social scientists to borrow the terms and concepts of physics and chemistry to bolster their own assertions or illusions of being scientific. Both literally and metaphorically, the theory of dissipative structures offers fascinating lessons about the dynamics of survival and development as an open system. Those dynamics are illustrated in figure A.4.

Some of the concepts invoked by Prigogine offer valuable metaphors for discussions of emotionality and the phenomenology of psychological change (chapters 7–12). I believe that episodes of intense emotional distress and disorder often reflect natural (and, yes, even healthy) expressions of an individual's struggles toward reorganization. Such struggles are not always successful, of course, but they may be viewed with substantially less fear and impatience (on the part of both clients and therapists) if they are construed as the activities of an open, developing system in search of a "more extensive balance" with its world. For the time being, however, it is important only to remember that developmental dynamics appear to be nonlinear and fundamentally based in the seeming chaos of systemic dis/re-organization.

F. HUMAN EVOLUTION

Current estimates place the birth of our universe at about 15 billion years ago—an expanse of time so incomprehensible to us as to require translation to human proportions. Such a translation is afforded by what is called the "cosmic calendar": a mathematical transformation in which these 15 billion years are compressed into an earthly year of 365 days. This transformation has been used by a number of writers on cosmology and evolution. In such a calendar, the Big Bang occurred in the first micromoment of New Year's Day and the second that is now passing represents the last micromoment of December 31. In this transformation, a *cosmic calendar day* is comprised of about 41 million earth years, and a *cosmic second* is 475 years. As shown in table A.2, the cosmic calendar offers a novel perspective on the time course of our universal evolution, including the relative recency and rapid proliferation of life on earth. Very soon after its cooling, the planet was teeming with life. The forms we find most interesting, however—ourselves and our mammalian predecessors—are also the most recent. Indeed, primates did not appear until the (cosmic) day before yesterday, human (hominid) forms are less than three hours old, and "modern" humans have yet to complete their second minute of existence. In less than two cosmic minutes, though, humans have literally transformed the planet. Our written records cover only the last nine seconds, and whatever we mean by "formal knowledge" and "consciousness" must be considered literally "newborn."

The evolutionary appearance and subsequent elaboration of the cell

Figure A.4   The Belousov-Zhabotinskii Reaction in Stages

SOURCE: Photographs courtesy of Fritz Goro.
NOTE: This chemical reaction occurs when malonic acid is oxidized by bromate in the presence of cerium ions. The stages are here depicted by columns, beginning at the left and moving downward (within columns) and left-to-right (across columns).

was a dramatic leap forward in the survival and proliferation of life on this planet. The simplest single cell—albeit lacking a nucleus and the division of intracellular metabolic labor—had achieved the monumental step of literally defining and maintaining its own integrity through the strategic use of a boundary (Churchman 1984). By creating and maintaining a membrane between itself and its world, the simple cell carved out a context for growth and development. More important than the membrane or boundary itself, however, were the *self-organizing processes* that allowed life forms to expand and develop themselves in co-evolution with their worlds. As discussed in chapter 6, the "self-replicating hypercycle" studied by Eigen and his colleagues appears to have played an important role in this evolutionary achievement. Simple hypercycles were probably the precursors of cells, and they are involved extensively in the maintenance and development of all subsequent life forms (Eigen and Schuster

Table A.2   The Cosmic Calendar

January 1		The Big Bang
May 1		Emergence of the Milky Way
September 9		Emergence of our solar system
September 14		Formation of Earth
September 25		First life forms on Earth
November 1		Sexual differentiation by microorganisms
December 16		First worms
December 19		First fish and vertebrates
December 21		First insects
December 22		First amphibians
December 23		First trees and reptiles
December 24		First dinosaurs
December 26		First mammals
December 28		Dinosaurs became extinct
December 29		First primates
December 31	9:06 P.M.	First hominids (*Australopithecus*)
	11:58:15	First "modern" humans (*Homo sapiens*)
	11:59:21	Emergence of agriculture
	11:59:35	First cities
	11:59:51	Invention of the alphabet
	11:59:56	Roman empire
	11:59:58	Crusades and Mayan civilization
	11:59:59	Renaissance and discovery of the New World
	12:00:00	1990

NOTE: The data are drawn primarily from Sagan (1977) and Jantsch (1980).

1977, 1978). As simple single cells evolved, they became more complex. Thus, for example, the DNA weight of a single human cell is about 16,000 times greater than that of a simple single-cell organism (Land 1973). The evolutionary development of the single cell is itself a microcosmic history of the self-organizing processes that afforded "higher" life forms.

With the emergence of the cell nucleus came more advanced organization and the beginnings of intracellular division of labor. Likewise with the appearance of early sexual differentiation, which allowed life to beget itself not only by simple replication but through genetic exchange. Although these sexual life forms were significantly more successful at reproductive survival than their predecessors, their increased viability meant that they were subject to the "new" phenomena of aging and ultimate death:

Sexuality can only represent one side of a principle the other side of which is *death* [of the individual organism]. . . . In purely vertical reproduction by asexual cell division, there is no natural death, only forced death. Amoebae do not die. The dividing cells do not age and continue to divide if the environmental conditions are favorable. The prokaryotes living today are still the same which populated the earth in the early phases of life. (Jantsch 1980, p. 126)

As Woody Allen has poignantly reminded us, love and death are companion processes.

The progression from simple to complex and unicellular to multicellular life also brought significant shifts in the relative balance of power between organism and environment. While the single-cell organism is hardly a passive participant in its own survival, its capacity to alter and use its own environment is limited relative to that of a complex multicellular organism. With increasing complexity and capacity came a dramatic shift toward adaptation *of* (rather than *to*) the ambient environment:

The harmony of a quiescent environment is disturbed greatly when a living being absorbs it, dismembers it, rearranges it, and transforms it into its own living form. The environment changes substantially more than the organism. As with biological systems, this active adapting of and transformation of the environment is actually the most prominent characteristic of both biological and psychological systems. (Land 1973, pp. 171–72)

A composition of many cells allowed the luxury of specialization within those cells, but specialization also placed increasing demands on the organism to develop the processes necessary for communication and coordination within its divisions of labor.

Neural Evolution and Encephalization

In the earliest differentiations of simple multicellular organisms, signs of cellular specialization are associated with the physical location of cells during the early development of the organism. A cup shape is common in these early stages, and two or three layers of cells are discernible: (1) an outside layer called the *ectoderm;* (2) an inside layer known as the *endoderm;* and—in later and more complex life forms—(3) a middle layer, the *mesoderm.* Corresponding in general to their physical location, cells in each of these early layers will specialize in serving the organism. The endoderm ("inner skin") layer will thus specialize in internal metabolic processes, particularly digestion; and the cells of the mesoderm ("middle skin") will afford movement and motor behavior. Cells from the early ectodermal ("outer skin") layer will eventually become the organism's "skin" and (in vertebrates) nervous system. Since we associate human complexity with a highly developed nervous system, the origins of the neuron are of particular interest. There is significance in the fact that the nervous system and the skin both originated from the ectoderm. As Montagu (1978) has pointed out, for example, it suggests that the skin might be considered an "external nervous system." He uses this linkage to organize research and theory on the role of touch in psychological well-being. Whatever its implications, it is clear that *our core and our boundaries have emerged from the same origins.*

Evolution of the Neuron. What is today known as the neuron began many millions of years ago as a *primitive sensorimotor unit.* These units are still apparent on the surface of some single-cell organisms (for example, protozoa, metazoa) where they serve the dual (and undifferentiated) functions of sensation *and* action. As shown in figure A.5, the primitive sensorimotor unit began as an onion-shaped entity with a pyramid-shaped extension that was sensitive to changes in local chemical concentrations. Changes in those chemical concentrations cause a contraction of the onion-shaped portion of the unit—the prototype of modern muscle—and, hence, a primitive movement of the organism. These early sensorimotor units were a major developmental advantage in affording coordinated sensitivity and action. They were the archetypal precursors of our capacities to feel and actively to engage with our worlds. In this early specialization, sensation and action were inseparable. *Feeling and doing do not emanate from separate biological origins; they share a common ancestry.*

The next evolutionary development in the emergence of the neuron was the differentiation of the sensory and motor components of the primitive unit. This was accomplished by a gradual elongation of the motor (muscular) subunit, resulting in what we now know as the *axon.* Thus, as Heinz von Foerster has noted, the "generative" (axonal) portions of modern human neurons reflect the legacy of "degenerated muscle fibers" that sacrificed their contractility in the service of internal communication (von Foerster 1984). As recent studies in neurobiology have shown, axons are involved in the transmission not only of discrete electrochemical signals but also of "slow wave" patterns and critical elements in the interdependence of the human nervous and endocrine systems (Bergland 1985; Eccles 1977; Granit 1977, 1982; Pribram 1971, 1982, 1986; Weimer 1977). Out of the differentiated sensorimotor unit emerged the *internuncial neuron,* a nerve cell with a specialized bridge between its sensory and motor portions. This development was contributed by the sensory portion of the former sensorimotor unit. Eventually developing immense operational speed and formidable interconnections, the internuncial neuron set the stage for higher-order levels of knowing.

Figure A.5   The Evolution of the Neuron

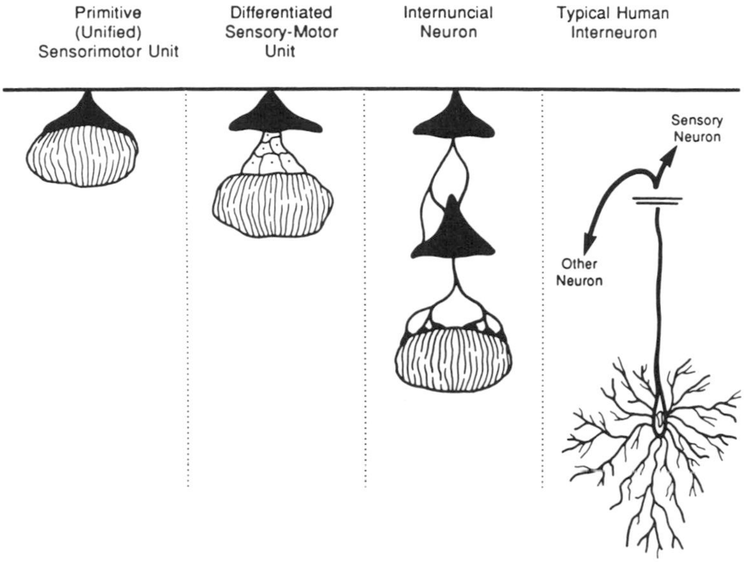

| Primitive (Unified) Sensorimotor Unit | Differentiated Sensory-Motor Unit | Internuncial Neuron | Typical Human Interneuron |

SOURCE: Adapted from von Foerster (1984)

Its ultimate successor, the modern *interneuron,* became the structurally dominant unit of the primate nervous system. The human neocortex, for example, which accounts for over 85 percent of the mature brain, is almost exclusively comprised of interneurons. Their interconnectedness is incomprehensible. Each of the estimated 30 billion neurons of the human brain (see appendix D) can have as many as 10,000 connections with other neurons. Thus, as noted in chapter 5, there are at least 100,000 times more interconnections among our neurons than there are connections with our sensory receptors. *We are, literally, more attuned to and engaged with our "inner selves" than to our external worlds.*

Encephalization and Systems Development. The earliest nervous *systems* were little more than indiscriminate nerve networks, and are still apparent in the coelenterates (hydra, jellyfish). These networks are relatively crude and chaotic systems, however, in that the activation of a single neuron excites the entire network and begets a response of the whole organism. There is no response discrimination and no fine motor control. Moreover, communication bottlenecks are common, and nerve impulse transmission is relatively slow. When the primitive nerve network was later eclipsed by the primitive nerve cord (as in flatworms), the nervous system was afforded its first differentiation as a specialized system. Soon after this development would follow the emergence of a functionally and structurally specialized "head" (Glezer, Jacobs, and Morgane 1988). The phenomenon of a differentiated nervous system has appeared only in organisms that are bilaterally symmetrical (those having mirror-image right and left sides), for reasons that may be related to the affordance of directed or controlled movement (see Polanyi 1958 for one interpretation). Isaac Asimov offers a readable synopsis of the argument:

An animal with no marked symmetry need have no preferred direction of movement. There is no reason why one particular leg of a starfish should take the lead in movement over any other. A creature with bilateral symmetry is usually longest in the direction of the plane of symmetry and tends to progress along that plane. Other directions of movement are possible, but one direction is preferred. If a bilaterally symmetric creature, by reason of its very shape and structure, adopts one preferred direction of movement, then one end of its body is generally breaking new ground as it moves. It is constantly entering a new portion of the environment. It is this end of the body which is the head. (1965, pp. 141–42)

The differentiation and enlargement of one end of the nerve cord is called *encephalization,* and humans are particularly impressed with their own heady development. What began as an enlargement and concentration of internal exchange and communication mechanisms in one end of the primitive nerve cord would eventually be dubbed the "crowning achievement" of evolutionary intelligence.

As encephalization progressed, further specializations emerged. In all vertebrates, for example, the neural tube exhibits three "swellings" in its early development. These swellings become centers of specialized development—*hindbrain, midbrain,* and *forebrain.* The hindbrain will eventually beget pons, medulla, and cerebellum, each serving critical functions in basic life support and coordinated movement. The midbrain will give rise to a small but important series of relay systems for internal communication, and the forebrain will engender the optic nerves and the neocortex.

Meanwhile, of course, much more than the nervous system was evolving. When mammals differentiated from reptiles about 165 million years ago, their rapid rise to dominance among life forms was associated with several significant increases in physical viability. Indeed, the progression from early to modern mammals reflects a wide range of developments in complexity and self-regulatory systems. *Homeostasis,* for example—the self-regulation of basic life support processes—is most highly developed among mammals. Operated by negative feedback loops and a sophisticated interaction of all bodily systems, homeostasis afforded us mammals more freedom to explore and exploit greater regions of our worlds. Such refinements were not, however, replacements of previous levels of organization so much as elaborations of them. This point is most aptly illustrated in the relatively recent recognition that every human being is the possessor/operator of four interrelated brains.

The Multiple Human Brain

However startling it may be to think that each human skull encases more than one brain, the evidence on this point is now substantial. The idea of multiple brains was first formalized by the psychobiologist Paul D. MacLean. He pointed out that, structurally and functionally, the human brain is comprised of three separate and relatively independent subbrains that reflect our evolutionary heritage.* Each of these brains has "its own sense of time and space and its own memory, motor, and other functions" (1973, p. 8). Enveloping each other in succession, these brains ultimately surround the *neural chassis* (hindbrain, midbrain, and spinal cord), which forms the foundation of basic life support (respiration, circulation, digestion, and so on). As successive elaborations of each preceding level, the three brains "add" increasing degrees of organization and self-preservation to the basically "vegetative" functions of the neural chassis. Figure A.6 shows Paul MacLean's model of the *triune brain* ("triune" means "three in one"; the fourth brain will be discussed on pages 433–35).

Figure A.6 The Triune Brain

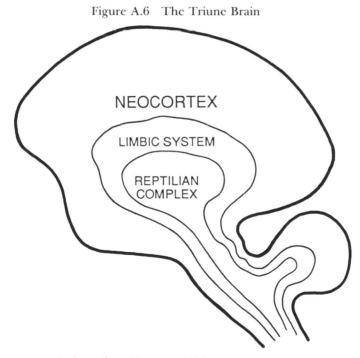

SOURCE: Redrawn from MacLean (1973)

*For a recent critique of oversimplifications and problems with this view, see A. Reiner (1990), "An explanation of behavior,"*Science* 250:303–5.

The Reptilian Complex. The *reptilian brain,* or *R-complex,* is the most ancient and primitive of the three brains described by MacLean. It evolved about 280 million years ago as a major development in early land-dwelling vertebrates. Reptiles dominated terrestrial life throughout the Mesozoic era (225 million to 65 million years ago), but most reptilian groups became extinct around the time that mammals rose to terrestrial dominance. The single greatest achievement of reptiles was their emergence from the watery environments that had constrained their predecessors (fish and amphibians). This was made possible by a modification of their scaly skin and the development of the amniote egg and internal fertilization. The reptilian brain was a major leap in neural evolution. Besides allowing life on land, the R-complex afforded an expanded repertoire of repetitive and ritualistic behaviors in the domains of migration, territoriality, aggression, and courtship. The reptilian system thus afforded primitive levels of genetically transmitted knowing, generally expressed in relatively inflexible and repetitive patterns of life-supporting behavior. Still guiding the lives of modern reptiles, this primitive brain relies almost exclusively on the sense of smell (olfaction) for its guidance through the environment, and its preferred form of defense is avoidance. When escape is impossible, reptiles deal with confrontations by threatening postures (such as enlargement, elevation of the head, sound generation) and biting.

From the perspective of human psychology, the most important achievement of the reptilian brain may have been its affordance of "homing . . . a recognized tendency among animals, after reaching out for food, for a mate, or whatever else, to return to a recognized frame of reference" (MacLean 1973, p. 10). The establishment of a frame of reference, if only in the autistic realm of inflexible repetition, may have been a precursor of later developments in human knowing. A home base imposed upon one's environment might well accommodate later exploratory ventures into that environment. Moreover, this primitive but powerful *active creation of order* may well have set the stage for the later human creation of "reality" (an orderly and temporally stable world).

Although the reptilian brain was a step forward relative to the more primitive neural chassis, its adaptive capacities were still limited. Because of its inflexibility, it was poor at handling novelty. This drawback is thought to have been a factor in the large-scale extinction of most reptilian groups just as mammals began to emerge. A number of environmental challenges during this era—including glaciation and possible fluctuations in ultraviolet radiation—may have taxed the reptilian brain beyond its capacities. Unable to break out of their ritualistic patterns at a time when environmental changes demanded novel problem solving, reptiles lost their terrestrial dominance to the "young upstart" mammals around 165 million years ago.

The Limbic System. It was with the evolution of mammals that our second brain first appeared as an overlapping neural fold engulfing and intertwining with the reptilian complex. This *paleomammalian* ("old mammal") brain—now better known as the *limbic system*—afforded dramatic improvements in adaptive flexibility:

The hallmarks of the mammalian level of organization are advanced reproduction and parental care, behavioral flexibility, and endothermy (the physiological maintenance of a relatively constant body temperature independent of that of the environment, allowing a high level of activity). Within the class, ecological diversity has resulted from adaptive specialization in food-getting, habitat preferences, and locomotion. (*Encyclopaedia Britannica*, 1981, vol. 11, p. 402)

The limbic brain serves its structural parents (the neural chassis and reptilian brain) by integrating and refining life-relevant behavior patterns (feeding, aggression, and reproduction). Thus, it did not replace or rule its predecessors, but instead collaborated with them as a higher-order emergence. Besides two subsystems that refined the reptilian sense of smell, the paleomammalian brain developed a specialized subsystem for vision, environmental orientation, and greater flexibility of action. Its refinements of the respiratory and circulatory systems allowed for a whole new order of neural functioning. In the mammal, there are also the first neural paths for sensing and responding to itself as well as to its environment, rendering "a functional bridge between the internal and external worlds," with "the tollgate regulating the flow of traffic . . . on the internal side of the bridge" (MacLean 1973, p. 54).

What the limbic system is best known for, however, is its introduction of emotional intensity and motivational complexity. A mistaken portrayal of early mammalian evolution is that it introduced "feelings" into living systems. The limited warrant for that generalization is that the active sensitivities and complexity of biological life were dramatically transformed in mammals. We should be careful, however, not to let our human feelings about feelings get in the way of our understanding of their development. Reptiles may not ostensibly care for their young or grieve over their dead, but their stubborn insistence on life over death can be meaningfully described as "passionate." Theories of emotionality have generally emphasized motivational systems in mammals and primates, and many also acknowledge the operation of primitive and powerful opponent processes at hierarchical levels of organization. In other words, knowing is evaluative, and the flow of our conscious experience is a succession of forms (contents) carved out of a background stream of dynamic sensitivities.

Not surprisingly, the leap in mammalian sensitivity was associated with emergent qualities in behavioral capacities. Anatomically, mammalian developments are attributed to the extensive interconnections between the limbic system and other body-brain systems—particularly the reticular activating system (which is involved in attention and overall alertness), the endocrine system (via the pituitary and the hypothalamus), and, in humans, the frontal cortex. This connectivity gives the limbic brain a fundamental role in the dynamic relations between old and new brains. All manner of approach/avoidance oscillations are fundamentally rooted in limbic processes, and studies of humans with limbic epilepsy suggest that this second brain modulates the full range of basic human feelings (hunger, thirst, apnea, nausea, fear, terror, anger, sadness, joy, and so on). All psychotropic drugs—whether therapeutic or recreational—act on limbic structures and processes.

Above and beyond the emotionality and behavioral flexibility afforded by the limbic system, it may well have provided the foundations for genuinely intentional life movement. Through structures like the amygdala and the hippocampus, for example, it may have enabled us to develop a functional memory system based on (and continuously updated by) individual experience. With early mammals and their later limbic elaborations we see dramatic improvements in reversible (flexible) learning, remembering, and anticipatory action. All of this emanated from a gut level of knowing, of course; but its capacity to mobilize and immobilize its owner—then and now—is truly awesome. Moreover, the early mammalian sensitivity to pain (which has more immediate relevance for survival than does pleasure) and its resourcefulness in avoiding pain were important developments.

To all of this may be added the emergence of a deepening sensitivity and devotion to offspring. From our human perspective, in fact, attention to the survival and nurturance of offspring may well have been the most significant mammalian innovation: parenting and socialization came to play central roles in primate and human evolution. During progressively longer periods of developmental dependency, offspring were not only protected and nourished but actively taught the lessons of their forebears. This extended preparation, which is longest in humans, had significant effects on the evolution of intimacy, the family, socialization, and language, as I shall discuss.

The paleomammalian brain was, then, a major development in neural complexity and integration. It seems to have been our first real thinking-and-feeling brain, a powerful venture beyond fixed reptilian patterns. With its complicated coordination of homeostatic life support, emotionality, learning, memory, and purposive action, the limbic system developed a primitive form of reflective intelligence. It was also a rich source of adaptive variations, pioneering the integration of inner and outer worlds and the beginnings of a time-binding memory/anticipation system. Mammals are a crafty and resourceful life form. Their flexible activity—made possible by their self-regulatory achievements—is also evident in the next major development in brain evolution.

The Neocortex. The *neomammalian* ("new mammal") brain, now commonly called the *neocortex,* developed relatively recently—somewhere around 50 million years ago—and is largest and most complex in the higher primates. It emerged from its reptilian and limbic predecessors as an early embryonic differentiation within the neural tube. Vertebrates "lower" than mammals have only a rudimentary cortex (originally a Latin term, which refers to the outer layer of an organ). What was immediately striking about this third brain was its rapid proliferation in primates—a growth that invited the concept of a "new" (neo) cortex, which accounts for 85 percent of the entire brain in *Homo sapiens.* The ratio of brain weight to body weight increases substantially as we ascend through primates and humans, but the relationship between this ratio and intelligence is not entirely straightforward (Jerison 1973, 1976; Passingham 1982). Although the human brain is about three times larger than would be predicted for any other primate our size, it would be misleading to suggest that this enlargement is solely due to proliferation of the neocortex. As shown in figure A.7, the relative proportions of different brain areas in humans reflect fairly widespread expansions. This figure shows the ratio of human brain area size to that predicted for a nonhuman primate of the same weight, but does not indicate the relative size of the frontal area of the brain—the area associated with intentionality, self-awareness, and higher mental organization. The frontal area in humans is over six times larger than that of other primates our size (Granit 1982). The dramatic co-evolution of the cortex and cerebellum and their ongoing interdependence have been noted by some "movement" and "body" therapies as well as by contemporary writers in self psychology (Cash and Pruzinsky 1990; Frick 1982).

Our pons and medulla are not much larger than would be predicted for a primate our size, but both our "paleocortex" and hippocampus are more than double their predicted sizes. Moreover, "it is in the extraordinary development of the cerebellum and the neocortex that the human brain is most specialized" (Passingham 1982, p. 83). These two areas are closely connected with one another (via the thalamus), and their interdependent collaborations figure prominently in our efforts toward adaptation. Movement and mentation are inseparable expressions of the same active, operational knowing processes.

The neocortex is generally considered the crowning achievement of neural evolution. Although this generalization overlooks the holistic complexity of a massively distributed heterarchical system, it would be foolish to deny the many human abilities uniquely associated with relative corticalization. It is inaccurate, however, to characterize the neocortex as the dominant or ruling brain. Reason and intellect, which are traditionally located in the neocortex, have fought a long (and relatively unsuccessful) battle for the control of our passions. We are well advised to learn something from that conflict. Part of the problem here stems from our

Figure A.7   Relative Brain Area Proportions (Ratio of Human Brain Area Size to That Predicted for a Nonhuman Primate of the Same Weight)

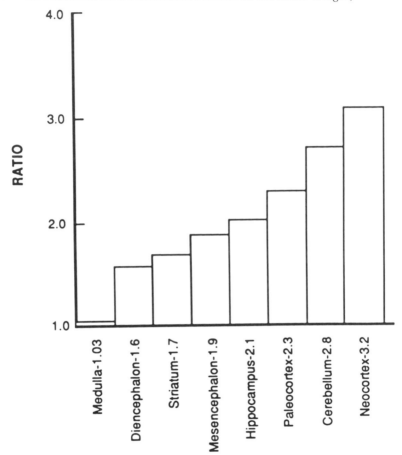

SOURCE: Adapted from Passingham (1982)

past infatuation with linear, ascending, and supplantive models of mind— what Peter Reynolds (1981) and others have called the *Victorian brain.* This model mistakenly assumes that rational, intellectual functions came to rule over the visceral "animal" from which they emerged. The impact of that model on twentieth-century psychology has yet to be fully appreciated. Reynolds points out, for example, that Freud was a student of Theodor Meynert, one of the principal proponents of the Victorian brain model; and that id, ego, and superego reflect an essentially evolutionary metatheory of individual psychological development (see also Masterton et al. 1976; Masterton, Hodos, and Jerison 1976).

The Specialized Hemispheres. The fourth and final human brain was actually a differentiation of the neocortex. Although MacLean has denied the need to invoke a fourth type of brain, the majority of modern neuroscientists have disagreed. Somewhere between 2 million and 14 million years ago, our hominid forebears developed and refined *bipedalism,* the capacity to walk on two legs. In doing so, they also wrought the phenomenon of *hemispheric specialization,* also known as *lateralization of function* (Corballis 1980; Davidson and Davidson 1980; Eccles 1977; Gazzaniga and LeDoux 1978; Geschwind and Galaburda 1987; Hamilton and Vermeire 1988; Jaynes 1977). Following the pioneering "split brain" research of Roger Sperry and others, it is now widely accepted that one (usually the left) hemisphere of the human neocortex specializes in higher-order symbolic processes (language, mathematics, and analytic logic), while the other (usually right) hemisphere is more adept at space-time relationships (rhythm, form, and synthetic operations). The reasons and the exclusiveness of this specialization are still being studied, but the essence of the generalization appears to be undisputed. What is particularly fascinating is the fact that the two hemispheres appear to function as independent "higher" brains with very different "styles" of operation. With your left (verbal/logical) hemisphere anesthetized, for example, you can sing but not speak; the reverse is true when the right hemisphere is asleep. Equally fascinating are the studies suggesting that aspects of our emotional experience may be complexly lateralized. In general, right hemispheric activity is associated with greater emotionality, and there is some evidence that negative emotions are related to activity in the right frontal region while positive emotions are more commonly associated with activity in the left frontal region (Buck 1986; Davidson 1984; LeDoux and Hirst 1986).

Research on hemispheric specialization has also pointed to the limitations and arrogance of our verbal left hemispheres. Studies have repeatedly shown, for example, that the human left hemisphere will fabricate explanations for feelings and body states emanating from right hemisphere activity. Because language is so powerfully involved in our constructions of knowledge and consciousness, however, we may be inclined to place more confidence in our fabrications than in the experiential mysteries they purport to explain:

We are faced, it seems, with a new problem in analyzing the person. The person is a conglomeration of selves—a sociological entity. Because of our cultural bias toward language and its use, as well as the richness and flexibility that it adds to our existence, the governor of these multiple selves comes to be the verbal system. Indeed, a case can be made that the entire process of maturing in our culture is the process of the verbal system's trying to note and eventually control the behavioral impulses of the many selves that dwell inside us. (Gazzaniga and LeDoux 1978, p. 161)

With the hominid specialization of the cerebral hemispheres, our brains became *quadune* ("four in one"). Even with this acknowledgment, however, our mental complexity may be understated. As shown in figure A.8, the dynamic balance of central and peripheral subdivisions in the human nervous system is itself complicated by still further differentiations among these parts. The left hemisphere literally developed its own language(s) and accelerated into symbolic knowing, never able to transfer its wisdom to its mute-but-masterful twin except through the actions and feelings of the body they share. The gap between head and heart is more than metaphorical, and the failure to recognize these (and other) gaps as expressions of neural complexity remains a major problem for theoretical psychology. Contrary to the claims of modern rationalism—including the rationalist cognitive therapies—thought does not dictate either feeling or action.

Each successive step in brain development involved an elaboration or refinement of prior capacities plus transformations afforded by neural reorganization, division of labor, and novel activities. Although human neocortical processes reflect a legacy of limbic and reptilian evolution, we have not retained all of our ancestors' capacities. Structural and functional sacrifices are readily apparent. We humans and other primates have a relatively poor sense of smell, for example, and are deaf to high frequency sound. Our visual systems are, on the other hand, very sensitive to color, depth, and distance; and our forelimbs and hands allow a degree of environmental manipulation unknown to our evolutionary forebears. These sacrifices and specializations were not "caused" by en-

Figure A.8   Major Structural Differentiations of the Human Nervous System

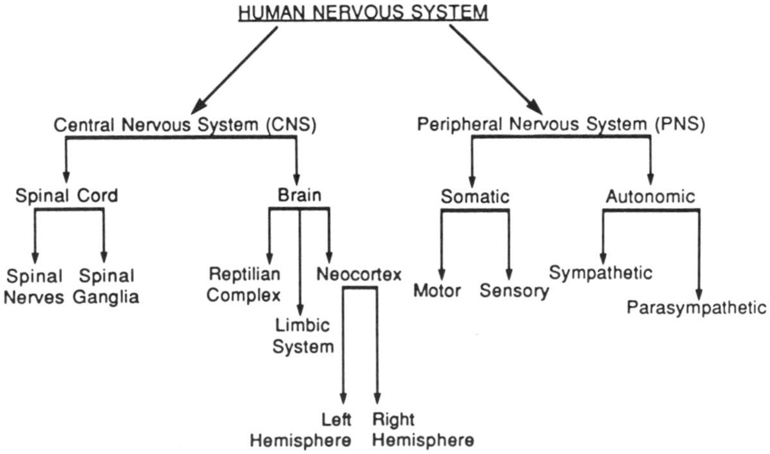

SOURCE: © 1989 M. J. Mahoney

largement of the neocortex any more than the latter was the simple result of the former. As noted in my discussion of cerebral primacy, to separate body from brain and mind from movement is both mistaken and misleading. Our bodies and brains co-evolved, and our four subbrains collaborate in a "coalitional" (decentralized) control of our actions (see chapter 5 and appendix D). While the left half of the neocortex may like to consider itself the "executive" brain, it does so only at the expense of appreciating the complexity of human neural organization.

Summary. The evolution of knowing systems—human and otherwise—is not synonymous with neural evolution. As much as our culture and time might incline us to view neurology as the base camp of psychology, the lessons of evolution have made it clear that structure and function have co-evolved, and that there is much more to human experience than the activities of an artificially isolated nervous system. From the beginnings of life as we know it, self-organizing units (individual organisms) have demonstrated an active engagement with their worldly neighborhoods, creating boundaries and then policing these dynamic borders in the interest of their own self-perpetuation. The major leaps in evolution—from precellular to cellular life, from unicellular to multicellular organisms, and from specialization to systems of systems—all reflect a proliferation of self-organizational processes. The role of the neuron and neural systems in this pageant has been powerfully facilitative. Traditional models in psychology would depict that role as primarily communicative, with nerve cells serving as messengers of input and output from and to the boundaries (periphery) and brains (center) of the organism. Recent developments in the cognitive sciences, however, challenge this oversimplification (see chapters 4–5). As their legacy in primitive muscle should have forecast, neurons and the nervous system they comprise are anything but passive conduits of experience. The human brain and its nervous system are pervasively active—indeed, proactive; and their evolutionary emergence cannot be meaningfully separated from that of the body they inhabit, both of which are embedded in formative physical and social environments (Steele 1989; Willis 1989).

Neoteny

In 1874, Ernst Haeckel, a professor of zoology at the University of Jena, announced what he called "the Law of Recapitulation" which maintained that "ontogeny recapitulates phylogeny"—or, in less technical terms, that every organism repeats its ancestral history during its own individual development. This law remained widely accepted in zoology for many years and is still often cited. There is indeed a remarkable resemblance between some of the early stages of human fetal development and the progression of neural evolution from simpler to more complex life forms (reptilian, amphibian, and so on). The problem with the law of recapitulation—first noted by the English biologist Walter Garstang in 1922—is that "ontogeny does not repeat phylogeny: it creates it" (1922, p. 81). Our physical transformations during embryonic development do not resemble a succession of pre-human *adult* life forms. On the contrary, the progression from human fetus to human adult shows a striking resemblance to the *embryonic* and *fetal* forms of our pre-human ancestors. In other words, we do not climb our evolutionary family tree via its adult branches so much as by staying progressively closer to an undifferentiated (and less specialized) common trunk. This is virtually the opposite of what is often implied when we allude to the law of recapitulation:

In recapitulation the embryonic descendant is alleged to resemble the adult ancestor; in fact Garstang found the reverse to be true, namely, that the adult descendant resembles the embryonic or fetal ancestor. To describe the process by which this occurred Garstang introduced the term paedomorphosis . . . meaning "formed like a child."

Garstang defined paedormorphosis as a mechanism whereby evolutionary advance is achieved in certain highly progressive species, including humans, by the retention in the adult of structures formerly found only in the fetal stages of the individuals of the species. This is neoteny, the reverse or opposite of recapitulation. (Montagu 1981, pp. 232–33)

Neoteny is now the preferred term for paedomorphosis and refers not only to the retention of fetal, neonate-like, juvenile characteristics into adulthood, but also to the general slowing of developmental rates.

Humans are unquestionably the most neotenous life form ever to have graced the planet. Even a cursory examination of physical structure will reveal how much we resemble the fetal and newborn stages of our primate relatives. Baby chimpanzees, gibbons, and other newborn simians look remarkably human. They are not, however, unfinished forms of us: we are literally developmentally retarded forms of them! We have managed to remain more "childlike" in both structure and function and to capitalize on the advantages of nonspecialized versatility. This has been accomplished by spreading our development over a larger proportion of our lifespan. We remain essentially dependent on one another, physically and symbolically; and—like *Peterpanthecus*—we delight in growing, but not in growing up. Throughout known human history, we have enshrined the innocence, spirit, and flexibility of youth, seldom recognizing that youth is not a time in one's life so much as a style of being. Our paradoxical goal in life, according to Montagu, is "to die young—as late as possible" (1981, p. 6). Unfortunately our cultural and personal myths about aging have not been particularly helpful in our quest toward that goal.

The "humanization" of our form clearly reflects progressively more successful approximations of the primate fetal form. Montagu puts it succinctly:

From *Homo erectus* . . . to modern man *(Homo sapiens sapiens)*, we proceed by a steplike process to shed one anthropoid trait after another: the large teeth, projecting jaws, cranial crests, massive eyebrow ridges and facial structures. Simply by stretching out the fetal stages of development of the brain, the trend is toward the retention of the structural traits of an ancestral fetus. (1981, p. 18)

Some of these "structural traits" were to afford significant changes in a variety of human experiences. The cranial flexure, for example, resulted in our head and eyes facing forward (ventrally). All mammalian embryos possess the cranial flexure—the head essentially at a right angle to the vertebral column; but the head usually rotates later in embryonic development, and the mammal is born with head and spine in linear alignment. The only exception is the human. Other changes in the neck and at the base of the skull make it easier to balance our heavy heads while standing, to move skillfully on two legs, and to therefore free our hands to help us knead and feel our environments.

The pubic flexure was also developmentally powerful. In other mammals the urogenital structures and the vaginal opening begin with a "downward" orientation but shift, during gestation, toward a backward direction. Humans are the only mammals to retain the fetal orientation of these structures—an orientation that affords (if not encourages) a face-to-face posture during sexual intercourse. The latter, in turn, may well have played a significant role in the evolution of human consciousness. Self-awareness appears to require exchanges with a similar but distinct other being (chapter 9). The emergence of face-to-face intimacy during sexual activity may well have accelerated and encouraged much of what we now hold dearest about human consciousness. Changes in our reproductive postures may have helped us see beyond ourselves phenomenologically, and our passionate awareness of each other may well have helped beget aspects of our awareness of ourselves.

Changes in the rate and timing of brain and body development were likewise to have effects that were structurally and functionally transformational. As we became progressively more neotenous, our embryonic brains began growing at increasingly faster rates and achieving larger sizes relative to our more slowly developing bodies. Childbirth became a literal "tight squeeze"; and even then, the brain was just beginning to expand. In the human embryo, neurons first appear around the eighteenth day after conception. Once they begin developing, however, their pace is startling. Current estimates suggest that neurons are generated at an average rate of 250,000 per minute throughout fetal growth (Cowan 1979). The fetal brain quadruples in weight during the last three months of pregnancy—gaining 2.2 milligrams per minute. When the newborn enters the buzzing, booming confusion of life outside the uterus, it is eight million times heavier than the original zygote. Although its brain is still only one fourth its adult mass, it accounts for 10 percent of the newborn's total body weight. This percentage will decrease to about 2 percent in adult maturity, but that 3-pound organ will still consume up to 10 percent of our calories and 25 percent of our oxygen supply.

The magnitude of developmental freedom afforded by our "fetalization" has only recently become widely acknowledged among life scientists. In addition to the many structural advances achieved during neotenization, we evolved a more powerful and intense web of social relationships. Besides being functionally dependent for so many years, the human child is (under ideal conditions) nurtured through a long and intense apprenticeship in the elusive art of living. No other young mammal is so diligently cared for, trained, or challenged; and—thanks to symbolic communication—no comparable system of cultural and personal transmission comes anywhere near the human phenomenon. With the blessings of a prolonged childhood, excellent educational systems, and a secure and nurturant home base, the human child can reach toward ever deeper expressions of learning. These blessings are not without their share of risks, however, in that prolonged dependency and a slower developmental pace leave extra room for neglect, abuse, and misguidance of those developing. Insecure or damaging emotional attachments and poor educational services may constrain or divert a "life in process," and our painful early vulnerabilities may figure prominently in how we have learned to cope and grow. If we are ever to reap more fully the harvest of neotenization, it will be when we have come to more deeply appreciate the preciousness of children and childhood (chapters 7–9).

Hominid Evolution

Speculations on the emergence of modern humans and their unique psychological skills are often themselves an intriguing display of the skills they strive to explain. Although there is now little doubt, for example, that absolute brain volume and the relative size of the neocortex increased significantly in the evolution of the higher primates and hominids (human forms), it has become increasingly clear that our emergence and uniqueness as a life form cannot be adequately captured by a brain-centered account. The nature of the complex forces—internal and external—contributing to our development as a unique life form are only now being appreciated. As Gould (1980b) and others have noted, billard ball determinism is inadequate as a metaphor for the mechanisms of influence operative with living organisms. Complex, self-organizing systems are inherently historical, and relatively small changes in their early (e.g.,

Table A.3 Probable Hominid Ancestry

Form	Approximate Era	Brain Volume	Encephalization Quotient	Special Features, Capacities
Homo sapiens	50,000–present	870–2,150 cc. Average: 1,400 cc.	6.93	Symbols, agriculture, community
Neanderthal	250,000–32,000	1,300 cc.		Ceremonies
Homo erectus	1.7–.5 million	815–1,225 cc. Average: 970 cc.	5.16–6.01	Fire, family
Homo habilis	2–1.5 million	750 cc	4.45	Improved manual dexterity, tools, hunting
Australopithecus	5–1.5 million	430–530 cc. Average: 480 cc.	3.40	Bipedalism, probably omnivorous
Ramapithecus	14–8 million	unknown	—	Some signs of neotenization
Orangutan, Chimpanzee, Gorilla	20 million	300–425 cc.	2.0–4.0	Frontal sinus, molecular variability

embryonic) development can have dramatic (and unpredictable) effects on their later activity and adaptability.

Such complexity of form and function are readily apparent in the emergence of the modern human (table A.3).* Current fossil evidence suggests that primates differentiated from other mammals about 75 million years ago. The later emergence of humanlike (hominid) forms has been estimated at roughly 5 million years ago. Our closest animal ancestors were the apes *(pongids)*, currently represented by the orangutan, gorilla, and chimpanzee. There is now growing consensus that hominids emerged from a family of small ape known as *Ramapithecus*. Fossils found in India, Turkey, Pakistan, and Kenya suggest that *Ramapithecus* lived between 8 million and 14 million years ago. Unfortunately, these fossils are fragmentary—amounting to no more than jaw segments—so that it is impossible to estimate confidently body and brain characteristics. The jaw segments do suggest a short muzzle, however, and this is believed to indicate a shift toward the flat face and enlarged brain later encountered among the hominids.

The Emergence of Australopithecus. The earliest known human ancestor was probably *Australopithecus,* a relatively small (90-pound) hominid be-

*For recent discussions of hominid evolution, see Kinzey 1987; Lewin 1988*a*, 1988*b;* Steele 1989; Stringer and Andrews 1988; and Willis 1989.

lieved to have lived between 5 million and 1.5 million years ago. Their remains have been found in southern and eastern Africa; the most famous are those of "Lucy" discovered in Ethiopia in 1974. It is now clear that Lucy and her Australopithecine peers were capable of standing erect and walking in a human manner. In an essay titled "Our Greatest Evolutionary Step," Gould argues that this sudden appearance of bipedalism represents "the great punctuation in human evolution" (Gould 1980*b*, p. 132). The mystery of its abrupt emergence has fueled many debates in evolutionary biology, particularly since it required major changes in anatomical structure and function of the pelvis and foot. It seems most likely that these changes took place at embryonic stages and were successfully propagated by the adaptive advantage they afforded. A prolongation of gestation and an overall slowing of development (intra- and extra-uterine) probably aided such structural/functional transformations, and there is now strong evidence corroborating a progressive retardation of developmental rates (neotenization) from the lower to the higher primates.

Besides being bipedal, there is reason to believe that *Australopithecus* may have made the shift from vegetarianism to the status of omnivore. This change would have afforded significant advantages in dietary protein and set the stage for the development of hunting. There is some evidence that *Australopithecus* may have engaged in hunting, but credit for pioneering this activity is usually reserved for *Homo habilis* (literally, "handy man"). The habilines also lived in east Africa between 2 million and 1.5 million years ago. Although they were only slightly larger than their Australopithecine counterparts (averaging perhaps 115 pounds), estimates of brain size derived from cranial volume suggest that the habilines had significantly larger brains (see table A.3). Wear patterns on their teeth indicate that they were definitely omnivorous. What is most striking about the habilines, however, is the fact they they were tool makers. Although it is likely that the Australopithecines used rocks, bones, and sticks as tools, the habilines were apparently the first actually to manufacture their own tools. The stone tools found with their remains were "primitive" in design and probably employed for cutting, scraping, and the manufacture of other tools. Some writers have noted that these tools were apparent extensions and improvements of the hand as an instrument for pounding, tearing, and so on. Combined with other fossil evidence, the tools suggest that the habilines actively hunted small and medium-sized animals, collected plant food, and perhaps scavenged the carcasses of already dead or injured game. Unfortunately, we do not know whether they found uses for animal skins and it is not clear that they retained their tools after use. There is no evidence of their having built shelters, and we do not know to what extent they used wood and other materials.

The next distinct hominid form was *Homo erectus* (literally, "upright man"—a label now anachronistic given the evidence of bipedalism among the Australopithecines). *Home erectus* lived between 1.7 million and half a million years ago and was apparently the first hominid to have spread beyond the warm and fertile terrain of southern and eastern Africa. Besides these areas in Africa, fossil remains of *Homo erectus* have been found in China, Java, France, Spain, Germany, and Hungary. In addition to being the first hominids to leave home, as it were, they were also the first to evidence knowledge of fire—knowledge that would have served them well in the colder northern climates. This is particularly true since *Home erectus* had to contend with the first of our four "ice ages." We can only conjecture that their fire was used primarily for heat and perhaps for cooking; there is no current evidence that they had discovered its other uses. *Homo erectus* had a significantly larger brain than *Homo habilis* despite being only slightly larger in body size (perhaps 120 pounds). Both had relatively high foreheads, indicating the possibility of growth in the frontal and prefrontal areas of the neocortex (to be discussed). The tools left behind by *Homo erectus* were larger and more carefully shaped than those of the habilines. They were also made from a wider variety of stony materials, and some experts believe *Homo erectus* had learned to retain these tools for repeated use. As they moved toward the cooler northern climates, the *Homo erectus* people became professional (rather than casual) hunters, relying more and more on larger animals for their dietary protein. There are now several sites where the remains of the hominids are mingled with those of their apparent prey—deer, horses, and even elephants. Although they may have been migratory—perhaps following herds of game as their mobile food source—the fire is believed to have established a semipermanent home base for group (and perhaps family) gathering. It is with *Homo erectus* that we first find evidence of cave dwelling, and some investigators have speculated that they were also capable of building primitive shelters from available woods and plants. If this were indeed the case, *Homo erectus* may have pioneered many of the early behaviors related to community, communication, and family life.

Sometime between 250,000 and 32,000 years ago, the hominid strain known as *Neanderthals* lived in Europe, the Middle East, and Asia. Their name derives from the fact that the first remains to be scientifically classified were found in a cave in the Neander valley of Germany. Other finds have since been reported in France, Italy, England, Israel, Gibraltar, and several sites in Asia. Besides living in caves, the Neanderthals apparently built hutlike structures and hunted big game (including bears, elephants, wooly mammoths, and rhinoceros). They had a brain almost as large as our own (table A.3) but retained the thick brow ridge (above the eyes) of the earlier hominids. Before their mysterious disappearance, they left signs not only of skillful adaptation but also of a developing consciousness. The Neanderthals were the first hominids to bury their dead, apparently with ceremonial rituals involving the interment of food, tools, and other artifacts (perhaps including flowers). These early human ceremonies are noteworthy for reflecting a consciousness of time and physical mortality.

Encephalization and Frontal Cortex Development.   Some authorities classify the Neanderthals as a separate species, and others include them among our own class of *Homo sapiens* ("knowing man"). In the former case, modern humans are given the recursive label *Homo sapiens sapiens* ("knowing knowing man" or, as some have rendered it, "man who knows he knows"). Whatever the classification or translation, it is now believed that humans have existed in the modern form for perhaps 50,000 years. One of our earlier European strains, *Cro-Magnon,* may have had a brain up to 100 cubic centimeters larger than our current model. It is apparent from their artifacts and habitats that the early sapiens were an intelligent and versatile life form. Their tools, for example, included awls, needles, spearheads, and a variety of instruments for facilitating hunting, fishing, food preparation, and the construction of shelters. In the excavations of Jericho, near the Dead Sea, it is clear that the farming of grains and domestication of small animals (such as goats) dates back at least 9,000 years. A socially stratified community of perhaps 2,000 people had existed there, and there are many other sites of comparable "pre-historic" civilizations scattered across the continents. Beyond agriculture, community, and a rapidly expanding technology, however, the major advance of the sapiens lay in their development and use of symbols. Although the foundations of gestural and verbal languages might well go back to *Homo erectus,* it was not until *Homo sapiens* that symbolic communication was elevated to its currently central role in ongoing cultural evolution.

In sum, although the exact time of emergence and the ancestry of the earliest hominids are still uncertain, we now have converging evidence of subsequent differentiations. Attempts to describe and understand their life styles and intelligence are, of course, highly conjectural. Nevertheless, a crude sketch of probable brain and behavioral evolution offers fascinating food for thought. The highlights of hominid progression suggest, for example, that bipedalism and the subsequent development of manual dexterity played a significant role in our evolution. *Australopithecus* may have learned how to use his or her hands and naturally occurring tools for everyday tasks, but it appears that *Homo habilis* was the first to begin making tools. This skill, combined with a probable increase in fleetness of foot, made the habilines more effective in food gathering, especially via hunting. It is also likely that the creative initiative of the habilines marked the beginnings of a pattern still evident today. Instead of being reactive residents of a challenging environment, the habilines literally took matters into their own hands and began to shape small parts of their world to fit their needs. This active strategy was probably a major step in the unceasing human preoccupation with technology and power. Moreover, it marked a dramatic increase in the mutual reciprocity and unfolding evolution of both life form and environs. Passingham has stressed this point in his analysis of primate and hominid technology:

> The key difference is that the hominids were not just moving into a new environment or reacting to changes in the natural world; they were also creating a new artificial environment of their own through cultural advance. This technical environment could change rapidly, because technology is passed from generation to generation by cultural and not by genetic transmission; advances in one generation make possible further progress in the next. Given that the hominids were not only creating a technical environment but also reacting to it, they were living in an environment that was rapidly changing. Such conditions would set up a high selection pressure for the neurological changes that would allow the capacity to cope with this cultural environment. (Passingham 1982, pp. 167–68)

In cultural evolution, the mistakes of past generations can also create unanticipated problems for their descendants.

Unfortunateley, we do not have any early hominid brains to subject to an anatomical inquiry. Using measures of cranial volume, however, we can estimate the absolute brain size of those hominids for whom we have relevant evidence. As we saw in table A.3, the hominid brain has tripled in size from *Australopithecus* to *Homo sapiens.* An even more sensitive index of relative brain size is the *encephalization quotient,* a measure developed by Jerison (1973, 1976, 1979) to convey the relative ratio of brain to body size among mammals. Figure A.9 shows the estimated encephalization quotients for the various hominid groups, with the dramatic jump from *Australopithecus* to *Homo habilis.* We do not have a cranium from which to estimate brain size in *Ramapithecus,* our probable simian ancestor, but our current simian relatives have encephalization quotients ranging from 2.0 to perhaps as high as 4.0.

As mentioned earlier, human frontal areas are enormous in both size and apparent importance. For more than half a century, neurobiologists have ventured speculations on the role of frontal lobe development in human evolution. Studies of the changing shape of the hominid skull and brain casing now offer crude but fascinating clues on recent brain growth, and suggest dramatic changes in the frontal (forehead) areas. *Australopithecus* probably had little or no forehead—certainly nothing like our high, flat variety. If we assume other parallels in brain orientation and anatomical coordinates, it appears that *Homo sapiens* has effected yet another dramatic change in the structural hardware of its brain. We now know that the frontal areas are involved in several "integrative" functions; our abilities to anticipate and plan, for example, depend on frontal lobe processes. Moreover, several *prefrontal* structures—those at the most forward and recursive edges of development—have important connections

Figure A.9   Relative Encephalization Among Hominids

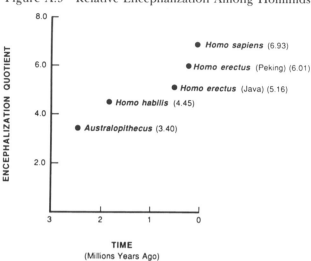

TIME
(Millions Years Ago)

SOURCE: Adapted from Passingham (1982)

with limbic and other subcortical areas. These connections were recognized by early practitioners of psychosurgery; hence, the prefrontal area became a favorite site of assault on the "agitated" chronic mental patient.

Current research in neuroscience suggests that frontal lobe functions include aspects of attention, perception, sensation, action, memory, strategic flexibility, and several other fundamental categories. Investigations of frontal lobe functions have been dominated, of course, by observations and tests performed after tumor or trauma to this area of the brain. Despite problems of methodology and inference, however, at least some prefrontal functions can be surmised. They include the following:

1. Integration of conceptual and practical knowledge (knowing "that" and knowing "how")
2. Sequential organization of action
3. Attentional maintenance ("concentration") with and without distraction
4. Balanced coordination of change/maintain strategies in patterned movement (thereby avoiding the extremes of random instability and rigid perseveration)
5. Self-awareness
6. Affective engagement and empathic perspective taking

Frontal lobe damage or dysfunction is often associated with separations of knowledge and action, poor planning skills, distractibility, random or perseverative behavior, limited self-awareness, and apathy.

Whatever the original pressures that afforded dramatic frontal and prefrontal development in *Homo sapiens,* it has been a richly harvested innovation. We are the hominids who came to know time and its complexities, and we are apparently still developing richer connections within our own neural architecture. Likewise, we have begun to reduce the gap between our conceptual and practical knowledge and to develop a deeper appreciation of our own role in the unfolding directions of our lives. Each of these developments appears to be related to frontal and prefrontal functions, and it has become apparent that we have only recently begun to fathom their overall significance in our adaptation.

In all of this talk about relative brain size, however, it is important to remember the complex reciprocity of brain and body evolution, not to mention the much greater impact of social and cultural variables as "downwardly causal" factors in the saga of human life. Our increasing sophistication in skilled movement, tool use, and the quest for fire, for example, were both causes and effects of neurological developments, all of which took place in increasingly social contexts even before we left the seas, the trees, and the savannas.

G. THINKING ABOUT FEELING: A BRIEF HISTORY

After more than half a century of relative neglect, the topic of emotionality has drawn considerable attention over the last two decades, as theorists and researchers have come to recognize its centrality to virtually all other aspects of human psychological functioning (Buck 1986; de Sousa 1987; Frijda 1988; Izard, Kagan, and Zajonc 1984; Langer 1953, 1967, 1972, 1982; Leventhal 1984; Mandler 1975, 1979, 1984; Panksepp 1982; Plutchik and Kellerman 1980; Rorty 1980; Scherer and Ekman 1984; Strongman 1973). Before discussing that centrality and some of the issues that challenge current attempts to understand human affect, I shall briefly reflect on past efforts to address feelings and their role in human experience.

Historically, affect and emotional processes (which I here use interchangeably) have been associated with the more base, primitive, and animal aspects of human nature. As such, they have been portrayed as major impediments to rationality and the pursuit of truth; and it is therefore not entirely surprising that, until relatively recently, scientific inquiries have avoided the study of experienced emotion.

Early Rationalist Influences

Plato's portrayal of the passions as "unruly" and "animalistic" contributed to the tradition of *rationalism* that Pythagoras had founded, and also encouraged the doctrine of *rational supremacy*, which I briefly discussed in my review of the cognitive sciences. Rationalist supremacy asserts that reason and rationality can and should control everything "below" them in the human organism, especially feelings and actions. The assumption that "as you think so shall you feel" laid the foundations for "the power of positive thinking" and what William James (1902) called the "religion of healthy mindedness" (Ehrenwald 1976; Ellenberger 1970). Although James considered many of its practitioners "moonstruck with optimism," he also believed that there was already impressive evidence of the positive effects of "healthy-minded attitudes, . . . the conquering efficacy of courage, hope, and trust, and a correlative contempt for doubt, fear, worry, and all nervously precautionary states of mind" (1958 [1902] p. 88). Although there were popular versions of these systems (Bain 1928; Carnegie 1948; Coue 1922; Dubois 1906, 1908, 1911; Janet 1898; Maltz 1960; and Peale 1960), it was not until the emergence of the *cognitive psychotherapies* that some of these assertions were to undergo formal scientific examination. Over all, those examinations have revealed that thought and image patterns can influence mood and affect, but that those patterns (1) are much more complex than prior theories have recognized and (2) are not so easily modified; and (3) that emotional experiences are neither dictated nor dominated by cognitive processes. In fact, I shall argue that the least promising cognitive psychotherapies are those that excessively emphasize "rational thinking" as a primary or exclusive strategy for emotional control (Mahoney 1988*a;* Mahoney and Lyddon 1988).

A spiritual variant of the doctrine of rational supremacy also held sway in the Asiatic religious philosophies of the first and second millennia B.C. In his Four Noble Truths, for example, Buddha argued that the source of all human suffering was "longing" and an attachment to the realm of the flesh. To be liberated from pain and achieve ultimate spiritual purity, he maintained that the individual must completely abandon such attachments and turn inward toward the true light of wisdom. The parallels between Platonic and Buddhist dualisms are striking, as are their assertions about the human body, its sensations, and, most important, its "passions." The latter, they agree, require vigilant control, suppression, displacement, discharge, or transcendence.

Also worth noting are the apparently contradictory values associated with the concepts of attachment and of ego, or self development in the history of Asian and European thought. Traditionally, Asian (and especially Buddhist) philosophies have encouraged *detachment* from the physical body and material world, as well as from personal identity (ego or self). European philosophies, on the other hand, have encouraged the development of personal identity and "ego strength," often through the flexible autonomy afforded by secure interpersonal *attachment.* Aspects of this contradiction may be illusory, however, given the different meanings of these terms in different times and cultures. (See chapter 9 and Marsella, DeVos, and Hsu 1985; White and Kirkpatrick 1985; and Wilber, Engler, and Brown 1986.)

The Moral Sentiments

Various assertions about emotionality and the passions have appeared in diverse writings in religion, philosophy, and the humanities throughout the last four thousand years (Langer 1967, 1972, 1982; Wiener 1974). The contributions of the Scottish moral philosophers are again note-worthy in a number of respects. Adam Smith's *Theory of Moral Sentiments* (1759) was a classic in both ethics and epistemology in its emphasis on the interdependence of feeling and human imagination and interpersonal sensitivity. Smith noted the powerful human capacity to imagine and experience the perspective of other human beings, this capacity being most evident in the form of a private witness—what Smith called "an impartial spectator"—to all conscious human action. Note the blending here of a special form of self-awareness (knowledge about self) that involves *metacognition* (knowledge about knowledge), social awareness (knowledge about others), and a shared sensitivity ("sentiment") that connects the self with the system. It was Smith's book, in fact, that in fluenced Adam Ferguson's *Essay on the History of Civil Society* (1767) and David Hume's *Enquiry Concerning the Principles of Morals* (1777) (Hamowy 1987; Harrison 1976; Heilbroner 1986; Hume 1969 [1739]). Immanuel Kant's *Foundations of the Metaphysics of Morals* (1938 [1785]) was also in-fluenced by these earlier writings.

Modern humanistic and existential theories of a "natural ethics" derive much from Smith's analyses of human conscience and moral conduct, as does the notion of the "looking-glass self" that has dominated twentieth-century theories of personal identity:

According to Smith, conscience is a product of social relationship. Our first moral sentiments are concerned with the actions of other people. Each of us judges as a spectator and finds himself judged by spectators. . . . "We suppose ourselves the spectators of our own behavior, and endeavor to imagine what effect it would, in this light, produce upon us. This is the only looking-glass by which we can, in some measure, with the eyes of other people, scrutinize the propriety of our own conduct (III.I.5)." The looking-glass requires imagination: Smith's impartial spectator is not the actual "man without" but an imagined "man within." (From the introduction to Smith 1976 [1759], pp. 15–16)

These thoughts would influence later ideas about the relations between social sensitivity (moral development) and self-knowledge, as well as the attempts to integrate social and personal development through vicarious learning and that vast expanse of theory, research, and practice devoted to self psychology (chapter 9).

But the social foundations and "individuating" functions of human emotions remained less popular themes of inquiry than their organic aspects. Research and theory in emotionality has long been dominated by the biological sciences, where the organs and juices of "raw feels" can be exposed to chemical assay. In a 1649 essay on "the passions of the soul," Descartes argued for a physiological explanation of emotionality in animals. Deviating from his dualistic separation of mind and body, however, he suggested that, in humans alone, emotions served to mediate mental and physical states. Darwin's *The Expression of the Emotions in Man and Animals* (1965 [1872]) was also influential in emphasizing the basic biological bases of emotional behavior, their (social) signaling functions, and the significance of the face as a central realm of emotional expression in primates (Reynolds 1987). Darwin was also responsible for some misguided efforts to classify mental health/illness on the basis of facial features.

As one of the pioneering voices of what would later be called "activation" or "arousal" theories of emotion, Herbert Spencer focused on the *intensity* of emotions and their proportional relation to the amount of bodily movement observed, with the smaller muscles (as of the face and hands) much more affected than the larger muscles. Spencer also popularized the metaphor of *spillover* in emotional theorizing, with "excess intensities" of arousal "spilling over" into nervous discharge, spontaneous physical activity, and recreational play. In the later research of experimental medicine and the biological sciences, the assumption of physiological primacy was maintained and elaborated, and the energy and balance metaphors long popular in other sciences continued to find expression in writings about human emotions.

The Cycles of Emotion in Psychology

The topic of emotionality has spawned a vast literature in psychology. The abundance of those writings should not obscure the fact, however, that interest in and perspectives on human affect have themselves exhibited cycles in the first century of scientific psychology. At the beginning of this century, affect, will, and "hedonic tone" were among the most central concerns of the new science. The most influential pioneers in theory, research, and practice—people like Wundt, James, Titchener, McDougall, Dewey, Breuer, and Freud—linked emotionality with instinct, motivation, learning, memory, consciousness, and purposive behavior.

Wundt and his colleagues, for example, recognized the need to distinguish sensations and feelings because the former seemed linear while the latter appeared bipolar. Wundt believed that affective "tone" permeated human consciousness, and that all acts of conscious cognition were preceded by feelings. His *tridimensional theory of emotion* (1907 [1896]) suggested three dimensions of bipolar affect: un/pleasant, excitement/calm, and relaxation/effort. If the last two polarities are combined, research on the dimensionality of human feelings has generally corroborated Wundt's pioneering insight (see figure A.10). Most modern theories of emotionality adopt a bipolar format, and research has shown moods and affective states to exhibit patternings consistent with a complex range of opponent processes. As it turns out, however, the "positive" and "negative" emotions appear to operate somewhat independently of one another, so that changes in one do not automatically result in changes in the other (Harter 1986; Larsen 1987; Russell 1979, 1980; Sandvik, Diener, and Larsen 1985; Schwartz and Garamoni 1986; Solomon 1980; Solomon and Corbit 1974; Warr, Barter, and Brownbridge 1983; Watson and Tellegen 1985; Yelen 1985; Zevon and Tellegen 1982).

The most famous debate in the psychological study of emotion was, of course, that associated with the James–Lange and Cannon–Bard perspectives. William James had offered a counterintuitive assertion that emotional experiences were not caused by the perception of an arousing stimulus, but rather by the perception of our own bodily changes and behaviors evoked by the aforementioned perception. James believed that we do not see a bear, experience fear, and then run away, but that we see a bear, run away, and then experience fear. A somewhat similar view was

Figure A.10   Spatial Representation of Emotions Along Dimensions of Valence and Activity

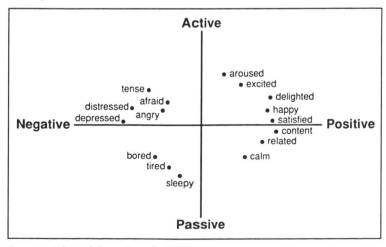

SOURCE: Adapted from Russell (1980)

independently offered by the Danish anatomist Carl Lange, which is why the two names are linked. The physiologist Walter B. Cannon later challenged this view, noting that physiological arousal is not differentially informative given that physiological activity seems very similar across the different emotions. Philip Bard later elaborated this point (hence the Cannon–Bard linkage). The technicalities of that debate are less relevant to our discussion than the subsequent breakthroughs in the study of the autonomic nervous system, the limbic system, and the reticular activating system (see appendices D and F; Hilgard 1987; LeDoux and Hirst 1986; Neiss 1988; Panksepp 1982; Plutchik and Kellerman 1980; Scherer and Ekman 1984; Strongman 1973). The "activation" and "arousal" theories of Elizabeth Duffy, Magda B. Arnold, and Donald B. Lindsley also reflected these developments.

When behaviorism emerged as the dominant perspective in experimental psychology, however, the research attention devoted to emotionality was considerably diminished. While there are important exceptions, for the most part psychological studies of emotion were subdued until after midcentury. There were even some predictions that the term *emotion* would eventually be abandoned by psychologists, a prediction almost realized outside the areas of psychobiology and human development (Campos and Barrett 1984). When the cognitive revolution emerged in the 1950s and later flourished, the neglect of emotionality was further amplified (chapter 3). Some social psychologists did attempt to link emotions with attitudes and behaviors—but in a way that made "cognitive equilibrium" the central mechanism of human motivation. Attempts to outline principles of learning and human psychological adaptation generally treated emotional processes as instinctually "hard-wired," physiological "epiphenomena," or the disorganizing "spillover" of nervous activity (Berkowitz 1978; Haber 1966; Hastorf and Isen 1982; Hilgard 1987; Rokeach 1972; Weiner 1972).

This is not to say that all psychologists were neglecting emotionality, or that their understanding was necessarily confined to a redefinition of emotions in accordance with their preferred theory of human experience. Besides the growing voice of the developmentalists (chapter 7), important contributions were being made by psychotherapy researchers and practitioners. Behaviorists, psychoanalysts, and humanists agreed, for example, that emotional distress was the most common "entry point" for psychological services, and concurred that "corrective emotional experiences" were an important ingredient in successful psychotherapy (Goldfried 1982). As some psychoanalysts, humanists, and gestalt therapists experimented with the power of intense emotional experience and expression, whole families of theories and treatments grew up around "body work" and emotionally "expressive" therapies (Boudewyns and Shipley 1983; Feder and Feder 1981; Feiss 1979; Gendlin 1978; Greenberg and Safran 1987; Herink 1980; Hill 1978; Jackins 1965; Janov 1970;

Keleman 1979; Lowen 1975; Mahrer 1978; Nichols and Zax 1977; Perls 1969; Perls, Hefferline, and Goodman 1951; Polster and Polster 1973; Reich 1942, 1949; Rolf 1977; Scheff 1979).

H. SELECTED PRIORITIES FOR SCIENCE, EDUCATION, AND SERVICE

I offer the following capsule recommendations, which are neither exclusive nor exhaustive, regarding future priorities in research, teaching, and training. Although I believe that science, education, and the training of professional practitioners are inseparable aspects of the same human project, I shall order my remarks in terms of these components.

Research Priorities

Science cannot be value-free. Try as they may (and have and will), scientists and philosophers will not be capable of either defending or developing value-neutral methods (Eger 1989; Weimer 1979). Indeed, all attempts to do so must necessarily reflect self-contradiction if only in their valuation of value-neutrality. Knowledge cannot be disentangled from the process of knowing, and all human knowing is based in value-generated processes (such as categories, contrasts, and the dynamic directives of attention). The ubiquity and influence of values in psychology and psychotherapy are particularly apparent (Kovel 1982; Prilleltensky 1989). This being the case, research priorities must also reflect judgments about more and less promising directions and methods of inquiry. Given past and present circumstances in the study and facilitation of human psychological development, four general themes deserve to be prioritized in future work.

First and perhaps foremost, energies should be directed at expanding traditional research methodologies to include qualitative, process-sensitive measures of human change. Some valuable work in this direction is already under way (for example, Gaston and Marmar, 1989; Neimeyer and Resnikoff 1982; Taylor and Bogdan, 1984; Hoshmand 1988). What is particularly important here is that future generations of researchers avoid the costly mistake of confining their inquiry methods to those now dominant in the field. Traditional factorial designs and inferential statistics can render valuable lessons about human change processes, but—if they remain exclusive in their dominance of psychological research (Shemberg, Keeley, and Blum 1989)—they can also hinder the development of other methods that may be more sensitive to individual and temporal patterns of development (Dar 1987). We need ways of measuring continuity and change, for example, from many levels, especially self-generating continuities in lifespan development (Caspi, Bem, and Elder 1989). These are not just measurement and methodological issues, of course: they reflect conceptual and contextual assumptions (Lerner and Tubman 1989). We also need to invest more energies in the development of phenomenological research. Measures of personal experience that are sensitive to both changes and continuities therein should be diligently explored.

The first priority was methodological—the need to move toward a focus on (de)stabilizing processes; and the second is both methodological and theoretical. Namely, we would be wise to explore and expand our understanding of individual differences and their role in the generation of different lifespan patterns. *Subject variances*, (differences among individuals) are too often disregarded as "error variances," and measures of central tendency (rather than of range or variance, for example) use algebraic averaging laws to transform differences into means (Bryk and Raudenbush 1988). A creative synthesis of idiographic (individual-focused) and nomothetic (group-focused) concepts and methodologies would be a valuable contribution to the field (Hermans 1988). In balancing our study of the individual with our search for generalizations, we also need to integrate our concepts of self and system. Studies in diversity should be encouraged, as should an exploratory spirit that looks at diversity as a powerful source of creativity and development. It will be by genuinely hearing the voices of feminist and minority scholars, for example, that we will most likely make our greatest strides in appreciating the values of human rights, ethnic and cultural heritage, and identity-making processes throughout the full range of oppression and affirmation (Crawford and Chaffin 1986; Crawford and Marecek 1989; López et al. 1989; Mascia-Lees, Sharpe, and Cohen 1989; Schiebinger 1989; Tuana 1989; Wohl 1989).

Relatedly, a third priority is the need for intensive longitudinal studies, preferably lifespan in length. We also need to be creative about the measures and meanings we use to study human lives in process, both individually and in relation to others (attachments and separations). This is not a time to be constrictive about acceptable forms of inquiry; encouragement is needed in the other direction. We need to know more about what it means to "know" another person's experience, and what it means to "understand" any given patterns within that experience. This is also where the experience of psychotherapy may teach us valuable lessons about the processes of personal change. And this leads to the fourth priority in further studies of such change.

Researchers in psychotherapy should expand their collaborative relationship with practitioners and their clients. Scientists and practitioners share more psychological characteristics than is often appreciated, and yet there are clear differences both among and between them (Conway 1988). Not everyone wants to be one or the other, however, and "scientist-practitioners" exhibit characteristics common to both emphases. Psychotherapy research will be most relevant to practice when it is incorporated into the actual complexities of that practice. The converse point is also true: practitioners will be optimally informed and most responsibly involved in furthering our understanding by actively participating in dialogues and studies about human change processes.

Educational Priorities

My comments here begin with the general issue of education as a value and meaningful human interaction as its primary process. It is not just psychotherapists and their clients who are changing and who might benefit from knowing some general principles about change processes. Our public school curricula should be active and engagingly process-focused. Besides respect for diversity and human rights, we would do well to educate (from the Latin *educere,* "to bring forth from within") our children in terms of human relatedness, self-esteem, and individual styles of adaptation. We would also be wise to expand the affective, social, and physical dimensions of education, at all levels. We need Teachers. We need "good" teachers who enjoy learning in the process of being engaged with the privilege of "touching the future" and in caring about the children and lives they touch.

In respect to the education of psychologists, our priorities and policies should be sensitive to changing trends in the field (Howard et al. 1986). At the undergraduate level, breadth and depth in the humanities and sciences should remain an ideal. Of particular relevance for those who might later become psychotherapists are courses in philosophy, world history, world religions, biology, anthropology, sociology, and literature. Interactive, expressive, and experiential course formats are also to be recommended. At the level of graduate education and professional training, the priorities are both more pressing and more complex. A constructive resolution of the split between scientists and practitioners is of paramount importance to the quality of work in both areas (Altman 1987; Holden 1988; Stricker and Keisner 1985). A broader, more human sense of *science* and a developmental, more inquiring sense of *practitioner* are both likely to better serve the ideal of the "scientist-practitioner" (Conway 1988). Although practitioner training may continue to grow as the primary function of graduate training (Peterson 1985), it would be tragic for both if science and service fail to make peace with their differences and fail to engage each other in constructive dialogue.

The single most pressing priority in the graduate education of psychotherapists, however, may well be the shift from a predominantly objectivist and authoritarian approach to mentorship toward one that is phenomenological and non-authoritarian (Carrere and Weiss 1988). Apprentices should be taught both to question and to respect authority, and to honor the relative importance of their person over their technique in the quality of their professional services (Lambert 1989). They should also be encouraged to feel and to care. Although personal therapy for the apprentice should not be forced, encouragement toward exploring that option should be programmatically expressed and subsidized (for example, by enlisting the services of local practitioners who offer confidential counsel to apprentices at reduced fees). A commitment to lifelong personal and professional development should be modeled and encouraged. Ethical and value issues should be addressed throughout training, with particular emphasis on competency, clients' rights, and professional ethics (American Psychological Association 1990; Borys and Pope 1989; Everstine et al. 1980; Fine and Ulrich 1988; Jordan and Meara 1990; Keith-Spiegel and Koocher 1985; Masterpasqua 1989; Miller and Thelen 1987; Pope, Tabachnick, and Keith-Spiegel 1988).

Finally, it is clear that graduate mentorship and clinical supervision constitute two categories of relationship that are central to the personal and professional development of the graduate student (Conway 1988; Guest and Beutler 1988). Developmental models of supervision merit expanded use and evaluation, particularly those that acknowledge the "parallel processes" of development in the counselor stimulated by his or her relationships with clients and clinical supervisors (Hess 1980; Holloway 1987; McNeill and Worthen 1989; Stoltenberg and Delworth 1987, 1988).

Priorities in Practice

The most important priorities for practitioners overlap with those already outlined under research and education. They begin with the need for greater participation on the part of practitioners in the study of human change and in the teaching and training of professional apprentices. This may require considerable initiative from all three areas as well as changes in policies that have previously discouraged full-time psychotherapists from sharing their experiences and ideas about helping (as in journal articles, books, collaborative research projects, teaching, and supervision). Future research questions and training policies should reflect the hard-won lessons of experienced and talented service providers (Lambert 1989). As mentioned earlier, studies of psychotherapists and their clients should also be expanded via methodologies and measures that encourage a synergistic collaborative effort of scientists, practitioners, and clients.

Finally, a major priority for practitioners is in the area of personal development and self-care. Given the impact of psychotherapist distress on the quality of services provided, this emphasis derives some warrant from ethical principles that make the well-being of the client a top priority. As we have seen, the well-being of the therapist also warrants such priority; and more attention should be given to possible means for encouraging self-care on the part of the helping professional. In particular, the sources of reluctance to seek personal counsel should be examined and addressed, and opportunities for confidential referral and consultation should be made easily accessible. The risks and responsibilities of being a mental health professional deserve continued study and emphasis, as do the unique privileges of the profession.

References

Aaronson, T. A. 1989. A critical review of psychotherapeutic treatments of the borderline personality: Historical trends and future directions. *Journal of Nervous and Mental Disease* 177: 511–28.

Abele, A. 1989. Psychodrama and social psychology: A theoretical analysis with respect to cognitive restructuring. *International Journal of Small Group Research* 5: 29–46.

Aber, J. L.; and Allen, J. P. 1987. Effects of maltreatment on young children's socioemotional development: An attachment theory perspective. *Developmental Psychology* 23: 406–14.

Adams, G. R.; Markstrom, C. A.; and Abraham, K. G. 1987. The relations among identity development, self-consciousness, and self-focusing during middle and late adolescence. *Developmental Psychology* 23: 292–97.

Adams, H. 1988. *The academic tribes,* 2d ed. Chicago: University of Illinois Press.

Adams-Webber, J. 1981. Fixed role therapy. In R. Corsini, ed., *Handbook of innovative psychotherapies.* New York: Wiley.

Adelman, G., ed. 1987. *Encyclopedia of neuroscience* 2 vols. Boston: Birkhäuser.

Adelmann, P. K.; and Zajonc, R. B. 1989. Facial efference and the experience of emotion. *Annual Review of Psychology* 40: 249–80.

Adler, A. 1979 [1928–37]. *Superiority and social interest,* 3d ed. New York: Norton.

Adler, A. 1988. The child's inner life and a sense of community. *Individual Psychology* 44: 417–23.

Adorno, T. W.; Frenkel-Brunswik, E.; Levinson, D. J.; and Sanford, R. N. 1950. *The authoritarian personality.* New York: Harper.

Agnew, N. McK.; and Brown, J. L. 1989a. Foundations for a model of knowing: I. Constructing reality. *Canadian Psychology* 30: 152–67.

Agnew, N. McK.; and Brown, J. L. 1989*b*. Foundations for a model of knowing: II. Fallible but functional knowledge. *Canadian Psychology* 30: 168–83.

Agnew, N. McK.; and Brown, J. L. 1989*c*. The rhythms of reality: Entrainment theory. *Canadian Psychology* 30: 193–201.

Agnew, N. McK.; and Pyke, S. W. 1978. *The science game,* 3d ed. Englewood Cliffs, N.J.: Prentice-Hall.

Ainsworth, M. D. S. 1979. Infant-mother attachment. *American Psychologist* 34: 932–37.

Ainsworth, M. D. S. 1985*a*. Patterns of infant-mother attachments: Antecedents and effects on development. *Bulletin of the New York Academy of Medicine* 61: 771–91.

Ainsworth, M. D. S. 1985*b*. Attachments across the life span. *Bulletin of the New York Academy of Medicine* 61: 792–812.

Ainsworth, M. D. S. 1989. Attachments beyond infancy. *American Psychologist* 44: 709–16.

Akamatsu, T. J. 1988. Intimate relationships with former clients: National survey of attitudes and behavior among practitioners. *Professional Psychology: Research and Practice* 19: 454–58.

Akhtar, S. 1989. Narcissistic personality disorder: Descriptive features and differential diagnosis. *Narcissistic Personality Disorder* 12: 505–29.

Aldwin, C. M.; Levenson, M. R.; Spiro, A. III; and Bossé, R. 1989. Does emotionality predict stress? Findings from the normative aging study. *Journal of Personality and Social Psychology* 56: 618–24.

Alexander, C. N.; and Langer, E. J., eds. 1989. *Higher stages of human development: Perspectives on adult growth.* Oxford: Oxford University Press.

Alexander, F. G.; and Selesnick, S. T. 1966. *The history of psychiatry.* New York: Harper and Row.

Allen, D. M. 1988. *Unifying individual and family therapies.* San Francisco: Jossey-Bass.

Allen, G. J. 1977. *Understanding psychotherapy: Comparative perspectives.* Champaign, Ill.: Research Press.

Allen, P. M. 1989. Towards a new science of human systems. *International Social Science Journal* 41: 81–91.

Allport, G. W. 1937. *Personality: A psychological interpretation.* New York: Holt, Rinehart and Winston.

Allport, G. W. 1942. *The use of personal documents in psychological science.* New York: Social Science Research Council.

Allport, G. W. 1955. *Becoming: Basic considerations for a psychology of personality.* New Haven, Conn.: Yale University Press.

Allport, G. W. 1961. *Pattern and growth in personality.* New York: Holt, Rinehart and Winston.

Allred, K. D.; and Smith, T. W. 1989. The hardy personality: Cognitive and physiological responses to evaluate threat. *Journal of Personality and Social Psychology* 56: 257–66.

Altman, I. 1987. Centripetal and centrifugal trends in psychology. *American Psychologist* 42: 1058–69.

American Academy of Physical Education. 1984. *Exercise and health.* Champaign, Ill.: Human Kinetics.

American Contextual Therapy Association. 1986. *Constructing the foundations for a more effective psychotherapy.* Berkeley, Calif.: The Contextual Therapy Center.

American Psychiatric Association. 1987. *Diagnostic and statistical manual of mental disorders,* 3d ed. revised. Washington, D. C.: American Psychiatric Association.

American Psychological Association. 1990. Ethical principles of psychologists. *American Psychologist* 45: 390–95.

Amsel, A. 1989. *Behaviorism, neobehaviorism, and cognitivism in learning theory: Historical and contemporary perspectives.* Hillsdale, N.J.: Erlbaum.

Armsel, A.; and Rashotte, M.E. 1984. *Mechanisms of adaptive behavior: Clark L. Hull's theoretical papers, with commentary.* New York: Columbia University Press.

Anderson, B. 1980. *Stretching.* Bolinas, Calif.: Shelter Publications.

Anderson, B. S.; and Zinsser, J. P. 1988. *A history of their own: Women in Europe from prehistory to the present,* vol. 1. New York: Harper and Row.

Anderson, J. R. 1980. *Cognitive psychology and its implications.* San Francisco: W. H. Freeman.

Anderson, J. R. 1983. *The architecture of cognition.* Cambridge, Mass.: Harvard University Press.

Anderson, J. R. 1985. *Cognitive psychology and its implications,* 3d ed. New York: W. H. Freeman.

Anderson, J. R. 1987. Methodologies for studying human knowledge. *Behavioral and Brain Sciences* 10: 467–505.

Anderson, J. R.; and Kosslyn, S. eds. 1984. *Tutorials in learning and memory: Essays in honor of Gordon Bower.* San Francisco: W. H. Freeman.

Andreasen, N. C. 1988. Brain imaging: Applications in psychiatry. *Science* 239: 1381–88.

Andrews, J. D. W. 1989. Integrating visions of reality: Interpersonal diagnosis and the existential vision. *American Psychologist* 44: 803–17.

Angell, J. R. 1911. Imageless thought. *Psychological Review* 18: 295–323.

Angus, L. E.; and Rennie, D. L. 1988. Therapist participation in metaphor generation: Collaborative and noncollaborative styles. *Psychotherapy* 25: 552–60.

Ansbacher, H. L.; and Ansbacher, R. R., eds. 1956. *The individual psychology of Alfred Adler.* New York: Harper and Row.

Anthony, E. J. 1987. Risk, vulnerability, and resilience: An overview. In E. J. Anthony and B. J. Cohler, eds., *The invulnerable child,* 3–48. New York: Guilford.

Anthony, E. J.; and Cohler, B. J., eds. 1987. *The invulnerable child.* New York: Guilford Press.

Antonovsky, A. 1979. *Health, stress and coping.* San Francisco: Jossey-Bass.

Apter, M. J. 1982. *The experience of motivation: The theory of psychological reversals.* New York: Academic Press.

Apter, M. J. 1989. *Reversal theory: Motivation, emotion and personality.* London: Routledge.

Arbib, M. A.; and Hesse, M. B. 1986. *The construction of reality.* Cambridge: Cambridge University Press.

Archard, D. 1984. *Consciousness and the unconscious.* LaSalle, Ill.: Open Court.

Arciero, G. 1989. Evolutionary epistemology and scientific psychology. Paper presented at the annual meeting of the American Association for the Advancement of Science, January 15, San Francisco.

Arendt, H. 1978. *The life of the mind.* New York: Harcourt Brace Jovanovich.

Argyle, M. 1987. *The psychology of happiness.* London: Methuen.

Aries, P.; and Duby, G., eds. 1987. *A history of private life. I: From pagan Rome to Byzantium,* P. Veyne, ed. Trans. A. Goldhammer. Cambridge, Mass.: Harvard University Press.

Aries, P.; and Duby, G. eds. 1988. *A history of private life. II: Revelations of the medieval world,* G. Duby, ed. Trans. A. Goldhammer. Cambridge, Mass.: Harvard University Press.

Aries, P.; and Duby, G. eds. 1989. *A history of private life. III: Passions of the Renaissance,* R. Chartier, ed. Trans. A. Goldhammer. Cambridge, Mass.: Harvard University Press.

Aries, P.; and Duby, G. eds. 1990. *A history of private life. IV: From the fires of revolution to the Great War,* M. Perrot, ed. Trans A. Goldhammer. Cambridge, Mass.: Harvard University Press.

Aries, P.; and Duby, G. eds. in press. *A history of private life. V: From the first world war to our times,* A. Prost and G. Vincent, eds. Trans A. Goldhammer. Cambridge, Mass.: Harvard University Press.

Arieti, S. 1967. *The intrapsychic self.* New York: Basic Books.

Arkowitz, H.; and Messer, S. B., eds. 1984. *Psychoanalytic therapy and behavior therapy: Is integration possible?* New York: Plenum.

Armsden, G. C. 1986. Coping strategies and quality of parent and peer attachment in late adolescence. Paper presented at the First Biennial Meeting of the Society for Research on Adolescence, March, Madison, Wis.

Armsden, G. C.; and Greenberg, M. T. 1986. The inventory of parent and peer attachment: Individual differences and their relationship to psychological well-being in adolescence. University of Washington. Manuscript.

Armstrong, J. G.; and Roth, D. M. 1989. Attachment and separation difficulties in eating disorders: A preliminary investigation. *International Journal of Eating Disorders* 8: 141–55.

Arnkoff, D. B. 1980. Psychotherapy from the perspective of cognitive theory. In M. J. Mahoney, ed., *Psychotherapy process: Current issues and future directions,* 339–61. New York: Plenum.

Aron, E.; and Aron, A. 1987. The influence of inner state on self-reported long-term happiness. *Journal of Humanistic Psychology* 27: 248–70.

Aronson, E. 1960. *The social animal.* New York: W. H. Freeman.

Ascher, L. M. 1989. *Therapeutic paradox.* New York: Guilford.

Aschoff, J., ed. 1981. *Handbook of behavioral neurobiology*. Vol. 4, *Biological rhythms*. New York: Plenum.

Ash, M. G.; and Woodward, W. R., eds. 1988. *Psychology in twentieth-century thought*. New York: Cambridge University Press.

Asimov, I. 1965. *The human brain*. New York: New American Library.

Assagioli, R. 1973. *The act of will*. New York: Penguin.

Atkinson, R. C.; and Shiffrin, R. M. 1968. Human memory: A proposed system and its control processes. In K. W. Spence and J. T. Spence, eds., *The psychology of learning and motivation*, vol. 2. New York: Academic Press.

Atlan, H. 1986. Connaissance scientifique et niveaux d'organisation. In H. Atlan, ed., *À tort et à raison*, 45–93. Paris: DuFeuil.

Atlan, H. 1987. Uncommon finalities. In W. I. Thompson, ed., *GAIA: A way of knowing*, 110–27. Great Barrington, Mass.: Lindisfarne.

Atlan, H.; Benezra, E.; Fogleman-Soulie, F.; Pellegrin, D.; and Weisbuch, G. 1986. Emergence of classification procedures in automata networks as a model for functional self-organization. *Journal of Theoretical Biology* 3: 371–80.

Attridge, D.; Bennington, G.; and Young, R., eds. 1987. *Post-structuralism and the question of history*. Cambridge: Cambridge University Press.

Averill, J. R. 1975. A semantic atlas of emotional concepts. *JSAS Catalogue of Selected Documents in Psychology* 5: 330–16.

Averill, J. R. 1986. The acquisition of emotions during adulthood. In R. Harré, ed., *The social construction of emotions*, 98–118. Oxford: Basil Blackwell.

Averill, J. R. 1988. Disorders of emotion. *Journal of Social and Clinical Psychology* 6: 247–68.

Ayala, F. J.; and Dobzhansky, T. 1974. *Studies in the philosophy of biology: Reduction and related problems*. Berkeley: University of California Press.

Baars, B. J., ed. 1986. *The cognitive revolution in psychology*. New York: Guilford.

Babcock, H. H., ed. 1988. Integrative psychotherapy. *Psychiatric Annals*, 18 (5): 267–308.

Babloyantz, A.; Salazar, J. M.; and Nicolis, C. 1985. Evidence of chaotic dynamics of brain activity during the sleep cycle. *Physics Letters* 111A: 152–56.

Bach, R. 1977. *Illusions: The adventures of a reluctant messiah*. New York: Dell.

Bachelard, G. 1968. *The philosophy of no*. Trans. G. C. Waterston. New York: Orion Press.

Bacon, F. 1960 [1620]. *Novum organum*. New York: Bobbs-Merrill.

Baillargeon, R. 1987. Object permanence in 3½- and 4½-month-old infants. *Developmental Psychology* 23: 655–64.

Bain, J. A. 1928. *Thought control in everyday life*. New York: Funk and Wagnalls.

Bainerd, C. J. 1978. The stage question in cognitive-developmental theory. *Behavioral and Brain Sciences* 2: 173–213.

Balay, J.; and Shevrin, H. 1988. The subliminal psychodynamic activation method. *American Psychologist* 43: 161–74.

Balch, S. H. 1989. Metaevolution and biocultural history. *Journal of Social and Biological Structures* 12: 303–18.

Baldwin, J. M. 1911 [1895]. *Mentai   lopment in the child and the race,* 3d ed. New York: Macmillan.

Baldwin, M. W.; and Holmes, J. G. 1987. Salient private audiences and awareness of the self. *Journal of Personality and Social Psychology* 52: 1–12.

Balint, M. 1950. On the termination of analysis. *International Journal of Psychoanalysis.* 31: 196–99.

Baltes, P. B. 1987. Theoretical propositions of life-span developmental psychology: On the dynamics between growth and decline. *Developmental Psychology* 23: 611–26.

Baltes, P. B.; Featherman, D. L.; and Lerner, R. M., eds. 1987. *Life-span development and behavior.* Hillsdale, N.J.: Erlbaum.

Band, E. B.; and Weisz, J. R. 1988. How to feel better when it feels bad: Children's perspectives on coping with everyday stress. *Developmental Psychology* 24: 247–53.

Bandura, A. 1969. *Principles of behavior modification.* New York: Holt, Rinehart and Winston.

Bandura, A. 1973. *Aggression: A social learning analysis.* Englewood Cliffs, N.J.: Prentice-Hall.

Bandura, A. 1977. Self-efficacy: Toward a unifying theory of behavioral change. *Psychological Review* 84: 191–215.

Bandura, A. 1978. The self system in reciprocal determinism. *American Psychologist* 33: 344–58.

Bandura, A. 1982. The psychology of chance encounters and life paths. *American Psychologist* 37: 747–55.

Bandura, A. 1986. *Social foundations of thought and action: A social cognitive theory.* Englewood Cliffs, N.J.: Prentice-Hall.

Bandura, A.; and Walters, R. H. 1963. *Social learning and personality development.* New York: Holt, Rinehart and Winston.

Bannister, D. 1975. Personal construct theory in psychotherapy. In D. Bannister, ed., *Issues and approaches in the psychological therapies.* New York: Wiley.

Bannister, R. C. 1987. *Sociology and scientism: The American quest for objectivity, 1880–1940.* Chapel Hill: University of North Carolina Press.

Barclay, C. R. 1986. Schematization of autobiographical memory. In D. C. Rubin, ed., *Autobiographical memory,* 82–99. Cambridge: Cambridge University Press.

Barker, S. L.; Funk, S. C.; and Houston, B. K. 1988. Psychological treatment versus nonspecific factors: A meta-analysis of conditions that engender comparable expectations for improvement. *Clinical Psychology Review* 8: 579–94.

Bar-Levav, R. 1988. *Thinking in the shadow of feelings.* New York: Simon & Schuster.

Barlow, D. H. 1988. *Anxiety and its disorders: The nature and treatment of anxiety and panic.* New York: Guilford.

Baron, R. S.; and Moore, D. L. 1987. The impact of exercise-induced arousal on the self-other memory effect. *Social Cognition* 5: 166–77.

Barrett, W. 1958. *Irrational man: A study in existential philosophy.* New York: Doubleday.

Barrett, W. 1967. *The illusion of technique.* New York: Doubleday.

Barrom, C. P.; Shadish, W. R., Jr.; and Montgomery, L. M. 1988. PhDs, PsyDs, and real-world constraints on scholarly activity: Another look at the Boulder Model. *Professional Psychology: Research and Practice* 19: 93–101.

Barron, J., ed. 1978. The relationship between the personality of the psychotherapist and his/her selection of a theoretical orientation to psychotherapy. *Psychotherapy: Theory, Research and Practice* 15: 307–415.

Barsalou, L. W. 1987. The instability of graded structure: Implications for the nature of concepts. In U. Neisser, ed., *Concepts and conceptual development: Ecological and intellectual factors in categorization,* 101–40. Cambridge: Cambridge University Press.

Bartlett, F. C. 1932. *Remembering.* Cambridge: Cambridge University Press.

Bartley, W. W. 1984 [1962]. *The retreat to commitment,* 2d ed. La Salle, Ill.: Open Court.

Bartley, W. W. 1987a. In defense of self-applicable critical rationalism. In G. Radnitzky and W. W. Bartley, eds., *Evolutionary epistemology, theory of rationality, and sociology of knowledge,* 279–312. La Salle, Ill.: Open Court.

Bartley, W. W. 1987b. Theories of rationality. In G. Radnitzky and W. W. Bartley, eds., *Evolutionary epistemology, theory of rationality, and sociology of knowledge,* 205–20. La Salle, Ill.: Open Court.

Bartley, W. W. 1987c. A refutation of the alleged refutation of comprehensively critical rationalism. In G. Radnitzky and W. W. Bartley, eds., *Evolutionary epistemology, theory of rationality, and sociology of knowledge,* 313–41. La Salle, Ill.: Open Court.

Bartley, W. W. 1987d. Philosophy of biology versus philosophy of physics. In G. Radnitzky and W. W. Bartley, eds., *Evolutionary epistemology, theory of rationality, and the sociology of knowledge,* 7–45. LaSalle, Ill.: Open Court.

Bateson, G. 1972. *Steps to an ecology of mind.* New York: Ballantine.

Bateson, G. 1979. *Mind and nature: A necessary unity.* New York: Bantam.

Bateson, P. 1985. Problems and possibilities in fusing developmental and evolutionary thought. In G. Butterworth, J. Rutkowska, and M. Scaife, eds., *Evolution and developmental psychology,* 3–21. Sussex, England: Harvester Press.

Batson, C. D. 1990. How social an animal? The human capacity for caring. *American Psychologist* 45: 336–46.

Baumeister, R. F. 1987. How the self became a problem: A psychological review of historical research. *Journal of Personality and Social Psychology* 52: 163–76.

Baumeister, R. F. 1990. Suicide as escape from self. *Psychological Review* 97: 90–113.

Baumeister, R. F.; and Scher, S. J. 1988. Self-defeating behavior patterns among normal individuals: Review and analysis of common self-destructive tendencies. *Psychological Bulletin* 104: 3–22.

Baumrind, D. 1989. The permanence of change and the impermanence of stability. *Human Development* 32: 187–95.

Bazerman, C. 1988. *Shaping written knowledge: The genre and activity of the experimental article in science.* Madison: University of Wisconsin Press.

Beavers, W. R.; and Kaslow, F. W. 1981. The anatomy of hope. *Journal of Marital and Family Therapy* 7: 119–26.

Bechtel, W. 1988. Connectionism and rules and representation systems: Are they compatible? *Philosophical Psychology* 1: 5–16.

Beck, A. T. 1963. Thinking and depression, I. Idiosyncratic content and cognitive distortion. *Archives of General Psychiatry* 9: 324–33.

Beck, A. T. 1967. *Depression: Clinical, experimental, and theoretical aspects.* New York: Hoeber.

Beck, A. T. 1970. Cognitive therapy: Nature and relation to behavior therapy. *Behavior Therapy* 1: 184–200.

Beck, A. T. 1976. *Cognitive therapy and the emotional disorders.* New York: International Universities Press.

Beck, A. T.; Emery, G.; and Greenberg, R. L. 1985. *Anxiety disorders and phobias: A cognitive perspective.* New York: Basic Books.

Beck, A. T.; Brown, G.; and Steer, R. A. 1989. Prediction of eventual suicide in psychiatric inpatients by clinical ratings of hopelessness. *Journal of Consulting and Clinical Psychology* 57: 309–10.

Beck, A. T.; Riskind, J. H.; Brown, G.; and Steer, R. A. 1988. Levels of hopelessness in DSM-III disorders: A partial test of content specificity in depression. *Cognitive Therapy and Research* 12: 459–69.

Beck, R. L.; and Munson, C. E. 1988. Family-of-origin experience in a psychotherapy training program. *Social Casework: The Journal of Contemporary Social Work* (January): 54–57.

Becker, E. 1973. *The denial of death.* New York: Free Press.

Beiser, M. 1974. Components and correlates of mental well-being. *Journal of Health and Social Behavior* 15: 320–27.

Beitman, B.; and Maxim, P. 1984. A survey of psychiatric practice: Implications for psychiatric training. *Journal of Psychoanalytic Education* 8: 149–53.

Belenky, M. F.; Clinchy, B. M.; Goldberger, N. R.; and Tarule, J. M. 1986. *Women's ways of knowing: The development of self, voice and mind.* New York: Basic Books.

Bellah, R. N.; Madsen, R.; Sullivan, W. M.; Swidler, A.; and Tipton, S. M. 1985. *Habits of the heart: Individualism and commitment in American life.* New York: Harper and Row.

Bellah, R. N.; Madsen, R.; Sullivan, W. M.; Swidler, A.; and Tipton, S. M., eds. 1987. *Individualism and commitment in American life: Readings on the themes of habits of the heart.* New York: Harper and Row.

Belsky, J.; and Nezworski, M. T., eds. 1987. *Clinical implications of attachment.* Hillsdale, N.J.: Erlbaum.

Bentall, R. P. 1990. The illusion of reality: A review and integration of psychological research on hallucinations. *Psychological Bulletin* 107: 82–95.

Ben-Zeev, A. 1988. The schema paradigm in perception. *Journal of Mind and Behavior* 9: 487–514.

Berger, B. G.; and Owen, D. R. 1988. Stress reduction and mood enhancement in four exercise modes: Swimming, body conditioning, hatha yoga, and fencing. *Research Quarterly for Exercise and Sport* 59: 148–59.

Berger, P. L. 1967. *The sacred canopy: Elements of a sociological theory of religion.* New York: Anchor.

Berger, P. L.; and Luckman, T. 1966. *The social construction of reality: A treatise in the sociology of knowledge.* Garden City, N.Y.: Anchor.

Bergin, A. E. 1971. The evaluation of therapeutic outcomes. In A. E. Bergin and S. L. Garfield, eds., *Handbook of psychotherapy and behavior change,* 1st ed., 217–70. New York: Wiley.

Bergin, A. E.; and Jensen, J. P. 1990. Religiosity of psychotherapists: A national survey. *Psychotherapy* 27: 3–7.

Bergin, A. E.; and Lambert, M. J. 1978. The evaluation of therapeutic outcomes. In S. L. Garfield and A. E. Bergin, eds., *Handbook of psychotherapy and behavior change,* 2d ed., 139–89. New York: Wiley.

Bergland, R. 1985. *The fabric of mind.* New York: Viking.

Berkowitz, L., ed. 1978. *Cognitive theories in social psychology.* New York: Academic Press.

Berlin, I. 1976. *Vico and Herder: Two studies in the history of ideas.* New York: Viking.

Berman, M. 1989. *Coming to our senses: Body and spirit in the hidden history of the west.* New York: Simon and Schuster.

Bernal, J. D. 1954. *The scientific and industrial revolutions.* Cambridge, Mass.: MIT Press.

Berner, P. 1988. Emotion, affect and mood: A terminological introduction. *Psychopathology* 21: 65–69.

Bernstein, P. P.; Duncan, S. W.; Gavin, L. A.; Lindahl, K. M.; and Ozonoff, S. 1989. Resistance to psychotherapy after a child dies: The effects of the death on parents and siblings. *Psychotherapy* 26: 227–32.

Bernstein, R. J. 1983. *Beyond objectivism and relativism: Science, hermeneutics, and praxis.* Philadelphia: University of Pennsylvania Press.

Bertalanffy, L. 1968. *General system theory.* New York: George Braziller.

Berzonsky, M. D. 1989. The self as a theorist: Individual differences in identity formation. *International Journal of Personal Construct Psychology* 2: 363–76.

Besharov, D. J. 1989. *Recognizing child abuse.* New York: Free Press.

Bettelheim, B. 1960. *The informed heart: Autonomy in a mass age.* Glencoe, Ill.: Free Press.

Bettelheim, B. 1982. Freud and the soul. *New Yorker,* 1 March, 52–93.

Beuter, A.; Larocque, D.; and Glass, L. 1989. Complex oscillations in a human motor system. *Journal of Motor Behavior* 21: 277–89.

Beutler, L. E. 1989. Differential treatment selection: The role of diagnosis in psychotherapy. *Psychotherapy* 26: 271–81.

Beutler, L. E.; Crago, M.; and Arizmendi, T. G. 1986. Therapist variables in psychotherapy process and outcome. In S. L. Garfield and A. E. Bergin, eds., *Handbook of psychotherapy and behavior change,* 3d ed., 257–310. New York: Wiley.

Bever, T. G.; Fodor, J. A.; and Garrett, M. 1968. A formal limit of associationism. In T. R. Dixon and D. L. Horton, eds., *Verbal behavior and general behavior therapy,* 582–85. Englewood Cliffs, N.J.: Prentice-Hall.

Bhatt, R. S.; Wasserman, E. A.; Reynolds, W. F.; and Knauss, K. S. 1988. Conceptual behavior in pigeons: Categorization of both familiar and novel examples from four classes of natural and artificial stimuli. *Journal of Experimental Psychology: Animal Behavior Processes* 14: 219–34.

Bienenstock, E. 1985. Dynamics of the central nervous system. In J. P. Aubin, D. Saari, and K. Sigmund, eds., *Dynamics of macrosystems*, 3–20. Berlin: Springer-Verlag.

Bienenstock, E.; Soulié, F. F.; and Weisbuch, G., eds. 1986. *Disordered systems and biological organization.* Berlin: Springer-Verlag.

Birren, J. E.; and Hateley, B. J. 1985. Guided autobiography: A special method of life review. In R. Blum and G. Simon, eds., *The art of life and family writing.* American Lives Endowment.

Birren, J. E., and Hedlund, B. 1987. Contributions of autobiography to developmental psychology. In N. Isenberg, ed., *Contemporary topics in developmental psychology*, 394–415. Englewood Cliffs, N.J.: Prentice-Hall.

Black, I. B.; Adler, J. E.; Dreyfus, C. F.; Friedman, W. F.; LaGamma, E. F.; and Roach, A. H. 1987. Biochemistry of information storage in the nervous system. *Science* 236: 1263–68.

Blackemore, C. and Greenfield, S., eds. 1987. *Mindwaves.* New York: Basil Blackwell.

Blackmore, J. 1979. On the inverted use of the terms 'realism' and 'idealism' among scientists and historians of science. *British Journal for the Philosophy of Science* 30: 125–34.

Blanchard, D. C.; and Blanchard, R. J. 1988. Ethoexperimental approaches to the biology of emotion. *Annual Review of Psychology* 39: 43–68.

Blanck, G.; and Blanck, R. 1974. *Ego psychology: Theory and practice*, vol. 1. New York: Columbia University Press.

Blanck, G.; and Blanck, R. 1979. *Ego psychology*, vol. 2. New York: Columbia University Press.

Blanco, S.; Guidano, V. F.; Mahoney, M. J.; and Reda, M. A. 1986. *The experimental use of mirror time in cognitive psychotherapy.* Paper presented at the annual meeting of the Italian Psychological Society, October, Milano.

Blashfield, R. K.; and McElroy, R. A. 1989. Ontology of personality disorder categories. *Psychiatric Annals* 19: 126–31.

Blatner, A. 1988. *Foundations of psychodrama: History, theory, and practice.* New York: Springer.

Blatner, A. 1989. *Acting-in: Practical applications of psychodramatic methods*, 2d ed. New York: Springer.

Bliss, S., ed. 1985. *The new holistic health handbook.* Lexington, Mass.: Stephen Greene.

Block, J. 1971. *Lives through time.* Berkeley, Calif.: Bancroft Books.

Block, J. H.; and Block, J. 1980. The role of ego-control and ego-resiliency in the organization of behavior. In W. A. Collins, ed., *Minnesota symposium on child psychology*, vol. 13, 39–101. Hillsdale, N.J.: Erlbaum.

Block, N., ed. 1980. *Readings in philosophy of psychology.* Cambridge, Mass.: Harvard University Press.

Bloom, L.; and Capatides, J. 1987. Expression of affect and the emergence of language. *Child Development* 58: 1513–22.

Blumenthal, A. L. 1975. A reappraisal of Wilhelm Wundt. *American Psychologist* 30: 1081–88.

Blumenthal, A. L. 1980. Wilhelm Wundt and early American psychology: A clash of cultures. In R. Rieber and K. Salzinger, eds., *Psychology: Theoretical-historical perspectives*, 25–42. New York: Academic Press.

Blumenthal, A. L. 1985. Wilhelm Wundt: Psychology as the propaedeutic science. In C. Buxton, ed., *Points of view of the history of modern psychology*, 19–50. New York: Academic Press.

Boakes, R. A. 1984. *From Darwin to behaviourism.* Cambridge: Cambridge University Press.

Boden, M. A. 1981. *Minds and mechanisms: Philosophical psychology and computational models.* Ithaca, N.Y.: Cornell University Press.

Bohm, D. 1980. *Wholeness and the implicate order.* Boston: Routledge and Kegan Paul.

Bolles, R. C. 1972. Reinforcement, expectancy, and learning. *Psychological Review* 79: 394–409.

Bolles, R. C. 1975. *Learning theory.* New York: Holt, Rinehart and Winston.

Bonner, J. T., ed. 1982. *Evolution and development.* New York: Springer-Verlag.

Boorstin, D. J. 1983. *The discoverers: A history of man's search to know his world and himself.* New York: Random House.

Borges, J. L. 1964. *Dreamtigers.* Trans. M. Boyer and H. Morland. Austin: University of Texas Press.

Boring, E. G. 1952a. The Gibsonian visual field. *Psychological Review* 59: 246–47.

Boring, E. G. 1952b. Visual perception as invariance. *Psychological Review* 59: 141–48.

Bornstein, M. H. 1985. How infant and mother jointly contribute to developing cognitive competence in the child. *Proceedings of the National Academy of Science,* 7470–73.

Bornstein, M. H. 1988. Mothers, infants, and the development of cognitive competence. In H. E. Fitzgerald, B. M. Lester, and M. W. Yogman, eds., *Theory and research in behavioral pediatrics,* vol. 4, 67–99.

Bornstein, M. H. 1989. Sensitive periods in development: Structural characteristics and causal interpretations. *Psychological Bulletin* 105: 179–97.

Bornstein, M. H.; and Sigman, M. D. 1986. Continuity in mental development from infancy. *Child Development* 57: 251–74.

Borys, D. S.; and Pope, K. S. 1989. Dual relationships between therapist and client: A national study of psychologists, psychiatrists, and social workers. *Professional Psychology: Research and Practice* 20: 283–93.

Boslough, J. 1985. *Stephen Hawking's Universe.* New York: William Morrow.

Boudewyns, P. A.; and Shipley, R. H. 1983. *Flooding and implosive therapy: Direct therapeutic exposure in clinical practice.* New York: Plenum Press.

Bower, G. H. 1970. Imagery as a relational organizer in associative learning. *Journal of Verbal Learning and Verbal Behavior* 9: 529–37.

Bower, G. H. 1981. Mood and memory. *American Psychologist* 36: 129–48.

Bower, G. H.; and Cohen, P. R. 1982. Emotional influences in memory and thinking: Data and theory. In M. S. Clark and S. T. Fiske, eds., *Affect and cognition: The 17th Annual Carnegie Symposium on Cognition.* Hillsdale, N.J.: Erlbaum.

Bower, G. H.; and Hilgard, E. R. 1981. *Theories of learning,* 5th ed. Englewood Cliffs, N.J.: Prentice-Hall.

Bowers, K. S. 1973. Situationism in psychology: An analysis and a critique. *Psychological Review* 80: 307–36.

Bowers, K. S. 1987. Revisioning the unconscious. *Canadian Psychology* 28: 93–104.

Bowers, K. S.; and Meichenbaum, D., eds. 1984. *The unconscious reconsidered.* New York: Wiley.

Bowlby, J. 1969. *Attachment and loss.* Vol. 1, *Attachment.* New York: Basic Books.

Bowlby, J. 1973. *Attachment and loss.* Vol. 2, *Separation: Anxiety and anger.* New York: Basic Books.

Bowlby, J. 1979. *The making and breaking of affectional bonds.* London: Tavistock.

Bowlby, J. 1980. *Attachment and loss.* Vol. 3, *Loss: Sadness and depression.* London: Hogarth Press.

Bowlby, J. 1985. The role of childhood experience in cognitive disturbance. In M. J. Mahoney and A. Freeman, eds., *Cognition and psychotherapy,* 181–99. New York: Plenum.

Bowlby, J. 1988. *A secure base,* New York: Basic Books.

Bowler, P. J. 1988. *Evolution: The history of an idea,* rev. ed. Berkeley: University of California Press.

Boyle, G. J. 1989. Factor structure of the Differential Emotions Scale and the Eight State Questionnaire revisited. *Irish Journal of Psychology* 10: 56–66.

Boynton, R. M. 1974. The visual system: Environmental information. In E. C. Carterette and M. Friedman, eds., *Handbook of perception,* vol. 1. New York: Academic Press.

Bradley, M. T.; MacDonald, P.; and Fleming, I. 1989. Amnesia, feelings of knowing, and the guilty knowledge test. *Canadian Journal of Behavioral Science* 21: 224–31.

Brainerd, C. J. 1978. The stage question in cognitive-developmental theory. *The Behavioral and Brain Sciences* 2: 173–213.

Brand, A. G. 1980. *Therapy in writing: A psycho-educational enterprise.* Lexington, Mass.: D.C. Heath.

Brand, A. G.; and Leckie, P. A. 1988. The emotions of professional writers. *Journal of Psychology* 122: 421–39.

Brandstädter, J. 1989. Personal self-regulation of development: Cross-sequential analyses of development-related control beliefs and emotions. *Developmental Psychology* 25: 96–108.

Bransford, J. D. 1971. The abstraction of linguistic ideas. *Cognitive Psychology* 2: 331–50.

Bransford, J. D. 1979. *Human cognition: Learning, understanding, and remembering.* Belmont, Calif.: Wadsworth.

Bransford, J. D.; and McCarrell, N. S. 1974. A sketch of a cognitive approach to comprehension: Some thoughts about understanding what it means to comprehend. In W. B. Weimer and D. S. Palermo, eds., *Cognition and the symbolic processes*, 189–229. vol. 1. Hillsdale, N.J.: Erlbaum.

Bransford, J. D.; and Franks, J. J. 1971. The abstraction of linguistic ideas. *Cognitive Psychology* 2: 331–50.

Braudel, F. 1979a. *The structures of everyday life.* Vol. 1, *The limits of the possible.* New York: Harper and Row.

Braudel, F. 1979b. *The structures of everyday life.* Vol. 2, *The wheels of commerce.* New York: Harper and Row.

Braudel, F. 1979c. *The structures of everyday life.* Vol. 3, *The perspective of the world.* New York: Harper and Row.

Breasted, J. H. 1930. *The Edwin Smith surgical papyrus.* 2 vols. Chicago: University of Chicago Press.

Breger, L.; and McGaugh, J. L. 1965. Critique and reformulation of "learning theory" approaches to psychotherapy and neurosis. *Psychological Bulletin* 63: 338–58.

Breger, L.; and McGaugh, J. L. 1966. Learning theory and behavior therapy: A reply to Rachman and Eysenck. *Psychological Bulletin* 65: 170–73.

Breger, L., ed. 1969. *Clinical-cognitive psychology: Models and integrations.* Englewood Cliffs, N.J.: Prentice-Hall.

Breger, L. 1974. *From instinct to identity: The development of personality.* Englewood Cliffs, N.J.: Prentice-Hall.

Brehm, J. W. 1966. *A theory of psychological reactance.* New York: Academic Press.

Breland, K.; and Breland, M. 1961. The misbehavior of organisms. *American Psychologist* 16: 681–84.

Brent, S. B. 1978. Prigogine's model for self-organization in nonequilibrium systems: Its relevance for developmental psychology. *Human Development* 21: 374–87.

Brent, S. B. 1984. *Psychological and social structures.* Hillsdale, N.J.: Erlbaum.

Brentano, F. 1973 [1874]. *Psychology from an empirical standpoint.* Trans. A. C. Rancurello. New York: Humanities Press.

Brentano, F. 1981 [1929]. *Sensory and noetic consciousness.* New York: Routledge and Kegan Paul.

Bretherton, I. 1984a. Representing the social world in symbolic play: Reality and fantasy. In I. Bretherton, ed., *Symbolic play: The development of social understanding.* New York: Academic Press.

Bretherton, I., ed. 1984b. *Symbolic play: The development of social understanding.* New York: Academic Press.

Bretherton, I. 1985. Attachment theory: Retrospect and prospect. In I. Bretherton and E. Waters, eds., *Growing points of attachment theory and research.* Chicago: University of Chicago Press.

Bretherton, I.; and Beeghly, M. 1982. Talking about internal states: The acquisition of an explicit theory of mind. *Developmental Psychology* 18: 906–21.

Bretherton, I.; and Waters, E., eds. 1985. *Growing points of attachment theory and research.* Chicago: University of Chicago Press.

Brewer, W. F. 1974a. The problem of meaning and the interrelations of the higher mental processes. In W. B. Weimer and D. S. Palermo, eds., *Cognition and the symbolic processes*, vol. 1, 263–98. Hillsdale, N.J.: Erlbaum.

Brewer, W. F. 1974b. There is no convincing evidence for operant or classical conditioning in adult humans. In W. B. Weimer and D. S. Palermo, eds., *Cognition and the symbolic process*, vol. 1, 1–42. Hillsdale, N.J.: Erlbaum.

Brewer, W. F. 1986. What is autobiographical memory? In D. C. Rubin, ed., *Autobiographical memory*, 25–49. Cambridge: Cambridge University Press.

Brewer, W. F. 1988. Memory for randomly sampled autobiographical events. In U. Neisser and E. Winograd, eds., *Remembering reconsidered: Ecological and traditional approaches to the study of memory*, 21–90. Cambridge: Cambridge University Press.

Brewer, W. F.; and Nakamura, G. V. 1984. The nature and functions of schemas. In R. S. Wyer and T. K. Srull, eds., *Handbook of social cognition*, vol. 1, 119–60. Hillsdale, N.J.: Erlbaum.

Brewin, C. R. 1989. Cognitive change processes in psychotherapy. *Psychological Review* 96: 379–94.

Bridges, K. M. B. 1932. *The social and emotional development of the pre-school child*. London: Kegan Paul.

Bridgman, P. W. 1927. *The logic of modern physics*. New York: Macmillan.

Briggs, J. P.; and Peat, F. D. 1984. *The looking glass universe: The emerging science of wholeness*. New York: Simon and Schuster.

Briggs, S. R.; and Cheek, J. M. 1988. On the nature of self-monitoring: Problems with assessment, problems with validity. *Journal of Personality and Social Psychology* 54: 663–78.

Brim, O. G. 1976. Life span development of the theory of oneself: Implications for child development. In H. W. Reese, ed., *Advances in child development and behavior*, vol. 11. New York: Academic Press.

Broad, C. D. 1925. *The mind and its place in nature*. New York: Routledge.

Broadbent, D. E. 1954. The role of auditory localization and attention in memory span. *Journal of Experimental Psychology* 47: 51–60.

Broadbent, D. E. 1958. *Perception and communication*. London: Pergamon Press.

Broadbent, D. E. 1985. A question of levels: Comments on McClelland and Rumelhart. *Journal of Experimental Psychology: General* 114: 189–92.

Brody, E. M.; and Farber, B. A. 1989. Effects of psychotherapy on significant others. *Professional Psychology: Research and Practice* 20: 116–22.

Bromberg, W. 1959. *The mind of man: A history of psychotherapy and psychoanalysis*. New York: Harper and Row.

Bronfenbrenner, U. 1974. Developmental research, public policy, and the ecology of childhood. *Child Development* 45: 1–5.

Bronowski, J. 1973. *The ascent of man*. Boston: Little, Brown.

Bronson, G. W. 1982. Structure, status, and characteristics of the nervous system at birth. In P. Stratton, ed., *Psychobiology of the human newborn*, 99–118. New York: Wiley.

Broughton, J. M. 1986. The psychology, history and ideology of the self. In K.

S. Larsen, ed., *Dialectics and ideology in psychology*, 128–64. Norwood, N.J.: Ablex.

Broughton, J.; and Honey, M., eds. 1988. Gender arrangements and nuclear threat: A discussion with Dorothy Dinnerstein. *Theoretical and Philosophical Psychology* 8: 27–40.

Brown, L. S. 1988. Harmful effects of posttermination sexual and romantic relationships between therapists and their former clients. *Psychotherapy* 25: 249–55.

Brown, L. S. 1990. Taking account of gender in the clinical assessment interview. *Professional Psychology: Research and Practice* 21: 12–17.

Brown, R.; and McNeill, D. 1966. The "tip of the tongue" phenomenon. *Journal of Verbal Learning and Verbal Behavior* 5: 325–37.

Brown, R. 1958. *Words and things.* Glencoe, Ill.: Free Press.

Brown, T.; and Weiss, L. 1987. Structures, procedures, heuristics, and affectivity. *Archives de Psychologie* 55: 59–94.

Brown, T. H.; Chapman, P. F.; Kairiss, E. W.; and Keenan, C. L. 1988. Long-term synaptic potentiation. *Science* 242: 724–28.

Bruce, D. 1985. The how and why of ecological memory. *Journal of Experimental Psychology: General* 114: 78–90.

Bruner, J. S. 1966. *Toward a theory of instruction.* New York: Norton.

Bruner, J. S. 1979. *On knowing: Essays for the left hand.* Cambridge, Mass.: Harvard University Press.

Bruner, J. S. 1986. *Actual minds, possible worlds.* Cambridge, Mass.: Harvard University Press.

Bruner, J. S.; Goodnow, J. J.; and Austin, G. A. 1956. *A study of thinking.* New York: Wiley.

Bruner, J. S.; Jolly, A.; and Sylva, K., eds. 1976. *Play—Its role in development and evolution.* New York: Basic Books.

Bruner, J. S.; and Postman, L. 1947a. Emotional selectivity in perception and reaction. *Journal of Personality* 16: 69–77.

Bruner, J. S.; and Postman, L. 1947b. Tension and tension-release as organizing factors in perception. *Journal of Personality* 15: 300–8.

Bruner, J. S.; and Postman, L. 1949. On perception of incongruity: A paradigm. *Journal of Personality* 18: 206–23.

Bryk, A. S.; and Raudenbush, S. W. 1988. Heterogeneity of variance in experimental studies: A challenge to conventional interpretations. *Psychological Bulletin* 104: 396–404.

Bryne, N. O.; and McCarthy, I. C. 1988. Moving statutes: Re-questing ambivalence through ambiguous discourse. *Irish Journal of Psychology* 9: 173–82.

Bubner, R. 1981. *Modern German philosophy.* Trans. E. Matthews. Cambridge: Cambridge University Press.

Buck, R. 1986. The psychology of emotion. In J. E. LeDoux and W. Hirst, eds., *Mind and brain: Dialogues in cognitive neuroscience*, 275–300. Cambridge: Cambridge University Press.

Buckley, K. W. 1989. *Mechanical man: John Broadus Watson and the beginnings of behaviorism.* New York: Guilford.

Buckley, W.; and Jones, B. J. eds. 1979. Sociobiology. *Behavioral Science* 24(1).

Buckley, P.; Karasu, T. B.; and Charles, E. 1981. Psychotherapists view their personal therapy. *Psychotherapy: Theory, Research and Practice* 18: 299–305.

Bugental, J. F. T. 1978. *Psychotherapy and process: The fundamentals of an existential-humanistic approach.* Reading, Mass.: Addison-Wesley.

Bugental, J. F. T. 1981. *The search for authenticity: An existential-analytic approach to psychotherapy.* New York: Irvington.

Bugental, J. F. T. 1987. *The art of the psychotherapist.* New York: Norton.

Bugental, J. F. T. 1988. What is "failure" in psychotherapy? *Psychotherapy* 25: 532–35.

Bugental, J. F. T.; and Bugental, E. K. 1984. A fate worse than death: The fear of changing. *Psychotherapy* 21: 543–49.

Bühler, C. 1935. The curve of life as studied in biographies. *Journal of Applied Psychology* 19: 405–9.

Buie, J. 1989. Turf battle heats up on many fronts. *APA Monitor* 20: 15–16.

Burke, K. 1962. *A rhetoric of motives.* Cleveland, Ohio: World Publishing.

Burke, K. 1965. *Permanence and change,* 2d ed. New York: Bobbs-Merrill.

Burke, K. 1966. *Language as symbolic action: Essays on life, literature, and method.* Berkeley: University of California Press.

Burke, K. 1973. *The philosophy of literary form: Studies in symbolic action,* 3d ed. Berkeley: University of California Press.

Burnkrant, R. E.; and Page, T. J., Jr. 1984. A modification of the Fenigstein, Scheier, and Buss Self-Consciousness Scales. *Journal of Personality Assessment* 48: 629–37.

Burrell, M. J. 1987. Cognitive psychology, epistemology, and psychotherapy: A motor-evolutionary perspective. *Psychotherapy* 24: 225–32.

Burt, J. J. 1984. Metahealth: A challenge for the future. In J. D. Matarazzo, ed., *Behavioral health,* 1239–45. New York: Wiley.

Buss, A. H. 1980. *Self-consciousness and social anxiety.* San Francisco: W. H. Freeman.

Buss, A. R. 1978. The structure of psychological revolutions. *Journal of the History of the Behavioral Sciences* 14: 57–64.

Buss, L. W. 1988. *The evolution of individuality.* Princeton, N.J.: Princeton University Press.

Butler, R. 1963. The life review: An interpretation of reminiscence of the aged. *Psychiatry* 26: 65–76.

Butler, R. 1980–81. The life review: An unrecognized bonanza. *International Journal of Aging and Human Development* 12: 35–38.

Butterfield, E. C.; Nelson, T. O.; and Peck, V. 1988. Developmental aspects of the feeling of knowing. *Developmental Psychology* 24: 654–663.

Butterworth, G.; Rutkowska, J.; and Scaife, M., eds. 1985. *Evolution and developmental psychology.* Sussex, England: Harvester Press.

Button, E., ed. 1985. *Personal construct theory and mental health.* London: Croom Helm.

Byrne, B. M. 1988. The Self Description Questionnaire III: Testing for equivalent factorial validity across ability. *Education and Psychological Measurement* 48: 397–406.

Byrne, B. M.; and Shavelson, R. J. 1986. On the structure of adolescent self-concept. *Journal of Educational Psychology* 78: 474–81.

Cacioppo, J. T.; Martzke, J. S.; Petty, R. E.; and Tassinary, L. G. 1988. Specific forms of facial EMG response index emotions during an interview: From Darwin to continuous flow hypothesis of affect-laden information processing. *Journal of Personality and Social Psychology* 54: 592–604.

Cacioppo, J. T.; and Tassinary, L. G. 1990. Inferring psychological significance from physiological signals. *American Psychologist* 45: 16–28.

Cacioppo, J. T.; Tassinary, L. G.; Stonebraker, T. B.; and Petty, R. E. 1987. Self-report and cardiovascular measures of arousal: Fractionation during residual arousal. *Biological Psychology* 25: 135–51.

Cairns, R. B.; Gariépy, J. L.; and Hood, K. E. 1990. Development, microevolution, and social behavior. *Psychological Review* 97: 49–65.

Calkins, M. W. 1915. The self in scientific psychology. *American Journal of Psychology* 26: 495–524.

Calkins, M. W. 1916. The self in recent psychology. *Psychological Bulletin* 13: 20–27.

Calkins, M. W. 1919. The self in recent psychology. *Psychological Bulletin* 16: 111–19.

Calkins, M. W. 1927. The self in recent psychology. *Psychological Bulletin* 24: 205–15.

Callaway, E.; and Thompson, S. 1953. Sympathetic activity and perception. *Psychosomatic Medicine* 15: 443–55.

Callebaut, W.; and Pinxten, R. 1987. *Evolutionary epistemology: A multiparadigm program.* Boston: Reidel.

Calvin, W. H. 1988. A global brain theory. *Science* 240: 1802–3.

Camaras, L. A.; Ribordy, S.; Hill, J.; Martino, S.; Spaccarelli, S.; and Stefani, R. 1988. Recognition and posing of emotional expressions by abused children and their mothers. *Developmental Psychology* 24: 776–81.

Campbell, D. T. 1959. Methodological suggestions from a comparative psychology of knowledge processes. *Inquiry* 2: 152–82.

Campbell, D. T. 1960. Blind variation and selective retention in creative thought as in other knowledge processes. *Psychological Review* 67: 380–400.

Campbell, D. T. 1974a. Evolutionary epistemology. In P. A. Schilpp, ed., *The philosophy of Karl Popper*, vol. 14, I and II, 413–63. La Salle, Ill.: Open Court. Reprinted in Radnitzky and Bartley 1987.

Campbell, D. T. 1974b. "Downward causation" in hierarchically organized biological systems. In F. J. Ayala and T. Dobzhansky, eds., *Studies in the philosophy of biology: Reduction and related problems*, 179–86. Berkeley: University of California Press.

Campbell, D. T. 1975. On the conflicts between biological and social evolution and between psychology and moral tradition. *American Psychologist* 30: 1103–26.

Campbell, D. T. 1987. Neurological embodiments of belief and the gaps in the fit of phenomena to noumena. In A. Shimony and D. Nails, eds., *Naturalistic epistemology: A symposium of two decades.* Dordrecht, Netherlands: D. Reidel.

Campbell, D. T. 1988. Fragments of the fragile history of psychological epistemology and theory of science. In B. Gholson, W. R. Shadish, R. A. Neimeyer, and A. C. Houts, eds., *Psychology of science and metascience,* pp. 21-46. Cambridge: Cambridge University Press.

Campbell, D. T. 1989. Being mechanistic/materialistic/realistic about the process of knowing. *Canadian Psychology* 30: 184–85.

Campbell, J. M.; Amerikaner, M.; Swank, P.; and Vincent, K. 1989. The relationship between the Hardiness Test and the Personal Orientation Inventory. *Journal of Research in Personality* 23: 373–80.

Campos, J. J.; and Barrett, K. C. 1984. Toward a new understanding of emotions and their development. In C. E. Izard, J. Kagan, and R. B. Zajonc, eds., *Emotions, cognition and behavior.* Cambridge: Cambridge University Press.

Campos, J. J.; Barrett, K. C.; Lamb, M.; Goldsmith, H.; and Sternbery, C. 1983. Socioemotional development. In P. H. Mussen, ed., *Handbook of child psychology.* Vol. 2, *Infancy and developmental psychology,* 783–915. New York: Wiley.

Campos, J. J.; Campos, R. G.; and Barrett, K. C. 1989. Emergent themes in the study of emotional development and emotion regulation. *Developmental Psychology* 25: 394–402.

Campos, J. J.; Hiatt, S.; Ramsay, D.; Henderson, C.; and Svejda, M. 1978. The emergence of fear on the visual cliff. In M. Lewis and L. A. Rosenblum, eds., *The development of affect,* pp. 149–82. New York: Plenum.

Canda, E. R. 1988. Therapeutic transformation in ritual, therapy, and human development. *Journal of Religion and Health* 27: 205–20.

Cantor, N.; and Mischel, W. 1977. Traits as prototypes: Effects on recognition memory. *Journal of Personality and Social Psychology* 35: 38–48.

Caplan, D., ed. 1982. *Biological studies of mental processes.* Cambridge, Mass.: MIT Press.

Caporael, L. R.; Dawes, R. M.; Orbell, J. M.; and van de Kragt, A. J. C. 1989. Selfishness examined: Cooperation in the absence of egoistic incentives. *Behavioral and Brain Sciences* 12: 683–739.

Capra, F. 1983. *The turning point.* New York: Bantam.

Carey, S. 1985*a*. Are children fundamentally different kinds of thinkers and learners than adults? In S. F. Chipman, J. W. Segal, and R. Glaser, eds., *Thinking and learning skills,* vol 2, 485–517. Hillsdale, N.J.: Erlbaum.

Carey, S. 1985*b*. *Conceptual change in childhood.* Cambridge, Mass.: MIT Press.

Carlsen, M. B. 1988. *Meaning-making: Therapeutic processes in adult development.* New York: Norton.

Carlson, G. A.; and Kashani, J. H. 1988. Phenomenology of major depression from childhood throughout adulthood: Analysis of three studies. *American Journal of Psychiatry* 145: 1222–25.

Carlson, R. 1971. Where is the person in personality research? *Psychological Bulletin* 75: 203–19.

Carlson, V.; Cicchetti, D.; Barnett, D.; and Braunwald, K. 1989. Disorganized/

disoriented attachment relationships in maltreated infants. *Developmental Psychology* 25: 525–31.

Carnegie, D. 1948. *How to stop worrying and start living.* New York: Simon and Schuster.

Carrere, R. A.; and Weiss, A. G. 1988. The relationship of the personal from graduate training to professional practice. *Journal of Phenomenological Psychology* 19: 147–57.

Carson, H. L. 1975. The genetics of speciation at the diploid level. *American Naturalist* 109: 83–92.

Carver, C. S.; and Scheirer, M. F. 1978. Self-focusing effects of dispositional self-consciousness, mirror presence, and audience presence. *Journal of Personality and Social Psychology* 36: 324–32.

Carver, C. S.; and Scheier, M. F. 1990. Origins and functions of positive and negative affect: A control-process view. *Psychological Review* 97: 19–35.

Casey, E. S. 1987. *Remembering: A phenomenological study.* Bloomington: Indiana University Press.

Casey, G.; and Moran, A. 1989. The computational metaphor and cognitive psychology. *Irish Journal of Psychology* 10: 143–61.

Cash, T. F.; and Pruzinsky, T., eds. 1990. *Body images: Development, deviance, and change.* New York: Guilford.

Caspi, A.; Bem, D. J.; and Elder, G. H., Jr. 1988. Moving away from the world: Life-course patterns of shy children. *Developmental Psychology* 24: 824–31.

Caspi, A.; Bem, D. J.; and Elder, G. H., Jr. 1989. Continuities and consequences of interactional styles across the life course. *Journal of Personality* 57: 375–406.

Cassano, G. B.; Petracca, A.; Perugi, G.; Toni, C.; Tundo, A.; and Roth, M. 1989. Derealization and panic attacks: A clinical evaluation of 150 patients with panic disorder/agoraphobia. *Comprehensive Psychiatry* 30: 5–12.

Cassidy, J. 1986. The ability to negotiate the environment: An aspect of infant competence as related to quality of attachment. *Child Development* 57: 331–37.

Cassirer, E. 1944. *An essay on man: An introduction to a philosophy of human culture.* New Haven, Conn.: Yale University Press.

Cassirer, E. 1955a. *The philosophy of symbolic forms.* Vol. 1, *Language.* New Haven, Conn.: Yale University Press.

Cassirer, E. 1955b. *The philosophy of symbolic forms.* Vol. 2, *Mythical thought.* New Haven, Conn.: Yale University Press.

Cassirer, E. 1957. *The philosophy of symbolic forms.* Vol. 3, *The phenomenology of knowledge.* New Haven, Conn.: Yale University Press.

Cautela, J. R. 1966. Treatment of compulsive behavior by covert sensitization. *Psychological Record* 16: 33–41.

Cautela, J. R. 1967. Covert sensitization. *Psychological Reports* 20: 459–68.

Cautela, J. R. 1971. Covert conditioning. In A. Jacobs and L. B. Sachs, eds., *The psychology of private events: Perspectives on covert response systems,* 109–30. New York: Academic Press.

Center for Applied Psychology. 1990. *Childswork—childsplay.* Philadelphia: Center for Applied Psychology.

Cernic, D.; and Longmire, L., eds. 1987. *Know thyself: Collected readings on identity.* New York: Paulist Press.

Chamberlain, A. F. 1911. *The child: A study in the evolution of man,* 2d ed. New York: Scribner.

Chamberlaine, C.; Barnes, S.; Waring, E. M.; Wood, G.; and Fry, R. 1989. The role of marital intimacy in psychiatric help-seeking. *Canadian Journal of Psychiatry* 34: 3–7.

Chambless, D. L.; and Gracely, E. J. 1989. Fear of fear and the anxiety disorders. *Cognitive Therapy and Research* 13: 9–20.

Chandler, M. 1987. The Othello effect: Essay on the emergence and eclipse of skeptical doubt. *Human Development* 30: 137–59.

Changeaux, J. P. 1985. *Neuronal man: The biology of mind.* New York: Pantheon.

Changeaux, J. P.; and Dehaene, S. 1989. Neuronal models of cognitive functions. *Cognition* 33: 63–109.

Changeaux, J. P.; and Konishi, M., eds. 1987. *The neural and molecular bases of learning.* New York: Wiley.

Charlesworth, W. R. 1986. Darwin and developmental psychology: 100 years later. *Human Development* 29: 1–35.

Cheal, D. 1987. "Showing them you love them": Gift giving and the dialectic of intimacy. *Sociological Review* 35: 150–69.

Cheal, D. 1988*a*. The postmodern origin of ritual. *Journal for the Theory of Social Behavior* 18: 268–90.

Cheal, D. 1988*b*. Relationships in time: Ritual, social structure, and the life course. *Studies in Symbolic Interaction* 9: 83–109.

Cheal, D. 1988*c*. The ritualization of family ties. *American Behavioral Scientist* 31: 632–43.

Chemtob, C. M.; Hamada, R. S.; Bauer, G.; Torigoe, R. Y.; and Kinney, B. 1988. Patient suicide: Frequency and impact on psychologists. *Professional Psychology: Research and Practice* 19: 416–20.

Chernin, K. 1985. *The hungry self: Women, eating, and identity.* New York: Harper and Row.

Cherry, E. C. 1953. Some experiments on the recognition of speech, with one and with two ears. *Journal of the Acoustical Society of America* 25: 975–79.

Chessick, R. D. 1978. The sad soul of the psychiatrist. *Bulletin of the Menninger Clinic* 42: 1–9.

Chessick, R. D. 1986. Heidegger for psychotherapists. *American Journal of Psychotherapy* 40: 83–95.

Chiari, G.; and Nuzzo, M. L. 1988. Embodied minds over interacting bodies: A constructivist perspective on the mind-body problem. *Irish Journal of Psychology* 9: 91–100.

Chodorow, N. 1978. *The reproduction of mothering.* Berkeley: University of California Press.

Chodorow, N. 1989. *Feminism and psychoanalytic theory.* New Haven, Conn.: Yale University Press.

Chomsky, N. 1956. Three models for the description of language. *IRE Transactions on Information Theory* IT-2(3): 113–24.

Chomsky, N. 1957. *Syntactic structures*. The Hague: Mouton.

Chomsky, N. 1959. Review of Skinner's *Verbal Behavior. Language* 35: 26–58.

Christman, J. 1988. Constructing the inner citadel: Recent work on the concept of autonomy. *Ethics* 99: 109–24.

Churchland, P. M. 1988. Perceptual plasticity and theoretical neutrality: A reply to Jerry Fodor. *Philosophy of Science* 55: 167–87.

Churchland, P. S. 1986. *Neurophilosophy*. Cambridge, Mass.: MIT Press.

Churchland, P. S.; and Sejnowski, T. J. 1988. Perspectives on cognitive neuroscience. *Science* 242: 741–45.

Churchman, P. M. 1984. *Matter and consciousness*. Cambridge, Mass.: MIT Press.

Cicchetti, D. 1987. Developmental psychopathology in infancy: Illustration from the study of maltreated youngsters. *Journal of Consulting and Clinical Psychology* 55: 837–45.

Cicchetti, D.; and Schneider-Rosen, K. 1986. An organizational approach to childhood depression. In M. Rutter, C. E. Izard, and P. B. Read, eds., *Depression in young people*. New York: Guilford.

Claiborn, C. D. 1982. Interpretation and change in counseling. *Journal of Counseling Psychology* 29: 439–53.

Clark, D. A. 1986. Factors influencing the retrieval and control of negative cognitions. *Behavior Research and Therapy* 24: 151–59.

Clark, J. M.; and Paivio, A. 1989. Observational and theoretical terms in psychology. *American Psychologist* 44: 500–12.

Clark, M. S.; and Reis, H. T. 1988. Interpersonal processes in close relationships. *Annual Review of Psychology* 39: 609–72.

Clarke, A. M.; and Clarke, A. D. B., eds. 1976. *Early experience: Myth and evidence*. New York: Free Press.

Clarke, K. M. 1989. Creation of meaning: An emotional processing task in psychotherapy. *Psychotherapy* 26: 139–48.

Coan, R. W. 1977. *Hero, artist, sage, or saint? A survey of views of what is variously called mental health, normality, maturity, self-actualization, and human fulfillment*. New York: Columbia University Press.

Coan, R. W. 1979. *Psychologists: Personal and theoretical pathways*. New York: Irvington.

Coan, R. W. 1987a. *Human consciousness and its evolution: A multidimensional view*. New York: Greenwood.

Coan, R. W. 1987b. Theoretical orientation in psychology and the traditions of Freud, Jung, and Adler. *Professional Psychology: Research and Practice* 18: 134–39.

Cofer, C. N. 1979. Human learning and memory. In E. Hearst, ed., *The first century of experimental psychology*, 322–69. Hillsdale, N.J.: Erlbaum.

Cohen, I. B. 1980. *The Newtonian revolution: With illustrations of the transformation of scientific ideas*. Cambridge: Cambridge University Press.

Cohen, L. B. 1979. Our developing knowledge of infant perception and cognition. *American Psychologist* 34: 894–99.

Cohen, L. H.; Sargent, M. M.; and Sechrest, L. B. 1986. Use of psychotherapy research by professional psychologists. *American Psychologist* 41: 198–206.

Cohen, S.; and Wills, T. A. 1985. Stress, social support, and the buffering hypothesis. *Psychological Bulletin* 98: 310–57.

Coles, M. G. H. 1989. Modern mind-brain reading: Psychophysiology, physiology, and cognition. *Psychophysiology* 26: 251–69.

Collingwood, R. G. 1946. *The idea of history.* Oxford: Oxford University Press.

Collins, W. A., ed. 1982. *The concept of development.* Hillsdale, N.J.: Erlbaum.

Committee on Women in Psychology, American Psychological Association. 1989. If sex enters into the psychotherapy relationship. *Professional Psychology* 20: 112–15.

Comparetti, A. M. 1981. The neurophysiologic and clinical implications of studies on fetal motor behavior. *Seminars in Perinatology* 5: 183–89.

Connors, G. S.; and Maisto, S. A. 1988. The alcohol expectancy construct: Overview and clinical applications. *Cognitive Therapy and Research* 12: 487–504.

Conway, F.; and Siegelman, J. 1978. *Snapping: America's epidemic of sudden personality change.* New York: Dell.

Conway, J. B. 1984. A place for discontent and tensions in psychology. *Canadian Psychology* 25: 96–104.

Conway, J. B. 1988. Differences among clinical psychologists: Scientists, practioners, and scientist-practioners. *Professional Psychology: Research and Practice* 19: 642–55.

Conway, J. B. 1989. *Epistemic values and psychologists: A world of individual differences.* University of Saskatchewan. Manuscript.

Cook, N. D. 1980. *Stability and flexibility: An analysis of natural systems.* New York: Pergamon.

Cook, T. D.; and Campbell, D. T. 1979. *Quasi-experimentation: Design and analysis issues for field settings.* Boston: Houghton Mifflin.

Cooper, A. M. 1989. Narcissism and masochism: The narcissistic-masochistic character. *Narcissistic Personality Disorder* 12: 541–52.

Corballis, M. C. 1989. Laterality and human evolution. *Psychological Review* 96: 492–505.

Corcoran, K.; and Fischer, J. 1987. *Measures for clinical practice: A sourcebook.* New York: Free Press.

Coren, S. 1986. An efferent component in the visual perception of direction and extent. *Psychological Review* 93: 391–410.

Cornsweet, D. M. 1969. Use of cues in the visual periphery under conditions of arousal. *Journal of Experimental Psychology* 80: 14–18.

Costa, P. T., Jr.; and McCrae, R. R. 1988*a.* From catalog to classification: Murray's needs and the five-factor model. *Journal of Personality and Social Psychology* 55: 258–65.

Costa, P. T., Jr.; and McCrae, R. R. 1988*b.* Personality in adulthood: A six-year longitudinal study of self-reports and spouse ratings on the NEO Personality Inventory. *Journal of Personality and Social Psychology* 54: 853–63.

Cota, A. A.; and Fekken, G. C. 1988. Dimensionality of the personal attributes questionnaire: An empirical replication. *Journal of Social Behavior and Personality* 3: 135–40.

Côté, J. E.; and Levine, C. 1988a. The relationship between ego identity status and Erikson's notions of institutionalized moratoria, value orientation state, and ego dominance. *Journal of Youth and Adolescence* 17: 81–99.

Côté, J. E.; and Levine, C. 1988b. A critical examination of the ego identity status paradigm. *Developmental Review* 8: 147–84.

Côté, J. E.; and Levine, C. 1988c. On critiquing the identity status paradigm: A rejoinder to Waterman. *Developmental Review* 8: 209–18.

Coué, E. 1922. *The practice of autosuggestion.* New York: Doubleday.

Cousins, S. D. 1989. Culture and self-perception in Japan and the United States. *Journal of Personality and Social Psychology* 56: 124–31.

Cowan, N. 1988. Evolving conceptions of memory storage, selective attention, and their mutual constraints within the human information-processing system. *Psychological Bulletin* 104: 163–91.

Cowan, W. M. 1979. The development of the brain. *Scientific American* 241(3): 112–33.

Cox, D. J.; Tisdelle, D. A.; and Culbert, J. P. 1988. Increasing adherence to behavioral homework assignments. *Journal of Behavioral Medicine* 11: 519–22.

Cox, M.; and Theilgaard, A. 1987. *Mutative metaphors in psychotherapy: The Aeolian mode.* London: Tavistock.

Craske, M. G.; and Barlow, D. H. 1988. A review of the relationship between panic and avoidance. *Clinical Psychology Review* 8: 667–85.

Craven, J. L. 1989. Meditation and psychotherapy. *Canadian Journal of Psychiatry* 34: 648–53.

Crawford, M.; and Chaffin, R. 1986. The reader's construction of meaning: Cognitive research on gender and comprehension. In E. Flynn and P. Schweickart, eds., *Gender and reading: Essays on readers, texts, and context.* Baltimore, Md.: Johns Hopkins University Press.

Crawford, M.; and Marecek, J. 1989. Psychology reconstructs the female: 1968–1988. *Psychology of Women Quarterly* 13: 147–65.

Crews, D. J.; and Landers, D. M. 1987. A meta-analytic review of aerobic fitness and reactivity to psychosocial stressors. *Medicine and Science in Sports and Exercise* 19: S114–S120.

Critchlow, B. 1986. The powers of John Barleycorn: Beliefs about the effects of alcohol on social behavior. *American Psychologist* 41: 751–64.

Csikszentmihalyi, M. 1975. *Beyond boredom and anxiety: The experience of games in work and play.* San Francisco: Jossey-Bass.

Csikszentmihalyi, M. 1988a. Motivation and creativity: Toward a synthesis of structural and energistic approaches to cognition. *New Ideas in Psychology* 6: 159–76.

Csikszentmihalyi, M. 1988*b*. Solving a problem is not finding a new one: A reply to Simon. *New Ideas in Psychology* 6: 183–86.

Csikszentmihalyi, M.; and Csikszentmihalyi, I. S., eds. 1988. *Optimal experience: Psychological studies of flow in consciousness.* Cambridge: Cambridge University Press.

Cunningham, J. G.; and Sterling, R. S. 1988. Developmental change in the understanding of affective meaning in music. *Motivation and Emotion* 12: 399–413.

Cunningham, M. R. 1988. What do you do when you're happy or blue? Mood, expectancies, and behavioral interest. *Motivation and Emotion* 12: 309–31.

Curti, M. 1974. Psychological theories in American thought. In P. P. Wiener, ed., *Dictionary of the history of ideas: Studies of selected pivotal ideas,* vol. 4, 16–30. New York: Scribner.

Cushman, P. 1990. Why the self is empty: Toward a historically situated psychology. *American Psychologist* 45: 599–611.

Cytryn, L.; McKnew, D. H.; Zahn-Waxler, C.; and Gershon, E. S. 1986. Developmental issues in risk research: The offspring of affectively ill parents. In M. Rutter, C. E. Izard, and P. B. Read, eds., *Depression in young people,* 163–88. New York: Guilford.

Dacey, J. S. 1989. Peak periods of creative growth across the lifespan. *Journal of Creative Behavior* 23: 224–47.

Dahlmayr, F. R. 1981. *Twilight of subjectivity.* Amherst: University of Massachusetts Press.

Daldrup, R. J.; Beutler, L. E.; Engle, D.; and Greenberg, L. S., eds. 1988. *Focused expressive psychotherapy: Freeing the overcontrolled patient.* New York: Guilford.

d'Aquili, E. G.; Laughlin, C. D. Jr.; and McManus. 1979. *The spectrum of ritual: A biogenetic structural analysis.* New York: Columbia University Press.

Dar, R. 1987. Another look at Meehl, Lakatos, and the scientific practices of psychologists. *American Psychologist* 42: 145–51.

Daro, D. 1988. *Confronting child abuse.* New York: Free Press.

Darwin, C. 1964 [1859]. *On the origin of species.* Cambridge, Mass.: Harvard University Press.

Darwin, C. 1965 [1872]. *The expression of the emotions in man and animals.* Chicago: University of Chicago Press.

Darwin, C. 1969. *The autobiography of Charles Darwin,* N. Barlow, ed. New York: Norton.

Dass, R. 1970. *The only dance there is.* New York: Anchor.

Dass, R. 1971. *Be here now.* New York: Crown.

Dass, R. 1978. *Journey of awakening: A meditator's guidebook.* New York: Bantam.

Dass, R.; and Gorman, P. 1985. *How can I help? Stories and reflections on service.* New York: Knopf.

Davidson, J. M.; and Davidson, R. J. 1980. *The psychobiology of consciousness.* New York: Plenum.

Davidson, L. 1988. Husserl's refutation of psychologism and the possibility of a phenomenological psychology. *Journal of Phenomenological Psychology* 19: 1–17.

Davidson, R. J. 1978. Specificity and patterning in biobehavioral systems: Implications for behavior change. *American Psychologist* 33: 430–36.

Davidson, R. J. 1984. Affect, cognition, and hemispheric specialization. In C. E. Izard, J. Kagan, and R. B. Zajonc, eds., *Emotions, cognition, and behavior*, 320–65. Cambridge: Cambridge University Press.

Davis, P. J.; and Hersh, R. 1986. *Descartes' dream: The world according to mathematics.* Boston: Houghton Mifflin.

Davis, P. J.; and Schwartz, G. E. 1987. Repression and the inaccessibility of affective memories. *Journal of Personality and Social Psychology* 52: 155–62.

Davis, R. C., ed. 1966. *Lacan and narration.* Baltimore, Md.: Johns Hopkins University Press.

Davisson, A. 1978. George Kelly and the American mind (or why has he been obscure for so long in the U.S.A. and whence the new interest?). In F. Fransella, ed., *Personal construct psychology 1977*, 25–33. London: Academic Press.

Davitz, J. R. 1969. *The language of emotions.* New York: McGraw-Hill.

Dawkins, R. 1976. *The selfish gene.* Oxford: Oxford University Press.

DeAngelis, T. 1987. A meeting of the minds: Kohutian, Horneyan schools call a halt to 'sibling rivalry.' *APA Monitor* 18: 22–23.

Deaux, K. 1984. From individual differences to social categories: Analysis of a decade's research on gender. *American Psychologist* 39: 105–16.

DeBord, J. B. 1989. Paradoxical interventions: A review of the recent literature. *Journal of Counseling and Development* 67: 394–98.

Deci, E. L. 1980. *The psychology of self-determination.* Lexington, Mass.: D. C. Heath.

Dell, P. F. 1982a. Beyond homeostasis: Toward a concept of coherence. *Family Process* 21: 21–41.

Dell, P. F. 1982b. In search of truth: On the way to clinical epistemology. *Family Process* 21: 407–14.

Dell, P. F. 1985. Understanding Bateson and Maturana: Toward a biological foundation for the social sciences. *Journal of Marital and Family Therapy* 13: 1–20.

Dell, P. F.; and Goolishian, H. A. 1981. Order through fluctuation: An evolutionary epistemology for human systems. *Australian Journal of Family Therapy* 2: 175–84.

DeLoache, J. S. 1987. Rapid change in the symbolic functioning of very young children. *Science* 238: 1556–57.

Delmonte, M. M. 1989. Existentialism and psychotherapy: A constructivist perspective. *Psychologia—An International Journal of Psychology in the Orient* 32: 81–90.

Dember, W. N. 1974. Motivation and the cognitive revolution. *American Psychologist* 29: 161–68.

DeMey, M. 1982. *The cognitive paradigm.* Boston: D. Reidel.

Dennett, D. C. 1978. *Brainstorms: Philosophical essays on mind and psychology.* Cambridge, Mass.: MIT Press.

Dennett, D. C. 1984. *Elbow room: The varieties of free will worth wanting.* Cambridge, Mass.: MIT Press.

Dennett, D. C. 1988. Précis of *The intentional stance. Behavioral and Brain Sciences* 11: 495–546.

Dent, J. K. 1978. *Exploring the psycho-social therapies through the personalities of effective therapists.* Washington, D.C.: U. S. Government Printing Office.

Depew, D. J.; and Weber, B. H. 1985. Innovation and tradition in evolutionary theory: An interpretive afterword. In D. J. Depew and B. H. Weber, eds., *Evolution at a crossroads: The new biology and the new philosophy of science,* 227–60. Cambridge, Mass.: MIT Press.

de Rivera, J. 1977. A structural theory of the emotions. *Psychological Issues* 10 No. 4, Monograph 40.

Derry, P. A.; and Kuiper, N. A. 1981. Schematic processing and self-reference in clinical depression. *Journal of Abnormal Psychology* 90: 286–97.

Descartes, R. 1955 [1649]. The passions of the soul. In E. S. Haldane and G. R. T. Ross, trans., *The philosophical works of Descartes,* vols. 1–2. New York: Dover.

De Shazer, S. 1984. The death of resistance. *Family Process* 23: 11–21.

de Sousa, R. 1987. *The rationality of emotion.* Cambridge, Mass.: MIT Press.

Deutsch, C. J. 1985. A survey of therapists' personal problems and treatment. *Professional Psychology: Research and Practice* 16: 305–15.

Deutsch, F. M.; Kroll, J. F.; Weible, A. L.; Letourneau, L. A.; and Goss, R. L. 1988. Spontaneous trait generation: A new method for identifying self-schemas. *Journal of Personality* 56: 327–53.

Deutsch, J. A.; and Deutsch, D. 1963. Attention: Some theoretical considerations. *Physiology and Behavior* 28: 1029–33.

DeWaele, J. P.; and Harré, R. 1979. Autobiography as a psychological method. In G. P. Ginsburg, ed., *Emerging strategies in social psychological research,* 177–224. New York: Wiley.

Dewey, J. 1981 [1934]. The live creature. In J. J. McDermott, ed., *The philosophy of John Dewey* 2 vols., 525–40. Chicago: University of Chicago Press.

Dewey, J. 1894. The theory of emotion: 1. Emotional attitudes. *Psychological Review* 1: 553–69.

Dewey, J. 1986. The reflex arc concept in psychology. *Psychological Review* 3: 357–70.

Digman, J. M. 1989. Five robust trait dimensions: Development, stability, and utility. *Journal of Personality* 57: 195–214.

Diener, E. 1984. Subjective well-being. *Psychological Bulletin* 95: 542–75.

Dienstbier, R. A. 1989. Arousal and physiological toughness: Implications for mental and physical health. *Psychological Review,* 96: 84–100.

Dilthey, W. 1976 [1883–]. *Selected writings.* Trans. and ed. H. P. Rickman. Cambridge: Cambridge University Press.

Dinkmeyer, D. C.; Dinkmeyer, D. C., Jr.; and Sperry, L. 1987. *Adlerian counseling and psychotherapy,* 2d ed. Columbus, Oh.: Merrill.

Dinnerstein, D. 1976. *The mermaid and the minotaur: Sexual arrangements and human malaise.* New York: Harper and Row.

Dixon, N. F. 1981. *Preconscious processing.* New York: Wiley.

Dixon, T. R.; and Horton, D. L., eds. 1968. *Verbal behavior and general behavior theory.* Englewood Cliffs, N.J.: Prentice-Hall.

Dobson, K. S., ed. 1988. *Handbook of cognitive-behavioral therapies.* New York: Guilford.

Dobzhansky, T. 1962. *Mankind evolving: The evolution of the human species.* New Haven, Conn.: Yale University Press.

Dobzhansky, T. 1967. *The biology of ultimate concern.* New York: New American Library.

Doctor, R. M.; Goldenring, J. M.; Chivian, E.; Mack, J.; Waletzky, J. P.; Lazaroff, C.; and Goss, T. 1988. Self-reports of Soviet and American children on worry about the threat of nuclear war. *Political Psychology* 9: 13–24.

Doepke, F. 1989. The step to individuation. *Synthese* 78: 129–40.

Doi, T. 1985. *The anatomy of self: The individual versus society.* Tokyo: Kodansha.

Doise, W. 1989. Constructivism in social psychology. *European Journal of Social Psychology* 19: 389–400.

Dollard, J.; and Miller, N. E. 1950. *Personality and psychotherapy: An analysis in terms of learning, thinking and culture.* New York: McGraw-Hill.

Dollinger, S. J. 1986. The need for meaning following disaster: Attributions and emotional upset. *Personality and Social Psychology Bulletin* 12: 300–10.

Doorslaer, M. V. 1988. Living constructivism. *Irish Journal of Psychology* 9: 195–99.

Dore, F. Y.; and Dumas, C. 1987. Psychology of animal cognition: Piagetian studies. *Psychological Bulletin* 102: 219–33.

Dosamantes-Alperson, E.; and Merill, N. 1980. Growth effects of experiential movement psychotherapy. *Psychotherapy: Theory, Research and Practice* 17: 63–68.

Dowd, E. T.; and Milne, C. R. 1986. Paradoxical interventions in counseling psychology. *Counseling Psychologist* 14: 237–82.

Dretske, F. I. 1981. *Knowledge and the flow of information.* Cambridge, Mass.: MIT Press.

Dreyfus, H. L.; and Dreyfus, S. E. 1988. *Mind over machine: The power of human intuition and expertise in the era of the computer.* New York: Free Press.

Driesch, H. 1914. *The problem of individuality.* London: Macmillan.

Dryden, W. 1988. *Therapists' dilemmas.* New York: Hemisphere.

Dryden, W.; and Spurling, L., eds. 1989. *On becoming a psychotherapist.* London: Tavistock/Routledge.

Dubé, R.; and Hébert, M. 1988. Sexual abuse of children under 12 years of age: A review of 511 cases. *Child Abuse and Neglect* 12: 321–30.

Dubois, P. 1906. *The influence of the mind on the body.* New York: Funk and Wagnalls.

Dubois, P. 1908. *The psychic treatment of nervous disorders.* New York: Funk and Wagnalls.

Dubois, P. 1911. *The education of self.* New York: Funk and Wagnalls.

Dubs, G. 1987. Psycho-spiritual development in Zen Buddhism: A study of resistance in meditation. *Journal of Transpersonal Psychology* 19: 19–86.

Duby, G., ed. 1988. *A history of private life: Revelations of the medieval world.* Cambridge: Harvard University Press.

Dudycha, G. J.; and Dudycha, M. M. 1941. Childhood memories: A review of the literature. *Psychological Bulletin* 38: 668–82.

Dukas, H.; and Hoffmann, B. eds. 1979. *Albert Einstein: The human side.* Princeton, N.J.: Princeton University Press.

Duke, J. T.; and Johnson, B. L. 1989. The stages of religious transformation: A study of 200 nations. *Review of Religious Research* 30: 209–24.

Dulany, D. E. 1962. The place of hypotheses and intentions: An analysis of verbal control in verbal conditioning. In C. W. Eriksen, ed., *Behavior and awareness,* 102–29. Durham, N.C.: Duke University Press.

Dulany, D. E. 1968. Awareness, rules, and propositional control: A confrontation with S-R behavior theory. In T. R. Dixon and D. L. Horton, eds., *Verbal behavior and general behavior theory,* 340–87. Englewood Cliffs, N.J.: Prentice-Hall.

Duncan, J. 1984. Selective attention and the organization of visual information. *Journal of Experimental Psychology: General* 113: 501–17.

Dupre, J., ed. 1987. *The latest on the best: Essays on evolution and optimality.* Cambridge, Mass.: MIT Press.

Durant, W. 1926. *The story of philosophy.* Garden City, N.Y.: Garden City Publishing.

Durant, W.; and Durant, A. 1935–75. *The story of civilization.* 11 vols. New York: Simon and Schuster.

Durant, W.; and Durant, A. 1970. *Interpretations of life: A survey of contemporary literature.* New York: Simon and Schuster.

Duval, S.; and Wicklund, R. A. 1972. *A theory of objective self-awareness.* New York: Academic Press.

D'Zurilla, T. J.; and Goldfried, M. R. 1971. Problem solving and behavior modification. *Journal of Abnormal Psychology* 78: 107–26.

Easter, S. S.; Barald, K. F.; and Carlson, B. M., eds. 1987. *From message to mind: Directions in developmental neurobiology.* Sunderland, Mass.: Sinauer.

Eaton, T. T.; Abeles, N; and Gutfreund, M. J. 1988. Therapeutic alliance and outcome: Impact of treatment length and pretreatment symptomatology. *Psychotherapy* 25: 536–42.

Ebbesson, S. O. E. 1984. Evolution and ontogeny of neural circuits. *The Behavioral and Brain Sciences* 7: 321–66.

Ebbinghaus, H. 1913 [1885]. *Memory: A contribution to experimental psychology.* Trans. H. A. Ruger and C. E. Bussenius. New York: Teachers College.

Eccles, J. C. 1977. *The understanding of the brain,* 2d ed. New York: McGraw-Hill.

Eckler, J. A.; and Weininger, O. 1989. Structural parallels between pretend play and narratives. *Developmental Psychology* 25: 736–43.

Edelman, G. M. 1987. *Neural Darwinism: The theory of neuronal group selection.* New York: Basic Books.

Edelson, M. 1963. *The termination of intensive psychotherapy.* Springfield, Ill.: Charles C. Thomas.

Edelwich, J.; and Brodsky, A. 1982. *Sexual dilemmas for the helping professional.* New York: Brunner/Mazel.

Edwards, P. W.; Zeichner, A.; Lawler, N.; and Kowalski, R. 1987. A validation study of the Harvey Imposter Phenomenon Scale. *Psychotherapy* 24: 256–59.

Egeland, B. 1988. Breaking the cycle of abuse: Implications for prediction and intervention. In K. Browne, C. Davies, and P. Stratton, eds., *Early prediction and prevention of child abuse,* 87–99. New York: Wiley.

Eger, M. 1989. The 'interests' of science and the problems of education. *Synthese* 81: 81–106.

Ehrenwald, J., ed. 1976. *The history of psychotherapy: From healing magic to encounter.* New York: Jason Aronson.

Eigen, M. 1971. Self-organization of matter and the evolution of biological macromolecules. *Naturwissenschaften* 58: 465–523.

Eigen, M.; and Schuster, P. 1977. The hypercycle: A principle of natural self-organization, Part A: Emergence of the hypercycle. *Naturwissenschaften* 64: 541–65.

Eigen, M.; and Schuster, P. 1978. The hypercycle: A principle of natural self-organization, Part B: The abstract hypercycle. *Naturwissenschaften* 65: 7–41.

Eigen, M.; and Schuster, P. 1979. *The hypercycle: A principle of natural self-organization.* New York: Springer.

Eigen, M.; and Winkler, R. 1981. *Laws of the game: How the principles of nature govern chance.* New York: Harper and Row.

Eimas, P. D.; and Galaburda, A. M. 1989. Some agenda items for a neurobiology of cognition: An introduction. *Cognition* 33: 1–23.

Eiseley, L. 1958. *Darwin's century: Evolution and the men who discovered it.* New York: Doubleday.

Eisenberg, N., ed. 1987. *Contemporary topics in developmental psychology.* New York: Wiley.

Eisenberg, N.; Schaller, M.; Fabes, R. A.; Bustamante, D.; Mathy, R. M.; Shell, R.; and Rhodes, K. 1988. Differentiation of personal distress and sympathy in children and adults. *Developmental Psychology* 24: 766–75.

Ekman, P., ed. 1972. *Darwin and facial expression: A century of research in review.* New York: Academic Press.

Ekman, P.; and Friesen, W. V. 1971. Constants across culture in the face and emotion. *Journal of Personality and Social Psychology* 17: 124–29.

Eldredge, N.; and Gould, S. J. 1972. Punctuated equilibria: an alternative to phyletic gradualism. In T. J. Schopf, M., ed., *Models in paleobiology,* 82–115. San Francisco: Freeman, Cooper & Co.

Eldredge, N.; and Tattersall, I. 1982. *The myths of human evolution.* New York: Columbia University Press.

Eliou, M. 1988. Women in the academic profession: Evolution or stagnation? *Higher Education* 17: 505–24.

Elkin, I.; Pilkonis, P. A.; Docherty, J. P.; and Sotsky, S. M. 1988a. Conceptual and methodological issues in comparative studies of psychotherapy and pharmacotherapy, I: Active ingredients and mechanisms of change. *American Journal of Psychiatry* 145: 909–17.

Elkin, I.; Pilkonis, P. A.; Docherty, J. P.; and Sotsky, S. M. 1988b. Conceptual and methodological issues in comparative studies of psychotherapy and pharmacotherapy, II: Nature and timing of treatment effects. *American Journal of Psychiatry* 145: 1070–76.

Elkisch, P. 1957. Psychological significance of the mirror. *Journal of the American Psychoanalytic Association* 5: 235–44.

Ellenberger, H. F. 1970. *The discovery of the unconscious.* New York: Basic Books.

Elliott, G. C. 1988. Gender differences in self-consistency: Evidence from an investigation of self-concept structure. *Journal of Youth and Adolescence* 17: 41–57.

Elliott, R.; and James, E. 1989. Varieties of client experience in psychotherapy: An analysis of the literature. *Clinical Psychology Review* 9: 443–67.

Ellis, A. 1962. *Reason and emotion in psychotherapy.* New York: Stuart.

Ellis, A. 1985*a*. Expanding the ABC's of rational-emotive therapy. In M. J. Mahoney and A. Freeman, eds., *Cognition and psychotherapy,* 313–23. New York: Plenum.

Ellis, A. 1985*b*. *Overcoming resistance: Rational-emotive therapy with difficult clients.* New York: Springer.

Ellis, A. 1986. Fanaticism that may lead to a nuclear holocaust. *Journal of Counseling and Development* 65: 146–50.

Ellis, A. 1988. Are there "rationalist" and "constructivist" camps of the cognitive therapies? A response to Michael Mahoney. *Cognitive Behaviorist* 10 (2): 13–17.

Ellis, L.; Miller, C.; and Widmayer, A. 1988. Content analysis of biological approaches in psychology: 1894 to 1985. *Sociology and Social Research* 72: 145–49.

Ellison, J. M.; Hughes, D. H.; and White, K. A. 1989. An emergency psychiatry update. *Hospital and Community Psychiatry* 40: 250–60.

Ellsworth, P. C.; and Smith, C. A. 1988. From appraisal to emotion: Differences among unpleasant feelings. *Motivation and Emotion* 12: 271–302.

Elsberg, C. A. 1945. The anatomy and surgery of the Edwin Smith surgical papyrus. *Journal of Mt. Sinai Hospital* 12: 141–51.

Elster, J., ed. 1985. *The multiple self.* Cambridge: Cambridge University Press.

Elvee, R. Q., ed. 1982. *Mind in nature.* New York: Harper and Row.

Emde, R. N. 1984. Levels of meaning for infant emotions: A biosocial view. In K. R. Scherer and P. Ekman, eds., *Approaches to emotion,* 77–107. Hillsdale, N.J.: Erlbaum.

Emde, R. N.; Harmon, R. J.; and Good, W. V. 1986. Depressive feelings in children: A transactional model for research. In M. Rutter, C. E. Izard, and P. B. Read, eds., *Depression in young people,* 135–60. New York: Guilford.

Emery, O. B.; and Csikszentmihalyi, M. 1981. An epistemological approach to psychiatry: On the psychology/psychopathology of knowledge. *Journal of Mind and Behavior* 2: 375–96.

Endler, N. S.; and Magnusson, D. 1976. *Interactional psychology and personality.* Washington, D.C.: Hemisphere.

Engel, S. 1988. Metaphors: How are they different for the poet, the child and the everyday adult? *New Ideas in Psychology* 6: 333–41.

Engler, J. 1983. Vicissitudes of the self according to psychoanalysis and Buddhism: A spectrum model of object relations development. *Psychoanalysis and Contemporary Thought* 6: 29–72.

Engler, J. 1986. Therapeutic aims in psychotherapy and meditation: Developmental stages in the representation of self. In K. Wilber, J. Engler, and D. P.

Brown, eds., *Transformations of consciousness: Conventional and contemplative perspectives on development* 17–51. Boston: New Science Library.

Epstein, S. 1973. The self-concept revisited: Or a theory of a theory. *American Psychologist* 28: 404–16.

Epstein, S. 1979. The stability of behavior: I. On predicting most of the people much of the time. *Journal of Personality and Social Psychology* 37: 1097–1126.

Epstein, S. 1980. The stability of behavior: II. Implications for psychological research. *American Psychologist* 35: 790–806.

Epstein, S.; and Erskine, N. 1983. The development of personal theories of reality from an interactional perspective. In D. Magnusson and V. L. Allen, eds., *Human development: An interactional perspective,* 133–47. New York: Academic Press.

Epstein, W., ed. 1987. The ontogenesis of perception. *Journal of Experimental Psychology: Human Perception and Performance* 13: 515–613.

Epting, F. R. 1984. *Personal construct counseling and psychotherapy.* New York: Wiley.

Érdi, P.; and Szentágothai, J. 1985. Neural connectivities: Between determinism and randomness. In J. P. Aubin, D. Saari, and K. Sigmund, eds., *Dynamics of macrosystems.* Berlin: Springer-Verlag.

Erikson, E. H. 1950. *Childhood and society.* New York: Norton.

Erikson, E. H. 1959. *Identity and the life cycle.* New York: Norton.

Erikson, E. H. 1968. *Identity: Youth and crisis.* New York: Norton.

Erwin, E. 1988. Cognitivist and behaviorist paradigms in clinical psychology. In D. B. Fishman, F. Rotgers, and C. M. Franks, eds., *Paradigms in behavior therapy: Present and promise,* 109–40. New York: Springer.

Estes, W. K. 1971. Reward in human learning: Theoretical issues and strategic choice points. In R. Glaser, ed., *The nature of reinforcement,* 16–36. New York: Academic Press.

Evans, M. B. 1988. The role of metaphor in psychotherapy and personality change: A theoretical reformulation. *Psychotherapy* 25: 543–51.

Everstine, L.; Everstine, D. S.; Heymann, G. M.; True, R. H.; Frey, D. H.; Johnson, H. G.; and Seiden, R. H. 1980. Privacy and confidentiality in psychotherapy. *American Psychologist* 35: 828–40.

Evoy, J. J. 1981. *The rejected: Psychological consequences of parental rejection.* University Park: Pennsylvania State University Press.

Exner, J. E., Jr. 1973. The self focus sentence completion: A study of egocentricity. *Journal of Personality Assessment* 37: 437–55.

Eysenck, H. J. 1965. The effects of psychotherapy: An evaluation. *Journal of Consulting Psychology* 16: 319–24.

Eysenck, H. J. 1988. Psychotherapy to behavior therapy: A paradigm shift. In D. B. Fishman, F. Rotgers, and C. M. Franks, eds., *Paradigms in behavior therapy: Present and promise,* 45–76. New York: Springer.

Fahlman, S. E.; and Hinton, G. E. 1987. Connectionist architectures for artificial intelligence. *Computer* 20: 100–9.

Fair, C. M. 1988. *Memory and central nervous organization.* New York: Paragon House.

Falmagne, R. J., ed. 1975. *Reasoning: Representation and process in children and adults.* Hillsdale, N.J.: Erlbaum.

Farber, B. A. 1983*a*. Dysfunctional aspects of the psychotherapeutic role. In B. A. Parker, ed., *Stress and burnout in the human service professions,* 97–118. New York: Pergamon.

Farber, B. A. 1983*b*. The effects of psychotherapeutic practice upon psychotherapists. *Psychotherapy: Theory, Research, and Practice* 20: 174–82.

Farber, B. A. 1983*c*. Psychotherapists' perceptions of stressful patient behavior. *Psychotherapy: Theory, Research, and Practice* 14: 697–705.

Farber, B. A. 1985. Clinical psychologists' perceptions of psychotherapeutic work. *Clinical Psychologist* 38: 10–13.

Farber, B. A. 1989. Psychological-mindedness: Can there be too much of a good thing? *Psychotherapy* 26: 210–20.

Farber, B. A.; and Heifetz, L. J. 1981. The satisfactions and stresses of psychotherapeutic work: A factor analytic study. *Professional Psychology: Research and Practice* 12: 621–30.

Faust, D. 1982. A needed component in prescriptions for science: Empirical knowledge of human cognitive limitations. *Knowledge* 3: 555–70.

Faust, D. 1984. *The limits of scientific reasoning.* Minneapolis: University of Minnesota Press.

Faust, D.; and Moates, D. R. 1987. Behavior modification and cognitive developmental communities. *Journal of Cognitive Psychotherapy: An International Quarterly* 1: 135–54.

Feather, B. W.; and Rhoads, J. M. 1972. Psychodynamic behavior therapy. *Archives of General Psychiatry* 26: 496–511.

Fechner, G. T. 1966 [1860]. *Elements of psychophysics.* Vol. 1. E. G. Boring and D. H. Howes, eds., H. E. Adler, trans. New York: Holt, Rinehart & Winston.

Feder, E.; and Feder, B. 1981. *The expressive arts therapies.* Englewood Cliffs, N.J.: Prentice-Hall.

Feher, M.; Naddaff, R.; and Tazi, N., eds. 1989. *Fragments for a history of the body,* 3 vols. Cambridge, Mass.: MIT Press.

Fein, G. G. 1981. Pretend play in childhood: An integrative review. *Child Development* 52: 1095–1118.

Feinberg, T. E.; Rifkin, A.; Schaffer, C.; and Walker, E. 1986. Facial discrimination and emotional recognition in schizophrenia and affective disorders. *Arch Gen Psychiatry* 43: 276–79.

Feiss, G. J. 1979. *Mind therapies—body therapies: A consumer's guide.* Millbrae, Calif.: Celestial Arts.

Feldman, J. A.; and Ballard, D. H. 1982. Connectionist models and their properties. *Cognitive Science* 6: 205–54.

Fenigstein, A.; Scheier, M. F.; and Buss, A. H. 1975. Public and private self-consciousness: Assessment and theory. *Journal of Consulting and Clinical Psychology* 43: 522–27.

Ferencz, B. B.; and Keyes, K., Jr. 1988. *Planethood: The key to your survival and prosperity.* Coos Bay, Oreg.: Vision Books.

Ferguson, A. 1980 [1767]. *An essay on the history of civil society.* New Brunswick, N.J.: Transaction Books.

Festinger, L. 1957. *A theory of cognitive dissonance.* Evanston, Ill.: Row, Peterson.

Feyerabend, P. K. 1981*a. Philosophical papers.* Vol. 1, *Realism, rationalism and scientific method.* Cambridge: Cambridge University Press.

Feyerabend, P. K. 1981*b. Philosophical papers.* Vol. 2, *Problems of empiricism.* Cambridge: Cambridge University Press.

Field, T. 1987. Interaction and attachment in normal and atypical infants. *Journal of Consulting and Clinical Psychology* 55: 853–59.

Field, T.; Healy, B.; Goldstein, S.; Perry, S.; and Bendell, D. 1988. Infants of depressed mothers show "depressed" behavior even with nondepressed adults. *Child Development* 59: 1569–79.

Field, T. M.; McCabe, P.; and Schneiderman, N., eds. 1988. *Stress and coping across development.* Hillsdale, N.J.: Erlbaum.

Field, T.; and Reite, M. 1985. The psychobiology of attachment and separation: A summary. In M. Reite and T. Field, eds., *Biology of social attachments and separation.* New York: Academic Press.

Fine, M. A.; and Ulrich, L. P. 1988. Integrating psychology and philosophy in teaching a graduate course in ethics. *Professional Psychology: Research and Practice* 19: 542–46.

Firrao, S. 1983. *The theory of self-organizing systems in physics, biology and psychology.* Milan: Cooperativa Edizioni Nuova Stampa.

Fischer, K. W. 1980. A theory of cognitive development: The control and construction of hierarchies of skills. *Psychological Review* 87: 477–531.

Fischer, K. W.; and Silvern, L. 1985. Stages and individual differences in cognitive development. *Annual Review of Psychology* 36: 613–48.

Fischer, R. 1987. On fact and fiction—The structures of stories that the brain tells to itself about itself. *Journal of Social and Biological Structures* 10: 343–51.

Fischer-Schreiber, I.; Ehrard, F. K.; Friedrichs, K.; and Diener, M. S. 1989. *The encyclopedia of eastern philosophy and religion.* Boston: Shambhala.

Fisher, D. D. V. 1990. Emotional construing: A psychobiological model. *International Journal of Personal Construct Psychology* 3: 183–203.

Fisher, L. M.; and Wilson, G. T. 1985. A study of the psychology of agoraphobia. *Behavior Research and Therapy* 23: 97–107.

Fishman, D. B.; Rotgers, F.; and Franks, C. M., eds. 1988. *Paradigms in behavior therapy: Present and promise.* New York: Springer.

Fiske, J. 1874. *Outlines of cosmic philosophy based upon the doctrine of evolution,* 2 vols. London: unknown.

Fiske, D. W.; and Schweder, R. A., eds. 1986. *Metatheory in social science: Pluralisms and subjectivities.* Chicago: University of Chicago Press.

Fitzgibbons, R. P. 1986. The cognitive and emotive uses of forgiveness in the treatment of anger. *Psychotherapy* 23: 629–33.

Flavell, J. H. 1979. Metacognition and cognitive monitoring: A new area of cognitive-developmental inquiry. *American Psychologist* 34: 906–11.

Flavell, J. H.; Flavell, E. R.; and Green, F. L. 1987. Young children's knowledge about the apparent-real and pretend-real distinctions. *Developmental Psychology* 23: 816–22.

Fleischer, J. A.; and Wissler, A. 1985. The therapist as patient: Special problems and considerations. *Psychotherapy* 22: 587–94.

Flew, A., ed. 1979. *A dictionary of philosophy.* New York: Macmillan.

Foa, E. B.; Steketee, G.; and Rothbaum, B. O. 1989. Behavioral/cognitive conceptualizations of post-traumatic stress disorder. *Behavior Therapy* 20: 155–76.

Fodor, J. A. 1981. *Representations: Philosophical essays on the foundations of cognitive science.* Cambridge, Mass.: MIT Press.

Fodor, J. A. 1987. *Psychosemantics.* Cambridge, Mass.: MIT Press.

Fodor, J. A.; and Pylyshyn, Z. W. 1988. Connectionism and cognitive architecture: A critical analysis. *Cognition* 28: 3–71.

Fogle, D. O. 1978. Learned helplessness and learned restlessness. *Psychotherapy* 15: 39–47.

Fogel, A.; and Thelen, E. 1987. Development of early expressive and communicative action: Reinterpreting the evidence from a dynamic systems perspective. *Developmental Psychology* 23: 747–61.

Fontana, A. F.; Kerns, R. D.; Blatt, S. J.; Rosenberg, R. L.; Burg, M. M.; and Colonese, K. L. 1989. Cynical mistrust and the search for self-worth. *Journal of Psychosomatic Research* 33: 449–56.

Ford, D. H. 1987. *Humans as self-constructing living systems: A developmental perspective on behavior and personality.* Hillsdale, N.J.: Erlbaum.

Ford, M. E.; and Thompson, R. A. 1985. Perceptions of personal agency and infant attachment: Toward a life-span perspective on competence development. *International Journal of Behavioral Development* 8: 377–406.

Forest, J. J. 1987. Effects on self-actualization of paperbacks about psychological self-help. *Psychological Reports* 60: 1243–46.

Forest, J. J. 1988. Exploring more on the effects of psychological self-help paperbacks. *Psychological Reports* 63: 891–94.

Foucault, M. 1965. *Madness and civilization: A history of insanity in the age of reason* Trans. R. Howard. New York: Random House.

Foucault, M. 1970. *The order of things: An archeology of the human sciences.* New York: Random House.

Foulkes, D. 1985. *Dreaming: A cognitive-psychological analysis.* Hillsdale, N.J.: Erlbaum.

Foulkes, D.; and Fleisher, S. 1975. Mental activity in relaxed wakefulness. *Journal of Abnormal Psychology* 75: 66–75.

Fox, M. 1979. *A spirituality named compassion and the healing of the global village, Humpty Dumpty and us.* Minneapolis, Minn.: Winston Press.

Fox, N. A.; and Davidson, R. J. 1988. Patterns of brain electrical activity during facial signs of emotion in 10-month-old infants. *Developmental Psychology* 24: 230–36.

Frank, J. D. 1961. *Persuasion and healing,* 1st ed. Baltimore, Md.: Johns Hopkins University Press.

Frank, J. D. 1973. *Persuasion and healing,* 2d ed. Baltimore, Md.: Johns Hopkins University Press.

Frank, J. D. 1985. Therapeutic components shared by all psychotherapies. In M. J. Mahoney and A. Freeman, eds., *Cognition and psychotherapy,* 49–79. New York: Plenum.

Frank, J. D. 1987. Psychotherapy, rhetoric, and hermeneutics: Implications for practice and research. *Psychotherapy* 24: 293–302.

Frank, J. D.; Hoehn-Saric, R.; Imber, S. D.; Liberman, B. L.; and Stone, A. R. 1978. *Effective ingredients of successful psychotherapy.* New York: Brunner/Mazel.

Frank, S. J.; Avery, C. B.; and Laman, M. S. 1988. Young adults' perceptions of their relationships with their parents: Individual differences in connectedness, competence, and emotional autonomy. *Developmental Psychology* 24: 729–37.

Frankfort, H.; Frankfort, H. A.; Wilson, J. A.; and Jacobsen, T. 1946. *Before philosophy: The intellectual adventure of ancient man.* Baltimore, Md.: Penguin.

Frankl, V. E. 1959. *Man's search for meaning: An introduction to logotherapy.* New York: Washington Square Press.

Frankl, V. E. 1978. *The unheard cry for meaning: Psychotherapy and humanism.* New York: Simon and Schuster.

Frankl, V. E. 1985. Logos, paradox, and the search for meaning. In M. J. Mahoney and A. Freeman, eds., *Cognition and psychotherapy,* 259–75. New York: Plenum.

Fransella, F. 1972. *Personal change and reconstruction: Research and treatment of stuttering.* London: Academic Press.

Franz, J. G. 1989 [1940]. The place of psychodrama in research. *International Journal of Small Group Research* 5: 131–41.

Freedman, R. 1988. *Bodylove.* New York: Harper and Row.

Frenkel, E. 1936. Studies in biographical psychology. *Character and personality* 5: 1–35.

Frenkel, H. M. 1963. *Fundamentals of the Frenkel mirror image projective technique.* New York: Psychological Library.

Frenkel, R. E. 1980. Mirror image therapy. In R. Herink, ed., *The psychotherapy handbook,* 381–84. New York: Meridien.

Freud, A. 1946. *The ego and the mechanisms of defense.* New York: International Universities Press.

Freud, S. 1953–1966 [1923]. The ego and the id. Vol. 19. In J. Strachey, ed., *The standard edition of the complete psychological works of Sigmund Freud,* 3–66. (23 vols.; J. Strachey, trans.) London: Hogarth Press.

Freud, S. 1958 [1930]. *Civilization and its discontents.* New York: Doubleday.

Freud, S. 1963 [1904]. On psychotherapy. In P. Rieff, ed., *Therapy and technique.* New York: Macmillan.

Freudenberger, H. J.; and Robbins, A. 1979. The hazards of being a psychoanalyst. *Psychoanalytic Review* 66: 275–95.

Frick, R. B. 1982. The ego and the vestibulocerebellar system: Some theoretical perspectives. *Psychoanalytic Quarterly* 51: 93–121.

Frick, W. B. 1982. Conceptual foundations of self-actualization: A contribution to motivation theory. *Journal of Humanistic Psychology* 22: 33–52.

Fridlund, A. J. In press. Evolution and facial action in reflex, emotion, and paralanguage. In P. K. Ackles, J. R. Jennings, and M. G. H. Coles, eds., *Advances in Psychophysiology,* vol. 4. Greenwich, Conn.: JAI Press.

Friedman, H.; Rohrbaugh, M.; and Krakauer, S. 1988. The time-line genogram: Highlighting temporal aspects of family relationships. *Family Process* 27: 293–303.

Friedman, H. S.; and Booth-Kewley, S. 1987. The "disease-prone personality": A meta-analytic view of the construct. *American Psychologist* 42: 539–55.

Friedman, M. 1967. *To deny our nothingness: Contemporary images of man.* Chicago: University of Chicago Press.

Friedman, M. 1974. *The hidden human image.* New York: Dell.

Friedman, M. 1982. Comment on the Rogers-May discussion of evil. *Journal of Humanistic Psychology* 22: 93–96.

Friedman, M. 1988. The healing dialogue in psychotherapy. *Journal of Humanistic Psychology* 28: 19–41.

Friedman, M. P.; Das, J. P.; and O'Connor, N. 1981. *Intelligence and learning.* New York: Plenum.

Friel, J.; and Friel, L. 1988. *Adult children: The secrets of dysfunctional families.* Deerfield Beach, Fla.: Health Communications.

Frijda, N. H. 1988. The laws of emotion. *American Psychologist* 5: 349–58.

Fromm, E. 1941. *Escape from freedom.* New York: Holt, Rinehart and Winston.

Fromm, E. 1956. *The art of loving.* New York: Harper.

Fromm-Reichmann, F. 1950. *Principles of intensive psychotherapy.* Chicago: The University of Chicago Press.

Fruggeri, L.; and Matteini, M. 1988. Larger systems? Beyond a dualistic approach to the process of change. *Irish Journal of Psychology* 9: 183–94.

Fryrear, J. L.; and Stephens, B. C. 1988. Group psychotherapy using masks and video to facilitate intrapersonal communication. *Arts in Psychotherapy* 15: 227–34.

Fuhriman, A.; Barlow, S. H.; and Wanlass, J. 1989. Words, imagination, meaning: Toward change. *Psychotherapy* 26: 149–56.

Fulghum, R. 1986. *All I really need to know I learned in kindergarten.* New York: Ballantine.

Fuller, S. 1988. *Social epistemology.* Bloomington: Indiana University Press.

Furth, H. G. 1987. *Knowledge as desire: An essay on Freud and Piaget.* New York: Columbia University Press.

Furumoto, L. 1989. The new history of psychology. In I. S. Cohen, ed., *The G. Stanley Hall Lecture Series,* vol. 9, 3–34. Washington, D. C.: American Psychological Association.

Gabel, S. 1989. Dreams as a possible reflection of a dissociated self-monitoring system. *Journal of Nervous and Mental Disease* 177: 560–68.

Gabriel, T. J. 1990. Alcohol and self-focus: A balanced placebo investigation. Ph.D. diss. University of California, Santa Barbara.

Gadamer, H. G. 1975. Hermeneutics and social science. *Cultural Hermeneutics* 2: 307–52.

Gadamer, H. G. 1976. *Philosophical hermeneutics* Trans. D. E. Linge. Berkeley: University of California Press.

Gadamer, H. G. 1981. *Reason in the age of science.* Trans. F. G. Lawrence. Cambridge, Mass.: MIT Press.

Gadamer, H. G. 1988. *Truth and method.* Trans. G. Barden and J. Cumming. New York: Crossroad.

Gallup, G. G. 1977. Self-recognition in primates: A comparative approach to the bidirectional properties of consciousness. *American Psychologist* 32: 329–38.

Gallup, G. G. 1982. Self-awareness and the emergence of mind in primates. *American Journal of Primatology* 2: 237–48.

Gallup, G. G. 1985. Do minds exist in species other than our own? *Neuroscience and Biobehavioral Reviews* 9: 631–41.

Galton, F. 1883. *Inquiries into human faculty and its development.* London: Dent.

Gara, M. A.; Rosenberg, S.; and Mueller, D. R. 1989. Perception of self and other in schizophrenia. *International Journal of Personal Construct Psychology* 2: 253–70.

Gardner, H. 1985. *The mind's new science: A history of the cognitive revolution.* New York: Basic Books

Gardner, R. A.; and Gardner, B. T. 1988. Feedforward versus feedbackward: An ethological alternative to the law of effect. *Behavioral and Brain Sciences* 11: 429–93.

Gardner, R. M.; Gallegos, V.; Martinez, R.; and Espinoza, T. 1989. Mirror feedback and judgments of body size. *Journal of Psychosomatic Research* 33: 603–7.

Garfield, S. L. 1986. Research on client variables in psychotherapy. In S. L. Garfield and A. E. Bergin, eds., *Handbook of psychotherapy and behavior change,* 3rd ed., 213–256. New York: Wiley.

Garfield, S. L. 1989. *The practice of brief psychotherapy.* London: Pergamon.

Garfield, S. L.; and Bergin, A. E. 1971. Personal therapy, outcome and some therapist variables. *Psychotherapy: Theory, Research and Practice* 8: 251–53.

Garfield, S. L.; and Bergin, A. E. 1978. *Handbook of psychotherapy and behavior change,* 2d ed. New York: Wiley.

Garfield, S. L.; and Bergin, A. E., eds. 1986. *Handbook of psychotherapy and behavior change,* 3d ed. New York: Wiley.

Garfield, S. L.; and Kurtz, R. 1976a. Clinical psychologists in the 1970s. *American Psychologist* 31: 1–9.

Garfield, S. L.; and Kurtz, R. 1976b. Personal therapy for the psychotherapist: Some findings and issues. *Psychotherapy: Theory, Research and Practice* 13: 188–92.

Garfield, S. L.; and Kurtz, R. 1977. A study of eclectic views. *Journal of Consulting and Clinical Psychology* 45: 78–83.

Garfinkel, H. 1985. *Studies in ethnomethodology.* New York: Basil Blackwell.

Garmezy, N.; and Masten, A. S. 1986. Stress, competence, and resilience: Common frontiers for therapist and psychopathologist. *Behavior Therapy* 17: 500–21.

Garmezy, N.; and Rutter, M. 1983. *Stress, coping and development.* New York: McGraw-Hill.

Garner, D. M.; and Garfinkel, P. E., eds. 1985. *Handbook of psychotherapy for anorexia nervosa and bulimia.* New York: Guilford.

Garstang, W. 1922. The theory of recapitulation: A critical restatement of the biogenetic law. *Journal of the Linnaean Society, Zoology* 35: 81–101.

Gaston, L.; and Marmar, C. R. 1989. Quantitative and qualitative analyses for psychotherapy research: Integration through time-series designs. *Psychotherapy* 26: 169–73.

Gazzaniga, M. S.; and LeDoux, J. E. 1978. *The integrated mind.* New York: Plenum.

Geertz, C. 1973. *The interpretation of cultures.* New York: Basic Books.

Gelman, R.; and Baillargeon, R. 1983. A review of some Piagetian concepts. In P. Mussen, ed., *Manual of child psychology*, 4th ed., vol. 3, *Cognitive development,* J. H. Flavell and E. M. Markham, eds., 167–230. New York: Wiley.

Gendlin, E. T. 1962. *Experiencing and the creation of meaning.* New York: Free Press.

Gendlin, E. T. 1978. *Focusing.* New York: Bantam.

Georgopoulos, A. P.; Lurito, J. T.; and Masey J. T. 1989. Mental rotation of the neuronal population vector. *Science* 243: 234–36.

Gergen, K. J. 1965. The effects of interaction goals and personalistic feedback on the presentation of self. *Journal of Personality and Social Psychology* 1: 413–24.

Gergen, K. J. 1971. *The concept of the self.* New York: Holt, Rinehart and Winston.

Gergen, K. J. 1985. The social constructionist movement in modern psychology. *American Psychologist* 40: 266–75.

Geschwind, N.; and Galaburda, A. M. 1987. *Cerebral lateralization: Biological mechanisms, associations, and pathology.* Cambridge, Mass.: MIT Press.

Gfeller, K. 1988. Musical components and styles preferred by young adults for aerobic fitness activities. *Journal of Music Therapy* 25: 28–43.

Gholson, B.; Shadish, W.; Neimeyer, R. A.; and Houts, A., eds. 1989. *Psychology of science and metascience.* Cambridge: Cambridge University Press.

Gibbons, F. X.; Smith, T. W.; Ingram, R. E.; Pearce, K.; Brehm, S. S.; and Schroeder, D. J. 1985. Self-awareness and self-confrontation: Effects of self-focused attention on members of a clinical population. *Journal of Personality and Social Psychology* 48: 662–75.

Giblin, P. 1989. Use of reading assignments in clinical practice. *American Journal of Family Therapy* 17: 219–28.

Gibson, E. J. 1969. *Principles of perceptual learning and development.* New York: Appleton-Century-Crofts.

Gibson, E. J. 1987. Introductory essay: What does infant perception tell us about theories of perception? *Journal of Experimental Psychology: Human Perception and Performance* 13: 515–23.

Gibson, E. J. 1988. Exploratory behavior in the development of perceiving, acting, and the acquiring of knowledge. *Annual Review of Psychology* 39: 1–41.

Gibson, E.; and Walk, R. 1960. The "visual cliff." *Scientific American* 202: 64–71.

Gibson, J. J. 1950. *The perception of the visual world.* Boston: Houghton Mifflin.

Gibson, J. J. 1966. *The senses considered as perceptual systems.* Boston: Houghton Mifflin.

Gibson, J. J. 1979. *The ecological approach to visual perception.* Boston: Houghton Mifflin.

Giffin, H. 1984. The coordination of meaning in the creation of a shared make-believe reality. In I. Bretherton, ed., *Symbolic Play: The development of social understanding,* 73–100. New York: Academic Press.

Gilbert, P. 1989. *Human nature and suffering.* Hillsdale, N.J.: Erlbaum.

Gilligan, C. 1982. *In a different voice: Psychological theory and women's development.* Cambridge, Mass.: Harvard University Press.

Gilligan, S. G.; and Bower, G. H. 1983. Reminding and mood-congruent memory. *Bulletin of the Psychonomic Society* 21: 431–34.

Gilligan, S. G.; and Bower, G. H. 1984. Cognitive consequences of emotional arousal. In C. Izard, J. Kagan, and R. Zajonc, eds., *Emotions, cognition, and behavior.* Cambridge: Cambridge University Press.

Ginsburg, H.; and Opper, S. 1969. *Piaget's theory of intellectual development.* Englewood Cliffs, N.J.: Prentice-Hall.

Glaser, S. R. 1980. Rhetoric and psychotherapy. In M. J. Mahoney, ed., *Psychotherapy process: Current issues and future directions,* 313–33. New York: Plenum.

Glass, C. R.; and Arnkoff, D. B. 1988. Common and specific factors in client descriptions of and explanations for change. *Journal of Integrative and Eclectic Psychotherapy* 7: 427–40.

Glasser, W. 1972. *The identity society.* New York: Harper and Row.

Glassman, M. 1988. Kernberg and Kohut: A test of competing psychoanalytic models of narcissism. *Journal of the American Psychoanalytic Association* 36: 597–625.

Gleick, J. 1987. *Chaos: Making a new science.* New York: Viking.

Glezer, I. I.; Jacobs, M. S.; and Morgane, P. J. 1988. Implications of the "initial brain" concept for brain evolution in Cetacea. *Behavioral and Brain Sciences* 11: 75–116.

Globus, G. G. 1989. Connectionism and the dreaming mind. *Journal of Mind and Behavior* 10: 179–96.

Glover, J. 1988. *I: The philosophy and psychology of personal identity.* London: Penguin.

Gluck, M. A.; and Rumelhart, D. E., eds. 1990. *Neuroscience and connectionist theory.* Hillsdale, N.J.: Erlbaum.

Glucksberg, S. 1989. Metaphors in conversation: How are they understood? Why are they used? *Metaphor and Symbolic Activity* 4: 125–43.

Glucksberg, S.; and Keysar, B. 1990. Understanding metaphorical comparisons: Beyond similarity. *Psychological Review* 97: 3–18.

Goffman, E. 1959. *The presentation of self in everyday life.* New York: Doubleday.

Goffman, E. 1963. *Stigma.* Englewood Cliffs, N.J.: Prentice-Hall.

Goffman, E. 1974. *Frame analysis.* New York: Harper and Row.

Goguen, J. A.; and Varela, F. J. 1979. Systems and distinctions: Duality and complementarity. *International Journal of General Systems* 5: 31–43.

Goldberg, A., ed. 1985. *Progress in self psychology,* vol. 1. New York: Guilford.

Goldberg, A. 1989. Self psychology and the narcissistic personality disorders. *Narcissistic Personality Disorder* 12: 731–39.

Goldberg, B. 1985. *The mirror and man.* Charlottesville: University Press of Virginia.

Goldberg, C. 1986. *On being a psychotherapist.* New York: Gardner.

Goldberg, S. 1988. Risk factors in infant-mother attachment. *Canadian Journal of Psychology* 42: 173–88.

Goldfried, M. R. 1980a. Toward the delineation of therapeutic change principles. *American Psychologist* 35: 991–99.

Goldfried, M. R., ed. 1980b. Some views on effective principles of psychotherapy. *Cognitive Therapy and Research* 4 (Whole No. 3).

Goldfried, M. R. 1982. *Converging themes in psychotherapy.* New York: Springer.

Goldfried, M. R.; Greenberg, L. S.; and Marmar, C. 1990. Individual psychotherapy: Process and outcome. *Annual Review of Psychology* 41: 659–88.

Goldfried, M. R.; and Robins, C. 1983. Self-schemas, cognitive bias, and the processing of learning experiences. In P. C. Kendall, ed., *Advances in cognitive-behavioral research and therapy,* vol. 2, 33–80. New York: Academic Press.

Goldman, A. I. 1986 *Epistemology and cognition.* Cambridge, Mass.: Harvard University Press.

Goldrosen, J.; and Beecher, J. 1987. *Remembering Buddy: The definitive biography.* New York: Penguin.

Goldschmid, M. L.; Stein, D. D.; Weissman, H. N.; and Sorrells, J. 1969. A survey of the training and practice of clinical psychologists. *Clinical Psychologist* 22: 89–94.

Goldschmidt, R. 1933. Some aspects of evolution. *Science* 78: 539–47.

Goldschmidt, R. 1940. *The material basis of evolution.* New Haven, Conn.: Yale University Press.

Goldstein, M. J. 1988. The family and psychopathology. *Annual Review of Psychology* 39: 283–99.

Goldstein, K. M.; and Blackman, S. 1978. *Cognitive style: Five approaches and relevant research.* New York: Wiley.

Goldstein, W. N. 1989. Update on psychodynamic thinking regarding the diagnosis of the borderline patient. *American Journal of Psychotherapy* 43: 321–42.

Goleman, D. 1977. *The varieties of meditative experience.* New York: Dutton.

Goleman, D. 1985. *Vital lies, simple truths: The psychology of self-deception.* New York: Simon and Schuster.

Golombek, H.; Marton, P.; Stein, B. A.; and Korenblum, M. 1989. Adolescent personality development: Three phases, three courses and varying turmoil. Findings from the Toronto Adolescent Longitudinal Study. *Canadian Journal of Psychiatry* 34: 500–504.

Gonçalves, O. F., ed. 1989a. *Advances in the cognitive therapies: The constructivist-developmental approach.* Lisbon: APPORT.

Gonçalves, O. F., ed. 1989b. *Constructive developmental approaches to cognitive therapies.* Porto, Portugal: APPORT.

Gonçalves, O. F. 1990. *Hermeneutics, constructivism and cognitive-behavioral therapies:*

From the object to the project. Paper presented to an international conference, "Constructivism in Psychotherapy," May 17–20, Memphis, Tenn.

Gonçalves, O. F.; and Ivey, A. E. 1987. The effects of unconscious presentation of information on therapist conceptualizations, intentions, and responses. *Journal of Clinical Psychology* 43: 237–45.

Good, G. E.; Dell, D. M.; and Mintz, L. B. 1989. Male role and gender role conflict: Relations to help seeking in men. *Journal of Counseling Psychology* 36: 295–300.

Goodman, D. S.; and Maultsby, M. C. 1974 *Emotional well-being through rational behavior training.* Springfield, Ill.: Charles C. Thomas.

Goodman, M.; and Teicher, A. 1988. To touch or not to touch. *Psychotherapy* 25: 492–500.

Goolishian, H. A.; and Winderman, L. 1988. Constructivism, autopoiesis and problem determined systems. *Irish Journal of Psychology* 9: 130–43.

Gorelick, K. 1989. Rapprochement between the arts and psychotherapies: Metapor the mediator. *Arts in Psychotherapy* 16: 149–55.

Gornick, V. 1983. *Woman and science: Portraits from a world of transition.* New York: Simon and Schuster.

Gottman, J. M.; and Katz, L. F. 1989. Effects of marital discord on young children's peer interaction and health. *Developmental Psychology* 25: 373–81.

Gottman, J. M.; and Krokoff, L. J. 1989. Marital interaction and satisfaction: A longitudinal view. *Journal of Consulting and Clinical Psychology* 57: 47–52.

Goudge, T. A. 1974. Evolutionism. In P. P. Wiener, ed., *Dictionary of the history of ideas,* vol. 2, 174–89. New York: Scribner.

Gould, S. J. 1977*a. Ontogeny and phylogeny.* Cambridge, Mass.: Harvard University Press.

Gould, S. J. 1977*b. Ever since Darwin: Reflections in natural history.* New York: Norton.

Gould, S. J. 1980*a.* Is a new and general theory of evolution emerging? *Paleobiology* 6: 119–30.

Gould, S. J. 1980*b. The panda's thumb: More reflections in natural history.* New York: Norton.

Gould, S. J. 1981. *The mismeasure of man.* New York: Norton.

Gould, S. J. 1982. Darwinism and the expansion of evolutionary theory. *Science* 216: 380–87.

Gould, S. J. 1989. Punctuated equilibrium in fact and theory. *Journal of Social and Biological Structures* 12: 117–36.

Gould, S. J.; and Eldredge, N. 1977. Punctuated equilibria: The tempo and mode of evolution reconsidered. *Paleobiology* 3: 115–51.

Gould, S. J.; and Lewontin, R. C. 1979. The spandrels of San Marco and the Panglossian paradigm: A critique of the adaptionist programme. *Proceedings of the Royal Society* 205: 581–98.

Gove, W. R., ed. 1982. *Deviance and mental illness.* Beverly Hills, Calif.: Sage.

Granit, R. 1977. *The purposive brain.* Cambridge, Mass.: MIT Press.

Granit, R. 1982. Reflections on the evolution of the mind and its environment. In R. Q. Elvee, ed., *Mind in nature,* 96–117. New York: Harper and Row.

Grant, V. 1963. *The origin of adaptations.* New York: Columbia University Press.

Greenberg, G.; and Tobach, E., eds. 1990. *Theories of the evolution of knowing.* Hillsdale, N.J.: Erlbaum.

Greenberg, J.; and Pyszczynski, T. 1986. Persistent high self-focus after failure and low self-focus after success: The depressive self-focusing style. *Journal of Personality and Social Psychology* 50: 1039–44.

Greenberg, L. S.; and Pinsof, W., eds. 1986. *The psychotherapeutic process.* New York: Guilford.

Greenberg, L. S.; and Safran, J. D. 1987. *Emotion in psychotherapy.* New York: Guilford.

Greenberg, L. S.; and Safran, J. D. 1989. Emotion in psychotherapy. *American Psychologist* 44: 19–29.

Greenberg, M. T.; Siegel, J. M.; and Leitch, C. J. 1983. The nature and importance of attachment relationships to parents and peers during adolescence. *Journal of Youth and Adolescence* 12: 373–86.

Greenberg, R. P.; and Staller, J. S. 1981. Personal therapy for therapists. *American Journal of Psychiatry* 138: 1467–71.

Greenspan, S.; and Greenspan, W. T. 1985. *First feelings: Milestones in the emotional development of your baby and child.* New York: Viking.

Greenwald, A. G. 1980. The totalitarian ego: Fabrication and revision of personal history. *American Psychologist* 35: 603–18.

Greenwald, A. G.; Klinger, M. R.; and Liu, T. J. 1989. Unconscious processing of dichoptically masked words. *Memory and Cognition* 17: 35–47.

Gregg, R. B. 1978. Kenneth Burke's prolegomena to the study of the rhetoric of form. *Communication Quarterly* 26: 3–13.

Gregory, R. L., ed. 1987. *The Oxford companion to the mind.* Oxford: Oxford University Press.

Grinker, R. R.; Werble, B.; and Drye, R. C. 1968. *The borderline syndrome: A behavioral study of ego functions.* New York: Basic Books.

Groddeck, G. 1949 [1923]. *The book of the it.* Trans. V. M. E. Collins. New York: Random House.

Groeger, J. A. 1986. Predominant and non-predominant analysis: Effects of level of presentation. *British Journal of Psychology* 77: 109–16.

Gross, C. G. 1987. Early history of neuroscience. In G. Adelman, ed., *Encyclopedia of neuroscience,* 843–46. Boston: Birkhäuser.

Grossmann, K. E.; and Grossmann, K. 1990. The wider concept of attachment in cross-cultural research. *Human Development* 33: 31–47.

Gruber, H. E. 1974. *Darwin on man.* New York: Dutton.

Gruber, H. E. 1985a. Divergence in evolution and individuality in development. In G. Butterworth, J. Rutkowska, and M. Scaife, eds., *Evolution and developmental psychology,* 133–47. Sussex, England: Harvester Press.

Gruber, H. E. 1985b. From epistemic subject to unique creative person at work. *Archives de Psychologie* 53: 167–85.

Grunebaum, H. 1983. A study of therapists' choice of a therapist. *American Journal of Psychiatry* 140: 1336–39.

Grusky, Z. 1987. The practice of psychotherapy: A search for principles in an ambiguous art. *Psychotherapy* 24: 1–6.

Guest, P. D.; and Beutler, L. E. 1988. Impact of psychotherapy supervision on therapist orientation and values. *Journal of Consulting and Clinical Psychology* 56: 653–58.

Guidano, V. F. 1984. A constructivist outline of cognitive processes. In M. A. Reda and M. J. Mahoney, eds., *Cognitive psychotherapies: Recent developments in theory, research, and practice*, 31–45. Cambridge, Mass.: Ballinger.

Guidano, V. F. 1987. *Complexity of the self: A developmental approach to psychopathology and therapy.* New York: Guilford.

Guidano, V. F. 1990. *The self in process: Toward a post-rationalist cognitive therapy.* New York: Guilford.

Guidano, V. F.; and Liotti, G. 1983. *Cognitive processes and emotional disorders.* New York: Guilford.

Guidano, V. F.; and Liotti, G. 1985. A constructivistic foundation for cognitive therapy. In M. J. Mahoney and A. Freeman, eds., *Cognition and psychotherapy*, 101–42. New York: Plenum.

Gunderson, J. G. 1984. *Borderline personality disorder.* Washington, D. C.: American Psychiatric Press.

Gurman, A. S. 1973. Effects of therapist and patient mood on the therapeutic functioning of high- and low-facilitative therapists. *Journal of Consulting and Clinical Psychology* 40: 48–58.

Gurman, A. S.; and Razin, A. M., eds. 1977. *Effective psychotherapy: A handbook of research.* London: Pergamon.

Gustafson, J. P. 1986. *The complex secret of brief psychotherapy.* New York: Norton.

Guthrie, F. R. 1935. *The psychology of learning.* New York: Harper and Row.

Gutsch, K. U.; Sisemore, D. A.; and Williams, R. L. 1984. *Systems of psychotherapy.* Springfield, Ill.: Charles C. Thomas.

Gutting, G., ed. 1980. *Paradigms and revolutions: Applications and appraisals of Thomas Kuhn's philosophy of science.* Notre Dame, Ind.: University of Notre Dame Press.

Guy, J. D. 1987. *The personal life of the psychotherapist.* New York: Wiley.

Guy, J. D.; and Liaboe, G. P. 1986. Personal therapy for the experienced psychotherapist: A discussion of its usefulness and utilisation. *Clinical Psychologist* 39: 20–23.

Guy, J. D.; Poelstra, P. L.; and Stark, M. J. 1989. Personal distress and therapeutic effectiveness: National survey of psychologists practicing psychotherapy. *Professional Psychology: Research and Practice* 20: 48–50.

Guy, J. D.; Stark, M. J.; and Poelstra, P. L. 1988. Personal therapy for psychotherapists before and after entering professional practice. *Professional Psychology: Research and Practice* 19: 474–76.

Haber, R. N., ed. 1966. *Current research in motivation.* New York: Holt, Rinehart and Winston.

Haber, R. N. 1983. The impending demise of the icon: A critique of the concept of iconic storage in visual information processing. *Behavioral and Brain Sciences* 6: 1–54.

Haeckel, E. 1874. *Anthropogenie.* Berlin: Georg Reimer.

Hale, G. A.; and Lewis, M. 1979. *Attention and cognitive development.* New York: Plenum.

Halleck, S. L. 1971. *The politics of therapy.* New York: Harper and Row.

Hamburg, P. 1988. House and psyche. *American Journal of Psychotherapy* 42: 107–23.

Hamilton, C. R.; and Vermeire, B. A. 1988. Complementary hemispheric specialization in monkeys. *Science* 242: 1691–94.

Hamilton, E. 1940. *Mythology.* Boston: Little, Brown.

Hamilton, N. G. 1989. A critical review of object relations theory. *American Journal of Psychiatry* 146: 1552–60.

Hamilton, V.; Bower, G. H.; and Frijda, N. H., eds. 1988. *Cognitive perspectives on emotion and motivation.* Dordrecht, Netherlands: Kluwer Academic Publishers.

Hamlyn, D. W. 1987. *A history of western philosophy.* New York: Viking Penguin.

Hammen, C. 1988. Self-cognitions, stressful events, and the prediction of depression in children of depressed mothers. *Journal of Abnormal Child Psychology* 16: 347–60.

Hamowy, R. 1987. *The Scottish Enlightenment and the theory of spontaneous order.* Carbondale: Southern Illinois University Press.

Hampden-Turner, C. 1981. *Maps of the mind: Charts and concepts of the mind and its labyrinths.* New York: Macmillan.

Handelsman, M. M.; and Galvin, M. D. 1988. Facilitating informed consent for outpatient psychotherapy: A suggested written format. *Professional Psychology: Research and Practice* 19: 223–25.

Handelsman, M. M.; Kemper, M. B.; Kesson-Craig, P.; McLain, J.; and Johnsrud, C. 1986. Use, content, and readability of written informed consent forms for treatment. *Professional Psychology: Research and Practice* 17: 514–18.

Hansen, R. D.; and Hansen, C. H. 1988. Repression of emotionally tagged memories: The architecture of less complex emotions. *Journal of Personality and Social Psychology* 55: 811–18.

Hansen, R. D.; and Hansen, C. H. 1989. Sympathetic arousal and self-attention: The accessibility of interoceptive and exteroceptive arousal cues. *Journal of Experimental Social Psychology* 25: 437–49.

Hanson, N. R. 1970. A picture theory of theory meaning. In R. G. Colodny, ed., *The nature and function of scientific theories: Essays in contemporary science and philosophy,* 233–74. Pittsburgh, Pa.: University of Pittsburgh Press.

Harcum, E. R. 1988. Defensive reactance of psychologists to a metaphysical foundation for integrating different psychologies. *Journal of Psychology* 122: 217–35.

Hardaway, R. A. 1990. Subliminally activated symbiotic fantasies: Facts and artifacts. *Psychological Bulletin* 107: 177–95.

Hareven, T. K.; and Masoaka, K. 1988. Turning points and transitions: Perceptions of the life course. *Journal of Family History* 13: 271–89.

Harland, R. 1987. *Superstructuralism: The philosophy of structuralism and post-structuralism.* London: Methuen.

Harlow, L. L.; Newcomb, M. D.; and Bentler, P. M. 1986. Depression, self-derogation, substance use, and suicide ideation: Lack of purpose in life as a mediational factor. *Journal of Clinical Psychology* 42: 5–21.

Harré, R. 1984. *Personal being: A theory for individual psychology.* Cambridge, Mass.: Harvard University Press.

Harré, R. 1987. Enlarging the paradigm. *New Ideas in Psychology* 5: 3–12.

Harris, D. B., ed. 1957. *The concept of development: An issue in the study of human behavior.* Minneapolis: University of Minnesota Press.

Harrison, J. 1976. *Hume's moral epistemology.* Oxford, England: Clarendon Press.

Hart, J. T. 1965. Memory and the feeling-of-knowing experience. *Journal of Educational Psychology* 56: 208–16.

Hart, S. N.; and Brassard, M. R. 1987. A major threat to children's mental health. *American Psychologist* 42: 160–65.

Harter, S. 1983. Developmental perspectives on the self-system. In E. M. Hetherington, ed., *Handbook of child psychology, Vol. 4: Socialization, personality, and social development,* 275–385. New York: Wiley.

Harter, S. 1986. Cognitive-developmental processes in the integration of concepts about emotions and the self. *Social Cognition* 4: 119–51.

Harter, S.; and Buddin, B. J. 1987. Children's understanding of the simultaneity of two emotions: A five-stage developmental acquisition sequence. *Developmental Psychology* 23: 388–99.

Hartman, L. M.; and Blankstein, K. R., eds. 1986. *Perception of self in emotional disorder and psychotherapy.* New York: Plenum.

Hartmann, H. 1958 [1939]. *Ego psychology and the problem of adaptation.* New York: International Universities Press.

Hartnett, J.; Simonetta, L.; and Mahoney, J. 1989. Perceptions of nonclinical psychologists toward clinical psychology and clinical psychologists. *Professional Psychology: Research and Practice* 20: 187–89.

Hartshorne, C.; and Peden, C. 1981. *Whitehead's view of reality.* New York: Pilgrim.

Hartup, W. W. 1989. Social relationships and their developmental significance. *American Psychologist* 44: 120–26.

Hastorf, A. H.; and Isen, A. M., eds. 1982. *Cognitive social psychology.* New York: Elsevier North-Holland.

Hatcher, S. L.; Huebner, D. A.; and Zakin, D. F. 1986. Following the trail of the focus in time-limited psychotherapy. *Psychotherapy* 23: 513–20.

Hatfield, G. 1988. Neuro-philosophy meets psychology: Reduction, autonomy, and physiological constraints. *Cognitive Neuropsychology* 5: 723–46.

Hatfield, E.; and Sprecher, S. 1986. *Mirror, mirror.* Albany: State University of New York Press.

Haugeland, J., ed. 1981. *Mind design: Philosophy, psychology, artificial intelligence.* Montgomery, Vt.: Bradford.

Haugeland, J. 1985. *Artificial intelligence: The very idea.* Cambridge, Mass.: MIT Press.

Havelock, E. A. 1976. *Origins of western literacy.* Ontario, Canada: Ontario Institute for Studies in Education.

Havelock, E. A. 1978. The alphabetization of Homer. In E. A. Havelock and J. P. Hershbell, eds., *Communication arts in the ancient world,* 3–21. New York: Hastings House.

Hawking, S. W. 1988. *A brief history of time: From the big bang to black holes.* New York: Bantam.

Hawkins, W. L.; French, L. C.; Crawford, B. D.; and Enzle, M. E. 1988. Depressed affect and time perception. *Journal of Abnormal Psychology* 97: 275–80.

Hayek, F. A. 1944. *The road to serfdom.* Chicago: University of Chicago Press.

Hayek, F. A. 1948. *Individualism and economic order.* Chicago: University of Chicago Press.

Hayek, F. A. 1952*a. The counter-revolution of science.* Glencoe, Ill.: Free Press.

Hayek, F. A. 1952*b. The sensory order.* Chicago: University of Chicago Press.

Hayek, F. A. 1964. The theory of complex phenomena. In M. Bunge, ed., *The critical approach to science and philosophy: Essays in honor of K. R. Popper.* New York: Free Press.

Hayek, F. A. 1967. *Studies in philosophy, politics, and economics.* Chicago: University of Chicago Press.

Hayek, F. A. 1973. *Law, legislation, and liberty.* Vol. 1, *Rules and order.* Chicago: University of Chicago Press.

Hayek, F. A. 1978. *New studies in philosophy, politics, economics, and the history of ideas.* Chicago: University of Chicago Press.

Hayek, F. A. 1979. *Law, legislation and liberty.* Vol. 3, *The political order of a free people.* Chicago: University of Chicago Press.

Hayek, F. A. 1982. *The Sensory Order* after 25 years. In W. B. Weimer and D. S. Palermo, eds., *Cognition and the symbolic processes,* vol. 2, 287–93. Hillsdale, N.J.: Erlbaum.

Hayes, S. C. 1987. A contextual approach to therapeutic change. In N. S. Jacobson, ed., *Psychotherapists in clinical practice: Cognitive and behavioral perspectives,* 327–87. New York: Guilford.

Hazan, C.; and Shaver, P. R. 1987. Romantic love conceptualized as an attachment process. *Journal of Personality and Social Psychology* 52: 511–24.

Hazan, C.; and Shaver, P. R. 1989. Love and work: An attachment-theoretical perspective. Cornell University. Manuscript.

Healy, D.; and Williams, J.M.G. 1988. Dysrhythmia, dysphoria, and depression: The interaction of learned helplessness and circadian dysrhythmia in the pathogenesis of depression. *Psychological Bulletin* 103: 163–78.

Hearst, E., ed. 1979. *The first century of experimental psychology.* Hillsdale, N.J.: Erlbaum.

Heath, A. E.; Neimeyer, G. J.; and Pedersen, P. B. 1988. The future of cross-cultural counseling: A Delphi poll. *Journal of Counseling and Development* 67: 27–30.

Hebb, D. O. 1949. *The organization of behavior.* New York: Wiley.

Hebb, D. O. 1975. Science and the world of imagination. *Canadian Psychology* 16: 4–11.

Heckhausen, J.; Dixon, R. A.; and Baltes, P. B. 1989. Gains and losses in development throughout adulthood as perceived by different adult age groups. *Developmental Psychology* 25: 109–21.

Hedges, L. V. 1987. How hard is hard science, how soft is soft science? *American Psychologist* 42: 443–55.

Heelàs, P.; and Lock, A., eds. 1981. *Indigenous psychologies: The anthropology of the self.* London: Academic Press.

Heelen, P. A. 1989. The new relevance of experiment: A postmodern problem. *Theoretical and Philosophical Issues in Psychology* 9: 11–19.

Heery, M. W. 1989. Inner voice experiences: An exploratory study of thirty cases. *Journal of Transpersonal Psychology* 21: 73–82.

Heidegger, M. 1962 [1927]. *Being and time.* New York: Harper and Row.

Heidegger, M. 1971 [1959]. *On the way to language.* Trans. P. D. Hertz. New York: Harper and Row.

Heider, F. 1946. Attitudes and cognitive organization. *Journal of Psychology* 21: 107–12.

Heilbroner, R. L., ed. 1986. *The essential Adam Smith.* New York: Norton.

Heimberg, R. G.; Klosko, J. S.; Dodge, C. S.; Shadick, R.; Becker, R. E.; and Barlow, D. H. 1989. Anxiety disorders, depression, and attributional style: A further test of the specificity of depressive attributions. *Cognitive Therapy and Research* 13: 21–36.

Heims, S. J. 1980. *John von Neumann and Norbert Wiener: From mathematics to the technologies of life and death.* Cambridge, Mass.: MIT Press.

Held, R.; and Hein, A. 1963. Movement-produced stimulation in the development of visually guided behaviour. *Journal of Comparative and Physiological Psychology* 56: 872–76.

Hellman, I. D.; and Morrison, T. L. 1987. Practice setting and type of caseload as factors in psychotherapist stress. *Psychotherapy* 24: 427–33.

Hellman, I. D.; Morrison, T. L.; and Abramowitz, S. I. 1987. Therapist experience and the stresses of psychotherapeutic work. *Psychotherapy* 24: 171–77.

Henley, T. B.; Johnson, M. G.; and Jones, E. M. 1989. Definitions of psychology. *Psychological Record* 39: 143–52.

Henry, W. E. 1966. Some observations on the lives of healers. *Human Development* 9: 47–56.

Henry, W. E.; Sims, J. H.; and Spray, S. L. 1973. *Public and private lives of psychotherapists.* San Francisco: Jossey-Bass.

Herink, R. 1980. *The psychotherapy handbook.* New York: New American Library.

Hermans, H. J. M. 1987. Self as an organized system of valuations: Toward a dialogue with the person. *Journal of Counseling Psychology* 34: 10–19.

Hermans, H. J. M. 1988. On the integration of nomothetic and idiographic research methods in the study of personal meaning. *Journal of Personality* 56: 785–812.

Hermans, H. J. M. 1989. The meaning of life as an organized process. *Psychotherapy* 26: 11–22.

Herrmann, D. J.; and Chaffim, R., eds. 1988. *Memory in historical perspective.* Heidelberg: Springer-Verlag.

Herrnstein, R. J. 1990. Rational choice theory: Necessary but not sufficient. *American Psychologist* 45: 356–67.

Herrnstein, R. J.; and Loveland, D. H. 1964. Complex visual concept in the pigeon. *Science* 146: 549–51.

Hersh, T. 1980. The phenomenology of belief systems. *Journal of Humanistic Psychology* 20: 57–68.

Hess, A. K., ed. 1980. *Psychotherapy supervision: Theory, research, and practice.* New York: Wiley.

Hetherington, E. M. 1989. Coping with family transitions: Winners, losers, and survivors. *Child Development* 60: 1–14.

Hetherington, E. M.; Lerner, R. M.; and Perlmutter, M., eds. 1988. *Child development in a life-span perspective.* Hillsdale, N.J.: Erlbaum.

Hettich, P. 1990. Journal writing: Old fare or nouvelle cuisine? *Teaching of Psychology* 17: 36–39.

Hibbard, L. S.; McGlone, J. S.; Davis, D. W.; and Hawkins, R. A. 1987. Three-dimensional representation and analysis of brain energy metabolism. *Science* 236: 1641–46.

Hick, J., ed. 1964. *The existence of God.* New York: Macmillan.

Higgins, E. T. 1987. Self-discrepancy: A theory relating self and affect. *Psychological Review* 94: 319–40.

Higgins, E. T. 1989. Knowledge accessibility and activation: Subjectivity and suffering from unconscious sources. In J. S. Uleman and J. A. Bargh, eds., *Unintended thought,* 75–123. New York: Guilford.

Hilgard, E. R. 1977. *Divided consciousness: Multiple controls in human thought and action.* New York: Wiley.

Hilgard, E. R. 1981. Imagery and imagination in American psychology. *Journal of Mental Imagery* 5: 5–19.

Hilgard, E. R. 1987. *Psychology in America: A historical survey.* San Diego, Calif.: Harcourt Brace Jovanovich.

Hill, A., ed. 1978. *A visual encyclopedia of unconventional medicine.* New York: Crown.

Hill, C. E. 1982. Counseling process research: Philosophical and methodological dilemmas. *Counseling Psychologist* 10: 7–19.

Hill, C. E.; Helms, J. E.; Tichenor, V.; Spiegel, S. B.; O'Grady, K. E.; and Perry, E. S. 1988. Effects of therapist response modes in brief psychotherapy. *Journal of Counseling Psychology* 35: 222–33.

Hill, K. A. 1978. Meta-analysis of paradoxical interventions. *Psychotherapy* 24: 266–70.

Hillis, D. 1985. *The connection machine.* Cambridge, Mass.: MIT Press.

Hillman, J. 1965 Betrayal. *Contributions to Jungian Thought* (Spring): 57–76.

Hillyard, S. A. 1985. Electrophysiology of human selective attention. *Trends in Neuroscience* 8: 400–405.

Hirst, W. 1986. The psychology of attention. In J. E. LeDoux and W. Hirst, eds., *Mind and brain: Dialogues in cognitive neuroscience,* 105–41. Cambridge: Cambridge University Press.

Hirst, W., ed. 1988. *The making of cognitive science.* Cambridge: Cambridge University Press.

Hobson, J. A. 1988. *The dreaming brain.* New York: Basic Books.

Hochberg, J. E. 1979. Sensation and perception. In E. Hearst, ed., *The first century of experimental psychology,* 88–142. Hillsdale, N.J.: Erlbaum.

Hochberg, J. E. 1981. On cognition in perception. Perceptual coupling and unconscious inference. *Cognition* 10: 127–34.

Hoehn-Saric, R. (1978). Emotional arousal, attitude change, and psychotherapy. In J. D. Frank, R. Hoehn-Saric, S. D. Imber, B. L. Liberman, and A. R. Stone, eds., *Effective ingredients of successful psychotherapy,* 73–106. New York: Brunner/Mazel.

Hofer, M. A. 1984. Relationships as regulators: A psychobiologic perspective on bereavement. *Psychosomatic Medicine* 46: 183–97.

Hoffding, H. 1900. *A history of modern philosophy,* Vol. 2. New York: Macmillan.

Hoffman, L. 1981. *Foundations of family therapy: A conceptual framework for systems change.* New York: Basic Books.

Hofstadter, D. R. 1979. *Gödel, Escher, Bach: An eternal golden braid.* New York: Basic Books.

Hofstadter, D. R. 1985. *Metamagical themas: Questing for the essence of mind and pattern.* New York: Basic Books.

Hofstadter, D. R.; and Dennett, D. C., eds., 1981. *The mind's I: Fantasies and reflections on self and soul.* New York: Basic Books.

Holden, C. 1988. Research psychologists break with APA. *Science* 241: 1036.

Holender, D. 1986. Semantic activation without conscious identification in dichotic listening, parafoveal vision, and visual masking: A survey and appraisal. *Behavioral and Brain Sciences* 9: 1–66.

Holender, D. 1987. Is the unconscious amenable to scientific scrutiny? *Canadian Psychology* 28: 120–32.

Hollander, R. D.; and Steneck, N. H. 1990. Science- and engineering-related ethics and values studies: Characteristics of an emerging field of research. *Science, Technology, and Human Values* 15: 84–104.

Hollon, S. D.; and Flick, S. N. 1988. On the meaning and methods of clinical significance. *Behavioral Assessment* 10: 197–206.

Hollon, S. D.; and Kriss, M. R. 1984. Cognitive factors in clinical research and practice. *Clinical Psychology Review* 4: 35–76.

Holloway, E. L. 1987. Developmental models of supervision: Is it development? *Professional Psychology: Research and Practice* 18: 209–16.

Holloway, E. L.; Freund, R. D.; Gardner, S. L.; Nelson, M. L.; and Walker, B. R. 1989. Relation of power and involvement to theoretical orientation in supervision: An analysis of discourse. *Journal of Counseling Psychology* 36: 88–102.

Holmes, R. 1986. The knower and the known. *Sociological Forum* 1: 610–31.

Holton, G. 1986. *The advancement of science, and its burdens.* Cambridge: Cambridge University Press.

Holub, E. A.; and Lee, S. S. 1990. Therapists' use of nonerotic physical contact: Ethical concerns. *Professional Psychology: Research and Practice* 21: 115–17.

Honzik, M. P. 1984. Life-span development. *Annual Review of Psychology* 35: 309–31.

Hook, S. 1958. *Determinism and freedom: In the age of modern science.* New York: Collier.

Hooper, S. L.; and Moulins, M. 1989. Switching of a neuron from one network to another by sensory-induced changes in membrane potentials. *Science* 244: 1587–89.

Hope, D. 1987. The healing paradox of forgiveness. *Psychotherapy* 24: 240–44.

Hope, M. 1988. *The psychology of ritual.* Dorset, England: Element Books.

Hornstein, G. A. 1986. *The Social Construction of Quantification in American Psychology, 1880–1930.* Paper presented at the Annual Meeting of the Society for the Social Study of Science, October, Pittsburgh, Pa.

Horney, K. 1945. *Our inner conflicts: A constructive theory of neurosis.* New York: Norton.

Hornyak, L. M.; and Baker, E. K., eds. 1989. *Experiential therapies for eating disorders.* New York: Guilford.

Horowitz, M. J. 1979. *States of mind: Analysis of change in psychotherapy.* New York: Plenum.

Horton, D. L.; and Mills, C. B. 1984. Human learning and memory. *Annual Review of Psychology* 35: 361–94.

Horvath, A. O.; and Greenberg, L. S. 1989. Development and validation of the working alliance inventory. *Journal of Counseling Psychology* 36: 223–33.

Hoshmand, L. L. S. T. 1989. Alternate research paradigms: A review and teaching proposal. *Counseling Psychologist* 17: 3–79.

Houk, J. C.; and Lehman, S. 1987. Control systems: Feedback, feedforward, and adaptive strategies. In G. Adelman, ed., *Encyclopedia of neuroscience,* vol. 1, 275–77. Boston: Birkhäuser.

Houlding, S.; and Holland, P. 1988. Contributions of a poetry writing group to the treatment of severely disturbed psychiatric inpatients. *Clinical Social Work Journal* 16: 194–200.

House, J. S.; Landis, K. R.; and Umberson, D. 1988. Social relationships and health. *Science* 241: 540–45.

Howard, A.; Pion, G. M.; Gottfredson, G. D.; Flattau, P. E.; Oskamp, S.; Pfafflin, S. M.; Bray, D. W.; and Burstein, A. G. 1986. The changing face of American psychology: A report from the Committee on Employment and Human Resources. *American Psychologist* 41: 1311–27.

Howard, G. S. 1986. *Dare we develop a human science?* Notre Dame, Ind.: Academic Publications.

Hsu, L. K. G. 1989. The gender gap in eating disorders: Why are the eating disorders more common among women? *Clinical Psychology Review* 9: 393–407.

Hudgins, M. K.; and Kiesler, D. J. 1987. Individual experiential psychotherapy: An analogue validation of the intervention module of psychodramatic doubling. *Psychotherapy* 24: 245–55.

Hughes, M.; and Demo, D. H. 1989. Self-perceptions of black Americans: Self-esteem and personal efficacy. *American Journal of Sociology* 95: 132–59.

Hui, C. H.; and Villareal, M. J. 1989. Individualism-collectivism and psychological needs: Their relationships in two cultures. *Journal of Cross-Cultural Psychology* 20: 310–23.

Hull, C. L. 1920. Quantitative aspects of the evolution of concepts: An experimental study. *Psychological Monographs* 28 (123).

Hull, C. L. 1943. *Principles of behavior.* New York: Appleton-Century.

Hull, D. L. 1978. A matter of individuality. *Philosophy of Science* 45: 335–60.

Hull, D. L. 1985. Darwinism as a historical entity: A historiographic proposal. In D. Kohn, ed., *The Darwinian Heritage,* 773–812. Princeton, N.J.: Princeton University Press.

Hull, D. L. 1988. *Science as a process: An evolutionary account of the social and conceptual development of science.* Chicago: University of Chicago Press.

Hume, D. 1947 [1779]. *Dialogues concerning natural religion.* Ed. N.K. Smith. New York: Bobbs-Merrill.

Hume, D. 1966 [1777]. *An enquiry concerning the principles of morals,* 2d ed. La Salle, Ill.: Open Court.

Hume, D. 1969 [1739]. *A treatise of human nature.* New York: Penguin.

Humphrey, G. 1951. *Thinking: An introduction to its experimental psychology.* London: Methuen.

Humphrey, L. L. 1986. Structural analysis of parent-child relationships in eating disorders. *Journal of Abnormal Psychology* 95: 395–402.

Hunsley, J. 1988. Conceptions and misconceptions about the context of paradoxical therapy. *Professional Psychology: Research and Practice* 19: 553–59.

Hunt, E. 1989. Cognitive science: Definition, status, and questions. *Annual Review of Psychology* 40: 603–29.

Hutchinson, M. G. 1985. *Transforming body image.* Freedom, Calif.: Crossing Press.

Hutchison, M. 1984. *The book of floating: Exploring the private sea.* New York: Quill.

Hutzell, R. R.; and Peterson, T. J. 1986. Use of the Life Purpose Questionnaire with an alcoholic population. *International Journal of the Addictions* 21: 51–57.

Ingram, R. E., ed. 1986. *Information processing approaches to clinical psychology.* New York: Academic Press.

Ingram, R. E. 1990a. Attentional nonspecificity in depressive and generalized anxious affective states. *Cognitive Therapy and Research* 14: 25–35.

Ingram, R. E. 1990b. Self-focused attention in clinical disorders: Review and a conceptual model. *Psychological Bulletin* 107: 156–76.

Isen, A. M.; and Daubman, K. A. 1984. The influence of affect on categorization. *Journal of Personality and Social Psychology* 47: 1206–17.

Iser, W. 1978. *The act of reading: A theory of aesthetic response.* Baltimore, Md.: John Hopkins University Press.

Ivey, A. E. 1986. *Developmental therapy.* San Francisco: Jossey-Bass.

Ivey, A. E.; and Gonçalves, O. F. 1988. Developmental therapy: Integrating development processes into clinical practice. *Journal of Counseling and Development* 66: 406–13.

Izard, C. E. 1978. On the ontogenesis of emotions and emotion-cognition relationships in infancy. In M. Lewis and L. A. Rosenblum, eds., *The development of affect*, 389–413. New York: Plenum.

Izard, C. E.; Kagan, J.; and Zajonc, R. B., eds. 1984. *Emotions, cognition, and behavior*. Cambridge: Cambridge University Press.

Izard, C. E.; and Schwartz, G. M. 1986. Patterns of emotion in depression. In M. Rutter, C. E. Izard, and P. B. Read, eds., *Depression in young people*, 33–70. New York: Guilford.

Izraeli, D. N. 1988. Burning out in medicine: A comparison of husbands and wives in dual-career couples. *Journal of Social Behavior and Personality* 3: 329–46.

Jackendoff, R. 1987. *Consciousness and the computational mind*. Cambridge, Mass.: MIT Press.

Jackins, H. 1965. *The human side of human beings: The theory of re-evaluation counseling*. Seattle, Wash.: Rational Island Publishers.

Jacob, E. 1987. Qualitative research traditions: A review. *Review of Educational Research* 57: 1–50.

Jacobs, M. K.; and Goodman, G. 1989. Psychology and self-help groups: Predictions on a partnership. *American Psychologist* 44: 536–45.

Jacobs, M. S. 1989. *American psychology in the quest for nuclear peace*. New York: Praeger.

Jacoby, L. L.; and Kelley, C. M. 1987. Unconscious influences of memory for a prior event. *Personality and Social Psychology Bulletin* 13: 314–36.

Jacoby, L. L.; and Whitehouse, K. 1989. An illusion of memory: False recognition influenced by unconscious perception. *Journal of Experimental Psychology: General* 118: 126–35.

Jacoby, L. L.; Woloshyn, V.; and Kelley, C. 1989. Becoming famous without being recognized: Unconscious influences of memory produced by dividing attention. *Journal of Experimental Psychology: General* 118: 115–25.

James, N. 1989. Emotional labour: Skill and work in the social regulation of feelings. *Sociological Review* 37: 15–42.

James, W. 1890. *The principles of psychology*, 2 vols. New York: Henry Holt & Co.

James, W. 1956 [1896]. *The will to believe*. New York: Dover.

James, W. 1958 [1902]. *The varieties of religious experience*. New York: New American Library.

Janet, P. 1889. *L'Automatisme psychologique*. Paris: Alcan.

Janet, P. 1898. *Neurosis and fixed ideas*. Paris: Alcan.

Jankowicz, A. D. 1987. Whatever became of George Kelly? Applications and implications. *American Psychologist* 42: 481–87.

Janov, A. 1970. *The primal scream*. New York: Dell.

Jansen, M.; and Barron, J. 1988. Introduction and overview: Psychologists' use of physical interventions. *Psychotherapy* 25: 487–91.

Jantsch, E. 1980. *The self-organizing universe: Scientific and human implications of the emerging paradigm of evolution*. New York: Pergamon.

Jantsch, E., ed. 1981. *The evolutionary vision: Toward a unifying paradigm of physical, biological, and sociocultural evolution*. Boulder, Colo.: Westview.

Jantsch, E.; and Waddington, C. H., eds. 1976. *Evolution and consciousness: Human systems in transition*. Reading, Mass.: Addison-Wesley.

Jaspers, K. 1951. Way to wisdom. Trans. R. Manheim. New Haven, Conn.: Yale University Press.

Jaynes, J. 1976. *The origin of consciousness in the breakdown of the bicameral mind*. Boston: Houghton Mifflin.

Jeannerod, M. 1985. *The brain machine: The development of neurophysiological thought*. Cambridge, Mass.: Harvard University Press.

Jenkins, J. J. 1974. Remember that old theory of memory? Well, forget it! *American Psychologist* 29: 785–95.

Jensen, J. P.; Bergin, A. E.; and Greaves, D. W. 1990. The meaning of eclecticism: New survey and analysis of components. *Professional Psychology: Research and Practice* 21: 124–30.

Jerison, H. J. 1973. *Evolution of the brain and intelligence*. New York: Wiley.

Jerison, H. J. 1976. Paleoneurology and the evolution of mind. *Scientific American* 234: 90–101.

Jerison, H. J. 1979. Brain, body and encephalization in early primates. *Journal of Human Evolution* 8: 615–35.

Jerome, J. 1980. *The sweet spot in time*. New York: Summit.

John, E. R.; Prichep, L. S.; Fridman, J.; and Easton, P. 1988. Neurometrics: Computer-assisted differential diagnosis of brain dysfunctions. *Science* 239: 162–69.

Johnson, F. 1985. The Western concept of self. In A. J. Marsella, G. DeVos, and F. L. K. Hsu, eds., *Culture and self: Asian and Western perspectives*, 91–138. New York: Tavistock.

Johnson, J. A.; Germer, C. K.; Efran, J. A.; and Overton, W. F. 1988. Personality as the basis for theoretical predilections. *Journal of Personality and Social Psychology* 55: 824–35.

Johnson, M. 1987. *The body in the mind: The bodily basis of meaning, imagination, and reason*. Chicago: University of Chicago Press.

Johnson, M.; and Stone, G. L. 1989. Logic and nurture: Gender differences in thinking about psychotherapy. *Professional Psychology: Research and Practice* 20: 123–27.

Johnson, M. H.; and Magaro, P. A. 1987. Effects of mood and severity on memory processes in depression and mania. *Psychological Bulletin* 101: 28–40.

Johnson, M. K. 1988. Reality monitoring: An experimental phenomenological approach. *Journal of Experimental Psychology: General* 117: 390–94.

Johnson, M. K.; Foley, M. A.; Suengas, A. G.; and Raye, C. L. 1988. Phenomenal characteristics of memories for perceived and imagined autobiographical events. *Journal of Experimental Psychology: General* 117: 371–76.

Johnson, N. S.; and Holloway, E. L. 1988. Conceptual complexity and obsessionality in bulimic college women. *Journal of Counseling Psychology* 35: 251–57.

Jonas, H. 1966. *The phenomenon of life: Toward a philosophical biology*. Chicago: University of Chicago Press.

Jones, B. L.; Lynch, P. P.; and Reesink, C. 1987. Children's conceptions of the earth, sun and moon. *International Journal of Science Education* 9: 43–53.

Jones, E. E.; and Davis, K. E. 1965. From acts to dispositions: The attribution process in person perception. In L. Berkowitz, ed., *Advances in experimental social psychology*, vol. 2. New York: Academic Press.

Jones, E. E.; Farina, A.; Hastorf, A. H.; Markus, H.; Miller, D. T.; and Scott, R. A. 1984. *Social stigma: The psychology of marked relationships.* New York: W. H. Freeman.

Jones, E. E.; Krupnick, J. L.; and Kerig, P. K. 1987. Some gender effects in a brief psychotherapy. *Psychotherapy* 24: 336–52.

Jones, G. V. 1989. Back to Woodworth: Role of interlopers in the tip-of-the-tongue phenomenon. *Memory and Cognition* 17: 69–76.

Jones, J. W. 1982. The delicate dialectic: Religion and psychology in the modern world. *Cross Currents* 31: 143–53.

Jones, R. A. 1977. *Self-fulfilling prophecies: Social, psychological, and physiological effects of expectancies.* Hillsdale, N.J.: Erlbaum.

Jordan, A. E.; and Meara, N. M. 1990. Ethics and the professional practice of psychologists: The role of virtues and principles. *Professional Psychology: Research and Practice* 21: 107–14.

Josselson, R. 1987. *Finding herself: Pathways to identity development in women.* San Francisco: Jossey-Bass.

Joyce, J. 1980 [1939]. *Finnegan's wake.* London: Faber & Faber.

Joyce-Moniz, L. 1985. Epistemological therapy and constructivism. In M. J. Mahoney and A. Freeman, eds., *Cognition and psychotherapy,* 143–79. New York: Plenum.

Joyce-Moniz, L. 1988. Self-talk, dramatic expression, and constructivism. In C. Perris, I. M. Bleckburn, and H. Perris, eds., *Cognitive psychotherapy: Theory and practice,* 276–305. Heidelberg, W. Germany: Springer-Verlag.

Joyce-Moniz, L. 1989. Structures, dialectics and regulation in applied constructivism: From developmental psychopathology to individual drama therapy. In O. F. Gonçalves, ed., *Advances in the cognitive therapies: The constructivist-developmental approach,* 45–89. Lisbon: APPORT.

Judge, L. C. 1988. *The therapeutic writing process: A case study.* Ph.D. diss., University of Texas, Austin.

Jung, C. G. 1957. *The undiscovered self.* New York: Mentor.

Jung, C. G. 1960–1979. *The collected works of C. G. Jung,* 2d ed., vols. 1–20; H. Read, M. Fordham, G. Adler, and W. McGuire, eds. Princeton, N.J.: Princeton University Press.

Jussim, L. 1986. Self-fulfilling prophecies: A theoretical and integrative review. *Psychological Review* 93: 429–45.

Kagan, J. 1976. Resiliency and continuity in psychological development. In A. M. Clarke and A. D. Clarke, eds., *Early experience: Myth and evidence,* 97–285. New York: Free Press.

Kagan, J. 1984. The idea of emotion in human development. In C. E. Izard, J.

Kagan, and R. B. Zajonc, eds., *Emotions, cognition, and behavior*, 38–72. Cambridge: Cambridge University Press.

Kagan, J. 1988. *The nature of the child.* New York: Basic Books.

Kagan, J.; Kearsley, R. B.; and Zelazo, P. R. 1978. *Infancy: Its place in human development.* Cambridge, Mass.: Harvard University Press.

Kahill, S. 1988. Symptoms of professional burnout: A review of the empirical evidence. *Canadian Psychology* 29: 284–97.

Kahneman, D. 1973. *Attention and effort.* Englewood Cliffs, N.J.: Prentice-Hall.

Kahneman, D.; Slovic, P.; and Tversky, A., eds. 1982. *Judgement under uncertainty: Heuristics and biases.* Cambridge: Cambridge University Press.

Kahneman, D.; and Treisman, A. M. 1984. Changing views of attention and automaticity. In R. Parasuraman and D. R. Davies, eds., *Varieties of attention*, 29–62. New York: Academic Press.

Kahneman, D.; and Tversky, A. 1973. On the psychology of prediction. *Psychological Review* 80: 237–51.

Kammerman, M. 1977. *Sensory isolation and personality change.* Springfield, Ill.: Charles C. Thomas.

Kant, I. 1929 [1781]. *The critique of pure reason.* Trans. N. K. Smith. New York: Macmillan.

Kant, I. 1938 [1785]. *Foundations of the metaphysics of morals.* Trans. O. Manthey-Zorn. New York: Appleton-Century-Crofts.

Kashani, J. H.; and Sherman, D. D. 1988. Childhood depression: Epidemiology, etiological models and treatment implications. *Integrative Psychiatry* 6: 1–8.

Kasschau, R. A.; Rehm, L. P.; and Ullmann, L. P., eds. 1985. *Psychology research, public policy and practice: Toward a productive partnership.* New York: Praeger.

Katz, A. N.; Paivio, A.; Marschark, M.; and Clark, J. M. 1988. Norms for 204 literary and 260 nonliterary metaphors on 10 psychological dimensions. *Metaphor and Symbolic Activity* 3: 191–214.

Kauffman, S. A. 1985. Self-organization, selective adaptation, and its limits: A new pattern of inference in evolution and development. In D. J. Depew and B. H. Weber, eds., *Evolution at a crossroads: The new biology and the new philosophy of science*, 169–207. Cambridge, Mass.: MIT Press.

Kaufman, A.; Baron, A.; and Kopp, R. E. 1966. Some effects of instructions on human operant behavior. *Psychological Monograph Supplements* 1: 243–50.

Kaufman, G. 1989. *The psychology of shame: Theory and treatment of shame-based syndromes.* New York: Springer.

Kaufmann, W. 1958. *Critique of religion and philosophy.* New York: Anchor.

Kaufmann, W. 1959. *The faith of a heretic.* New York: McGraw-Hill.

Kaufmann, W., ed. 1961. *Religion from Tolstoy to Camus.* New York: Harper and Row.

Kaye, M. E. 1987. *The effects of brief flotation REST on physiological, cognitive, and mood measures.* Ph. D. diss., Pennsylvania State University.

Kazantzakis, N. 1960 [1927]. *The saviors of God: Spiritual exercises.* Trans. K. Friar. New York: Simon and Schuster.

Kazdin, A. E. 1978. *History of behavior modification.* Baltimore, Md.: University Park Press.

Kazdin, A. E. 1989. Developmental psychopathology: Current research, issues, and directions. *American Psychologist* 44: 180–87.

Keeley, S. M.; Shemberg, K. M.; and Zaynor, L. 1988. Dissertation research in clinical psychology: Beyond positivism? *Professional Psychology: Research and Practice* 19: 216–22.

Keeney, B. P. 1983. *Aesthetics of change.* New York: Guilford.

Kegan, R. 1982. *The evolving self: Problem and process in human development.* Cambridge: Harvard University Press.

Keil, F. C. 1981. Constraints on knowledge and cognitive development. *Psychological Review* 88: 197–227.

Keinan, G.; Almagor, M.; and Ben-Porath, Y. S. 1989. A reevaluation of the relationship between psychotherapeutic orientation and perceived personality characteristics. *Psychotherapy* 26: 218–26.

Keith-Spiegel, P.; and Koocher, G. P. 1985. *Ethics in psychology: Professional standards and cases.* New York: Random House.

Keleman, S. 1979. *Somatic reality.* Berkeley, Calif.: Center Press.

Keller, E. F. 1983. *A feeling for the organism: The life and work of Barbara McClintock.* New York: W. H. Freeman.

Keller, E. F. 1985. *Reflections on gender and science.* New Haven, Conn.: Yale University Press.

Kelly, E. L. 1961. Clinical psychology—1960: Report on survey findings. *Newsletter: Division of Clinical Psychology of the American Psychological Association* 14 (1): 1–11.

Kelly, E. L.; Goldberg, L. R.; Fiske, D. W.; and Kilkowski, J. M. 1978. Twenty-five years later: A follow-up study of the graduate students in clinical psychology assessed in the VA Selection Research Project. *American Psychologist* 33: 746–55.

Kelly, G. A. 1955. *The psychology of personal constructs.* New York: Norton.

Kelso, J. A. S.; and Schoner, G. 1988. Self-organization of coordinate movement patterns. *Human Movement Science* 7: 27–46.

Kemp-Wheeler, S. M.; and Hill, A. B. 1988. Semantic priming without awareness: Some methodological considerations and replications. *Quarterly Journal of Experimental Psychology* 40: 671–92.

Kendall, P. C.; and Hollon, S. D., eds. 1981. *Assessment strategies for cognitive-behavioral interventions.* New York: Academic Press.

Kendall, P. C.; and Watson, D., eds. 1989. *Anxiety and depression.* New York: Academic Press.

Kenny, V.; and Gardner, G. 1988. Constructions of self-organising systems. *Irish Journal of Psychology* 9: 1–24.

Kernberg, O. F. 1967. Borderline personality organization. *Journal of the American Psychoanalytic Association* 15: 641–685.

Kernberg, O. F. 1968. The treatment of patients with borderline personality organization. *International Journal of Psychoanalysis* 49: 600–19.

Kernberg, O. F. 1975. *Borderline conditions and pathological narcissism.* New York: Jason Aronson.

Kernberg, O. F. 1976. *Object relations theory and clinical psychoanalysis.* New York: Jason Aronson.

Kernberg, O. F. 1989a. An ego psychology object relations theory of the structure and treatment of pathologic narcissism: An overview. *Psychiatric Clinics of North America* 12: 723–29.

Kernberg, O. F. 1989b. The narcissistic personality disorder and the differential diagnosis of antisocial behavior. *Psychiatric Clinics of North America* 12: 553–70.

Kerr, M. E.; and Bowen, M. 1988. *Family evaluation.* New York: Norton.

Ketterer, M. W. 1985. Awareness I: The natural ecology of subjective experience and the mind-brain problem revisited. *Journal of Mind and Behavior* 6: 469–514.

Ketterer, M. W. 1987. *Cognizance of chronic negative emotion ("stress") and stressors in the Type A CAD/CHD patient: The phenomenological imperative.* Oklahoma College of Osteopathic Medicine and Surgery. Manuscript.

Kiesler, D. J. 1966. Some myths of psychotherapy research and the search for a paradigm. *Psychological Bulletin* 64: 114–20.

Kiesler, D. J. 1973. *The process of psychotherapy.* Chicago: Aldine.

Kihlstrom, J. F. 1987. The cognitive unconscious. *Science* 237: 1445–52.

Kilburg, R. R. 1988. Psychologists and physical interventions: Ethics, standards, and legal implications. *Psychotherapy* 25: 516–31.

Kilburg, R. R.; Nathan, P. E.; and Thoreson, R. W., eds. 1986. *Professionals in distress: Issues, syndromes, and solutions in psychology.* Washington, D. C.: American Psychological Association.

Kilgore, L. C. 1988. Effect of early childhood sexual abuse on self and ego development. *Social Casework: The Journal of Contemporary Social Work* 224–30.

Killeen, P. 1984. Emergent behaviorism. *Behaviorism* 12: 25–39.

Kilpatrick, W. 1975. *Identity and intimacy,* New York: Dell.

Kim, H.; and Baron, R. S. 1988. Exercise and the illusory correlation: Does arousal heighten stereotypic processing? *Journal of Experimental Social Psychology* 24: 366–80.

Kimble, G. A. 1984. Psychology's two cultures. *American Psychologist* 39: 833–39.

King, R. K. 1989. An emerging profession. *Massage Therapy Journal* 28: 5–6.

Kinzey, W. G., ed. 1987. *The evolution of human behavior: Primate models.* Albany: State University of New York Press.

Kipper, D. A. 1989. Psychodrama research and the study of small groups. *International Journal of Small Group Research* 5: 4–27.

Kirk, G. S.; Raven, J. E.; and Schofield, M., eds. 1983. *The presocratic philosophers.* Cambridge: Cambridge University Press.

Kitcher, P. 1985. *Vaulting ambition: Sociobiology and the quest for human nature.* Cambridge, Mass.: MIT Press.

Kitcher, P. 1987. Precis of *Vaulting Ambition: Sociobiology and the Quest for Human Nature. Behavioral and Brain Sciences* 10: 61–100.

Kitcher, P. 1988. Marr's computational theory of vision. *Philosophy of Science* 55: 1–24.

Klass, E. T. In press. Guilt, shame, and embarrassment: Cognitive-behavioral approaches. In H. Leitenberg, ed., *Handbook of Social Anxiety.* New York: Plenum.

Klatzky, R. L. 1984. *Memory and awareness: An information-processing perspective.* New York: W. H. Freeman.

Klein, D. B. 1977. *The unconscious: Invention or discovery?* Santa Monica, Calif.: Goodyear Publishing.

Klein, D. C. 1988. The power of appreciation. *American Journal of Community Psychology* 16: 305–24.

Klein, D. N.; Harding, K.; Taylor, E. B.; and Dickstein, S. 1988. Dependency and self-criticism in depression: Evaluation in a clinical population. *Journal of Abnormal Psychology* 97: 399–404.

Klein, E.; and Erickson, D., eds. 1987. *About men: Reflections on the male experience.* New York: Poseidon.

Klein, J. 1987. *Our need for others and its roots in infancy.* London: Tavistock.

Klein, M. 1932. *The psychoanalysis of children.* London: Hogarth.

Klein, M. H.; Dittmann, A. T.; Parloff, M. B.; and Gill, M. M. 1969. Behavior therapy: Observations and reflections. *Journal of Consulting and Clinical Psychology* 33: 259–66.

Kleinginna, P. R.; and Kleinginna, A. M. 1988. Current trends toward convergence of the behavioristic, functional, and cognitive perspectives in experimental psychology. *Psychological Record* 36: 369–92.

Kleinke, C. L. 1978. *Self-perception: The psychology of personal awareness.* San Francisco: W. H. Freeman.

Kleinke, C. L. 1986. Gaze and eye contact: A research review. *Psychological Bulletin* 100: 78–100.

Klemke, E. D., ed. 1981. *The meaning of life.* New York: Oxford University Press.

Kliegl, R.; Smith, J.; and Baltes, P. B. 1989. Testing-the-limits and the study of adult age differences in cognitive plasticity of a mnemonic skill. *Developmental Psychology* 25: 247–56.

Kline, M. 1985. *Mathematics and the search for knowledge.* Oxford: Oxford University Press.

Klinger, E. 1971. *Structure and functions of fantasy.* New York: Wiley.

Klinger, E. 1977. *Meaning and void: Inner experience and the incentives in people's lives.* Minneapolis: University of Minnesota Press.

Knight, R. P. 1953. Borderline states. *Bulletin of the Menninger Clinic* 17: 1–12.

Knorr-Cetina, K. D. 1981. *The manufacture of knowledge: An essay on the constructivist and contextual nature of science.* New York: Pergamon.

Knorr-Cetina, K; and Mulkay, M. 1983. *Science observed: Perspectives on the social study of science.* London: Sage.

Kobasa, S. C.; Maddi, S. R.; and Kahn, S. 1982. Hardiness and health: A prospective study. *Journal of Personality and Social Psychology* 42: 168–77.

Kobasa, S. C.; Maddi, S. R.; Puccetti, M. C.; and Zola, M. A. 1985. Effectiveness of hardiness, exercise and social support as resources against illness. *Journal of Psychosomatic Research* 29: 525–33.

Koch, S., ed. 1959. *Psychology: A study of science.* New York: McGraw-Hill.

Koch, S. 1964. Psychology and emerging conceptions of knowledge as unitary. In T. W. Wann, ed., *Behaviorism and phenomenology,* 1–41. Chicago: University of Chicago Press.

Köhler, W. 1925 [1917]. *The mentality of apes.* Trans. E. Winter. New York: Harcourt Brace.

Kohonen, T. 1984. *Self-organization and associative memory.* Berlin: Springer-Verlag.

Kohut, H. 1966. Forms and transformations of narcissism. *Journal of American Psychoanalytic Association* 5: 389–407.

Kohut, H. 1971. *The analysis of the self.* New York: International University Press.

Kohut, H. 1977. *The restoration of the self.* New York: International University Press.

Kolb, B. 1989. Brain development, plasticity, and behavior. *American Psychologist* 44: 1203–12.

Kolbenschlag, M. 1988. *Lost in the Land of Oz: The search for identity and community in American life.* New York: Harper and Row.

Kolodny, A. 1988. Dancing between left and right: Feminism and the academic minefield in the 1980s. *Feminist Studies* 14: 453–66.

Komada, K. A. 1988. Psychology and women's studies: Epistemological dilemma or opportunity? *Theoretical and Philosophical Psychology* 8: 40–47.

Kopp, C. B. 1989. Regulation of distress and negative emotions: A developmental view. *Developmental Psychology* 25: 343–54.

Kopp, S. B. 1978. *An end to innocence.* New York: Bantam.

Kopp, S. B. 1972. *If you meet the Buddha on the road, kill him!* New York: Bantam.

Kopp, S. B. 1976. *Guru: Metaphors from a psychotherapist.* New York: Bantam.

Kosslyn, S. M. 1980. *Image and mind.* Cambridge, Mass.: Harvard University Press.

Kottler, J. A. 1986. *On being a psychotherapist.* San Francisco: Jossey-Bass.

Kottler, J. A.; and Blau, D. S. 1989. *The imperfect therapist: Learning from failure in therapeutic practice.* San Francisco: Jossey-Bass.

Kovel, J. 1982. Values, interests, and psychotherapy. *American Journal of Psychoanalysis* 42: 109–19.

Kozulin, A. 1986. The concept of activity in Soviet psychology: Vygotsky, his disciples and critics. *American Psychologist* 41: 264–74.

Kraemer, D. L.; and Hastrup, J. L. 1988. Crying in adults: Self-control and autonomic correlates. *Journal of Social and Clinical Psychology* 6: 53–68.

Kraemer, G. W. 1985. Effects of differences in early social experience on primate neurobiological-behavioral development. In M. Reite and T. Field, eds., *Biology of social attachments and separation,* 35–161. New York: Academic Press.

Kramer, R. 1989. Windows of vulnerability or cognitive illusions? Cognitive processes and the nuclear arms race. *Journal of Experimental Social Psychology* 25: 79–100.

Krantz, D. L. 1987. Psychology's search for unity. *New ideas in Psychology* 3: 329–39.

Krantz, D. S.; Grunberg, N. E.; and Baum, A. 1985. Health psychology. *Annual Review of Psychology* 36: 349–83.

Krasnegor, N. A.; Blass, E. M.; Hofer, M. A.; and Smotherman, W. P., eds. 1987. *Perinatal Development.* New York: Academic Press.

Krasner, L.; and Houts, A. C. 1984. A study of the "value" systems of behavioral scientists. *American Psychologist* 39: 840–50.

Kravitz, E. A. 1988. Hormonal control of behavior: Amines and the biasing of behavioral output in lobsters. *Science* 241: 1775–81.

Kreilkamp, T. 1976. *The corrosion of the self: Society's effect on people.* New York: New York University Press.

Kreitler, H.; and Kreitler, S. 1976. *Cognitive orientation and behavior.* New York: Springer.

Krenz, C.; and Sax, G. 1986. What quantitative research is and why it doesn't work. *American Behavioral Scientist* 30: 58–69.

Kreppner, K.; and Lerner, R. M., eds. In press. *Family systems and life-span development.* Hillsdale, N.J.: Erlbaum.

Kris, A. O. 1982. *Free association: Method and process.* New Haven, Conn.: Yale University Press.

Krishnamurti, J. 1964. *Think on these things.* New York: Harper and Row.

Kroger, J.; and Haslett, S. J. 1988. Separation-individuation and ego identity status in late adolescence: A two-year longitudinal study. *Journal of Youth and Adolescence* 17: 59–79.

Krueger, D. W. 1989. *Body self and psychological self.* New York: Brunner/Mazel.

Kruglanski, A. W.; and Jaffe, Y. 1983. The lay epistemic model in cognitive therapy. In M. Rosenbaum, C. M. Franks, and Y. Jaffe, eds., *Perspectives on behavior therapy in the eighties.* New York: Springer.

Kugler, L. K. (1987). Jacques Lacan: Postmodern depth psychology and the birth of the self-reflexive subject. In P. Young-Eisendrath and J. A. Hall, eds., *The book of the self,* 173–84. New York: New York University Press.

Kuhl, J. 1987. Action control: The maintenance of motivational states. In F. Halisch and J. Kuhl, eds., *Motivation, intention, and volition,* 279–95. Berlin: Springer-Verlag.

Kuhl, J.; and Helle, P. 1986. Motivational and volitional determinants of depression: The degenerated-intention hypothesis. *Journal of Abnormal Psychology* 95: 247–51.

Kuhl, P. K.; and Meltzoff, A. N. 1982. The bimodal perception of speech in infancy. *Science* 218: 1138–41.

Kuhn, T. S. 1957. *The Copernican revolution: Planetary astronomy in the development of Western thought.* Cambridge, Mass.: Harvard University Press.

Kuhn, T. S. 1962. *The structure of scientific revolutions.* Chicago: University of Chicago Press.

Kuhn, T. S. 1970a. Logic of discovery or psychology of research? In I. Lakatos and A. Musgrave, eds., *Criticism and the growth of knowledge,* 1–23. Cambridge: Cambridge University Press.

Kuhn, T. S. 1970b. Reflections on my critics. In I. Lakatos and A. Musgrave, eds., *Criticism and the growth of knowledge,* 231–78. Cambridge: Cambridge University Press.

Kuhn, T. S. 1977. *The essential tension.* Chicago: University of Chicago Press.

Kuiper, N. A.; and Derry, P. A. 1982. Depressed and nondepressed content self-reference in mild depressives. *Journal of Personality* 50: 67–80.

Kuipers, L.; and Bebbington, P. 1988. Expressed emotion research in schizophrenia: Theoretical and clinical implications. *Psychological Medicine* 18: 893–909.

Kukla, A. 1989. Nonempirical issues in psychology. *American Psychologist* 44: 785–94.

Kulik, J. A.; Sledge, P.; and Mahler, H. I. M. 1986. Self-confirmatory attribution, egocentrism, and the perpetuation of self-beliefs. *Journal of Personality and Social Psychology* 50: 587–94.

Kulpe, O. 1909 [1893]. *Outlines of psychology*, 3rd ed. Trans. E. B. Titchener. New York: Macmillan.

Kurtz, R. 1986. *Hakomi therapy*. Boulder, Colo.: The Hakomi Institute.

Kurtzman, H. S. 1987. Deconstruction and psychology: An introduction. *New Ideas in Psychology* 5: 33–71.

Kuykendall, D.; Keating, J. P.; and Wagaman, J. 1988. Assessing affective states: A new methodology for some old problems. *Cognitive Therapy and Research* 12: 279–94.

Labott, S. M.; and Martin, R. B. 1987. The stress-moderating effects of weeping and humor. *Journal of Human Stress* 13: 159–64.

Labott, S. M.; and Martin, R. B. 1988. Weeping: Evidence for a cognitive theory. *Motivation and Emotion* 12: 205–16.

Lacan, J. 1977. *Écrits: A selection*. Trans. A. Sheridan. New York: Norton.

Lacan, J. 1978. *The four fundamental concepts of psychoanalysis*. Trans. A. Sheridan. New York: Norton.

Lacey, J. I. 1959. Psychophysiological approaches to the evaluation of psychotherapeutic process and outcome. In E. A. Rubenstein and M. B. Parloff, eds., *Research in Psychotherapy*, vol. 1, 160–208. Washington, D. C.: American Psychological Association.

Laderman, C. 1987. The ambiguity of symbols in the structure of healing. *Social Science Medicine* 24: 293–301.

Lafferty, P.; Beutler, L. E.; and Crago, M. 1989. Differences between more and less effective psychotherapists: A study of select therapist variables. *Journal of Consulting and Clinical Psychology* 57: 76–80.

Lakatos, I. 1970. Falsification and the methodology of scientific research programmes. In I. Lakatos and A. Musgrave, eds., *Criticism and the growth of knowledge*, 91–196. Cambridge: Cambridge University Press.

Lakatos, I.; and Musgrave, A., eds. 1970. *Criticism and the growth of knowledge*. Cambridge: Cambridge University Press.

Lakoff, G. 1987. *Women, fire, and dangerous things: What categories reveal about the mind*. Chicago: University of Chicago Press.

Lakoff, G.; and Johnson, M. 1980. *Metaphors we live by*. Chicago: University of Chicago Press.

Laliotis, D. A.; and Grayson, J. H. 1985. Psychologist heal thyself: What is available for the impaired psychologist? *American Psychologist* 40: 84–96.

Lambert, M. J. 1989. The individual therapist's contribution to psychotherapy process and outcome. *Clinical Psychology Review* 9: 469–85.

Lamper, N. 1988. The incredible lightness of listening. *Pilgrimage* 14: 23–28.

Land, G. T. L. (1973). *Grow or die: The unifying principle of transformation.* New York: Dell.

Landfield, A. W. 1971. *Personal construct systems in psychotherapy.* Chicago: Rand McNally.

Landfield, A. W.; and Leitner, L. M., eds. 1980. *Personal construct psychology: Psychotherapy and personality.* New York: Wiley.

Lane, R. D.; and Schwartz, G. E. 1987. Levels of emotional awareness: A cognitive-developmental theory and its application to psychopathology. *American Journal of Psychiatry* 144: 133–43.

Lang, P. J. 1979. A bio-informational theory of emotional imagery. *Psychophysiology* 16: 495–512.

Langer, S. K. 1953. *Feeling and form.* New York: Scribner.

Langer, S. K. 1967. *Mind: An essay on human feeling,* vol. 1. Baltimore, Md.: Johns Hopkins University Press.

Langer, S. K. 1972. *Mind: An essay on human feeling,* vol. 2. Baltimore, Md.: Johns Hopkins University Press.

Langer, S. K. 1982. *Mind: An essay on human feeling,* vol. 3. Baltimore, Md.: Johns Hopkins University Press.

Langer, W. L., ed., 1980. *An encyclopedia of world history,* 5th ed. Boston: Houghton Mifflin.

Lapsley, D. K.; and Power, F. C., eds. 1987. *Self, ego and identity: Integrative approaches.* New York: Springer-Verlag.

Larkin, L. 1987. Identity and fear of success. *Journal of Counseling Psychology* 34: 38–45.

Larsen, R. J. 1987. The stability of mood variability: A spectral analytic approach to daily mood assessments. *Journal of Personality and Social Psychology* 52: 1195–1204.

Larsen, R. J.; and Cowan, G. S. 1988. Internal focus of attention and depression: A study of daily experience. *Motivation and Emotion* 12: 237–49.

Larson, D. 1980. Therapeutic schools, styles and schoolism: A national survey. *Journal of Humanistic Psychology* 20: 3–20.

Lasch, C. 1979. *The culture of narcissism: American life in an age of diminishing expectations.* New York: Norton.

Lashley, K. S. 1942. An examination of the "continuity theory" as applied to discriminative learning. *Journal of General Psychology* 26: 241–65.

Lashley, K. S. 1950. In search of the engram. *Symposia of the Society for Experimental Biology* 4: 454–82.

Lashley, K. 1951. The problem of serial order in behavior. In L. Jeffress, ed., *Cerebral Mechanisms in Behavior.* New York: Wiley.

Laszlo, E. 1983. *Systems science and world order: Selected studies.* Oxford, England: Pergamon.

Laszlo, E. 1987. *Evolution: The grand synthesis.* Boston: New Science Library.

Latour, B.; and Woolgar, S. 1979. *Laboratory life: The social construction of scientific facts.* London: Sage.

Lax, R. F.; Bach, S.; and Burland, J. A., eds. 1986. *Self and object constancy: Clinical and theoretical perspectives.* New York: Guilford.

Lazarus, A. A. 1971. *Behavior therapy and beyond.* New York: McGraw-Hill.

Lazarus, A. A. 1976. *Multimodal behavior therapy.* New York: Springer.

Lazarus, A. A. 1977. Has behavior therapy outlived its usefulness? *American Psychologist* 32: 550–54.

Lazarus, A. A.; and Davison, G. C. 1971. Clinical innovation in research and practice. In A. E. Bergin and S. L. Garfield, eds., *Handbook of psychotherapy and behavior change,* vol. 1, 196–213. New York: Wiley.

Lazarus, R. S. 1982. Thoughts on the relations between emotion and cognition. *American Psychologist* 37: 1019–24.

Lazarus, R. S. 1984. On the primacy of cognition. *American Psychologist* 39: 124–29.

Lazarus, R. S. 1987. Response to Bowers: Revisioning the unconscious. *Canadian Psychology* 28: 105–6.

Leahy, R. L., ed. 1985. *The development of the self.* New York: Academic Press.

LeDoux, J. E. 1986. The neurobiology of emotion. In J. E. LeDoux and W. Hirst, eds., *Mind and brain: Dialogues in cognitive neuroscience.* Cambridge: Cambridge University Press.

LeDoux, J. E.; and Hirst, W., eds. 1986. *Mind and brain: Dialogues in cognitive neuroscience.* Cambridge: Cambridge University Press.

Ledwidge, B. 1978. Cognitive behavior modification: A step in the wrong direction? *Psychological Bulletin* 85: 353–75.

Lee, M. 1989. When is an object not an object? The effect of 'meaning' upon the copying of line drawings. *British Journal of Psychology* 80: 15–37.

Legrenzi, P. 1971. Discovery as a means of understanding. *Quarterly Journal of Experimental Psychology* 23: 417–22.

Leichtman, M. 1989. Evolving concepts of borderline personality disorders. *Bulletin of the Menninger Clinic* 53: 229–49.

Leigh, B. C. 1989. In search of the seven dwarves: Issues of measurement and meaning in alcohol expectancy research. *Psychological Bulletin* 105: 361–73.

Leitner, L. 1987. Crisis of the self: The terror of personal evolution. In R. A. Neimeyer and G. J. Neimeyer, eds., *Personal construct therapy casebook,* 39–56. New York: Springer.

Leplin, J., ed. 1984. *Scientific realism.* Berkeley: University of California Press.

Lerner, H. G. 1985. *The dance of anger.* New York: Harper and Row.

Lerner, H. G. 1989. *Women in therapy.* New York: Harper and Row.

Lerner, R. M. 1984. *On the nature of human plasticity.* Cambridge: Cambridge University Press.

Lerner, R. M.; and Busch-Rossnagel, N. A. 1981. Individuals as producers of their development: Conceptual and empirical bases. In R. M. Lerner and N. A. Busch-Rossnagel, eds., *Individuals as producers of their development: A lifespan perspective,* 1–36. New York: Academic Press.

Lerner, R. M.; and Tubman, J. G. 1989. Conceptual issues in studying continuity and discontinuity in personality development across life. *Journal of Personality* 57: 343–73.

Leslie, A. M. 1987. Pretense and representation: The origins of "Theory of Mind." *Psychological Review* 94: 412–26.

Lester, D. 1989. Suicide among psychologists and a proposal for the American Psychological Association. *Psychological Reports* 64: 65–66.

Leva, L. M. 1984. Cognitive behavioral therapy in the light of Piagetian theory. In M. A. Reda and M. J. Mahoney, eds., *Cognitive psychotherapies: Recent developments in theory, research, and practice,* 233–50. Cambridge, Mass.: Ballinger.

Leventhal, H. 1984. A perceptual motor theory of emotion. In K. R. Scherer and P. Ekman, eds., *Approaches to emotion,* 271–91. Hillsdale, N.J.: Erlbaum.

Levine, F. J.; and Kravis, R. 1987. Psychoanalytic theories of the self: Contrasting clinical approaches to the new narcissism. In P. Young-Eisendrath and J. A. Hall, eds., *The book of the self,* 306–30. New York: New York University Press.

Levine, S. 1979. *A gradual awakening.* Garden City, N.Y.: Anchor.

Levins, R.; and Lewontin, R. 1985. *The dialectical biologist.* Cambridge, Mass.: Harvard University Press.

Levinson, D. J. 1986. A conception of adult development. *American Psychologist* 41: 3–13.

Levy, B. S.; and Farber, B. A. 1986. Clinical implications of adolescent introspection. *Psychotherapy* 23: 570–77.

Levy, L. H. 1963. *Psychological interpretation.* New York: Holt, Rinehart and Winston.

Levy, M. B.; and Davis, K. E. 1988. Lovestyles and attachment styles compared: Their relations to each other and to various relationship characteristics. *Journal of Social and Personal Relationships* 5: 439–71.

Lewin, K. 1931. The conflict between Aristotelian and Galilean modes of thought in contemporary psychology. *Journal of General Psychology* 5: 141–77.

Lewin, R. 1987. The earliest "humans" were more like apes. *Science* 236: 1061–63.

Lewin, R. 1988a. Modern human origins under close scrutiny. *Science* 239: 1240–41.

Lewin, R. 1988b. New views emerge on hunters and gatherers. *Science* 240: 1146–48.

Lewin, R. 1988c. A lopsided look at evolution. *Science* 241: 291–93.

Lewis, M. 1987. Social development in infancy and early childhood. In J. D. Osofsky, ed., *Handbook of infant development,* 2d ed., 419–555. New York: Wiley.

Lewis, M.; and Brooks-Gunn, J. 1979. *Social cognition and the acquisition of self.* New York: Plenum.

Lewis, M.; and Rosenbaum, L. A., eds. 1974. *The effect of the infant on its caregiver.* New York: Wiley.

Lewis, M.; and Rosenbaum, L. A. 1978. *The development of affect.* New York: Plenum.

Lewis, M.; Sullivan, M. W.; Stanger, C.; and Weiss, M. 1989. Self development and self-conscious emotions. *Child Development* 60: 145–56.

Lewis, M.; Sullivan, M. W.; and Vasen, A. 1987. Making faces: Age and emotion differences in the posing of emotional expressions. *Developmental Psychology* 23: 690–97.

Lewis, M. I.; and Butler, R. N. 1974. Life review therapy: Putting memories to work in individual and group psychotherapy. *Geriatrics* 29: 165–73.

Lewis, R. L.; Dlugokinski, E. L.; Caputo, L. M.; and Griffin, R. B. 1988. Children at risk for emotional disorders: Risk and resource dimensions. *Clinical Psychology Review* 8: 417–40.

Lewis, W. A.; and Evans, J. W. 1986. Resistance: A reconceptualization. *Psychotherapy* 23: 426–33.

Lewontin, R. 1978. Adaptation. *Scientific American* 239: 156–69.

Libet, B. 1985. Unconscious cerebral initiative and the role of conscious will in voluntary action. *Behavioral and Brain Sciences* 8: 529–66.

Lichtman, R. 1986. Constructionalism and reductionism: A reply to Ingleby. *New Ideas in Psychology* 4: 273–80.

Lieberman, M.; and Falk, J. 1971. The remembered past as a source of data for research in the life cycle. *Human Development* 14: 132–41.

Lifton, R. J. 1976. *The life of the self.* New York: Basic Books.

Light, D. 1980. *Becoming psychiatrists: The professional transformation of self.* New York: Norton.

Linehan, M. M. 1988. Perspectives on the interpersonal relationship in behavior therapy. *Journal of Integrative and Eclectic Psychotherapy* 7: 278–90.

Links, P. S.; Steiner, M.; and Mitton, J. 1989. Characteristics of psychosis in borderline personality disorder. *Psychopathology* 22: 188–93.

Linville, P. W. 1985. Self-complexity and affective extremity: Don't put all of your eggs in one cognitive basket. *Social Cognition* 3: 94–120.

Linville, P. W. 1987. Self-complexity as a cognitive buffer against stress-related illness and depression. *Journal of Personality and Social Psychology* 52: 663–76.

Liotti, G. 1984. Cognitive therapy, attachment theory, and psychiatric nosology: A clinical and theoretical inquiry into their interdependence. In M. A. Reda and M. J. Mahoney, eds., *Cognitive psychotherapies: Recent developments in theory, research, and practice,* 211–32. Cambridge, Mass.: Ballinger.

Liotti, G. 1987. The resistance to change of cognitive structures: A counter-proposal to psycholanalytic metapsychology. *Journal of Cognitive Psychotherapy: An International Quarterly* 1: 87–104.

Liotti, G.; and Reda, M. 1981. Some epistemological remarks on behavior therapy, cognitive therapy, and psychoanalysis. *Cognitive Therapy and Research* 5: 231–36.

Lipsitt, L. P. 1979. Critical conditions in infancy: A psychological perspective. *American Psychologist* 34: 973–80.

Lisberger, S. G. 1988. The neural basis for learning of simple motor skills. *Science* 242: 728–35.

Livingston, P., ed. 1984. *Disorder and order.* Saratoga, Calif.: ANMA Libri.

Llewelyn, S. P. 1988. Psychological therapy as viewed by clients and therapists. *British Journal of Clinical Psychology* 27: 223–37.

Locke, E. A. 1980. Behaviorism and psychoanalysis: Two sides of the same coin. *Objectivist Forum* 1: 10–15.

Locker, A.; and Coulter, N. A., Jr. 1977. A new look at the description and prescription of systems. *Behavioral Science* 22: 197–206.

Loevinger, J. 1976. *Ego development.* San Francisco: Jossey-Bass.

Loevinger, J. 1987. The concept of self or ego. In P. Young-Eisendrath and J. A. Hall, eds., *The book of the self,* 88–94. New York: New York University Press.

LoGerfo, M. 1980–81. Three ways of reminiscence in theory and practice. *International Journal of Aging and Human Development* 12: 39–46.

Lombardi, W. J.; Higgins, E. T.; and Bargh, J. A. 1987. The role of consciousness in priming effects on categorization: Assimilation versus contrast as a function of awareness of the priming task. *Personality and Social Psychology Bulletin* 13: 411–29.

Lombardo, T. J. 1987. *The reciprocity of perceiver and environment: The evolution of James J. Gibson's ecological psychology.* Hillsdale, N. J.: Erlbaum.

London, P. 1964. *The modes and morals of psychotherapy.* New York: Holt, Rinehart and Winston.

London, P. 1969. *Behavior control.* New York: Harper and Row.

London, P. 1972. The end of ideology in behavior modification. *American Psychologists* 27: 913–20.

Long, A. A. 1974. Psychological ideas in antiquity. In P. P. Wiener, ed., *Dictionary of the history of ideas: Studies of selected pivotal ideas,* vol. 4, 1–9. New York: Scribner.

Longino, H. E. 1988. Science, objectivity, and feminist values. *Feminist Studies* 14: 561–74.

López, S. R.; Grover, P.; Holland, D.; Johnson, M. J.; Kain, C. D.; Canel, K.; Mellins, C. A.; and Rhyne, M. C. 1989. Development of culturally sensitive psychotherapists. *Professional Psychology: Research and Practice* 20: 369–76.

Lorenz, F. N. 1963. Deterministic non-periodic flows. *Journal of Atmospheric Science* 20: 131–41.

Loring, M.; and Powell, B. 1988. Gender, race and DSM-III: A study of the objectivity of psychiatric diagnostic behavior. *Journal of Health and Social Behavior* 29: 1–22.

Lorr, M.; Shi, A. Q.; and Youniss, R. P. 1989. A bipolar multifactor conception of mood states. *Personality and Individual Differences* 10: 155–59.

Lovejoy, C. O. 1981. The origin of man. *Science* 211: 341–50.

Lovejoy, C. O. 1988. Evolution of human walking. *Scientific American* (November): 118–25.

Loveland, K. A. 1986. Discovering the affordances of a reflecting surface. *Developmental Review* 6: 1–24.

Lowen, A. 1975. *Bioenergetics.* New York: Coward, McCann and Geoghegan.

Lowen, A. 1983. *Narcissism: Denial of the true self.* New York: Macmillan.

Lubin, B. 1962. Survey of psychotherapy training and activities of psychologists. *Journal of Clinical Psychology* 18: 252–56.

Luborsky, L.; Crits-Christoph, P.; McLellan, A. T.; Woody, G.; Piper, W.; Liberman, B.; Imber, S.; and Pilkonis, P. 1986. Do therapists vary much in their success? Findings from four outcome studies. *American Journal of Orthopsychiatry* 56: 501–12.

Luborsky, L.; Crits-Christoph, P.; Mintz, J.; and Auerbach, A. 1988. *Who will benefit from psychotherapy? Predicting therapeutic outcomes.* New York: Basic Books.

Luborsky, L.; and Singer, B. 1975. Comparative studies of psychotherapy. *Archives of General Psychiatry* 32: 995–1008.

Lubusko, A.; and Forest, J. 1989. Memory for information in self-help psychology books. *Psychological Reports* 65: 891–96.

Luce, G. G. 1971. *Biological rhythms in human and animal physiology.* New York: Dover.

Lucock, M. P.; and Salkovskis, P. M. 1988. Cognitive factors in social anxiety and its treatment. *Behaviour Research and Therapy* 26: 297–302.

Lukes, S. 1974. Types of individualism. In P. P. Wiener, ed., *Dictionary of the history of ideas: Studies of selected pivotal ideas,* vol. 2, 594–604. New York: Scribner.

Luria, A. R. 1981. *Language and cognition.* New York: Wiley.

Lyddon, W. J. 1987. Emerging views of health: A challenge to rationalist doctrines of medical thought. *Journal of Mind and Behavior* 8: 365–94.

Lyddon, W. J. 1989. Root metaphor theory: A philosophical framework for counseling and psychotherapy. *Journal of Counseling and Development* 67: 442–48.

Lyman, B.; and Waters, J. C. E. 1986. The experiential loci and sensory qualities of various emotions. *Motivation and Emotion* 10: 25–37.

Lynch, J. J. 1977. *The broken heart: The medical consequences of loneliness.* New York: Harper and Row.

Lyons, N. P. 1983. Two perspectives: On self, relationships, and morality. *Harvard Educational Review* 53: 125–45.

McAdams, D. P. 1988. Biography, narrative, and lives: An introduction. *Journal of Personality* 56: 1–18.

McAdams, D. P.; Lensky, D. B.; Daple, S. A.; and Allen, J. 1988. Depression and the organization of autobiographical memory. *Journal of Social and Clinical Psychology* 7: 332–49.

McCain, G.; and Segal, E. M. 1973. *The game of science,* 2d ed. Monterey, Calif.: Brooks/Cole.

McCarthy, C. 1975. *Inner companions.* Washington, D. C.: Acropolis.

McCarthy, I. C.; and Byrne, N. O. 1988. Mis-taken love: Conversations on the problem of incest in an Irish context. *Family Process* 27: 181–99.

McCauley, R. N. 1987. The role of theories in a theory of concepts. In U. Neisser, ed., *Concepts and conceptual development: Ecological and intellectual factors in categorization,* 288–309. Cambridge: Cambridge University Press.

McClelland, J. L.; and Rumelhart, D. E. 1985. Distributed memory and the representation of general and specific information. *Journal of Experimental Psychology: General* 114: 159–88.

Maccoby, E. E. 1988. Gender as a social category. *Developmental Psychology* 24: 755–65.

Maccoby, E. E.; and Jacklin, C. N. 1974. *The psychology of sex differences.* Palo Alto, Calif.: Stanford University Press.

McConnaughy, E. A. 1987. The person of the therapist in psychotherapeutic practice. *Psychotherapy* 24: 303–14.

McCrae, R. R.; and Costa, P. T., Jr. 1987. Validation of the five-factor model of personality across instruments and observers. *Journal of Personality and Social Psychology* 52: 81–90.

McCrae, R. R.; and Costa, P. T., Jr. 1989. The structure of interpersonal traits: Wiggins's circumplex and the five-factor model. *Journal of Personality and Social Psychology* 56: 586–95.

McCulloch, W. S. 1965. *Embodiments of mind.* Cambridge, Mass.: MIT Press.

McCulloch, W. S.; and Pitts, W. 1943. A logical calculus of the ideas immanent in nervous activity. *Bulletin of Mathematical Biophysics, 5,* 115–133.

McDermott, J. J., ed. 1981. *The philosophy of John Dewey,* 2 vols. Chicago: University of Chicago Press.

MacDevitt, J. W. 1987. Therapists' personal therapy and professional self-awareness. *Psychotherapy* 24: 693–703.

Mace, W. M. 1974. Ecologically stimulating cognitive psychology: Gibsonian perspectives. In W. B. Weimer and D. S. Palermo, eds., *Cognition and the symbolic processes,* 137–64. Hillsdale, N. J.: Erlbaum.

Mace, W. M. 1977. James J. Gibson's strategy for perceiving: Ask not what's inside your head, but what your head's inside of. In R. Shaw and J. Bransford, eds., *Perceiving, acting, and knowing: Toward an ecological psychology,* 43–65. Hillsdale, N. J.: Erlbaum.

McFarland, D., ed. 1987. *The Oxford companion to animal behavior.* Oxford: Oxford University Press.

McFarlane, J.; Martin, C. L.; and Williams, T. M. 1988. Mood fluctuations: Woman versus men and menstrual versus other cycles. *Psychology of Women Quarterly* 12: 201–23.

McGaugh, J. L. 1990. Significance and remembrance: The role of neuromodulatory systems. *Psychological Science* 1: 15–25.

McGeoch, J. A. 1932. Forgetting and the law of disuse. *Psychological Review* 39: 352–70.

McGeoch, J. A. 1933. Review of "Remembering" by F. C. Bartlett. *Psychological Bulletin* 30: 774–76.

McGovern, M. P.; Newman, F. L.; Kopta, S. M. 1986. Metatheoretical assumptions and psychotherapy orientation: Clinician attributions of patients' problem causality and responsibility for treatment outcome. *Journal of Consulting and Clinical Psychology* 54: 476–81.

McGuinness, C. 1989. Visual imagery: The question of representation. *Irish Journal of Psychology* 10: 188–200.

McGuire, M. T.; and Essock-Vitale, S. M. 1982. Psychiatric disorders in the context of evolutionary biology: The impairment of adaptive behaviors during the exacerbation and remission of psychiatric illnesses. *The Journal of Nervous and Mental Disease* 170: 9–20.

McGuire, M. T.; and Troisi, A. 1987. Physiological regulation—deregulation and psychiatric disorders. *Ethology and Sociobiology* 8: 9S–25S.

McGuire, M. T.; Essock-Vitale, S. M.; and Polsky, R. H. 1981. Psychiatric disorders in the context of evolutionary biology: An ethological model of behavioral changes associated with psychiatric disorders. *The Journal of Nervous and Mental Disease* 169: 687–704.

McKeachie, W. J. 1974. The decline and fall of the laws of learning. *Educational Researcher* 3: 7–11.

MacLean, P. D. 1973. *A triune concept of the brain and behaviour.* Toronto: University of Toronto Press.

McLennan, J.; Gotts, G. H.; and Omodei, M. M. 1988. Personality and relationship dispositions as determinants of subjective well-being. *Human Relations* 41: 593–602.

MacLeod, C.; and Mathews, A. 1988. Anxiety and the allocation of attention to threat. *Quarterly Journal of Experimental Psychology* 44: 653–70.

McMullin, R. E. 1986. *Handbook of cognitive therapy techniques.* New York: Norton.

McNair, D. M.; and Lorr, M. 1964. An analysis of professed psychotherapeutic techniques. *Journal of Consulting Psychology* 6: 165–67.

Macnamara, J. 1982. Meaning. In W. B. Weimer and D. S. Palermo, eds., *Cognition and the symbolic processes,* vol. 2, 35–61. Hillsdale, N. J.: Erlbaum.

McNamara, K.; and Richard, K. M. 1989. Feminist identity development: Implications for feminist therapy with women. *Journal of Counseling and Development* 68: 184–89.

McNeill, B. W.; and Worthen, V. 1989. The parallel process in psychotherapy supervision. *Professional Psychology: Research and Practice* 20: 329–33.

McWhinney, W. 1984. Alternative realities: Their impact on change and leadership. *Journal of Humanistic Psychology* 24: 7–38.

Maddi, S. R.; Hoover, M.; and Kobasa, S. C. 1982. Alienation and exploratory behavior. *Journal of Personality and Social Psychology* 42: 884–90.

Maddux, J. E.; Norton, L. W.; and Leary, M. R. 1988. Cognitive components of social anxiety: An investigation of the integration of self-presentation theory and self-efficacy theory. *Journal of Social and Clinical Psychology* 6: 180–90.

MacDonald, G. F.; Cove, J. L.; Laughlin, C. D.; and McManus, J. 1989. Mirrors, portals, and multiple realities. *Zygon* 24: 39–64.

Madison, G. B. 1988. *The hermeneutics of postmodernity.* Bloomington: Indiana University Press.

Magnusson, D. 1987. *Individual development from an interactional perspective.* Hillsdale, N. J.: Erlbaum.

Magnusson, D.; and Allen, V. L. 1983. *Human development: An interactional perspective.* New York: Academic Press.

Magoon, A. J. 1977. Constructivist approaches in educational research. *Review of Educational Research* 47: 651–93.

Mahler, M. 1968. *On human symbiosis and the vicissitudes of individuation.* New York: International University Press.

Mahler, M. 1972. On the first three subphases of the separation-individuation process. *International Journal of Psychoanalysis* 53: 333–38.

Mahler, M.; Pine, F.; and Bergman, A. 1975. *The psychological birth of the human infant.* New York: Basic Books.

Mahoney, M. J. 1974. *Cognition and behavior modification.* Cambridge, Mass.: Ballinger.

Mahoney, M. J. 1976. *Scientist as subject: The psychological imperative.* Cambridge, Mass.: Ballinger.

Mahoney, M. J. 1977*a*. Publication prejudices: An experimental study of confirmatory bias in the peer review system. *Cognitive Therapy and Research* 1: 165–75.

Mahoney, M. J. 1977*b*. Reflections on the cognitive-learning trend in psychotherapy. *American Psychologist* 32: 5–13.

Mahoney, M. J. 1979*a*. Psychology of the scientist: An evaluative review. *Social Studies of Science* 9: 349–75.

Mahoney, M. J. 1979*b*. Cognitive and non-cognitive views in behavior modification. In P. O. Sjoden, S. Bates, and W. S. Dockens, eds., *Trends in behavior therapy,* 39–54. New York: Plenum.

Mahoney, M. J., ed. 1980*a*. *Psychotherapy process: Current issues and future directions.* New York: Plenum.

Mahoney, M. J. 1980*b*. Psychotherapy and the structure of personal revolutions. In M. J. Mahoney, ed., *Psychotherapy process: Current issues and future directions,* 157–80. New York: Plenum.

Mahoney, M. J. 1980*c*. *Abnormal psychology: Perspectives on human variance.* San Francisco: Harper and Row.

Mahoney, M. J. 1982. Publication, politics, and scientific progress. *Behavioral and Brain Sciences* 5: 220–21.

Mahoney, M. J. 1983. Knowledge and power, privilege and privacy: Reflections on the boundaries of studying powerful persons and institutions. *Newsletter of the Society for the Advancement of Social Psychology* 9: 16–22.

Mahoney, M. J. 1984*a*. Psychoanalysis and behaviorism: The yin and yang of determinism. In H. Arkowitz and S. Messer, eds., *Psychoanalytic and behavior therapy: Is integration possible?* 303–25. New York: Plenum.

Mahoney, M. J. 1984*b*. Behaviorism and individual psychology: Contacts, conflicts, and future directions. In T. J. Reinelt, Z. Otalora, and H. Kappus, eds., *Contacts of individual psychology with other forms of therapy,* 70–82. Munich: Ernst Reinhardt Verlag.

Mahoney, M. J. 1984*c*. Integrating cognition, affect, and action: A comment. *Cognitive Therapy and Research* 8: 585–89.

Mahoney, M. J. 1984*d*. Behaviorism, cognitivism, and human change processes. In M. A. Reda and M. J. Mahoney, eds., *Cognitive psychotherapies: Recent developments in theory, research, and practice,* 3–30. Cambridge, Mass.: Ballinger.

Mahoney, M. J. 1985*a*. Open exchange and epistemic progress. *American Psychologist* 40: 29–39.

Mahoney, M. J. 1985*b*. Citation classic: *Cognition and Behavior Modification. Current Contents: Social and Behavioral Sciences.* 17: 16.

Mahoney, M. J. 1985*c*. Psychotherapy and human change processes. In M. J.

Mahoney and A. Freeman, eds., *Cognition and psychotherapy*, 3–48. New York: Plenum.

Mahoney, M. J. 1986*a*. The tyranny of technique. *Counseling and Values* 30: 169–74.

Mahoney, M. J. 1986*b*. Paradoxical intention, symptom prescription, and principles of therapeutic change. *Counseling Psychologist* 14: 283–90.

Mahoney, M. J. 1987. Scientific publication and knowledge politics. *Journal of Social Behavior and Personality* 2: 165–76.

Mahoney, M. J. 1988*a*. The cognitive sciences and psychotherapy: Patterns in a developing relationship. In K. S. Dobson, ed., *The handbook of cognitive-behavioral therapies*, 357–86. New York: Guilford.

Mahoney, M. J. 1988*b*. Constructive metatheory: I. Basic features and historical foundations. *International Journal of Personal Construct Psychology* 1: 1–35.

Mahoney, M. J. 1988*c*. Constructive metatheory: II. Implications for psychotherapy. *International Journal of Personal Construct Psychology* 1: 299–315.

Mahoney, M. J. 1988*d*. Rationalism and constructivism in clinical judgment. In D. C. Turk and P. Salovey, eds., *Reasoning, inference, and judgment in clinical psychology*, 155–81. New York: Free Press.

Mahoney, M. J. 1989*a*. Participatory epistemology and psychology of science. In B. Gholson, R. A. Neimeyer, A. Houts, and W. Shadish, eds., *Psychology of science and metascience*, 138–64. Cambridge: Cambridge University Press.

Mahoney, M. J. 1989*b*. Sport psychology. In I. S. Cohen, ed., *The G. Stanley Hall lecture series*, vol. 9, 97–134. Washington, D. C.: American Psychological Association.

Mahoney, M. J. 1989*c*. Scientific psychology and radical behaviorism: Important distinctions based in scientism and objectivism. *American Psychologist* 44: 1372–77.

Mahoney, M. J. 1989*d*. Cognitive and behavioral contributions to the modern synthesis in psychology. Paper presented to the 23rd meeting of the Association for the Advancement of Behavior Therapy, 4 November, Washington, D. C.

Mahoney, M. J. 1989*e*. Holy epistemology! Construing the constructions of the constructivists. *Canadian Psychology* 30: 187–88.

Mahoney, M. J. 1990*a*. Psychotherapy and the body in the mind. In T. F. Cash and T. Pruzinsky, eds., *Body images: Development, deviance, and change*, 316–33. New York: Guilford.

Mahoney, M. J. 1990*b*. Representations of self in cognitive psychotherapies. *Cognitive Therapy and Research* 14: 229–40.

Mahoney, M. J.; and Arnkoff, D. B. 1978. Cognitive and self-control therapies. In S. L. Garfield and A. E. Bergin, eds., *Handbook of psychotherapy and behavior change*, vol. 2, 689–722. New York: Wiley.

Mahoney, M. J.; and Craine, M. 1988. *Development and psychotherapy as viewed by psychotherapists: A national survey*. University of California, Santa Barbara. Manuscript.

Mahoney, M. J.; and DeMonbreun, B. G. 1977. Psychology of the scientist: An analysis of problem-solving bias. *Cognitive Therapy and Research* 1: 229–38.

Mahoney, M. J.; and Eiseman, S. C. 1989. The object of the dance. In W. Dryden and L. Spurling, eds., *On becoming a psychotherapist,* 17–32. London: Croom Helm.

Mahoney, M. J.; and Freeman, A., eds. 1985. *Cognition and psychotherapy.* New York: Plenum.

Mahoney, M. J.; and Gabriel, T. J. 1987. Psychotherapy and the cognitive sciences: An evolving alliance. *Journal of Cognitive Psychotherapy: An International Quarterly* 1: 29–59.

Mahoney, M. J.; and Gabriel, T. J. 1990. Essential tensions in psychology: Longitudinal data on cognitive and behavioral ideologies. *Journal of Cognitive Psychotherapy: An International Quarterly* 4: 5–21.

Mahoney, M. J.; and Kazdin, A. E. 1979. Cognitive behavior modification: Misconceptions and premature evacuation. *Psychological Bulletin* 86: 1044–49.

Mahoney, M. J.; and Lyddon, W. J. 1988. Recent developments in cognitive approaches to counseling and psychotherapy. *Counseling Psychologist* 16: 190–234.

Mahoney, M. J.; and Meyers, A. W. 1989. Anxiety and athletic performance. In D. Hackfort and C. D. Spielberger, eds., *Anxiety in sports: An international perspective,* 77–94. Washington, D. C.: Hemisphere.

Mahoney, M. J.; and Nezworski, T. 1985. Cognitive-behavioral approaches to children's problems. *Journal of Abnormal Child Psychology* 13: 467–76.

Mahoney, M. J.; and Thoresen, C. E. 1974. *Self-control: Power to the person.* Monterey, Calif.: Brooks/Cole.

Mahoney, M. J.; Craine, M.; and Gabriel, T. J. 1987. Physiological correlates of mirror self-focus. University of California, Santa Barbara. Unpublished raw data.

Mahoney, M. J.; Lyddon, W. J.; and Alford, D. J. 1989. The rational-emotive theory of psychotherapy. In M. E. Bernard and R. DiGiusepe, eds., *Inside rational-emotive therapy,* 69–94. New York: Academic Press.

Mahoney, M. J.; Norcross, J. C.; Prochaska, J. O.; and Missar, C. D. 1989. Psychological development and optimal psychotherapy: Converging perspectives among clinical psychologists. *Journal of Integrative and Eclectic Psychotherapy* 8: 251–63.

Mahoney, M. J.; Miller, H. M.; and Arciero, G. 1990 In press. Constructive metatheory and the nature of mental representation. *Journal of Mental Imagery.*

Mahrer, A. R. 1978. *Experiencing: A humanistic theory of psychology and psychiatry.* New York: Brunner/Mazel.

Mahrer, A. R. 1985. *Psychotherapeutic change: An alternative approach to meaning and measurement.* New York: Norton.

Mahrer, A. R. 1986. *Therapeutic experiencing.* New York: Norton.

Mahrer, A. R. 1989. The case for fundamentally different existential-humanistic psychologies. *Journal of Humanistic Psychology* 29: 249–62.

Mahrer, A. R.; Nadler, W. P.; Sterner, I.; and White, M. V. 1989. Patterns of organization and sequencing of "good moments" in psychotherapy sessions. *Journal of Integrative and Eclectic Psychotherapy* 8: 125–39.

Main, M.; and Cassidy, J. 1988. Categories of response to reunion with the parent at age 6: Predictable from infant attachment classifications and stable over a 1-month period. *Developmental Psychology* 24: 415–26.

Main, M.; and Goldwyn, R. In press. Interview-based adult attachment classifications: Related to infant-mother and infant-father attachments. *Developmental Psychology*.

Main, M.; and Solomon, J. 1986. Discovery of an insecure disorganized/disoriented attachment pattern. In T. B. Brazelton and M. Yogman, eds., *Affective development in infancy*, 95–124. Norwood, N.J.: Ablex.

Malatesta, C. Z.; and Izard, C. E., eds. 1984. *Emotion in adult development*. London: Sage.

Malcolm, J. 1980. *Psychoanalysis: The impossible profession*. New York: Random House.

Malde, S. 1988. Guided autobiography: A counseling tool for older adults. *Journal of Counseling and Development* 66: 290–93.

Malsburg, C.; and Bienenstock, E. 1986. Statistical coding and short-term synaptic plasticity: A scheme for knowledge representation in the brain. In E. Beinenstock, F. F. Soulie, and G. Weisbuch, eds., *Disordered systems and biological organization*, 247–70. Berlin: Springer-Verlag.

Malthus, T. 1926 [1798]. *An essay on the principles of population*. London: Macmillan.

Maltz, M. 1960. *Psycho-cybernetics*. Englewood Cliffs, N.J.: Prentice-Hall.

Mancuso, J. C.; and Adams-Webber, J. R. 1982. *The construing person*. New York: Praeger.

Mancuso, J. C.; and Shaw, L. G. 1988. *Cognition and personal structure: Computer access and analysis*. New York: Greenwood.

Mandel, H. P. 1981. *Short-term psychotherapy and brief treatment techniques: An annotated bibliography 1920–1980*. New York: Plenum.

Mandelbrot, B. 1977. *The fractal geometry of nature*. New York: Freeman.

Mandeville, B. 1924 [1728]. *The fable of the bees*. Trans. F. B. Kaye. Oxford: Oxford University Press.

Mandler, G. 1975. *Mind and emotion*. New York: Wiley.

Mandler, G. 1979. Emotion. In E. Hearst, ed., *The first century of experimental psychology*, 275–321. Hillsdale, N.J.: Erlbaum.

Mandler, G. 1984. *Mind and body: Psychology of emotion and stress*. New York: Norton.

Mandler, J. M. 1988. How to build a baby: On the development of an accessible representational system. *Cognitive Development* 3: 113–36.

Manicas, P. T. 1987. *A history and philosophy of the social sciences*. New York: Basil Blackwell.

Mann, L. M.; Sher, K. J.; and Chassin, L. 1987. Alcohol expectancies and the risk for alcoholism. *Journal of Consulting and Clinical Psychology* 55: 411–17.

Mann, L. S.; Wise, T. N.; Segall, E. A.; Goldberg, R. L.; and Goldstein, D. M. 1988. Borderline symptom inventory: Assessing inpatient and outpatient borderline personality disorders. *Psychopathology* 21: 44–50.

Marcel, A. J. 1983a. Conscious and unconscious perception: Experiments on visual masking and word recognition. *Cognitive Psychology* 15: 197–237.

Marcel, A. J. 1983b. Conscious and unconscious perception: An approach to the relations between phenomenal experience and perceptual processes. *Cognitive Psychology* 15: 238–300.

Marcia, J. E. 1966. Development and validation of ego-identity status. *Journal of Personality and Social Psychology* 5: 551–58.

Margolis, J. 1987. *Science without unity: Reconciling the human and natural sciences.* Oxford, England: Basil Blackwood.

Markowitz, J. S.; Weissman, M. M.; Ouellette, R.; Lish, J. D.; and Klerman, G. L. 1989. Quality of life in panic disorder. *Archives of General Psychiatry* 46: 984–92.

Markus, H. 1977. Self-schemata and processing information about the self. *Journal of Personality and Social Psychology* 35: 63–78.

Markus, H.; and Nurius, P. 1986. Possible selves. *American Psychologist* 41: 954–69.

Marlatt, G. A.; and Gordon, J. R., eds. 1985. *Relapse prevention: Maintenance strategies in the treatment of addictive behaviors.* New York: Guilford.

Marmor, J. 1975. *Psychiatrists and their patients: A national study of private office practice.* Washington, D. C.: American Psychiatric Association.

Marmor, J.; and Woods, S. M., eds. 1980. *The interface between the psychodynamic and behavior therapies.* New York: Plenum.

Marr, D. 1982. *Vision: A computational investigation into the human representation of visual information.* San Francisco: W. H. Freeman.

Marsella, A. J.; DeVos, G.; and Hsu, F. L. K., eds. 1985. *Culture and self: Asian and Western perspectives.* London: Tavistock.

Marsh, H. W.; and O'Neill, R. 1984. Self description questionnaire III: The construct validity of multidimensional self-concept ratings by late adolescents. *Journal of Educational Measurement* 21: 153–74.

Martin, I.; and Levey, A. B. 1985. Conditioning, evaluations and cognitions: An axis of integration. *Behavior Research and Therapy* 23: 167–75.

Martin, J. 1989. A rationale and proposal for cognitive-meditational research on counseling and psychotherapy. *Counseling Psychologist* 17: 111–35.

Martin, J.; Slemon, A. G.; Hiebert, B.; Hallberg, E. T.; and Cummings, A. L. 1989. Conceptualizations of novice and experienced counselors. *Journal of Counseling Psychology* 36: 395–400.

Martin, J. R. 1989. Ideological critiques and the philosophy of science. *Philosophy of Science* 56: 1–22.

Maruyama, M. 1963. The second cybernetics: Deviation-amplifying mutual causal processes. *American Scientist* 51: 164–79.

Maruyama, M. 1977. Heterogenistics: An epistemological restructuring of biological and social sciences. *Acta Biotheoretica* 26: 120–36.

Marx, J. L. 1988. Evolution's link to development explored. *Science* 240: 880–82.

Marx, M. H.; and Hillix, W. A. 1963. *Systems and theories in psychology.* New York: McGraw-Hill.

Mascia-Lees, F. E.; Sharpe, P.; and Cohen, C. B. 1989. The postmodernist turn in anthropology: Cautions from a feminist perspective. *Journal of Women in Culture and Society* 15: 7–33.

Mascolo, M. F.; and Mancuso, J. C. 1990. Functioning of epigenetically evolved emotion systems: A constructive analysis. *International Journal of Personal Construct Psychology* 3: 205–22.

Maslow, A. H. 1962. *Toward a psychology of being.* Princeton, N.J.: Van Nostrand.

Massaro, D. W. 1988. Some criticisms of connectionist models of human performance. *Journal of Memory and Language* 27: 213–34.

Masterpasqua, F. 1989. A competence paradigm for psychological practice. *American Psychologist* 44: 1366–71.

Masterson, J. F. 1981. *The narcissistic and borderline disorders.* New York: Brunner/Mazel.

Masterson, J. F. 1988. *The search for the real self: Unmasking the personality disorders of our age.* New York: Free Press.

Masterson, J. F.; and Klein, R., eds. 1988. *Psychotherapy of the disorders of the self: The Masterson approach.* New York: Brunner/Mazel.

Masterton, R. B.; Campbell, C. B.; Bitterman, M. E.; and Hotton, N., eds. 1976. *Evolution of brain and behavior in vertebrates.* Hillsdale, N.J.: Erlbaum.

Masterton, R. B.; Hodos, W.; and Jerison, H. 1976. *Evolution, brain, and behavior: Persistent problems.* Hillsdale, N.J.: Erlbaum.

Matarazzo, J. D.; Weiss, S. M.; Herd, J. A.; Miller, N. E.; and Weiss, S. M., eds. 1984. *Behavioral health: A handbook of health enhancement and disease prevention.* New York: Wiley.

Matson, F. W. 1971. Matson replies to Skinner. *Humanist* 31: 2.

Matson, F. W., ed. 1973. *Without/within: Behaviorism and humanism.* Monterey, Calif.: Brooks/Cole.

Matson, W. I. 1965. *The existence of God.* Ithaca, N.Y.: Cornell University Press.

Matsumoto, D.; Kudoh, T.; Scherer, K.; and Wallbott, H. 1988. Antecedents of and reactions to emotions in the United States and Japan. *Journal of Cross-Cultural Psychology* 19: 267–86.

Maturana, H. R. 1970. *Biology of cognition.* BCL Report 9.0. University of Illinois Biological Computer Laboratory, Urbana.

Maturana, H. R. 1975. The organization of the living: A theory of the living organization. *International Journal of Man-Machine Studies* 7: 313–32.

Maturana, H. R. 1977. Biology of language: The epistemology of reality. In R. W. Rieber, ed., *The neuropsychology of language,* 27–63. New York: Plenum.

Maturana, H. R. 1978. Biology of language: The epistemology of reality. In G. A. Miller and E. Lenneberg, eds., *Psychology and biology of language and thought.* New York: Academic Press.

Maturana, H. R. 1980. Biology of cognition. In H. R. Maturana and F. J. Varela, eds., *Autopoiesis and cognition: The realization of the living.* Boston: Reidel.

Maturana, H. R. 1987. Everything is said by an observer. In W. I. Thompson, ed., *GAIA: A way of knowing,* 65–82. Great Barrington, Mass.: Lindisfarne.

Maturana, H. R. 1988 *Reality: The search for objectivity, or the quest for a compelling argument.* University of Chile, Santiago. Manuscript.

Maturana, H. R. 1989. *Emotion and the origin of the human.* Workshop presented at the International Conference at the Frontiers of Family Therapy, May 18–20, Brussels. Audiotape.

Maturana, H. R.; and Varela, F. G., eds. 1980. *Autopoiesis and cognition: The realization of the living.* Boston: Reidel.

Maturana, H. R.; and Varela, F. J. 1987. *The tree of knowledge: The biological roots of human understanding.* Boston: Shambhala.

Maultsby, M. C. 1984. *Rational behavior therapy.* Englewood Cliffs, N.J.: Prentice-Hall.

Mauro, R. 1988. Opponent processes in human emotions? An experimental investigation of hedonic contrast and affective interactions. *Motivation and Emotion* 12: 333–51.

Maxwell, G. 1970. Theories, perception, and structural realism. In R. G. Colodny, ed., *The nature and function of scientific theories: Essays in contemporary science and philosophy,* 3–34. Pittsburgh, Pa.: University of Pittsburgh Press.

May, R. 1982. The problem of evil: An open letter to Carl Rogers. *Journal of Humanistic Psychology* 22: 10–21.

May, R. 1986. Transpersonal psychology. *APA Monitor* 17(5):2.

May, R. 1989. Answers to Ken Wilber and John Rowan. *Journal of Humanistic Psychology* 29: 244–48.

May, R.; Angel, E.; and Ellenberger, H. F. 1958. *Existence: A new dimension in psychiatry and psychology.* New York: Basic Books.

Mayer, J. D. 1986. How mood influences cognition. In N. E. Sharkey, ed., *Advances in cognitive sciences,* 290–314. Chichester, England: Ellis Horwood.

Mayer, J. D.; and Bremer, D. 1985. Assessing mood with affect-sensitive tasks. *Journal of Personality Assessment* 49: 95–99.

Mayer, J. D.; and Gaschke, Y. N. 1988. The experience and meta-experience of mood. *Journal of Personality and Social Psychology* 55: 102–11.

Mayer, J. D.; Mamberg, M. H.; and Volanth, A. J. 1988. Cognitive domains of the mood system. *Journal of Personality* 56: 453–86.

Mayer, J. D.; and Salovey, P. 1988. Personality moderates the interaction of mood and cognition. In K. Fiedler and J. Forgas, eds., *Affect, cognition and social behavior,* 87–99. Toronto: C. J. Hogrefe.

Mayer, J. D.; and Volanth, A. J. 1985. Cognitive involvement in the mood response system. *Motivation and Emotion* 9: 261–75.

Mayer, R. E. 1983. *Thinking, problem solving, and cognition.* San Francisco: W. H. Freeman.

Mayeroff, M. 1971. *On caring.* New York: Harper and Row.

Mayerson, N. H.; and Rhodewalt, F. 1988. Role of self-protective attributions in the experience of pain. *Journal of Social and Clinical Psychology* 6: 203–18.

Mayr, E. 1982. *The growth of biological thought: Diversity, evolution, and inheritance.* Cambridge, Mass.: Belknap.

Mayr, E. 1988. *Toward a new philosophy of biology: Observations of an evolutionist.* Cambridge, Mass.: Harvard University Press.

Meaney, M. J.; Aitken, D. H.; van Berkel, C.; Bhatnagar, S.; and Sapolsky, R. B. 1988. Effect of neonatal handling on age-related impairments associated with the hippocampus. *Science* 239: 766–68.

Medawar, P. B. 1981. *The uniqueness of the individual,* 2d ed. New York: Dover.

Medawar, P. B. 1984. *Pluto's Republic.* Oxford: Oxford University Press.

Mednick, M. T. 1989. On the politics of psychological constructs: Stop the bandwagon, I want to get off. *American Psychologist* 44: 1118–23.

Meehl, P. E. 1978. Theoretical risks and tabular asterisks: Sir Karl, Sir Ronald, and the slow progress of soft psychology. *Journal of Consulting and Clinical Psychology* 46: 806–34.

Mehler, J.; Garrett, M.; and Walker, E., eds. 1982. *Perspectives on mental representation.* Hillsdale, N.J.: Erlbaum.

Mehrabian, A.; and Russell, J. A. 1974. *An approach to environmental psychology.* Cambridge, Mass.: MIT Press.

Meichenbaum, D. 1977. *Cognitive behavior modification.* New York: Plenum.

Melges, F. T.; and Swartz, M. S. 1989. Oscillations of attachment in borderline personality disorder. *American Journal of Psychiatry* 146: 1115–20.

Mellor, C. S. 1988. Depersonalisation and self perception. *British Journal of Psychiatry* 153: 15–19.

Melzack, R. 1989. Phantom limbs, the self and the brain. *Canadian Psychology* 30: 1–16.

Meltzoff, A. N. 1985a. Immediate and deferred imitation in fourteen- and twenty-four-month-old infants. *Child Development* 56: 62–72.

Meltzoff, A. N. 1985b. The roots of social and cognitive development: Models of man's original nature. In T. M. Field and N. A. Fox, eds., *Social perception in infants,* 1–30. Norwood, N.J.: Ablex.

Meltzoff, A. N.; and Borton, R. W. 1979. Intermodal matching by human neonates. *Nature* 282: 403–4.

Meltzoff, A. N.; and Moore, M. K. 1977. Imitation of facial and manual gestures by human neonates. *Science* 198: 75–78.

Meltzoff, A. N.; and Moore, M. K. 1983. Newborn infants imitate adult facial gestures. *Child Development* 54: 702–9.

Melville, S. W. 1986. *Philosophy beside itself: On deconstruction and modernism.* Minneapolis: University of Minnesota Press.

Mendelson, J. 1979. The Habermas-Gadamer debate. *New German Critique* 18: 44–73.

Merikangas, K. R.; Weissman, M. M.; Prusoff, B. A.; and John, K. 1988. Assortative mating and affective disorders: Psychopathology in offspring. *Psychiatry* 51: 48–57.

Merleau-Ponty, M. 1962. *Phenomenology of perception.* Trans. C. Smith. London: Routledge and Kegan Paul.

Merluzzi, T. V.; Glass, C. R.; and Genest, M., eds. 1981. *Cognitive assessment.* New York: Guilford.

Messer, S. B. 1986. Behavioral and psychoanalytic perspectives at therapeutic choice points. *American Psychologist* 41: 1261–72.

Messer, S. B. 1988. Psychoanalytic perspectives on the therapist-client relationship. *Journal of Integrative and Eclectic Psychotherapy* 7: 268–77.

Messer, S. B.; Sass, L. A.; and Woolfolk, R. L., eds. 1988. *Hermeneutics and psychological theory: Interpretive perspectives on personality, psychotherapy, and psychopathology.* New Brunswick, N.J.: Rutgers University Press.

Messer, S. B.; and Winokur, M. 1980. Some limits to the integration of psychoanalytic and behavior therapy. *American Psychologist* 35: 818–27.

Meyer, G. J.; and Shack, J. R. 1989. Structural convergence of mood and personality: Evidence for old and new directions. *Journal of Personality and Social Psychology* 57: 691–706.

Meyer, J. D.; and Fink, C. M. 1989. Psychiatric symptoms from prescription medications. *Professional Psychology: Research and Practice* 20: 90–96.

Meyer, M. S. 1988. Ethical principles of psychologists and religious diversity. *Professional Psychology: Research and Practice* 19: 486–87.

Miall, D. S. 1986. Emotion and the self: The context of remembering. *British Journal of Psychology* 77: 389–97.

Miall, D. S. 1989. Anticipating the self: Toward a personal construct model of emotion. *International Journal of Personal Construct Psychology* 2: 185–98.

Migdal, J. S. 1988. Individual change in the midst of social and political change. *Social Science Journal* 25: 125–39.

Mikhailov, F. T. 1976. *The riddle of the self.* New York: International Publishers.

Mill, J. S. 1988 [1869]. *The subjection of women,* S. M. Okin, ed. Indianapolis, Ind.: Hackett Publishing.

Miller, A. 1988. Toward a typology of personality styles. *Canadian Psychology* 29: 263–83.

Miller, A. I. 1984. *Imagery in scientific thought.* Cambridge, Mass.: MIT Press.

Miller, D. J.; and Thelen, M. H. 1987. Confidentiality in psychotherapy: History, issues and research. *Psychotherapy* 24: 704–11.

Miller, G. A. 1951. *Language and communication.* New York: McGraw-Hill.

Miller, G. A. 1956. The magical number seven plus or minus two: Some limits on our capacity for processing information. *Psychological Review* 63: 81–97.

Miller, G. A.; Galanter, E.; and Pribram, K. H. 1960. *Plans and the structure of behavior.* New York: Holt.

Miller, J. 1983. *States of mind.* New York: Pantheon.

Miller, L. K.; and Schyb, M. 1989. Facilitation and interference by background music. *Journal of Music Therapy* 26: 42–54.

Miller, M. L.; and Thayer, J. F. 1988. On the nature of self-monitoring: Relationships with adjustment and identity. *Personality and Social Psychology Bulletin* 14: 544–53.

Miller, N. E. 1935. The influence of past experience upon the transfer of subsequent training. Ph. D. diss., Yale University.

Minsky, M. L. 1987. *The society of mind.* New York: Simon and Schuster.

Minsky, M. L.; and Papert, S. A. 1988 [1969]. *Perceptrons,* 2d ed. Cambridge, Mass.: MIT Press.

Minton, S. C. 1989. *Body and self: Partners in movement.* Champaign, Ill.: Human Kinetics.

Miró, M. 1989. Knowledge and society: An evolutionary outline. In O. F. Gonçalves, ed., *Advances in the cognitive therapies: The constructive-developmental approach,* 111–28. Lisbon: APPORT.

Mischel, T., ed. 1971. *Cognitive development and epistemology.* New York: Academic Press.

Mischel, W. 1969. Continuity and change in personality. *American Psychologist* 24: 1012–18.

Mischel, W. 1973. Toward a cognitive social learning reconceptualization of personality. *Psychological Review* 80: 252–83.

Mischel, W. 1979. On the interface of cognition and personality: Beyond the person-situation debate. *American Psychologist* 34: 740–54.

Mischel, W. 1980. George Kelly's anticipation of psychology. In M. J. Mahoney, ed., *Psychotherapy process: Current issues and future directions,* 85–87. New York: Plenum.

Mitchell, J. D. 1987. Dance/movement therapy in a changing health care system. *American Journal of Dance Therapy* 10: 4–10.

Mitroff, I. I. 1974. *The subjective side of science.* New York: Elsevier Science.

Monod, J. 1971. *Chance and necessity.* New York: Knopf.

Montagu, A. 1978. *Touching: The human significance of the skin,* 2d ed. New York: Harper and Row.

Montagu, A. 1981. *Growing young.* New York: McGraw-Hill.

Moore, C. 1968. *The status of the individual in East and West.* Honolulu: University of Hawaii Press.

Moore, D. 1987. Parent-adolescent separation: The construction of adulthood by late adolescents. *Developmental Psychology* 23: 298–307.

Moore, J. 1987. The roots of the family tree: A review of four books on the history and nature of behaviorism. *Psychological Record* 37: 449–70.

Morawski, J. G., ed. 1988. *The rise of experimentation in American psychology.* New Haven, Conn.: Yale University Press.

Moreno, J. 1946. *Psychodrama,* vol. 1. New York: Beacon House.

Moreno, J. 1959. *Psychodrama,* vol. 2. New York: Beacon House.

Moreno, J. 1962. *Psychodrama,* vol. 3. New York: Beacon House.

Morgan, W. P. 1985a. Selected psychological factors limiting performance: A mental health model. In D. H. Clarke and H. M. Eckert, eds., *Limits of human performance,* 70–80. Champaign, Ill.: Human Kinetics.

Morgan, W. P. 1985b. Psychogenic factors and exercise metabolism: A review. *Medicine and Science in Sports and Exercise* 17: 94–100.

Morgan, W. P. 1985c. Affective beneficence of vigorous physical activity. *Medicine and Science in Sports and Exercise* 17: 94–100.

Morgan, W. P.; and Pollock, M. L. 1977. Psychologic characterization of the elite distance runner. *Annals of the New York Academy of Science* 301: 382–403.

Morin, A.; and Deblois, S. 1989. Gallup's mirrors: More than an operationalization of self-awareness in primates. *Psychological Reports* 65: 287–91.

Morin, E. 1981. Self and autos. In M. Zeleny, ed., *Autopoiesis: A theory of living organization.* New York: Elsevier North-Holland.

Morris, C. 1972. *The discovery of the individual 1050–1200.* London: Camelot Press.

Morrison, R. L.; Bellack, A. S.; and Bashore, T. R. 1988. Perception of emotion among schizophrenic patients. *Journal of Psychopathology and Behavioral Assessment* 10: 319–32.

Morrow-Bradley, C.; and Elliott, R. 1986. Utilization of psychotherapy research by practicing psychotherapists. *American Psychologist* 41: 188–97.

Mosig, Y. D. 1989. Wisdom and compassion: What the Budda taught. *Theoretical and Philosophical Psychology* 9: 27–36.

Moss, R. 1981. *The I that is We*. Millbrae, Calif.: Celestial Arts.

Mountcastle, V. 1978. An organizing principle for cerebral function: The unit module and the distributed system. In G. Edelman and V. Mountcastle, eds., *The Mindful Brain*. Cambridge, Mass.: MIT Press.

Moustakas, C. E. 1981. *Rhythms, rituals and relationships*. Detroit, Mich.: Center for Humanistic Studies.

Moustakas, C. E., ed. 1956. *The self: Explorations in personal growth*. New York: Harper and Row.

Mowrer, O. H. 1960a. *Learning theory and behavior*. New York: Wiley.

Mowrer, O. H. 1960b. *Learning theory and the symbolic processes*. New York: Wiley.

Mueller, F. L. 1974. Psychological schools in European thought. In P. P. Wiener, ed., *Dictionary of the history of ideas: Studies of selected pivotal ideas*, vol. 4, 10–16. New York: Scribner.

Mumford, L. 1956. *The transformations of man*. New York: Collier.

Muran, J. C.; and DiGiuseppe, R. A. 1990. Towards a cognitive formulation of metaphor use in psychotherapy. *Clinical Psychology Review* 10: 69–85.

Murphy, G. 1949. *Historical introduction to modern psychology*, rev. ed. New York: Harcourt, Brace and World.

Murphy, G.; and Murphy, L. B., eds. 1968. *Asian psychology*. New York: Basic Books.

Murray, H. A. 1938. *Explorations in personality*. New York: Oxford University Press.

Nagy, S.; and Nix, C. L. 1989. Relations between preventive health behavior and hardiness. *Psychological Reports* 65: 339–45.

Nalimov, V. V. 1982. *Realms of the unconscious: The enchanted frontier*. Philadelphia, Pa.: ISI Press.

National Research Council. 1988. *The behavioral and social sciences: Achievements and opportunities*. Washington, D. C.: National Academy Press.

Natsoulas, T. 1988. Sympathy, empathy, and the stream of consciousness. *Journal for the Theory of Social Behavior* 18: 169–95.

Natsoulas, T. 1989a. The ecological approach to perception: The place of perceptual content. *American Journal of Psychology* 102: 443–76.

Natsoulas, T. 1989b. Understanding William James's conception of consciousness with the help of Gerald E. Myers. *Imagination, Cognition and Personality* 8: 323–44.

Necker, L. A. 1832. Observations on some remarkable phenomena seen in Switzerland: And an optical phenomenon which occurs on viewing of a crystal or geometrical solid. *Philosophical Magazine* 3 (1): 329–37.

Needleman, J. 1982. *The heart of philosophy*. New York: Collier.

Neimeyer, G. J.; and Neimeyer, R. A., eds. 1990. *Advances in personal construct psychology,* vol. 1. Greenwich, Conn.: JAI Press.

Neimeyer, G. J.; and Resnikoff, A. 1982. Qualitative strategies in counseling research. *Counseling Psychologist* 10: 75–85.

Neimeyer, R. A. 1985*a.* Personal constructs in clinical practice. In P. C. Kendall, ed., *Advances in cognitive-behavioral research and therapy,* vol. 2, 275–339. New York: Academic Press.

Neimeyer, R. A. 1985*b. The development of personal construct psychology.* Lincoln: University of Nebraska Press.

Neimeyer, R. A.; and Neimeyer, G. J., eds. 1987. *Personal construct therapy casebook.* New York: Springer.

Neiss, R. 1988. Reconceptualizing arousal: Psychobiological states in motor performance. *Psychological Bulletin* 103: 345–66.

Neisser, U. 1967. *Cognitive psychology.* New York: Appleton-Century-Crofts.

Neisser, U. 1976. *Cognition and reality.* San Francisco: W. H. Freeman.

Neisser, U. 1980. Three cognitive psychologies and their implications. In M. J. Mahoney, ed., *Psychotherapy process: Current issues and future directions,* 363–67. New York: Plenum.

Neisser, U. 1981. James J. Gibson. *American Psychologist* 36: 214–15.

Neisser, U. 1987*a.* From direct perception to conceptual structure. In U. Neisser, ed., *Concepts and conceptual development: Ecological and intellectual factors in categorization,* 1–24. Cambridge: Cambridge University Press.

Neisser, U., ed. 1987*b. Concepts and conceptual development: Ecological and intellectual factors in categorization.* Cambridge: Cambridge University Press.

Neisser, U. 1988. Five kinds of self-knowledge. *Philosophical Psychology* 1: 35–59.

Neisser, U.; and Winograd, E., eds. 1988. *Remembering reconsidered: Ecological and traditional approaches to the study of memory.* Cambridge: Cambridge University Press.

Nelson, K.; and Seidman, S. 1984. Playing with scripts. In I. Bretherton, ed., *Symbolic Play: The development of social understanding,* 45–71. New York: Academic Press.

Nelson, K. E. 1988. The ontogeny of memory for real events. In U. Neisser and E. Winograd, eds., *Remembering reconsidered: Ecological and traditional approaches to the study of memory,* 244–76. Cambridge: Cambridge University Press.

Nelson, K. E.; and Nelson, K. 1978. Cognitive pendulums and their linguistic realization. In K. E. Nelson, ed., *Children's language,* vol. 1, 223–85. New York: Gardner.

Nesselroade, J. R.; and Ford, D. H. 1987. Methodological considerations in modeling living systems. In M. E. Ford and D. H. Ford, eds., *Humans as self-constructing living systems: Putting the framework to work,* 47–79. Hillsdale, N.J.: Erlbaum.

Neugarten, B. L. 1977. Personality and aging. In J. E. Birren and K. W. Schaie, eds., *Handbook of the psychology of aging,* 626–49. New York: Van Nostrand Reinhold.

Neumann, E. 1954. *The origins and history of consciousness.* Trans. R. F. C. Hull. Princeton, N.J.: Princeton University Press.

Neuringer, A. J. 1969. Animals respond for food in the presence of free food. *Science* 166: 399–401.

Neuringer, A. J. 1970. Many responses per food reward with free food present. *Science* 169: 503–4.

Newcomb, M. D. 1989. Assessment of nuclear anxiety among American students: Stability over time, secular trends, and emotional correlates. *Journal of Social Psychology* 129: 591–608.

Newcomb, M. D.; and Harlow, L. L. 1986. Life events and substance use among adolescents: Mediating effects of perceived loss of control and meaninglessness in life. *Journal of Personality and Social Psychology* 51: 564–77.

Newell, A.; Shaw, J. C.; and Simon, H. A. 1958. Elements of a theory of human problem solving. *Psychological Review* 65: 151–66.

Newell, A.; and Simon, H. A. 1956. The Logic Theory Machine: A complex information processing system. *IRE Transactions on Information Theory* IT-2(3): 61–79.

Nichols, M. P. 1987. *The self in the system: Expanding the limits of family therapy.* New York: Brunner/Mazel.

Nichols, M. P.; and Zax, M. 1977. *Catharsis in psychotherapy.* New York: Gardner.

Nisbett, R. E.; and Ross, L. 1980. *Human inference: Strategies and shortcomings of social judgement.* Englewood Cliffs, N.J.: Prentice-Hall.

Nisbett, R. E.; and Wilson, T. D. 1977. Telling more than we can know: Verbal reports on mental processes. *Psychological Review* 84: 231–59.

Norcross, J. C., ed. 1986. *Handbook of eclectic psychotherapy.* New York: Brunner/Mazel.

Norcross, J. C., ed. 1987. *Casebook of eclectic psychotherapy.* New York: Brunner/Mazel.

Norcross, J. C.; and Guy, J. D. 1989. Ten therapists: The process of becoming and being. In W. Dryden and L. Spurling, eds., *On becoming a psychotherapist,* 215–39. London: Tavistock/Routledge.

Norcross, J. C.; and Prochaska, J. O. 1982. A national survey of clinical psychologists: Affliations and orientations. *Clinical Psychologist* 35 (3): 1, 4–6.

Norcross, J. C.; and Prochaska, J. O. 1983. Clinicians' theoretical orientations: Selection, utilization, and efficacy. *Professional Psychology: Research and Practice* 14: 197–208.

Norcross, J. C.; and Prochaska, J. O. 1986a. Psychotherapist heal thyself—I. The psychological distress and self-change of psychologists, counselors, and lay persons. *Psychotherapy: Theory, Research and Practice* 23: 102–11.

Norcross, J. C.; and Prochaska, J. O. 1986b. Psychotherapist heal thyself—II. The self-initiated and therapy-facilitated change of psychological distress. *Psychotherapy: Theory, Research and Practice* 23: 345–56.

Norcross, J. C.; and Prochaska, J. O. 1988. A study of eclectic (and integrative) views revisited. *Professional Psychology: Research and Practice* 19: 170–74.

Norcross, J. C.; Prochaska, J. O.; and Gallagher, K. M. In press. Clinical psychologists in the 1980s, II: Theory, research and practice. *Clinical Psychologist.*

Norcross, J. C.; Strausser, D. J.; and Faltus, F. J. 1988. The therapist's therapist. *American Journal of Psychotherapy* 42: 53–66.

Norcross, J. C.; Strausser-Kirtland, D. J.; and Missar, C. D. 1988. The processes and outcomes of psychotherapists' personal treatment experiences. *Psychotherapy* 25: 36–43.

Norcross, J. C.; and Wogan, M. 1983. American psychotherapists of diverse persuasions: Characteristics, theories, practices, and clients. *Professional Psychology: Research and Practice* 14: 529–39.

Norcross, J. C.; and Wogan, M. 1987. Values in psychotherapy: A survey of practitioners' beliefs. *Professional Psychology: Research and Practice* 18: 5–7.

Norman, D. A. 1969. *Memory and attention.* New York: Wiley.

Norman, D. A. 1980a. Twelve issues for cognitive science. In D. A. Norman, ed., *Perspectives on cognitive science: Talks from the La Jolla Conference.* Hillsdale, N.J.: Erlbaum.

Norman, D. A., ed. 1980b. *Perspectives on cognitive science: Talks from the La Jolla Conference.* Hillsdale, N.J.: Erlbaum.

Nowack, K. M. 1989. Coping style, cognitive hardiness, and health status. *Journal of Behavioral Medicine* 12: 145–57.

Nurius, P. S. 1986. Reappraisal of the self-concept and implications for counseling. *Journal of Counseling Psychology* 33: 429–38.

Nurius, P. S.; Lovell, M.; and Edgar, M. 1988. Self-appraisals of abusive parents. *Journal of Interpersonal Violence* 3: 458–67.

Oakley, D. A. 1983. The varieties of memory: A phylogenetic approach. In A. Mayes, ed., *Memory in animals and humans,* 20–82. New York: Van Nostrand Reinhold.

Oates, J.; and Sheldon, S., eds. 1988. *Cognitive development in infancy.* Hillsdale, N.J.: Erlbaum.

O'Connor, M. J.; Sigman, M.; and Brill, N. 1987. Disorganization of attachment in relation to maternal alcohol consumption. *Journal of Consulting and Clinical Psychology* 55: 831–36.

O'Donnell, J. M. 1985. *The origins of behaviorism: American psychology, 1870–1920.* New York: New York University Press.

O'Grady, D.; and Metz, J. R. 1987. Resilience in children at high risk for psychological disorder. *Journal of Pediatric Psychology* 12: 3–23.

Öhman, A. 1986. Face the beast and fear the face: Animal and social fears as prototypes for evolutionary analyses of emotion. *Psychophysiology* 23: 123–45.

Olby, R. C.; Cantor, G. N.; Christie, J. R. R.; and Hodge, M. J. S., eds. 1990. *Companion to the history of modern science.* London: Routledge.

Oler, C. H. 1989. Psychotherapy with Black clients' racial identity and locus of control. *Psychotherapy* 26: 233–41.

Olney, J. 1972. *Metaphors of self: The meaning of autobiography.* Princeton, N.J.: Princeton University Press.

O'Mahony, J. F. 1984. Knowing others through the self—influence of self-perception on perception of others: A review. *Current Psychological Research and Reviews* 3: 48–62.

O'Mahony, J. F. 1986. Development of self-relatedness in descriptions of others over adolescence. *Journal of Personality* 54: 494–505.

Omer, H.; and London, P. 1988. Metamorphosis in psychotherapy: End of the systems era. *Psychotherapy* 25: 171–79.

Onians, R. B. 1951. *The origins of European thought about the body, the mind, the soul, the world, time, and fate.* Cambridge: Cambridge University Press.

Orbach, S. 1978. *Fat is a feminist issue.* New York: Berkley.

Orbach, S. 1982. *Fat is a feminist issue: II.* New York: Berkley.

Orlinsky, D. E. 1989. Researchers' images of psychotherapy: Their origins and influence on research. *Clinical Psychology Review* 9: 413–41.

Orlinsky, D. E.; and Howard, K. I. 1975. *Varieties of psychotherapeutic experience.* New York: Teachers College Press.

Orlinsky, D. E.; and Howard, K. I. 1977. The therapist's experience of psycho-therapy. In A. S. Gurman and A M. Razdin, eds., *Effective psychotherapy: A hand-book of research,* 566–89. New York: Pergamon.

Orlinsky, D. E.; and Howard, K. I. 1986. Process and outcome in psychotherapy. In S. L. Garfield and A. E. Bergin, eds., *Handbook of psychotherapy and behavior change,* 3d ed., 311–81. New York: Wiley.

Orlinsky, D. E.; and Howard, K. I. 1987. A generic model of psychotherapy. *Journal of Integrative and Eclectic Psychotherapy* 6: 6–16.

Orlofsky, J.; and Frank, M. 1986. Personality structure as viewed through early memories and identity status in college men and women. *Journal of Personality and Social Psychology* 50: 580–86.

Ornstein, D. S. 1989. Ergodic theory, randomness, and "chaos." *Science* 243: 182–86.

Ornstein, R.; and Ehrlich, P. 1989. *New world, new mind.* New York: Double-day.

Osborn, M. 1972. Archetypal metaphor in rhetoric: The light-dark family. In R. L. Scott and B. L. Brock, eds., *Methods of rhetorical criticism: A twentieth century perspective,* 383–99. New York: Harper and Row.

Osgood, C. E. 1952. The nature and measurement of meaning. *Psychological Bulletin* 49: 197–237.

Osgood, C. E.; Suci, G. J.; and Tannenbaum, P. H. 1957. *The measurement of meaning.* Urbana: The University of Illinois Press.

Osherson, D. N.; Stob, M.; and Weinstein, S. 1986. *Systems that learn.* Cambridge, Mass.: MIT Press.

Osofsky, J. D., ed. 1987. *Handbook of infant development,* 2d ed. New York: Wiley.

Otani, A. 1989. Client resistance in counseling: Its theoretical rationale and taxonomic classification. *Journal of Counseling and Development* 67: 458–61.

Overton, W. F. 1976. The active organism in structuralism. *Human Development* 19: 71–86.

Oyama, S. 1985. *The ontogeny of information: Developmental systems and evolution.* London: Cambridge University Press.

Pagels, H. 1988. *The dreams of reason: The computer and the rise of the sciences of complexity.* New York: Simon and Schuster.

Palermo, D. S. 1971. Is a scientific revolution taking place in psychology? *Science Studies* 1: 135–55.

Palermo, D. S. In press. *Coping with uncertainty: Behavioral and developmental perspectives.* Hillsdale, N.J.: Erlbaum.

Palmer, R. E. 1969. *Hermeneutics: Interpretation theory in Schleiermacher, Dilthey, Heidegger, and Gadamer.* Evanston, Ill.: Northwestern University Press.

Panksepp, J. 1982. Toward a psychobiological theory of emotions. *Behavioral and Brain Sciences* 5: 407–67.

Panksepp, J. 1986. The psychobiology of prosocial behaviors: Separation distress, play, and altruism. In E. Zahn-Waxler, E. M. Cummings, and R. Iannotti, eds., *Altruism and aggression: Biological and social origins,* 19–57. Cambridge: Cambridge University Press.

Panksepp, J.; and Clynes, M. 1988. *Emotions and psychopathology.* New York: Plenum.

Panksepp, J.; Siviy, S. M.; and Normansell, L. A. 1985. Brain opioids and social emotions. In M. Reite and T. Field, eds., *Biology of social attachments and separation,* 3–49. New York: Academic Press.

Papert, S. A. 1982. *Mindstorms.* New York: Basic Books.

Parasuraman, R.; and Davies, D. R., eds. 1984. *Varieties of attention.* New York: Academic Press.

Parker, B. A., ed. 1983. *Stress and burnout in the human service systems.* New York: Pergamon.

Parkes, C. M.; and Stevenson-Hinde, J., eds. 1982. *The place of attachment in human behavior.* New York: Basic Books.

Parkinson, C. I.. 1985. *Breakthroughs: A chronology of great achievements in science and mathematics 1200–1930.* Boston: G. K. Hall.

Parrot, W. G.; and Sabini, J. 1989. On the "emotional" qualities of certain types of cognition: A reply to arguments for the independence of cognition and affect. *Cognitive Therapy and Research* 13: 49–65.

Pascual-Leone, J. 1984. Attention, dialectic and mental effort: Toward an organismic theory of life stages. In M. L. Commons, F. A. Richards, and C. Armon, eds., *Beyond formal operations: Late adolescent and adult cognitive development.* New York: Praeger.

Pascual-Leone, J. 1987. Organismic processes for neo-Piagetian theories: A dialectical causal account of cognitive development. *International Journal of Psychology* 22: 531–70.

Passingham, R. 1982. *The human primate.* San Francisco: W. H. Freeman.

Paterson, R. J.; and Moran, G. 1988. Attachment theory, personality development, and psychotherapy. *Clinical Psychology Review* 8: 611–36.

Pattee, H. H. 1973. *Hierarchy theory: The challenge of complex systems.* New York: George Braziller.

Pattee, H. H. 1977. Dynamic and linguistic modes of complex systems. *International Journal of General Systems* 3: 259–66.

Pattee, H. H. 1978. The complementarity principle in biological and social structures. *Journal of Biological and Social Structures* 1: 191–200.

Pattee, H. H. 1979. The complementarity principle and the origin of macromolecular information. *BioSystems* 11: 217–26.

Pattee, H. H. 1981. Symbol-structure complementarity in biological evolution. In E. Jantsch, ed., *The evolutionary vision.* Boulder, Colo.: Westview.

Patterson, C. H. 1984. Empathy, warmth, and genuineness in psychotherapy: A review of reviews. *Psychotherapy* 21: 431–38.

Patterson, C. H. 1989. Eclecticism in psychotherapy: Is integration possible? *Psychotherapy* 26: 157–61.

Pattison, J. E. 1973. Effects of touch on self-exploration and the therapeutic relationship. *Journal of Consulting and Clinical Psychology* 40: 170–75.

Pauly, P. J. 1987. *Controlling life: Jacques Loeb and the engineering ideal in biology.* Oxford: Oxford University Press.

Payne, R.; and Firth-Cozens, J., eds. 1987. *Stress in health professionals.* New York: Wiley.

Peale, N. V. 1960. *The power of positive thinking.* Englewood Cliffs, N.J.: Prentice-Hall.

Peebles, M. J. 1980. Personal therapy and ability to display empathy, warmth, and genuineness in psychotherapy. *Psychotherapy* 17: 252–62.

Peele, S. 1985. *The meaning of addiction.* Lexington, Mass.: D. C. Heath.

Pelham, B. W.; and Swann, W. B. 1989. From self-conceptions to self-worth: On the sources and structure of global self-esteem. *Journal of Personality and Social Psychology* 57: 672–80.

Pennebaker, J. W.; and Beall, S. K. 1986. Confronting a traumatic event: Toward an understanding of inhibition and disease. *Journal of Abnormal Psychology* 95: 274–81.

Pepper, S. C. 1942. *World hypotheses: A study in evidence.* Berkeley: University of California Press.

Perlmuter, L. C.; and Monty, R. A., eds. 1979. *Choice and perceived control.* Hillsdale, N.J.: Erlbaum.

Perloff, L. S. 1983. Perceptions of vulnerability to victimization. *Journal of Social Issues* 39: 41–61.

Perls, F. S. 1969. *Gestalt therapy verbatim.* Lafayette, Calif.: Real People.

Perls, F. S.; Hefferline, R.; and Goodman, P. 1951. *Gestalt therapy.* New York: Dell.

Perry, J., ed. 1975. *Personal identity.* Berkeley: University of California Press.

Pessoa, F. 1974. *Selected poems,* 2d ed. Trans. J. Griffin. London: Penguin.

Petersen, A. C.; and Hamburg, B. A. 1986. Adolescence: A developmental approach to problems and psychopathology. *Behavior Therapy* 17: 480–99.

Peterson, D. R. 1985. Twenty years of practitioner training in psychology. *American Psychologist* 40: 441–51.

Phillips, B. N. 1989. Role of the practitioner in applying science to practice. *Professional Psychology: Research and Practice* 20: 3–8.

Piaget, J. 1926. *The language and thought of the child.* New York: Harcourt, Brace.

Piaget, J. 1928. *Judgement and reasoning in the child.* New York: Harcourt, Brace.

Piaget, J. 1929. *The child's conception of the world.* New York: Harcourt, Brace.

Piaget, J. 1930. *The child's conception of physical causality.* New York: Harcourt, Brace.

Piaget, J. 1932. *The moral judgement of the child.* London: Kegan Paul.

Piaget, J. 1950. *The psychology of intelligence.* New York: Harcourt, Brace.

Piaget, J. 1970. *Psychology and epistemology: Towards a theory of knowledge.* New York: Viking.

Piaget, J. 1981. *Intelligence and affectivity: Their relationship during child development.* Ed. and Trans. T. A. Brown and C. E. Kaegi. Palo Alto, Calif.: Annual Reviews.

Piaget, J. 1987a. *Possibility and necessity.* Vol. 1, *The role of possibility in cognitive development.* Trans. H. Feider. Minneapolis: University of Minnesota Press.

Piaget, J. 1987b. *Possibility and necessity.* Vol. 2, *The role of necessity in cognitive development.* Trans. H. Feider. Minneapolis: University of Minnesota Press.

Piaget, J.; and Inhelder, B. 1963. *The psychology of the child.* New York: Basic Books.

Pick, H. L. 1988. Some theoretical issues confronting developmental psychologists. *Theoretical and Philosophical Psychology* 8: 57–58.

Piliavin, J. A.; and Charing, H. 1988. What *is* the factorial structure of the private and public self-consciousness scales? *Personality and Social Psychology Bulletin* 14: 587–95.

Pilkonis, P. A. In press. Personality prototypes among depressives: Themes of dependency and autonomy. *Journal of Personality Disorders.*

Pine, F. 1989. Motivation, personality organization, and the four psychologies of psychoanalysis. *Journal of the American Psychoanalytic Association* 37: 31–64.

Pingleton, J. P. 1989. The role and function of forgiveness in the psychotherapeutic process. *Journal of Psychology and Theology* 17: 27–35.

Pinker, S., ed. 1985. *Visual cognition.* Cambridge, Mass.: MIT Press.

Pinker, S.; and Mehler, J., eds. 1988. *Connections and symbols.* Cambridge, Mass.: MIT Press.

Pinkley, R.; Laprelle, J.; Pyzczynski, T.; and Greenberg, J. 1988. Depression and the self-serving search for consensus after success and failure. *Journal of Social and Clinical Psychology* 6: 235–44.

Piolat, M. 1988. Estimation of self-change by adults: Effect of temporal reference point and self-image comparison mode. *European Bulletin of Cognitive Psychology* 8: 281–92.

Piotrowski, C.; and Keller, J. W. 1984. Psychodiagnostic testing in APA-approved clinical psychology programs. *Professional Psychology: Research and Practice* 15: 450–56.

Pipp, S.; Fischer, K. W.; and Jennings, S. 1987. Acquisition of self- and mother-knowledge in infancy. *Developmental Psychology* 23: 86–96.

Pirandello, L. 1987 [1904]. *The late Mattia Pascal.* Trans. N. Simbrowski. New York: Hippocrene.

Pistole, M. C. 1989. Attachment in adult romantic relationships: Style of conflict resolution and relationship satisfaction. *Journal of Social and Personal Relationships* 6: 505–10.

Plakun, E. M. 1989. Narcissistic personality disorder: A validity study and comparison to borderline personality disorder. *Psychiatric Clinics of North America* 12: 603–20.

Plato. 1907. *The dialogues of Plato*, 2 vols. Trans. B. Jowett. New York: Scribner.

Plous, S.; and Zimbardo, P. G. 1986. Attributional biases among clinicians: A comparison of psychoanalysts and behavior therapists. *Journal of Consulting and Clinical Psychology* 54: 568–70.

Plutchik, R.; and Kellerman, H. 1980. *Emotion: Theory, research, and experience*, vol. 1. New York: Academic Press.

Poincaré, H. 1905. *Science and hypothesis*. New York: Science Press.

Poincaré, H. 1929 [1907]. *The foundations of science*. New York: Science House.

Polanyi, M. 1951. *The logic of liberty*. Chicago: University of Chicago Press.

Polanyi, M. 1958. *Personal knowledge: Towards a post-critical philosophy*. Chicago: University of Chicago Press.

Polanyi, M. 1966. *The tacit dimension*. New York: Doubleday.

Polster, E.; and Polster, M. 1973. *Gestalt therapy integrated*. New York: Brunner/Mazel.

Polti, G. 1921. *The thirty-six dramatic situations*. Trans. L. Ray. Boston: The Writer.

Pomerantz, J. R.; and Pristach, E. A. 1989. Emergent features, attention, and perceptual glue in visual form perception. *Journal of Experimental Psychology: Human Perception and Performance* 15: 635–49.

Pompa, L. 1975. *Vico: A study of the 'New Science.'* Cambridge: Cambridge University Press.

Pool, R. 1989*a*. Ecologists flirt with chaos. *Science* 243: 310–13.

Pool, R. 1989*b*. Is it healthy to be chaotic? *Science* 243: 604–7.

Pope, H. G.; and Hudson, J. I. 1989. Are eating disorders associated with borderline personality disorder? A critical review. *International Journal of Eating Disorders* 8: 1–9.

Pope, K. S. 1985. Fantasy. In G. Stricker and R. H. Keisner, eds., *From research to clinical practice*, 375–400. New York: Plenum.

Pope, K. S. 1987. Preventing therapist-patient sexual intimacy: Therapy for a therapist at risk. *Professional Psychology: Research and Practice* 18: 624–28.

Pope, K. S. 1988. How clients are harmed by sexual contact with mental health professionals: The syndrome and its prevalence. *Journal of Counseling and Development* 67: 222–26.

Pope, K. S.; Keith-Spiegel, P.; and Tabachnick, B. G. 1986. Sexual attraction to clients: The human therapist and the (sometimes) inhuman training system. *American Psychologist* 41: 147–58.

Pope, K. S.; and Singer, J. L. 1978. *The stream of consciousness: Scientific investigations into the flow of human experience*. New York: Plenum.

Pope, K. S.; Tabachnick, B. G.; and Keith-Spiegel, P. 1988. Good and poor practices in psychotherapy: National survey of beliefs of psychologists. *Professional Psychology: Research and Practice* 19: 547–52.

Popper, K. R. 1962. *Conjectures and refutations*. New York: Harper.

Popper, K. R., ed. 1972*a*. *Objective knowledge: An evolutionary approach*. London: Oxford University Press.

Popper, K. R. 1972*b* [1966]. Of clouds and clocks. In K. R. Popper, ed., *Objective knowledge: An evolutionary approach,* 206–55. London: Oxford University Press.

Popper, K. R. 1974. Campbell on the evolutionary theory of knowledge. In P. A. Schilpp, ed., *The philosophy of Karl Popper,* 1059–65. La Salle, Ill.: Open Court. Reprinted in Radnitzky and Bartley, 1987.

Popper, K. R. 1978. Natural selection and the emergence of mind. *Dialectica* 22: 339–55.

Popper, K. R. 1982*a*. *The open universe: An argument for indeterminism.* Totowa, N.J.: Rowman and Littlefield.

Popper, K. R. 1982*b*. The place of mind in nature. In R. Q. Elvee, ed., *Mind in nature,* 31–59. New York: Harper and Row.

Popper, K. R. 1983. *Realism and the aim of science.* Totowa, N.J.: Rowman and Littlefield.

Popper, K. R.; and Eccles, J. C. 1977. *The self and its brain: An argument for interactionism.* New York: Springer.

Posner, M. I. 1982. Cumulative development of attentional theory. *American Psychologist* 37: 168–79.

Posner, M. I.; and Keele, S. W. 1968. On the genesis of abstract ideas. *Journal of Experimental Psychology* 77: 353–63.

Posner, M. I.; and Marin, O. S. M., eds. 1985. *Mechanisms of attention,* vol. 11. Hillsdale, N.J.: Erlbaum.

Posner, M. I.; and Shulman, G. L. 1979. Cognitive science. In E. Hearst, ed., *The first century of experimental psychology,* 370–405. Hillsdale, N.J.: Erlbaum.

Posner, M. I.; and Snyder, C. R. R. 1975. Attention and cognitive control. In R. L. Solso, ed., *Information processing and cognition,* 55–85. Hillsdale, N.J.: Erlbaum.

Post, R. M.; Roy-Byrne, P. P.; and Uhde, T. W. 1988. Graphic representation of the life course of illness in patients with affective disorder. *American Journal of Psychiatry* 145: 844–48.

Postman, L. 1951. Towards a general theory of cognition. In J. H. Rohrer and M. Sherif, eds., *Social psychology at the crossroads.* New York: Harper.

Powell, J. L.; and Brand, A. G. 1987. The development of an emotions scale for writers. *Educational and Psychological Measurement* 47: 329–38.

Powell, W. E. 1987. The "ties that bind": Relationships in life transitions. *Social Casework: The Journal of Contemporary Social Work* 69: 556–62.

Powers, W. T. 1973. *Behavior: The control of perception.* Chicago: Aldine.

Prather, H. 1970. *Notes to myself.* New York: Bantam.

Pribram, K. H. 1971. *Languages of the brain: Experimental paradoxes and principles in neuropsychology.* Englewood Cliffs, N.J.: Prentice-Hall.

Pribram, K. H. 1977. Some comments on the nature of the perceived universe. In R. Shaw and J. Bransford, eds., *Perceiving, acting, and knowing: Toward an ecological psychology,* 83–101. Hillsdale, N.J.: Erlbaum.

Pribram, K. H. 1982. Reflections on the place of brain in the ecology of mind. In W. B. Weimer and D. S. Palermo, eds., *Cognition and the symbolic processes,* Vol. 2, 361–81. Hillsdale, N.J.: Erlbaum.

Pribram, K. H. 1986. The cognitive revolution and mind/brain issues. *American Psychologist* 41: 507–20.

Pribram, K. H. 1990. *Brain and perception: Holonomy and structure in figural processing.* Hillsdale, N.J.: Erlbaum.

Price, R. 1987. Dissociative disorders of the self: A continuum extending into multiple personality. *Psychotherapy* 24: 387–91.

Priel, B.; and Schonen, S. de 1986. Self-recognition: A study of a population without mirrors. *Journal of Experimental Child Psychology* 41: 237–50.

Prigogine, I. 1980. *From being to becoming: Time and complexity in the physical sciences.* San Francisco: W. H. Freeman.

Prigogine, I.; and Stengers, I. 1984. *Order out of chaos: Man's new dialogue with nature.* New York: Bantam.

Prilleltensky, I. 1989. Psychology and the status quo. *American Psychologist* 44: 795–802.

Prince, M. 1906. *The dissociation of personality.* London: Longmans Effren.

Prochaska, J. O. 1984. *Systems of psychotherapy: A transtheoretical analysis.* Homewood, Ill.: Dorsey.

Prochaska, J. O.; Nash, J. M.; and Norcross, J. C. 1986. Independent psychological practice: A national survey of full-time practitioners. *Psychotherapy in Private Practice* 4 (3): 57–66.

Prochaska, J. O.; and Norcross, J. C. 1983a. Contemporary psychotherapists: A national survey of characteristics, practices, orientations, and attitudes. *Psychotherapy: Theory, Research and Practice* 20: 161–73.

Prochaska, J. O.; and Norcross, J. C. 1983b. Psychotherapists' perspectives on treating themselves and their clients for psychic distress. *Professional Psychology: Research and Practice* 14: 642–55.

Prochaska, J. O.; Norcross, J. C.; and Hambrecht, M. 1988. *Treating ourselves vs. treating our clients: A replication with alcohol abuse.* Manuscript under review.

Proffitt, D. R. 1976. *Demonstrations to investigate the meaning of everyday experience.* Doctoral dissertation, The Pennsylvania State University.

Proffit, D. R.; and Halwes, T. 1982. Categorical perception: A contractual approach. In W. B. Weimer and D. S. Palermo, eds., *Cognition and the symbolic processes,* vol. 2, 295–319. Hillsdale, N.J.: Erlbaum.

Progoff, I. 1975. *At a journal workshop.* New York: Dialogue House Library.

Progoff, I. 1980. *The practice of process meditation.* New York: Dialogue House Library.

Pruzinsky, T. 1984. *The influence of the body in the development and change of the self.* Department of Psychiatry, University of Virginia. Manuscript.

Purves, D. 1988. *Body and brain: A trophic theory of neural connections.* Cambridge, Mass.: Harvard University Press.

Purzner, K. 1988. Psychoanalysis as therapeutic crisis induction: Affect and emotion as a prerequisite of radical change. *Psychopathology* 21: 143–48.

Pylyshyn, Z. W. 1979. Imagery theory: Not mysterious—just wrong. *Behavioral and Brain Sciences* 2: 561–62.

Pylyshyn, Z. W. 1980. Cognition and computation: Issues in the foundations of cognitive science. *Behavioral and Brain Sciences* 3: 154–69.

Pylyshyn, Z. W. 1981. The imagery debate: Analogue media versus tacit knowledge. *Psychological Review* 88: 15–16.

Pylyshyn, Z. W. 1984. *Computation and cognition: Toward a foundation for cognitive science*. Cambridge, Mass.: MIT Press.

Quay, H. C.; and Werry, J. S., eds. 1986. *Psychopathological disorders of childhood*, 3d ed. New York: Wiley.

Rachlin, H. 1970. *Introduction to modern behaviorism*. San Francisco: W. H. Freeman.

Rachlin, H. 1988. Molar behaviorism. In D. B. Fishman, F. Rotgers, and C. M. Franks, eds., *Paradigms in behavior therapy: Present and promise*, 77–105. New York: Springer.

Rachlin, H. 1989. *Judgement, decision, and choice: A cognitive/behavioral synthesis*. San Francisco: W. H. Freeman.

Rachman, S. 1980. Emotional processing. *Behaviour Research and Therapy* 18: 51–60.

Radhakrishnan, S.; and Moore, C. A., eds. 1957. *A source book in Indian philosophy*. Princeton, N.J.: Princeton University Press.

Radke-Yarrow, M. 1989. Developmental and contextual analysis of continuity. *Human Development* 32. 204–9.

Radnitzky, G. 1987a. In defense of self applicable critical rationalism. In G. Radnitzky and W. W. Bartley, eds., *Evolutionary epistemology, theory of rationality, and sociology of knowledge*, 279–312. La Salle, Ill.: Open Court.

Radnitzky, G., ed. 1987b. *Centripetal forces in the sciences*, vol. 1. New York: Paragon House.

Radnitzky, G.; and Bartley, W. W., eds. 1987. *Evolutionary epistemology, theory of rationality, and the sociology of knowledge*. La Salle, Ill.: Open Court.

Raff, R. A.; and Raff, E. C., eds. 1987. *Development as an evolutionary process*. New York: Liss.

Ragins, B. R.; and Sundstrom, E. 1989. Gender and power in organizations: A longitudinal perspective. *Psychological Bulletin* 105: 51–88.

Raimy, V. 1975. *Misunderstandings of the self*. San Francisco: Jossey-Bass.

Rainer, T. 1978. *The new diary: How to use a journal for self-guidance and expanded creativity*. Los Angeles: Jeremy P. Tarcher.

Rando, T. A. 1985. Creating therapeutic rituals in the psychotherapy of the bereaved. *Psychotherapy* 22: 236–40.

Raquepaw, J. M.; and Miller, R. S. 1989. Psychotherapist burnout: A componential analysis. *Professional Psychology: Research and Practice* 20: 32–36.

Raskin, D. E.; and Klein, Z. E. 1976. Losing a symptom through keeping it: A review of paradoxical treatment techniques and rationale. *Archives of General Psychiatry* 33: 548–55.

Rathunde, K. 1988. Optimal experience and the family context. In M. Csikszentmihalyi, and I. S. Csikszentmihalyi, eds., *Optimal experience*, 342–63. Cambridge: Cambridge University Press.

Reason, P.; and Rowan, J., eds. 1981. *Human inquiry: A source book of new paradigm research.* New York: Wiley.

Reda, M. A. 1986. *Sistemi cognitivi complessi e psicoterapia.* Rome: Nuova Italia Scientifica.

Reda, M. A.; and Mahoney, M. J., eds. 1984. *Cognitive psychotherapies: Recent developments in theory, research, and practice.* Cambridge: Ballinger.

Redfearn, J. W. T. 1987. Terminology of ego and self: From Freud(ians) to Jung(ians). In P. Young-Eisendrath and J. A. Hall, eds., *The book of the self,* 384–403. New York: New York University.

Reed, J. 1989. A psychologist of the '20s. *Science* 244: 1386–87.

Reese, W. L. 1980. *Dictionary of philosophy and religion: Eastern and Western thought.* Atlantic Highlands, N.J.: Humanities Press.

Reich, W. 1942. *The function of the orgasm.* New York: Orgone Institute.

Reich, W. 1949. *Character analysis.* New York: Noonday.

Reik, T. 1949. *Listening with the third ear: The inner experience of a psychoanalyst.* New York: Farrar, Straus.

Reilly, R. 1989. On the relationship between connectionism and cognitive science. *Irish Journal of Psychology* 10: 162–87.

Reinelt, T.; Otalora, Z.; and Kappus, H., eds. 1984. *Contacts of individual psychology with other forms of therapy.* Munich: Ernst Reinhardt Verlag.

Reiser, M. F. 1984. *Mind, brain, body: Toward a convergence of psychoanalysis and neurobiology.* New York: Basic Books.

Reiser, M. F. 1989. The future of psychoanalysis in academic psychiatry: Plain talk. *Psychoanalytic Quarterly* 58: 185–209.

Rescorla, R. A. 1988. Pavlovian conditioning: It's not what you think it is. *American Psychologist* 43: 151–60.

Restle, F. 1980. The seer of Ithaca. *Contemporary Psychology* 25: 291–92.

Reynolds, D. K. 1980. *The quiet therapies.* Honolulu: The University Press of Hawaii.

Reynolds, P. C. 1981. *On the evolution of human behavior: The argument from animals to man.* Berkeley: University of California Press.

Rheingold, H. L. 1985. Development as the acquisition of familiarity. *Annual Review of Psychology* 36: 1–17.

Rhodewalt, F.; and Agustsdottir, S. 1986. Effects of self-presentation on the phenomenal self. *Journal of Personality and Social Psychology* 50: 47–55.

Riccelli, P. T.; Antila, C. E.; Dale, J. A.; and Klions, H. L. 1989. Depressive and elative mood inductions as a function of exaggerated versus contradictory facial expressions. *Perceptual and Motor Skills* 68: 443–52.

Rice, L. N.; and Greenberg, L. S. 1984. *Patterns of change.* New York: Guilford.

Rich, A. 1978. *The dream of a common language: Poems 1974–1977.* New York: Norton.

Richards, N. 1988. Forgiveness. *Ethics* 99: 77–97.

Richards, R. J. 1987. *Darwin and the emergence of evolutionary theories of mind and behavior.* Chicago: University of Chicago Press.

Richter, F. M. 1986. Nonlinear behavior. In D. W. Fiske and R. A. Schweder, eds.,

Metatheory in social science: Pluralisms and subjectivities, 284–92. Chicago: University of Chicago Press.

Ricks, D. F. 1974. Supershrink: Methods of a therapist judged successful on the basis of adult outcomes of adolescent patients. In D. F. Ricks, M. Roff, and A. Thomas, eds., *Life history research in psychopathology.* Minneapolis: University of Minnesota Press.

Ricoeur, P. 1981. *Hermeneutics and the human sciences.* Trans. J. B. Thompson. Cambridge, Mass.: Cambridge University Press.

Rieber, R. W., ed. 1983. *Dialogues on the psychology of language and thought.* New York: Plenum.

Rieder, C.; and Cicchetti, D. 1989. Organizational perspective on cognitive control functioning and cognitive-affective balance in maltreated children. *Developmental Psychology* 25: 382–93.

Rippere, V.; and Williams, R., eds. 1985. *Wounded healers: Mental health workers' experiences of depression.* New York: Wiley.

Roberts, W. A.; and Mazmanian, D. S. 1988. Concept learning at different levels of abstraction by pigeons, monkeys, and people. *Journal of Experimental Psychology: Animal Behavior Processes* 14: 247–60.

Robey, K. L.; Cohen, B. D.; and Gara, M. A. 1989. Self-structure in schizophrenia. *Journal of Abnormal Psychology* 98: 436–42.

Robins, L. N. 1988. The composite international diagnostic interview. *Archives of General Psychiatry* 45: 1069–77.

Robinson, D. L.; and Petersen, S. E. 1986. The neurobiology of attention. In J. E. LeDoux and W. Hirst, eds., *Mind and brain: Dialogues in cognitive neuroscience*, 142–78. Cambridge: Cambridge University Press.

Robinson, D. N. 1981. *An intellectual history of psychology*, rev. ed. New York: Macmillan.

Robles, R.; Smith, R.; Carver, C. S.; and Wellens, A. R. 1987. Influence of subliminal visual images on the experience of anxiety. *Personality and Social Psychology Bulletin* 13: 399–410.

Rock, I. 1983. *The logic of perception.* Cambridge, Mass.: MIT Press.

Rock, I. 1984. *Perception.* New York: Scientific Books.

Rodrigue, J. R.; Olson, K. R.; and Markley, R. P. 1987. Induced mood and curiosity. *Cognitive Therapy and Research* 2: 101–6.

Rogers, C. R. 1957. The necessary and sufficient conditions of therapeutic personality change. *Journal of Consulting Psychology* 21: 95–103.

Rogers, C. R. 1982. Reply to Rollo May's letter to Carl Rogers. *Journal of Humanistic Psychology* 22: 85–89.

Rogers, C. R.; and Skinner, B. F. 1956. Some issues concerning the control of human behavior: A symposium. *Science* 124: 1057–66.

Rogers, T. B.; Kuiper, N. A.; and Kirker, W. S. 1977. Self-reference and the encoding of personal information. *Journal of Personality and Social Psychology* 35: 677–88.

Roitblat, H. L. 1982. The meaning of representation in animal memory. *Behavioral and Brain Sciences* 5: 353–406.

Rokeach, M. 1972. *Beliefs, attitudes and values: A theory of organization and change.* San Francisco: Jossey-Bass.

Rokeach, M.; and Ball-Rokeach, S. J. 1989. Stability and change in American value priorities 1968–1981. *American Psychologist* 44: 775–84.

Roland, A. 1988. *In search of self in India and Japan.* Princeton, N.J.: Princeton University Press.

Rolf, I. D. 1977. *Rolfing: The integration of human structures.* New York: Harper and Row.

Romanyshyn, R. D. 1981. Science and reality: Metaphors of experience and experience as metaphorical. In R. S. Valle and R. von Eckartsberg, eds., *The metaphors of consciousness,* 3–19. New York: Plenum.

Ronningstam, E.; and Gunderson, J. 1989. Descriptive studies on narcissistic personality disorder. *Narcissistic Personality Disorder* 12: 585–601.

Rorty, R. 1979. *Philosophy and the mirror of nature.* Princeton, N.J.: Princeton University Press.

Rorty, A. O., ed. 1980. *Explaining emotions.* Berkeley, Calif.: University of California Press.

Rosch, E.; and Mervis, C. 1975. Family resemblances: Studies in the internal structure of categories. *Cognitive Psychology* 7: 573–605.

Rose, K. J. 1988. *The body in time.* New York: Wiley.

Rosen, G. M. 1987. Self-help treatment books and the commercialization of psychotherapy. *American Psychologist* 42: 46–51.

Rosen, H. 1985. *Piagetian dimensions of clinical relevance.* New York: Columbia University Press.

Rosen, N. A.; and Wyer, R. S. 1972. Some further evidence for the "Socratic effect" using a subjective probability model of cognitive organization. *Journal of Social Psychology* 24: 420–24.

Rosen, S., ed. 1982. *My voice will go with you: The teaching tales of Milton H. Erickson.* New York: Norton.

Rosenberg, M. 1979. *Conceiving the self.* New York: Basic Books.

Rosenberg, M. 1988. Self-objectification: Relevance for the species and society. *Sociological Forum* 3: 548–65.

Rosenberg, R.; and Gara, M. A. 1985. The multiplicity of personal identity. In P. Shaver, ed., *Self, situations, and social behavior: Review of personality and social psychology,* vol. 6, 87–113. Beverly Hills, Calif.: Sage.

Rosenblatt, F. 1962. *Principles of neurodynamics.* New York: Spartan Books.

Rosenblueth, A.; Wiener, N.; and Bigelow, J. 1943. Behavior, purpose, and teleology. *Philosophy of Science* 10: 18–24.

Rosenfield, I. 1988. *The invention of memory: A new view of the brain.* New York: Basic Books.

Rosenthal, C. J.; and Marshall, V. W. 1988. Generational transmission of family ritual. *American Behavioral Scientist* 31: 669–84.

Rosin, S. A.; and Knudson, R. M. 1986. Perceived influence of life experiences on clinical psychologists' selection and development of theoretical orientations. *Psychotherapy* 23: 357–67.

Ross, C. A. 1989. *Multiple personality disorder: Diagnosis, clinical features and treatment.* New York: Wiley.

Ross, C. A.; Heber, S.; Norton, G. R.; and Anderson, G. 1989. Somatic symptoms in multiple personality disorder. *Psychosomatics* 30: 154–60.

Ross, C. A.; Norton, R.; and Wozney, K. 1989. Multiple personality disorder: An analysis of 236 cases. *Canadian Journal of Psychiatry* 34: 413–18.

Ross, M. 1989. Relation of implicit theories to the construction of personal histories. *Psychological Review* 96: 341–57.

Rossi, E. L. 1973. Psychological shocks and creative moments in psychotherapy. *American Journal of Clinical Hypnosis* 16: 9–22.

Rotter, J. B. 1966. Generalized expectancies for internal versus external control of reinforcement. *Psychological Monographs* 80 (Whole No. 609).

Rouse, W. B.; and Morris, N. M. 1986. On looking into the black box: Prospects and limits in the search for mental models. *Psychological Bulletin* 100: 349–63.

Rousseau, J. J. 1979 [1762]. *Emile: Or, on education.* Trans. A. Bloom. New York: Basic Books.

Rowan, J. 1989. Two humanistic psychologies or one? *Journal of Humanistic Psychology* 29: 224–29.

Royce, J. R. 1964. *The encapsulated man: An interdisciplinary essay on the search for meaning.* Princeton, N.J.: Van Nostrand.

Rubin, D. C., ed., 1986. *Autobiographical memory.* Cambridge: Cambridge University Press.

Rubin, D. C. 1988. Go for the skill. In U. Neisser and E. Winograd, eds., *Remembering reconsidered: Ecological and traditional approaches to the study of memory,* 374–82. Cambridge: Cambridge University Press.

Rubin, D. C.; Wetzler, S. E.; and Nebes, R. D. 1986. Autobiographical memory across the lifespan. In D. C. Rubin, ed., *Autobiographical memory,* 202–21. Cambridge: Cambridge University Press.

Rumelhart, D. E.; McClelland, J. L.; and The PDP Research Group. 1986a. *Parallel distributed processing: Explorations in the microstructure of cognition.* Vol. 1, *Foundations.* Cambridge, Mass.: MIT Press.

Rumelhart, D. E.; McClelland, J. L.; and The PDP Research Group. 1986b. *Parallel distributed processing: Explorations in the microstructure of cognition.* Vol. 2, *Psychological and biological models.* Cambridge, Mass.: MIT Press.

Runyan, W. M. 1984. *Life histories and psychobiography: Explorations in theory and method.* Oxford: Oxford University Press.

Ruse, M. 1986. *Taking Darwin seriously: A naturalistic approach to philosophy.* New York: Basil Blackwell.

Russell, B. 1945. *A history of western philosophy.* New York: Simon and Schuster.

Russell, B. 1957. *Why I am not a Christian.* New York: Simon and Schuster.

Russell, B. 1967. *The autobiography of Bertrand Russell.* London: George Allen and Unwin.

Russell, J. A. 1979. Affective space is bipolar. *Journal of Personality and Social Psychology* 37: 345–56.

Russell, J. A. 1980. A circumplex model of affect. *Journal of Personality and Social Psychology* 39: 1161–78.

Russell, J. A. 1983. Pancultural aspects of the human conceptual organization of emotions. *Journal of Personality and Social Psychology* 45: 1281–88.

Russo, N. F. 1990. Overview: Forging research priorities for women's mental health. *American Psychologist* 45: 368–73.

Rutter, M. 1971. Parent-child separation: Psychological effects on the children. *Journal of Child Psychology and Psychiatry* 12: 233–60.

Rutter, M. 1981. *Maternal deprivation reassessed.* New York: Penguin.

Rutter, M. 1986. The developmental psychopathology of depression: Issues and perspectives. In M. Rutter, C. E. Izard, and P. B. Read, eds., *Depression in young people,* 3–30. New York: Guilford.

Rutter, M. 1987. The role of cognition in child development and disorder. *British Journal of Medical Psychology* 60: 1–16.

Rutter, M.; Izard, C. E.; and Read, P. B., eds. 1986. *Depression in young people.* New York: Guilford.

Rychlak, J. F. 1968. *A philosophy of science for personality theory.* Boston: Houghton Mifflin.

Rychlak, J. F. 1977. *The psychology of rigorous humanism.* New York: Wiley.

Rychlak, J. F. 1988. Following the Skinnerian example: In search of a science of psychology beyond the black box computer. *Theoretical and Philosophical Psychology* 8: 2–12.

Ryle, A. 1982. *Psychotherapy: A cognitive integration of theory and practice.* London: Academic Press.

Ryle, A. 1984. How can we compare different psychotherapies? Why are they all effective? *British Journal of Medical Psychology* 57: 261–64.

Ryle, G. 1949. *The concept of mind.* New York: Barnes and Noble.

Safran, J. D; and Greenberg, L. S. 1987. Affect and the unconscious: A cognitive perspective. In R. Stern, ed., *Theories of the unconscious and theories of the self,* 191–212. Hillsdale, N.J.: Analytic Press.

Safran, J. D.; Greenberg, L. S.; and Rice, L. N. 1988. Integrating psychotherapy research and practice: Modeling the change process. *Psychotherapy* 25: 1–17.

Safran, J. D.; Vallis, T. M.; Segal, Z. V.; and Shaw, B. F. 1986. Assessment of core cognitive processes in cognitive therapy. *Cognitive Therapy and Research* 10: 509–26.

Sagan, C. 1977. *The dragons of Eden.* New York: Ballantine.

Sahakian, W. S. 1976. *Learning: Systems, models, and theories,* 2d ed. Chicago: Rand McNally.

Sahley, T. L.; and Panksepp, J. 1987. Brain opioids and autism: An updated analysis of possible linkages. *Journal of Autism and Developmental Disorders* 17: 210–16.

Salovey, P.; and Birnbaum, D. 1989. Influence of mood on health-relevant cognitions. *Journal of Personality and Social Psychology* 57: 539–51.

Salter, A. 1949. *Conditioned reflex therapy.* New York: Capricorn.

Salthe, S. N. 1985. *Evolving hierarchical systems: Their structure and representation.* New York: Columbia University Press.

Salthe, S. N. 1989. Self-organization of/in hierarchically structured systems. *Systems Research* 6: 199–208.

Samelson, F. 1988. A new scholarship. *Science* 243: 1837.

Sameroff, A. J. 1983. Developmental systems: Contexts and evolution. In W. Kessen, ed., *Handbook of child psychology.* Vol. 1, *History, theory, and methods,* 237–94. New York: Wiley.

Sampson, E. E. 1985. The decentralization of identity: Toward a revised concept of personal and social order. *American Psychologist* 40: 1203–11.

Sampson, E. E. 1988. The debate on individualism: Indigenous psychologies of the individual and their role in personal and societal functioning. *American Psychologist* 43: 15–22.

Sandell, R. 1987. Assessing the effects of psychotherapy. *Psychotherapy and Psychosomatics* 47: 29–64.

Sanderson, W. C.; Rapee, R. M.; and Barlow, D. H. 1989. The influence of an illusion of control on panic attacks induced via inhalation of 5.5% carbon dioxide-enriched air. *Archives of General Psychiatry* 46: 157–62.

Sandvik, E.; Diener, E.; and Larsen, R. J. 1985. The opponent process theory and affective reactions. *Motivation and Emotion* 9: 407–18.

Sanford, N. 1966. *Self and society: Social change and individual development.* New York: Atherton.

Sapadin, L. A. 1988. Friendship and gender: Perspectives of professional men and women. *Journal of Social and Personal Relationships* 5: 387–403.

Saper, Z.; and Forest, J. 1987. Personality variables and interest in self-help books. *Psychological Reports* 60: 563–66.

Sarbin, T. R. 1962. A preface to a psychological analysis of the self. *Psychological Review* 59: 11–22.

Sarnat, H. B.; and Netsky, M. G. 1981. *Evolution of the nervous system,* 2d ed. New York: Oxford University Press.

Sartorius, N.; Nielsen, J. A.; and Stromgren, E., eds. 1989. Changes in the frequency of mental disorder over time. *Acta Psychiatrica Scandinavica* 79 Supplementum No. 348.

Sass, L. A. 1988*a*. The self and its vicissitudes: An "archaeological" study of the psychoanalytic avant-garde. *Social Research* 55: 551–607.

Sass, L. A. 1988*b*. The land of unreality: On the phenomenology of the schizophrenic break. *New Ideas in Psychology* 6: 223–42.

Satir, V. 1972. *Peoplemaking.* Palo Alto, Calif.: Science and Behavior Books.

Saussure, F. de 1959 [1916]. *Course in general linguistics.* Trans. W. Baskin. New York: Philosophical Library.

Sayre, K. M. 1986. Intentionality and information processing: An alternative model for cognitive science. *Behavioral and Brain Sciences* 9: 121–66.

Scarborough, E.; and Furumoto, L. 1987. *Untold lives: The first generation of American women psychologists.* New York: Columbia University Press.

Scarr, S. 1982. Development is internally guided, not determined. *Contemporary Psychology* 27: 852–53.

Scarr, S. 1985. Constructing psychology: Making facts and fables for our times. *American Psychologist* 40: 499–512.

Scarr, S.; Phillips, D.; and McCartney, K. 1990. Facts, fantasies and the future of child care in the United States. *Psychological Science* 1: 26–35.

Schacht, T. E. 1984. The varieties of integrative experience. In H. Arkowitz and S. B. Messer, eds., *Psychoanalytic therapy and behavior therapy: Is integration possible?* 107–31. New York: Plenum.

Schacht, T. E. 1985. DSM-III and the politics of truth. *American Psychologist* 40: 513–21.

Schachter, D. L. 1986. The psychology of memory. In J. E. LeDoux and W. Hirst, eds., *Mind and brain: Dialogues in cognitive neuroscience,* 189–214. Cambridge: Cambridge University Press.

Schanberg, S. M.; and Field, T. M. 1987. Sensory deprivation stress and supplemental stimulation in the rat pup and preterm human neonate. *Child Development* 58: 1431–47.

Scheerer, E. 1988. Towards a history of cognitive science. *International Social Science Journal* 40: 7–19.

Scheff, T. J., ed. 1975. *Labeling madness.* Englewood Cliffs, N.J.: Prentice-Hall.

Scheff, T. J., ed. 1979. *Catharsis in healing, ritual, and drama.* Berkeley: University of California Press.

Scheffler, I. 1967. *Science and subjectivity.* Indianapolis, Ind.: Bobbs-Merrill.

Scheibe, K. E. 1988. Metamorphoses in the psychologist's advantage. In J. G. Morawski, ed., *The rise of experimentation in American psychology,* 52–71. New Haven, Conn.: Yale University Press.

Scher, J., ed. 1962. *Theories of the mind.* New York: Free Press.

Scherer, K. R. 1984. On the nature and function of emotion: A component process approach. In K. R. Scherer and P. Ekman, eds., *Approaches to emotion,* 293–317. Hillsdale, N.J.: Erlbaum.

Scherer, K. R.; and Ekman, P., eds. 1984. *Approaches to emotion.* Hillsdale, N.J.: Erlbaum.

Schiebinger, L. 1989. *Women in the origins of modern science.* Cambridge, Mass.: Harvard University Press.

Schilcher, F. von; and Tennant, N. 1984. *Philosophy, evolution and human nature.* Boston: Routledge and Kegan Paul.

Schneider, W. 1987. Connectionism: Is it a paradigm shift for psychology? *Behavior Research Methods, Instruments, and Computers* 19: 73–83.

Schofield, W. 1964. *Psychotherapy: The purchase of friendship.* Englewood Cliffs, N.J.: Prentice-Hall.

Schöner, G.; and Kelso, J. A. S. 1988. Dynamic pattern generation in behavioral and neural systems. *Science* 239: 1513–20.

Schultz, D. P. 1965. *Sensory restriction: Effects of behavior.* New York: Academic Press.

Schutz, A.; and Luckmann, T. 1973. *The structures of the life-world.* Evanston, Ill.: Northwestern University Press.

Schwartz, G. E. 1988. From behavior therapy to cognitive behavior therapy to systems therapy: Toward an integrative health science. In D. B. Fishman, F. Rotgers, and C. M. Franks, eds., *Paradigms in behavior therapy: Present and promise,* 294–320. New York: Springer.

Schwartz, R. M.; and Garamoni, G. L. 1986. A structural model of positive and negative states of mind: Asymmetry in the internal dialogue. In P. C. Hendall, ed., *Advances in cognitive-behavioral research and therapy,* 1–62. New York: Academic Press.

Schweber, S. 1980. Darwin and the political economists. *Journal of the History of Biology* 13: 195–289.

Schweder, R. A.; and LeVine R. A. 1984. *Cultural theory: Essays on mind, self and emotion.* Cambridge: Cambridge University Press.

Scogin, F.; Jamison, C.; and Gochneaur, K. 1989. Comparative efficacy of cognitive and behavioral bibliotherapy for mildly and moderately depressed older adults. *Journal of Consulting and Clinical Psychology* 57: 403–7.

Scott, C. D.; and Hawk, J., eds. 1986. *Heal thyself: The health of health care professionals.* New York: Brunner/Mazel.

Segal, J.; and Yahraes, H. 1978. *A child's journey: Forces that shape the lives of our young.* New York: McGraw-Hill.

Segal, L. 1986. *The dream of reality: Heinz von Foerster's constructivism.* New York: Norton.

Segal, M. M. 1988. Neural network programs. *Science* 241: 1107–8.

Segal, Z. V.; Hood, J. E.; Shaw, B. F.; and Higgins, E. T. 1988. A structural analysis of the self-schema construct in major depression. *Cognitive Therapy and Research* 12: 471–85.

Sejnowski, T. J.; Koch, C.; and Churchland, P. S. 1988. Computational neuroscience. *Science* 241: 1299–1306.

Seligman, M. E. P. 1989. Research in clinical psychology: Why is there so much depression today? In I. S. Cohen, ed., *The G. Stanley Hall lecture series,* vol. 9, 79–96. Washington, D. C.: American Psychological Association.

Seligman, M. E. P. 1970. On the generality of the laws of learning. *Psychological Review* 77: 406–18.

Servos, J. W. 1987. Biology as power. *Science* 237: 305.

Seznec, J. 1974. Myth in antiquity. In P. P. Wiener, ed., *Dictionary of the history of ideas: Studies of selected pivotal ideas,* vol. 3, 272–94. New York: Scribner.

Shadish, W. R. 1986. Planned critical multiplism: Some elaborations. *Behavioral Assessment* 8: 75–103.

Shaffer, L. F. 1953. Of whose reality I cannot doubt. *American Psychologist* 8: 608–23.

Shafranske, E. P.; and Malony, H. N. 1990. Clinical psychologists' religious and spiritual orientations and their practice of psychotherapy. *Psychotherapy* 27: 72–78.

Shannon, C. E.; and Weaver, W. 1949. *The mathematical theory of communication.* Urbana: University of Illinois Press.

Shanon, B. 1984. *Meno:* A cognitive psychological view. *British Journal of Philosophy and Science* 35: 129–47.

Shanon, B. 1987. On the place of representations in cognition. In D. N. Perkins, J. Lochhead, and J. Bishop, eds., *Thinking: The second international conference,* 33–49. Hillsdale, N.J.: Erlbaum.

Shanon, B. 1988*a.* Semantic representation of meaning: A critique. *Psychological Bulletin* 104: 70–83.

Shanon, B. 1988*b.* Remarks on the modularity of mind. *British Journal of Philosophy of Science* 39: 331–52.

Shapere, D. 1974. On the relations between compositional and evolutionary theories. In F. J. Ayala and T. Dobzhansky, eds., *Studies in the philosophy of biology: Reduction and related problems,* 187–204. Berkeley: University of California Press.

Shapiro, T. 1989. Psychoanalytic classification and empiricism with borderline personality disorder as a model. *Journal of Consulting and Clinical Psychology* 57: 187–94.

Shaver, P. R., ed. 1985. *Self, situations, and social behavior: Review of personality and social psychology.* Beverly Hills, Calif.: Sage.

Shaver, P. R.; and Hazan, C. 1988. A biased overview of the study of love. *Journal of Social and Personal Relationships* 5: 473–501.

Shaver, P. R.; Schwartz, J.; Kirson, D.; and O'Connor, C. 1987. Emotion knowledge: Further exploration of a prototype approach. *Journal of Personality and Social Psychology* 52: 1061–86.

Shaw, M. L. G. 1980. *On becoming a personal scientist: Interactive computer elicitation of personal models of the world.* London: Academic Press.

Shaw, R.; and Bransford, J. 1977. *Perceiving, acting, and knowing: Toward an ecological psychology.* Hillsdale, N.J.: Erlbaum.

Shaw, R.; and McIntyre, M. 1974. Algoristic foundations to cognitive psychology. In W. B. Weimer and D. S. Palermo, eds., *Cognition and the symbolic processes,* vol. 1, 305–62. Hillsdale, N. J.: Erlbaum.

Shaw, R.; and Pittenger, J. 1977. Perceiving the face of change in changing faces: Implications for a theory of object perception. In R. Shaw and J. Bransford, eds., *Perceiving, acting, and knowing: Toward an ecological psychology,* 103–32. Hillsdale, N. J.: Erlbaum.

Shaw, R.; Turvey, M. R.; and Mace, W. 1982. Ecological psychology: The consequence of a commitment to realism. In W. B. Weimer and D. S. Palermo, eds., *Cognition and the symbolic processes,* vol. 2, 159–226. Hillsdale, N.J.: Erlbaum.

Shelton, J. L.; and Ackerman, J. M. 1974. *Homework in counseling and psychotherapy.* Springfield, Ill.: Charles C. Thomas.

Shemberg, K.; Keeley, S. M.; and Blum, M. 1989. Attitudes toward traditional and nontraditional dissertation research: Survey of directors of clinical training. *Professional Psychology: Research and Practice* 20: 190–92.

Shepard, R. N. 1975. Form, formation, and transformation of internal representations. In R. Solso, ed., *Information processing and cognition: The Loyola symposium,* 87–122. Hillsdale, N.J.: Erlbaum.

Shepard, R. N. 1987a. Evolution of a mesh between principles of the mind and regularities of the world. In J. Dupre, ed., *The latest on the best: Essays on evolution and optimality,* 251–75. Cambridge: MIT Press.

Shepard, R. N. 1987b. Toward a universal law of generalization for psychological science. *Science* 237: 1317–23.

Sheridan, A. 1980. *Michel Foucault: The will to truth.* London: Tavistock.

Sherif, M.; and Cantril, H. 1947. *The psychology of ego-involvement.* New York: Wiley.

Sherrington, C. S. 1906. *The integrative action of the nervous system.* Silliman Lectures. New Haven: Yale University Press.

Sherrington, C. S. 1940. *Man on his nature.* Gifford Lectures. Cambridge: Cambridge University Press.

Sherwood, A.; Allen, M. T.; Murrell, D.; and Obrist, P. A. 1988. Motor preparation aspects of cardiovascular reactivity to psychological challenge. *International Journal of Psychophysiology* 6: 263–272.

Shevrin, H.; and Dickman, S. 1980. The psychological unconscious: A necessary assumption for all psychological theory? *American Psychologist* 35: 421–34.

Shoham-Salomon, V.; Avner, R.; and Neeman, R. 1989. You're changed if you do and changed if you don't: Mechanisms underlying paradoxical interventions. *Journal of Consulting and Clinical Psychology* 57: 590–98.

Silverman, H. J. 1987. *Inscriptions.* London: Routledge and Kegan Paul.

Simek-Downing, L., ed. 1989. *International psychotherapy: Theories, research, and cross-cultural implications.* New York: Praeger.

Simon, H. A. 1988. Creativity and motivation: A response to Csikszentmihalyi. *New Ideas in Psychology* 6: 177–81.

Simon, L. R. 1986. *Cognition and affect: A developmental psychology of the individual.* New York: Prometheus.

Simons, A. D.; McGowan, C. R.; Epstein, L. H.; Kupfer, D. J.; and Robertson, R. J. 1985. Exercise as a treatment for depression: An update. *Clinical Psychology Review* 5: 553–68.

Singer, J. A.; and Salovey, P. 1988. Mood and memory: Evaluating the network theory of affect. *Clinical Psychology Review* 8: 211–51.

Singer, J. L. 1966. *Daydreaming.* New York: Random House.

Singer, J. L. 1974. *Imagery and daydream techniques in psychotherapy and behavior modification.* New York: Academic Press.

Singer, J. L.; and Pope, K. S., eds. 1978. *The power of human imagination: New methods in psychotherapy.* New York: Plenum.

Siviy, S. M.; and Panksepp, J. 1987. Sensory modulation of juvenile play in rats. *Developmental Psychobiology* 20: 39–55.

Sizemore, C. C. 1989. *A mind of my own.* New York: William Morrow.

Skafte, D. 1987. Video in groups: Implications for a social theory of the self. *International Journal of Group Psychotherapy* 37: 389–402.

Skarda, C. A.; and Freeman, W. J. 1987. How brains make chaos in order to make sense of the world. *Behavioral and Brain Sciences* 10: 161–95.

Skinner, B. F. 1948. *Walden Two.* New York: Macmillan.

Skinner, B. F. 1953. *Science and human behavior.* New York: Macmillan.

Skinner, B. F. 1957. *Verbal behavior.* New York: Appleton-Century-Crofts.

Skinner, B. F. 1959. *Cumulative record.* New York: Appleton-Century-Crofts.

Skinner, B. F. 1969. *Contingencies of reinforcement: A theoretical analysis.* New York: Appleton-Century-Crofts.

Skinner, B. F. 1971. *Beyond freedom and dignity.* New York: Knopf.

Skinner, B. F. 1974. *About behaviorism.* New York: Knopf.

Skinner, B. F. 1977. Why I am not a cognitive psychologist. *Behaviorism* 5: 1–10.

Skinner, B. F. 1987. What happened to psychology as the science of behavior? *American Psychologist* 42: 780–86.

Skinner, Q., ed. 1985. *The return of grand theory in the human sciences.* Cambridge: Cambridge University Press.

Smith, A. 1776. *The wealth of nations.* London: J. M. Dent and Sons.

Smith, A. 1976 [1759]. *The theory of moral sentiments.* Indianapolis, Ind.: Liberty Classics.

Smith, D. 1982. Trends in counseling and psychotherapy. *American Psychologist* 37: 802–9.

Smith, H. 1988. The crisis in philosophy. *Behaviorism* 16: 51–56.

Smith, L. D. 1986. *Behaviorism and logical positivism.* Palo Alto, Calif.: Stanford University Press.

Smith, M. B. 1978. Perspectives on selfhood. *American Psychologist* 33: 1053–63.

Smith, M. L.; and Glass, G. V. 1977. Meta-analysis of psychotherapy outcome studies. *American Psychologist* 32: 752–60.

Smith, M. O. 1969. History of the motor theories of attention. *Journal of General Psychology* 80: 243–57.

Smith, P. B.; and Pederson, D. R. 1988. Maternal sensitivity and patterns of infant-mother attachment. *Child Development* 59: 1097–1101.

Smith, V. A. 1980. Patient contacts outside therapy. *Canadian Journal of Psychiatry* 25: 297–302.

Smolensky, P. 1988. On the proper treatment of connectionism. *Behavioral and Brain Sciences* 11: 1–74.

Smollar, J.; and Youniss, J. 1989. Transformations in adolescents' perceptions of parents. *International Journal of Behavioral Development* 12: 71–84.

Smotherman, W. P.; and Robinson, S. R. 1990. The prenatal origins of behavioral organization. *Psychological Science* 1: 97–106.

Snow, C. P. 1964. *The two cultures and a second look.* Cambridge: Cambridge University Press.

Snyder, C. R. 1988. From defenses to self-protection: An evolutionary perspective. *Journal of Social and Clinical Psychology* 6: 155–58.

Snyder, C. R.; and Fromkin, H. L. 1980. *Uniqueness: The human pursuit of difference.* New York: Plenum.

Snyder, C. R.; and Higgins, R. L. 1988. Excuses: Their effective role in the negotiation of reality. *Psychological Bulletin* 104: 23–35.

Snyder, M. 1987. *Public appearances, private realities: The psychology of self-monitoring.* New York: W. H. Freeman.

Snyder, S.; Pitts, W. M.; and Pokorny, A. D. 1986. Selected behavioral features of patients with borderline personality traits. *Suicide and Life-Threatening Behavior* 16: 28–39.

Sober, E. 1984. *The nature of selection: Evolutionary theory in philosophical focus.* Cambridge, Mass.: MIT Press.

Sogon, S.; and Masutani, M. 1989. Identification of emotion from body movements: A cross-cultural study of Americans and Japanese. *Psychological Reports* 65: 35–46.

Sokolov, E. M. 1963. Higher nervous functions: The orienting reflex. *Annual Review of Psychology* 25: 545–80.

Solomon, G. F. 1987. Psychoneuroimmunology. In G. Adelman, ed., *Encyclopedia of neuroscience,* vol. 2, 1001–4. Boston: Birkhäuser.

Solomon, R. L. 1980. The opponent-process theory of acquired motivation: The costs of pleasure and the benefits of pain. *American Psychologist* 35: 691–712.

Solomon, R. L.; and Corbit, J. D. 1974. An opponent-process theory of motivation: I. Temporal dynamics of affect. *Psychological Review* 81: 119–45.

Sonstroem, R. J.; and Morgan, W. P. 1989. Exercise and self-esteem: Rationale and model. *Medicine and Science in Sports and Exercise* 21: 329–37.

Soper, B.; and Rosenthal, G. 1988. The number of neurons in the brain: How we report what we do not know. *The Teaching of Psychology* 15: 153–55.

Sparrow, C. 1982. The Lorenz equations: Bifurcations, chaos, and strange attractors. *Applied Mathematical Series, 41.* New York: Springer-Verlag.

Spencer, H. 1897 [1855]. *Principles of psychology,* 4th ed. New York: Appleton.

Spencer-Brown, G. 1972. *Laws of form.* New York: Julian.

Spengemann, W. C. 1980. *The forms of autobiography: Episodes in the history of a literary genre.* New Haven, Conn.: Yale University Press.

Sperling, G. 1960. The information available in brief visual presentations. *Psychological Monographs* 74 (Whole No. 498).

Sperry, R. W. 1988. Psychology's mentalist paradigm and the religion/science tension. *American Psychologist* 43: 607–13.

Spiegel, S. B.; and Hill, C. E. 1989. Guidelines for research on therapist interpretation: Toward greater methodological rigor and relevance to practice. *Journal of Counseling Psychology* 36: 121–29.

Spielberger, C. D.; and DeNike, L. D. 1966. Descriptive behaviorism versus cognitive theory in verbal operant conditioning. *Psychological Review* 73: 306–26.

Spiro, R. J. 1977. Remembering information from text: The "state of schema" approach. In R. C. Anderson, R. J. Spiro, and W. E. Montague, eds., *Schooling and the acquisition of knowledge,* 137–65. Hillsdale, N.J.: Erlbaum.

Spitz, R. A. 1945. Hospitalism. In *The psychoanalytic study of the child,* vol. 1, New York: International Universities Press.

Spitz, R. A. 1946. Hospitalism. A follow-up report. In *The psychoanalytic study of the child,* vol. 2, New York: International Universities Press.

Spivak, G.; and Shure, M. B. 1974. *Social adjustment of young children: A cognitive approach to solving real-life problems.* San Francisco: Jossey-Bass.

Sroufe, L. A. 1979. The coherence of individual development: Early care, attachment, and subsequent developmental issues. *American Psychologist* 34: 834–41.

Sroufe, L. A. 1984. The organization of emotional development. In K. R. Scherer and P. Ekman, eds., *Approaches to emotion,* 109–28. Hillsdale, N.J.: Erlbaum.

Sroufe, L. A. 1987. The role of infant-caregiver attachment in development. In J. Belsky and M. T. Nezworski, eds., *Clinical implications of attachment.* Hillsdale, N.J.: Erlbaum.

Sroufe, L. A.; and Cooper, R. G. 1988. *Child development: Its nature and course.* New York: Free Press.

Sroufe, L. A.; and Jacobvitz, D. 1989. Diverging pathways, developmental transformations, multiple etiologies and the problem of continuity in development. *Human Development* 32: 196–203.

Sroufe, L. A.; and Rutter, M. 1984. The domain of developmental psychopathology. *Child Development* 55: 17–29.

Sroufe, L. A.; and Waters, E. 1976. The ontogenesis of smiling and laughter: A perspective on the organization of development in infancy. *Psychological Review* 3: 173–89.

Staats, A. W. 1983. *Psychology's crisis of disunity: Philosophy and method for a unified science.* New York: Praeger.

Staats, A. W. 1988. Paradigmatic behaviorism, unified positivism, and paradigmatic behavior therapy. In D. B. Fishman, F. Rotgers, and C. M. Franks, eds., *Paradigms in behavior therapy: Present and promise,* 211–53. New York: Springer.

Staddon, J. E. R.; and Simmelhag, V. L. 1971. The "superstition" experiment: A reexamination of its implications for the principles of adaptive behavior. *Psychological Review* 78: 3–43.

Stampfl, T. G.; and Levis, D. J. 1967. Essentials of implosive therapy. *Journal of Abnormal Psychology* 72: 496–503.

Starker, S. 1988a. Do-it-yourself therapy: The prescriptions of self-help books by psychologists. *Psychotherapy* 25: 142–46.

Starker, S. 1988b. Psychologists and self-help books: Attitudes and prescriptive practices of clinicians. *American Journal of Psychotherapy* 42: 448–55.

Starr, P. 1982. *The social transformation of American medicine.* New York: Basic Books.

Staub, E. 1988. The evolution of caring and nonaggressive persons and societies. *Journal of Social Issues* 44: 81–100.

Stebbins, G. L.; and Ayala, F. J. 1981. Is a new evolutionary synthesis necessary? *Science* 213: 967–71.

Steele, J. 1989. Hominid evolution and primate social cognition. *Journal of Human Evolution* 18: 421–32.

Stengers, I. 1985. Genealogies de l'auto-organisation. *Cahiers du Centre de Recherche d'Epistemologie et Autonomie* 8: 7–104.

Stent, G. S. 1985. Hermeneutics and the analysis of complex biological systems. In D. J. Depew and B. H. Weber, eds., *Evolution at a crossroads: The new biology and the new philosophy of science,* 209–25. Cambridge, Mass.: MIT Press.

Stephen, F. J. 1874. *Liberty, equality, fraternity,* 2d ed. London: Smith, Elder.

Steppacher, R. C.; and Mausner, J. S. 1973. Suicide in professionals: A study of male and female psychologists. *American Journal of Epidemiology* 98: 435–45.

Stern, A. 1938. Psychoanalytic investigation of and therapy in the border line group of neuroses. *Psychoanalytic Quarterly* 7: 467–89.

Stern, D. B. 1983. Unformulated experience. *Contemporary Psychoanalysis* 19: 71–99.

Stern, D. N. 1985. *The interpersonal world of the infant.* New York: Basic Books.

Stern, R., ed. 1987. *Theories of the unconscious and theories of the self.* Hillsdale, N.J.: Analytic Press.

Stern, W. 1911. *Differential psychology.* Leipzig: Barth.

Sternberg, R. J. 1988. Mental self-government: A theory of intellectual styles and their development. *Human Development* 31: 197–224.

Sternberg, R. J.; and Barnes, M. L., eds. 1988. *The psychology of love.* New Haven, Conn.: Yale University Press.

Stevenson, L., ed. 1981. *The study of human nature.* Oxford: Oxford University Press.

Stewart, A. J.; Franz, C.; and Layton, L. 1988. The changing self: Using personal documents to study lives. *Journal of Personality* 56: 41–74.

Stewart, A. J.; and Healy, J. M., Jr. 1989. Linking individual development and social changes. *American Psychologist* 44: 30–42.

Stiles, W. B.; and Shapiro, D. A. 1989. Abuse of the drug metaphor in psychotherapy process-outcome research. *Clinical Psychology Review* 9: 521–43.

Stiles, W. B.; Shapiro, D. A.; and Elliott, R. 1986. "Are all psychotherapies equivalent?" *American Psychologist* 41: 165–80.

Stoltenberg, C. D.; and Delworth, U. 1987. *Supervising counselors and therapists: A developmental approach.* San Francisco: Jossey-Bass.

Stoltenberg, C. D.; and Delworth, U. 1988. Developmental models of supervision: It is development—Response to Holloway. *Professional Psychology: Research and Practice* 19: 134–37.

Stone, H.; and Winkelman, S. 1985. *Embracing our selves.* Marina del Rey, Calif.: Devorss.

Stone, I. F. 1988. *The trial of Socrates.* Boston: Little, Brown.

Stone, M. H., ed. 1986. *Essential papers on borderline disorders: One hundred years at the border.* New York: New York University Press.

Straker, G. 1987. Conflicts of theory and views of human nature: The case of Kernberg versus Kohut. *South African Journal of Psychology* 17: 76–78.

Stratton, V. N.; and Zalanowski, A. H. 1989. The effects of music and paintings on mood. *Journal of Music Therapy* 26: 30–41.

Strauman, T. J.; and Higgins, E. T. 1987. Automatic activation of self-discrepancies and emotional syndromes: When cognitive structures influence affect. *Journal of Personality and Social Psychology* 53: 1004–14.

Strauss, A.; Schatzman, L.; Bucher, R.; Ehrlick, D.; and Sabshin, M. 1964. *Psychiatric ideologies and institutions.* New Brunswick, N.J.: Transaction.

Strauss, J.; and Ryan, R. M. 1987. Autonomy disturbances in subtypes of anorexia nervosa. *Journal of Abnormal Psychology* 96: 254–58.

Stricker, G.; and Keisner, R. H., eds. 1985. *From research to clinical practice: The implications of social and developmental research for psychotherapy.* New York: Plenum.
Strickland, B. R. 1989. Internal-external control expectancies: From contingency to creativity. *American Psychologist* 44: 1–12.
Stringer, C. B.; and Andrews, P. 1988. Genetic and fossil evidence for the origin of modern humans. *Science* 239: 1263–68.
Strongman, K. T. 1973. *The psychology of emotion.* New York: Wiley.
Strouse, J., ed. 1974. *Women and analysis: Dialogues on psychoanalytic views of femininity.* New York: Viking.
Strupp, H. H. 1955. The effect of the psychotherapist's personal analysis upon his techniques. *Journal of Consulting Psychology* 19: 197–204.
Strupp, H. H. 1973. On the basic ingredients of psychotherapy. *Journal of Consulting and Clinical Psychology* 41: 1–8.
Strupp, H. H. 1976. The nature of the therapeutic influence and its basic ingredients. In A. Burton, ed., *What makes behavior change possible?* 96–112. New York: Brunner/Mazel.
Strupp, H. H. 1978. The therapist's theoretical orientation: An overrated variable. *Psychotherapy: Research and Practice* 15: 314–17.
Strupp, H. H. 1986. Psychotherapy: Research, practice, and public policy (How to avoid dead ends). *American Psychologist* 41: 120–30.
Strupp, H. H. 1989. Psychotherapy: Can the practitioner learn from the researcher? *American Psychologist* 44: 717–24.
Su, T.; London, E. D.; and Jaffe, J. H. 1988. Steroid binding at sigma receptors suggests a link between endocrine, nervous, and immune systems. *Science* 240: 219–21.
Suedfeld, P. 1980. *Restricted environmental stimulation: Research and clinical applications.* New York: Wiley.
Suh, C. S.; O'Malley, S. S.; Strupp, H. H.; and Johnson, M. E. 1989. The Vanderbilt Psychotherapy Process Scale (VPPS). *Journal of Cognitive Psychotherapy: An International Quarterly* 3: 123–33.
Suleiman, S.; and Crossman, I. 1980. *The reader in the text.* Princeton, N.J.: Princeton University Press.
Sullivan, H. S. 1954. *The psychiatric interview.* New York: Norton.
Suls, J.; and Fletcher, B. 1985. Self-attention, life stress, and illness: A prospective study. *Psychosomatic Medicine* 47: 469–81.
Suls, J.; and Greenwald, A., eds. 1983. *Psychological perspectives on the self.* Hillsdale, N.J.: Erlbaum.
Sundland, D. M.; and Barker, E. N. 1967. The orientations of psychotherapists. *Journal of Consulting Psychology* 26: 201–12.
Sutherland, M. 1988. Women in higher education: Effects of crises and change. *Higher Education* 17: 479–90.
Swann, W. B.; and Read, S. J. 1981a. Acquiring self-knowledge: The search for feedback that fits. *Journal of Personality and Social Psychology* 41: 1119–28.
Swann, W. B.; and Read, S. J. 1981b. Self-verification processes: How we sustain our self-conceptions. *Journal of Experimental Social Psychology* 17: 351–72.

Szamosi, G. 1986. *The twin dimensions: Inventing time and space.* New York: McGraw-Hill.

Szasz, T. S. 1970. *The manufacture of madness: A cooperative study of the inquisition and the mental health movement.* New York: Harper and Row.

Szentágothai, J.; and Érdi, P. 1989. Self-organization in the nervous system. *Journal of Social and Biological Structures* 12: 367–84.

Talbert, F. S.; and Pipes, R. B. 1987. Informed consent for psychotherapy: Content analysis of selected forms. *Professional Psychology: Research and Practice* 18: 131–32.

Tarman, V. I. 1988. Autobiography: The negotiation of a lifetime. *International Journal of Aging and Human Development* 27: 171–91.

Taylor, S. E. 1990. Health psychology. *American Psychologist* 45: 40–50.

Taylor, S. E.; and Brown, J. D. 1988. Illusion and well-being: A social psychological perspective on mental health. *Psychological Bulletin* 103: 193–210.

Taylor, S. J.; and Bogdan, R. 1984. *Introduction to qualitative research methods,* 2d ed. New York: Wiley.

Tellegen, A.; and Atkinson, G. 1974. Openness to absorbing and self-altering experiences ("Absorption"), a trait related to hypnotic susceptibility. *Journal of Abnormal Psychology* 83: 208–77.

Termine, N. T.; and Izard, C. E. 1988. Infants' responses to their mothers' expressions of joy and sadness. *Developmental Psychology* 24: 223–29.

Thatcher, R. W.; Walker, R. A.; and Guidice, S. 1987. Human cerebral hemispheres develop at different rates and ages. *Science* 236: 1110–13.

Thayer, R. E. 1989. *The biopsychology of mood and arousal.* Oxford: Oxford University Press.

Thelen, E. 1988. Dynamical approaches to the development of behavior. In J. A. S. Kelso, A. J. Mandell, and M. F. Shlesinger, eds., *Dynamic patterns in complex systems.* Singapore: World Scientific Publishers.

Thelen, E. 1989a. Conceptualizing development from a dynamical systems perspective. Paper presented at the Society for Research in Child Development, April 26–27, Kansas City, Mo.

Thelen, E. 1989b. Self-organization in developmental processes: Can systems approaches work? In M. Gunnar and E. Thelen, eds., *Systems and development: The Minnesota symposium in child psychology,* vol. 22. Hillsdale, N.J.: Erlbaum.

Thelen, E. In press. Dynamical systems and the generation of individual differences. In J. Colombo and J. W. Fagen, eds., *Individual differences in infancy: Reliability, stability, and prediction.* Hillsdale, N.J.: Erlbaum.

Thigpen, C. H.; and Cleckly, H. 1957. *The three faces of Eve.* New York: McGraw-Hill.

Thom, R. 1975. *Structural stability and morphogenesis: An outline of a general theory of models.* Reading, Pa.: Benjamin.

Thomas, J. A.; and Stock, W. A. 1988. The concept of happiness: A multidimensional scaling investigation. *International Journal of Aging and Human Development* 27: 141–54.

Thomas, L. 1974. *The medusa and the snail.* New York: Viking.

Thompson, D. W. 1917. *On growth and form.* Cambridge: Cambridge University Press.

Thompson, E. H. 1989. Recovery networks and patient interpretations of mental illness. *Journal of Community Psychology* 17: 5–17.

Thompson, S. C. 1981. Will it hurt less if I can control it? A complex answer to a simple question. *Psychological Bulletin* 90: 89–101.

Thompson, W. I. 1981. *The time falling bodies take to light.* New York: St. Martin's Press.

Thoresen, C. E.; and Mahoney, M. J. 1974. *Behavioral self-control.* New York: Holt, Rinehart & Winston.

Thoreson, R. W.; Miller, M.; and Krauskopf, C. J. 1989. The distressed psychologist: Prevalence and treatment considerations. *Professional Psychology: Research and Practice* 20: 153–58.

Thorndike, E. L. 1898. Animal intelligence: An experimental study of the associative processes in animals. *Psychological Review, Monograph Supplements* 2 (Serial No. 8).

Thorndike, E. L.; and Lorge, I. 1944. *The teacher's word book of 30,000 words.* New York: Teachers College.

Thorndyke, P. W. 1984. Applications of schema theory in cognitive research. In J. Anderson and S. Kosslyn, eds., *Tutorials in learning and memory: Essays in honor of Gordon Bower,* 167–92. San Francisco: W. H. Freeman.

Tichenor, V.; and Hill, C. E. 1989. A comparison of six measures of working alliance. *Psychotherapy* 26: 195–99.

Tiedemann, D. 1897 [1787]. *Tiedemann's Beobachtungen uber die Entwicklung der Seelenthatigkeit bei Kindern.* ed. W. Rein. Altenburg: Bonded.

Tillich, P. 1952. *The courage to be.* New Haven, Conn.: Yale University Press.

Timberlake, W.; and Allison, J. 1974. Response deprivation: An empirical approach to instrumental performance. *Psychological Review* 81: 146–64.

Titchener, E. G. 1895. Simple reactions. *Mind* 4: 74–81.

Tolman, E. C. 1932. *Purposive behavior in animals and men.* New York: Appleton-Century.

Tomlin, E. W. F. 1963. *The Oriental philosophers: An introduction.* New York: Harper and Row.

Traub, R. D.; Miles, R.; and Wong, R. K. S. 1989. Model of the origin of rhythmic population oscillations in the hippocampal slice. *Science* 243: 1319–25.

Travers, J. A., ed. 1986. *Psychotherapy and the selfless patient.* New York: Harrington Press.

Treisman, A. M. 1969. Strategies and models of selective attention. *Psychological Review* 76: 282–99.

Treisman, A. M.; and Gelade, G. 1980. A feature integration theory of attention. *Cognitive Psychology* 12: 97–136.

Treisman, A. M.; and Paterson, R. 1984. Emergent features, attention, and object perception. *Journal of Experimental Psychology: Human Perception and Performance* 10: 12–31.

Trevarthen, C. 1982. The primary motives for cooperative understanding. In G.

Butterworth and P. Light, eds., *Social cognition: Studies of the development of under-standing.* Chicago: University of Chicago Press.

Trevarthen, C. 1984. Emotions in infancy: Regulators of contact and relation-ships with persons. In K. R. Scherer and P. Ekman, eds. *Approaches to emotion,* 129–57. Hillsdale, N.J.: Erlbaum.

Triandis, H. C. 1989. The self and social behavior in differing cultural contexts. *Psychological Review* 96: 506–20.

Trick, L.; and Katz, A. N. 1986. The domain interaction approach to metaphor processing: Relating individual differences and metaphor characteristics. *Metaphor and Symbolic Activity* 1: 185–213.

Tronick, E. Z. 1989. Emotions and emotional communication in infants. *American Psychologist* 44: 112–19.

Trull, T. J.; Widiger, T. A.; and Guthrie, P. 1990. Categorical versus dimensional status of borderline personality disorder. *Journal of Abnormal Psychology* 99: 40–48.

Tuana, N., ed. 1989. *Feminism and science.* Bloomington: Indiana University Press.

Tucker, L. A. 1983a. Effect of weight training on self-concept: A profile of those most influenced. *Research Quarterly for Exercise and Sport* 54: 389–97.

Tucker, L. A. 1983b. Muscular strength and mental health. *Journal of Personality and Social Psychology* 45: 1355–60.

Tuckman, B. W. 1988. The scaling of mood. *Educational and Psychological Measurement* 48: 419–27.

Tulku, T. 1977. *Gesture of balance.* Berkeley, Calif.: Dharma Publishing.

Tulving, E. 1972. Episodic and semantic memory. In E. Tulving and W. Donald-son, eds., *Organization of memory.* New York: Academic Press.

Tulving, E. 1983. *Elements of episodic memory.* New York: Oxford University Press.

Tulving, E. 1984. Precis of elements of episodic memory. *The Behavioral and Brain Sciences* 7: 223–68.

Tulving, E. 1985. How many memory systems are there? *American Psychologist* 40: 385–98.

Tulving, E. 1990. Priming and human memory systems. *Science* 247: 301–6.

Tuma, J. M. 1989. Mental health services for children. *American Psychologist* 44: 188–99.

Turing, A. M. 1950. Computing machinery and the mind. *Mind* 59: 433–60.

Turk, D. C.; Meichenbaum, D.; and Genest, M. 1983. *Pain and behavioral medicine: A cognitive-behavioral perspective.* New York: Guilford.

Turk, D. C.; and Salovey, P., eds. 1988. *Reasoning, inference, and judgment in clinical psychology.* New York: Free Press.

Turkkan, J. S. 1989. Classical conditioning: The new hegemony. *Behavioral and Brain Sciences* 12: 121–79.

Turner, V. 1974. *Dramas, fields and metaphors.* Ithaca, N.Y.: Cornell University Press.

Turvey, M. T. 1974. Constructive theory, perceptual systems, and tacit knowl-edge. In W. B. Weimer and D. S. Palermo, eds., *Cognition and the symbolic processes,* vol. 1, 165–80. Hillsdale, N.J.: Erlbaum.

Turvey, M. T.; and Shaw, R. 1979. The primacy of perceiving: An ecological reformulation of perception as a point of departure for understanding memory. In L. G. Nilsson, ed., *Perspectives on memory research: Essays in honor of Uppsala University's 500th Anniversary.* Hillsdale, N.J.: Erlbaum.

Tuttman, S. 1988. Psychoanalytic concepts of "the self." *Journal of the American Academy of Psychoanalysis* 16: 209–19.

Tuttman, S.; Kaye, C.; and Zimmerman, M., eds. 1981. *Object and self: A developmental approach.* New York: International Universities Press.

Tversky, A.; and Kahneman, D. 1971. Belief in the law of small numbers. *Psychological Bulletin* 76: 105–10.

Tversky, A.; and Kahneman, D. 1974. Judgement under uncertainty: Heuristics and biases. *Science* 183: 1124–31.

Ugland, J. H. 1989. Health as a value: Implications for practice. *Professional Psychology: Research and Practice* 20: 415–16.

Ulanowics, R. E. 1989. A phenomenology of evolving networks. *Systems Research* 6: 1–9.

Underwood, B. J. 1957. Interference and forgetting. *Psychological Review* 64: 49–60.

Unger, R. K.; Draper, R. D.; and Pendergrass, M. L. 1986. Personal epistemology and personal experience. *Journal of Social Issues* 42: 67–79.

Uttal, D. H.; and Perlmutter, M. 1989. Toward a broader conceptualization of development: The role of gains and losses across the life span. *Developmental Review* 9: 101–32.

Vaihinger, H. 1924 [1911]. *The philosophy of 'as if.'* Berlin: Reuther and Reichard.

Vaillant, G. E. 1983. *The natural history of alcoholism.* Cambridge, Mass.: Harvard University Press.

Valentine, T. 1988. Upside-down faces: A review of the effect of inversion upon face recognition. *British Journal of Psychology* 79: 471–91.

Valle, R. S.; and Halling, S., eds. 1989. *Existential-phenomenological perspectives in psychology: Exploring the breadth of human experience.* New York: Plenum.

Valle, R. S.; and von Eckartsberg, R. 1981. *The metaphors of consciousness.* New York: Plenum.

Van Den Bergh, O.; and Eelen, P. 1984. Unconscious processing and emotion. In M. A. Reda and M. J. Mahoney, eds., *Cognitive psychotherapies: Recent developments in theory, research, and practice,* 173–209. Cambridge, Mass.: Ballinger.

van der Hart, O. 1981. *Rituals in psychotherapy: Transition and continuity.* New York: Irvington.

van der Hart, O.; and Ebbers, J. 1981. Rites of separation in strategic psychotherapy. *Psychotherapy: Theory, Research and Practice* 18: 188–94.

Varela, F. J. 1979. *Principles of biological autonomy.* New York: Elsevier North-Holland.

Varela, F. J. 1984. The creative circle: Sketches on the natural history of circularity. In P. Watzlawick, ed., *The invented reality: Contributions to constructivism,* 309–323. New York: Norton.

Varela, F. J. 1986. *The science and technology of cognition: Emergent directions.* Florence: Hopeful Monster.

Varela, F. J. 1987. Laying down a path in walking. In W. I. Thompson, ed., *GAIA: A way of knowing,* 48–64. Great Barrington, Mass.: Lindisfarne.

Varela, F. J.; Maturana, H. R.; and Uribe, R. 1974. Autopoiesis: The organization of living systems, its characterization and a model. *Bio-Systems* 5: 187–96.

Varela, F. J.; and Singer, W. 1987. Neuronal dynamics in the visual cortico-thalamic pathway revealed through binocular rivalry. *Experimental Brain Research* 66: 10–20.

Varghese, F. T. 1988. The phenomenology of psychotherapy. *American Journal of Psychotherapy* 42: 389–403.

Verene, D. P. 1981. *Vico's science of imagination.* Ithaca, N.Y.: Cornell University Press.

Vermeij, G. J. 1987. *Evolution and escalation: An ecological history of life.* Princeton, N.J.: Princeton University Press.

Vico, G. 1948 [1725]. *The new science.* Trans. T. G. Bergin and M. H. Fisch. Ithaca, N.Y.: Cornell University Press.

Viney, L. L. 1987. *Interpreting the interpreters.* Malabar, Fla.: Robert E. Kreiger.

Viney, W. 1989. The cyclops and the twelve-eyed toad. William James and the unity-disunity problem in psychology. *American Psychologist* 44: 1261–65.

Vining, D. R. 1986. Social versus reproductive success: The central theoretical problem of human sociobiology. *The Behavioral and Brain Sciences* 9: 167–216.

Vitaliano, P. P.; Katon, W.; Russo, J.; Maiuro, R. D.; Anderson, K.; and Jones, M. 1987. Coping as an index of illness behavior in panic disorder. *Journal of Nervous and Mental Disease* 175: 78–84.

Von Bertalanffy, L. 1967. *Robots, men and minds: Psychology in the modern world.* New York: George Braziller.

von der Malsburg, C.; and Bienenstock, E. 1986. Statistical coding and short-term synaptic plasticity: A scheme for knowledge representation in the brain. In E. Bienenstock, F. F. Soulié, and G. Weisbuch, eds., *Disordered systems and biological organization,* 247–70. Berlin: Springer-Verlag.

von Foerster, H. 1984. On constructing a reality. In P. Watzlawick, ed., *The invented reality: Contributions to constructivism,* 41–61. New York: Norton.

von Glaserfeld, E. 1979. Radical constructivism and Piaget's concept of knowledge. In F. B. Murray, ed., *The impact of Piagetian theory on education, philosophy, psychiatry, and psychology,* 109–22. Baltimore, Md.: University Park Press.

von Glaserfeld, E. 1984. An introduction to radical constructivism. In P. Watzlawick, ed., *The invented reality: Contributions to constructivism,* 18–40. New York: Norton.

von Glaserfeld, E. 1988. The reluctance to change a way of thinking. *Irish Journal of Psychology* 9: 83–90.

von Glaserfeld, E. 1989. Cognition, construction of knowledge, and teaching. *Synthese* 80: 121–40.

von Neumann, J. 1951. The general and logical theory of automata. In L. A. Jefress, ed., *Cerebral mechanisms in behavior.* New York: Wiley.

Vosniadou, S.; and Brewer, W. F. 1987. Theories of knowledge restructuring in development. *Review of Educational Research* 57: 51–67.

Vygotsky, L. S. 1962 [1934]. *Thought and language.* Cambridge, Mass.: MIT Press.

Vygotsky, L. S. 1978. *Mind in society: The development of higher psychological processes.* Cambridge, Mass.: Harvard University Press.

Wachs, T. D.; and Gruen, G. E. 1982. *Early experience and human development.* New York: Plenum.

Wachtel, P. L. 1977. *Psychoanalysis and behavior therapy: Toward an integration.* New York: Basic Books.

Wachtel, P. L., ed. 1982. *Resistance: Psychodynamic and behavioral approaches.* New York: Plenum.

Wachtel, P. L. 1987. *Action and insight.* New York: Guilford.

Wachter, K. W. 1988. Disturbed by meta-analysis? *Science* 241: 1407–8.

Wachterhauser, B. R., ed. 1986. *Hermeneutics and modern philosophy.* Albany: State University of New York Press.

Wachtershauser, G. 1987. Light and life: On the nutritional origins of sensory perception. In G. Radnitzky and W. W. Bartley, eds., *Evolutionary epistemology, theory of rationality, and the sociology of knowledge,* 121–38. La Salle, Ill.: Open Court.

Waddington, C. H. 1940. *Organisers and genes.* London: Allen and Unwin.

Waddington, C. H., ed. 1968–72. *Towards a theoretical biology,* 4 vols. Edinburgh: Edinburgh University Press.

Waggoner, J. E.; and Palermo, D. S. 1989. Betty is a bouncing bubble: Children's comprehension of emotion-descriptive metaphors. *Developmental Psychology* 25: 152–63.

Wahler, R. G.; and Dumas, J. E. 1989. Attentional problems in dysfunctional mother-child interactions: An interbehavioral model. *Psychological Bulletin* 105: 116–30.

Waldrop, M. M. 1988*a.* The quantum wave function of the universe. *Science* 242: 1248–50.

Waldrop, M. M. 1988*b.* Toward a unified theory of cognition. *Science* 241: 27–29.

Waldrop, M. M. 1989. PARC brings Adam Smith to computing. *Science* 244: 145–46.

Wallace, A. R. 1864. The origin of human races and the antiquity of man deduced from the theory of 'natural selection.' *Anthropological Review* 2: clvii–clxxxvii.

Wallace, A. R. 1905. *My life,* 2 vols. New York: Dodd, Mead.

Wallach, M. A.; and Wallach, L. 1983. *Psychology's sanction for selfishness: The error of egoism in theory and therapy.* Salt Lake City, Utah: W. H. Freeman.

Wallerstein, R. S. 1989. The psychotherapy research project of the Menninger Foundation: An overview. *Journal of Consulting and Clinical Psychology* 57: 195–205.

Walsh, R. N. 1976. Reflections on psychotherapy. *Journal of Transpersonal Psychology* 8: 100–11.

Walsh, R. N. 1984. *Staying alive: The psychology of human survival.* Boston: New Science Library.

Walsh, R. N. 1989. Psychological chauvinism and nuclear holocaust: A response to Albert Ellis and defense of non-rational emotive therapies. *Journal of Counseling and Development* 67: 338–40.

Walsh, R. N. 1989*b*. Toward a psychology of human survival: Psychological approaches to contemporary global threats. *American Journal of Psychotherapy* 43: 158–80.

Walsh, R. N.; and D. H. Shapiro, eds. 1983. *Beyond health and normality: Explorations of exceptional psychological well-being.* New York: Van Nostrand Reinhold.

Walsh, R. N.; and Vaughan, F., eds. 1980. *Beyond ego: Transpersonal dimensions in psychology.* Los Angeles: J. P. Tarcher.

Walsh, R. N.; and Vaughan, F. 1983. Towards an integrative psychology of well-being. In R. Walsh and D. H. Shapiro, eds., *Beyond health and normality: Explorations of exceptional psychological well-being,* 388–432. New York: Van Nostrand Reinhold.

Waltz, D. L.; and Pollack, J. B. 1985. Massively parallel parsing: A strongly interactive model of natural language interpretation. *Cognitive Science* 9: 51–71.

Wampler, L. D.; and Strupp, H. H. 1976. Personal therapy for students in clinical psychology: A matter of faith? *Professional Psychology: Research and Practice* 7: 195–201.

Wandersman, A.; Poppen, P. J.; and Ricks, D. F., eds. 1976. *Humanism and behaviorism: Dialogue and growth.* New York: Pergamon.

Waring, E. M.; and Chelune, G. J. 1983. Marital intimacy and self-disclosure. *Journal of Clinical Psychology* 39: 183–90.

Waring, E. M.; Tillman, M. P.; Frelick, L.; Russell, L.; and Weisz, G. 1980. Concepts of intimacy in the general population. *Journal of Nervous and Mental Disease* 168: 471–74.

Warr, P. 1978. A study of psychological well-being. *British Journal of Psychology* 69: 111–21.

Warr, P.; Barter, J.; and Brownbridge, G. 1983. On the independence of positive and negative affect. *Journal of Personality and Social Psychology* 44: 644–51.

Washburn, M. F. 1926. *Movement and mental imagery: Outlines of a motor theory of the complexer mental processes.* Boston: Houghton Mifflin.

Washburn, S. L.; and Moore, R. 1980. *Ape into human: A study of human evolution.* Boston: Little, Brown.

Waskow, I.; and Parloff, M. 1975. *Psychotherapy change measures.* Washington, D.C.: U. S. Government Printing Office.

Wasserman, E. A.; Kiedinger, R. E.; and Bhatt, R. S. 1988. Conceptual behavior in pigeons: Categories, subcategories, and pseudocategories. *Journal of Experimental Psychology: Animal Behavior Processes* 14: 235–46.

Watkins, C. E., Jr.; Lopez, F. G.; Campbell, V. L.; and Himmell, C. D. 1986. Contemporary counseling psychology: Results of a national survey. *Journal of Counseling Psychology* 33: 301–9.

Watkins, M. 1986. *Invisible guests: The development of imaginal dialogues.* New York: Analytic Press.

Watkins, M. 1988. Imagination and peace: On the inner dynamics of promoting peace activism. *Journal of Social Issues* 44: 39–57.

Watson, D. 1988. The vicissitudes of mood measurement: Effects of varying descriptors, time frames, and response formats on measures of positive and negative affect. *Journal of Personality and Social Psychology* 55: 128–41.

Watson, D.; and Clark, L. A. 1984. Negative affectivity: The disposition to experience aversive emotional states. *Psychological Bulletin* 96: 465–90.

Watson, D.; and Clark, L. A. 1988. Positive and negative affectivity and their relation to anxiety and depressive disorders. *Journal of Abnormal Psychology* 97: 346–53.

Watson, D.; and Pennebaker, J. W. 1989. Health complaints, stress, and distress: Exploring the central role of negative affectivity. *Psychological Review* 96: 234–54.

Watson, D.; and Tellegen, A. 1985. Toward a consensual structure of mood. *Psychological Bulletin* 98: 219–35.

Watson, J. B. 1913. Psychology as the behaviorist views it. *Psychological Review* 20: 158–77.

Watson, J. B. 1924. *Behaviorism.* New York: Norton.

Watson, J. B. 1928. *The psychological care of the infant and child.* New York: Norton.

Watson, L. E., ed. 1979. *Light from many lamps.* New York: Simon and Schuster.

Watson, R. I. 1963. *The great psychologists.* Philadelphia, Pa.: Lippincott.

Watts, A. 1966. *The book: On the taboo against knowing who you are.* New York: Random House.

Watts, F. N. 1989. Attentional strategies and agoraphobic anxiety. *Behavioral Psychotherapy* 17: 15–26.

Watzlawick, P. 1978. *Change: The language of therapeutic communication.* New York: Basic Books.

Watzlawick, P., ed. 1984. *The invented reality: Contributions to constructivism.* New York: Norton.

Watzlawick, P.; Weakland, J.; and Fisch, R. 1974. *Change: Principles of problem formation and problem resolution.* New York: Norton.

Webb, M. E. 1988. A new history of Hartley's *Observations on Man. Journal of the History of the Behavioral Sciences* 24: 202–11.

Webb, M. E. 1989. The early medical studies and practice of Dr. David Hartley. *Bulletin of the History of Medicine* 63: 618–36.

Wegner, D. M.; and Giuliano, T. 1980. Arousal-induced attention to self. *Journal of Personality and Social Psychology* 38: 719–26.

Wegner, D. M.; and Vallacher, R. R., eds. 1980. *The self in social psychology.* New York: Oxford University Press.

Weil, A. 1983. *Health and healing: Understanding conventional and alternative medicine.* Boston: Houghton Mifflin.

Weimer, W. B. 1973. Psycholinguistics and Plato's paradoxes of the *Meno. American Psychologist* 28: 15–33.

Weimer, W. B. 1974a. Overview of a cognitive conspiracy. In W. B. Weimer and

D. S. Palermo, eds., *Cognition and the symbolic processes,* vol. 1, 415–42. Hillsdale, N.J.: Erlbaum.

Weimer, W. B. 1974*b*. The history of psychology and its retrieval from historiography: I. The problematic nature of history. *Science Studies* 4: 235–58.

Weimer, W. B. 1974*c*. The history of psychology and its retrieval from historiography: II. Some lessons for the methodology of scientific research. *Science Studies* 4: 367–96.

Weimer, W. B. 1977. A conceptual framework for cognitive psychology: Motor theories of mind. In R. Shaw and J. Bransford, eds., *Perceiving, acting, and knowing,* 267–311. Hillsdale, N.J.: Erlbaum.

Weimer, W. B. 1979. *Notes on the methodology of scientific research.* Hillsdale, N.J.: Erlbaum.

Weimer, W. B. 1980. Psychotherapy and philosophy of science: Examples of a two-way street in search of traffic. In M. J. Mahoney, ed., *Psychotherapy process: Current issues and future directions,* 369–93. New York: Plenum.

Weimer, W. B. 1982*a*. Ambiguity and the future of psychology: *Meditations Leibniziennes.* In W. B. Weimer and D. S. Palermo, eds., *Cognition and the symbolic processes,* vol. 2, 331–360. Hillsdale, N.J.: Erlbaum.

Weimer, W. B. 1982*b*. Hayek's approach to the problems of complex phenomena: An introduction to the theoretical psychology of *The Sensory Order.* In W. B. Weimer and D. S. Palermo, eds., *Cognition and the symbolic processes,* vol. 2, 241–285. Hillsdale, N.J.: Erlbaum.

Weimer, W. B. 1983. CCR is not completely confused rhetoric (and there is no need to "pan" it). In International Cultural Foundation, ed., *Proceedings of the 11th international conference on the unity of the sciences,* 1101–15. New York: International Cultural Foundation Press.

Weimer, W. B. 1987. Spontaneously ordered complex phenomena and the unity of the moral sciences. In G. Radnitzky, ed., *Centripetal forces in the universe,* 257–96. New York: Paragon House.

Weimer, W. B.; and Palermo, D. S., eds. 1974. *Cognition and the symbolic processes,* vol. 1. Hillsdale, N.J.: Erlbaum.

Weimer, W. B.; and Palermo, D. S., eds. 1982. *Cognition and the symbolic processes,* vol. 2. Hillsdale, N.J.: Erlbaum.

Weiner, B. 1972. *Theories of motivation: From mechanism to cognition.* Chicago: Rand McNally.

Weiner, H. 1965. Real and imagined cost effects upon human fixed-interval responding. *Psychological Reports* 17: 659–62.

Weiner, M. L. 1975. *The cognitive unconscious: A Piagetian approach to psychotherapy.* Davis, Calif.: International Psychological Press.

Weiner, M. L. 1985. *Cognitive-experiential therapy: An integrative ego psychotherapy.* New York: Brunner/Mazel.

Weinstein, N. D. 1989. Effects of personal experience on self-protective behavior. *Psychological Bulletin* 105: 31–50.

Weisskopf, V. F. 1979. *Knowledge and wonder: The natural world as man knows it,* 2d ed. Cambridge, Mass.: MIT Press.

Weitzman, B. 1967. Behavior therapy and psychotherapy. *Psychological Review* 74: 300–17.

Wellman, H. M.; and Estes, D. 1986. Early understanding of mental entities: A reexamination of childhood realism. *Child Development* 57: 910–23.

Welwood, J. 1979. Befriending emotion: Self-knowledge and transformation. *Journal of Transpersonal Psychology* 11: 141–160.

Werner, E. E. 1986. Resilient offspring of alcoholics: A longitudinal study from birth to age 18. *Journal of Studies on Alcohol* 47: 34–40.

Werner, H. 1948. *The comparative psychology of mental development.* New York: International Universities Press.

Werner, H. 1957. The concept of development from a comparative and organismic point of view. In D. B. Harris, ed., *The concept of development: An issue in the study of human behavior,* 125–48. Minneapolis: University of Minnesota Press.

Wertheimer, M. 1912. Experimentelle studien uber das sehen von bewegung. *Zeitschrift fur Psychologie* 60: 321–78.

Wertheimer, M. 1945. *Productive thinking.* New York: Harper and Row.

Wertheimer, M. 1988. Obstacles to the integration of competing theories in psychology. *Philosophical Psychology* 1: 131–37.

West, M. O.; and Prinz, R. J. 1987. Parental alcoholism and childhood psychopathology. *Psychological Bulletin* 102: 204–18.

West, M.; Sheldon, A.; and Reiffer, L. 1989. Attachment theory and brief psychotherapy: Applying current research to clinical interventions. *Canadian Journal of Psychiatry* 34: 369–75.

Westen, D. 1986. What changes in short-term psychodynamic psychotherapy? *Psychotherapy* 23: 501–12.

Wethington, E.; and Kessler, R.C. 1986. Perceived support, received support, and adjustment to stressful life events. *Journal of Health and Social Behavior* 27: 78–89.

Wheeler, J. A. 1982. Bohr, Einstein, and the strange lesson of the quantum. In R. Q. Elvee, ed., *Mind in Nature,* 1–30. New York: Harper and Row.

Whitbourne, S. K. 1989. Psychological treatment of the aging individual. *Journal of Integrative and Eclectic Psychotherapy* 8: 161–73.

Whitcher, S. J.; and Fisher, J. D. 1979. Multidimensional reaction to therapeutic touch in a hospital setting. *Journal of Personality and Social Psychology* 37: 87–96.

White, D. J. 1981. *The construction of an instrument to measure written content in personal journals.* Doctoral dissertation, University of California, Santa Barbara.

White, D. J.; and Atkinson, D. R. 1980. College counselors' use of writing assignments as a treatment strategy. *Journal of Counseling Services* 4: 4–11.

White, G. M.; and Kirkpatrick, J. 1985. *Person, self and experience: Exploring Pacific ethnopsychologies.* Berkeley: University of California Press.

White, M.; and Epston, D. 1990. *Narrative means to therapeutic ends.* New York: Norton.

White, P. A. 1988. Knowing more about what we can tell: 'Introspective access' and casual report accuracy 10 years later. *British Journal of Psychology* 79: 13–45.

White, P. A.; and Younger, D. P. 1988. Differences in the ascription of transient internal states to self and other. *Journal of Experimental Social Psychology* 24: 292–309.

White, R. W., ed. 1963. *The study of lives: Essays on personality in honor of Henry A. Murray.* New York: Prentice-Hall.

Whitehead, A. N. 1957. *Process and reality.* New York: Macmillan.

Whitehead, A. N.; and Russell, B. 1913. *Principia mathematica,* 3 vols. Cambridge: Cambridge University Press.

Whitfield, M. D. 1980. Emotional stresses on the psychotherapist. *Canadian Journal of Psychiatry* 25: 292–96.

Whorf, B. L. 1956. *Language, thought and reality.* Cambridge, Mass.: MIT Press.

Wickens, C. 1980. The structure of attentional processes. In R. S. Nickerson, ed., *Attention and performance,* vol. 8. Hillsdale, N.J.: Erlbaum.

Wickens, C. 1984. Processing resources in attention. In R. Parasuraman and D. R. Davies, eds., *Varieties of attention.* New York: Academic Press.

Wicklund, R. A. 1974. *Freedom and reactance.* New York: Wiley.

Wiener, N. 1948. *Cybernetics.* New York: Wiley.

Wiener, P. P., ed. 1974. *Dictionary of the history of ideas: Studies of selected pivotal ideas.* New York: Scribner.

Wilber, K. 1981. *Up from Eden. A transpersonal view of human evolution.* Boston: Shambhala.

Wilber, K. 1989a. Let's nuke the transpersonalists: A response to Albert Ellis. *Journal of Counseling and Development* 67: 332–40.

Wilber, K. 1989b. Two humanistic psychologies? *Journal of Humanistic Psychology* 29: 230–43.

Wilber, K.; Engler, J.; and Brown, D. P. 1986. *Transformations of consciousness: Conventional and contemplative perspectives on development.* Boston: New Science Library.

Wilkinson, S. J. 1981. Constructs, counterfactuals and fictions: Elaborating the concept of possibility in science. In H. Bonarius, R. Holland, and S. Rosenberg, eds., *Personal construct psychology: Recent advances in theory and practice,* 39–46. New York: Macmillan.

Williams, J. M. G.; and Scott, J. 1988. Autobiographical memory in depression. *Psychological Medicine* 18: 689–95.

Williams, S. L.; Kinney, P. J.; and Falbo, J. 1989. Generalization of therapeutic changes in agoraphobia: The role of perceived self-efficacy. *Journal of Consulting and Clinical Psychology* 57: 436–42.

Williamson, C. 1975. *The changer and the changed.* Oakland, Calif.: Olivia Records.

Willis, C. 1987. Legal and ethical issues of touch in dance/movement therapy. *American Journal of Dance Therapy* 10: 41–53.

Willis, D. 1989. *The hominid gang: Behind the scenes in the search for human origins.* New York: Viking.

Willison, B. G.; and Masson, R. L. 1986. The role of touch in therapy: An adjunct to communication. *Journal of Counseling and Development* 64: 497–500.

Willits, F. K.; and Crider, D. M. 1988. Health rating and life satisfaction in the later middle years. *Journal of Gerontology* 43: S172–76.

Willmuth, L. R. 1986. A retrospective evaluation—Darwin comes to American psychiatry: Evolutionary biology and Adolf Meyer. *Journal of Social Biological Structures* 9: 279–87.

Wilson, E. O. 1975. *Sociobiology: The new synthesis.* Cambridge, Mass.: Harvard University Press.

Wilson, J. P.; Harel, Z.; and Kahana, B., eds. 1988. *Human adaptations to extreme stress.* New York: Plenum.

Wilson, P. J. 1980. *Man: The promising primate.* New Haven, Conn.: Yale University Press.

Windelband, W. 1894. *History and science.* Strassburg: Heitz and Mündel.

Winnicott, D. W. 1965. *The family and individual development.* London: Tavistock.

Winnicott, D. W. 1971. *Playing and reality.* London: Tavistock.

Winograd, T. 1980. What does it mean to understand language? *Cognitive Science* 4: 209–41.

Winograd, T.; and Flores, F. 1986. *Understanding computers and cognition: A new foundation for design.* Reading, Mass.: Addison-Wesley.

Winstead, B. A.; Derlega, V. J.; Lewis, R. J.; and Margulis, S. T. 1988. Understanding the therapeutic relationship as a personal relationship. *Journal of Social and Personal Relationships* 5: 109–25.

Wise, S. P., ed. 1987. *Higher brain functions: Recent explorations of the brain's emergent properties.* New York: Wiley-Interscience.

Wise, S. P.; and Desimone, R. 1988. Behavioral neurophysiology: Insights into seeing and grasping. *Science* 242: 736–41.

Wogan, M.; and Norcross, J. C. 1985. Dimensions of therapeutic skills and techniques: Empirical identification, therapist correlates, and predictive utility. *Psychotherapy* 22: 63–74.

Wohl, J. 1989. Integration of cultural awareness into psychotherapy. *American Journal of Psychotherapy* 43: 343–55.

Wolf, D. P.; Rygh, J.; and Altshuler, J. 1984. Agency and experience: Actions and states in play narratives. In I. Bretherton, ed., *Symbolic Play: The development of social understanding.* New York: Academic Press.

Wolff, P. H. 1987. *The development of behavioral states and the expression of emotions in early infancy.* Chicago: University of Chicago Press.

Wollman, N., ed. 1985. *Working for peace.* San Luis Obispo, Calif.: Impact Publishers.

Wolpe, J. 1958. *Psychotherapy by reciprocal inhibition.* Palo Alto, Calif.: Stanford University Press.

Wolpe, J. 1978. Cognition and causation in human behavior and its therapy. *American Psychologist* 33: 437–46.

Wong, P. T. P. 1989. Personal meaning and successful aging. *Canadian Psychology* 30: 516–25.

Woodcock, A.; and Davis, M. 1978. *Catastrophe theory.* New York: Avon.

Woodruff-Pak, D. S. 1989. Aging and intelligence: Changing perspectives in the twentieth century. *Journal of Aging Studies* 3: 91–118.

Woolfolk, R. L. 1988. The self in cognitive behavior therapy. In D. B. Fishman, F. Rotgers, and C. M. Franks, eds., *Paradigms in behavior therapy: Present and promise,* 168–84. New York: Springer.

Woolfolk, R. L.; and Richardson, F. C. 1984. Behavior therapy and the ideology of modernity. *American Psychologist* 39: 777–86.

Woolgar, S., ed. 1988. *Knowledge and reflexivity.* London: Sage.

Worell, J. 1988. Women's satisfaction in close relationships. *Clinical Psychology Review* 8: 477–98.

Wright, R.; and Spielberger, C. D. 1989. *Psychiatry declares war on psychology.* Washington, D. C.: Association for the Advancement of Psychology.

Wrightsman, L. S. 1981. Personal documents as data in conceptualizing adult personality development. *Personality and Social Psychology Bulletin* 7: 367–85.

Wundt, W. 1907 [1896]. *Outlines of psychology,* 7th ed. Trans. C. H. Judd. Leipzig: Engelmann.

Wundt, W. 1908–1911 [1874]. *Principles of physiological psychology,* 6th ed., 3 vols. Leipzig: Engelmann.

Wundt, W. 1912. *An introduction to psychology.* New York: Macmillan.

Wylie, R. C. 1989. *Measures of self-concept.* Lincoln: University of Nebraska Press.

Wysocki, J.; Chemers, M. M.; and Rhodewalt, F. 1987. Situational demand and self-reports of stress and illness: The moderating influence of self-monitoring. *Basic and Applied Social Psychology* 8: 249–58.

Yankelovich, D. 1981. *New rules: Searching for self-fulfillment in a world turned upside down.* New York: Bantam.

Yardley, K. M.; and Honess, T., eds. 1987. *Self and identity.* New York: Wiley.

Yarrow, L. J. 1979. Emotional development. *American Psychologist* 34: 951–57.

Yee, C. M.; and Miller, G. A. 1988. Emotional information processing: Modulation of fear in normal and dysthymic subjects. *Journal of Abnormal Psychology* 97: 54–63.

Yelen, D. R. 1985. Opponent-process theory: The interaction of trials, intertrial interval, and the presence of evoking stimuli. *Bulletin of the Psychonomic Society* 23: 25–27.

Yogman, M. W.; and Brazelton, T. B. 1986. *In support of families.* Cambridge, Mass.: Harvard University Press.

Yorke, J.; and Li, T. 1975. Period three implies chaos. *American Mathematical Monthly* 82: 985–92.

Young, M. B. 1988. Understanding identity disruption and intimacy: One aspect of post-traumatic stress. *Contemporary Family Therapy* 10: 30–43.

Young-Eisendrath, P.; and Hall, J. A., eds. 1987. *The book of the self: Person, pretext, and process.* New York: New York University Press.

Yu-Ian, F. 1934. *A history of Chinese philosophy,* 2 vols. Princeton, N.J.: Princeton University Press.

Zajonc, R. B. 1980. Feeling and thinking: Preferences need no inferences. *American Psychologist* 35: 151–75.

Zajonc, R. B. 1984. On the primacy of affect. *American Psychologist* 39: 117–23.

Zajonc, R. B.; and Markus, H. 1984. Affect and cognition: The hard interface. In C. E. Izard, J. Kagan, and R. B. Zajonc, eds., *Emotions, cognition, and behavior,* 73–102. Cambridge: Cambridge University Press.

Zajonc, R. B.; Murphy, S. T.; and Inglehart, M. 1989. Feeling and facial efference: Implications of the vascular theory of emotion. *Psychological Review* 96: 395–416.

Zanarini, M. C.; Gunderson, J. G.; and Frankenburg, F. R. 1989. Axis I phenomenology of borderline personality disorder. *Comprehensive Psychiatry* 30: 149–56.

Zautra, A. J.; Guarnaccia, C. A.; and Reich, J. W. 1988. Factor structure of mental health measures for older adults. *Journal of Consulting and Clinical Psychology* 56: 514–19.

Zeeman, E. C. 1976 Catastrophe theory. *Scientific American* 237: 65–83.

Zeeman, E. C. 1977. *Catastrophe theory: Selected papers 1972–1977.* Reading, Pa.: Benjamin.

Zeig, J. K., ed. 1987. *The evolution of psychotherapy.* New York: Brunner/Mazel.

Zeleny, M. 1980. *Autopoiesis, dissipative structures, and spontaneous social orders.* Washington, DC: American Association for the Advancement of Science.

Zeleny, M. 1981. *Autopoiesis: A theory of living organization.* New York: Elsevier North-Holland.

Zevon, M. A.; and Tellegen, A. 1982. The structure of mood change: An idiographic/nomothetic analysis. *Journal of Personality and Social Psychology* 43: 111–22.

Zimmerman, J. E. 1964. *Dictionary of classical mythology.* New York: Bantam.

Zinberg, N. E. 1984. *Drug, set, and setting.* New Haven, Conn.: Yale University Press.

Zivin, G., ed. 1979. *The development of self-regulation through private speech.* New York: Wiley.

Zubek, J. P., ed. 1969. *Sensory deprivation: Fifteen years of research.* New York: Appleton-Century-Crofts.

Zuriff, G. E. 1985. *Behaviorism: A conceptual reconstruction.* New York: Columbia University Press.

Zuriff, G. E. 1986. Precis of *Behaviorism: A conceptual reconstruction. Behavioral and Brain Sciences* 9: 687–723.

Zuroff, D. C.; and Mongrain, M. 1987. Dependency and self-criticism: Vulnerability factors for depressive affective states. *Journal of Abnormal Psychology* 96: 14–22.

Zusne, L. 1987. Contributions to the history of psychology: XLIV. Coverage of contributors in histories of psychology. *Psychological Reports* 61: 343–50.

Index